FERGUSON

CAREER RESOURCE GUIDE TO

Grants, Scholarships, and Other Financial Resources

VOLUME 1

Ferguson

An imprint of Infobase Publishing

Ferguson Career Resource Guide to Grants, Scholarships, and Other Financial Resources

Copyright © 2007 by Infobase Publishing

Ferguson
An imprint of Infobase Publishing
132 West 31st Street
New York, NY 10001

ISBN-10: 0-8160-6491-1
ISBN-13: 978-0-8160-6491-5

Library of Congress Cataloging-in-Publication Data

Ferguson career resource guide to grants, scholarships, and other financial resources.
    p. cm.
  Includes bibliographical references and index.
  ISBN 0-8160-6491-1 (alk. paper)
 1. Student aid—United States. 2. Scholarships—United States. 3. Grants-in-aid—United States. I. J.G. Ferguson Publishing Company.
  LB2337.4.F47 2007
  378.3—dc22   2006017904

Text design by David Strelecky
Cover design by Salvatore Luongo

Printed in the United States of America

VB MSRF 10 9 8 7 6 5 4 3 2 1

This book is printed on acid-free paper.

CONTENTS

VOLUME 2

PART I
INTRODUCTION AND OVERVIEW

FOREWORD

Brad Barnett, Senior Associate Director of Financial Aid and Scholarships, James Madison University
President (2005–06), Virginia Association of Student Financial Aid Administrators

It has been said that death and taxes are the only constants in life. Well, I believe you can add one more item to this list—a college education is expensive.

There was a time when college did not cost as much as it does today, but the reality is that if you want to secure a higher-education degree you must pay for it. You might ask yourself: "Can I make college affordable?" Rest assured, it is possible to make the dream of a college education a reality. In fact, I am living proof of it.

I wasn't always a financial aid officer or president of the Virginia Association of Student Financial Aid Administrators (VASFAA). At one time, I was a boy with a dream of going to college, a boy from a background that made it unlikely that this would happen.

The short version of my story is that my mother and father divorced when I was very young. Both my parents have been married three times, and my mother's second husband died when I was a senior in high school. So, if you are reading this book and thinking that your family situation is one that lends itself towards not going to college, think again. The majority of my childhood was spent in a household with an annual income below the poverty line. There was even a point in my childhood when my mother, brother, stepfather, and I lived in a tent.

Don't get me wrong, the one constant I had from both of my parents despite everything was love and support. That was never in question, and I learned a great deal from my childhood. I love my parents dearly, and I know they feel the same way about me. But, growing up in the woods of Arkansas, with poverty-level income, in a split family where neither parent had attended college did not make the odds of me going to college good. However, both my parents wanted me to attend college. In fact, after my mother's second husband died, she decided to go to college. She secured a bachelor's degree, two master's degrees, and is now extremely successful. And, yes, she used financial aid to help pay for her education.

So, how did I pay for college? I benefited immensely from scholarship aid while attending Southern Arkansas University (SAU) for my undergraduate degree. My situation was one where the scholarship dollars came from SAU, but I found out about them through my church. My choir director at church had knowledge of choir scholarships offered at SAU. He encouraged me to audition, and the end result was that I received a full-tuition scholarship.

The financial aid officer at SAU was also a huge help in assisting me when applying for federal aid and securing federal grant dollars to help with expenses my scholarships did not cover. In the end, I graduated from SAU only having to take out a $1,000 Perkins Loan for the entire four years. Of course, there was more to it than just getting money. Growing up, my mother taught me the value of a dollar and that if you don't have the money to buy something, then chances are you don't need it. So, I stayed away from loan money as much as possible and "lived within my means." Because of that, I graduated basically debt free, which gave me a fabulous start to life after college.

A few years later, I decided to return to school to pursue a graduate degree at the Medical College of Virginia at Virginia Commonwealth University. I received a graduate assistantship in the financial aid office that paid for all of my tuition and gave me 20 hours a week of paid work. I found out about this opportunity by simply walking into the financial aid office to ask about applying for aid. Just like my undergraduate career, I was able to secure significant aid directly from the college. I took out a bit more loan money in graduate school, in part because I got married while I was pursuing my degree and my wife was also a student at the time. However, we took out as little as possible, so we graduated with a minimal amount of debt.

The point of my personal story is to say that whatever your circumstances, college can be affordable. Financial aid is typically available if you do the work to find it. Talking with people you know in churches, civic organizations, and high schools is a great way to start your private scholarship search. Taking advantage of free scholarship searches on the Internet can be beneficial by getting people to look for you by simply answering a few questions about your interests and background. Using books like this one to learn about what is available is also a good place to start your research.

I will be the first to admit that if you are someone who needs money to attend college, like I did, it will be a bit more difficult to walk away debt free now. College costs have continued to rise annually at a rate higher than the general rate of inflation. The federal government has not provided a significant increase in grant dollars in several years, and many states have only seen small increases in available grant aid from their own legislative bodies. The fact is, grant aid from government sources are not keeping pace with college costs.

I have spent the better part of my professional career helping students find ways to pay for college, and the good news is that there are still ways to help make college more affordable.

In an ideal world, you have started saving for college early—very early. If you are a student reading this book, then hopefully you started saving for college when you landed your first summer job. If you are a parent, then in a perfect world you started saving for your children's education as soon as they were born. If you are a new parent, welcome your child into the world, hug your spouse, and then head off to see your financial planner or visit a bank to open a college savings plan. Early savings and planning are the best approaches to saving for college. This book will give you some insight into several avenues you can take to start that process.

However, if college is right around the corner and you are just beginning to think about how to pay for it, then your options are a bit more limited. In most cases you will now be dependent on the financial aid you can secure from the federal and state governments, college, and private resources. You have your work cut out for you in making sure all available options are covered, but this is not an insurmountable task. Millions of students each year attend college utilizing solely these avenues to pay for college.

The process of finding aid can be confusing, but there are many college financial aid officers out there who are willing to assist you. Additionally, this book will provide you some insight into sources of funding that you might be able to utilize to pay for college.

The most legwork you will probably have to do is in the realm of private scholarships. There are millions of dollars available from countless resources. If you put enough time and energy into this process, you could come away with

some funds from this effort. I have seen several students enter college with up to a dozen private scholarships that they secured by doing a lot of research and submitting numerous scholarship applications.

When you begin the process of finding private scholarships, it is important to understand that most of the time you will apply for many more scholarships than you will actually receive. The competition can be steep. It is also possible that you will receive no awards, but, remember, you don't have a chance of receiving any unless you apply.

Securing financial aid to help pay for college is only half of the issue when it comes to ensuring that college is affordable. How much you spend is the other half. There are certain required costs that go along with a college education (e.g., tuition and mandatory fees, books, and room and board costs if you live on campus). However, what a student spends above that is determined by individual spending habits, and this is where a lot of students get into trouble. Credit cards, unnecessary loans, poor budgeting skills, and the freedom of being out from under a parent's watchful eye can lead to early financial problems.

I am a big believer in financial literacy for students. Parents, if you have not taught your children money-management skills and how to properly budget, please do so immediately before it is too late. Students, if you have never created a budget, I suggest that you develop the skills to do so before you get into financial trouble.

As a result of the continuing increase in college costs and governmental grant aid not keeping pace with costs, those of us in the financial aid field are seeing an increasing number of students taking out loans to pay for college. It has reached the point where in many cases the loans offered through the federal aid programs are still not enough, so students are going to private sources for what we typically call an "alternative" or "private" loan.

Additionally, colleges are becoming more creative in how they spend institutional dollars, and in many cases are allocating millions more in aid than in prior years to address this issue. In some cases, families are dipping into their savings, even retirement funds, to help pay for college. Congress has provided tax breaks for college costs, authorized 529 Plans to help families save for college, and increased the savings limit for the Coverdell Education Savings Plan to help encourage saving for college, but paying for college can still be challenging for those who are not able to take advantage of these options.

College can be expensive, so don't make it harder on yourself than necessary. Do the research and apply for all sources of federal, state, and institutional aid available. If you learn how to properly manage your money and locate free sources of aid by using tools like this book, you should be able to limit your debt so your postcollege life can be more enjoyable and less of a financial struggle.

Brad Barnett received a bachelor of science degree from Southern Arkansas University, with a major in psychology and a minor in business. He then received a master of science degree in rehabilitation counseling, specializing in mental health, from the Medical College of Virginia at Virginia Commonwealth University. He has *been involved in the financial aid and/or rehabilitation professions for the past 14 years, currently serving as the senior associate director of financial aid and scholarships for James Madison University, Harrisonburg, Virginia. Prior to this, he served as an assistant director of the financial aid office at Virginia Commonwealth University. He was the 2005–06 president of the Virginia Association of Student Financial Aid Administrators. He has served on a variety of association committees and has conducted numerous workshops and presentations on topics such as financial aid and money management for non–financial aid professionals.*

INTRODUCTION

The importance of higher education is increasing, and so is the cost of obtaining it. In the last decade, tuition at public and private four-year colleges has increased by 54 and 37 percent, respectively, according to The College Board. To find the pathway to personal and professional success, students must determine the education they need and find a way to receive and afford that education. College or graduate school costs can seem overwhelming, but don't lose heart. There are ways to find dollars for college. In fact, there are many options. *Ferguson Career Resource Guide to Grants, Scholarships, and Other Financial Resources* is a directory of tools to help you pay for college tuition and related expenses. It features financial assistance resources (scholarships, grants, awards, loans, and other programs), helpful essays, and Web sites and print resources that will help you plan and pay for your college education. This book will help you learn how and where to look for financial aid, and what kinds of aid are available.

Looking for financial aid can seem confusing, but take it one step at a time and you'll soon be an expert. The steps outlined below will get you started.

STEP 1: DETERMINE YOUR FINANCIAL NEED

First, determine whether you actually need financial aid. Use the formula that colleges and funding sources use to determine financial need: the cost of attendance minus the expected family contribution (EFC). The cost of attendance includes the cost of schooling (tuition, fees, books, and supplies) plus living expenses (room and board, travel, and incidental expenses). Every school can supply an estimated average cost of attendance. The expected family contribution (EFC) is based on family income and expense information you provide on the Free Application for Federal Student Aid (FAFSA). Subtract the EFC from the cost of attendance at a particular educational institution to determine what your financial need would be if you attended that school. It is important to note that while all colleges who award federal aid are required to

use the FAFSA and EFC derived from that document to award those funds, some colleges may require additional documents to determine need for institutional aid. For example, several private colleges require students to also complete the College Scholarship Service Profile in addition to the FAFSA.

If the financial need formula shows that you do not need aid, you may have saved yourself a lot of time and work. Even if you do not need financial aid, read the section below on scholarships, grants, and fellowships (financial aid that you do not have to repay). You may qualify for awards based on particular skills or interests.

STEP 2: CONTACT FINANCIAL AID OFFICES

If you determine that you do need financial aid, start looking right away. Finding the many kinds of aid that may be available to you takes time and energy. Starting early can improve your chances of obtaining aid. Get off to a good start by contacting the financial aid offices of the schools you are considering. The financial aid packages different colleges offer you may be a determining factor in your final selection. Each college or university has its own requirements, and failing to learn about them can slow down or jeopardize your financial aid. To learn as much as you can about each school's financial aid process, ask a financial aid officer the following questions:

- What types of financial aid do you offer?
- What are your guidelines for requesting financial aid?
- What application materials do you require?
- What are the deadlines for submitting financial aid requests?
- What effect will my request for financial aid have on my admission?
- Will your school be able to cover my total financial need?

- Will the school cover my financial need for four years?
- When will you notify me of my eligibility for financial aid?
- What other sources of aid should I know about?

Get to know the aid administrators. Tell them about any unusual circumstances or expenses you have. They may be able to help you. Each school has its own procedures and forms, but most (including any school that awards federal aid) of them also use the Free Application for Federal Student Aid. You should also visit the Web sites of colleges and universities to learn more about available financial aid options.

STEP 3: COMPLETE THE FAFSA

The Free Application for Federal Student Aid (FAFSA) is the form you must complete to apply for federal assistance of any kind. Complete the FAFSA first, and complete it as soon after January 1 as possible. Note that you will have to provide tax return information on your FAFSA. While it is ideal to complete your federal and state tax returns before you fill out your FAFSA, do not wait to submit your FAFSA if your parents' tax return is not available; instead, submit estimated tax information with the FAFSA. It is imperative that you meet the priority filing deadlines at your chosen schools so as not to miss out on receiving the best aid package possible. In some cases, missing the priority filing could cost you thousands of dollars in grant assistance. Applications are accepted as of January 1 each year, and the earlier you apply, the better your chances of receiving what you need. If you apply late, you will miss out on aid that has already been awarded. It can take several weeks to process the application.

Experts suggest that students submit the FAFSA whether they think they qualify for aid or not. Many colleges and universities use it in their aid decisions. Some forms of private assistance are only available after you have been rejected for federal aid. The FAFSA form is available in high schools and colleges, by telephone (800-4-FED-AID), and online (http://www.fafsa.ed.gov).

STEP 4: LEARN ABOUT THE TYPES OF FINANCIAL AID

In addition to the excellent resources available in this book, information about student aid is available in the reference section of the library. Look under "financial aid" or "student aid." The Internet also has a wealth of financial aid information. Some helpful Web sites are mentioned at the end of this book. (If you do not have a computer, use one at your local library or school.) All of these resources can help you learn more about the three basic kinds of financial aid:

- Money you don't have to pay back (grants, scholarships, awards, fellowships).
- Money you must pay back (loans).
- Money you earn as you go (military tuition assistance programs, work-study programs, employer tuition reimbursement programs).
- You may need to combine more than one type of financial aid to cover all of the costs of higher education, so learn about, consider, and apply for as many forms of aid as you can.

Money You Do Not Have to Pay Back

First, look for sources of funds you do not have to pay back. They fall into four categories: grants, scholarships, awards, and fellowships.

Grants

Grants are monetary awards that do not have to be repaid. There are three kinds: grants based on financial need, grants based on financial need that also require applicants to meet other non-financially based criterion, and grants that support a specific project.

- **Grants Based on Financial Need.** The federal government sponsors two grants that are based entirely on financial need: the Pell Grant and the Federal Supplemental Educational Opportunity Grant (FSEOG). Both require that applicants submit the FAFSA in order to be considered. To apply for the Pell and FSEOG grants, consult *Funding Education Beyond High School: The Guide to Federal Student Aid* of the U.S. Department of Education. This publication is available for download at http://studentaid.ed.gov/students/publications/student_guide/2006-2007/index.html.
- **Grants Based on Financial Need That Also Require Applicants to Meet Other Non–Financially Based Criterion.** Two new grants were created by the Higher Education Reconciliation Act of 2005: the Academic Competitiveness Grant (for first- and second-year undergraduates) and the National Science and Mathematics

Access to Retain Talent Grant, also known as the National SMART Grant (for third- and fourth-year undergraduates). Students must be Pell Grant-eligible to apply for these new grants, as well as meet other eligibility requirements (such as minimum GPA and interest in a particular field of study. For more information on the Academic Competitiveness Grant and the National Science and Mathematics Access to Retain Talent Grant, visit http://studentaid.ed.gov/PORTALSWebApp/students/english/NewPrograms.jsp.

- Grants That Support a Specific Project. The federal government and other organizations offer funds to support research in specific areas. The sponsor generally requires that applicants submit grant proposals for evaluation. This type of grant is most common in applications for graduate study. Contact the U.S. Department of Education for more information on these grants.

Scholarships

Scholarships are usually short-term monetary awards. Like grants, they do not have to be repaid. Scholarships are offered by a variety of providers. Each scholarship provider sets the criteria for application, which can range from financial need to special hobbies and interests to academic excellence. This is an area in which creative thinking and research can help you find dollars. Think of all of the kinds of scholarships for which you may be eligible.

First, consider your major and minor subjects. Some organizations offer scholarships especially for students who are entering certain fields such as biology, health care, or computer science. Next, think about your hobbies, talents, and interests. Your ability in sports, music, or creative writing, or your interest in the environment or in helping others might help finance your education. Find all of the scholarships for which you might qualify and apply for as many as you can.

Awards

Awards are generally given in recognition of achievement, either to a promising young individual moving up in his or her career field or to an experienced professional for a lifetime of achievement. Many awards include a monetary stipend; others don't grant any money at all but are valuable recognition by one's peers and excellent resume-builders.

Fellowships

Fellowships generally are offered at the graduate, post-graduate, or doctoral level, often for research projects or dissertation assistance.

Money That Must Be Paid Back

Few individuals who need financial aid can put together enough scholarships to pay for school entirely with "free money." Most students also need loans. Whether loans are federal, state, or private, they must be paid back.

The largest sources of student financial aid in the United States are the government's Federal Student Aid Office Programs. They account for 70 percent of all student financial aid. All federal loans require the completion of the FAFSA. The government makes loans to students and to parents. See "Federal Financial Aid Programs and Offices" in Section IV of this book for more information on government loan programs.

Funds are also available from Federal Family Education Loan Program-participating state guaranty agencies, as well as state-sponsored loan programs. To find available educational loans in your home state, log on to the U.S. Department of Education's Web site, http://wdcrobcolp01.ed.gov/Programs/EROD/org_list.cfm?category_cd=SGA, for links to your state's guaranty agency.

Private loans are also available from a wide variety of banks and other financial entities. Major student loan providers include the National Education Loan Network and SallieMae.

For more on loans, read the essay, "Applying for Student Loans" in Part II.

Money That Is Paid While Attending School

Many colleges, universities, and other organizations offer alternate forms of financial aid. Some require students to work to earn the financial aid. Others give students credit on different bases.

Military Service Benefits

Branches of the U.S. military offer a number of tuition assistance programs. See "Military Scholarships" in Part III of this book for more information on tuition assistance programs offered by the Air Force, Army, Coast Guard, Marines, and Navy.

Work-Study Programs

Work-study programs allow you to earn money by working while you go to school. These programs may involve work on or off campus. Work-study programs are available through colleges and universities, private sources, state sources, and the Federal Work-Study Program. Ask financial aid counselors about opportunities at the schools you are considering. For information on the Federal Work-Study Program, see the current edition of *Funding Education Beyond High School: The Guide to Federal Student Aid*, which is published by the U.S. Department of Education.

Employer Tuition Support

If you are working, ask whether your employer has an educational assistance program. Many employers recognize the importance of helping employees advance. An added advantage to employer-provided educational assistance is that up to $5,250 received for courses, both undergraduate and graduate level, is exempt from taxes. Visit the Internal Revenue Service's Web site for additional information (http://www.irs.gov/publications/p970/ch11.html).

HOW TO USE THIS BOOK

Ferguson Career Resource Guide to Grants, Scholarships, and Other Financial Aid Resources is organized to help readers quickly locate resources in their particular interest area, as well as their level of education. The book has four parts: Part I, "Introduction and Overview" (the section you are reading now); Part II, "Essays;" Part III, "Directory;" and Part IV, "Further Resources."

Part II, "Essays," offers thoughtful commentary on key financial aid- and college-related issues. Topics of interest include how to choose a major, how to choose a college, essay-writing tactics for financial aid and admissions essays, savings plans for colleges, military scholarships, work-study options, athletic scholarships, student loan programs, and financial aid options for students with disabilities. In addition, a financial aid planning timeline and a college planning timeline are also included in this section.

Part III, "Directory," is the largest section of the book. It features thousands of financial aid resources in its three main subsections: "Financial Aid by Major," "Student Profile–Based Financial Aid," and "Other Types of Financial Aid."

The "Financial Aid by Major" section is further organized into federal and state financial aid resources, financial aid resources by major field of study [business, education, engineering/computer science/mathematics, media arts, medicine/health care, open to all majors, performing arts, science, social sciences, visual arts/design, and vocational education. Each section is divided into aid for undergraduate education, followed by aid for graduate education.

The "Student Profile–Based Financial Aid" section features specialized undergraduate and graduate financial aid resources for dependents of veterans; lesbian, gay, bisexual, and transgender students; minorities; people with disabilities; theological studies and students of specific religious denominations; United Negro College Fund scholarships; and women.

"Other Types of Financial Aid" provides information on aid from a variety of sources, such as athletic scholarships, early awareness programs, military scholarships, and study abroad programs.

Each entry in the Directory section of this book is organized in the following manner: name of organization, street address, telephone number (if available), e-mail address (if available), URL (if available), and descriptive overview of financial aid offered by the organization.

The descriptive overview of financial aid offered by the organization features the following components to help you learn more about each award:

- **Scholarship Name**
- **Academic Area.** This section lists the major field of study that is required to be eligible for the award. More than 250 majors are listed in this book. (For a complete list of majors, see the end of this article.) Note: some financial aid is available to students pursuing majors in any field. In this instance, the word "open" is used to denote that students in any major may apply for the award.
- **Age Group.** This section tells you the academic level at which the funds can be used. For example, financial aid classified under "undergraduate students" must be used for undergraduate study, although it is important to note that this designation does not exclude high school students (in certain cases) from applying for the funds; it just means that the funds can only be used at the undergraduate level. Aid classified under "graduate students" or "medical students" must be used at these respective academic levels.
- **Eligibility.** This section details the requirements necessary to be considered for funds. Criteria include grade level (high school seniors, college sophomores, graduate students, etc), grade point average, ACT/SAT scores, U.S. citizenship,

residence in a particular state, minority status, disability status, and extracurricular activities. Some organizations have very specific eligibility requirements, others just a few. To ensure that you are eligible for a specific award, it is always a good idea to contact the organization providing the award for complete requirements.

- **Application Process.** This section tells you how to apply for the funds, whether it be by completing the Free Application for Federal Student Aid, downloading a scholarship application at an association's Web site, submitting an audition tape, or contacting a scholarship coordinator for details. In addition, this section provides (when available) a list of other materials that you may be required to submit with your application, such as academic transcripts, ACT/SAT scores, letters of recommendation, proof of enrollment or acceptance at a college or university, samples of artwork, birth certificate, essays, financial documents, resume, curriculum vita, and so on.

- **Amount.** This section details the dollar amount of the award. It is important to keep in mind that award lengths vary. Some financial aid is available only for one year, while other awards may be renewed annually for up to four or five years if the recipient meets renewal requirements. Unless otherwise stipulated, this section lists award amounts for one-time use or one year of academic study. Contact the award provider to learn if the award you are interested in is available for more than one year and the renewal requirements. It is important to note that dollar amounts may also vary based on the availability of funding. Be sure to contact the award provider for current award amounts.

- **Deadline.** This section lists, when available, the deadline for submitting your application and all supporting documents. It is important to keep in mind that deadlines change year to year and some types of financial aid do not have deadlines. Contact the award provider for the latest information on deadlines.

Part IV: Further Resources includes detailed listings of federal and state financial aid programs and offices; helpful books, magazines, and Web sites about financial aid and college planning; and three indexes: geographic location, academic major, organization name.

MAJORS

The following is a complete of the majors covered by the financial aid resources listed in this book. Following each major in parentheses is the name of the section in Part III in which you can find financial aid resources related to your major of interest. Also refer to the majors index to at the end of this book to find the exact page numbers for specific financial aid listings.

(Business)
Actuarial science (Business)
Advertising (Business)
Aerospace (Engineering/Computer Science/Mathematics)
African American studies (Social Sciences)
Agricultural economics (Science)
Agriculture (Science)
Agronomy (Science)
Anthropology (Social Sciences)
Aquaculture (Vocational Education)
Archaeology (Social Sciences)
Architecture (Engineering/Computer Science/ Mathematics)
Assessment (Social Sciences)
Astronomy (Science)
Athletics (administration) (Athletics)
Athletics (equipment management) (Athletics)
Athletics (journalism) (Athletics)
Athletics (open) (Athletics)
Athletics (training) (Athletics)
Athletics (turfgrass science) (Athletics)
Automation (Vocational Education)
Automotive (Vocational Education)
Aviation (Vocational Education)
Aviation (maintenance) (Vocational Education)
Behavioral sciences (Social Sciences)
Biochemistry (Science)
Bioinformatics (Science)
Biology (Science)
Biophysics (Science)
Broadcasting (Media Arts)
Business (open) (Business)
Business administration (Business)
Chemistry (Science)
Classical studies (Social Sciences)
Communications science (Media Arts)
Computer science (Engineering/Computer Science/ Mathematics)
Construction trades (Vocational Education)
Cosmetology (Vocational Education)
Counseling (Social Sciences)

Court reporting (Vocational Education)
Criminal justice (Social Sciences)
Culinary arts (Vocational Education)
Disability services (Social Sciences)
Disability studies (Social Sciences)
Earth science (Science)
Economics (Social Sciences)
Education (Education)
Electrical energy (Engineering/Computer Science/
    Mathematics)
Engineering (aerospace/aviation) (Engineering/Computer Science/Mathematics)
Engineering (agricultural) (Engineering/Computer Science/Mathematics)
Engineering (architectural) (Engineering/Computer Science/Mathematics)
Engineering (audio) (Engineering/Computer Science/Mathematics)
Engineering (automotive) (Engineering/Computer Science/Mathematics)
Engineering (biological) (Engineering/Computer Science/Mathematics)
Engineering (chemical) (Engineering/Computer Science/Mathematics)
Engineering (civil) (Engineering/Computer Science/Mathematics)
Engineering (computer) (Engineering/Computer Science/Mathematics)
Engineering (construction) (Engineering/Computer Science/Mathematics)
Engineering (cost) (Engineering/Computer Science/Mathematics)
Engineering (electrical) (Engineering/Computer Science/Mathematics)
Engineering (fire protection) (Engineering/Computer Science/Mathematics)
Engineering (geological) (Engineering/Computer Science/Mathematics)
Engineering (industrial) (Engineering/Computer Science/Mathematics)
Engineering (manufacturing) (Engineering/Computer Science/Mathematics)
Engineering (marine) (Engineering/Computer Science/Mathematics)
Engineering (materials science) (Engineering/Computer Science/Mathematics)
Engineering (mechanical) (Engineering/Computer Science/Mathematics)
Engineering (mining) (Engineering/Computer Science/Mathematics)

Engineering (nondestructive testing) (Engineering/Computer Science/Mathematics)
Engineering (nuclear) (Engineering/Computer Science/Mathematics)
Engineering (ocean) (Engineering/Computer Science/Mathematics)
Engineering (open) (Engineering/Computer Science/Mathematics)
Engineering (optical) (Engineering/Computer Science/Mathematics)
Engineering (petroleum) (Engineering/Computer Science/Mathematics)
Engineering (plastics) (Engineering/Computer Science/Mathematics)
Engineering (safety) (Engineering/Computer Science/Mathematics)
Engineering (structural) (Engineering/Computer Science/Mathematics)
Engineering (transportation) (Engineering/Computer Science/Mathematics)
Engineering (water supply and treatment) (Engineering/Computer Science/Mathematics)
Engineering technology (Engineering/Computer Science/Mathematics)
English/literature (Social Sciences)
Enology and viticulture (Vocational Education)
Entomology (Science)
Entrepreneurism (Business)
Environmental science (Science)
Equestrian studies (Vocational Education)
Ethnic studies (Social Sciences)
Family and consumer science (Vocational Education)
Fashion (Visual Arts/Design)
Film/television (Performing Arts)
Finance (Business)
Fire science (Vocational Education)
Food sciences (Science)
Foreign languages (Social Sciences)
French studies (Social Sciences)
Funeral services (Vocational Education)
Geochemistry (Science)
Geography (Social Sciences)
Geology (Science)
Geophysics (Science)
Geosciences (Science)
Golf course management (Athletics)
Government (Social Sciences)
Graphic design (Visual Arts/Design)
Greek studies (Social Sciences)
History (Social Sciences)

Horticulture (Vocational Education)
Hospitality (Vocational Education)
Human resources (Business)
Humanities (Social Sciences)
Hydrology (Science)
Illustration (Visual Arts/Design)
Industrial hygiene (Vocational Education)
Industrial technology (Vocational Education)
Information technology (Engineering/Computer Science/Mathematics)
Insurance (Business)
Interior design (Visual Arts/Design)
International studies (Social Sciences)
Islamic studies (Social Sciences)
Italian studies (Social Sciences)
Jewelry design (Visual Arts/Design)
Journalism (Media Arts)
Labor relation (Social Sciences)
Landscape architecture (Visual Arts/Design)
Law (Social Sciences)
Library science (Social Sciences)
Life sciences (Science)
Linguistics (Social Sciences)
Management (Business)
Management (Business)
Marine sciences (Science)
Mathematics (Engineering/Computer Science/Mathematics)
Media arts (Media Arts)
Medicine (audiology) (Medicine/Health Care)
Medicine (biomedical sciences) (Medicine/Health Care)
Medicine (chiropractic) (Medicine/Health Care)
Medicine (clinical laboratory science) (Medicine/Health Care)
Medicine (dental assisting) (Medicine/Health Care)
Medicine (dental hygiene) (Medicine/Health Care)
Medicine (dentistry) (Medicine/Health Care)
Medicine (education) (Medicine/Health Care)
Medicine (endocrinology) (Medicine/Health Care)
Medicine (gastroenterology and nutrition) (Medicine/Health Care)
Medicine (health physics) (Medicine/Health Care)
Medicine (information management) (Medicine/Health Care)
Medicine (kinesiology) (Medicine/Health Care)
Medicine (laboratory science) (Medicine/Health Care)
Medicine (management) (Medicine/Health Care)
Medicine (medical technology) (Medicine/Health Care)
Medicine (mental health) (Medicine/Health Care)
Medicine (neuroscience) (Medicine/Health Care)

Medicine (open) (Medicine/Health Care)
Medicine (optometry) (Medicine/Health Care)
Medicine (orthotics and prosthetics) (Medicine/Health Care)
Medicine (pedorthics) (Medicine/Health Care)
Medicine (phlebotomy) (Medicine/Health Care)
Medicine (physician assisting) (Medicine/Health Care)
Medicine (physician) (Medicine/Health Care)
Medicine (podiatry) (Medicine/Health Care)
Medicine (psychiatry) (Medicine/Health Care)
Medicine (radiological science) (Medicine/Health Care)
Medicine (research) (Medicine/Health Care)
Medicine (school health) (Medicine/Health Care)
Medicine (sonography) (Medicine/Health Care)
Medicine (surgery) (Medicine/Health Care)
Medicine (veterinary and medical technology) (Medicine/Health Care)
Medicine (veterinary) (Medicine/Health Care)
Meteorology (Science)
Microbiology (Science)
Military
Mortuary science (Vocational Education)
Native American studies (Social Sciences)
Natural resources (Science)
Naval sciences (Engineering/Computer Science/Mathematics)
Nuclear science (Engineering/Computer Science/Mathematics)
Nursing (anesthesia) (Medicine/Health Care)
Nursing (assisted living) (Medicine/Health Care)
Nursing (critical care) (Medicine/Health Care)
Nursing (developmental disabilities) (Medicine/Health Care)
Nursing (education) (Medicine/Health Care)
Nursing (emergency care) (Medicine/Health Care)
Nursing (gerontology) (Medicine/Health Care)
Nursing (holistic) (Medicine/Health Care)
Nursing (licensed practical nursing) (Medicine/Health Care)
Nursing (midwifery) (Medicine/Health Care)
Nursing (neonatal) (Medicine/Health Care)
Nursing (nephrology) (Medicine/Health Care)
Nursing (neuroscience) (Medicine/Health Care)
Nursing (nurse practitioner) (Medicine/Health Care)
Nursing (oncology) (Medicine/Health Care)
Nursing (open) (Medicine/Health Care)
Nursing (psychiatric) (Medicine/Health Care)
Nursing (rehabilitation) (Medicine/Health Care)
Nursing (school) (Medicine/Health Care)

Nursing (substance abuse and mental health) (Medicine/Health Care)
Nursing (surgical) (Medicine/Health Care)
Nursing (women's health) (Medicine/Health Care)
Occupational health and safety (Vocational Education)
Oceanography (Science)
Open
Parapsychology (Social Sciences)
Performing Arts (choreography) (Performing Arts)
Performing Arts (dance) (Performing Arts)
Performing Arts (music-classical) (Performing Arts)
Performing Arts (music-composition) (Performing Arts)
Performing Arts (music-directing) (Performing Arts)
Performing Arts (music-open) (Performing Arts)
Performing Arts (music-instrumental) (Performing Arts)
Performing Arts (music-religious) (Performing Arts)
Performing Arts (open) (Performing Arts)
Performing Arts (theatre) (Performing Arts)
Performing Arts (voice) (Performing Arts)
Pharmaceutical sciences (Medicine/Health Care)
Philosophy (Social Sciences)
Photography (Visual Arts/Design)
Photojournalism (Media Arts)
Physical education (Education)
Physical sciences (Science)
Physics (Science)
Physiology (Medicine/Health Care)
Planning (Social Sciences)
Political science (Social Sciences)
Printing (Vocational Education)
Psychology (Social Sciences)
Public health (Medicine/Health Care)
Public policy (Social Sciences)
Public relations (Business)
Publishing (Media Arts)
Pulp and paper (Vocational Education)
Railroad sciences (Vocational Education)

Range management (Science)
Real estate (Vocational Education)
Rehabilitation (Medicine/Health Care)
Religion (Social Sciences)
Risk management (Business)
Satellite technology (Engineering/Computer Science/Mathematics)
Science (open) (Science)
Scuba (Vocational Education)
Social sciences (open) (Social Sciences)
Social work (Social Sciences)
Sociology (Social Sciences)
Special education (Education)
Speech pathology (Medicine/Health Care)
Sports turf administration (Athletics)
Statistics (Engineering/Computer Science/Mathematics)
Surveying (Vocational Education)
Technology (Engineering/Computer Science/Mathematics)
Therapy (art) (Medicine/Health Care)
Therapy (horticulture) (Medicine/Health Care)
Therapy (music) (Medicine/Health Care)
Therapy (occupational) (Medicine/Health Care)
Therapy (physical) (Medicine/Health Care)
Transportation (Vocational Education)
Visual arts (ceramics) (Visual Arts/Design)
Visual arts (crafts) (Visual Arts/Design)
Visual arts (folk art) (Visual Arts/Design)
Visual arts (history) (Visual Arts/Design)
Visual arts (open) (Visual Arts/Design)
Visual arts (painting) (Visual Arts/Design)
Visual arts (photography) (Visual Arts/Design)
Visual arts (sculpting) (Visual Arts/Design)
Vocational education (Vocational Education)
Wellness (strength and conditioning) (Vocational Education)
Welsh studies (Social Sciences)
Women's studies (Social Sciences)
Writing (Social Sciences)

PART II
ESSAYS

COLLEGE PLANNING TIMELINE

Now that you've made the decision to attend college, don't sit back and wait until the end of your high school career to put this goal into motion. There are many things you can do right now to prepare for college. Use the following timeline of suggested activities, objectives, and strategies to help you turn your dream of a college education into a reality.

FRESHMAN YEAR

- Take a college preparatory curriculum that includes plenty of writing classes. Also, take a language class, as many colleges require their incoming freshman to have a certain number of language credits.
- Get good grades. This will ensure you a spot in your school's honor roll as well as a higher class rank—college admission departments view both favorably.
- Get involved in extracurricular activities. Join a school club or sports team, or run for student government. Not only will this provide you an avenue for meeting new friends, but you'll also prove to college admissions officers that you were able to successfully balance academics with outside interests.
- Get to know your school counselor. Review your class schedule, and decide which classes to take next semester. Inform your counselor of your plans to attend college.
- Start thinking about careers that might interest you. Sign up for a job-shadowing program to learn more about a specific career. You can also learn more about career options by visiting the U.S. Department of Labor Web site, http://www.bls.gov/oco.
- Interested in attending a state school? A community college? A private college? A religious institution? Determine what you want and don't want from your college experience and begin assembling a list of colleges that match your criteria. Visit CollegeBoard's Web site, http://apps.collegeboard.com/search/index.jsp, to search for colleges by area, size, or other affiliation.
- Read, read, read! You'll increase your vocabulary and thank yourself you did come SAT or ACT time. Visit the American Library Association's Web site (http://www.ala.org/ala/librariesandyou/recomreading/recomreading.htm) for a sample of suggested reading lists appropriate for your grade level.
- Start saving money for college. You may still be too young to hold a part-time job, but you can start adding to your college fund with money earned from babysitting, doing household chores, and from allowance and gifts. Show your parents you are serious about helping fulfill your college dream.
- Start building your extracurricular background as a means to make yourself well rounded when it comes to applying to colleges and seeking financial aid. For example, if you hope to win an athletic scholarship, now is a good time to join a school sport. Enroll in art or dance classes if you hope to win a performance arts scholarship. In addition, community service always looks good to admissions and financial aid officials.

SOPHOMORE YEAR

Fall

- At the beginning of the school year, ask your guidance counselor to provide you with registration information and testing dates for the PLAN (http://www.act.org/plan) and PSAT (http://www.collegeboard.com/student/testing/psat/about.

html). These tests will help you prepare for the ACT and SAT, respectively—college entrance tests that are used by colleges and universities to gauge admission.

- Ask your guidance counselor to review your class schedule and suggest any necessary classes for next semester.
- Enroll in Advanced Placement (AP) classes if you are eligible to do so. AP classes are beneficial for two reasons: they provide the chance for a higher grade point average, and possible college credit. For more information on AP classes, visit http://apcentral.collegeboard.com.
- Get a part-time job or volunteer—both are great ways to earn community service points and make valuable contacts.
- Around December, you should receive your PLAN and/or PSAT scores. Meet with your counselor to review your scores, and explore ways to improve on them.
- Discuss college costs with your family. Are they able to help financially? Have they enrolled in a college savings plan?

Winter

- Begin researching colleges by attending college fairs, surfing the Internet, and by word of mouth. Keep yourself organized by starting a filing system for each college's brochure. Visit the Web site of the National Association for College Admission Counseling (http://www.nacacnet.org) for a list of college fairs near you.
- Keep a file to record your talents. Athletes should keep newspaper clippings of game reviews, artists should have a portfolio of their work, and writers should keep a file of their published work.
- Register for SAT Subject Tests. Subjects Tests center on different academic subjects such as math, English, foreign language, and sciences such as biology and chemistry. Colleges use the Subject Tests as another factor in admissions and to advise students about course selection. Testing dates and subjects vary, so be sure to check with your school's guidance office for the latest dates and testing centers. Visit http://www.collegeboard.com/student/testing/sat/about/SATII.html for more information.

Summer

- Read, read, read!
- Sign up for summer classes that cover subjects that you find particularly challenging. Many community colleges offer classes to high school students who need to hone certain skills, such as math or writing.
- Visit your local library to access reference books and study guides that will help you prepare for college entrance exams.

JUNIOR YEAR

Fall

- Develop a short list of schools that you would like to attend. Discuss the list, as well as your intended major of study and future career goals, with your counselor. Can your counselor recommend any specific colleges to help you achieve these goals? (Perhaps a well-known art school, a top journalism program, or a college known for its excellent faculty and internship program in your field of study.) Also, have your counselor review the classes you plan on taking this year. Make sure you are on target academically.
- If you are eligible for Advanced Placement (http://apcentral.collegeboard.com) classes, take them to boost your GPA, impress college admission departments, and hopefully, earn some college credit!
- Attend college fairs and financial aid information meetings, which are usually scheduled at this time of the year. Many times you can meet with college representatives who can provide more information on admission requirements and available financial aid. Visit http://www.nacacnet.org for a list of college fairs in your area.
- Beware of financial aid information meetings that are not conducted by college financial aid administrators or high schools. Some companies host these fairs and advertise them as "free," but then ask for payment to secure their services for additional assistance in getting through the financial aid process. In most cases, you can get all of the information about financial aid that you need free from a college financial aid officer or high school guidance

office. Spending money for this type of assistance is generally not necessary.

- Begin researching the ins and outs of financial aid. Become familiar with the different types of loans, scholarships, and other forms of financial funding. The *Student Guide,* which provides an overview of financial aid from the federal government, is a great place to start. You can download a copy by visiting http://studentaid.ed.gov/students/publications/student_guide/index.html, or order a print copy by calling 800-433-3243.
- Continue researching all possible scholarships. You can use a scholarship search engine such as the one provided by CollegeNET.com (http://www.collegenet.com/about/index_html), or ask your guidance counselor to direct you to scholarships for which you may be qualified. You should also discuss financial aid with your family. Do your parents' employers or any organizations they support offer scholarships or other financial aid? (Your parents can check with their company benefits office or the organizational headquarters regarding possible sources of college funding.) (Note: In most cases, it is a good idea to steer clear of fee-based scholarship services. A wealth of free information on financial aid is available on the Internet, through professional associations and colleges and universities, through your guidance counselors, and at the library. Beware of fee-based scholarship services that do not provide what they promise, as well as other scholarship scams as you conduct your research. Visit http://www.ftc.gov/bcp/conline/edcams/scholarship and http://www.finaid.org/scholarships/scams.phtml for more information on how to avoid scholarship scams.)
- Stay focused on your studies.
- Stay involved with your extracurricular activities.

Winter

- Register for the SAT (http://www.collegeboard.com) and/or the ACT (http://www.act.org). These exams are offered throughout the school year. Make sure to allow enough time to properly study for them. If you are unsure about how well you are prepared for these exams, you may want to enroll for a review course offered by many organizations nationwide.

Such courses will identify your weak subjects, review trouble areas, and offer practice exams. One major test-preparation organization is Kaplan, Inc. Visit its Web site, http://www.kaplan.com, for more information.

Spring

- Use this time wisely by scheduling campus visits to colleges that you'd like to attend. Call ahead and arrange for an on-campus tour, where you can sit in on a class, stay in a dorm, tour libraries and other facilities, and meet financial aid and admissions officials. Don't forget to tour the campus neighborhood—can you see yourself living here for the next four years?
- Athletes planning to play sports at National Collegiate Athletic Association (NCAA)-affiliated colleges should check with the association regarding adding their name to the NCAA Initial-Eligibility Clearinghouse, which makes student-athletes' grades and games statistics known to colleges throughout the United States. Visit http://www.ncaaclearinghouse.net/ncaa/NCAA/general/index_general.html for more information.
- Continue to narrow your list of colleges. Visit CollegeBoard's Web site, http://apps.collegeboard.com/search/index.jsp, to search for colleges by area, size, or other affiliation.

Summer

- Get a summer job. It's a great way to save money for college and gain practical work experience as well. If you plan on becoming a nurse, perhaps you can get a part-time job working in a hospital or nursing home. If you want to be a lawyer, you can work as a clerk at a law office. You get the idea.
- Arrange tours of colleges on your list that you have not yet visited.
- Investigate military options as a way to fund your college education.
- You may want to take a writing workshop to hone your college application essay-writing skills. Check to see if your local community college, park district, or library offers such courses.

Teen Ink.com posts college essays written by students all over the United States at its Web site, http://teenink.com/College/Essays.html. Read them to get inspiration for your own work. You may also want to visit the Web sites of colleges you are considering—they often post the best essays of the past year.

SENIOR YEAR

Be prepared for a busy year! Not only will you have to stay on top of your class work and exams, but you'll be overwhelmed with the details, paperwork, and deadlines of getting your college applications and financial aid forms turned in on time. Are you ready?

Fall

- Inform your counselor of your final college choices. Make a checklist of what each college needs—transcripts, application, letters of recommendation, essays, etc.—in order to process your application.
- Contact schools directly to request their applications. Does the college accept the Common Application (which allows you to apply to nearly 300 colleges with one application)? If so, log on to http://www.commonapp.org to download a copy. Note deadlines for each school, as well as special documents needed for the Common Application.
- Obtain a copy of your official school transcripts. Review and make any necessary corrections.
- Register for the SAT (http://www.collegeboard. com) and/or the ACT (http://www.act.org) exams, if necessary.
- Aspiring college athletes should begin to send out athletic packages containing game tapes, clippings, statistics, and a schedule of upcoming home games to college coaches.
- Ask your teachers, employers, or coaches for letters of recommendation. Give them plenty of time (at least three weeks) to write their letters.
- Begin writing your application essays.

Late Fall/Winter

- Submit completed applications for consideration for early admission.

- Meet with your family to discuss the Free Application for Federal Student Aid (FAFSA) process. Organize all of the financial information that you will need to submit with the application. You may want to ask your parents to file their income tax from the past year as soon as possible. Visit http://www.fafsa.ed.gov for more information.
- Submit any remaining college applications before winter break

January

- Submit your completed FAFSA as soon after January 1 as possible.
- Register for the SAT Subject Tests (http://www. collegeboard.com/student/testing/sat/about/ SATII.html), if necessary.
- Meet with your counselor regarding possible scholarships and other financial aid possibilities.
- Keep tabs on your applications. Send additional information, if necessary.
- Monitor the status of your FAFSA and Student Aid Report (SAR). The SAR should be available within a month following your FAFSA submission. Use your PIN to access your FAFSA information. Contact the Federal Student Aid Information Center at 800-433-3243 if you have any questions.
- Continue to research possible scholarships. Complete all scholarship applications.
- Study! Study! Study! It may be tempting to sit back and coast the rest of your senior year, but colleges will monitor any sudden changes in your grades.

Spring

- Wait for letters of college acceptance.
- Wait for letters announcing your scholarship and grant awards. Continue to apply for scholarships that have later deadlines.
- Review the financial aid package and award offers you receive. The amount of financial assistance you receive from each college and government sources should factor into your final college choice.
- Many schools mandate May 1 as the final day to accept an offer of admission. Complete any paperwork that may be needed to finalize your

acceptance. Make your first school deposit at this time, if necessary.

- Notify other schools of your choice.
- Some students are accepted by colleges on a probationary basis. If this is the case for you, speak with an admissions representative from your college to learn what criteria must be met before the start of the school year. It could be as simple as keeping up your GPA or taking classes during the summer to boost your knowledge of a particular subject.
- Finalize receipt of scholarships, grants, and other sources of financial aid.
- Be aware of the final tuition amount, including fees, housing costs, books, etc. Take advantage of a school payment plan, if available.
- Graduate from high school!

Summer

- Complete information needed to apply for housing, roommate assignment, and school orientation.
- Get to know your roommate via e-mail or a phone call.
- Work part time to save money for college expenses.
- Enjoy your last summer before starting college!
- Start making a list of things you will need to take to school.
- Start packing.
- Head to college! Good luck, have fun, and continue to work hard in your studies.

FINANCIAL PLANNING FOR YOUR COLLEGE EDUCATION: A HIGH SCHOOL TIMELINE

As a high school freshman or sophomore, you may think it is too early to begin planning how to finance your college education. But as college tuition continues to increase rapidly and competition for financial aid grows, it is important that you treat your financial education (learning about college costs, types of financial aid available, etc.) as importantly as you view your academic studies. In short, the sooner you start preparing for the financial demands of college, the better off you will be. This essay provides useful tips on the steps you should be taking during each year of high school.

FRESHMAN YEAR
Research Average College Costs

Even though you still have your entire high school career ahead of you, it's never too early to consider college. It's a good idea to start considering whether you want to attend a state university or private school and, if you plan to attend a state school, whether you will be attending a school in your state or one that is located in another state. The type of school that you attend, as well as its location, will be key factors in determining financial costs for you and your family. For example, The College Board reports that tuition at four-year private colleges was $21,235 in 2005–06, as compared to $5,491 at four-year public colleges. This may encourage you to attend a public school to save money on tuition. But if you attend a public school that is not in your state of residence, you will be charged higher tuition than a student who actually lives in that state. For example, tuition for Illinois residents who attend the University of Illinois was only $3,521 per semester in 2005–06, but was a whopping $10,564 per semester for students who resided out of state.

This is not to say you should only consider attending public institutions within your state. Rather, you should have a complete picture when planning your financial strategy. If you already have some schools in mind, visit their Web sites or contact their admission offices for more information. Many Web sites provide information on college costs; check out Section IV of this book for an annotated list of financial aid Web sites. Besides the Internet, other research tools that you can use include your school's guidance office, college fairs, and the experiences of friends and family.

DETERMINE YOUR FAMILY'S FINANCIAL STATUS

Now is the time to discuss your college plans with your parents. Let them know you are aware of the benefits of a college education, and are determined to pursue a degree. Ask your parents the following questions:

- Will they be able to help you pay for college?
- Have they invested in a college fund such as a State 529 savings plan, pre-paid tuition plan, Coverdell Education Saving Account, or the Roth IRA? Visit http://www.savingforcollege.com or http://www.collegesavings.org for more information on these common, college savings options.
- Are your parents willing to take out a loan to help with your college expenses?

Duly informed, you will have a clearer picture of your true financial status. Keep in mind your parents' amount of help may be limited, especially if you have siblings already enrolled in college or who will soon be college bound.

SOPHOMORE YEAR
Start Saving for College by Getting a Part-Time Job

One great way to start saving for your college education is by getting a part-time job. How much will you earn watching television or hanging out with friends after school or on the weekends? Zero dollars. Part-time employment will not only add to your college savings, it will teach you the valuable lesson of budgeting your time efficiently. It also looks good on a college application. Many employers will work around a student's school schedule, or give preference for weekend hours. Look for employment in areas you enjoy—caddying at a golf course, retail work at a store you frequent, or hosting at an eatery frequented by students. If you find work you enjoy, chances are you will view it as a positive experience, rather than a chore. However, if you worry about making good grades with a tough class load this year, you may want to consider summer employment instead.

Take Advanced Placement (AP) Classes

Are you eligible for AP classes? If so, you would be wise to take them. They may have a tougher curriculum and require higher expectations, but AP classes in math, English, history, language, or science have a double bonus: they can earn you a point higher for your total grade point average, and potential class exemption in college.

Learn More about Financial Aid Options and Scholarships

According to the American Council of Education, more than 8 million college students receive some form of financial aid annually. Use the Internet to familiarize yourself with the difference between subsidized and unsubsidized loans or school-based and private scholarships. Check out http://www.collegeanswer.com/paying/scholarship_search/pay_scholarship_search.jsp for free access to a nationwide award database sponsored by College Answer and Scholarship Experts.

JUNIOR YEAR
Begin Aggressively Researching Applicable Scholarships and Financial Aid

Most students add to their total amount of college money with federal loans and grants, but funding can also be gained through scholarship awards. The key is finding them. Where are the scholarship dollars? The largest amounts come from the schools themselves. Start researching scholarships suited to your financial needs, talents, or academic standing at any of the colleges you are considering. Some schools also award scholarships within a particular college or specific major. If you know which school you plan to attend, inquire with the school's financial aid department, or log onto the school's Web site for scholarship details such as eligibility, application procedures, deadlines, and other requirements.

Begin Close to Home

Ask you guidance counselor for help in researching scholarships earmarked for residents of your local town, county, or state. Does your village board reward students with good grades and exemplary citizenship? Does your particular state have scholarships or grants set aside for their residents? The state of Delaware, for instance, has many incentives and financial assistance programs available only to students residing in state. Visit http://www.doe.state.de.us/high-ed/scholarships.htm to see this state's offerings. Contact your state's education department to learn more about special offers to residents. Your local library should also hold a wealth of information regarding scholarships and other forms of state-funded financial aid.

There are also numerous national competitions from corporate sponsors, such as the Xerox Corporation (offers combination scholarship and internship, http://www.xerox.com), the Walt Disney Company Foundation (scholarship, plus incidental allowance, http://www.ja.org/programs/programs_schol_dis.shtml) and Wal-Mart Stores, Inc. (public and employee scholarships, http://www.walmartfoundation.org/wmstore/goodworks/scripts/index.jsp). Do a scholarship search on the Internet for a participating list of businesses, and all details on each program. Also visit http://www.nationalmerit.org/sponsorship.php for more details on National Merit Scholarships sponsored by more than 300 businesses, corporations, and company foundations.

Don't forget scholarships awarded to members of certain organizations such as social and religious groups, unions, professional and special interest groups, as well as the military. Depending on the scholarship, recipients or their parent should have membership in the organization. The Knights of Columbus, for example, offers an annual scholarship for members with intent to study at a Catholic college or university. (http://www.kofc.org/members/scholarships/index.cfm)

Many employers have special scholarships designated to employees or children of employees. Your parents should inquire with the human resource department or company Web site to gather more details. Your current part-time job could also be a source for additional college money. Many employers have scholarships for outstanding student employees, such as McDonald's Corporation. They designate an annual $1,000 scholarship for its college-bound employees per state, in addition to a national McScholar of the Year award worth $5,000. (http://www.mcdonalds.com/usa/good/people/scholarship.html)

It's important to note that not all scholarships are academic in nature. Others stress community service, athletic or artistic ability, or ethnic pride. One example is the United Negro College Fund (UNCF). The oldest minority assistance organization in the nation, the UNCF provides financial and technical assistance to deserving minorities, as well as operating support to 39 historically black colleges and universities in the United States. For more information, visit http://www.uncf.org. Still other scholarships are based on future career aspirations, or living with a disability. The site, http://www.heath.gwu.edu, for example, provides information and links to disability-related scholarships.

Become Familiar with Available Grants and Student Loans at Both the State and Federal Level

According to the U.S. Department of Education, more than $67 billion dollars are disbursed annually to students in the form of loans, grants, and other campus-based aid. Visit http://www.studentaid.ed.gov for more information. Here is a quick summary of available federal aid:

Federal Pell Grants
Eligibility: financial need
Maximum amount: $4,050
Other details: Students do not repay grants; amount of grant money will depend on cost of school and student's status

Federal Student Loans (Subsidized, Unsubsidized, PLUS programs)
Eligibility: Subsidized loans are financially based. Unsubsidized loans are offered to all. PLUS loans are offered to parents of dependent college students.
Maximum amount: Varies according to financial need and status
Other details: Payment schedules and interest rates vary for each loan

Campus-Based Aid Programs (Federal Supplemental Educational Opportunity Grant, Work-Study, and Perkins)
Eligibility: financial need, will vary depending on total amount of aid student receives.

Should You Invest in the Services of a Professional Financial Aid Consultant?

Such consultants offer their services, for a fee, to search for scholarships that fit your needs. Some even offer to act as mediators between the applicant and awarding organiza-tion. Save your money. Your high school guidance counselor, members of the college admission and financial aid departments, and your parents can do the job—for free. Besides, it's doubtful school officials and foundation organizers would be willing to discuss such sensitive information with anyone other than the student.

SENIOR YEAR
Complete the Free Application for Federal Student Aid (FAFSA)

The Free Application for Federal Student Aid (FAFSA) serves as a common application for all federally funded financial assistance. Many states and schools also use the FAFSA as part of their non-federal aid programs. The late fall months are a good time to tackle the FAFSA. Though the final deadline for the school year falls in the summer (actual dates will vary from year to year), the earlier you turn in a completed FAFSA the better, as funding is given out on a first-come, first-served basis. Attempt to file soon after January 1 of the year for which you are requesting aid. (Note: Any applications sent to the U.S. Department of Education before January 1 will be considered ineligible) Applications are still accepted via mail, but file electronically if possible. To do so, you will need a personal identification number, or PIN, which will enable you to track your application status, and will serve as an electronic signature. Your PIN is necessary to electronically apply for any type of financial aid and to check on the status of paper claims. Log on to http://www.pin.ed.gov/PINWebApp/appinstr.jsp to apply for your PIN online. You will receive e-mail notification of your number in about four hours, as opposed to seven to 10 days via regular mail.

You must also be aware of these other FAFSA steps:

- You'll need to assemble important information about yourself and your family such as Social Security numbers, a copy of your driver's license, income tax records, bank statements, and investment records. If you are not a U.S. citizen, you will also need a copy of your alien registration record or permanent resident card. Males who have reached the age of 18 must also provide proof of Selective Service registration.
- A completed FAFSA application can be sent electronically or in paper format. Note: An electronic submission can be processed seven to 10 days faster than a hard copy submission.
- Once your FAFSA is processed, you will receive a Student Aid Report (SAR). The SAR calcu-

lates the amount the government believes your family will be able to contribute to your education—this is your Expected Family Contribution (EFC). The SAR is also automatically sent to the schools you indicated as your top choices. (You are given a choice of up to six schools to receive your SAR. You can, however, indicate more schools to receive your information for processing. Refer to http://www.fafsa.ed.gov/faq014.htm#faq014_5 for more information.)

■ Each school, using your SAR and EFC information, will create a financial aid award package. Your package will list all eligible forms of financial aid and their total amount. You are not obliged to accept all aid possibilities. It would be wise to visit http://www.fafsa.ed.gov for details on the application process and for information on how to monitor the process step by step.

Complete All Scholarship Applications

Verify each scholarship's date of deadline, as each program will have different timelines. You should hear word of awards sometime in the spring.

Keep Track of Your Money

Keep a running tally of college money—both savings already in the bank (college fund, savings, parental contribution) and potential funding (anticipated awards and loans). Listing sources of funding will not only keep you organized, it will inspire you to work harder.

List All Possible Ways to Cut College Costs

Do the following to reduce your college costs:

■ **Take Advanced Placement (AP) exams.** Take AP exams to receive exemptions from some college courses. This will free up your college schedule for other classes or lighten your class load. Verify that your exam scores will count toward college credit. Your guidance counselor will be able to provide assistance on this matter.

■ **Take College Level Examination Program (CLEP) exams.** The College Level Examination Program differs from AP exams, in that it awards credit towards your college degree. CLEP exams cover general subjects such as science or math, or a particular subject such as a foreign language. Contact your college of choice to see if it offers CLEP exams.

■ **Consider attending a community college.** Consider attending a local community college for the first year or two of your college career. You can save money two ways: by completing your core classes at a less expensive institution, and living at home to save on dorm fees and other living expenses.

■ **Consider commuting to college.** You can save thousands of dollars in dorm fees by attending a four-year college located near your home.

■ **Reciprocity and Two-for-One.** Do you wish to attend a state school, but are wary of its nonresident tuition? Many state-funded schools offer reciprocity to students who reside in neighboring states or have intention to reside in the state after graduation. Also, if a sibling already attends a state university, your family may qualify for a two-for-one tuition package. Find out if these offers are available by contacting the admission offices of the colleges in which you are interested in attending.

■ **"Be All You Can Be."** The United States Armed Forces offer generous college financial programs, up to $50,000 in some cases, to those who sign up for active duty. You can choose to serve your term before or after obtaining your college degree. Research your options by visiting http://rotc.com or http://www.military.com.

■ **Volunteer.** Consider giving your time and service in exchange for college financial assistance. Organizations such as the Peace Corps (http://www.peacecorps.gov) and AmeriCorps (http://www.americorps.org) work with communities to build housing, provide health and education programs, and participate in homeland security projects. Learn more about these programs by visiting their Web sites.

CHOOSING A COLLEGE

Some students know from the start of high school exactly what college they want to attend, whether it is a lifelong dream to attend their parent's alma mater, an Ivy League school, or a community college just down the street. For the majority of students, however, choosing a college will probably be among the hardest decisions they will ever make. There are many factors to consider before picking the ultimate school. Here are some questions to ponder that may prove helpful as you choose a college.

WHAT TYPE OF COLLEGE IS RIGHT FOR YOU?

Community Colleges

For some students, the two-year associate degree awarded by community colleges is sufficient to help them achieve their desired career goal. There are plenty of career options available for those who obtain a two-year degree and who do not go on to a four-year college. These include opportunities in health care, computer science, engineering technology, fashion, hospitality, and many other career fields.

Others choose community colleges as a way to prepare for a four-year college, save money, or learn more about educational options if they are unsure of their career choice.

Students whose grade point average or college entrance score is not on par with the expectations of a university often use their time at a community college to improve their grades, obtain more experience in a particular area, or prepare themselves to study courses at the college level.

Many students also opt to take core classes at community colleges and transfer course credit toward a bachelor's degree at another school. In order to make the most of their educational dollars, many students take advantage of the lower cost per credit hour (compared to larger schools) charged at community college. Another financial plus: many students live at home during their community college days, which saves on boarding fees.

If this is your plan of action, make sure your credits will indeed be transferable—don't waste your time and money on classes that won't be recognized by four-year colleges and universities.

If you are undecided on a course of study, then perhaps a two-year community college is your best option. Attending a community college will give you the opportunity to take a variety of classes and find out exactly where your interests and talents lie.

Vocational Schools

Vocational, or trade, schools teach students the skills needed to perform a particular job, such as automotive repair or plumbing. Vocational schools are either nonprofit or proprietary institutions and are found throughout the nation. It should be noted that many vocational school programs, such as hair and beauty, are not eligible for financial aid or funding from some student college savings programs.

Four-Year Colleges and Universities

In addition to offering baccalaureate and graduate degrees, four-year colleges and universities typically provide more comprehensive facilities and a broader range of majors than those offered at two-year colleges. These types of colleges can be divided into two categories: public and private. State and local governments subsidize public institutions, allowing for lower tuition costs. Private schools do not rely on government funding and must rely on tuition, grants, and endowments. Private schools can be further defined by the special interest they serve. For example, Loyola University, with its many campuses nationwide, is known for its Jesuit Catholic affiliation. Morehouse College and Spelman College, both located in Atlanta, Georgia, hold reputations as leading institutions of learning for African-American men and women, respectively, although both schools are open to students from all races. Mount Holyoke College in Massachusetts and Saint Mary's College in Indiana are examples of women-only colleges.

WHAT ACADEMIC PROGRAMS DOES THE SCHOOL OFFER?

This is the basic, most important question to ask when gathering your long list of colleges. Identify the major you plan to declare. Are you planning to study business? Then you'll want to include schools with a stellar reputation for their business program. Interested in a writing career? You'll want to find schools with strong creative writing or journalism programs. If you are undecided, but leaning toward liberal arts, then it wouldn't make sense to include the Massachusetts Institute of Technology, which is internationally known for its programs in science and technology.

Though a school's reputation is important, it shouldn't be the final factor when weighing your decision. Instead, determine if the school has the program to fit your goals. You can receive just as fine an education at a small college as you would at a large state university. The key point is finding out what path will be most beneficial to you.

WHAT ARE THE ADMISSION REQUIREMENTS?

If the school's average SAT score is 1300, and yours is only 900, you may want to think twice about adding the school to your dream list. Unless you wow the admissions board with a prize-winning college essay, you will want to consider schools with admission requirements you can meet. In certain cases, schools will offer admission to students with low college entrance scores—if they have a high grade point average or vice versa. Athletics, or participation in extracurricular activities, can also play a role in college acceptance. In these cases, the student is offered probationary admission, meaning they need to keep their grades at a certain level until graduation from high school, or attend remedial classes during the summer.

CAN YOU AFFORD IT?

Affordability is another important topic. The tuition difference between public and private schools is huge. According to The College Board, in 2005–06, average tuition at public four-year institutions was $5,491. Average tuition at private four-year institutions was $21,235. Although private schools cost more than public schools, this is not to say that private schools, or even public schools outside of your state of residence (which charge higher tuition), should be kept off limits. Many private schools offer a higher amount of financial aid in order to attract qualified students who may

be wary of high tuition costs. And many students, after exhausting every available aid package, grant, and scholarship, find themselves turning to student loans in order to finance their education. The question to ask: Is attending this school the best way to reach my goal regardless of the cost? If the answer is yes, add it to your list now and worry about the financing after you are accepted.

Scholarships, academic and athletic, are other variables in the affordability debate. For example, if your heart is set on studying at a Big 10 college, but a smaller, lesser-known, but equally qualified college offers you a sizable scholarship, that may change your decision—right? Accepting the scholarship and admission to the smaller school will still provide you with a strong education, as well as reduce your total financial burden come graduation time.

WHERE DO YOU WANT TO STUDY?

Location, for some students, is key to college planning. College is not just about studying a particular discipline, but also a time for personal growth and experience. Some students attracted to the activities and excitement of the big city desire schools located in large cities such as Los Angeles or Chicago. Others prefer the quiet and small town charm that often comes with a rural college. Still others see college as an opportunity to relocate to a long admired area such as University of California-San Diego's oceanside campus, New York University's metropolitan campus, or perhaps a place totally unlike where they grew up.

HOW IMPORTANT IS COLLEGE AND CLASS SIZE?

Campus size is also an important factor to consider. State universities often have large, rambling campuses, as well as locations off-site. Do you mind having to walk long distances—or in some cases, bike—to get to your class? Some large universities even hold classes at other campus locations. Or would you rather have the convenience of having classes in one or two buildings on the cozy, but charming campus, of a smaller college?

Experience has a lot to do with class size preference. Did you attend a private high school with a small student body? If so, you may have some adjustments to make when attending a large multicampus university. It's not uncommon for hundreds of students to be enrolled in freshman-level classes. Were you part of a graduating class of 1,500? If so, it may take some time to adjust to a smaller student-to-teacher ratio, where quiet, nonparticipating students are easily singled out. What type of learning environment is best for you?

WHAT ABOUT YOUR FELLOW STUDENTS?

You will want to do some research on the college's student demographics. What is the male/female ratio? What is the number of undergraduate versus graduate students? Does the school have student diversity?

You'll also want to know the retention rate of the college—the number of students returning after the first year of college. The higher the retention rate, the better. If students transfer or leave the college, you'll want to ask the reasons why. If the college offers a four-year degree, find out the percentage of students who pursue a graduate degree or other professional education. Most colleges maintain a student profile that can be accessed on its Web site. If not, you can contact the school's office of student affairs for the latest profile statistics.

WHAT KIND OF FACILITIES DOES THE COLLEGE OFFER?

You will want to consider the type of classrooms and libraries located on campus, and depending on your intended major, science and computer laboratories, theaters, and art studios as well.

If you plan to live on campus, you will want to research your options. How far are the dormitories from classroom buildings? Are residence halls co-ed, or are there options for female-only or male-only housing? Students with a physical disability should be especially cognizant of these issues; you'll want to learn about wheelchair accessibility in dorm rooms as well as public spaces, distance to classrooms, and elevator access. Does the school offer a virtual tour on its Web site? If so, take it. You'll get a feel for the campus—from educational facilities to the student center—without ever leaving your house.

WHAT ABOUT CAMPUS LIFE?

No one, not even your parents, expects you to study 24 hours a day. College life should offer a range of extracurricular activities ranging from intramural sports to political clubs to Greek life. Again, the question to ask is, what is important to you? Organized sports, a fitness center, or perhaps a ski club will be important school assets to students who are athletic or just enjoy exercising. For some students at large universities and colleges, fraternities and sororities are a way to meet fellow students with the same interests or goals. Perhaps religion plays an especially strong role in your life. In that case, you would want to learn about houses of worship, student religious groups, and the overall role that religion plays (if any) on your campus.

NARROWING YOUR CHOICES

Once you create your dream list of colleges and universities, it's time to narrow down to three or four—or more if you're willing to complete applications and pay the fees. Attend college fairs in your area to find out about schools on your list, or perhaps learn about schools in which you are not aware. College fairs are held several times a year; ask your guidance counselor for upcoming dates in your area, or look for advertisements in your local paper. Visit http://test.nacacnet.org/MemberPortal/Events/CollegeFairs for more information on college fairs in your area.

You can also use the Internet to learn about colleges. Some popular college search Web sites include http://nces.ed.gov/globallocator and http://www.petersons.com/ugchannel/code/searches/srchCrit1.asp?path=ug.fas.college. You simply enter information about yourself (such as your interests and GPA) and what you are looking for in a college (size, location, and programs). The search will then list all colleges located within the boundaries you set. As you begin to accumulate information on each college—brochures, application forms, financial aid information, statistics gathered from the Internet—stay organized by creating a separate file or folder for each school.

Once you have narrowed your college list to a manageable number, create a list of the pros and cons for each school. One school may have a great business program, but hardly any campus life to offer. Another has an equally known program, but few on-campus residence halls. Still another is offering you a sizable scholarship. Once you have written down each point, review your list; the schools with the most negatives should be removed from your list.

At this time, you should also talk to your family about your choices. Consider your parents' opinions, especially if they are going to help foot the educational bill. If you have siblings, ask them for their input, also. Perhaps they attended or know someone who attended one of the colleges on your list. What better way to find out about a school than from someone who has already gone there?

CAMPUS VISITS

All the research in the world is no substitute for actually seeing the colleges that interest you. Arrange campus visits as early as possible. The summer before senior year is the perfect time for visiting distant campuses. Save weekends or school holidays to visit colleges near your community. Before visiting a college, you will want to arrange for a formal campus tour online, or by calling the school's visitor coordinator. Campus tours will include visits to different classroom buildings, residence halls, libraries, and student centers. Make time to explore on your own to get a feel for the college's atmosphere. Schedule an appointment with the admission counselor and financial aid counselor, as well as a department staff of your intended major. Now is the time to ask pertinent questions. If possible, attend a class so you can experience how students and teachers interact with each other. Allow extra time to visit the area surrounding the campus. Are there restaurants and stores within walking distance? What about public transportation? Can you be part of this "community" for the next four to five years? Take notes on each visit and include them in your files.

After reviewing each college file, you can eliminate the schools that did not prove favorable after the campus visit. Send a completed application to the schools left on your short list, and wait, wait, wait. Hopefully, that "fat letter" of acceptance will come your way!

ADDITIONAL RESOURCES

American Association of Community Colleges
http://www.aacc.nche.edu
The association offers a list of two-year technical and vocational institutions at its Web site.

CampusTours.com
http://www.campustours.com
Visit this Web site to take virtual tours of thousands of colleges and universities throughout the United States. In addition to the tours, information on enrollment, tuition, majors, admission requirements, and athletics is provided.

Community College Web
http://www.mcli.dist.maricopa.edu/cc
This Web site provides a searchable database of nearly 1,300 community colleges that is searchable by geographical region, alphabetical order, and keyword.

ECampusTours.com
https://www.ecampustours.com
This Web site offers 360-degree virtual tours of hundreds of colleges and universities, as well as information on college planning, financial aid, and careers.

National Association of College Admission Counseling
http://test.nacacnet.org/MemberPortal/Events/CollegeFairs
Visit the association's Web site for a list of national college fairs.

National Center for Education Statistics
http://nces.ed.gov/globallocator
The Center's Web site offers a comprehensive college search engine. You can search by college name, location, and type of institution.

Peterson's College Planner: Student Edition
http://www.petersons.com/ugchannel/code/searches/srchCrit1.asp?path=ug.fas.college
The "Find a School" section offers a searchable database of thousands of colleges and universities. Information on location, enrollment, SAT/ACT scores, tuition, and level of admission difficulty is provided for each institution.

CHOOSING A COLLEGE MAJOR

Choosing a college major represents one of the first important life decisions you will make as a young adult. Don't let this scare you, though; think of it as the beginning of a new phase in your life. This new phase will be full of self-discovery and personal exploration. Determining the right college major is a journey. Along the way you will learn more about who you are and who you want to be. Few people know exactly what they want to major in when they begin college. Those who claim to know usually discover new interests in college that cause them to rethink their options. You'll find that those options seem endless.

In *Choosing Your College Major: How to Chart Your Ideal Path,* Dr. Randall S. Hansen states that the most important piece of advice he gives to students who are choosing a major is this: Don't panic. After all, choosing your college major represents a big step in your life, but you always have options, and you can always expand upon what you learn as you go along. It is a fact that college life will help you discover your true interests. And more than half of all students will change their majors at least once, according to the National Research Center for College and University Admissions.

SO WHAT ARE YOU GOING TO DO WITH YOUR LIFE?

Chances are you have been facing this question, in one form or another, ever since you were little. And your response has likely changed since your kindergarten days. Your interests have grown with you, and now it is time to think about those interests and how they will influence your job prospects. If you are still in high school, a good place to start is with your guidance counselor. He or she should have materials to help you take inventory of your interests. While some experts caution that traditional "interest inventory" activities are not reliable enough to base "major" decisions on, they do serve at least one good purpose—they make you start thinking about what you really like and don't like to do. So while you should never

let any test dictate your future, take it for what it is—a good place to start the self-analysis process.

Students who are already in college will find that their college career centers offer interest inventory assessments as well. You can also find online assessments—most of which charge a fee. Careerkey.com offers one such personality test that you can complete online for a modest price. A more expensive assessment is available at DiscoverYourPersonality.com. Many more can be found by doing a simple online search. Ultimately, it is up to you to decide if you think such an assessment is worth taking. Just be sure to keep in mind that if you do pay for such an assessment, the results should be only a guiding factor in your search for a major.

Your values, goals, and your motivations for what you want out of a job and career also play a large role in choosing a college major. In other words, what are you looking for in a career? Do you view your future career as a means of achieving status? Is money a motivator? Or are you seeking something that contributes to the well-being of society, but will probably never make you rich?

DEVELOP A STRATEGY

Choosing a college major involves strategizing. Your motivations and goals play a big role in this process. Will your major be a stepping stone towards a graduate degree? If so, you may want to think about the undergraduate options for entrance into medical school, law school, or a graduate program in another area. According to *Choosing and Using Your Major*, published by University Career Service at the University of Virginia, this is an important consideration. Will your college career end in four years, or are you preparing for an advanced education? The other two strategies this publication emphasizes are choosing a major that helps you develop as a human being and devising a marketable combination of majors and minors that will be most beneficial to you in the current marketplace. A combination of these two strategies should contribute to your marketability as a well-rounded applicant.

Finally, you should closely examine your abilities when you are in this initial stage of research. If you hated math in high school and struggled to get a passing grade, majoring in a math-intensive field like engineering might not be a good match for you. On the other hand, if you excelled in English classes and found your classes to be both stimulating and rewarding, you might choose to look into careers that involve communication. Whatever your academic strengths and weaknesses, you should have a basic idea as to your learning capabilities and your aptitudes for different subject matter. Your high school counselors or your college adviser are good sources of help in this area as well. Since they will have knowledge of your scholastic aptitude, make an effort to discuss any questions or concerns you have about your strengths or weaknesses in a subject area. They can help you understand the types of courses that will be best suited for you.

Once you've narrowed your options to a few majors that you would like to explore in depth, there is still a lot of research to be done. You have a list of possible majors at this point, so it's time to find out more about them. There are many, many publications available that offer a wealth of information on choosing college majors. First, take a look at your college's course catalog and the individual curriculums for the majors you are interested in. If the courses look intriguing, that's a good sign. Even if some of them look a little scary, don't despair—you should expect to be challenged in your courses. After all, the goal is to strive to enrich your experience in a subject matter. You aren't expected to be an expert when you are just beginning.

At this stage you should also visit your library or bookstore. The number of publications out there describing college majors is enormous. Books such as The Princeton Review's *Guide to College Majors* provide additional information about college majors that you won't find in your college's course catalog. You'll discover fun facts about the major and potential careers and salary ranges. Of added value are related majors that you might want to explore. This can really prove valuable if you are still contemplating the pros and cons of a major because you might find that you've overlooked a related major that better suits your interests. The U.S. Bureau of Labor Statistics' *Occupational Outlook Handbook* (available online at http://www.bls.gov/oco) is also a good resource. Here you will find out about current salary ranges and projected job opportunities in all fields. For example, if you are thinking of going into teaching and you want to make sure that there is going to be a need for teachers in four or five years, this is the resource to consult.

TALK TO YOUR FRIENDS, FAMILY, TEACHERS, AND OTHER PROFESSIONALS

The human factor also plays a critical role in this big decision, so be sure to connect with peers, professors, family, and professionals. This is extremely important. You really should strive to base this first big decision about a college major on a well-rounded and thoroughly researched process. However, you don't want to base your decision on what looks good on paper, or solely on what *you* think.

Your peers offer a great source of support. After all, they are going through the same thing that you are. Talk to them about their career goals and how they are approaching the process of deciding on a major. Just knowing that you are not alone in this experience helps ease the stress. Your peers can also motivate you to become involved in more activities as well. In fact, students advise that becoming involved in as many extracurricular activities and student organizations that interest you is one of the best ways to find your true passions. Simply put, if you're interested in something, college is the place to dive in and give it a try. No other place will offer you so many social opportunities pertaining to such a diversified group of topics. Join, join, join. It's the only way to discover things about yourself that you'd never discover without trying.

Additionally, your family provides unique insight into who you are. Nobody knows you like they do. While you want to make sure that you make up your own mind and are not pushed to do something you don't want to do, listening to and considering their opinions is usually a smart move.

College professors and advisers are also important sources of guidance. If you are serious about a major, make an appointment to talk with the department head of the major. It is professors' jobs to teach students about what their field has to offer. Don't be shy or assume someone is too busy to talk to you. To the contrary! Most professors love to tell you all about their field and why it is so exciting to them. They'll also be able to give you good advice as to the opportunities that exist for graduates. They will know what recent graduates are doing and might even be able to put you in contact with some. After all, a recent graduate can tell you the real-world implications of working in an entry-level job in a given field.

This leads us to consider professionals at all levels in a field. If you go about this from a reverse perspective— knowing the jobs or careers in which you are interested, but still unsure about the best major to pursue—make a phone call or send an e-mail to the companies you want to work for or the professionals themselves. Your college should also be able to provide you with alumni contacts who will be happy to discuss their careers with you. They have been in your shoes at one time in their lives, so who better to speak with? Set up a time to visit with them in their place of employment. You might even request to shadow them for a day to learn even more about their jobs. Speaking to professionals in a field can be very helpful, particularly in that it will teach you that there are many paths to a given career. For example, you might assume that the account executive you speak to at an advertising firm has a degree in marketing or business, only to find out he or she majored in education in college.

This point brings up something that should ease your mind. *Choosing and Using Your Major* puts it this way: The relationship of college majors to career fields varies. It isn't true that you are locking yourself into a career field with any given major. Now, that is not to say that some careers don't require specific majors. Obviously if you want to be a marine biologist, you must study marine biology. Or if you want to become an engineer, you must study engineering. Yet there are many careers that have much less rigid requirements. And many college majors don't lead to any one specific job or career. Often your leadership activities outside of the college classroom or your volunteer and internship experience will make you a strong candidate for a job—no matter your college major. This is all the more reason to make your college experience a well-rounded one.

Your journey begins right now. You are reading and thinking about your college major at this very moment. You have learned, however, that there is no need to panic. Many students start college undecided about a major, and that is perfectly normal. You have plenty of time to explore introductory courses before making that official declaration. Declaring a major sometime around your third or fourth semester of college won't cause you any lost time or money. In fact, you'll probably save some paperwork by not declaring too early—and having to change! As Dr. Hansen points out in *Choosing a College Major: How to Chart Your Ideal Path*, studies show that most people change *careers* four or five times during their lifetimes. In other words, you'll face many important decisions in your lifetime. Yes, choosing your college major represents your first big decision as an adult, but it is only the first of many. And you can't go wrong with pursuing something that makes you happy.

ADDITIONAL RESOURCES

The Career Key
http://www.careerkey.org
This online career assessment is available for a small fee.

The College Board
http://www.collegeboard.com/csearch/majors_careers/profiles
The College Board offers a Major & Career Profiles section on its Web site, which provides a detailed overview of majors and careers, including questions to ask when searching for college programs, recommended high school classes, typical college classes, degree requirements, and career options.

Occupational Outlook Handbook
http://www.bls.gov/oco
The *Occupational Outlook Handbook* provides comprehensive information on careers, including job duties, educational requirements, earnings, and employment outlook. It is available in print and online.

The Princeton Review
http://www.princetonreview.com/college/default.asp
The Princeton Review provides an overview of hundreds of majors, as well as a Career Quiz, at its Web site.

What Can I Do With a Major in…?
http://www.uncwil.edu/stuaff/career/Majors
http://www3.ashland.edu/services/cardev/cdm-major.html
http://www.utexas.edu/student/careercenter/careers
http://www.asu.edu/studentaffairs/career/Students/ChoosingAMajor/whatcanIdowith.htm
http://career.utk.edu/students/majors.asp
Many colleges and universities provide helpful information to students interested in learning more about educational and career options as they relate to a specific major. The Web sites listed above are good examples of such resources. You can find additional Web sites by performing a Web search using the following phrase: "What Can I Do With a Major in… (add the major of your choice)?" While content differs by Web site, most of these sites offer an overview of the major and a list of necessary personal skills, related careers, typical employers, professional organizations, and Web links for further study.

WRITING COLLEGE ADMISSIONS AND SCHOLARSHIP ESSAYS

When your application is up for committee review, will it stand out from the rest of the pack? Not a chance—if based only on transcripts and test scores. Every other high school student has, like you, been busy earning top grades, participating in extracurricular activities, and scoring high marks on the SAT and ACT. Your transcripts have been recorded, and unless you plan to retake your college entrance exams, there is no chance of improving your scores. Even letters of recommendation are up to the discretion of the teachers or employers writing them. At this point, the only part of the application process that you can control is the essay. Your essay is only as good as the effort you put forth.

The essay is the one part of your application (whether you are applying to college or a scholarship) that will give the judging committee a sense of who you are, as if they are meeting you, if only through your words. Here are some tips to make that first impression a winner.

KNOW THE RULES

Every application is different. Make sure you know the "rules" mandated by each governing body before you turn in your application. Things to keep in mind:

- Know the due date, and give yourself ample time to complete the application.
- Understand the nature of the essay question. If the prompt asks for your opinion on capital punishment, don't rehash your state's stand on it. Rather, do you agree or disagree with the issue? Can you elaborate on how you came to this decision?
- Does your essay need a title?
- Have you stayed within the allotted page or word count? Are you running 500 words over the specified word count? If so, then edit your essay to fit the requirements. Otherwise, committee judges may disqualify an overly wordy submission. The same holds true if your essay falls under the minimum word count.
- Double check for specified font size, line spacing, and margins.
- Think twice before turning in a handwritten essay. Not only will a printed essay look neater, it will also be easier to read. If you don't have access to a computer and printer, ask a friend to type it for you, or use the computer at your school or local library.
- If you are applying for financial aid, make sure you fit the award. Every organization has special criteria students must meet in order to win a scholarship. If you find you need to reinvent your personality or values to fit the organization's pre-set idea of a scholar, then move on. Chances are you can find another scholarship better suited to you and your goals.

READ PAST ESSAYS

It's a good idea to read past award-winning essays for inspiration and to get a feel for what judges deem worthy. There are several great Web sites that post students' college essays from all over the United States. Check out http://www.teenink.com/College/Essays.html, where you can read current essay topics ranging from high school popularity to knitting to an experience with a life-altering illness. Some corporate sponsors will post scholarship winners' essays on their site or, at the very least, a personal profile of the winner. Check out http://target.com/target_group/community_giving/index.jhtml for a sample profile.

University Web sites can be another source of inspiration. Connecticut College, for example, posts essays that their admission and financial aid committees found to be especially creative and noteworthy. Visit http://www.conncoll.edu/admissions/essays for a list of students' work that won them a coveted "fat letter" of acceptance.

KNOW THE ORGANIZATION AND ITS JUDGES

If you are applying for scholarships or other financial aid from a professional association or company, you need to learn about the organization's values and work. Assigned essay topics are not random questions compiled by the funding organization. Rather, they specify some sort of connection between the student and the organization's work or values. For example, the Target Corporation prides itself in forging close ties to the community and sponsoring many voluntary activities. It makes sense then that the recent essay topic posed to students vying for its $25,000 All-Around Scholarship focused on that topic—their own personal record of volunteer service. The software giant Microsoft asks scholarship candidates to write about their technical passion outside of the classroom setting. You can do your research by visiting the Web site of each organization.

Some university Web sites may also provide a list of faculty members assigned to the financial aid or scholarship committee. A little investigative work may yield a special interest or position you can use to connect to the judging committee.

WRITING THE STATEMENT OF PURPOSE

Many college admissions essays take shape as a statement of purpose. This style does not rely on an answer to a standard question such as "who is your favorite poet," or "if you had 1 million dollars . . ." Instead it tells of your life so far and your interests and achievements in high school. It provides you with an opportunity to boast of your successes!

Don't just list your good qualities; incorporate them into a story. Tell the judges who or what inspired you along the way. Provide a particular instance to breathe life into your essay. For example, an illness in your family led you to volunteer at a local hospital, which in turn sparked an interest in a future career in medicine. Meeting a dedicated civic leader inspired you to pursue study in government or public policy. Covering a local election for your journalism class encouraged you to pursue a career as a newspaper reporter. Write your essay to portray your personal qualities and interests as unique. Details and purpose will not only engage a reader to want to finish the essay, they will serve to make you memorable. After all, when award time comes, you will want to be remembered. To read more about Statement of Purpose essays, visit http://statementofpurpose.com/whatis.html.

DOS AND DON'TS OF WRITING AN ESSAY

There are right and wrong ways to do everything, and essays are no exception. Keep the following points in mind as you write your essay.

- **Use a great introduction.** Grab the attention of your reader with your opening sentence. Pose a question, or start with a dramatic line or famous quote.
- **Be yourself.** As stated before, the point of an essay is to give the judges a better picture of you. In the case of a college application, are you someone who can make a contribution to the school's student body? If you are applying for financial aid, are you worthy of this scholarship? Are you someone who echoes the values and goals of the corporate sponsor or association?
- **Be original.** Don't borrow other peoples' anecdotes and experiences. Be yourself. Come up with anecdotes or experiences that will personalize your essay, and set it apart from the rest of the applicants. It is a lot easier to write about something you know, and care about deeply, than other peoples' experiences.
- **Answer the question correctly.** If the essay portion of the application asks you to identify the most inspirational person you've met, don't write paragraphs on Abraham Lincoln. Unless you have a time machine in your garage, you've never personally met him.
- **Don't overuse the thesaurus.** Your chances of being accepted to a college or winning a scholarship don't increase with each $100 word used. Consider using more nouns and verbs instead of a slew of adjectives. They will make your writing more crisp, vivid, and interesting.
- **Use imagery.** Don't just tell us you worked as a kids' summer camp counselor. Paint a picture of what the campgrounds looked like, the activities you organized, and the personality of the kids assigned to your group.
- **Wrap it up right.** A good conclusion is as important as your introduction. Don't settle for a mere summary of your essay. Closing words such as "in conclusion" and "therefore" have become cliché. Did you learn something profound from your experience as a summer counselor? Did this experience change your outlook or life goals? Your essay will appear more polished if

your closing statement ties into your opening thoughts in a creative manner.

- **Have others read your essay.** Recruit as many people as possible to read and critique your essay. If possible, ask people to read your essay aloud. You will be surprised by how many mistakes you can catch when you actually hear a passage, instead of merely reading the words.

- **Write. Rest. Revise.** Allow yourself plenty of time so you can let your essay "rest" a day or so before attempting a revision. With a fresh approach, you may come up with another angle or different descriptive word. Also, you may catch mistakes missed during your first read.

STUCK? GET PAST WRITER'S BLOCK!

Even the best writers experience writer's block! Here are some suggestions from http://www.statementofpurpose.com to help you get started on an award-winning essay.

- **Find a topic that you are passionate about.** It could be something controversial such as abortion versus the right to life, or a less touchy subject such as your favorite sport. It could be something personal such as your volunteer work at a local shelter. Regardless of the topic, if you believe in it wholeheartedly, chances are your feelings will be reflected in your writing.

- **Evaluate your role models.** What traits do they possess that earn your respect and admiration? Sure, you can name prominent people in the news, but don't forget to look closer to home— your family and friends, teachers, and even employers. Did your grandparents immigrate to the United States in hopes of a better life? Tell their story and how their decision changed your destiny. By finding this connection, you are giving the judges a glimpse of your life and your own interesting story.

- **Short on ideas?** No ideas on what to write about yourself? Talk with family and friends, even your teachers. Sometimes it's helpful to have an outsider describe how they perceive you and your goals.

- **Evaluate your life experiences.** Can you pinpoint the moment you decided you wanted to become a nurse? Or a chemist? Or an artist? Write about that moment!

- **Write about your diversity.** Have you struggled with your ethnicity, gender, a disability, or financial need? Tell your story and spotlight how you overcame your difference, or used your particular diversity to your advantage.

CONSIDER PROFESSIONAL HELP

You may want to invest in a professional editing service. One such service is EssayEdge.com (http://www.essayedge.com), a fee-based, Internet editing resource. This organization only uses Harvard-educated editors—from a variety of industry backgrounds—to read and edit students' admissions and scholarship essays. Though they make necessary corrections and suggest rewrites to improve content and grammar, editors are adamant about maintaining the original tone of students' work. In addition to helping students with admissions and scholarship essays, EssayEdge.com's services also include work with essays needed for law school, medical school, and graduate school applications. Their fee is determined by the word count of the original essay, with prices ranging from just under $50 to $300 on up; turnaround time is 24 to 48 hours from the time the unedited essay is electronically submitted. According to EssayEdge.com, 80 percent of its nearly 9,000 customers in 2004–05 were accepted into their top-choice college. There are numerous editing services located nationwide. Check your local phone book or the Internet to find one to match your needs.

Is it worth the cost to use a professional editing service? Perhaps—especially if your writing style, or that of your parents and your friends, is not up to par. Remember, however, that you will be using your own funds to raise your chances of admission or winning or receiving access to college money.

WHAT ARE THE JUDGES LOOKING FOR?

Most organizations review applications in similar ways— weeding out candidates until they get to the top tier of students. Here is an easier way to visualize their scrutiny, according to http://www.scholarshiphelp.org:

- *Phase one:* All applications are checked to see if properly completed and sent with required transcripts and letters of recommendation. Sloppy applications or those lacking important information may be sent back to the student or, at the discretion of the screener, eliminated. Conducted by administrative staff.

- *Phase two:* Academic achievement is measured and ranked. Applicants with high GPAs and test scores are kept as possible candidates. Conducted by administrative staff, and possibly some members of the judging committee.
- *Phase three:* At this point in the process, all candidates are now equal, regardless of their class ranking or SAT scores. The only variable is a well-written essay. Judges are not just looking for a tally sheet of activity memberships or achievements. They want to know what kind of person you are. What are your interests? Your goals for the future? How have your life experiences formed your personality and ideals so far? Of course interpretation of your essay is subjective to the individual judge, what he or she values as relevant, perhaps even his or her mood at the initial time of reading. If your essay touches a chord with one judge and not the others, your message may move that one judge to argue in your favor.

THE LATE APPLICATION

The deadline for your application is quickly approaching, and your essay is nowhere near completion. Should you give up on this opportunity for college admission or financial help? Of course not. While most institutions are very strict about their deadlines, exceptions are sometimes made. Perhaps you can send your application in two parts: personal data and letters of recommendation, followed by the essay a few days later. Notify the proper office to explain your situation, and give good reason for the anticipated delay. It's certainly worth a shot.

ADDITIONAL RESOURCES

EssayEdge.com

http://www.essayedge.com

EssayEdge is a fee-based, Internet editing resource. Visit its Web site for the following free resources: sample essays, advice on writing essays and asking for recommendations, a college search engine, and an essay-writing course.

ScholarshipHelp.org

http://www.scholarshiphelp.org

For tips on writing scholarship essays and the application process, visit ScholarshipHelp's Web site.

StatementofPurpose.com

http://statementofpurpose.com/index.html

This Web site provides comprehensive advice on writing the Statement of Purpose.

TeenInk.com

http://www.teenink.com/College/Essays.html

The essay section of this Web site features nearly 400 samples of top-quality college essays.

APPLYING FOR STUDENT LOANS

After receiving federal- and state-sponsored financial aid, grants, scholarships, and money from college savings plans, many students are still unable to meet the rising cost of college. Student loan programs, funded by the federal government, state government, or private lenders, can help students and their families borrow money to help with educational costs. Read on to learn what is available for your situation.

FEDERAL LOANS
Stafford Loans

The Stafford Loan program is the largest source of government financial aid available to undergraduate and graduate students. There are two types of Stafford Loans—the William D. Ford Direct Loan Program, referred to as the Direct Loan Program (FFDL), and the Federal Family Educational Loan Program, commonly referred to as the FFEL Program. Both have the same eligibility requirements and differ only in the source of funding and payment options. The Direct Loan Program offers student and parent loans with funding directly from the federal government. The FFEL Program (referred to as Stafford Loans or Federal Stafford Loans) receives its funding from financial institutions, such as banks, credit unions, or a savings and loan. Schools participate in either the FFDL or FFEL program. Regardless of which program the school uses, the eligibility criteria for loans are the same. The main difference is the funding source. For the purposes of this section of the book, any reference to "Stafford Loans" refers to loans from the Direct Loan Program or the FFEL Program, unless specifically stated otherwise.

Stafford Loans can be further identified as subsidized or unsubsidized. Subsidized Stafford Loans are based on financial need; the federal government pays interest on the loan until six months after the student ceases being enrolled at least half-time and begins payment on the account. Unsubsidized loans do not have financial requirements and begin to accrue interest as soon as the loan is disbursed.

The amount of money available is substantial. Students can borrow anywhere from $2,625 to $18,500 annually, depending on their academic year of study. (Note: In July 2007, these amounts will increase to $3,500 to $20,500, respectively.) Interest rates are fixed at 6.8 percent annually. [Note: In the past, an origination fee (a certain percentage of the loan) was charged by the government or the lending agent to help with the cost of the loan. Through July 1, 2006, a maximum 2 percent fee will continue to be charged for the FFEL. The percentage will gradually decrease until July 1, 2010, when it is completely eliminated. Although, FFEL lenders have the option of charging a lesser fee, many FFEL lenders are waiving the fees entirely. A 3 percent fee will be charged for the FFDL through July 1, 2007. The percentage will gradually decrease until July 1, 2010, when it becomes fixed at 1 percent. Loan disbursements, which are generally made twice an academic year, are made directly to the school to pay for charges on the student's account. These charges could be tuition, fees, room and board, books, or other charges the student may be able to put on the account. (Note: Students who are enrolled for just one semester typically receive a one-time disbursement.) Any remaining funds can be paid to the student for other educational expenses, or kept on account for the next academic year. However, the student must provide the school with authorization to keep a refund on the account for future charges.

Students have 10 to 30 years to pay Stafford Loans. Deferment may be granted if the student can prove certain situations such as enrollment at approved secondary school programs (at least half-time status), approved fellowships, or unemployment. Participation in a volunteer or work program after graduation can cancel a portion of a Stafford Loan. Visit http://studentaid.ed.gov/students/publications/student_guide/index.html or http://www.staffordloan.com for more information.

PLUS Loans

Two Federal PLUS Loans are available: the Parent PLUS Loan and the Graduate PLUS Loan.

Parents can seek financial assistance with a Parent PLUS Loan. This is an unsubsidized loan. Parents must pass a credit check and have a dependent child enrolled at least half time at an approved college or university. There are two types of Parent PLUS Loans similar to the Stafford Loan: Direct PLUS Loans and Federal Family Education Loan Program (FFEL) Plus Loans. Each loan is identical in its requirements, interest, and repayment options; only the lending house differs. Parents can only apply for either a Direct PLUS Loan or a FFEL PLUS Loan, but not to both. However, similar to the Stafford Loan programs, the college will choose to participate in the Direct Loan Program or FFEL Program, and parents must apply for a Parent PLUS from the program the school uses.

Applicants who have trouble passing the credit check requirements can still qualify for a PLUS Loan with the help of a guarantor or endorser. The total loan amount peaks at the full tuition cost, minus any other funding from other sources—loans, grants, and scholarships. The interest rate for PLUS Loans is fixed: 8.5 percent for FFELP PLUS Loans (that are provided by banks) and 7.9 percent for Direct PLUS Loans (that are provided by the federal government). (Note: there is a chance that federal legislation may standardize these interest rates; check with your financial aid counselor about the latest legislation regarding interest rates.) . A fee, up to 4 percent of the total loan, is charged to help with the cost of the loan. Interest on the loan begins as soon as the first disbursement payment is made; parents have 60 days to begin payment after full disbursement. PLUS Loan disbursements are made directly to the school in two payments. The first is applied to tuition, room and board, and fees; the other is allotted to other educational expenses. Any remaining funds can be received by the parents, endorsed to the student, or kept on account for the next academic year. For more information, visit http://studentaid.ed.gov/students/publications/student_guide/2006-2007/index.html or http://www.parentplusloan.com.

Federal Graduate PLUS Loan are available to graduate students with an acceptable credit history. Graduate students may borrow funds up to the total cost of their education (minus any financial aid received). Applicants must be enrolled at least half time and U.S. citizens or noncitizen permanent residents. The interest rate for Graduate PLUS Loans is fixed at 8.5 percent. A loan origination fee and a guarantee fee may be charged. Contact your loan provider for more information.

Perkins Loans

Students with financial hardship may take out a low-interest Perkins Loan. The school acts as the lender for this loan, using funds appropriated by the federal government, with a share coming from the school itself. Undergraduates may borrow up to $4,000 a year and graduate students up to $6,000 a year at 5 percent interest. There is no fee to apply for this type of loan. Funding for this program is awarded on a first-come, first-served basis, so it is important to apply for this loan early. Funds are disbursed twice yearly, either directly to your school accounts, or sent to you in the form of a check. (Note: Students who are enrolled for just one semester typically receive a one-time disbursement.)

Students are given up to 10 years to repay a Perkins loan, with the first payment due within nine months after the student ceases to be enrolled at least half time. Depending on the circumstances, a deferment or forbearance may be granted. Interest will continue to accrue, without the monthly payments. Perkins loans may be cancelled if the student agrees to participate in work or volunteer programs after graduation. Visit http://studentaid.ed.gov/students/publications/student_guide/index.html for more information on Perkins Loans.

STATE LOANS

There are also funds available from FFELP-participating state guaranty agencies. For example, the Illinois Student Assistance Commission (ISAC) offers numerous financial aid packages to in-state students, as well as college savings plans and prepaid tuition plans. If you live in Illinois, visit http://www.collegezone.com for more information on available financial aid available from the ISAC. To find available educational loans in your home state, log on to the U.S. Department of Education's Web site, http://wdcrobcolp01.ed.gov/Programs/EROD/org_list.cfm?category_cd=SGA, for links to your state's guaranty agency. (Note: Not all states offer loan programs; check with your state's department of education or student assistance commission for details.)

PRIVATE LOANS

After receiving grants, scholarships, and the maximum federal and state sponsored loans available to them, students may still fall short of the funding needed to finance a college education. In these cases, they may want to apply for a private student loan, also known as alternative education loan. Eligibility requirements such as past credit history, U.S. citizenship or permanent residency status, school, or field of study can also affect assigned interest rates and fees. Since these loans carry higher interest rates and fees, some of which change during the grace period vs. the repayment period, students should consider private loans only after exhausting other financing options. Use the Internet to search for private loan programs, or ask your school's guidance office for help in acquiring the perfect loan for your needs. Here are some available programs:

National Education Loan Network

The National Education Loan Network (NelNet), offering private and federal loans, as well as consolidation loans, is one of the country's largest lenders with about $3 billion in student loan programs. It offers undergraduates up to $120,000; graduate students, $180,000; with no limit loans for students enrolled in medical or other health care studies. NelNet loans allow 20 to 25 years for repayment, depending on the loan type and amount. For more information, visit http://www.nelnet.net.

SallieMae

SallieMae is a major provider of all types of educational loans—federal, private, and consolidation loans. This company currently owns or manages 9 billion student loans. Qualified students can borrow anywhere from $100,000 to $220,000 depending on their status, field of study, and chosen institution. Loans carry a variable interest rate, with a fee based on 0 to 6 percent of the total amount borrowed. Borrowers have 15 to 20 years to repay their loan. One program offered by SallieMae is the Community College Loan, available for students pursuing an associate degree or Title IV certification program. A minimum of $1,000 up to the total cost of tuition, less other aid money, is available for qualified students. For more information, visit http://www.salliemae.com.

APPLYING FOR A STUDENT LOAN

Your first step in applying for a federal student loan is completing the Free Application for Federal Student Aid (FAFSA); information given on the FAFSA will generate a Student Aid Report (SAR). The academic institution uses the student's SAR information to determine the loan amount. The FAFSA, and personal identification number application, can be submitted online or in hard copy format. Completing a FAFSA is important, even if you are not anticipating a federal loan, since many state agencies and schools consider FAFSA and SAR information when allotting funding. Note that a FAFSA must be submitted annually. Also, keep aware of pressing deadlines since some federal dollars (Perkins Loan, Federal Supplemental Educational Opportunity Grant) are limited and there aren't always enough funds to provide an award to all eligible applicants. Once the budget is spent, you'll have to wait until next year, or find funding elsewhere.

IT'S TIME TO PAY . . .

Payment arrangements depend on the type of loan. Some loans stipulate that payment begins after the first disbursement; others hold off payments until a short time after graduation, but begin to accrue interest on the principal until then. Some loans do not accrue interest until after graduation. Payments on a loan are done on a monthly basis; arrangements can be to receive a monthly statement, automatic withdrawal from a checking account, or online payment. Be aware of all details—some private loans carry a penalty if a loan is paid off ahead of schedule.

CANCELING A LOAN AND LOAN FORGIVENESS

Some students are able to cancel certain loans or earn money towards educational expenses by participating in work or volunteer programs or other opportunities. Any funding received is considered taxable income for that particular year. Here are a few options to consider if you would like to cancel a loan or seek loan forgiveness:

Volunteer Programs

Service in AmeriCorps is one way to earn college money. The network of AmeriCorps volunteers works with a variety of nonprofit organizations, public agencies, and faith-based groups to provide educational and health assistance, public safety, and environmental duties. Eligible volunteers can receive up to $4,725 for one year of AmeriCorps service to pay college tuition and other educational expenses at an accredited school or certification program. Part-time AmeriCorps volunteers are eligible to receive partial funding. The money can also be designated to pay off qualified existing student loans—most federal and state loans, except PLUS loans. Payments are made directly to the school or lender and are considered taxable income. Visit http://www.americorps.gov/about/ac/index.asp for more information. Also, you can search the Internet for other similar volunteer programs.

Military Options

A tour of duty with the armed forces, active or reserve, can help you earn educational funding. Here are some examples:

- **The Montgomery GI Bill—Active Duty** (MGIB AD) offers up to 36 months of educational benefits for full-time students enrolled in an accredited college or university. Eligibility includes completion of at least two years of active duty in any branch of the U.S. military (or four years in the Selected Reserve), or an honorable discharge. Applicants must also have a high school diploma, GED, or in some cases 12 hours of college credit, and have made a monthly contribution into the program for 12 months during service. Don't wait too long to take advantage of these funds—the MGIB AD is available only up to 10 years after formal separation from military service. Visit http://www.gibill.com or http://www.gibill.va.gov for more details.
- The **Survivors' and Dependents' Educational Assistance Program** is available to dependents of U.S. veterans who have died or were disabled during service, are currently detained by a foreign power, or identified as missing in action. Eligibility requirements depend on the relationship to the veteran. Visit http://www.gibill.va.gov/pamphlets/CH35/CH35_Pamphlet_General.htm for complete details.

Teaching

Teachers working full- or part-time can cancel a portion, 15 to 30 percent, of their Perkins or Stafford Loans. The total amount of forgiveness depends on the length of service—a minimum of one year, with the largest amount awarded to teachers serving at least five years. Schools must serve elementary or secondary students from low-income families. Learn more by visiting the Web site (http://www.aft.org) of the American Federation of Teachers.

Heal or Advise

Health and legal professionals can also participate in a variety of loan forgiveness programs located throughout the United States and abroad. Many of these programs require doctors, nurses, therapists, and lawyers to practice in underserved, rural communities or economically disadvantaged areas. Visit the American Association of Medical Colleges Web site, http://www.aamc.org/students/financing/repayment/start.htm, to find a medically geared loan repayment program, or the Web site (http://www.equaljusticeworks.org) of Equal Justice Works for more information.

Consolidating Loans

What is a consolidation loan? It's a total or partial combination of student loans into one new loan, regardless of lender or original loan type. The benefit of consolidating students loans is twofold: the convenience of one monthly payment and, in most cases, a much lower interest rate. Student loans may be consolidated using loans from the federal government or state guaranty agencies. Visit http://loanconsolidation.ed.gov/borrower/bapply.shtml for more information on Federal Direct Consolidation Loans.

Defaulting on a Student Loan

Some students have difficulty paying their student loans due to unemployment, sickness, or an unfinished degree. This poses serious consequences that may be irreversible. A defaulted student loan is sent to a collection agency, which will make every effort to collect. Collection methods include garnishing wages and withholding Social Security benefits or income tax refunds. Professionals such as doctors, nurses, and lawyers will be denied reapplication for licensure. The most serious, and hardest to correct, is the black mark a defaulted loan will place on your credit history. Is it worth it? For information on how to avoid default, or ways to correct a defaulted loan, please visit http://www.ed.gov/offices/OSFAP/DCS/index.html.

ADDITIONAL RESOURCES

American Association of Medical Colleges
http://www.aamc.org/students/financing/repayment/start.htm
Visit this Web site for a list of state and private loan repayment/forgiveness programs for physicians.

AmeriCorps
1201 New York Avenue, NW
Washington, DC 20525
202-606-5000, 202-606-3472 (TTY)
questions@americorps.org
http://www.americorps.gov/about/ac/index.asp
Contact AmeriCorps for information on receiving college funding in exchange for volunteer service.

Equal Justice Works
2120 L Street, NW, Suite 450
Washington, DC 20037-1541
202-466-3686
mail@equaljusticeworks.org
http://www.equaljusticeworks.org

Contact Equal Justice Works for information on loan forgiveness programs for lawyers.

Federal Direct Consolidation Loans Information Center

800-557-7392
loan_consolidation@mail.eds.com
http://loanconsolidation.ed.gov/borrower/bapply.shtml
Contact the center for information on Federal Direct Consolidation Loans.

Federal Student Aid Information Center

http://studentaid.ed.gov/PORTALSWebApp/students/english/index.jsp
Contact the Federal Student Aid Information Center for comprehensive information on federal student aid programs.

Free Application for Federal Student Aid (FAFSA)

800-433-3243, 800-730-8913 (TTY)
http://www.fafsa.ed.gov
Visit the FAFSA's Web site to learn more about submitting the application online or via regular mail.

Funding Education Beyond High School: The Guide to Federal Student Aid

http://studentaid.ed.gov/students/publications/student_guide/2006-2007/index.html
Funding Education Beyond High School: The Guide to Federal Student Aid provides comprehensive resource on grants, loans, and work-study programs that are available from the U.S. Department of Education.

Montgomery G.I. Bill

http://www.gibill.com or http://www.gibill.va.gov
Visit these Web sites to learn more about education benefits for military service.

National Education Loan Network (Nelnet)

http://www.nelnet.net
Nelnet is one of the largest private education lenders in the United States.

SallieMae

http://www.salliemae.com
SallieMae is one of the largest private education lenders in the United States.

Student Loan Network

877-328-1565
http://www.staffordloan.com
Visit the Student Loan Network's Web site for information on Stafford Loans. Note: This is a private organization that is not affiliated with the federal government.

U.S. Department of Education: Addressing Your Defaulted Student Loan

http://www.ed.gov/offices/OSFAP/DCS/index.html
Visit this Web site for information on what to do if you default on a federally sponsored loan.

U.S. Department of Education: State Guaranty Agencies

http://wdcrobcolp01.ed.gov/Programs/EROD/org_list.cfm?category_cd=SGA
This Web site provides a list of state guaranty agencies.

U.S. Department of Veterans Affairs: Survivors' and Dependents' Educational Assistance Program

http://www.gibill.va.gov/pamphlets/CH35/CH35_Pamphlet_General.htm
Visit this Web site for information on the Survivors' and Dependents' Educational Assistance Program.

WORK-STUDY PROGRAMS

After adding up scholarships, loans, and a variety of other financial aid, many students still find themselves short when it comes to paying their college tuition, not to mention daily living expenses. In such cases, students can turn to college work-study programs—part-time employment geared to accommodate a student's academic schedule—to help make ends meet. Here are some programs available to students.

FEDERAL WORK-STUDY (FWS) PROGRAM

Eligible schools are allocated federal funds to provide employment to eligible students at the undergraduate and graduate levels. Currently, 3,400 universities and colleges nationwide participate in the FWS program. Eligible students must show financial need, and annual FWS earnings cannot exceed their maximum federal work-study award, an amount determined by submitting the Free Application for Federal Student Aid (FAFSA). Undergraduates are paid hourly at minimum wage or more, depending on the skills needed for the particular job; graduate students are often given an annual salary. Work hours must be arranged to accommodate a student's class schedule and cannot exceed 19 hours per week. Students are matched to jobs that relate to their major, or they provide community service. Employers contribute 25 percent of the student's salary.

Jobs can be located on or off campus. Campus jobs may include food service, providing security, or departmental research assistance. Other jobs involve student services such as library work, tutoring, or campus social and health services. Schools participating in the FWS program must direct at least 7 percent of their funding to off-campus jobs in local communities. Such jobs strive to better the life or environment of residents, many of whom reside in low-income neighborhoods. Students may serve as summer camp counselors, tutor preschool or elementary children, provide literacy work for new immigrants, work in child-care centers, or assist in area hospitals, clinics, and nursing homes. They may also participate in conservation programs such as helping to save wetlands or restoring historical sites.

STATE WORK-STUDY (SWS) PROGRAMS

State-funded work-study programs are also available to eligible students. Employment is ideally linked with a student's course of study. Financial need is necessary to be eligible for all of these programs, though other requirements vary by state. Most programs require U.S. citizenship (or legal immigrant status) and proven state residency; priority funding is awarded to students who have full-time status. Students must also not have any student loans in default.

Program awards are set up by the financial aid office of each school, but may vary depending on how much money is allocated by the state. For example, students participating in Minnesota's SWS program can earn up to $1,500 annually. In Pennsylvania, however, students can earn up to $7,200 a year, half during the school year and the remainder during the summer. Students employed under the SWS program work part time during the school year (about 10 to 15 hours a week); this number increases to full time during summer break.

Students can work on campus or off, in jobs similar to those provided by the FWS program. Some work-study programs can function as internships, especially if they are linked to a student's major.

PART-TIME EMPLOYMENT, NON–WORK-STUDY

Many colleges and universities also offer part-time jobs to students who are not participating in a federal- or state-funded program. In these cases, students need not demonstrate financial need, only a desire to work. Jobs are located on campus, but in a variety of settings. For example, at Saint Xavier University, located in Chicago,

Illinois, students can work in the groundskeeping department maintaining campus grounds and gardens, or they can check student identification cards at the athletic center, or work as lab assistants in the department of nursing. At the University of California-San Diego, students can work part time at the university book store stocking shelves, staffing the retail desk, or helping students find the correct textbook and supplies. Students with sales experience and computer knowledge can work in computer sales or support. They might help customers with hardware and software questions and purchases, and stock merchandise. Both jobs pay about $7.50 an hour, with work schedules of up to 19 hours per week.

APPLYING FOR THE JOB

For federal or state work-study programs, your first step in the job search process is submitting the FAFSA to determine your amount of federal work-study award. Employment opportunities for such programs, as well as part-time non–work-study jobs, can be found at your school's financial aid office or student employment center. You can also research job opportunities in the classified section of your campus newspaper, local newspaper, or department newsletter. Let your teachers, guidance counselor, and friends know you are interested in employment—they may be privy to jobs before they are posted to the general student body. You can also search your school's Web site for available job opportunities and descriptions.

The key is to start early, as many work-study jobs are filled quickly, and awarded on a first-come, first-served basis. Federal work-study jobs are posted in August. If you don't find your dream job in the beginning of the semester, don't despair. Job opportunities can become available during the middle of the school year due to vacancies, or as need arises. Don't be afraid to be choosy when it comes to accepting a position. It's as important to find a job that fits with your school schedule and course load, and gives important work experience, as it is to find one that provides financial benefits.

ADDITIONAL RESOURCES
Information for Financial Aid Professionals Library
http://www.ifap.ed.gov/IFAPWebApp/topicPag.jsp
Visit this site to learn about the Federal Work-Study
    Program, potential off-campus employers and their
    requirements, and student eligibility.

U.S. Department of Education
http://web99.ed.gov/GTEP/Program2.nsf/
    9f7174e36cc662958525645d005843b9/edc608c712d
    fa15f852563bc00540460?OpenDocument
This site offers information regarding the Federal Work-
    Study Program, including program description and
    student eligibility requirements.

GETTING THE MOST OUT OF COLLEGE SAVINGS PLANS

Expect to pay anywhere from $42,000 to $107,000 for a four-year college or university education, according to The College Board. Does paying for college seem unattainable? Think again. Never before have there been so many possibilities when it comes to saving for college. There are federal- and state-funded programs, as well as privately funded savings plans, available to accommodate every tax bracket and level of contribution. Read on to learn about some of the major college savings plans. Regardless of your financial status, it's important to take advantage of at least one of these programs—the benefits of a college education are truly priceless.

STATE SAVINGS 529 PLANS

529 Plans are so named after Internal Revenue Code Section 529, which allows each state to create its own college savings plan or prepaid tuition plan. The purpose of each plan is to help families save money for future college expenses tax-free during its accumulation period.

College Savings Plans

More than 30 institutional providers offer some type of state 529 College Savings Plan, with each one managed by a participating investment firm. Some well-known firms include Fidelity Investments, Putnam, Alliance Capital, and T. Rowe Price. Firms act as plan managers for the account, meaning they have control over how the funds are invested and managed. College savings accounts are given different names according to each plan manager. Some well-known accounts include Tomorrow's Scholar, NextGen College Investing Plan, and College Save.

The person opening the account is considered the owner, and has control over the management of the funds, as well as the power to withdraw funds. The owner may also choose to change management, or firm, if they are not satisfied with the return of the investment. By law, accounts may not move from one manager to another more than one time per year. The owner may name or change beneficiaries for the account. Relation to the owner does not matter when naming a beneficiary, but does when changing beneficiary status.

Plans differ by state. For example, some state plans are available only to those claiming state residency. Other plans are open to out of state residents, but charge a broker's commission to such accounts. Some states have rules concerning taxable withdrawals, while others do not. Enrollment fees, advisor and management fees, and fund expenses are other details that vary by state. While each state has its own level of maximum funding, most average about $225,000 per account; sufficient estimates to fund a five-year college education at even the most expensive private college. Check with your state to determine your particular cap and tax rules.

529 College Savings Plans may only receive cash contributions; physical assets, stocks and bonds, or other investments may not be included. Also, account funds may only be used toward education expenses at qualified institutions in order for withdrawals to remain tax-free. Schools—two-year, four-year, and trade or vocational schools—are deemed eligible if they participate in federal student aid programs. Besides tuition, expenses include room and board, school or athletic fees, books, and other supplies. If the beneficiary chooses not to pursue a college degree, the owner may name a new beneficiary to the account. The owner may also request an account refund; but doing so will result in a sizable tax penalty of about 10 percent.

For more information on this type of plan, visit http://www.collegesavings.org/faq/529savings.htm.

Prepaid Tuition Plans

The 529 Prepaid Tuition Plan allows for the purchase of tuition credit or certificates—often through monthly contributions—at today's prices to be presented when the beneficiary is ready to enter college. This plan is linked to participating state-funded schools, but some states allow credits to be used at select in-state private schools or out-of-state public schools. The individual purchasing the account is designated as owner, and has power to control the funds including withdrawals and refunds, and naming the beneficiary. Anyone can make contributions to a prepaid tuition plan.

Many people choose a prepaid plan to lock in a tuition price. If a one-year tuition credit is purchased at today's prices for a newborn, that beneficiary is entitled to one year of college at that cost regardless of the school's tuition price 18 years later. Drawbacks to this plan? Only tuition costs are covered; expenses for room and board, fees, or supplies must be met by other means. Many schools also enforce a time limit for students to finish their degrees. Keep in mind the value of each credit or certificate will vary from school to school. For example, a 10 percent tuition credit may be worth more at one institution or less at another, depending on the school's final tuition amount. More importantly, investing in a prepaid tuition plan does not guarantee school acceptance. Despite these obstacles, many families are drawn to this type of program. In fact, its popularity has forced some states to put a hold on new enrollees.

For more information on this type of plan, visit http://www.collegesavings.org/faq/529prepaid.htm.

FEDERAL SAVINGS PLANS

The federal government offers the Coverdell Education Savings Account and the Education Savings Bond Program.

Coverdell Education Savings Account

The Coverdell Education Savings Account (ESA) is a federal savings program to help parents and students save for all education-related expenses. This program was originally referred to as Education IRA, but renamed to honor one of its congressional advocates, Senator Paul Coverdell of Georgia. The owner of the account is referred to as the "custodian"; the "beneficiary" is the future recipient of the funds. Beneficiaries must be under the age of 18, or have a special need. The custodian cannot be named as a beneficiary of the same account.

Funds are distributed once the beneficiary becomes of age. If applied towards tuition at an eligible educational institution, or for related expenses, money is tax-free. However, if a balance remains in the fund after tuition is paid, then the amount is taxable to the beneficiary, including an additional 10 percent penalty tax. Exceptions to the penalty tax include receipt of a scholarship, or the beneficiary's death or disablement. Any balance in the fund must be disbursed within one month of the beneficiary's 30th birthday. Any earnings from the fund will be taxable, including an additional 10 percent tax. This tax can be avoided if the balance is rolled over to another family member's Coverdell ESA.

There are limitations to the Coverdell ESA. The account does not have a maximum cap, but can receive no more than $2,000 a year in contributions. Anyone can contribute to this account, including the beneficiary, but must meet income limitations. According to the Internal Revenue Service, a contributor's income should be less than $110,000 (modified adjusted gross income), or $220,000 if filing jointly.

What if the designated beneficiary decides not to pursue a college education, or chooses a noneligible school, such as a beauty school or nail academy? The custodian could then choose to roll over the account's balance into another family member's ESA, or use the funds to pay for another beneficiary's private elementary or high school tuition and expenses.

For more information on Coverdell Education Savings Accounts, visit http://www.irs.gov/taxtopics/tc310.html or http://www.irs.gov/newsroom/article/0,,id=107636,00.html.

Education Savings Bond Program

The Education Savings Bond Program, also known as the Tax-Free Interest for Education Program, comes in the form of U.S. Savings bonds. These bonds are a very safe form of investment because the U.S. federal government backs them. Bonds must be a Series EE or I and can be purchased from any bank, savings and loan, or through employer programs.

Series EE bonds purchased before May 2005 earn an adjustable interest rate; those purchased in May 2005 and after earn a fixed interest rate. Paper EE Bonds are sold at half the face value; electronic EE Bonds are sold at face value. Series I Bonds earn a flexible interest rate and are sold at face value. The interest-earning period for both types of bonds is 30 years. The bonds must be owned for at least one year before redemption. Penalties exist for bonds that are cashed in within five years of ownership.

The purchaser is considered the owner of the bond. There is no need to name the beneficiary, or the reason for purchase, at the time of purchase. In fact, mature bonds can be used for purposes other than education, but the interest will be subject to tax. To avoid this tax, the bond must be used to pay for all educational expenses—tuition and fees—at approved colleges and universities or vocational schools. Room and board, books, and such expenses are not covered. Eligible institutions are those that participate in federally assisted programs.

Be sure to purchase bonds in small denominations, as any funds not used for educational purposes are taxable. Visit http://savingsbonds.gov/indiv/products/eebonds_glance.htm and http://savingsbonds.gov/indiv/products/ibonds_glance.htm for more information.

Private or Custodial Accounts

UGMA/UTMA Accounts (accounts created under the Uniform Gifts to Minors or Uniform Transfers to Minors Acts) are examples of custodial accounts. The greatest incentive to this type of program is its tax savings. UGMAs and UTMAs unearned incomes are taxed at the child's income tax bracket—usually at 5 to 10 percent—once the child reaches 14. Until then, a portion of the account's income is taxed according to the parent's tax bracket, the remaining at the lower minor's bracket. The limit of tax-free contribution is pretty high—up to $11,000 annually for a single tax payer, and up to $22,000 for couples.

The true owner of a UGMA or UTMA is the designated child on the account. While the child is a minor, the custodian (usually a parent) maintains control of the account, and can choose the direction and type of investment. However, once the child reaches majority (as mandated by the state of residence) the funds are made available. This may, at times, cause potential problems. For example, the child's goal may differ from the parent's. Even if the parent planned the account to pay for a child's college education, the child may choose to use the money to open a business, travel, invest, or use it for less desirable purposes. Visit the Web sites of private financial aid providers, such as Franklin Templeton Investments (http://www.franklintempleton.com), for more information on UGMA/UTMA accounts.

A **Roth IRA** is another example of a custodial account. While considered a retirement plan, many Roth IRAs are earmarked for future college expenses. Contributions are made with after-tax income, freeing any growth earnings and fund distributions as taxable income. Annual contributions must not exceed $4,000 (or $5,000 for those over age 50) as of 2006. It also has annual income caps on eligibility—$110,000 for single tax filers, $160,000 for married joint filers. Visit http://www.rothira.com or http://www.fairmark.com/rothira/roth101.htm for more details.

AFFINITY PROGRAMS

Consumers are urged to make purchases from affiliated vendors in order to receive monthly rebates. These rebates can be deposited into 529 Plans managed by the program, or an existing college savings plan. Affinity programs should not be used as a primary savings plan; the rebate percentages are just too small. Rather, they should be used as a way to accelerate your savings fund.

The **BabyMint** (http://www.babymint.com) and **Upromise** (http://www.upromise.com) programs offer college savings plans for serious shoppers. The strategy here is simple: shop at participating merchants and get a percentage (up to 50 percent) of your total purchase back to apply to a 529 or ESA of your choice. Earn an additional 1 percent of your total purchase if you use the BabyMint credit card or Upromise Citicard. This credit will be applied by the affinity programs directly to their 529 Plan, your designated college savings plan, or be sent to you on a monthly basis. Upromise is the larger of the two programs, with more than 30,000 participating vendors including nationwide retail chains and restaurants, grocery stores, gas stations, vacation vendors, and magazines. Purchase can be made in the stores themselves, through catalogs, or online. Family members and friends can also contribute their Upromise credits or BabyMint dollars to your savings plan. Referrals resulting in memberships can also add to your plan—up to 1 percent of your referral's monthly account total.

BabyMint also offers a Tuition Rewards Program where your rebates are matched by participating private colleges and universities. For example, if your rebate account holds $1,000, it would be worth $2,000 at a BabyMint-affiliated college. Money accrued through this program can only be applied to tuition; room and board, fees, books, and miscellaneous expenses must be paid via other means. Currently, 150 institutions are on board. Even if your school of choice is not on the list, you can still use your BabyMint money as planned, though less the matching funds.

ADDITIONAL RESOURCES

BabyMint
888-427-1099
service@babymint.com
http://www.babymint.com
Contact BabyMint for more information on its college savings program.

College Savings Plans Network
http://www.collegesavings.org
Those interested in learning more about 529 College Savings Plans will find this Web site a helpful resource. The Web site lets users choose their state from a drop-down list and gives state-specific savings plan options.

Internal Revenue Service
800-829-1040
http://www.irs.gov
Contact the IRS for more information on Coverdell
    Education Savings Accounts.

Savingforcollege.com
http://www.savingforcollege.com
Teaching individuals everything they need to know
    about 529 Savings Plans is the primary objective of
    this independent Web site, which provides overviews
    and news relating to saving for college, but does not
    try to sell anything other than extended use of its
    compiled material. For a monthly fee, users can gain
    access to detailed information (though this fee-based
    service is primarily geared for tax professionals).
    Parents, however, can compare 529 Plans, 529 Plan

ratings, find a 529 professional in a directory, read the
latest 529 news, and more—for free.

U.S. Department of the Treasury
Series EE and I
Bureau of the Public Debt
Division of Customer Assistance
PO Box 1328
Parkersburg, WV 26106-1328
http://savingsbonds.gov/indiv/indiv.htm
Contact the U.S. Department of the Treasury for more
    information on its Education Savings Bond Program.

Upromise
http://www.upromise.com
Contact Upromise for more information on its college
    savings program.

THE INS AND OUTS OF ATHLETIC SCHOLARSHIPS

Students who excel in sports have another way to fund their college education—athletic scholarships. In addition to the traditional forms of financial options such as federal, state, and private loans, grants, and scholarships, they are eligible for scholarships earmarked for athletic ability. Top student-athletes are offered financial assistance to attend school and compete in athletics—from well-known sports such as football and basketball, to less mainstream sports such as fencing and sailing.

WHO FUNDS ATHLETIC SCHOLARSHIPS?

Athletic, or sports, scholarships are funded by private organizations and colleges and universities under the guidance of various athletic associations of which the schools belong.

Athletic scholarships provided by private organizations are funded by private companies and are not governed by any athletic associations. These scholarships reward students who excel in a variety of sports, and some are specific to gender or disability.

Colleges and universities offer athletic scholarships to talented high school athletes in a variety of sports. Most colleges and universities with a sports program belong to an athletic association whose purpose is to govern competition between schools and to advocate for the best interests of student athletes.

College Athletic Associations

The three main college athletic associations that provide scholarships to students are the National Collegiate Athletic Association, the National Association of Intercollegiate Athletics, and the National Junior College Athletic Association.

National Collegiate Athletic Association

The National Collegiate Athletic Association (NCAA) is by far the largest athletic association with member schools throughout the United States. The NCAA sets up recruiting guidelines and schedules, and stipulates the number and amount of scholarships each school may offer. Participating schools are grouped into three divisions according to the size of their sports program. Divisions I and II schools offer athletic scholarships; Division III schools do not.

- **Division I.** Schools within this division have huge athletic programs, many of which receive national television coverage. Division I schools are further categorized into I-A or I-AA schools with requirements for the number of home games, scheduling criteria, and stadium attendance. Division I schools offer sports scholarship amounts as set by the NCAA; they offer a number of full scholarships. Division I-A schools are required to offer full tuition scholarships for a number of roster spots for football, men's basketball, and women's basketball. Other sports do not have this stipulation. Some examples of Division I schools? The University of Illinois, the University of Southern California, the University of Notre Dame, and Pennsylvania State University.
- **Division II.** Division II schools' athletic programs work within a set budget similar to other college departments. This budget is awarded to students according to need and/or performance. Although the NCAA allows a specific amount of scholarship funding, many colleges choose not to give out the maximum amount, or divide the money among several team members. Students must often subsidize their scholarship money with a combination of other funding—student loans, grants, and other scholarships. Examples of Division II schools include Northern Kentucky University, Central Missouri State University, and North Dakota State University.
- **Division III.** Schools participating at this level do not offer athletic scholarships, only those based on merit.

National Association of Intercollegiate Athletics
The National Association of Intercollegiate Athletics is the governing body for many smaller colleges in the United States, about 350 in all. Sports budgets at such schools tend to be smaller as compared to those with NCAA Division I, which translates to fewer or smaller athletic scholarships. Member schools include Aquinas College, Eastern Oregon University, Fresno Pacific University, and Ursuline College.

National Junior College Athletic Association
The National Junior College Athletic Association (NJCAA) is the organizing body of more than 500 member junior college schools nationwide. NJCAA schools offer full or partial tuition in 23 sports. Some students playing for NJCAA-level teams often try out for NCAA-level teams once they have earned their two-year degrees. Member schools include Atlantic Cape Community College, Bismarck State College, and Lewis & Clark Community College.

CREATING AN ATHLETIC RESUME

Elite student athletes are often strongly courted by college recruiters to participate in their programs. What should you do if representatives from Big Ten schools aren't attending your home games or visiting you at home? Take action and put yourself in the spotlight! Put together an athletic resume package to highlight your talents on the court, as well as off. Here are some key points to hit:

- Your cover letter should be addressed to the head coach of your desired sport program and the school by name. This will show you've actually done your research instead of simply putting together a mass mailing.
- Include information regarding your academic history. Besides your GPA, and ACT or SAT scores, list all Advanced Placement classes you've taken. Show the coach you'll be able to survive the school's curriculum as well as the workouts.
- List all of your extracurricular activities—that means honor societies, social or special interest clubs, community service, and part-time jobs. Do you have other talents besides an overpowering fastball? If you play an instrument, paint, or sing in the choir, include this information on your resume. Let the coach know you are talented in more ways than on the field.
- List all high school sports teams in which you've participated. Put together a game tape or DVD

highlighting games and key plays. Your game tape can also include practice sessions or scrimmages—anything that will show you in action.
- Give your personal and athletic statistics such as age, height and weight, and team position, as well as season statistics. Also, an athletic resume is probably the only type of resume that allows inclusion of a photo without appearing tacky. Really, the coaches want to know what you look like.
- Include newspaper clippings from your school or local paper that make mention of your ability. List any sports awards or honors you have received, be it a Scholar-Athlete award or MVP of the state championship game.
- Ask your high school coach for a letter of recommendation.
- If possible, include a sports schedule of upcoming games and their locations. If the school is highly interested in you, it may send a representative to see you in action.

Since many sports programs need to have their early intent choices in place by the end of September or October for the following year, industry veterans recommend that you send resume packages out by the end of your sophomore or the beginning of your junior year in high school. University and college coaches receive thousands of resumes annually, which far outnumber the available positions on a team. Give yourself the advantage by sending out as many copies of your resume as possible—at least 25, but more is better. Send resume packages to every school you are interested in attending, and keep your eyes peeled for new schools that might fit the bill.

THE ATHLETIC TIMELINE

Like anything worthwhile, vying for an athletic scholarship takes time, effort, and precision planning. A year-by-year preparation timeline will keep you from fumbling your scholarship prospects.

Freshman Year

Build your academic muscles by enrolling in core classes, as well as a college-bound curriculum. Play your favorite sport or join a high school team.

Sophomore Year

Continue to concentrate on your classes, and perhaps begin to take elective classes. If you are eligible for honors classes, take them. They will help boost your total GPA, and they'll look impressive on your athletic resume. Now is the time to begin your college research. Find out which schools are appealing not only for their sports program, but for what they can offer academically. If possible, attend a college game or two. It's a great way to get a feel for the atmosphere of collegiate-level competition.

The summer between sophomore and junior year is a good time to start sending out your athletic resumes. Some students choose to use the services of a professional athletic recruiter, though the fee they charge won't necessarily improve your chances of obtaining a scholarship. Your efforts, coupled with the help of your guidance counselor and high school coach can yield the same results.

Junior Year

This is going to be a busy year! If you haven't already done so, you should send out any remaining athletic resumes and register with the NCAA Initial-Eligibility Clearinghouse. The Clearinghouse is important because it will make your statistics, both academic and athletic, known to prospective schools nationwide. (Visit http://www. ncaaclearinghouse.net/ncaa/NCAA/common/index. html for more information.) Academically, keep up with your studies and prepare to take your college entrance exams. Research colleges and make on-campus visits. Be sure to apply for scholarships that are not sports-related. Chances are, even with an athletic scholarship, you will need extra financial to help meet the cost of college. Apply for every scholarship, grant, and student loan you possibly can. Athletically, you will want to play your best every game—you'll never know who's watching!

On July 1, after you complete your junior year of high school, you can begin formal contact with college coaches and members of college athletics departments. Any contact before this date must be made by correspondence or via phone.

Senior Year

Send out your senior sports fall schedule to your short list of colleges as soon as possible. You'll want to give recruiters every opportunity to see you play. You may be given a verbal agreement for scholarship funding, or asked to give a verbal agreement to play for a particular college team, or. It's important to note that such agreements are just that—verbal. Unless it's in writing, it can be rescinded at any time.

Find out the National Letter of Intent (NLI) deadline for your particular sport. (Visit http://www.national-letter. org for more information on the NLI). The NLI is a binding agreement between the student athlete and college; if you sign an NLI, you commit to playing on a college's team for one year. As a result, other schools must respect this agreement, and cease all recruitment. The NLI was originally designed to prevent strong recruitment tactics by schools vying for the same student athlete. It also protects the student by ensuring, once the NLI is signed, a spot on the team's roster. In the past, a student's sports scholarship could be legally given to another player with superior skills. All NCAA Division I and most Division II schools participate in the NLI. Check the NLI Web site for all details of the agreement, and signing requirements.

Study hard—it's almost graduation time!

DIFFERENT LOCKER ROOMS, SAME RULES OF THE GAME

Title IX of the Education Amendments Act of 1972 brought about equality in the way men and women received federally funded educational resources—and changed the world of women's collegiate sports. Title IX gives women more choices in individual and team sports, locker rooms and facilities that are equal in quality to those used by male athletes, and more opportunities to receive athletic scholarships. Visit http://www1.ncaa.org/membership/ed_outreach/gender_equity/faq.html#apply for more information on this important federal law.

IS PURSUING A SPORTS SCHOLARSHIP THE BEST WAY TO PAY FOR COLLEGE?

If this is your only hope for college money, then the answer is no. Most student athletes lucky enough to receive a sports scholarship still find themselves in need financially and must turn to traditional forms of financial aid.

If you are lucky enough to be offered a sports scholarship, be ready to work hard. College sports are played on a much higher level than what you may have been used to in high school. If you were the team star, be prepared to relinquish the title. You will most likely be just one of many of the biggest, fastest, and strongest student athletes from the nation vying for a spot on the starting team. Along with your studies, you'll be expected to participate in team practices, meetings, and conditioning exercises. Travel to away games (if your performance warrants a seat on the bus or plane) will certainly add to the pressure of completing schoolwork or studying for exams. Students who can't meet the expectations of making a passing grade or stellar athletic performance may risk losing their scholarship. However, if you are able to handle the pressures of college and excel in your sport, then the answer is an absolute yes.

ADDITIONAL RESOURCES

For more information on athletic associations, sports programs and schedules, and eligibility requirements, contact the following organizations:

National Association of Intercollegiate Athletics
23500 West 105th Street
Olathe, KS 66061
913-791-0044
http://naia.collegesports.com

National Collegiate Athletic Association
700 West Washington Street, PO Box 6222
Indianapolis, IN 46206-6222
317-917-6222
http://www.ncaa.org

National Junior College Athletic Association
1755 Telstar Drive, Suite 103
Colorado Springs, CO 80920
719-590-9788
http://www.njcaa.org

FinAid.com
http://www.finaid.org/otheraid/sports.phtml
Provides concise information on scholarships and financial aid for student athletes. Also provides links to athletic associations and a variety of private sports scholarships.

National Collegiate Athletic Association (NCAA) Initial-Eligibility Clearinghouse
http://www.ncaaclearinghouse.net/ncaa/NCAA/common/index.html
Visit this Web site for information on how to register with the NCAA Initial-Eligibility Clearinghouse.

National Letter of Intent
http://www.national-letter.org
Visit this Web site for information on the National Letter of Intent.

***NextStep* Magazine.com**
http://www.nextstepmagazine.com
Provides helpful information on the process of athletic recruitment, as well as insightful essays on the dos and don'ts of applying for an athletic scholarship.

THE INS AND OUTS OF MILITARY SCHOLARSHIPS

Many students turn to the military as a way to finance their college education, receive relevant work training, and serve their country at the same time. Some students even choose to stay in the service after meeting their commitments, and spend their entire careers in the military. Read on to learn more about educational financing options provided by the U.S. military, state and local government, and private organizations.

U.S. SERVICE ACADEMIES

Each branch of the military maintains its own four-year school of higher learning. Students enrolled in each academy receive full tuition, with a monthly stipend for four years, and study a concentration of courses toward a bachelor's of science. Training at this level is demanding, and many well-known politicians, world leaders, and business executives are among these institutions' alumnae. Entrance, or appointment, to a military academy is highly competitive, allowing only students with the highest GPAs and college entrance scores. Most academies also rely on a student's recommendation from a member of the U.S. Congress or academy official.

What will you learn? Students at service academies study a core curriculum heavy on science, engineering, and mathematics, along with physical training and military leadership. Students at the Coast Guard Academy also study courses in naval architecture or marine environmental science.

After graduation from the Air Force or Navy/Marine academy, students must complete a five-year tour of active duty. Graduates of the Army academy must complete a minimum of five years of active duty. Graduates of the Coast Guard's Officer Candidate School must complete three years of active duty. Students graduate with the rank of second lieutenant in the Army, Air Force, or Marines, and as ensigns in the Navy or Coast Guard.

For more information on U.S. military academies, visit the following Web sites:

- U.S. Air Force Academy (http://www.usafa. af.mil)
- U.S. Coast Guard Academy (http://www.cga. edu)
- U.S. Military Academy (Army, http://www.usma. edu)
- U.S. Naval Academy (Navy and Marine Corps, http://www.usna.edu/homepage.php)

RESERVE OFFICERS' TRAINING CORPS (ROTC)

Students taking this route receive full or partial funding of their college education, plus expenses for books, fees, and a monthly stipend. ROTC scholarships are merit based. ROTC programs are offered as an elective program at many colleges and universities throughout the United States as a means to recruit, educate, and train qualified students as commissioned officers. Each branch maintains admissions guidelines, applications, and list of participating schools at their respective Web sites. The following sections provide a breakdown of ROTC programs by service branch.

Air Force ROTC

To be eligible for this program, students must be U.S. citizens and between the ages of 17 to 31 (from the date their commission begins). Candidates must pass a medical exam, be physically fit, and have correctible vision. They must also hold a high school diploma or the equivalent, and have acceptable ACT or SAT scores. In addition to regular college course work, cadets must also take courses in military training, leadership labs, and physical training.

Commitment varies with a student's major and required training. Most graduates are required to serve a four-year commitment as an officer on active duty. Pilots must commit to 10 years after pilot training; navigators, six years after training; and aviation battle managers, six years after training.

The Air Force offers three types of ROTC scholarships:

- Type 1: Four-year scholarships paying full tuition, and $600 for books. Students accepting Type 1 scholarships major in computer, electrical, or environmental engineering. Only 5 percent of all scholarships fall into this category.
- Type 2: Three-year scholarships centering in the technical fields. Scholarships include tuition, fees up to $15,000, and $600 for books. If the student intends to enroll at a university where tuition exceeds the limit, they can choose to pay the difference. About 10 percent of scholarships awarded fall in this category.
- Type 7: Full-college tuition up to $9,000, plus a $600 allowance per year for books. Students must choose universities or colleges whose tuition falls within this range—they are not allowed to pay for the difference.

For more information on the Air Force ROTC, visit http://www.afrotc.com.

Army ROTC

In order to qualify for Army ROTC, students should be citizens of the United States, be between the ages of 17 and 26, meet physical standards, and meet certain educational requirements—high school diploma or GED, high school GPA of at least 2.5, and minimum SAT (920) and SAT (19) scores.

In addition to their usual college course load each semester, students, or cadets, are required to take one military science or related class per semester. During the first two years of college, cadets participate in the ROTC Basic Course where they learn military skills as well as leadership skills. No commitment to military service is required at this time, allowing many students to fully explore this career/educational option. During the last two years of college, cadets take advanced courses in military tactics, team organization, military planning and decision-making. Cadets graduating from the Army ROTC must commit to at least three to four years of full-time duty. Some cadets may choose to serve a longer, part-time commitment in the Army Reserve or National Guard, allowing them the opportunity to pursue a nonmilitary career full time.

Two-, three-, and four-year scholarships of up to $20,000 (plus allowances for books and fees) are available.

For more information on Army ROTC, visit http://www.goarmy.com/rotc.

Navy and Marine ROTC

The Navy and Marine branches of the military are served by the Navy ROTC (NROTC). Candidates must meet academic and physical standards including U.S. citizenship, age requirements (17 to 23), high school diploma or the equivalent, and qualified college entrance scores. In addition to their normal college course load, NROTC students, referred to as midshipmen, take calculus, physics, English grammar and composition, and classes in national security and American military affairs.

Midshipmen receive four years of full tuition, including books, fees, and a monthly stipend. NROTC scholarships for technical degrees such as engineering, computer science, or physics can award five years of full tuition.

NROTC graduates are commissioned as ensigns and have a military obligation of eight years—four years of active duty, and the remaining four as selective reserve, or inactive ready-reserve. For more information, https://www.nrotc.navy.mil.

OTHER PROGRAMS

Other military programs can also provide educational assistance in exchange for time in service. Here are some popular military programs:

Montgomery GI Bill

The Montgomery GI Bill (MGIB) is an education incentive for those enlisted in all branches of the military. Service men and women have the option of "buying" into this financial service during their tour of duty, with a monthly deduction of $100 from their pay for the first 12 months of duty. In return, the MGIB provides up to 36 months of benefits, with final benefit amounts dependent on the length of service. Money from the MGIB can be used toward educational expenses at accredited universities, colleges, technical schools, and vocational schools. Currently, veterans with two years of service can receive $840 monthly, or $30,240 lifetime. Those with three or more years of service can receive $1,034 a month, or $37,224 lifetime. Service in the Reserves and National Guard can also qualify you for educational funding. MGIB benefits must be taken no later than 10 years after the last tour of duty. Immediate family members of veterans may also be able to benefit from the MGIB. More detailed information on the MGIB can be found by contacting the various military branches or by visiting http://www.gibill.com.

Military College Funds

Military College Funds (MCFs) are available to enlisted personnel for help in paying for college. Because aid provided by MCFs are usually used to supplement, or boost, funding received from the MGIB, this program is often referred to as "kicker." MCFs are an option selected at the time of enlistment; participation in the MGIB is necessary to be eligible for these funds. Funds from this program are awarded based on merit—those eligible must earn above-average scores on military qualification exams. Other important requirements include status (nonofficers only) and participation in a military occupational specialty. The amount of funding received from a MCF depends on the branch of military, as well as the length of duty (two to four years). Military College Fund benefits expire 10 years after separation from the military.

Tuition Assistance

Some branches of the military provide tuition assistance to eligible personnel and reserves. Studies can be pursued via online courses or during leave time. Money from this program is not a loan, but rather a payment toward an associate or bachelor's degree. The amount of funding varies from branch to branch—the Air Force offers up to $3,500 per year; Navy, $3,000 annually; and the Marines and Coast Guard, up to $4,500 annually. The Army does not have a separate tuition assistance program; it offers funding through the Montgomery GI Bill and its College Fund. Many students use the tuition assistance program, along with the MGIB program, to fund their college education. Eligibility requirements and service commitments vary according to each military branch. For more information, visit each branch's Web site.

Student Repayment Program

This is an incentive offered to highly qualified service personnel at the time of enlistment; those signing up for the program cannot participate in the MGIB. Personnel must also be eligible for certain military occupational specialties in order to qualify for this program. The amount the military will pay for a student's loan is in accordance to the number of years in service. The loan in question must originate from an accredited source and must not be in default. The total amount of repayment varies from branch to branch—the Army and Navy will pay up to $65,000 versus the Air Force's limit of $10,000. For more information, contact the various military branches.

NON-MILITARY OPTIONS
State and Local Government

State and local governments also offer college funding to active, reserve, and retired members of the military and their dependents. Visit the military financial aid section of this book for a list of available programs.

Private Organizations

Veterans' organizations, professional associations, and colleges and universities offer financial aid to active, reserve, and retired members of the military and their dependants. Examples of such organizations include the Army Aviation Association of America (http://www.quad-a.org), Coast Guard Mutual Assistance (http://www.cgmahq.org), the Fleet Reserve Association (http://www.fra.org), the Horatio Alger Association of Distinguished Americans (https://www.horatioalger.com), and the Navy-Marine Corps Relief Society (http://www.nmcrs.org). Visit the military financial aid section of this book for a list of available programs.

IS THE MILITARY RIGHT FOR ME?

The educational rewards of joining the military are appealing. For some, it may be the best way to fund a college education. Read on to weigh the pros and cons of a military education.

PROS
- Great way to pay for college.
- Good job training and work experience.
- Good physical training.
- Opportunity to travel and experience other countries and cultures.
- Provides life direction and discipline.
- Great military benefits for self and family.
- Paves the path for a military career.

CONS
- The commitment service is long and unavoidable.
- Pay is not that good for enlisted servicemen.
- There is little freedom regarding personal decisions.
- The military lifestyle may be too strict and rigid for some.
- There is always the threat of war and risk of injury or even death.

ADDITIONAL RESOURCES

For information about the Reserve Officer Training Corps, contact the following organizations:

Air Force Reserve Officer Training Corps (AFROTC)
AFROTC Admissions
551 East Maxwell Boulevard
Maxwell AFB, AL 36112-5917
866-423-7682
http://www.afrotc.com

Army Reserve Officer Training Corps (ROTC)
U.S. Army ROTC Cadet Command
Ft. Monroe, VA 23651
800-USA-ROTC
atccps@usacc.army.mil
http://www.goarmy.com/rotc

Montgomery GI Bill
http://www.gibill.com
Visit this Web site for more information on the
    Montgomery GI Bill.

For more information about the many educational opportunities and programs offered by all branches of the military, their eligibility requirements, and service commitments, contact the following braches of the military:

U.S. Air Force
http://www.airforce.com

U.S. Army
http://www.goarmy.com

U.S. Coast Guard
http://www.gocoastguard.com

U.S. Marines
http://www.marines.com

U.S. Navy
http://www.navy.com

Military.com
http://www.military.com
This site provides thorough information regarding educational opportunities offered by all branches of the military. Learn about specific programs, scholarships, and commitment and eligibility requirements.

Naval Reserve Officers Training Corps
Red Cross, Naval Education and Training Professional
    Development
Building 853
Pensacola, FL 32501
800-NAV-ROTC
PNSC_NROTC.scholarship@navy.mil
https://www.nrotc.navy.mil

FINANCIAL AID FOR STUDENTS WITH DISABILITIES

The percentage of first-year college students who report having a disability has more than tripled since the late 1970s. A rise in the awareness and diagnosis of learning disabilities accounts for some of this tremendous enrollment jump. More significantly, however, students with disabilities who would have been steered away from college in the past now recognize that it's a great way to prepare for an interesting career and to take fuller control of their lives.

Heading off to college ranks right up there as one of life's major transitions. For the disabled student, it's particularly important to start laying the foundation for a good college experience early. Here are some tips to help you get into the school of your choice, locate a variety of financial aid options, and make a smooth transition once you're on campus.

STARTING NOW

You can't start preparations too soon. Even if you're only in the ninth or tenth grade, it's time to begin considering your options. Talk with school counselors or independent-living-center counselors about careers that pique your interest. Sign up for college-prep courses or consider taking a few college-level classes at a community college. Tackling tough courses now will make it easier once you're in college. And purchase the best computer you can afford, since they've become a necessity on most campuses. You should also obtain extensive documentation from medical professionals regarding your disability (in addition to the information that is found in your Individualized Education Program). This documentation will be necessary for you to obtain many accommodations when you are in college.

Doing well on precollege exams such as the SAT (http://www.collegeboard.com/ssd/student/index.html) and ACT (http://www.act.org/aap/disab/index.html) is also going to give you a head start on getting into the college of your choice. If you need any sort of test-taking accommodations, don't be shy about asking for them.

If you're disappointed with your score and feel you can improve on it, consider retaking the exam.

CHOOSING A SCHOOL

You've decided what kind of career or degree program interests you. Now it's time to make a list of schools that offer those programs. Your high school counselor will have some suggestions, but you should also do your own research on colleges and universities by using reference books and the Internet, and talking to people who have been to college about their experiences. Don't forget to consider two-year colleges. It is estimated that 60 percent of all students with disabilities choose two-year colleges.

After you've made a preliminary list of schools that offer your chosen course of study, start narrowing the list based on other criteria. One of the things you'll need to decide is how important a school's disability services are to you. By law, all colleges must be accessible to students with disabilities; so many students with disabilities consider available disability services as just one factor in their decision-making process. They also consider qualities such as the availability of a desired major, private versus public institution, cost, setting, class size, research facilities, two-year versus four-year, and so on. Yet a number of students believe that the strength of a college's disability services can have a huge impact on their academic success or failure.

Whatever the criteria on which you ultimately base your decision, you'll definitely want to inquire about disability services at all of the colleges on your list. One of the most important things you can do is to prepare a list of questions for potential colleges and universities regarding your needs and how they will address them. After you come up with your questions, share your list with your parents, teachers, counselors, and case managers in case they have any additional suggestions. Having as many people as possible who are familiar with you review your list of questions will help ensure that your questions are comprehensive and address all of your needs. Some general topics to cover in your questions:

- How much money does the school spend on its disability services?
- Is financial support available for continuing services?
- What's the enrollment of disabled students on campus?
- What is the graduation rate for students with disabilities?
- Is the staff knowledgeable about my disability?
- What services does the school offer?
- How can I obtain any services that I need that the school does not currently provide?
- What equipment and assistive technology is available, where is it, how often will I have access to it, and how will I be trained on it, if necessary.
- How are services or equipment funded? Will I be expected to pay for any portion of it?
- What types of accommodations will be made for me as I attend class, prepare assignments, and take exams?

If you anticipate living on campus while you attend school, ask about residential options:

- How accessible are they for me? Inquire about the layout of campus, taking into consideration the buildings you are most likely to live in and attend classes in, especially if you have a physical disability:
- How easily will I be able to maneuver between buildings?
- Are all buildings accessible to me?
- Are all of the classrooms accessible to me? If not, how likely is it that all of my classes can be held in accessible areas?
- What type of public transportation is available on campus and in the surrounding community? Is it accessible to me?
- Does the university offer transportation for disabled students?
- Are there any support groups or mentoring options on campus for students with disabilities?

When you find an institution that you are interested in, take the time to meet with staff from the school's office that coordinates disability services. Try to get a feel for the personnel of the office: how helpful they are, how com-fortable you are with them. While your overall impression of them should not be the only reason you decide whether or not to attend that institution, you should have a clear idea of what you can or cannot expect from them, and factor that into your planning process. Be sure to attend any orientations or programs for prospective students with disabilities that the school may have. Besides being informative, they will also serve to introduce you to other students with disabilities who might have already encountered some of the same obstacles that you have, and might be able to offer useful suggestions. They will also provide you with an opportunity to forge friendships with others who are facing many of the same things you are, as you anticipate your postsecondary education options.

FINDING THE FUNDS

If you're worried about how to pay for college, you're not alone. Every three years, the HEATH Resource Center, a national clearinghouse on postsecondary education for individuals with disabilities, publishes a statistical profile on first-year college students with disabilities. Among its findings, the 2001 study showed that students with disabilities are more likely than their peers without disabilities to be significantly concerned about paying for their education. The good news is that with some perseverance, you can find financial aid that will cover, or at least offset, the expense of college.

One of the sources that many college students with disabilities depend on is Vocational Rehabilitation (VR), a government-funded program. The purpose of VR is to help individuals with disabilities maximize their employment, economic self-sufficiency, and integration into society. It's very important to contact your local VR office as early as possible. If you're a junior in high school, you should apply now to find out if you're eligible for assistance. Once VR determines your eligibility, you'll begin meeting with a counselor who will help you map out a long-term career plan. In most states, VR will pay for tuition, books, reader and interpreter services, and technological aids or devices.

It's unlikely, however, that all of your expenses will be covered by VR. You'll need to look into funding from other sources, too, such as grants, scholarships, loans, and work-study. The benefit of grants and scholarships is that they do not have to be repaid. Some scholarships are given to specific disability populations (contact the HEATH Resource Center for a partial list). However, these scholarships are usually limited and in small amounts ranging from $500 to $1,000. Some colleges and universities also offer scholarships for students with disabilities, so it's important to contact disability services at the colleges you're considering. For a broader choice of scholarships, consider those that have nothing to do with your disability, but depend instead on your career goals, military experience, ethnic background, religious affiliation, extracurricular activities, and so forth. To search for current scholarships, see the "Directory" portion of this book (which includes financial aid resources for students with disabilities, as well as general financial aid). You can also research scholarships on the Internet (see "Further Resources" for specific Web sites) and at your local or school library.

Loans are a form of financial aid that must be repaid over an extended period of time after you finish college. Work-study allows you to work to earn money to cover your college expenses. One of the best sources of information about loans and work-study programs is the financial aid officer at each college to which you apply.

Other sources of financial assistance for students with disabilities include Supplemental Security Income (http://www.ssa.gov/notices/supplemental-security-income), a federal program that provides assistance to people who are aged, blind, or disabled and have little or no income, and Social Security Disability Insurance (http://www.ssa.gov/dibplan/index.htm), which assists certain students who have been employed, who have a parent who has filed for Social Security, or who have a deceased parent. Discuss these options with your VR counselor or contact the Social Security administration office.

Here are some final thoughts about applying for financial aid: You'll be dealing with reams of paperwork. It's vital that you meet the deadlines and provide accurate information. Ask someone to proofread your forms and applications. During the application process, contact the colleges' financial aid offices to confirm that your data is being processed. It doesn't hurt to ask your VR counselor to stay in touch with the colleges, too.

NOW YOU'RE IN COLLEGE!

One of the most important differences between high school and college for a person who is disabled is the manner in which his or her needs are addressed and served. In college, you are your own advocate, you are responsible for making your needs known. In high school, the educational system creates your Individualized Education Program (IEP) for you, identifies which services you need, and you can expect to receive the necessary support and services. In college, there is no IEP; you must request the same services that were previously identified and provided for you. In high

school, classes are modified for you according to your disability; in college they are not. Prepare yourself for this and create strategies to deal with the difference. You can request certain modifications, but the actual course work requirements will not be modified. Consider things like assistive technology or using a facilitator in class to assist with note taking. These are things you may be required to fund yourself, so it's a good idea to research how you'll do this while you're still in high school.

The 1973 Rehabilitation Act and 1990 Americans with Disabilities Act states: "No otherwise qualified individual with a disability shall, solely by reason of his/her disability, be excluded from participation in, be denied the benefits of, or be subjected to discrimination under any program or activity of a public entity." But, despite these laws, it is up to you to advocate for your rights under the law.

No matter how excellent a college or university is at providing accommodations for disabled students, you know better than anyone what your needs are. So it's up to you to make requests. Some accommodations are simple, such as a student with low vision asking to be seated in the front row. Other accommodations require creativity, like the student with a learning disability who asks a professor to incorporate tactile demonstrations into her instruction. Getting to know other students with disabilities on campus will give you a chance to share ideas and accommodation strategies.

Shifting into self-advocacy can be a dramatic change for students who have previously relied on counselors, parents, or teachers to handle matters for them. Students with disabilities find that one of their biggest adjustments is learning to speak up for themselves. Because they were assisted via an IEP in high school, they may have never talked about their disability and how it affects them academically. It's a good idea to start practicing these types of conversations before you get to college.

Learning how to be a self-advocate is, in itself, a powerful skill, something you should aspire to gain from your time in college. You'll need to remind yourself of that occasionally when you face obstacles along the way to getting your degree and pursuing a rewarding career.

ADDITIONAL RESOURCES
ACT Inc.
Services for Students With Disabilities
http://www.act.org/aap/disab/index.html
ACT Inc. provides reasonable accommodations to
    students with disabilities who are taking the ACT
    Assessment.

Association on Higher Education and Disabilities (AHEAD)

PO Box 540666
Waltham, MA 02454
781-788-0003 (TTY)
ahead@ahead.org
http://www.ahead.org
AHEAD is an organization that addresses the need for upgrading the quality of services and support available to persons with disabilities in postsecondary education. It provides a variety of useful brochures to disabled students at a low cost.

Beacon College

105 East Main Street
Leesburg, FL 34748
352-787-7660
http://www.beaconcollege.edu
Beacon is the only accredited college in the United States with a program exclusively for students with learning disabilities that offers a baccalaureate of arts degree.

College and Career Programs for Deaf Students

Gallaudet University
800 Florida Avenue, NE
Washington, DC 20002
http://gri.gallaudet.edu/ccg/index.html
At this Web site, you'll find excellent information that is intended for deaf students but is applicable to other disabilities as well.

The College Board

Services for Students With Disabilities
PO Box 6226
Princeton, NJ 08541-6226
609-771-7137
ssd@info.collegeboard.org
http://www.collegeboard.com/ssd/student/index.html
The College Board offers testing accommodations (SAT Reasoning and Subject Tests, Advanced Placement Tests, PSAT/NMSQT) for students with disabilities. It also offers a scholarship search engine (http://apps.collegeboard.com/cbsearch_ss/welcome.jsp), which lists awards that total more than $3 billion. You can search by specific major and a variety of other criteria.

CollegeNET

http://mach25.collegenet.com/cgi-bin/M25/index
The CollegeNET Web site features a scholarship database of more than 600,000 scholarships worth more than $1.6 billion. You can search by keyword or by creating a personality profile of your interests.

DO-IT

University of Washington
PO Box 355670
Seattle, WA 98195-5670
206-685-3648 (Voice/TTY), 888-972-3648 (Voice/TTY)
doit@u.washington.edu
http://www.washington.edu/doit
DO-IT (Disabilities, Opportunities, Internetworking, and Technology) works to increase the participation of individuals with disabilities in academic programs and careers. It offers a variety of useful publications and resources, including College: You Can Do It!, College Funding Strategies for Students with Disabilities, and Preparing for College: An Online Tutorial.

FastWeb LLC

444 North Michigan Avenue, Suite 3100
Chicago, IL 60611
800-FASTWEB
http://www.fastweb.com
The FastWeb Web site is an excellent source of information for planning for college and beyond. It includes information on admissions, scholarships, and financial aid, and tips on college life. It offers a free search of the nation's largest database of local, national, and college-specific scholarships.

Federal Trade Commission

600 Pennsylvania Avenue, Northwest
Washington, DC 20580
202-326-2222
http://www.ftc.gov/bcp/conline/edcams/scholarship
Contact the Federal Trade Commission to report fraud and for tips on avoiding scholarships scams.

FinAid

http://www.finaid.org
FinAid is an excellent Web site that focuses on financial aid. It offers calculators to help determine total school costs and financial need, and links to free financial aid searches. It also reviews many books on financial aid for undergraduates and for graduates.

Funding Your Education

Federal Student Aid Information Center
PO Box 84
Washington, DC 20044-0084

800-433-3243
http://studentaid.ed.gov/students/publications/FYE/
   index.html
This is a free booklet for students from the U.S.
   Department of Education. It is available in both
   English and Spanish.

HEATH Resource Center
2121 K Street, NW, Suite 220
Washington, DC 20037
202-973-0904 (Voice/TTY), 800-544-3284
askheath@gwu.edu
http://www.heath.gwu.edu
The HEATH Resource Center is the American
   Council on Education's national clearinghouse
   on postsecondary education for people with
   disabilities. Its Web site features useful publications
   (such as Financial Aid for Students with Learning
   Disabilities and Creating Options: A Resource on
   Financial Aid for Students With Disabilities) and
   articles written by disabled students.

Institute on Disability / UCED
10 West Edge Drive, Suite 101
Durham, N.H. 03824
603-862-4320 (Voice/TTY)http://www.iod.unh.edu
The institute seeks to "provide a coherent university-
   based focus for the improvement of knowledge,
   policies, and practices related to the lives of persons
   with disabilities and their families." It publishes
   Postsecondary Education: A Choice for Everyone,
   which provides tips on preparing for college while in
   high school, an overview of the differences between
   high school and college for students with disabilities,
   and advice on choosing the right college.

Landmark College
River Road South
Putney, VT 05346
802-387-6718
http://www.landmarkcollege.org
Landmark College is one of the few colleges in the United
   States that is designed exclusively for students with
   dyslexia, attention deficit hyperactivity disorder, or
   other specific learning disabilities.

National Center on Secondary Education and Transition
Institute on Community Integration
University of Minnesota
150 Pillsbury Drive, SE, 6 Pattee Hall

Minneapolis MN 55455
612-624-2097
ncset@umn.edu
http://www.ncset.org
The center provides support and information to
   students with disabilities who are pursuing higher
   education and other postsecondary options.

National Technical Institute for the Deaf
Rochester Institute of Technology
52 Lomb Memorial Drive
Rochester, NY 14623
585-475-6400 (Voice/TTY)
ntidmc@rit.edu
http://www.ntid.rit.edu
Affiliated with the Rochester Institute of Technology,
   the National Technical Institute for the Deaf is the
   world's largest technological college for students
   who are deaf or hard of hearing.

Parent Advocacy Coalition for Educational Rights (PACER) Center
8161 Normandale Boulevard
Minneapolis, MN 55437
952-838-9000 (Voice), 952-838-0190 (TTY)
pacer@pacer.org
http://www.pacer.org
This is a national network of parents that advocates
   educational opportunities for young people and
   adults with disabilities.

Scholarship America
One Scholarship Way
PO Box 297
St. Peter, MN 56082
507-931-1682, 800-537-4180
http://www.scholarshipamerica.org
Scholarship America works through its local Dollars for
   Scholars chapters throughout the country. In 2003,
   it awarded more than $29 million in scholarships to
   more than 35,000 students.

Scholarships.com LLC
473 Central Avenue, Suite 6
Highland Park, Illinois 60035
847-432-1700
http://www.scholarships.com
Scholarships.com offers a free college scholarship
   search engine (although you must register to use it)
   and financial aid information.

Social Security Administration

Benefits for People With Disabilities
6401 Security Boulevard
Baltimore, MD 21235
800-772-1213, 800-325-0778 (TTY)
http://www.ssa.gov/disability
Contact the Social Security Administration for more
  information on financial aid options available
  through its Supplemental Security Income and
  Social Security Disability Insurance programs.

Talent Search and Educational Opportunity Centers

U.S. Department of Education
400 Maryland Avenue, SW
Washington, DC 20202
http://www.ed.gov/programs/trioeoc
http://www.ed.gov/programs/triotalent/index.html
These programs provide counseling and other services
  to disadvantaged students and students with

disabilities. The programs can help to negotiate
financial assistance with postsecondary institutions.

Vocational Rehabilitation Offices

To find one in your community:

- Look under the "State Government" pages of
  the phone book.
- Check with the local health and human services office.
- Call your local independent living center.

Request a list from the National Rehabilitation
  Information Center, 4200 Forbes Boulevard, Suite
  202, Lanham, MD 20706, 800-346-2742 or 301-459-
  5984 (TTY), naricinfo@heitechservices.com, http://
  www.naric.com.

IS GRADUATE SCHOOL RIGHT FOR YOU?

You've almost completed your undergraduate educa-tion, and the question nags at you: "Should I enter the job market or should I go on to grad school?" This essay provides an overview of graduate degrees, admis-sions and personal requirements, financial aid options, and advice on how to decide if continuing on to graduate school is the best option for you.

TYPES OF GRADUATE DEGREES

There are two types of graduate degrees—the master's and doctorate. Students enter master's degree programs after they earn their undergraduate degree, and doctoral pro-grams after they earn their master's degree.

A master's degree is awarded after completion of advanced study in a particular field. Such programs typically last about two or three years. The most popular degrees conferred are master of arts (M.A.) degrees and master of science (M.S.) degrees. Other master's degrees are awarded in fine arts, library science, and business.

During the first year of a master's program, expect to take foundation course work required for your particular degree. Different professors will supervise your work, but a faculty adviser will monitor your overall performance. During this time you will begin to narrow your academic focus within your major.

More required course work will follow in the second year, but much of your time will be spent on your master's thesis or research paper, which highlights your expertise in a particular subject area or specialty, or in preparation for a comprehensive examination or final project.

A doctorate is the highest academic degree, lasting anywhere from three to eight years. Three types of doctor-ate degrees are awarded.

- The doctor of philosophy (Ph.D.) is the most common type of **research doctorate.** Candi-dates in this program usually pursue careers in research or academics after graduation and are regarded as experts in their field of study. Ph.D.

programs can last anywhere from three to more than seven years of study. During the first three years or so, depending on the doctoral program, expect to complete required course work in your major. You might obtain a research appointment working with professors in your field of inter-est, or be assigned teaching duties at the under-graduate level. You will be expected to develop a thesis or complete a series of exams before allowed to continue in the program. Your doc-toral dissertation will be the main focus of your remaining years in the program. Much time will be spent researching and writing your disserta-tion as proof you have mastered knowledge in a particular field or specialty. Teaching duties may still exist, though they will be supervised less by faculty; lessons of your own design may be used to teach these classes. Your doctoral program will conclude with the successful presentation and defense of your dissertation before a com-mittee of faculty members.

- **Professional doctorates,** lasting about three to four years, include thorough study in a particular field, practical experience, original research and thesis (required for certain professional doctor-ates), and examination for licensure. Some fields that require professional doctorates include medicine, law, veterinary medicine, and dental science. For example, students working toward a medical degree will spend their early years of study completing necessary course work, such as anatomy, physiology, genetics, and studies in neuroscience. The remaining years consist of various rotations where medical students inter-act with patients under the supervision of doc-tors, nurses, and other medical professionals.

- **Honorary doctorates** are awarded to individu-als who have made an impressive contribution to a particular field. For example, actor Bill Cosby, a longtime advocate of education, holds honorary doctorates from the University of Cincinnati and Wilkes University, in addition to earning a doctorate in education from the University of Massachusetts.

DO YOU HAVE WHAT IT TAKES TO ENTER GRADUATE SCHOOL?

The requirements for applying to graduate school almost mirror those for an undergraduate program. Here is a general overview of what will usually be required:

- **Graduate Record Examination.** Applicants to most programs must take a standardized entrance exam for graduate school consideration. Those applying for graduate study must take the Graduate Record Examination (GRE). General Test GREs test the student on such areas as critical thinking, analytical thinking, verbal reasoning, and quantitative reasoning skills. The GRE also offers optional Subject Tests that gauge a student's knowledge of a particular subject, or major, as learned during their undergraduate years. Subjects include biochemistry, cell, and molecular biology; biology; chemistry; computer science; literature in English; mathematics; physics; and psychology. Some programs do not require GRE scores for admission, so be sure to review admission criteria for the schools that interest you.
- **Standardized examinations for professional doctorate programs** include the Graduate Management Admission Test (GMAT), the Medical College Admission Test (MCAT), the Law School Admission Test (LSAT), and the Dental Admission Test (DAT)
- **Transcripts.** Graduate schools are selective and place great emphasis on a student's undergraduate grade point average; only high-ranking students are admitted. However, the level of courses you take as an undergraduate will also count as much as your final GPA. After all, an A in artistic welding will not hold as much weight as an A in organic chemistry, especially if you are hoping for admission to a top medical school program. Be sure to review your school transcripts for accuracy, and make any necessary corrections before submitting them to different graduate schools.
- **Application,** including a personal statement.
- **Letters of recommendation.** Ask for letters of recommendation from those who know you

well. The letters should attest to your character and study and work ethic, as well as your past academic achievements.
- **Interview.** Many schools require a personal interview before granting admission, perhaps due to fierce competition for few positions in a graduate program. This is also one final judging moment to see if the applicant "matches" the application as well as the program desired.

STAYING POWER

Your application, test scores, and transcripts pass muster—you're officially a graduate student! Now the stakes are higher, the atmosphere more serious, the competition fiercer as compared to your undergrad days. Be prepared for some major changes:

- Did you have the reputation of being one of the smartest students in your undergraduate class? Good, because you'll be spending the next two years or more with similar company. Graduate programs typically only accept 10 percent of total applicants per year, so they can be quite selective with their admissions. You'll need to work harder and be more competitive in order to keep up with your peers.
- Classes taught at the graduate-level are given letter grades of A, B, or C—with no grade curve allowed. Students with a C-average in any subject will be required to repeat the course. Class size will be considerably smaller and more active, giving students more opportunity to raise questions, contribute to discussions, and present their own interpretation of class topics. This may be a disadvantage to shy students whose lack of class participation may have gone unnoticed in larger undergraduate lectures and classes.
- Expect the workload to be quite heavy, and you will receive less time to complete assignments. Professors will assign more reading, writing, and research, in addition to other expected tasks such as moderating undergraduate classes, grading papers and exams, departmental research duties, fieldwork, and attending conferences. Avoid feeling overwhelmed by learning to work quickly and efficiently, multi-task, and prioritize different assignments and duties.
- Practical experience is required of all graduate students. Medical students are required to

rotate through various departments of a hospital; master's of psychology candidates often do a semester or two of testing and evaluation within their desired specialty; master's of art candidates often teach classes at the undergraduate level. This form of fieldwork is important since it gives graduate students the opportunity to implement information and skills taught in class, and network for future employment possibilities.

- You will be assigned an adviser to help you through graduate school. Advisers will provide suggestions on which courses to take, review your papers and research, and monitor your progress as a student. Advisers often tap their best students for help with important research projects and publications. This relationship can be beneficial to your future career—a good mentor/student connection can provide valuable work experience, a network of professional contacts, and an ally during educational struggles.

CAN YOU AFFORD GRADUATE SCHOOL?

Very few people are able to afford graduate school without some sort of financial assistance. Here are some options on how to fund your graduate education:

Fellowships

Fellowships are essentially merit-based scholarships awarded to promising students by the government, schools, or private organizations. Students are paid to continue their studies in a field approved or supported by the originator of the fellowship. In addition to paid tuition, fellows are provided an annual stipend, living allowance, and other benefits.

Research Assistantships/Teacher Assistantships

Graduate students can help pay for their education by becoming a research assistant (RA) or teacher assistant (TA). RAs and TAs work within their particular department by teaching classes at the undergraduate level, grading research papers, proctoring exams, assisting in laboratories and libraries, moderating study groups, performing research, and handling other duties as needed by departmental faculty. In exchange, RAs and TAs receive a modest annual stipend from the department. Funding is provided by the school, and is at the discretion of faculty members.

Loans

Unless you are independently wealthy, chances are you will turn to a number of available government loan programs. In fact, according to a recent National Postsecondary Student Aid Study, 95 percent of medical students undertake student loans to finance medical school. Recipients of fellowships and/or scholarships must often resort to student loans to help them make ends meet.

Your Workplace

Companies often provide their employees full or partial tuition reimbursement so that they may attend graduate programs, especially if it will help improve job performance or productivity. Contact your company's human resources department to find out if this is part of your benefits package.

WHAT'S IT WORTH?

You're in a graduate program to advance your intellect, master a field of interest, and perform good deeds for all humankind. That said, is there real money to be made with a graduate degree? It all depends on your specialty. Certain industries require an advanced degree in order to get licensure, such as law or medicine. Then there are industries that usually require an advanced degree, especially if the specialty, such as engineering or counseling, is highly competitive. Others, such as teachers, nurses, accountants, or journalists have numerous employment opportunities with simply a four-year, or in some cases, a two-year degree. However, salaries are higher, and career advancements faster for those with a graduate degree. A 2005 survey conducted by the National Association of Colleges and Employers provides a good example of the benefits of graduate education for mechanical engineers. A mechanical engineer with a bachelor's degree earned $50,286 in 2005, but those with master's degrees and doctorates earned $59,880 and $68,299, respectively.

College is not for everyone, and to a greater degree, the same holds true for graduate school. Here are some questions to ask yourself before committing to graduate education:

- What is my main objective in applying to graduate school? Do I want to learn more about my field? Do I want to be more competitive in the job market? Am I simply undecided about what to do next?
- Do I like the academic environment?

- Am I prepared for the hard work and dedication expected of me?
- Do I like to learn new things?
- Can I survive in a competitive atmosphere?
- Am I self-motivated?
- How will I finance my graduate education?
- Can I manage to live on a tight budget while in graduate school?
- Is a graduate degree an absolute necessity for my career goals?
- Am I willing to focus mainly on my studies and research for the near future?
- If working toward a Ph.D., will I be happy teaching or conducting research for the majority of my working years?

ADDITIONAL RESOURCES

About.com: Graduate School
http://gradschool.about.com
This Web site covers every imaginable topic regarding graduate school and features advice from people who have been in the trenches—graduates of master's and doctorate programs! Subjects covered include the admission process, recommendation letters, and the pros and cons of earning an advanced degree. The site also sponsors a lively forum where discussions range from educational burnout to raising a low GPA.

GradSchools.com
http://www.gradschools.com
This site is considered one of the most comprehensive sources of graduate school information available online. You can search for graduate programs nationwide by school or discipline, as well as create a personalized student profile, which allows school recruiters to contact you.

National Association of Graduate-Professional Students (NAGPS)
209 Pennsylvania Avenue, SE
Washington, DC 20003
202-543-0812
office@nagps.org
http://www.nagps.org
The NAGPS acts as an advocate for graduate and professional students. It also serves as a clearinghouse for student organizations, services, employment opportunities, and events of interest.

Petersons.com
http://www.petersons.com
This Web site provides useful tips on how to get started in your search for the best graduate school and program. It provides a planning timeline to keep you organized, as well as an online practice exam for a variety of standardized tests needed for admittance into graduate and professional schools.

The Princeton Review
http://princetonreview.com
The Princeton Review gives sound advice on how to choose a graduate school and program, financing options, and the ins and outs of the graduate school admission process.

School Guide Publications
http://www.graduateguide.com
This company publishes a variety of college guides aimed at high school students focused on pursuing postsecondary education. One publication, Graduate School Guide, provides a detailed listing of graduate schools and programs located throughout the country, as well as financing options, important standardized testing dates, and student interest response cards.

PART III
DIRECTORY

FINANCIAL AID BY MAJOR

BUSINESS—UNDERGRADUATE

The following financial aid resources are available to students who are interested in studying business and related fields at the undergraduate level.

Alice L. Haltom Educational Fund
PO Box 1794
Houston, TX 77251
contact@alhef.org
http://www.alhef.org
Scholarship Name: Alice L. Haltom Educational Fund. *Academic Area: Management. *Age Group: Undergraduate students. *Eligibility: Applicants must be actively pursuing an education for a career in information and records management. The scholarship is also available to graduate students. *Application Process: Applicants must submit a completed application, a personal statement, three letters of recommendation, and official transcripts. Visit the fund's Web site to download an application. *Amount: $1,000 to $2,000. *Deadline: May 1.

American Public Transportation Foundation
Attn: Pamela Boswell
1666 K Street, NW, Suite 1100
Washington, DC 20006
202-496-4803
pboswell@apta.com
http://www.apta.com/services/human_resources/program_guidelines.cfm
Scholarship Name: Dan M. Reichard Jr. Scholarship. *Academic Area: Business administration, management. *Age Group: Undergraduate students. *Eligibility: Applicants must demonstrate dedication to pursuing careers in the business administration/management area of the transit industry. They also must be enrolled in a fully accredited institution, maintain at least a 3.0 GPA (B) in course work that is relevant to the industry or required of a degree program, and either be employed by or demonstrate a strong interest in entering the public transportation industry. College sophomores (30 hours or more satisfactorily completed), juniors, and seniors may apply for scholarships. The scholarship is also available to graduate students. *Application Process: Applicants must submit a completed application, a letter of nomination, an essay, three letters of recommendation, a copy of completed FAFSA form, official transcripts, verification of enrollment, and a copy of the college's fee schedule. Visit the foundation's Web site to download an

application. *Amount: $2,500 minimum. *Deadline: June 17.

Colorado Society of CPAs Educational Foundation
Attn: Gena Mantz, Scholarship Coordinator
7979 East Tufts Avenue, Suite 1000
Denver, CO 80237-2845
303-773-2877, 800-523-9082
gmantz@cocpa.org
http://www.cocpa.org/student_faculty/scholarships.asp
Scholarship Name: General College Scholarship. *Academic Area: Accounting. *Age Group: Undergraduate students. *Eligibility: Applicants must be declared accounting majors who are attending a Colorado college or university and who have completed at least eight semester hours of accounting courses (with at least one at an intermediate level). They also must demonstrate academic achievement by maintaining at least a 3.0 GPA. The scholarship is also available to graduate students. *Application Process: Applicants should submit a completed application along with transcripts. Visit the society's Web site to download an application. *Amount: $1,000. *Deadline: June 30 and November 30.

Colorado Society of CPAs Educational Foundation
Attn: Gena Mantz, Scholarship Coordinator
7979 East Tufts Avenue, Suite 1000
Denver, CO 80237-2845
303-773-2877, 800-523-9082
gmantz@cocpa.org
http://www.cocpa.org/student_faculty/scholarships.asp
Scholarship Name: General High School Scholarship. *Academic Area: Accounting. *Age Group: Undergraduate students. *Eligibility: Applicants must be Colorado high school seniors who are enrolled in the upcoming summer or fall semester at a Colorado community college or Colorado college or university that offers a program (or transferable credit) in accounting. Applicants must demonstrate academic achievement with a GPA of at least 3.0. Students also must be enrolled in at least six semester or quarter hours. *Application Process: Applicants should submit a completed application along with transcripts and ACT or SAT scores. Visit

the society's Web site to download an application. *Amount: $1,000. *Deadline: March 1.

Colorado Society of CPAs Educational Foundation

Attn: Gena Mantz, Scholarship Coordinator
7979 East Tufts Avenue, Suite 1000
Denver, CO 80237-2845
303-773-2877, 800-523-9082
gmantz@cocpa.org
http://www.cocpa.org/student_faculty/scholarships.asp
Scholarship Name: Gordon Scheer College Scholarship. *Academic Area: Accounting. *Age Group: Undergraduate students. *Eligibility: Applicants must be declared accounting majors who are attending a Colorado college or university and who have completed at least eight semester hours of accounting courses (with at least one at an intermediate level). They also must demonstrate academic achievement by maintaining at least a 3.0 GPA. The scholarship is also available to graduate students. *Application Process: Applicants should submit a completed application along with transcripts and a letter of reference from an accounting professor. Visit the society's Web site to download an application. *Amount: $1,250. *Deadline: June 30.

Electronic Document Systems Foundation

Attn: EDSF Scholarship Awards
608 Silver Spur Road, Suite 280
Rolling Hills Estates, CA 90274-3616
310-265-5510
info@edsf.org
http://www.edsf.org/scholarships.cfm
Scholarship Name: Electronic Document Systems Foundation Document Communication Scholarship Program. *Academic Area: Business, computer science, engineering (open), graphic design. *Age Group: Undergraduate students. *Eligibility: Applicants must be full-time students who are committed to pursuing a career in the field of electronic document communication in the areas of: document preparation, production and/or document distribution, including 1:1 marketing; graphic communication and arts; e-commerce; imaging science, printing, web authoring, electronic publishing, computer science, engineering, or telecommunications. Applicants must also maintain a minimum 3.0 GPA. The scholarship is also available to graduate students. *Application

Process: Applicants must submit 10 copies of a completed application package. Applicants must include a covering letter, their academic details, two half- to full-page essays, a list of their extracurricular professional and academic activities, transcripts, two letters of recommendation, and samples of creative work (optional) in their application packets. Visit the foundation's Web site for further details. *Amount: Varies. *Deadline: May 15.

Florida Institute of CPAs Educational Foundation

Attn: Betsy Wilson, Scholarship Coordinator
325 West College Avenue, PO Box 5437
Tallahassee, FL 32301
850-224-2727, ext. 200
wilsonb@ficpa.org
http://www1.ficpa.org/ficpa/Visitors/Careers/EdFoundation/Scholarships/Available
Scholarship Name: Florida Institute of CPAs Educational Foundation Scholarship. *Academic Area: Accounting. *Age Group: Undergraduate students. *Eligibility: Applicants must be declared accounting majors in their fourth or fifth year at a college or university in Florida. A complete list of eligible schools is posted on the foundation's Web site. The scholarship is also available to graduate students. *Application Process: Applicants should contact their school's accounting scholarship chairperson in January to receive updated information and an application. To find out who this chairperson is at your school, contact the foundation's scholarship coordinator. An application and a transcript should be submitted to the school's accounting scholarship chairperson, who, along with other faculty, will select applicants to submit to the foundation. *Amount: Awards vary. *Deadline: March 15.

Government Finance Officers Association

Attn: Scholarship Committee
203 North LaSalle Street, Suite 2700
Chicago, IL 60601-1210
312-977-9700
scholarships@gfoa.org
http://www.gfoa.org/services/scholarships.shtml
Scholarship Name: Frank L. Greathouse Government Accounting Scholarship. *Academic Area: Accounting, finance. *Age Group: Undergraduate students. *Eligibility: Applicants must be full-time undergraduate students preparing for a career in state and local government finance. They also must

be completing at least their junior year of study at the time of award distribution and be citizens or permanent residents of the U.S. or Canada. The scholarship is also available to graduate students. *Application Process: Applicants must submit a completed application, a proposed career plan, transcripts, a resume, and a letter of recommendation (from an academic advisor or department chair). Visit the association's Web site to download an application. *Amount: $3,500. *Deadline: February 3.

Government Finance Officers Association
Attn: Scholarship Committee
203 North LaSalle Street, Suite 2700
Chicago, IL 60601-1210
312-977-9700
scholarships@gfoa.org
http://www.gfoa.org/services/scholarships.shtml
Scholarship Name: George A. Nielsen Public Investor Scholarship. *Academic Area: Business administration, finance. *Age Group: Undergraduate students. *Eligibility: Applicants must be employees of a local government or public entity planning to enroll in an undergraduate program in public administration, finance, or business administration. They also must have been employed by a state, local government, or other public entity for at least one year, as well as be citizens or permanent residents of the United States or Canada. The scholarship is also available to graduate students. *Application Process: Applicants must submit a completed application, a statement describing their work experience, transcripts, a resume, and an employer's letter of recommendation. Visit the association's Web site to download an application. *Amount: $2,500 to $5,000. *Deadline: February 3.

Institute of Management Accountants Inc.
Attn: Susan Bender
10 Paragon Drive
Montvale, NJ 07645-1718
800-638-4427, ext. 1543
students@imanet.org
http://www.imanet.org/ima/docs/3400/3352.pdf
Scholarship Name: Stuart Cameron and Margaret McLeod Memorial Scholarship. *Academic Area: Accounting, finance. *Age Group: Undergraduate students. *Eligibility: Applicants should be full- or part-time students residing in the U.S. or Puerto Rico

who are active student participants in the institute. They also must maintain a minimum 2.8 GPA. One outstanding applicant from the pool of Memorial Education Fund Scholarship applicants will be awarded this scholarship. The scholarship is also available to graduate students. *Application Process: Applicants should submit a completed application along with a one-page resume, a personal statement, and proof of enrollment in a program in management accounting, financial management, or information technology. Visit the institute's Web site to download an application. *Amount: $5,000, plus an all-expenses-paid trip to the institute's annual conference. *Deadline: February 15.

Institute of Management Accountants Inc.
Attn: Liz Brueck
10 Paragon Drive
Montvale, NJ 07645-1718
800-638-4427, ext. 1543
students@imanet.org
http://www.imanet.org/ima/docs/3400/3352.pdf
Scholarship Name: Memorial Education Fund Scholarship. *Academic Area: Accounting, finance. *Age Group: Undergraduate students. *Eligibility: Applicants should be full- or part-time students residing in the U.S. or Puerto Rico who are active student participants of the institute. They also must maintain a minimum 2.8 GPA and be IMA student members. The scholarship is also available to graduate students. *Application Process: Applicants should submit a completed application along with a one-page resume, a personal statement, and proof of enrollment in a program in management accounting, financial management, or information technology. Visit the institute's Web site to download an application. *Amount: $1,000 to $2,500. *Deadline: February 15.

Junior Achievement (JA)
Walt Disney Company Foundation Scholarship
One Education Way
Colorado Springs, CO 80906
888-4-JA-ALUM
scholarships@ja.org
http://studentcenter.ja.org/aspx/PayCollege/ScholarshipSearch.aspx
Scholarship Name: Walt Disney Company Foundation Scholarship. *Academic Area: Business administration. *Age Group: Undergraduate students. *Eligibility:

Applicants must be high school seniors, graduating before June 30, and have excellent academic and extracurricular credentials. Only exceptional applicants are encouraged to apply. Applicants must also have completed the JA Company Program or JA Economics Program. *Application Process: Applicants must submit a completed application, official transcripts, SAT/ACT scores, and three letters of recommendation. Visit the JA Web site to download an application. *Amount: Four-year full tuition scholarship. *Deadline: February 1.

National Society of Accountants (NSA) Scholarship Foundation
Attn: Susan E. Noell
1010 North Fairfax Street
Alexandria, VA 22314-1574
703-549-6400, ext. 1312, 800-966-6679, ext. 1312
snoell@nsacct.org
http://www.nsacct.org/foundation.asp?id=430
Scholarship Name: NSA Student Scholarship. *Academic Area: Accounting. *Age Group: Undergraduate students. *Eligibility: Applicants must be undergraduates enrolled in a degree program at an accredited two- or four-year college or university and be majoring in accounting with a "B" or better average. They must also be U.S. or Canadian citizens. High school students are not eligible to apply. *Application Process: Applicants must submit a completed application along with official, sealed transcripts, and letters of recommendation. Visit the society's Web site to download an application. *Amount: $500 to $2,000. *Deadline: March 10.

Phi Chi Theta Educational Foundation
Attn: Mary Ellen Lewis, Scholarship Committee Chair
1886 South Poplar Street
Denver, CO 80224-2271
303-757-2535
FoundationScholarship@phichitheta.org
http://www.phichitheta.org/foundation/foundation.htm
Scholarship Name: Phi Chi Theta Educational Foundation Scholarships. *Academic Area: Business (open), economics. *Age Group: Undergraduate students. *Eligibility: Applicants must be members of Phi Chi Theta in good standing who have completed at least one semester or two quarters of college work and enrolled in classes for the upcoming year. The scholarship is also available to graduate students. *Application Process: Applicants should submit a completed application along with an essay, a

statement of their career goals, a description of their contributions to Phi Chi Theta, a list of school and community involvement areas, official transcripts, and two letters of recommendation. Visit the foundation's Web site to download an application. *Amount: $500 to $1,000. *Deadline: May 1.

Public Relations Society of America Foundation
33 Maiden Lane, 11th Floor
New York, NY 10038-5150
212-460-1424
foundation@prsa.org
http://www.prsa.org/_About/prsafoundation/scholarships.asp
Scholarship Name: Gary Yoshimura Scholarship. *Academic Area: Public relations. *Age Group: Undergraduate students. *Eligibility: Applicants must be members of the Public Relations Student Society of America. *Application Process: Applicants must submit an essay on a designated topic. Contact the society for essay guidelines and application details. *Amount: $2,400. *Deadline: Varies.

Public Relations Society of America Foundation
33 Maiden Lane, 11th Floor
New York, NY 10038-5150
212-460-1424
foundation@prsa.org
http://www.prsa.org/_About/prsafoundation/scholarships.asp
Scholarship Name: Public Relations Society of America Champions/Betsy Plank Scholarship Program. *Academic Area: Public relations. *Age Group: Undergraduate students. *Eligibility: Applicants must be Public Relations Students Society of America (PRSSA) members in their junior or senior year in college. They must also demonstrate commitment and leadership in PRSSA and the public relations professions. *Application Process: Contact the society for application details. *Amount: Varies. *Deadline: Varies.

Society for Human Resource Management (SHRM) Foundation
SHRM Student Awards
1800 Duke Street
Alexandria, VA 22314-3499
800-283-SHRM
SHRMStudent@shrm.org
http://www.shrm.org/students/ags_published/CMS_003099.asp

Scholarship Name: Dr. Lisa Burke, SPHR Scholarship. *Academic Area: Human resources. *Age Group: Undergraduate students. *Eligibility: Applicants must be enrolled as undergraduate students and have completed their sophomore years majoring in human resources or related subject. Applicants also must be national student members of the SHRM, maintain a minimum C average, and pay more than 50 percent of their college expenses. *Application Process: Applicants must submit two copies of a completed application, one official transcript, and four copies of the following: resume, personal statement, and three letters of recommendation. Contact the foundation to obtain an application. *Amount: $1,000. *Deadline: March 1.

Society for Human Resource Management (SHRM) Foundation
Contact: Sandi Peyton, SHRM Foundation Administrator
Attn: Scholarship Selection Committee
1800 Duke Street
Alexandria, VA 22314
703-535-6020
speyton@shrm.org
http://www.shrm.org/students/ags_published/CMS_003104.asp
Scholarship Name: SHRM Foundation Scholarship. *Academic Area: Human resources. *Age Group: Undergraduate students. *Eligibility: Applicants must be SHRM national student members. Undergraduate applicants must have maintained at least a 3.0 GPA and completed at least 55 semester hours of course work in a human resources (HR) major or HR emphasis area, including at least one human resources management course. The scholarship is also available to graduate students. *Application Process: Applicants must submit three copies of a completed application, a resume, and two letters of recommendation. Applicants must also submit original transcripts (one only). *Amount: $2,500. *Deadline: October 15.

Society of Satellite Professionals International
Attn: Tamara Bond, Membership Director
The New York Information Technology Center
55 Broad Street, 14th Floor
New York, NY 10004
212-809-5199
tbond@sspi.org
http://www.sspi.org/displaycommon.cfm?an=1&subart iclenbr=56

Scholarship Name: Society of Satellite Professionals International Scholarship Program. *Academic Area: Satellite technology. *Age Group: High school seniors, undergraduate students, graduate students. *Eligibility: Applicants must demonstrate academic and leadership achievement, commitment to pursuing education and career opportunities in the satellite industry or a field making direct use of satellite technology, and show potential for a significant contribution to the satellite communications industry. *Application Process: The application process has been divided into two parts. Applicants who successfully pass stage one of the application process will be invited to apply for stage two. To apply for stage one, applicants should submit a completed application along with current transcripts. Information about stage two of the process will be provided to applicants who pass stage one. Visit the society's Web site to download an application. *Amount: $2,000 to $5,000. *Deadline: February 28 (for stage one).

Virginia Society of Certified Public Accountants
Attn: Molly Wash, Scholarship Coordinator
VSCPA Educational Foundation
PO Box 4620
Glen Allen, VA 23058
800-733-8272
foundation@vscpa.com
http://www.vscpa.com/CPAStudent_Zone/Awards_and_Scholarships/Undergrad_Scholarship.aspx
Scholarship Name: Virginia Society of Certified Public Accountants Undergraduate Scholarship. *Academic Area: Accounting. *Age Group: Undergraduate students. *Eligibility: Applicants must be U.S. citizens who are enrolled in an accredited Virginia college or university with the intent to pursue a bachelor's degree in accounting. They also should have completed at least three hours of accounting and be registered for at least three more. Applicants should also be maintaining at least a 3.0 GPA. *Application Process: Applicants should submit a completed application along with an essay, a letter of recommendation from a faculty member, a resume, transcripts, and any additional documentation that proves enrollment in additional accounting credit hours. Visit the society's Web site to download an application. *Amount: Awards vary. *Deadline: April 17.

BUSINESS—GRADUATE

The following financial aid resources are available to students who are interested in studying business and related fields at the graduate level.

Alice L. Haltom Educational Fund
PO Box 1794
Houston, TX 77251
contact@alhef.org
http://www.alhef.org
Scholarship Name: Alice L. Haltom Educational Fund. *Academic Area: Management. *Age Group: Graduate students. *Eligibility: Applicants must be actively pursuing an education for a career in information and records management. The scholarship is also available to undergraduate students. *Application Process: Applicants must submit a completed application, a personal statement, three letters of recommendation, and official transcripts. Visit the fund's Web site to download an application. *Amount: $1,000 to $2,000. *Deadline: May 1.

Colorado Society of CPAs Educational Foundation
Attn: Gena Mantz, Scholarship Coordinator
7979 East Tufts Avenue, Suite 1000
Denver, CO 80237-2845
303-773-2877, 800-523-9082
gmantz@cocpa.org
http://www.cocpa.org/student_faculty/scholarships.asp
Scholarship Name: General College Scholarship. *Academic Area: Accounting. *Age Group: Graduate students. *Eligibility: Applicants must be declared accounting majors who are attending a Colorado college or university and who have completed at least eight semester hours of accounting courses (with at least one at an intermediate level). They also must demonstrate academic achievement by maintaining at least a 3.0 GPA. The scholarship is also available to undergraduate students. *Application Process: Applicants should submit a completed application along with transcripts. Visit the society's Web site to download an application. *Amount: $1,000. *Deadline: June 30; November 30.

Colorado Society of CPAs Educational Foundation
Attn: Gena Mantz, Scholarship Coordinator
7979 East Tufts Avenue, Suite 1000
Denver, CO 80237-2845
303-773-2877, 800-523-9082
gmantz@cocpa.org
http://www.cocpa.org/student_faculty/scholarships.asp
Scholarship Name: Gordon Scheer College Scholarship. *Academic Area: Accounting. *Age Group: Graduate students. *Eligibility: Applicants must be declared accounting majors who are attending a Colorado college or university and who have completed at least eight semester hours of accounting courses (with at least one at an intermediate level). They also must demonstrate academic achievement by maintaining at least a 3.0 GPA. The scholarship is also available to undergraduate students.*Application Process: Applicants should submit a completed application along with transcripts and a letter of reference from an accounting professor. Visit the society's Web site to download an application. *Amount: $1,250. *Deadline: June 30.

Florida Institute of CPAs (FICPA) Educational Foundation
Attn: Betsy Wilson, Scholarship Coordinator
325 West College Avenue
Tallahassee, FL 32301
850-224-2727, ext. 200, 800-342-3197
wilsonb@ficpa.org
http://www1.ficpa.org/ficpa/Visitors/Careers/EdFoundation/Scholarships/Available
Scholarship Name: FICPA Educational Foundation Scholarship. *Academic Area: Accounting. *Age Group: Graduate students. *Eligibility: Applicants must be declared accounting majors in their fourth or fifth year at a college or university in Florida. A complete list of eligible schools is posted on the foundation's Web site. The scholarship is also available to undergraduate students. *Application Process: Applicants should contact their school's accounting scholarship chairperson in January to receive updated information and an application. To find out who this chairperson is at their school, they should contact the foundation's scholarship coordinator. An application and a transcript should be submitted to the school's accounting scholarship chairperson, who will then select applicants to submit to the foundation. *Amount: Awards vary. *Deadline: March 15.

Government Finance Officers Association
Scholarship Committee
203 North LaSalle Street, Suite 2700

Chicago, IL 60601-1210
312-977-9700
http://www.gfoa.org/services/scholarships.shtml
Scholarship Name: Daniel B. Goldberg Scholarship.
   *Academic Area: Finance. *Age Group: Graduate
   students. *Eligibility: Applicants must be currently
   enrolled full time in graduate programs that
   prepare students for careers in state and local
   government finance. They also must be citizens or
   permanent residents of the United States or Canada.
   *Application Process: Applicants must submit a
   completed application, a statement detailing their
   proposed career plan, transcripts, a resume, and
   a letter of recommendation (from their academic
   advisor or dean). Visit the association's Web site
   to download an application. *Amount: $10,000.
   *Deadline: February 3.

Government Finance Officers Association
Scholarship Committee
Chicago, IL 60601-1210
312-977-9700
http://www.gfoa.org/services/scholarships.shtml
Scholarship Name: Frank L. Greathouse Government
   Accounting Scholarship. *Academic Area: Finance.
   *Age Group: Graduate students. *Eligibility:
   Applicants must be full-time graduate students
   preparing for a career in state and local government
   finance. They also must be citizens or permanent
   residents of the United States or Canada. The
   scholarship is also available to undergraduate
   students. *Application Process: Applicants must
   submit a completed application, a statement
   detailing their proposed career plan, transcripts,
   a resume, and a letter of recommendation (from
   academic advisor or department chair). Visit the
   association's Web site to download an application.
   *Amount: $3,500. *Deadline: February 3.

Government Finance Officers Association
Scholarship Committee
203 North LaSalle Street, Suite 2700
Chicago, IL 60601-1210
312-977-9700
http://www.gfoa.org/services/scholarships.shtml
Scholarship Name: George A. Nielsen Public Investor
   Scholarship. *Academic Area: Business, finance. *Age
   Group: Graduate students. *Eligibility: Applicants
   must be employees of a local government or
   public entity planning to enroll in a graduate

program in public administration, finance, or
business administration. A state, local government,
or other public entity also must have employed
them for at least one year, and they must be
citizens or permanent residents of the United
States or Canada. The scholarship is also available
to undergraduate students. *Application Process:
Applicants must submit a completed application,
a statement describing their work experience,
transcripts, a resume, and an employer's letter of
recommendation. Visit the association's Web site to
download an application. *Amount: $2,500 to $5,000.
*Deadline: February 3.

Government Finance Officers Association
Scholarship Committee
203 North LaSalle Street, Suite 2700
Chicago, IL 60601-1210
312-977-9700
http://www.gfoa.org/services/scholarships.shtml
Scholarship Name: Public Employee Retirement
   Research and Administration Scholarship. *Academic
   Area: Business, finance, social sciences. *Age Group:
   Graduate students. *Eligibility: Applicants must
   be full- or part-time students enrolled in graduate
   programs in public administration, finance, business,
   or social sciences. They also must aim to prepare for
   a career in state and local government, focusing on
   public-sector retirement benefits, and be citizens or
   permanent residents of the United States or Canada.
   *Application Process: Applicants must submit a
   completed application, a statement detailing their
   proposed career plan, transcripts, a resume, and a
   letter of recommendation (from an academic advisor
   or dean). Visit the association's Web site to download
   an application. *Amount: $4,000. *Deadline:
   February 3.

Institute of Management Accountants (IMA)
Attn: Liz Brueck
10 Paragon Drive
Montvale, NJ 07645-1760
800-638-4427, ext. 1543
membersupport@imanet.org
http://www.imanet.org/ima/docs/3400/3352.pdf
Scholarship Name: Memorial Education Fund
   Scholarship. *Academic Area: Accounting, finance,
   information technology. *Age Group: Graduate
   students. *Eligibility: Applicants should be full- or
   part-time students residing in the United States or

Puerto Rico who are active student participants of the IMA. They also must maintain a minimum 2.8 GPA. The scholarship is also available to undergraduate students. *Application Process: Applicants should submit a completed application along with a one-page resume, a personal statement, two letters of recommendation, and proof of enrollment in a program in management accounting, financial management, or information technology. Visit the institute's Web site to download an application. *Amount: $1,000 to $2,500. *Deadline: February 15.

Institute of Management Accountants (IMA)

Attn: Liz Brueck
10 Paragon Drive
Montvale, NJ 07645-1760
800-638-4427, ext. 1543
membersupport@imanet.org
http://www.imanet.org/ima/docs/3400/3352.pdf
Scholarship Name: Stuart Cameron and Margaret McLeod Memorial Scholarship. *Academic Area: Accounting, finance, information technology. *Age Group: Graduate students. *Eligibility: Applicants should be full- or part-time students residing in the United States or Puerto Rico who are active student participants in the IMA. They also must maintain a minimum 2.8 GPA. One outstanding applicant from the pool of Memorial Education Fund Scholarship applicants will be awarded this scholarship. The scholarship is also available to undergraduate students. *Application Process: Applicants should submit a completed application along with a one-page resume, a personal statement, two letters of recommendation, and proof of enrollment in a program in management accounting, financial management, or information technology. Visit the institute's Web site to download an application. *Amount: $5,000, plus all expenses paid for a trip to the IMA's annual conference. *Deadline: February 15.

Phi Chi Theta Educational Foundation

Attn: Scholarship Committee
1886 South Poplar Street
Denver, CO 80224
303-757-2535
FoundationScholarship@phichitheta.org
http://www.phichitheta.org/foundation/programs.htm
Scholarship Name: Phi Chi Theta Educational Foundation Scholarship. *Academic Area: Business, economics. *Age Group: Graduate students. *Eligibility: Applicants must be members of Phi Chi Theta in good standing,

have completed at least one semester or two quarters of college work in the United States, and be enrolled in classes for the upcoming year. The scholarship is also available to undergraduate students. *Application Process: Applicants should submit a completed application along with an essay, a statement of their career goals, a description of their contributions to Phi Chi Theta, a list of school and community involvement areas, official transcripts, and two letters of recommendation. Visit the foundation's Web site to download an application. *Amount: $500 to $1,000. *Deadline: May 1.

Society for Human Resource Management (SHRM) Foundation

Scholarship Selection Committee
1800 Duke Street
Alexandria, VA 22314
703-535-SHRM
http://www.shrm.org/students/ags_published/CMS_003104.asp
Scholarship Name: Society for Human Resource Management Foundation Scholarship. *Academic Area: Human resources. *Age Group: Graduate students. *Eligibility: Applicants must be SHRM national student members. They must be enrolled in a master's degree program pursuing an emphasis area in human resources and have completed at least 12 hours of graduate course work with at least a 3.5 GPA. The scholarship is also available to undergraduate students. *Application Process: Applicants must submit three copies of a completed application, a resume, and two letters of recommendation. They also must submit original transcripts (one only). *Amount: $5,000. *Deadline: October 15.

Society of Satellite Professionals International (SSPI)

Attn: Tamara Bond, Membership Director
The New York Information Technology Center
55 Broad Street, 14th Floor
New York, NY 10004
212-809-5199, ext. 16
tbond@sspi.org
http://www.sspi.org/displaycommon.cfm?an=1&subart iclenbr=56
Scholarship Name: SSPI Scholarship Program. *Academic Area: Broadcasting, business, law, government, meteorology, satellite technology. *Age Group: Graduate students. *Eligibility: Applicants must demonstrate academic and leadership achievement, commitment to pursuing education

and career opportunities in the satellite industry or a field making direct use of satellite technology, and show potential for a significant contribution to the satellite communications industry. The scholarship is also available to high school seniors and undergraduate students. *Application Process: The application process is divided into two parts. Applicants who successfully pass stage one of the application process will be invited to apply for stage two. To apply for stage one, applicants should submit a completed application along with current transcripts. Information about stage two of the process will be provided to applicants who pass stage one. Visit the society's Web site to download an application. *Amount: $2,000 to $5,000. *Deadline: February 28 (for stage one).

Virginia Society of Certified Public Accountants
Attn: Molly Wash, Scholarship Coordinator
VSCPR Educational Foundation Inc.

PO Box 4620
Glen Allen, VA 23058-4620
800-733-8272
foundation@vscpa.com
http://www.vscpa.com/CPAStudent_Zone/Awards_and_Scholarships/VSCPA_Grad_Scholarship.aspx

Scholarship Name: Graduate Scholarship. *Academic Area: Accounting. *Age Group: Graduate students. *Eligibility: Applicants must be U.S. citizens who are enrolled in an accredited Virginia college or university graduate degree program in accounting. They also must demonstrate academic achievement by maintaining at least a 3.0 GPA as undergraduate students. *Application Process: Applicants should submit a completed application along with an essay, a letter of recommendation from a faculty member, a resume, and transcripts. Visit the society's Web site to download an application. *Amount: Awards vary. *Deadline: April 17.

EDUCATION—UNDERGRADUATE

The following financial aid resources are available to students who are interested in studying education and related fields at the undergraduate level.

Academy of Television Arts and Sciences
Fred Rogers Memorial Scholarship
c/o Michele Fowble
5220 Lankershim Boulevard
North Hollywood, CA 91601-3109
818-754-2802
http://www.emmys.tv/foundation/rogersscholar.php
Scholarship Name: Fred Rogers Memorial Scholarship.
    *Academic Area: Education, film/video, media
    arts (open). *Age Group: Undergraduate students.
    *Eligibility: Applicants must be undergraduates
    at accredited colleges or universities who are
    pursuing degrees in early childhood education,
    child development/child psychology, film/television
    production, media arts, music, or animation.
    Applicants must have the ultimate goal of working
    in the field of children's media. Particular attention
    will be given to student applicants from inner
    city or rural communities. The scholarship is also
    available to graduate students.*Application Process:
    Applicants must submit a completed application,
    a personal statement, transcripts, and two letters
    of recommendation. Visit the academy's Web site
    to download an application. *Amount: $10,000.
    *Deadline: January 31.

**American Alliance for Health, Physical Education,
    Recreation and Dance (AHPERD)**
Attn: Deb Callis
1900 Association Drive
Reston, VA 20191-1598
708-476-3400, 800-213-7193, ext 405
dcallis@aahperd.org
http://www.aahperd.org/aahperd/template.
    cfm?template=presidents_scholarships.html
Scholarship Name: Ruth Abernathy Presidential
    Scholarship. *Academic Area: Dance, physical
    education, recreation, wellness. *Age Group:
    Undergraduate students. *Eligibility: Applicants
    must be current members of the AHPERD (or join
    at time of application) who are majoring in the
    field of health, physical education, recreation, or
    dance. They also must be full-time students with a
    junior or senior status at a baccalaureate-granting
    college or university, maintain a 3.5 out of 4.0
    GPA, demonstrate exceptional leadership abilities,

and participate in community service activities.
    The scholarship is also available to graduate
    students. *Application Process: Applicants should
    submit a completed application along with a
    photocopy of their AAHPERD membership card
    or membership application form, three letters
    of recommendation, official transcripts from all
    college work completed, and a short biographical
    sketch. Materials should be mailed to the
    appropriate district contact. Visit the alliance's
    Web site to download an official application and
    to determine your district contact. *Amount:
    $1,000 (undergraduates), plus a three-year
    AAHPERD membership. *Deadline: October 15.

American Association of Physics Teachers
Attn: Programs Department
One Physics Ellipse
College Park, MD 20740
301-209-3344
aapt-prog@aapt.org
http://www.aapt.org/Grants/lotze.cfm
Scholarship Name: Barbara Lotze Scholarship for
    Future Teachers. *Academic Area: Education.
    *Age Group: Undergraduate students. *Eligibility:
    Applicants must be enrolled in a two- or four-year
    college (or high school seniors who are accepted
    into one), intend on becoming high school physics
    teachers, and U.S. citizens who can demonstrate
    academic achievement. *Application Process:
    Applicants must submit a completed application
    along with transcripts, a letter stating why they
    should be considered for the scholarship, and
    a copy of their birth certificate (or other proof
    of citizenship). Visit the association's Web site
    to download an application. *Amount: $2,000.
    *Deadline: December 1.

California Teachers Association (CTA)
CTA Scholarship Committee
Human Rights Department, c/o Manuel Ayan
PO Box 921
Burlingame, CA 94011-0921
650-697-1400
http://www.cta.org/InsideCTA/ScholarshipsWorkshops/
    ScholarshipsWorkshops.htm

Scholarship Name: CTA Scholarship for Members. *Academic Area: Education. *Age Group: Undergraduate students. *Eligibility: Applicants must be current and active CTA members, demonstrate high academic achievement, and be full-time students in an accredited institution of higher education. *Application Process: Applicants must submit a completed application, two letters of recommendation, CTA membership verification, and official transcripts. Visit the association's Web site to download an application. *Amount: $2,000. *Deadline: January 27.

California Teachers Association (CTA)
CTA Scholarship Committee
Human Rights Department, c/o Manuel Ayan
PO Box 921
Burlingame, CA 94011-0921
650-697-1400
http://www.cta.org/InsideCTA/ScholarshipsWorkshops/ScholarshipsWorkshops.htm
Scholarship Name: L. Gordon Bittle Memorial Scholarship for Student CTA (SCTA). *Academic Area: Education. *Age Group: Undergraduate students. *Eligibility: Applicants must be full-time students enrolled in an undergraduate or graduate degree program who wish to pursue a career in public education. They also must maintain at least a 3.5 GPA in high school or demonstrate high academic achievement in college. Applicants must be active members of the Student CTA. The scholarship is also available to graduate students. *Application Process: Applicants must submit a completed application, two letters of recommendation, SCTA membership verification, and official transcripts. Visit the association's Web site to download an application. *Amount: $2,000. *Deadline: January 27.

Hawaii Education Association (HEA)
1649 Kalakaua Avenue
Honolulu, HI 96826
808-949-6657, 866-653-9372
hea.office@heaed.com
http://www.heaed.com/HEA_Scholarships.html
Scholarship Name: Student Teacher Scholarship. *Academic Area: Education. *Age Group: Undergraduate students. *Eligibility: Applicants must be the children of HEA members (parent(s) must have been members for at least one year) or members of the HEA themselves (for at least one year) who are ready to begin their student teaching experience. *Application Process: Applicants should submit a completed application along with college transcripts, a 300-word personal statement, a financial aid form, and one recommendation from a college faculty member. Visit the association's Web site to download an application. *Amount: $3,000. *Deadline: April 1.

Indiana State Teachers Association (ISTA)
ISTA Scholarships
150 West Market Street, Suite 900
Indianapolis, IN 46204-2875
317-263-3400, 800-382-4037
http://www.ista-in.org/sam.cfm?xnode=1467
Scholarship Name: Educator Scholarship. *Academic Area: Education. *Age Group: Undergraduate students. *Eligibility: Applicants must be graduating Indiana high school seniors who are planning to attend a college or university to pursue a teaching license. They also must have a parent or legal guardian who is an active member of the ISTA and demonstrate academic achievement, community involvement, co-curricular activity involvement, and leadership ability. *Application Process: Applicants should submit a completed application along with current official high school transcripts, three letters of recommendation, and a typed essay (topic outlined on the application). Visit the association's Web site to download an application. *Amount: $1,000. *Deadline: March 3.

International Technology Education Association (ITEA)
Foundation for Technology Education
FTE Undergraduate Scholarship
1914 Association Drive, Suite 201
Reston, VA 20191-1539
703-860-2100
bmongold@iteaconnect.org
http://www.iteaconnect.org/I3d.html
Scholarship Name: Foundation for Technology Undergraduate Scholarship. *Academic Area: Education. *Age Group: Undergraduate students. *Eligibility: Applicants must be members of the ITEA and current, full-time undergraduate students majoring in technology education teacher preparation. They also must be freshmen, sophomores, or juniors at the time of application and maintain at least a 2.5 GPA. *Application Process:

Applicants must submit four copies of a letter of application, a resume, transcripts, and three faculty letters of recommendation. Visit the association's Web site for further application details. *Amount: $1,000. *Deadline: December 1.

International Technology Education Association (ITEA)

ITEA/EEA-Ship Undergraduate Scholarship
1914 Association Drive, Suite 201
Reston, VA 20191-1539
703-860-2100
bmongold@iteaconnect.org
http://www.iteaconnect.org/I3a.html
Scholarship Name: International Technology Education Association/EEA-Ship Undergraduate Scholarship. *Academic Area: Education. *Age Group: Undergraduate students. *Eligibility: Applicants must be members of the ITEA and current, full-time undergraduate students majoring in technology education teacher preparation. They also must be freshmen, sophomores, or juniors at the time of application and maintain at least a 2.5 GPA. *Application Process: Applicants must submit four copies of a letter of application, a resume, transcripts, and three faculty letters of recommendation. Visit the association's Web site for further application details. *Amount: $1,000. *Deadline: December 1.

International Technology Education Association (ITEA)

Foundation for Technology Education (FTE)
Litherland/FTE Scholarship
1914 Association Drive, Suite 201
Reston, VA 20191-1539
703-860-2100
bmongold@iteaconnect.org
http://www.iteaconnect.org/I3b.html
Scholarship Name: Litherland/Foundation for Technology Education Scholarship. *Academic Area: Education. *Age Group: Undergraduate students. *Eligibility: Applicants must be members of the ITEA and current, full-time undergraduate students majoring in technology education teacher preparation. They also must be freshmen, sophomores, or juniors at the time of application and maintain at least a 2.5 GPA. *Application Process: Applicants must submit four copies of a letter of application, a resume, transcripts, and three faculty

letters of recommendation. Visit the association's Web site for further application details. *Amount: $1,000. *Deadline: December 1.

Iowa State Education Association (ISEA)

Attn: Scholarship Committee
777 Third Street
Des Moines, IA 50309
515-471-8000, 800-445-9358
http://www.isea.org/members/scholarships.htm
Scholarship Name: Iowa State Education Association Education Scholarship. *Academic Area: Education. *Age Group: Undergraduate students. *Applicants must be the sons or daughters of ISEA members who have completed at least 60 semester hours of their undergraduate degree in education. Applicants must also be members of the National Education Association or a similar state student organization in the state where the applicants are attending college. *Application Process: Applicants should submit a completed application along with transcripts and a written statement detailing their intentions of becoming a teacher. Applicants should contact the ISEA state headquarters or UniServ unit (contact information located on ISEA's Web site) to request an application. *Amount; $1,000. *Deadline: February 1.

Maryland Agriculture Teachers Association (MATA)

Attn: Ms. Jamie Picardy, MATA Consultant
403 Oakington Road, PO Box 536
Havre de Grace, MD 21078
410-939-9030, 800-205-9737
jpicardy@maefonline.com
http://iaa.umd.edu/MATA/elcScholars.htm
Scholarship Name: Elmer L. Cooper Scholarship. *Academic Area: Agriculture, education. *Age Group: Undergraduate students. *Eligibility: Applicants must be high school seniors. There are two scholarships available in this program. One is for a high school senior who intends on becoming an agriculture teacher, and the other is for an outstanding FFA member who intends on majoring in any area of agriculture. *Application Process: Applicants should contact the association to receive an application. *Amount: Awards vary. *Deadline: Contact the association for deadline information.

National Cattlemen's Foundation

Attn: Beef Industry Scholarship
9110 East Nichols Avenue, Suite 300

Centennial, CO 80112
303-850-3347
ncf@beef.org
http://www.nationalcattlemensfoundation.org/
SCHOLARSHIP.aspx
Scholarship Name: Beef Industry Scholarship. *Academic Area: Agriculture, communications, education. *Age Group: Undergraduate students. *Eligibility: Applicants must be enrolled full time in a two- or four-year institution of higher learning with an intent on majoring in a field related to the beef industry—education, communications, production, or research. They must also demonstrate commitment to the beef industry through classes, internships, or life experiences. High school seniors may also apply for this scholarship. *Application Process: Applicants should submit a completed application along with a one-page letter expressing career goals, two letters of recommendation, and a 750-word essay. *Visit the association's Web site to download an application. *Amount: $1,500, plus expenses paid to attend the organization's annual convention and trade show. *Deadline: September 30.

National Institute for Labor Relations Research

Attn: Future Teachers Scholarships
5211 Port Royal Road, Suite 510
Springfield, VA 22151
703-321-9606
research@nilrr.org
http://www.nilrr.org/scholarships.htm
Scholarship Name: Applegate/Jackson/Parks Future Teacher Scholarship. *Academic Area: Education. *Age Group: Undergraduate students. *Eligibility: Applicants must be college students majoring in education who demonstrate academic achievement and an interest in the work of the institute. The scholarship is also available to graduate students. *Application Process: Applicants should submit a completed application, transcripts (or letter of college acceptance), and a 500-word essay on the principles of voluntary unionism. Applications should be submitted between October 1 and December 31. Visit the institute's Web site to download an application. *Amount: $1,000. *Deadline: December 31.

National Oceanic Atmospheric Administration (NOAA)

NOAA/Hollings Scholarship
Oak Ridge Institute for Science and Education

PO Box 117, MS 36
Oak Ridge, TN 37831-0117
202-482-3384
noaa.education@noaa.gov
http://www.orau.gov/noaa/HollingsScholarship
Scholarship Name: Ernest F. Hollings Scholarship Program. *Academic Area: Agriculture, biology, computer science, education, engineering (open), life sciences, marine sciences, mathematics, physical sciences, social sciences. *Age Group: Undergraduate students. *Eligibility: Applicants must be full-time undergraduate students, studying one of the aforementioned academic areas, who will be juniors in the fall academic term at an accredited college/university in the United States or U.S. territories. They also must be U.S. citizens and maintain at least a 3.0 GPA. *Application Process: Applicants must submit a completed application, two reference forms (to be completed and submitted by referees), and official transcripts. Visit the NOAA's Web site to download an application. *Amount: Up to $8,000. *Deadline: May 23.

Phi Delta Kappa (PDK) International

Scholarship Programs
PO Box 789
Bloomington, IN 47402-0789
800-766-1156
information@pdkintl.org
http://www.pdkintl.org/awards/pros_eds.htm
Grant Name: Grant for Prospective Educators. *Academic Area: Education. *Age Group: Undergraduate students. *Eligibility: Applicants must be undergraduate PDK members who are education majors or current high school seniors whose intended college major is education. *Application Process: Applicants must submit a completed application along with a 500-word (or less) essay, academic transcript, and two letters of reference. Visit PDK's Web site to download an application. *Amount: $500 to $5,000. *Deadline: February 1.

Society of Physics Students (SPS)

SPS Scholarship Committee
One Physics Ellipse
College Park, MD 20740
301-209-3007
sps@aip.org
http://www.spsnational.org/programs/spsscholarships.
htm

Scholarship Name: Society of Physics Students Future Teacher Scholarship. *Academic Area: Education, physics. *Age Group: Undergraduate students. *Eligibility: Applicants must be college juniors or seniors who demonstrate a high level of scholarship and active participation in SPS programs. They also must be participating in a teacher education program and plan to pursue a career in physics education. *Application Process: Applicants should submit a completed application along with official transcripts, two letters of recommendation, and a statement from an advisor verifying participation in a teacher education program. Visit the society's Web site to download an application. *Amount: $2,000. *Deadline: February 15.

EDUCATION—GRADUATE

The following financial aid resources are available to students who are interested in studying education and related fields at the graduate level.

Academy of Television Arts & Sciences
Fred Rogers Memorial Scholarship
Attn: Michele Fowble
5220 Lankershim Boulevard
North Hollywood, CA 91601-3109
818-754-2802
http://www.emmys.tv/foundation/rogersscholar.php
Scholarship Name: Fred Rogers Memorial Scholarship. *Academic Area: Education, film/video, media arts. *Age Group: Graduate students. *Eligibility: Applicants must be graduates students at accredited colleges or universities who are pursuing degrees in early childhood education, child development/child psychology, film/television production, media arts, music, or animation. Applicants must have the ultimate goal of working in the field of children's media. Particular attention will be given to student applicants from inner city or rural communities. The scholarship is also available to undergraduate students. *Application Process: Applicants must submit a completed application, a personal statement, transcripts, and two letters of recommendation. Visit the academy's Web site to download an application. *Amount: $10,000. *Deadline: January 31.

American Association of School Administrators
801 North Quincy Street, Suite 700
Arlington, VA 22203
703-875-0706
skeller@aasa.org
http://www.aasa.org/awards/content.cfm?ItemNumber=2175
Scholarship Name: Educational Administration Scholarship. *Academic Area: Education. *Age Group: Graduate students. *Eligibility: Applicants must be graduate students intending to pursue public school superintendency as a career. *Application Process: Applicants must submit one original and six photocopies of a completed application, a personal statement, and three letters of recommendation. Candidates must be recommended by a dean and at least one faculty member. Visit the association's Web site in May to download an application. *Amount: $2,000. *Deadline: September 30.

California Agricultural Teachers' Association (CATA)
PO Box 834
Elk Grove, CA 95759-0834
916-714-2970
http://www.calagteachers.org/Applications/ScholarshipApplication.doc
Scholarship Name: California Agricultural Teachers' Association Scholarship. *Academic Area: Education. *Age Group: Graduate students. *Eligibility: Applicants must be fifth-year post-baccalaureate students who are completing teacher certification requirements to become agriculture teachers. Applicants must also become members of the CATA while they are student teaching. *Application Process: Applicants should submit a completed application along with a description of their leadership or service activities, an essay on why they want to teach agriculture, resume, a description of how they are funding their student teaching experience, two letters of recommendation, and unofficial transcripts. One photocopied complete set of these materials should be submitted along with the originals. Visit the association's Web site to download an application. *Amount: $500. *Deadline: May 15.

National Institute for Labor Relations Research
Attn: Future Teachers Scholarships
5211 Port Royal Road, Suite 510
Springfield, VA 22151
703-321-9606
research@nilrr.org
http://www.nilrr.org/scholarships.htm
Scholarship Name: Applegate/Jackson/Parks Future Teacher Scholarship. *Academic Area: Education. *Age Group: Graduate students. *Eligibility: Applicants must be college students majoring in education who demonstrate academic achievement and an interest in the work of the institute. The scholarship is also available to undergraduate students. *Application Process: Applicants should submit a completed application, transcripts (or letter of college acceptance), and a 500-word essay on the principles of voluntary unionism. Applications should be submitted between October 1 and December 31. Visit the institute's Web site to download an application. *Amount: $1,000. *Deadline: December 31.

ENGINEERING/COMPUTER SCIENCE/ MATHEMATICS—UNDERGRADUATE

The following financial aid resources are available to students who are interested in studying engineering, computer science, mathematics, and related fields at the undergraduate level.

American Ground Water Trust
Scholarship Application
PO Box 1796
Concord, NH 03302
603-228-5444
http://www.agwt.org/scholarships.htm
Scholarship Name: Amtrol Inc. Scholarship. *Academic Area: Engineering (water supply and treatment). *Age Group: Undergraduate students. *Eligibility: Applicants must be high school seniors intending on pursuing a career in a ground water-related field. *Application Process: Applicants should submit a completed application along with two letters of recommendation and a 500-word essay on "Ground Water: An Important Environmental and Economic Resource for America." Visit the organization's Web site to download an application. *Amount: $1,000 to $2,000. *Deadline: June 1.

American Ground Water Trust
Scholarship Application
PO Box 1796
Concord, NH 03302
603-228-5444
http://www.agwt.org/scholarships.htm
Scholarship Name: Baroid Scholarship. *Academic Area: Engineering (water supply and treatment). *Age Group: Undergraduate students. *Eligibility: Applicants must be high school seniors entering their freshman year in a full-time academic program of study at a four-year accredited university or college, intending on pursuing a career in a ground water-related field. They must either have completed a science/environmental project in high school that directly involved ground water resources, or had an out-of-school experience related to the environment and natural resources. They also must be U.S. citizens or legal residents of the U.S., with a minimum 3.0 GPA. *Application Process: Applicants should submit a completed application along with two letters of recommendation and a 500-word essay on "Ground Water: An Important Environmental

and Economic Resource for America." Applicants should also submit a 300-word description about their high school ground water project and/or practical environmental work experience Visit the organization's Web site to download an application. *Amount: $1,000 to $2,000. *Deadline: June 1.

American Ground Water Trust
Scholarship Application
PO Box 1796
Concord, NH 03302
603-228-5444
http://www.agwt.org/scholarships.htm
Scholarship Name: Ben Everson Scholarship. *Academic Area: Engineering (water supply and treatment). *Age Group: Undergraduate students. *Eligibility: Applicants must be high school seniors entering their freshman year in a full-time academic program of study at a four-year accredited university or college, intending on pursuing a career in a ground water-related field. They must either have completed a science/environmental project in high school that directly involved ground water resources, or had an out-of-school experience related to the environment and natural resources. They also must be U.S. citizens or legal residents of the U.S., with a minimum 3.0 GPA. *Application Process: Applicants should submit a completed application along with two letters of recommendation and a 500-word essay on "Ground Water: An Important Environmental and Economic Resource for America." Applicants should also submit a 300-word description about their high school ground water project and/or practical environmental work experience. Visit the organization's Web site to download an application. *Amount: $2,500. *Deadline: June 1.

American Ground Water Trust
Scholarship Application
PO Box 1796
Concord, NH 03302

6603-228-544

http://www.agwt.org/scholarships.htm

Scholarship Name: Thomas M. Stetson Scholarship. *Academic Area: Engineering (water supply and treatment). *Age Group: Undergraduate students. *Eligibility: Applicants must be high school seniors entering their freshman year in a full-time academic program of study at a four-year accredited university or college, intending on pursuing a career in a ground water-related field. They must either have completed a science/environmental project in high school that directly involved ground water resources, or had an out-of-school experience related to the environment and natural resources. They also must be U.S. citizens or legal residents of the United States, with a minimum 3.0 GPA, and must be attending a college or university located west of the Mississippi River. *Application Process: Applicants should submit a completed application along with two letters of recommendation and a 500-word essay on "Ground Water: An Important Environmental and Economic Resource for America." Applicants should also submit a 300-word description about their high school ground water project and/or practical environmental work experience. Visit the organization's Web site to download an application. *Amount: $1,000. *Deadline: June 1.

American Helicopter Society/Vertical Flight Foundation

217 North Washington Street

Alexandria, VA 22314-2538

703-684-6777

staff@vtol.org

http://www.vtol.org/VFFSchoForm.pdf

Scholarship Name: Vertical Flight Foundation Engineering Scholarship. *Academic Area: Engineering (aerospace/aviation). *Age Group: Undergraduate students. *Eligibility: Applicants must be full-time students in accredited schools of engineering and be enrolled through the following full academic year. The scholarship is also available to graduate students. *Application Process: Applicants must submit a completed application, official transcripts, and a letter of recommendation. Visit the foundation's Web site to download an application. *Amount: $1,000 to $4,000. *Deadline: February 1.

American Institute of Aeronautics and Astronautics (AIAA) Foundation

1801 Alexander Bell Drive, Suite 500

Reston, VA 20191-4344

703-264-7500, 800-639-AIAA

http://www.aiaa.org/content.cfm?pageid=226

Scholarship Name: AIAA Foundation Undergraduate Scholarship Program. *Academic Area: Engineering (open), science (open). *Age Group: Undergraduate students. *Eligibility: Applicants must be college sophomores, juniors, and seniors, have completed at least one quarter or semester of academic work, maintain a 3.3 GPA, be pursuing some field of science or engineering encompassed by the technical activities of the AIAA, and must be or become an AIAA student member. *Application Process: Applicants should submit a completed application along with three letters of recommendation, transcripts, and an essay. Visit the association's Web site for essay topics and to download an application. *Amount: $2,000 to $2,500. *Deadline: January 31.

American Institute of Chemical Engineers (AIChE)

Attn: AIChE Awards Administrator

3 Park Avenue

New York, NY 10016-5901

212-591-7107

awards@aiche.org

http://students.aiche.org/pdfs/othmernat.pdf

Scholarship Name: AIChE/Donald F. & Mildred Topp Othmer National Scholarship Award. *Academic Area: Engineering (chemical). *Age Group: Undergraduate students. *Eligibility: Applicants must be AIChE national student members and be nominated by their student chapter advisor. The student chapter advisor makes his or her nomination based on the applicant's academic record, participation in their AIChE chapter, and personal statement. Applicants must have completed approximately 50 percent of their degree requirements and course work. *Application Process: The student chapter advisor must submit a completed nomination form, a letter of nomination, and a personal statement from the nominee. Visit the institute's Web site to download a nomination form. *Amount: $1,000. *Deadline: May 10.

American Institute of Chemical Engineers (AIChE)

Attn: AIChE Awards Administrator

3 Park Avenue

New York, NY 10016-5901
212-591-7107
awards@aiche.org
http://students.aiche.org/pdfs/mcketta_schol.pdf
Scholarship Name: John J. McKetta Undergraduate
Scholarship. *Academic Area: Engineering
(chemical). *Age Group: Undergraduate students.
*Eligibility: Applicants must be chemical engineering
undergraduate students (incoming juniors or seniors
only), planning careers in the chemical engineering
process industries. They also must maintain a
minimum 3.0 GPA. It is preferred that applicants be
student members of the AIChE and demonstrate
leadership or activity in either their AIChE student
chapter or other university-sponsored campus
activities. Applicants must attend Accreditation Board
for Engineering and Technology accredited schools in
the United States, Canada, and Mexico. *Application
Process: Applicants must submit a completed
application, official transcripts, a two-page essay,
student advisors' nomination forms, and two letters of
recommendation (in English). Visit the institute's Web
site to download an application. *Amount: $5,000.
*Deadline: May 12.

American Nuclear Society (ANS)
Attn: Scholarship Coordinator
555 North Kensington Avenue
LaGrange Park, IL 60526
708-352-6611
http://www.ans.org/honors/scholarships
Scholarship Name: ANS Incoming Freshman
Scholarship. *Academic Area: Engineering (nuclear).
*Age Group: Undergraduate students. *Eligibility:
Applicants must be graduating high-school seniors
who have enrolled, full time, in college courses and
are pursuing science, mathematics, and/or technical
courses with an interest in working in nuclear
science and technology. Applicants should also
demonstrate a high level of academic achievement.
*Application Process: Applicants should submit a
completed application along with official transcripts
with seal and two confidential reference forms. All
application materials must be mailed in one packet.
Visit the society's Web site to download an official
application. *Amount: $2,000. *Deadline: April 1.

American Nuclear Society (ANS)
Attn: Scholarship Coordinator
555 North Kensington Avenue

LaGrange Park, IL 60526
708-352-6611
http://www.ans.org/honors/scholarships
Scholarship Name: ANS Undergraduate Scholarships.
*Academic Area: Engineering (nuclear). *Age Group:
Undergraduate students. *Eligibility: Applicants
must be college sophomores, juniors, or seniors and
U.S. citizens (or possess a permanent resident visa).
Four scholarship will be awarded to undergraduate
students who have completed one year in a course
of study leading to a degree in nuclear science,
nuclear engineering, or a nuclear-related field and
who will be sophomores in the upcoming academic
year. A maximum of 21 scholarships will be awarded
to students who have completed two or more
years and will be entering as juniors or seniors.
*Application Process: Applicants should submit a
completed application along with official transcripts
with seal, a letter of recommendation from
sponsoring organization, and three confidential
reference forms. All application materials must be
mailed in one packet. Visit the society's Web site to
view a list of individual undergraduate scholarships
and additional requirements by scholarship.
Some scholarships require additional essays. An
application form can also be downloaded from the
society's Web site. *Amount: Awards vary. *Deadline:
February 1.

American Public Transportation Foundation
1666 K Street, NW, Suite 1100
Washington, DC 20006
202-496-4800
pboswell@apta.com
http://www.apta.com/services/human_resources/
program_guidelines.cfm
Scholarship Name: Louis T. Klauder Scholarship.
*Academic Area: Engineering (electrical),
engineering (mechanical). *Age Group:
Undergraduate students. *Eligibility: Applicants
must demonstrate a dedication to pursuing careers
in the rail transit industry as electrical or mechanical
engineers. They also must be enrolled in a fully
accredited institution, maintain at least a 3.0 GPA
(B) in course work that is relevant to the industry
or required of a degree program, and either be
employed by or demonstrate a strong interest
in entering the public transportation industry.
College sophomores (30 hours or more satisfactorily
completed), juniors, and seniors, or those seeking

advanced degrees may apply for scholarships. *Application Process: Applicants must submit a completed application, a letter of nomination, an essay, three letters of recommendation, a copy of their completed FAFSA form, official transcripts, verification of enrollment, and a copy of their academic fee schedule. Visit the foundation's Web site to download an application. *Amount: $2,500 minimum. *Deadline: June 17.

American Public Transportation Foundation

1666 K Street, NW, Suite 1100
Washington, DC 20006
202-496-4800
pboswell@apta.com
http://www.apta.com/services/human_resources/
  program_guidelines.cfm
Scholarship Name: Parsons Brinckerhoff-Jim Lammie Scholarship. *Academic Area: Engineering (transportation). *Age Group: Undergraduate students. *Eligibility: Applicants must demonstrate a dedication to pursuing public transportation engineering careers. They also must be enrolled in a fully accredited institution, maintain at least a 3.0 GPA (B) in course work that is relevant to the industry or required of a degree program, and either be employed by or demonstrate a strong interest in entering the public transportation industry. College sophomores (30 hours or more satisfactorily completed), juniors, and seniors, or those seeking advanced degrees may apply for scholarships. *Application Process: Applicants must submit a completed application, a letter of nomination, an essay, three letters of recommendation, a copy of a completed FAFSA form, official transcripts, verification of enrollment, and a copy of their academic fee schedule. Visit the foundation's Web site to download an application. *Amount: $2,500 minimum. *Deadline: June 17.

American Society for Nondestructive Testing (ASNT)

PO Box 28518
1711 Arlingate Lane
Columbus, OH 43228-0518
800-222-2768
http://www.asnt.org/keydocuments/awards/
  engineering.htm
Scholarship Name: ASNT Engineering Undergraduate Award. *Academic Area: Engineering (nondestructive testing). *Age Group: Undergraduate students.

*Eligibility: Applicants must be undergraduate students enrolled in an engineering program at a university accredited by the Accreditation Board for Engineering and Technology or its equivalent and choosing nondestructive testing as a field of specialization. *Application Process: Applicants must submit a nomination form, a nominating letter, official transcripts, three letters of recommendation from faculty members, and a personal statement. Visit the society's Web site to download a nomination form. *Amount: $3,000. *Deadline: December 15.

American Society for Nondestructive Testing (ASNT)

PO Box 28518
1711 Arlingate Lane
Columbus, OH 43228
800-222-2768
http://www.asnt.org/keydocuments/awards/oliver.htm
Scholarship Name: Robert B. Oliver ASNT Scholarship. *Academic Area: Technology (nondestructive testing). *Age Group: Undergraduate students. *Eligibility: Applicants must be enrolled in an undergraduate degree, associate degree, or postsecondary certificate program that includes studies in nondestructive testing. *Application Process: Applicants must submit a completed application, four copies of an original manuscript on nondestructive testing, a transcript detailing nondestructive course work that they have taken, official transcripts, and letter from a school official verifying enrollment. Visit the society's Web site to download an application. *Amount: $2,500. *Deadline: February 15.

American Society of Agricultural and Biological Engineers (ASABE) Foundation

Attn: Administrator
ASABE Foundation Scholarship Fund
2950 Niles Road
St. Joseph, MI 49085-9659
269-429-0300
hq@asabe.org
http://www.asabe.org/membership/students/
  foundation.html
Scholarship Name: ASABE Foundation Scholarship. *Academic Area: Engineering (agricultural), engineering (biological). *Age Group: Undergraduate students. *Eligibility: Applicants must be college sophomores and juniors, student members of the

ASABE, and enrolled in an Accreditation Board for Engineering and Technology- or Canadian Engineering Accreditation Board-accredited degree program in the United States or Canada. They also must maintain at least a 2.5 GPA, attest to the need for financial aid, and be able to verify that graduation from their agricultural or biological degree program assures eligibility for the Professional Engineer (PE) licensing examination. *Application Process: Applicants should submit a letter that formally requests the ASABE Foundation Scholarship; the letter should include the student's ASABE member number and document the accreditation of the engineering program. The letter should also state the student's GPA, expected graduation date, and include proof that the degree program assures eligibility for the PE licensing examination. Visit the society's Web site for additional information. *Amount: $1,000. *Deadline: March 15.

American Society of Agricultural and Biological Engineers (ASABE) Foundation
ASABE Student Engineer of the Year Scholarship
2950 Niles Road
St. Joseph, MI 49085-9659
269-429-0300
hq@asabe.org
http://www.asabe.org/membership/students/engscholar.html
Scholarship Name: ASABE Student Engineer of the Year Scholarship. *Academic Area: Engineering (agricultural), engineering (biological). *Age Group: Undergraduate students. *Eligibility: Applicants must have completed at least one full year of undergraduate study and must not be a graduating senior in the semester/term in which they are applying. They also must be majoring in an agricultural/biological engineering curriculum that is accredited by the Accreditation Board for Engineering and Technology or the Canadian Engineering Accreditation Board, student members of the ASABE, and maintain a GPA of at least 3.0. Applicant should demonstrate excellence in scholarship and outstanding character. *Application Process: Applicants should submit a completed application along with the signature of the department head and an essay, not exceeding 500 words, addressing the subject: "My Goals in the Engineering Profession." Visit the society's Web site for additional information. *Amount: $1,000. *Deadline: March 15.

American Society of Agricultural and Biological Engineers (ASABE) Foundation
John L. and Sarah G. Merriam Scholarship Fund
2950 Niles Road
St. Joseph, MI 49085-9659
269-429-0300
hq@asabe.org
http://www.asabe.org/membership/merriam.html
Scholarship Name: John L. and Sarah G. Merriam Scholarship. *Academic Area: Engineering (agricultural), engineering (biological). *Age Group: Undergraduate students. *Eligibility: Applicants must be college sophomores or juniors, student members of the ASABE with a biological or agricultural engineering major (emphasis of study in soil and water), and have at least a 2.5 GPA. Applicant's curriculum should be accredited by the Accreditation Board for Engineering and Technology or the Canadian Engineering Accreditation Board. *Application Process: Applicants should submit a letter that formally requests consideration for the Merriam Scholarship. The letter should include the applicant's ASABE member number, the name of the accredited engineering program that the applicant is attending, and the student's grade point average. It should also explain why the applicant has selected the soil and water discipline as his or her focus of study. Visit the society's Web site for additional information. *Amount: $1,000. *Deadline: March 15.

American Society of Agricultural and Biological Engineers (ASABE) Foundation
Attn: Administrator
Adams Scholarship Fund
2950 Niles Road
St. Joseph, MI 49085-9659
269-429-0300
hq@asabe.org
http://www.asabe.org/membership/students/grant1.html
Scholarship Name: William J. Adams Jr. and Marijane E. Adams Scholarship. *Academic Area: Engineering (agricultural), engineering (biological). *Age Group: Undergraduate students. *Eligibility: Applicants must have completed at least one full year of undergraduate study and must not be a graduating senior in the semester/term in which they are applying. They also must be majoring in an agricultural/biological engineering curriculum that is accredited by the Accreditation Board for Engineering and Technology

or the Canadian Engineering Accreditation Board, have a special interest in agricultural machinery product design and development, demonstrate financial need, and maintain a GPA of at least 2.5. *Application Process: Applicants should submit a letter that formally states interest in the Adams Scholarship and includes his or her ASABE member number. The following criteria should be verified in the letter: the extent of the applicant's financial need and why the applicant has selected the design and development of new agricultural machinery products as the area of focus for his or her degree. Applicants should limit their letter to no more than two pages. Visit the society's Web site for additional information. *Amount: $1,000. *Deadline: March 15.

American Society of Certified Engineering Technicians (ASCET)

PO Box 239
Wesson, MS 39191
601-643-9079
general-manager@ascet.org
http://www.ascet.org/AidArt.htm
Grant Name: Joseph C. Johnson Memorial Grant. *Academic Area: Engineering technology. *Age Group: Undergraduate students. *Eligibility: Applicants must be majoring in engineering technology and maintain at least a 3.0 GPA on a 4.0 scale. They also must be ASCET members and U.S. citizens or legal residents. Applicants in a two-year program should apply in the first year to receive the grant for their second year. Applicants in a four-year program who apply in the third year may receive the grant for their fourth year. Applicants must be qualified for financial aid under the Federal College Work-Study Program. *Application Process: Applicants must submit a completed application, verification of financial need (from their financial aid office or dean/registrar of engineering technology), transcripts, and three letters of recommendation. Contact the ASCET to request an application. *Amount: $750. *Deadline: Varies.

American Society of Certified Engineering Technicians (ASCET)

PO Box 239
Wesson, MS 39191
601-643-9079
general-manager@ascet.org
http://www.ascet.org/AidArt.htm

Scholarship Name: Joseph M. Parish Memorial Grant. *Academic Area: Engineering technology. *Age Group: Undergraduate students. *Eligibility: Applicants must be majoring in engineering technology and maintain at least a 3.0 GPA on a 4.0 scale. They also must be ASCET student members and U.S. citizens or legal residents. Applicants in a two-year program should apply in the first year to receive the grant for their second year. Applicants in a four-year program who apply in the third year may receive the grant for their fourth year. Applicants must be qualified for financial aid under the Federal College Work-Study Program. *Application Process: Applicants must submit a completed application, verification of financial need (from their financial aid office or dean/registrar of engineering technology), and transcripts. Contact the ASCET to request an application. *Amount: $500. *Deadline: Varies.

American Society of Certified Engineering Technicians (ASCET)

PO Box 239
Wesson, MS 39191
601-643-9079
general-manager@ascet.org
http://www.ascet.org/AidArt.htm
Grant Name: Small Cash Grant Program. *Academic Area: Engineering technology. *Age Group: Undergraduate students. *Eligibility: Applicants must be high school seniors in the last five months of the academic year who will be enrolled in an engineering technology curriculum no later than six months following selection for award. Applicants must also be ASCET members with passing grades in their present curriculum. *Application Process: Applicants must submit a completed application, transcripts, and a letter of recommendation. Contact the ASCET to request an application. *Amount: $100. *Deadline: Varies.

American Society of Mechanical Engineers (ASME)

Attn: Maisha Phillips, Coordinator, Student Development
Three Park Avenue
New York, NY 10016-5990
212-591-8131
phillipsm@asme.org
http://www.asme.org/education/enged/aid/scholar.htm
Scholarship Name: ASME Scholarship. *Academic Area: Engineering (mechanical). *Age Group: Undergraduate students. *Eligibility: Applicants must be high school seniors, undergraduate, or

graduate students pursuing degrees and careers in mechanical engineering. They must also be ASME members. Eligibility requirements vary. Visit the society's Web site to obtain specific scholarship eligibility requirements. *Application Process: Online applications are available from February 1 through March 15. Only ASME members can apply by using their registered e-mail address and membership number to log in. Contact the society for further application details. *Amount: $1,000 to $10,000. *Deadline: March 15.

American Society of Mechanical Engineers (ASME) Auxiliary

Attn: Alverta E. Cover
5425 Caldwell Mill Rd
Birmingham, AL 35242
205-991-6109
covera@asme.org
http://www.asme.org/auxiliary/scholarshiploans

Scholarship Name: American Society of Mechanical Engineers Auxiliary Undergraduate Scholarship. *Academic Area: Engineering (mechanical). *Age Group: Undergraduate students. *Eligibility: Applicants must apply in their junior years and demonstrate financial need, ASME participation, and academic achievement. They also must be U.S. citizens and be enrolled in a U.S. school in an Accreditation Board for Engineering and Technology accredited mechanical engineering department. *Application Process: Applicants must submit a completed application, three letters of recommendation, and official transcripts. Visit the society's Web site to download an application. *Amount: $2,000. *Deadline: March 15.

American Society of Naval Engineers

1452 Duke Street
Alexandria, VA 22314-3458
703-836-6727
dwoodbury@navalengineers.org
http://www.navalengineers.org/Programs/Scholarships/sc_info.htm

Scholarship Name: American Society of Naval Engineers Scholarship. *Academic Area: Engineering (ocean/naval). *Age Group: Undergraduate students. *Eligibility: Applicants must be applying for the scholarship for use during their last year of undergraduate study. They also must be U.S. citizens who demonstrate academic achievement, exemplary work history, financial need, extracurricular involvement, and a high degree of interest in naval engineering. The scholarship is also available to graduate students. *Application Process: Applicants should submit a completed application along with three signed and sealed letters of recommendation and official, sealed transcripts. Visit the association's Web site to download an official application. *Amount: $2,500 (undergraduate students). *Deadline: February 15.

American Society of Safety Engineers (ASSE) Foundation

Attn: Scholarships
1800 East Oakton Street
Des Plaines, IL 60018
847-699-2929
mgoranson@asse.org
http://www.asse.org

Scholarship Name: American Society of Safety Engineers Foundation Scholarship. *Academic Area: Engineering (safety). *Age Group: Undergraduate students. *Eligibility: Applicants must be student members of the ASSE. This Society offers a variety of scholarships with varying eligibility requirements. Visit the Society's Web site to view a list of available scholarships and specific eligibility requirements. Scholarships are also available to graduate students. *Application Process: Applicants should submit a completed application along with supporting materials, including a 300-word personal statement about their career goals and why they are seeking a degree in a safety-related field. Visit the society's Web site to download an application. *Amount: Awards vary. *Deadline: December 1.

Armed Forces Communications and Electronics Association (AFCEA) Educational Foundation

Attn: Norma Corrales, Director, Scholarships and Awards Program
4400 Fair Lakes Court
Fairfax, VA 22033-3899
703-631-6149, 800-336-4583, ext. 6149
scholarship@afcea.org
http://www.afcea.org/education/scholarships/undergraduate/pub1.asp

Scholarship Name: AFCEA Distance Learning/Online Scholarship. *Academic Area: Computer science, engineering (aerospace), engineering (chemical), engineering (computer), engineering (electrical), physics, mathematics. *Age Group: Undergraduate students. *Eligibility: Applicants must be U.S. citizens currently enrolled in full-time distance learning or online programs majoring in mathematics, physics, electrical, chemical, systems or computer engineering, and computer science. Applicants must have completed at least 30 semester hours of study (or equivalent) to be eligible to apply. Applicants must also have completed at least two semesters of calculus. *Application Process: Applicants must submit a completed application. Applications are available on the foundation's Web site each December. *Amount: $1,000. *Deadline: June 1.

Armed Forces Communications and Electronics Association (AFCEA) Educational Foundation
Attn: Fred H. Rainbow, Vice President and Executive Director
4400 Fair Lakes Court
Fairfax, VA 22033-3899
703-631-6149, 800-336-4583, ext. 6149
scholarship@afcea.org
http://www.afcea.org/education/scholarships/undergraduate/pub3.asp
Scholarship Name: AFCEA Lockheed Martin Orincon IT Scholarship. *Academic Area: Computer science, engineering (aerospace), engineering (chemical), engineering (computer), engineering (electrical), physics, mathematics. *Age Group: Undergraduate students. *Eligibility: Applicants must be U.S. citizens attending an accredited four-year college or university in the greater San Diego, California area. Applicants must be enrolled full time as sophomores or juniors majoring in electrical, computer, chemical, systems or aerospace engineering, computer science, physics, or mathematics. Applicants must also maintain at least a 3.5 GPA. Students enrolled in distance learning or online programs are not eligible to apply. *Application Process: Applicants must submit a completed application, at least two letters of recommendation, and official transcripts. Applications are available on the foundation's Web site each January. *Amount: $3,000. *Deadline: May 1.

Armed Forces Communications and Electronics Association (AFCEA) Educational Foundation
Attn: Fred H. Rainbow, Vice President and Executive Director
4400 Fair Lakes Court
Fairfax, VA 22033-3899

703-631-6149, 800-336-4583, ext. 6149
scholarship@afcea.org
http://www.afcea.org/education/scholarships/undergraduate/pub2.asp
Scholarship Name: General John A. Wickham Scholarship. *Academic Area: Computer science, engineering (aerospace), engineering (chemical), engineering (computer), engineering (electrical), physics, mathematics. *Age Group: Undergraduate students. *Eligibility: Applicants must be U.S. citizens attending an accredited four-year college or university. They also must be enrolled full-time as sophomores or juniors majoring in electrical, computer, chemical, systems or aerospace engineering, computer science, physics, or mathematics and maintain at least a 3.5 GPA. Students enrolled in distance learning or online programs are not eligible to apply. *Application Process: Applicants must submit a completed application, at least two letters of recommendation, and official transcripts. Applications are available on the foundation's Web site each January. *Amount: $2,000. *Deadline: May 1.

Armed Forces Communications and Electronics Association (AFCEA) Educational Foundation
Attn: Fred H. Rainbow, Vice President and Executive Director
4400 Fair Lakes Court
Fairfax, VA 22033-3899
703-631-6149, 800-336-4583, ext. 6149
scholarship@afcea.org
http://www.afcea.org/education/scholarships/undergraduate/Bragunier.asp
Scholarship Name: William E. "Buck" Bragunier Scholarship for Outstanding Leadership. *Academic Area: Computer science, engineering (aerospace), engineering (chemical), engineering (computer), engineering (electrical), physics, mathematics. *Age Group: Undergraduate students. *Eligibility: Applicants must be U.S. citizens attending an accredited four-year college or university in the greater San Diego, California area. Applicants must also demonstrate academic excellence and a commitment to university and/or local community leadership. They also must be enrolled full time as sophomores or juniors majoring in electrical, computer, chemical, systems or aerospace engineering, computer science, physics, or mathematics and maintain at least a 3.5 GPA.

Students enrolled in distance learning or online programs are not eligible to apply. *Application Process: Applicants must submit a completed application, at least two letters of recommendation, and official transcripts. Applications are available on the foundation's Web site each January. *Amount: $2,000. *Deadline: May 1.

ASM Materials Education Foundation
c/o National Merit Scholarship Corporation
1560 Sherman Avenue, Suite 200
Evanston, IL 60201-4897
847-866-5100
CustomerService@asminternational.org
http://www.asminternational.org/Content/
    NavigationMenu/ASMFoundation/MeritScholarships/
    merit.htm
Scholarship Name: ASM Materials Education Foundation National Merit Scholarship. *Academic Area: Engineering (materials science). *Age Group: Undergraduate students. *Eligibility: Applicants must indicate an interest in materials science and engineering as National Merit Semi-Finalists in high school. *Application Process: Contact the National Merit Scholarship Corporation to obtain application details. *Amount: $1,000. *Deadline: Contact the National Merit Scholarship Corporation.

ASM Materials Education Foundation
Scholarship Program
9639 Kinsman Road
Materials Park, OH 44073-0002
440-338-5151
CustomerService@asminternational.org
http://www.asminternational.org/Content/
    NavigationMenu/ASMFoundation/
    UndergraduateScholarships/Undergraduate.htm
Scholarship Name: ASM Materials Education Foundation Undergraduate Scholarship Program. *Academic Area: Engineering (materials science). *Age Group: Undergraduate students. *Eligibility: Applicants must be student members of ASM International. They also must have intended or declared majors in metallurgy or materials science engineering and have completed at least one year of college. Applicants majoring in related science or engineering disciplines will be considered if they demonstrate a strong academic emphasis and interest in materials science. Applicants for the need-based G.A. Roberts, N.J. Grant, W.P. Woodside,

and J. Haniak Scholarships must have junior or senior standing in the fall at an accredited North American university. International students are only eligible to apply for scholarships that are not need-based. *Application Process: Applicants must submit a completed application, a personal statement, transcripts, two letters of recommendation, and a current photo. Visit the society's Web site to download an application. *Amount: Varies. *Deadline: May 1.

Associated General Contractors (AGC) of America
AGC Education and Research Foundation
2300 Wilson Boulevard, Suite 400
Arlington, VA 22201
703- 837-5342
sladef@agc.org
http://www.agc.org/page.ww?section=AGC+Foundatio
    n&name=James+L.+Allhands+Student+Essay+Com
    petition
Contest Name: James L. Allhands Student Essay Competition. *Academic Area: Construction trades, engineering (construction). *Age Group: Undergraduate students. *Eligibility: Applicants must be senior-level students in four- or five-year Accreditation Board for Engineering Technology or American Council for Construction Education-accredited university construction management or construction-related engineering programs. *Application Process: Applicants must submit one original and two copies of an essay (no longer than 10 pages) and an essay abstract. Visit the foundation's Web site in July to download an application. *Amount: $300 to $1,000. *Deadline: November 1.

Association for Computing Machinery (ACM)
ACM Local Activities
1515 Broadway, 17th Floor
New York, NY 10036
upe@acm.org
http://www.acm.org/chapters/stu/upe/upe_award.html
Scholarship Name: UPE ACM Student Chapter Scholarship Award. *Academic Area: Computer science. *Age Group: Undergraduate students. *Eligibility: Applicants must be full-time students who are ACM members and members of the ACM student chapter at their academic institution. They also must have a GPA above 3.5. The scholarship is also available to graduate students.

*Application Process: Applicants should submit a completed application along with three letters of recommendation, official transcripts, and a statement of participation in the ACM student chapter at the applicant's academic institution. Visit the society's Web site to download an application form. *Amount: $1,000. *Deadline: June 30.

Association for the Advancement of Cost Engineering (AACE) International

Attn: Charla Miller
209 Prairie Avenue, Suite 100
Morgantown, WV 26501
304-296-8444, 800-858-COST
cmiller@aacei.org
http://www.aacei.org/education/scholarship.shtml
Scholarship Name: AACE International Undergraduate Scholarship. *Academic Area: Business administration, construction trades, engineering (agricultural), engineering (architectural), engineering (chemical), engineering (civil), engineering (cost), engineering (electrical), engineering (industrial), engineering (manufacturing), engineering (mechanical), engineering (mining). *Age Group: Undergraduate students. *Eligibility: Applicants must be currently enrolled full-time students who have achieved at least second-year academic standing in a program related to cost engineering/cost management. *Application Process: Applicants should submit a completed application along with transcripts, a list of extracurricular activities, and an essay on the value of study in cost engineering. Visit the association's Web site to download an application. *Amount: Awards vary. *Deadline: Varies.

Association of Engineering Geologists (AEG)

Attn: Paul Santi, Department of Geology and Geological Engineering
Colorado School of Mines
Berthoud Hall
Golden, CO 80401
303-273-3108
psanti@mines.edu
http://www.aegfoundation.org/index2.php
Scholarship Name: Marliave Fund/Scholarship. *Academic Area: Engineering (geological). *Age Group: Undergraduate students. *Eligibility: Applicants must be seniors who are presently enrolled full time in a college or university degree

program that is directly applicable to engineering geology or geological engineering. They also must be student members of the AEG. The scholarship is also available to graduate students. *Application Process: Applicants must submit a completed application form along with official transcripts of all undergraduate work, copies of pertinent publications and abstracts, three letters of reference, and a statement of career goals. Visit the association's Web site to download an application. The application package must be submitted through the applicant's major professor, AEG student chapter advisor, or department chair. *Amount: Awards vary. *Deadline: April 15.

Association of Engineering Geologists (AEG)

Attn: Robert A. Larson, Martin L. Stout Scholarship Committee Chair
13376 Azores Avenue
Sylmar, CA 91342
818-362-0363
ralarson@rampageusa.com
http://www.aegfoundation.org/index2.php
Scholarship Name: Martin L. Stout Scholarship. *Academic Area: Engineering (geological). *Age Group: Undergraduate students. *Eligibility: Applicants should be undergraduate geology majors in their sophomore through senior year with an environmental or engineering geology emphasis. Student membership in the AEG is required at the time of the award. If you are not currently a student member, you may submit a membership application and dues to AEG Headquarters with a copy included with your scholarship application. The scholarship is also available to graduate students. *Application Process: Applicants should submit an original completed application form along with four photocopies. Confidential evaluations submitted on the Appraisal of Applicant Form are required from each of two professors who have knowledge of the applicant's achievements. These forms must accompany the application in envelopes sealed by the professors. Visit the association's Web site to download an application. *Amount: $1,000. *Deadline: February 1.

Casualty Actuarial Society (CAS)

Attn: CAS Trust Scholarship Coordinator
4350 North Fairfax Drive, Suite 250
Arlington, VA 22203

703-276-3100

tlarock@casact.org

http://www.casact.org/academ/scholarship.htm

Scholarship Name: CAS Trust Scholarship Program.
*Academic Area: Mathematics. *Age Group:
Undergraduate students. *Eligibility: Applicants
must be U.S. or Canadian citizens or permanent
residents who have been admitted as full-time
students to U.S. or Canadian colleges or universities.
Applicants also must have demonstrated high
scholastic achievement and strong interest in
mathematics or mathematics-related fields.
Preference will be given to applicants who have
passed an actuarial exam and who have not yet
won either this or another Society of Actuaries or
CAS scholarship. *Application Process: Applicants
must submit a completed application, an essay,
two nomination forms, and official transcripts. Visit
the trust's Web site to download an application.
*Amount: $1,500. *Deadline: May 1.

EasyAid.com

PO Box 124

Youngtown, AZ 85363

computerscholarship@easyaid.com

http://www.easyaid.com/computer

Scholarship Name: Computer Science Scholarship.
*Academic Area: Computer science. *Age Group:
Undergraduate students. *Eligibility: Applicants must
be attending a postsecondary institution and majoring
in a computer-related discipline. The scholarship
is also available to graduate students. *Application
Process: Applicant must apply via EasyAid.com. Mailed
submissions are not accepted. Applicants should
submit their personal contact information and an essay
that answers the question, "What is the greatest impact
that computers have had on the world in the last 15
years?" Visit the company's Web site to apply. *Amount:
$500. *Deadline: March 15.

Electronic Document Systems Foundation (EDSF)

Attn: EDSF Scholarship Awards

608 Silver Spur Road, Suite 280

Rolling Hills Estates, CA 90274-3616

310-265-5510

info@edsf.org

http://www.edsf.org/scholarships.cfm

Scholarship Name: EDSF Document Communication
Scholarship Program. *Academic Area: Business,
computer science, engineering (open), graphic

design. *Age Group: Undergraduate students.
*Eligibility: Applicants must be full-time students
who are committed to pursuing a career in the
field of electronic document communication in the
areas of: document preparation, production and/or
document distribution, including 1:1 marketing;
graphic communication and arts; e-commerce;
imaging science, printing, web authoring, electronic
publishing, computer science, engineering, or
telecommunications. Applicants must also maintain a
minimum 3.0 GPA. The scholarship is also available to
graduate students. *Application Process: Applicants
must submit 10 copies of a completed application
package. Applicants must include a covering letter,
their academic details, two half- to full-page essays, a
list of their extracurricular professional and academic
activities, transcripts, two letters of recommendation,
and samples of creative work (optional) in their
application packets. Visit the foundation's Web site for
further details. *Amount: Varies. *Deadline: May 15.

Experimental Aircraft Association (EAA)

EAA Scholarship Department

PO Box 3086

Oshkosh, WI 54903-3086

920-426-6823

scholarships@eaa.org

http://www.eaa.org/education/scholarships

Scholarship Name: David Alan Quick Scholarship.
*Academic Area: Engineering (aeronautical),
engineering (aerospace). *Age Group:
Undergraduate students. *Eligibility: Applicants
must be college juniors or seniors in good
standing who are pursuing degrees in aerospace
or aeronautical engineering. Applicants must be
well rounded and involved in school/community
activities and aviation. Applicants must also be
current members of the EAA or recommended
by a current EAA member. *Application Process:
Applicants must visit the association's Web site
to submit an online application. *Amount: Varies.
*Deadline: March 1.

Experimental Aircraft Association (EAA)

EAA Scholarship Department

PO Box 3086

Oshkosh, WI 54903-3086

920-426-6823

scholarships@eaa.org

http://www.eaa.org/education/scholarships

Scholarship Name: Hansen Scholarship. *Academic Area: Engineering (aeronautic), engineering (aerospace). *Age Group: College students. *Eligibility: Applicants must be students in good academic standing enrolled in an accredited college, university, or technical college pursuing a degree in aerospace or aeronautical engineering. Applicants must demonstrate financial need. Applicants must be well rounded and involved in school/community activities and aviation. Applicants must also be current members of EAA or recommended by a current EAA member. *Application Process: Applicants must visit the Association's Web site to submit an online application. *Amount: $1,000. *Deadline: March 1.

Experimental Aircraft Association (EAA)
EAA Scholarship Department
PO Box 3086
Oshkosh, WI 54903-3086
920-426-6823
scholarships@eaa.org
http://www.eaa.org/education/scholarships
Scholarship Name: Payzer Scholarship. *Academic Area: Biological sciences, engineering (open), mathematics, and physical sciences. *Age Group: Undergraduate students. *Eligibility: Applicants must be accepted or enrolled in an accredited college, university, or postsecondary school that emphasizes technical information. Applicants must be majoring in and pursuing a professional career in engineering, mathematics, or the physical or biological sciences. Applicants must be well rounded and involved in school/community activities and aviation. Applicants must also be current members of EAA or recommended by a current EAA member. *Application Process: Applicants must visit the Association's Web site to submit an online application. *Amount: $5,000. *Deadline: March 1.

Fluid Power Educational Foundation
3333 North Mayfair Road, Suite 211
Milwaukee, WI 53222
414-778-3364
info@fpef.org
http://www.fpef.org/Education/scholar.html
Scholarship Name: Fluid Power Educational Foundation Scholarships. *Academic Area: Engineering (open), engineering (manufacturing), and technology. *Age Group: Undergraduate students. *Eligibility: Applicants must be planning to or attending a Fluid

Power Key School. Visit the foundation's Web site to review a Key School Directory. High school seniors and college students may apply for this scholarship. *Application Process: Applicants must contact their school, college, or university for application details. The applicant's educational institution submits the required forms on behalf of the student it selects. *Amount: Varies. *Deadline: Varies.

Institute of Electrical and Electronics Engineers (IEEE)
IEEE EMBS Executive Office
445 Hoes Lane, PO Box 1331
Piscataway, NJ 08855-1331
732-981-3433
emb-exec@ieee.org
http://www.ieee.org/portal/site/mainsite/menuite m.818c0c39e85ef176fb2275875bac26c8/index. jsp?&pName=corp_level1&path=membership/ students/awards&file=sc_meddesign. xml&xsl=generic.xsl
Contest Name: Engineering in Medicine and Biology Society (EMBS) Undergraduate Student Design Competition. *Academic Area: Engineering (biological). *Eligibility: Applicants must be IEEE EMBS undergraduate student members. *Application Process: Applicants must design and build an original device or product not currently offered on the market that applies engineering principles and technology to problems in medicine and biology. Design entries of 10 pages or less should be submitted with a title page, applicant's name, address, telephone, school name, abstract or summary background, purpose and scope, discussion of technical description with analysis support, conclusion, and specifications. A separate verification of project success must be supported either with videotape and/or photographs. Visit the institute's Web site for further application details. *Amount: $100 to $300. *Deadline: June 1.

Institute of Industrial Engineers (IIE)
3577 Parkway Lane, Suite 200
Norcross, GA 30092
800-494-0460
cs@iienet.org
http://www.iienet.org/public/articles/index.cfm?Cat=525
Scholarship Name: IIE Undergraduate Scholarships. *Academic Area: Engineering (industrial). *Age Group: Undergraduate students. *Eligibility: Applicants must be active institute members. New

member applications must be completely processed prior to the end of September in order for students to be eligible. Applicants must be enrolled full time in undergraduate industrial engineering programs and must maintain a minimum 3.4 GPA. Visit the institute's Web site for specific scholarship eligibility requirements. *Application Process: Applicants may not apply directly for any scholarships except the IIE Council of Fellows Undergraduate Scholarship. Applicants must be nominated by IIE department heads. Visit the institute's Web site for further application/nomination details and to download nomination forms. *Amount: Up to $4,000. *Deadline: November 15.

Intel International Science & Engineering Fair (ISEF)
Science Service
1719 N Street, NW
Washington, DC 20036
202-785-2255
http://www.sciserv.org/isef
Contest Name: Intel International Science & Engineering Fair. *Academic Area: Engineering (open). *Age Group: Undergraduate students. *Eligibility: Applicants must be high school students who compete in a local fair that's affiliated with Intel ISEF and be selected to represent that fair at Intel ISEF. Contact Science Service, founders of the ISEF, or visit their Web site to find affiliated local fairs. Application Process: Visit the Science Service-Intel ISEF Web site to obtain application details. *Amount: Up to $50,000. *Deadline: Contact Science Service for details.

Institute of Management Accountants (IMA) Inc.
Attn: Liz Brueck
Scholarship Selection Committee
10 Paragon Drive
Montvale, NJ 07645-1718
800-638-4427, ext. 1543
membersupport@imanet.org
http://www.imanet.org/ima/docs/3400/3352.pdf
Scholarship Name: IMA Memorial Education Fund Scholarship. *Academic Area: Accounting, finance, information technology. *Age Group: Undergraduate students. *Eligibility: Applicants should be full- or part-time students residing in the United States or Puerto Rico who are active student participants of the institute. They also must maintain a minimum 2.8 GPA. The scholarship is also available to graduate

students. *Application Process: Applicants should submit a completed application along with a one-page resume, a personal statement, and proof of enrollment in a program in management accounting, financial management, or information technology. Visit the institute's Web site to download an application. *Amount: $1,000 to $2,500. *Deadline: February 15.

Institute of Management Accountants (IMA) Inc.
Attn: Liz Brueck
Scholarship Selection Committee
10 Paragon Drive
Montvale, NJ 07645-1718
800-638-4427, ext. 1543
membersupport@imanet.org
http://www.imanet.org/ima/docs/3400/3352.pdf
Scholarship Name: Stuart Cameron and Margaret McLeod Memorial Scholarship. *Academic Area: Accounting, finance, information technology. *Age Group: Undergraduate students. *Eligibility: Applicants should be full- or part-time students residing in the United States or Puerto Rico who are active student participants in the institute. They also must maintain a minimum 2.8 GPA. One outstanding applicant from the pool of Memorial Education Fund Scholarship applicants will be awarded this scholarship. The scholarship is also available to graduate students. *Application Process: Applicants should submit a completed application along with a one-page resume, a personal statement, and proof of enrollment in a program in management accounting, financial management, or information technology. Visit the institute's Web site to download an application. *Amount: $5,000, plus an all-expenses-paid trip to the institute's annual conference. *Deadline: February 15.

The Minerals, Metals & Materials Society (TMS)
TMS Student Awards Program
184 Thorn Hill Road
Warrendale, PA 15086
724-776-9000, ext. 259
students@tms.org
http://www.tms.org/Students/AwardsPrograms/Scholarships.html
Scholarship Name: TMS Student Awards Program. *Academic Area: Engineering (materials science). *Age Group: Undergraduate students. *Eligibility: Applicants must be sophomores or juniors, members

of the Material Advantage student program, enrolled full-time in metallurgical/materials science engineering program at a qualified college or university. Additional eligibility requirements may apply depending on the scholarship for which applicants are applying. Contact the Society for further details. Some scholarships are also available to graduate students.*Application Process: Applicants must submit a completed application, a personal statement, transcripts, and three official recommendation forms. Applicants may apply for up to three of the six scholarship programs. Visit the society's Web site to download an application and recommendation forms. *Amount: Varies. *Deadline: May 15.

National Aeronautics and Space Administration (NASA)

NASA Headquarters
NASA Education Program
Office of Education
Code N
Washington, DC 20546-0001
202-358-0103
http://education.nasa.gov/divisions/higher/overview/ F_pathfinder_scholarship.html
Scholarship Name: NASA Science and Technology Scholarship Program. *Academic Area: Computer science, engineering (open), life sciences, mathematics, and physical sciences. *Age Group: Undergraduate students. *Eligibility: Applicants must be undergraduate students pursuing degrees in engineering, mathematics, computer science, physical science, or life science. *Application Process: Contact the NASA Education Program for details. *Amount: Up to $20,000. *Deadline: Varies.

National Fire Protection Association

Attn: Christine Ellis
1 Batterymarch Park
Quincy, MA 02169-7471
617-770-3000
cellis@nfpa.org
http://www.nfpa.org/itemDetail.asp?categoryID=1076& itemID=25796&URL=Learning/Public%20Education/ Scholarships,%20awards,%20grants/ Other%20scholarships
Scholarship Name: Frank J. Fee Jr. Award. *Academic Area: Engineering (fire protection). *Age Group: Undergraduate students. *Eligibility: Scholarship will

be awarded to students enrolled in the Department of Fire Protection Engineering at the University of Maryland. Scholarship will be granted based upon the student's academic record, fire protection interest, and academic potential. *Application Process: Contact the association or the University of Maryland Undergraduate Advising Office (301-405-3992) for details. *Amount: $5,000. *Deadline: April 1.

National Fire Protection Association

Attn: Christine Ellis
1 Batterymarch Park
Quincy, MA 02169-7471
617-770-3000
cellis@nfpa.org
http://www.nfpa.org/itemDetail.asp?categoryID=1076& itemID=25796&URL=Learning/Public%20Education/ Scholarships,%20awards,%20grants/ Other%20scholarships
Scholarship Name: Percy Bugbee Scholarship. *Academic Area: Engineering (fire protection). *Age Group: Undergraduate students. *Eligibility: Scholarship will be awarded to students at Worcester Polytechnic Institute who demonstrate excellence in academic achievement and intend to perform a thesis or graduate project activity aimed at improving fire protection engineering methods. *Application Process: Contact the association or a Worcester Polytechnic Institute (508-831-5000) departmental advisor for details. *Amount: $5,000. *Deadline: April 1.

National Oceanic and Atmospheric Administration (NOAA)

NOAA/Hollings Scholarship
Oak Ridge Institute for Science and Education
PO Box 117, MS 36
Oak Ridge, TN 37831-0117
202-482-3384
noaa.education@noaa.gov
http://www.orau.gov/noaa/HollingsScholarship
Scholarship Name: Ernest F. Hollings Undergraduate Scholarship Program. *Academic Area: Marine science. *Age Group: Undergraduate students. *Eligibility: Applicants must be undergraduate students studying ocean and marine sciences who will be juniors in the fall academic term at an accredited college/university in the United States or U.S. territories. Applicants must also be U.S. citizens and maintain at least a 3.0 GPA. *Application Process:

Applicants must submit a completed application, two reference forms (to be completed and submitted by referees), and official transcripts. Visit the NOAA's Web site to download an application. *Amount: Up to $8,000. *Deadline: May 23.

National Stone, Sand and Gravel Association
Barry K. Wendt Scholarship Program
1605 King Street
Alexandria, VA 22314
703-525-8788
info@NSSGA.org
http://www.nssga.org/careerscholarships/scholarships.cfm
Scholarship Name: Barry K. Wendt Commitment Award and Scholarship. *Academic Area: Engineering (open). *Age Group: Undergraduate students. *Eligibility: Applicants must be students from engineering schools who plan to pursue careers in the aggregates industry. *Application Process: Applicants must submit a completed application, a letter of recommendation (academic), and a personal statement. One additional letter of recommendation from an employer should be included if the applicant has work experience in the aggregate industry. Visit the association's Web site to download an application. *Amount: Varies. *Deadline: April 30.

National Security Agency (NSA)
PRISP Application
9800 Savage Road, Suite 6779
Ft. George G. Meade, MD 20755-6779
410-854-4725
http://www.nsa.gov/careers/students_4.cfm
Scholarship Name: Pat Roberts Intelligence Scholars Program (PRISP). *Academic Area: Computer science, engineering (computer), engineering (electrical), foreign languages. *Age Group: Undergraduate students. *Eligibility: Applicants must maintain a full course load and a minimum overall GPA of 3.0 for the duration of their participation in the program. They must also be eligible to obtain a high-level security clearance. Upon successful completion of senior year and graduation, students will have an employment obligation to the NSA equal to 1.5 times the length of educational support provided. Visit the agency's Web site for additional specific eligibility requirements for each category. The program is also open to graduate students. *Application Process: Applicants should submit a resume online during open season. The

resume must include the following: name, complete address, e-mail address, phone number(s), name and address of college, college major, unweighted GPA, class size and rank, extracurricular activities, and leadership positions held. Additionally, the following materials must be mailed: a one-page essay, unofficial transcripts, and a description of the undergraduate program with an outline of current and anticipated courses. Visit the agency's Web site for additional application information for individual scholarships. *Amount: Up to $25,000. *Deadline: October 30.

National Security Agency (NSA)
STOKES Application
9800 Savage Road, Suite 6779
Ft. George G. Meade, MD 20755-4725
410-854-4725
http://www.nsa.gov/careers/students_4.cfm
Scholarship Name: The Stokes Educational Scholarship Program. *Academic Area: Computer science, engineering (computer), engineering (electrical), foreign languages, mathematics. *Age Group: Undergraduate students. *Eligibility: Applicants must be high school seniors or undergraduate students, U.S. citizens, and have a minimum SAT score of 1600 or ACT score of 25 and at least a 3.0 GPA out of 4.0. Applicants must work during the summer at the NSA in areas related to their course of study. Selected winners are required to work for the NSA after college graduation for at least one-and-one-half times the length of study. Applicants must maintain at least a 3.0 GPA on a 4.0 scale each semester after their freshman year. *Application Process: Applicants must submit a resume online during open season and submit, by mail, a letter of recommendation from a teacher, counselor, or advisor, a one-page essay, and an official high school or college transcript. Applicants should also submit a photocopy of their SAT/ACT scores and up to three pages of supplemental information, if desired. Visit the agency's Web site for additional information in specific major categories. *Amount: Full tuition. *Deadline: November 30.

National Society of Professional Engineers (NSPE)
Attn: Erin Garcia Reyes, Practice Division Manager
1420 King Street
Alexandria, VA 22314-2794
703-684-2800
ed@nspe.org
http://www.nspe.org/scholarships/sc1-pei.asp

Scholarship Name: Professional Engineers in Industry Scholarship. *Academic Area: Engineering (open). *Age Group: Undergraduate students. *Eligibility: Applicants must be college sophomores, juniors, or seniors sponsored by a NSPE/PEI member. Students who are children, dependents, or relatives of NSPE members are given preference in the scholarship selection process. Students must have completed a minimum of two semesters or three quarters of undergraduate engineering studies in a program accredited by the Accreditation Board for Engineering and Technology and have a minimum GPA of 2.5. The scholarship is also available to graduate students. *Application Process: Applicants should submit a completed application along with two letters of recommendation from professors, transcripts, a resume, and a list of professional organizations in which they participates. Visit the society's Web site to download an application. *Amount: $2,500. *Deadline: April 1.

Salute to Education Inc.

PO Box 833425
Miami, FL 33283
305-476-7709
steinfo@stescholarships.org
http://www.stescholarships.org/SC_categories.html

Scholarship Name: Salute to Education Mathematics/Computer Science Scholarship. *Academic Area: Computer science, mathematics. *Age Group: Undergraduate students. *Eligibility: Applicants must be graduating high school seniors who attend a Miami-Dade or Broward County, Florida, high school and who also reside in one of these counties. They must also be legal residents of the United States, have a minimum weighted GPA of 3.0, demonstrate a commitment to service by participating in at least one school or community organization, and intend to pursue a college degree at an accredited institution after graduation. Applicants should have demonstrated exemplary performance in all advanced courses in trigonometry, calculus, business, marketing, and computer science. They should also be involved in math clubs, academic competitions, and peer tutoring. *Application Process: Applicants must apply online. Supporting materials should be mailed as detailed on the online application. *Amount: $1,000. *Deadline: Visit the organization's Web site for updated deadline information.

Society for Mining, Metallurgy, and Exploration (SME)

Attn: Mary O'Shea, Scholarship Coordinator
8307 Shaffer Parkway
Littleton, CO 80127
303-973-9550, 800-763-3132
http://www.smenet.org/education/Students/sme_scholarships.cfm

Scholarship Name: Coal and Energy Division Scholarship. *Academic Area: Engineering (mining). *Age Group: Undergraduate students. *Eligibility: Applicants must be SME student members in good standing, currently enrolled in a mining or mineral engineering program accredited by the Accreditation Board for Engineering and Technology, and have completed their sophomore year. They also must be recommended by their departmental chairperson. Applicants must also be engaged in coal-related activities. *Application Process: Applicants should contact the scholarship coordinator via an online form to receive an application. Visit the society's Web site for further information. *Amount: Up to $1,500. *Deadline: October 30.

Society for Mining, Metallurgy, and Exploration (SME)

Attn: Mary O'Shea, Scholarship Coordinator
8307 Shaffer Parkway
Littleton, CO 80127
303-973-9550, 800-763-3132
http://www.smenet.org/education/Students/sme_scholarships.cfm

Scholarship Name: Environmental Division Scholarship. *Academic Area: Engineering (mining), environmental science. *Age Group: Undergraduate students. *Eligibility: Applicants must be SME student members in good standing, currently enrolled in an Accreditation Board for Engineering and Technology accredited course of study, and have completed their sophomore year. They also must be recommended by their departmental chairperson. *Application Process: Applicants should contact the scholarship coordinator via online form to receive an application. Visit the society's Web site for further information. *Amount: Up to $2,000. *Deadline: October 30.

Society for Mining, Metallurgy, and Exploration (SME)

Attn: Mary O'Shea, Scholarship Coordinator
8307 Shaffer Parkway

Littleton, CO 80127
303-973-9550, 800-763-3132
http://www.smenet.org/education/Students/sme_
scholarships.cfm
Scholarship Name: Eugene P. Pfleider Memorial
Scholarship. *Academic Area: Engineering (mining).
*Age Group: Undergraduate students. *Eligibility:
Applicants must be SME student members in good
standing, currently enrolled in a postsecondary
program, and have completed their sophomore
year. Applicants must also be recommended by their
departmental chairperson. *Application Process:
Applicants should contact the scholarship coordinator
via an online form to receive an application. Visit the
society's Web site for further information. *Amount:
$1,000. *Deadline: November 30.

**Society for Mining, Metallurgy, and Exploration
(SME)**
Attn: Mary O'Shea, Scholarship Coordinator
8307 Shaffer Parkway
Littleton, CO 80127
303-973-9550, 800-763-3132
http://www.smenet.org/education/Students/sme_
scholarships.cfm
Scholarship Name: Gerald V. Henderson Industrial
Minerals Memorial Scholarship. *Academic Area:
Economics, engineering (mining), geology. *Age
Group: Undergraduate students. *Eligibility:
Applicants must be SME student members in good
standing, currently enrolled in an Accreditation Board
for Engineering and Technology accredited course
of study, and have completed their sophomore
year. They also must be recommended by the
departmental chairperson. *Application Process:
Applicants should contact the scholarship coordinator
via an online form to receive an application. Visit the
society's Web site for further information. *Amount:
Up to $2,000. *Deadline: October 15.

**Society for Mining, Metallurgy, and Exploration
(SME)**
Attn: Mary O'Shea, Scholarship Coordinator
8307 Shaffer Parkway
Littleton, CO 80127
303-973-9550, 800-763-3132
http://www.smenet.org/education/Students/sme_
scholarships.cfm
Scholarship Name: Mineral & Metallurgical Processing
Division Scholarship. *Academic Area: Engineering

(materials science). *Age Group: Undergraduate
students. *Eligibility: Applicants must be SME
student members in good standing, currently
enrolled in an Accreditation Board for Engineering
and Technology accredited course of study,
and have completed their sophomore year. The
applicant's degree program must include course
work in minerals processing, hydrometallurgy and/or
metallurgical engineering. Applicants must also be
recommended by their departmental chairperson.
*Application Process: Applicants should contact the
scholarship coordinator via an online form to receive
an application. Visit the society's Web site for further
information. *Amount: $1,000 to $2,000. *Deadline:
October 7.

**Society for the Advancement of Material and Process
Engineering (SAMPE)**
1161 Park View Drive, Suite 200
Covina, CA 91724-3751
626-331-0616, 800-562-7360
jimbell864@aol.com
http://www.sampe.org/studentp.html
Scholarship Name: Undergraduate Awards
Program. *Academic Area: Engineering (materials
science), engineering (technology). *Age Group:
Undergraduate students. *Eligibility: Applicants
must be SAMPE student chapter members and
either college freshmen, sophomores, or juniors.
*Application Process: Applicants should submit a
completed application along with transcripts and
a one-page, signed statement demonstrating their
knowledge of material processing technologies as
related to their interests. Visit the society's Web site
to download an application and to view additional
information about the categories in which an
applicant can apply. *Amount: $750 to $2,000.
*Deadline: February 1.

Society of Automotive Engineers (SAE)
SAE Engineering Scholarships
400 Commonwealth Drive
Warrendale, PA 15096-0001
724-776-4970
scholarships@sae.org
http://students.sae.org/awdscholar/scholarships
Scholarship Name: SAE Undergraduate Scholarships.
*Academic Area: Engineering (automotive). *Age
Group: Undergraduate students. *Eligibility:
Applicants must aim to pursue a postsecondary

degree and career in engineering. Eligibility requirements vary depending on the specific scholarship for which applicants are applying. Visit the society's Web site for details on eligibility requirements. High school seniors and undergraduate students may apply for these scholarships. *Application Process: Applicants must submit a completed application, official transcripts, education and employment record, and a personal statement. Visit the association's Web site for further application details and to download an application. *Amount: Varies. *Deadline: Varies.

Society of Manufacturing Engineers (SME) Education Foundation

Scholarship Review Committee
One SME Drive, PO Box 930
Dearborn, MI 48121
313-425-3300, 800-733-4763, ext. 3300
foundation@sme.org
http://www.sme.org/cgi-bin/smeefhtml.pl?/foundation/
  scholarships/fsfccsa.htm&&&SEF&

Scholarship Name: E. Wayne Kay Community College Scholarship. *Academic Area: Engineering (manufacturing). *Age Group: Undergraduate students. *Eligibility: Applicants must be graduating high school seniors or full-time undergraduate students enrolled in a degree program in manufacturing or a closely related field at a two-year community college or trade school in the United States or Canada. They also must maintain a 3.0 GPA on a 4.0 scale. *Application Process: Applicants must submit a completed application, an application cover sheet, a personal statement, resume, official transcripts, and two letters of recommendation. Visit the society's Web site to download an application. A variety of other related scholarships are also available at the state and local level. Contact the SME Education Foundation for details. *Amount: $1,000. *Deadline: February 1.

Society of Manufacturing Engineers (SME) Education Foundation

Scholarship Review Committee
One SME Drive, PO Box 930
Dearborn, MI 48121
313-425-3300, 800-733-4763, ext. 3300
foundation@sme.org
http://www.sme.org/cgi-bin/smeefhtml.pl?/foundation/
  scholarships/schl_briefly.html&&&SEF&#seniors

Scholarship Name: E. Wayne Kay High School Scholarship. *Academic Area: Engineering (manufacturing). *Age Group: Undergraduate students. *Eligibility: Applicants must be graduating high school students in their senior year who commit to enroll in a manufacturing engineering or technology program at an accredited college or university as a full time freshman. They also must maintain a 3.0 GPA on a 4.0 scale. *Application Process: Applicants must submit a completed application, an application cover sheet, a personal statement, a resume, official transcripts, and two letters of recommendation. Visit the society's Web site to download an application. A variety of other related scholarships are also available at the state and local level. Contact the SME Education Foundation for details. *Amount: Up to $2,500. *Deadline: February 1.

Society of Naval Architects and Marine Engineers

601 Pavonia Avenue
Jersey City, NJ 07306
201-798-4800, 800-798-2188
efaustino@sname.org
http://www.sname.org/scholarships_graduate.htm

Scholarship Name: Undergraduate Scholarship. *Academic Area: Architecture, engineering (ocean/naval). *Age Group: Undergraduate students. *Eligibility: Applicants must be society members (at least one year prior to application) and attend a U.S. or Canadian college or university. Graduate students are also eligible for this scholarship. *Application Process: Applicants should request an application by e-mail from the scholarship chair. Along with a completed application, applicants should submit any additional supporting materials requested on the application. Visit the society's Web site for additional application information. *Amount: Up to $12,000. *Deadline: February 1.

Society of Petroleum Engineers Inc.

Professional Development Coordinator
222 Palisades Creek Drive, PO Box 833836
Richardson, TX 75083-3836
972-952-9393, 800-456-6863, ext. 359
http://www.spe.org/spe/jsp/basic/0,2396,1104_12167_
  0,00.html

Scholarship Name: Gus Archie Memorial Scholarship. *Academic Area: Engineering (petroleum). *Age Group: Undergraduate students. *Eligibility: Applicants must be high school seniors, achieve an SAT score of at least 1200 or an ACT score of at least 27, and show intent to enroll in a program in an accredited petroleum engineering program. To renew the scholarship, the student must maintain a 3.0/4.0 GPA and must be enrolled in at least 14 credit hours per semester. *Application Process: Applicants should submit a completed application along with a statement of intent to pursue petroleum engineering. Visit the society's Web site to download an application. *Amount: $5,000, renewable for three additional years. *Deadline: April 30.

Society of Plastics Engineers Foundation
14 Fairchild Drive
Brookfield, CT 06804
203-740-5447
foundation@4spe.org
http://www.4spe.org/foundation/scholarships.php
Scholarship Name: General Scholarship. *Academic Area: Engineering (plastics). *Age Group: Undergraduate students. *Eligibility: Applicants must be attending two- or four-year colleges or universities as full-time students and demonstrate an interest in the plastics industry. They also must enroll in classes that would be beneficial to a career in the plastics industry, such as plastics engineering, polymer science, chemistry, physics, chemical engineering, mechanical engineering, and industrial engineering. Applicants must also demonstrate financial need. *Application Process: Applicants should submit a completed application along with three recommendations, transcripts, and a one- to two-page statement telling why the applicant is applying for the scholarship, his or her qualifications, and educational and career goals. Visit the foundation's Web site to download an application. *Amount: Up to $4,000. *Deadline: January 15.

Society of Satellite Professionals International (SSPI)
Attn: Tamara Bond, Membership Director
The New York Information Technology Center
55 Broad Street, 14th Floor
New York, NY 10004
212-809-5199, ext. 16
tbond@sspi.org
http://www.sspi.org/displaycommon.cfm?an=1&subart
    iclenbr=56
Scholarship Name: SSPI Scholarship Program. *Academic Area: Satellite technology. *Age Group: Undergraduate students. *Eligibility: Applicants must

demonstrate academic and leadership achievement, commitment to pursuing education and career opportunities in the satellite industry or a field making direct use of satellite technology, and show potential for a significant contribution to the satellite communications industry. High school seniors, undergraduate students, and graduate students may apply. Applicants must be matriculated or accepted in an accredited college or university program at the time of scholarship award. *Application Process: The application process is divided into two parts. Applicants who successfully pass stage one of the application process will be invited to apply for stage two. To apply for stage one, applicants should submit a completed application along with current transcripts. Information about stage two of the process will be provided to applicants who pass stage one. Visit the society's Web site to download an application. *Amount: $2,000 to $5,000. *Deadline: February 18 (for stage one).

SPIE-The International Society for Optical Engineering
SPIE Scholarship Committee
PO Box 10
Bellingham, WA 98227-0010
360-676-3290, ext. 659
scholarships@spie.org
http://www.spie.org/CommunityServices/
    StudentsAndEducators/index.cfm?fuseaction=Scho
    larships
Scholarship Name: SPIE Scholarship. *Academic Area: Engineering (optical). *Age Group: Undergraduate students. *Eligibility: Applicants must be enrolled full-time in an undergraduate optics, photonics, imaging, optoelectronics program or related discipline at an educational institution for the academic year in which the award will be used (not applicable to high school students). Applicants must be SPIE student members and either high school seniors or undergraduate and graduate students *Application Process: Applicants must submit a completed application, two letters of recommendation, an essay, and an Annual Scholarship Award Report (if reapplying). Visit the society's Web site to download an application. *Amount: Varies. *Deadline: January 6.

Triangle Education Foundation (TEF)
Attn: Chairman, TEF Scholarship & Loan Committee
120 South Center Street

Plainfield, IN 46168
317-837-9641
scholarships@triangle.org
http://www.triangle.org/tef/programs/scholarships
Scholarship Name: Triangle Education Foundation Scholarship. *Academic Area: Engineering (open). *Age Group: Undergraduate students. *Eligibility: Applicants must be undergraduate student members who are currently studying engineering and other hard sciences. Applicants must demonstrate financial need and active involvement in their chapters on campus or in the community. Most scholarships require a minimum GPA of 3.0 on a 4.0 scale. Eligibility requirements vary. Visit the foundation's Web site for specific scholarship eligibility requirements. The scholarship is also available to graduate students. *Application Process: Applicants must submit a completed application, two letters of recommendation, and transcripts. Visit the foundation's Web site to download an application. *Amount: $1,000 to $5,000. *Deadline: February 15.

Virginia Society of Professional Engineers
5206 Markel Road, Suite 300
Richmond, VA 23230
804-673-4545
vspe@aol.com
http://www.vspe.org/FrameEdu.htm
Scholarship Name: Virginia Society of Professional Engineers Scholarship. *Academic Area: Engineering (open). *Age Group: Undergraduate students. *Eligibility: Applicants must be students attending one of the eight engineering schools in Virginia and demonstrate academic excellence. *Application Process: The scholarship is rotated among the schools, and the dean of the school makes the recommendation to the society. Contact the society to obtain further application details. *Amount: $1,000. *Deadline: Varies.

ENGINEERING/COMPUTER SCIENCE/ MATHEMATICS—GRADUATE

The following financial aid resources are available to students who are interested in studying engineering, computer science, mathematics, and related fields at the graduate level.

American Helicopter Society/Vertical Flight Foundation
217 North Washington Street
Alexandria, VA 22314-2538
703-684-6777
staff@vtol.org
http://www.vtol.org/VFFSchoForm.pdf
Scholarship Name: Vertical Flight Foundation Engineering Scholarship. *Academic Area: Engineering (aerospace/aviation). *Age Group: Graduate students. *Eligibility: Applicants must be full-time students in accredited schools of engineering and be enrolled through the following full academic year. The scholarship is also available to undergraduate students. *Application Process: Applicants must submit a completed application, official transcripts, and a letter of recommendation. Visit the foundation's Web site to download an application. *Amount: $1,000 to $4,000. *Deadline: February 1.

American Institute of Aeronautics and Astronautics (AIAA) Foundation
1801 Alexander Bell Drive, Suite 500
Reston, VA 20191-4344
703-264-7500, 800-639-AIAA
http://www.aiaa.org/content.cfm?pageid=227
Scholarship Name: AIAA Graduate Scholarship. *Academic Area: Engineering (aerospace/aviation). *Age Group: Graduate students. *Eligibility: Applicants should indicate, by their approved department research, an interest in research related to aeronautics or astronautics. They also must have completed at least one quarter or semester of academic work, maintain a 3.3 GPA, and be or become an AIAA student member. *Application Process: Applicants should submit a completed application along with three letters of recommendation, transcripts, and an essay. Visit the association's Web site for essay topics and to download an application. *Amount: $5,000 and $10,000. *Deadline: January 31.

American Nuclear Society (ANS)
Attn: Scholarship Coordinator
555 North Kensington Avenue
LaGrange Park, IL 60526
708-352-6611
http://www.ans.org/honors/scholarships
Scholarship Name: ANS Graduate Scholarships. *Academic Area: Engineering (nuclear), nuclear science. *Age Group: Graduate students. *Eligibility: Applicants must be U.S. citizens or possess a permanent resident visa and must be graduate students enrolled in programs (in the United States) leading to an advanced degree in nuclear science, nuclear engineering, or a nuclear-related field. *Application Process: Applicants should submit a completed application along with official transcripts with seal, a letter of recommendation from a sponsoring organization, and three confidential reference forms. All application materials must be mailed in one packet. Visit the society's Web site to view a list of individual graduate scholarships and additional requirements by scholarship. An application form can also be downloaded from the society's Web site. *Amount: Awards vary. *Deadline: February 1.

American Public Transportation Foundation
1666 K Street, NW, Suite 1100
Washington, DC 20006
202-496-4803
pboswell@apta.com
http://www.apta.com/services/human_resources/ program_guidelines.cfm
Scholarship Name: Louis T. Klauder Scholarship. *Academic Area: Engineering (electrical), engineering (mechanical). *Age Group: Graduate students. *Eligibility: Applicants must demonstrate dedication to pursuing careers in the rail transit industry as electrical or mechanical engineers, be enrolled in a fully accredited institution, maintain at least a 3.0 GPA (B) in course work that is relevant to the industry or required of a degree program, and either be employed by or demonstrate a strong interest in entering the public transportation industry. The

scholarship is also available to undergraduate students. *Application Process: Applicants must submit a completed application, a letter of nomination, an essay, three letters of recommendation, a copy of their completed FAFSA form, official transcripts, verification of enrollment, and a copy of their fee schedule for academic study. Visit the foundation's Web site to download an application. *Amount: $2,500 minimum. *Deadline: June 17.

American Public Transportation Foundation
1666 K Street, NW, Suite 1100
Washington, DC 20006
202-496-4803
pboswell@apta.com
http://www.apta.com/services/human_resources/
    program_guidelines.cfm
Scholarship Name: Parsons Brinckerhoff-Jim Lammie Scholarship. *Academic Area: Engineering (transportation). *Age Group: Graduate students. *Eligibility: Applicants must demonstrate dedication to pursuing public transportation engineering careers, enrolled in a fully accredited institution, maintain at least a 3.0 GPA (B) in course work that is relevant to the industry or required of a degree program, and either be employed by or demonstrate a strong interest in entering the public transportation industry. The scholarship is also available to undergraduate students. *Application Process: Applicants must submit a completed application, a letter of nomination, an essay, three letters of recommendation, a copy of their completed FAFSA form, official transcripts, verification of enrollment, and a copy of their fee schedule for academic study. Visit the foundation's Web site to download an application. *Amount: $2,500 minimum. *Deadline: June 17.

American Society of Mechanical Engineers (ASME)
Attn: Maisha Phillips, Coordinator, Student Development
Three Park Avenue
New York, NY 10016
212-591-8131
phillipsm@asme.org
http://www.asme.org/education/enged/aid/scholar.htm
Scholarship Name: ASME Scholarship Program. *Academic Area: Engineering (mechanical). *Age Group: Graduate students. *Eligibility: Applicants must be graduate students pursuing degrees and careers in mechanical engineering. They must

also be ASME members. Eligibility requirements vary by scholarship. Visit the society's Web site to obtain specific scholarship eligibility requirements. Scholarships are also available to high school seniors and undergraduate students. *Application Process: Online applications are from February 1 through March 15. Only ASME members can apply by using their registered e-mail address and membership number to log in. Contact the society for further application details. *Amount: $1,000 to $10,000. *Deadline: Varies.

American Society of Mechanical Engineers (ASME) Auxiliary
Attn: Warren Leonard
Three Park Avenue
New York, NY 10016
212-591-7846
LeonardW@asme.org
http://www.asme.org/auxiliary/scholarshiploans
Scholarship Name: ASME Auxiliary Graduate Scholarship Program. *Academic Area: Engineering (mechanical). *Age Group: Graduate students. *Eligibility: Applicants must be pursuing a master's or doctoral degree in mechanical engineering and demonstrate financial need, ASME participation, and academic achievement. They also must be U.S. citizens (except for the Rice-Cullimore Scholarship) and be enrolled in a U.S. school in an Accreditation Board for Engineering Technology accredited mechanical engineering department. *Application Process: Applicants must submit a completed application, three letters of recommendation, and official transcripts. Visit the society's Web site to download an application. *Amount: $2,000. *Deadline: March 15.

American Society of Naval Engineers (ASNE)
1452 Duke Street
Alexandria, VA 22314-3458
703-836-6727
dwoodbury@navalengineers.org
http://www.navalengineers.org/Programs/Scholarships/
    sc_info.htm
Scholarship Name: ASNE Scholarship. *Academic Area: Engineering (ocean/naval). *Age Group: Graduate students. *Eligibility: Applicants must be applying for the scholarship for one year of graduate study. Applicants must be U.S. citizens who demonstrate

academic achievement, an exemplary work history, financial need, extracurricular involvement, and a high degree of interest in naval engineering. They also must be members of the ASNE. The scholarship is also available to undergraduate students. *Application Process: Applicants should submit a completed application along with three signed and sealed letters of recommendation and official, sealed transcripts. Visit the association's Web site to download an official application. *Amount: $3,500. *Deadline: February 15.

American Society of Safety Engineers (ASSE) Foundation
Attn: Scholarships
1800 East Oakton Street
Des Plaines, IL 60018
847-699-2929
mgoranson@asse.org
http://www.asse.org
Scholarship Name: American Society of Safety Engineers Foundation Scholarship. *Academic Area: Engineering (safety). *Age Group: Graduate students. *Eligibility: This society offers a variety of scholarships with varying eligibility requirements. Visit the society's Web site to view a list of available scholarships and specific eligibility requirements. Applicants for all scholarships must be student members of the ASSE. Scholarships are also available for undergraduate students. *Application Process: Applicants should submit a completed application along with supporting materials, including a 300-word personal statement about their career goals and why they are seeking a degree in a safety-related field. Visit the society's Web site to download an application. *Amount: Awards vary. *Deadline: December 1.

Association for Computing Machinery (ACM)
ACM Local Activities
1515 Broadway, 17th Floor
New York, NY 10036
upe@acm.org
http://www.acm.org/chapters/stu/upe/upe_award.html
Scholarship Name: UPE ACM Student Chapter Scholarship Award. *Academic Area: Computer science. *Age Group: Graduate students. *Eligibility: Applicants must be full-time students who are ACM members and members of the ACM student chapter at their academic institution. They also must have a GPA above 3.5. The scholarship is also available to undergraduate students. *Application Process: Applicants should submit a completed application along with three letters of

recommendation, official transcripts, and a statement of participation in the ACM student chapter at their academic institution. Visit the association's Web site to download an application form. *Amount: $1,000. *Deadline: June 30.

Association for the Advancement of Cost Engineering (AACE) International
Attn: Charla Miller
209 Prairie Avenue, Suite 100
Morgantown, WV 26501
304-296-8444, 800-858-COST
cmiller@aacei.org
http://www.aacei.org/education/scholarship.shtml
Scholarship Name: AACE International Graduate Scholarship. *Academic Area: Business administration, construction trades, engineering (agricultural), engineering (architectural), engineering (chemical), engineering (civil), engineering (cost), engineering (electrical), engineering (industrial), engineering (manufacturing), engineering (mechanical), engineering (mining). *Age Group: Graduate students. *Eligibility: Applicants should be currently enrolled full-time students who are pursuing graduate study in a program related to cost engineering/cost management. These programs include: agricultural engineering, architectural engineering, building construction, business administration, chemical engineering, civil engineering, industrial engineering, manufacturing engineering, mechanical engineering, mining engineering, electrical engineering, and quantity surveying. *Application Process: Applicants should submit a completed application along with transcripts, a list of extracurricular activities, and an essay on the value of study in cost engineering. Visit the association's Web site to download an application. *Amount: Awards vary. *Deadline: Varies.

Association of Engineering Geologists (AEG)
Attn: Paul Santi, Department of Geology and Geological Engineering
Colorado School of Mines
Berthoud Hall
Golden, CO 80401
303-273-3108
psanti@mines.edu
http://www.aegfoundation.org/index2.php
Scholarship Name: Marliave Fund/Scholarship. *Academic Area: Engineering (general). *Age Group: Graduate students. *Eligibility: Applicants

must be presently enrolled full time in a college or university degree program that is directly applicable to engineering geology or geological engineering. They also must also be student members of the Association of Engineering Geologists. *Application Process: Applicants must submit a completed application form along with official transcripts of all undergraduate and graduate work, copies of pertinent publications and abstracts, three letters of reference, and a statement of their career goals. Visit the association's Web site to download an application. The application package must be submitted through the applicant's major professor, AEG student chapter advisor, or department chair. *Amount: Awards vary. *Deadline: April 15.

Association of Engineering Geologists (AEG)

Attn: Robert A. Larson, Martin L. Stout Scholarship
    Committee Chair
13376 Azores Avenue
Sylmar, CA 91342
818-362-0363
ralarson@rampageusa.com
http://www.aegfoundation.org/index2.php
Scholarship Name: Martin L. Stout Scholarship.
    *Academic Area: Engineering (geological). *Age
    Group: Graduate students. *Eligibility: Applicants
    should be graduate students with an environmental or
    engineering geology emphasis. Student membership
    in the AEG is required at the time of the award. Current
    non-members may submit a membership application
    and dues to AEG headquarters with a copy included
    with the scholarship application. The scholarship
    is also available to undergraduate students.
    *Application Process: Applicants should submit an
    original completed application form along with four
    photocopies. Confidential evaluations submitted
    on the appraisal of applicant form are required
    from each of two professors who have knowledge
    of the applicant's achievements. These forms must
    accompany the application in envelopes sealed by
    the professors. Visit the association's Web site to
    download an application. *Amount: $1,000. *Deadline:
    February 1.

Audio Engineering Society Educational Foundation
    Inc.

60 East 42nd Street, Room 2520
New York, NY 10165
212-661-8528
http://www.aes.org/education/edu_foundation.html

Grant Name: Audio Engineering Society Educational Foundation Graduate Student Grant. *Academic Area: Engineering (audio). *Age Group: Graduate students. *Eligibility: Applicants must have successfully completed an undergraduate degree program (typically four years) at a recognized college or university, with a demonstrated commitment to audio engineering or a related field. They also must be accepted into a graduate academic program leading to a master's or higher degree. *Application Process: Applicants should submit a completed application, the first three pages of which include essays on past achievements and future plans, and a list of references that should be filled out by the applicant. The final two pages should be copied in duplicate and sent to the recommending faculty members or other persons more familiar with the qualifications of the applicant. Visit the association's Web site to download an application. *Amount: Awards vary. *Deadline: May 15.

EasyAid.com

PO Box 124
Youngtown, AZ 85363
computerscholarship@easyaid.com
http://www.easyaid.com/computer
Scholarship Name: Computer Science Scholarship.
    *Academic Area: Computer science. *Age Group:
    Graduate students. *Eligibility: Applicants must
    be attending a postsecondary institution and
    majoring in a computer-related discipline. The
    scholarship is also available to undergraduate
    students. *Application Process: Applicant must
    apply via EasyAid.com. Mailed submissions are not
    accepted. Applicants should submit their personal
    contact information, and an essay that addresses
    the question, "What is the greatest impact that
    computers have had on the world in the last 15
    years?" Visit the company's Web site to apply.
    *Amount: $500. *Deadline: March 15.

Institute of Industrial Engineers (IIE)

3577 Parkway Lane, Suite 200
Norcross, GA 30092
800-494-0460
cs@iienet.org
http://www.iienet.org/public/articles/index.cfm?Cat=525
Scholarship Name: IIE Graduate Scholarship. *Academic
    Area: Engineering (industrial). *Age Group: Graduate
    students. *Eligibility: Applicants must be enrolled
    full time in a graduate industrial engineering

program and maintain a minimum 3.4 GPA. They also must be active institute members. New member applications must be completely processed prior to the end of September in order for students to be eligible. Visit the institute's Web site for specific scholarship eligibility requirements. *Application Process: Applicants may not apply directly for the scholarship. Applicants must be nominated by IIE department heads. Visit the institute's Web site for further application/nomination details and to download nomination forms. *Amount: Up to $4,000. *Deadline: November 15 (for nomination form).

Institute of Transportation Engineers
1099 14th Street, NW, Suite 300 West
Washington, DC 20005-3438
202-289-0222
ite_staff@ite.org
http://www.ite.org/education/Harold_F_Hammond.asp
Scholarship Name: Harold F. Hammond Scholarship. *Academic Area: Engineering (transportation). *Age Group: Graduate students. *Eligibility: Applicants must be planning to pursue a master's degree in transportation engineering, with principal course work in traffic engineering, geometric design, and/or transportation planning. Applicants must have, or will have, earned a bachelor's degree by December and be qualified for unconditional admission to the graduate study program at their chosen host university. They also must begin graduate study in transportation on a full-time basis by January. *Application Process: Applicants must submit a completed application, an essay, a resume, a prospective course list, four reference forms, official transcripts, and a FAFSA report. Visit the institute's Web site to download an application and reference form. *Amount: $3,000. *Deadline: April 1.

Institute of Transportation Engineers
1099 14th Street, Suite 300 West
Washington, DC 20005-3438
202-289-0222
aoneill@ite.org
http://www.ite.org/education/scholarships.asp
Fellowship Name: Institute of Transportation Engineers Fellowships. *Academic Area: Engineering (transportation). *Age Group: Graduate students. *Eligibility: Applicants should demonstrate academic achievement and be attending a full-time graduate program in transportation within 12 months of the closing date of their application. Applicants should visit the institute's Web site for additional eligibility requirements for individual fellowships. *Application Process: Applicants should submit a completed application along with an essay discussing their career objectives and reasons for pursuing a graduate degree in transportation. They also must submit three letters of recommendation. Visit the institute's Web site to download an application. *Amount: Awards vary. *Deadline: April 1.

Medical University of South Carolina
Attn: Ms. Nancy Carder, Special Programs Office
165 Cannon Street, #402D
PO Box 250851
Charleston, SC 29425
843-792-1469
cardern@musc.edu
http://www.musc.edu/specialprograms/Templates/Fellowship.htm
Fellowship Name: Nuclear Engineering and Health Physics Fellowship. *Academic Area: Engineering (nuclear). *Age Group: Graduate students. *Eligibility: Applicants should have an undergraduate degree in the physical sciences, life sciences, or engineering. Applicants should also be U.S. citizens or permanent residents with at least one full year of graduate study remaining and attend a participating university. Visit the organization's Web site for a list of participating universities. *Application Process: Applicants should submit a completed application along with three letters of reference, official transcripts, and official GRE scores. Fellowship awardees are required to serve one three-month practicum. Visit the organization's Web site to download an application. *Amount: A $1,700 monthly stipend. *Deadline: January 31.

The Minerals, Metals & Materials Society (TMS)
TMS Student Awards Program
184 Thorn Hill Road
Warrendale, PA 15086
724-776-9000, ext. 259
students@tms.org
http://www.tms.org/Students/AwardsPrograms/Scholarships.html
Scholarship Name: International Symposium on Superalloys Scholarship. *Academic Area: Engineering (materials science). *Age Group: Graduate students. *Eligibility: Applicants must be "majoring in metallurgical and/or materials science and engineering with an emphasis on all aspects

of the high-temperature, high-performance materials used in the gas turbine industry and all other applications." They must also be members of the Material Advantage student program and enrolled full time in a metallurgical/materials science engineering program at a qualified college or university. The scholarship is also available to undergraduate students. *Application Process: Applicants must submit a completed application, a personal statement, transcripts, and three official recommendation forms. Visit the society's Web site to download an application and recommendation forms. *Amount: $2,000 plus $500 in travel reimbursements. *Deadline: March 15.

National Fire Protection Association
Attn: Christine Ellis
1 Batterymarch Park
Quincy, MA 02169-7471
617-984-7244
cellis@nfpa.org
http://www.nfpa.org/categoryList.asp?categoryID=205&
    URL=Learning/Public%20Education/Scholarships,%2
    0awards,%20grants
Scholarship Name: David B. Gratz Scholarship.
    *Academic Area: Engineering (fire protection).
    *Age Group: Graduate students. *Eligibility:
    Applicants must be full- or part-time graduate
    students enrolled in fire science or fire
    engineering programs outside the U.S. or Canada
    who exhibit scholarship achievement, leadership
    qualities, concern for others/volunteerism, and
    contributions to international/national fire
    safety activities. *Application Process: Once
    nominated by their institution, applicants must
    submit a completed application, a personal
    statement, undergraduate and graduate
    transcripts, nomination letter(s), and a letter of
    recommendation. Visit the association's Web site
    to download an application. *Amount: $5,000
    minimum. *Deadline: April 1.

National Fire Protection Association
Attn: Christine Ellis
1 Batterymarch Park
Quincy, MA 02169-7471
617-984-7244
cellis@nfpa.org
http://www.nfpa.org/categoryList.asp?categoryID=205&
    URL=Learning/Public%20Education/Scholarships,%2
    0awards,%20grants

Scholarship Name: John L. Jablonsky Scholarship.
    *Academic Area: Engineering (fire protection). *Age
    Group: Graduate students. *Eligibility: Applicants
    must be full- or part-time graduate students enrolled
    in a fire protection engineering program in the
    United States or Canada who exhibit scholarship
    achievement, leadership qualities, concern for
    others/volunteerism, and intention to pursue a
    career in fire safety engineering. *Application
    Process: Once nominated by their institution,
    applicants must submit a completed application, a
    personal statement, undergraduate and graduate
    transcripts, nomination letter(s), and a letter of
    recommendation. Visit the association's Web site
    to download an application. *Amount: $5,000
    minimum. *Deadline: April 1.

National Security Agency (NSA)
Graduate Training Program
9800 Savage Road, Suite 6779
Ft. George G. Meade, MD 20755-6779
410-854-4725
http://www.nsa.gov/careers/students_4.cfm
Scholarship Name: Graduate Training Program.
    *Academic Area: Engineering (computer),
    engineering (electrical). *Age Group: Graduate
    students. *Eligibility: Applicants must be U.S.
    citizens who have majored as an undergraduate
    in engineering, computer science, or information
    operations, have a minimum 3.5 GPA (on a 4.0 scale),
    and are willing to relocate to Monterey, California,
    or Dayton, Ohio. Preferences may be stated, but are
    not guaranteed. Upon completion of the master's
    program, program participants will be assigned to a
    permanent, full-time position at NSA headquarters in
    Ft. George G. Meade, Maryland. *Application Process:
    Applicants are applying for full-time employment
    with the NSA, during which time they will be
    attending graduate school. Applicants must agree to
    work for the NSA for a minimum of three times the
    length of paid schooling. Contact the NSA for further
    information about the application process. *Amount:
    Full-time salary, plus all tuition paid. *Deadline:
    November 30.

National Security Agency (NSA)
PRISP Application
9800 Savage Road, Suite 6779
Ft. George G. Meade, MD 20755-6779
410-854-4725
http://www.nsa.gov/careers/students_4.cfm

Scholarship Name: Pat Roberts Intelligence Scholars Program (PRISP). *Academic Area: Computer science, engineering (computer), engineering (electrical), foreign languages. *Age Group: Graduate students. *Eligibility: Applicants must maintain a full course load and a minimum overall GPA of 3.0 for the duration of their participation in the program. They must also be eligible to obtain a high-level security clearance. Upon successful completion of senior year and graduation, students will have an employment obligation to NSA equal to 1.5 times the length of educational support provided. Visit the agency's Web site for additional specific eligibility requirements for each category. The scholarship is also available to undergraduate students. *Application Process: Applicants should submit a resume online during open season. The resume must include the following: name, complete address, e-mail address, phone number(s), name and address of college, college major, unweighted GPA, class size and rank, extracurricular activities, and leadership positions held. Additionally, the following materials must be mailed: a one-page essay, unofficial transcripts, and a description of the graduate program with an outline of current and anticipated courses. Visit the agency's Web site for additional application information for individual scholarships. *Amount: Up to $25,000. *Deadline: October 30.

National Society of Professional Engineers (NSPE)
Attn: Erin Garcia Reyes, Practice Division Manager
1420 King Street
Alexandria, VA 22314-2794
703-684-2800
ed@nspe.org
http://www.nspe.org/scholarships/sc1-pei.asp
Scholarship Name: Professional Engineers in Industry Scholarship. *Academic Area: Engineering (open). *Age Group: Graduate students. *Eligibility: Applicants must be sponsored by a NSPE/PEI member. Students who are children, dependents, or relatives of NSPE members are given preference in the scholarship selection process. Students must be enrolled in graduate study in a program accredited by the Accreditation Board for Engineering and Technology. Applicants must also have a minimum GPA of 2.5. The scholarship is also available to undergraduate students.*Application Process: Applicants should submit a completed application along with two letters of recommendation from

professors, transcripts, a resume, and a list of professional organizations in which they participate. Visit the society's Web site to download an application. *Amount: $2,500. *Deadline: April 1.

Society of Automotive Engineers (SAE)
Yanmar/SAE Scholarship
SAE Award & Scholarship Program Staff
400 Commonwealth Drive
Warrendale, PA 15096-0001
724-776-4970
scholarships@sae.org
http://students.sae.org/awdscholar/scholarships
Scholarship Name: Yanmar/Society of Automotive Engineers Scholarship. *Academic Area: Engineering (automotive). *Age Group: Graduate students. *Eligibility: Applicants must be citizens of North America (United States, Canada, Mexico) and full-time students enrolled in a graduate engineering or related science program. They also must be pursuing a course of study or research related to the conservation of energy in transportation, agriculture and construction, and power generation. Emphasis will be placed on research or study related to the internal combustion engine. The scholarship is also available to undergraduate students. *Application Process: Applicants must submit an online application and send official transcripts to the SAE. Visit the society's Web site to submit an online application. *Amount: $2,000. *Deadline: April 1.

Society of Naval Architects and Marine Engineers
601 Pavonia Avenue
Jersey City, NJ 07306
201-798-4800, 800-798-2188
efaustino@sname.org
http://www.sname.org/scholarships_graduate.htm
Scholarship Name: Graduate Scholarship. *Academic Area: Architecture, engineering (ocean/marine). *Age Group: Graduate students. *Eligibility: Applicants must be society members (at least one year prior to application) and must attend a United States or Canadian college or university. *Application Process: Applicants should request an application by e-mail from the scholarship chair. Along with a completed application, applicants should submit GRE scores and any additional supporting materials requested on the application. Visit the society's Web site for additional application information. *Amount: Up to $12,000. *Deadline: February 1.

Society of Satellite Professionals International (SSPI)
Attn: Tamara Bond, Membership Director
The New York Information Technology Center
55 Broad Street, 14th Floor
New York, NY 10004
212-809-5199, ext. 16
tbond@sspi.org
http://www.sspi.org/displaycommon.cfm?an=1&subart
    iclenbr=56
Scholarship Name: SSPI Scholarship Program.
    *Academic Area: Satellite technology. *Age
    Group: Graduate students. *Eligibility: Applicants
    must demonstrate academic and leadership
    achievement, a commitment to pursuing education
    and career opportunities in the satellite industry
    or a field making direct use of satellite technology,
    and show potential for a significant contribution
    to the satellite communications industry. The
    scholarship is also available to undergraduate
    students. *Application Process: The application
    process is divided into two parts. Applicants who
    successfully pass stage one of the application
    process will be invited to apply for stage two. To
    apply for stage one, applicants should submit
    a completed application along with current
    transcripts. Information about stage two of the
    process will be provided to applicants who pass
    stage one. Visit the society's Web site to download
    an application. *Amount: $2,000 to $5,000.
    *Deadline: February 28 (for stage one).

**SPIE-The International Society for Optical
    Engineering**
SPIE Scholarship Committee
PO Box 10
Bellingham, WA 98227-0010
360-676-3290, ext. 659
scholarships@spie.org
http://www.spie.org/CommunityServices/
    StudentsAndEducators/index.cfm?fuseaction=
    Scholarships

Scholarship Name: SPIE Scholarship. *Academic
    Area: Engineering (optical). *Age Group: Graduate
    students. *Eligibility: Applicants must be enrolled
    full-time in a graduate optics, photonics, imaging,
    optoelectronics program or related discipline at
    an educational institution for the academic year
    in which the award will be used. They also must
    be SPIE student members. The scholarship is also
    available to high school seniors and undergraduate
    students. *Application Process: Applicants must
    submit a completed application, two letters of
    recommendation, an essay, and annual scholarship
    award report (if reapplying). Visit the society's Web
    site to download an application. *Amount: Varies.
    *Deadline: January 6.

Triangle Education Foundation (TEF)
Attn: Chairman, TEF Scholarship & Loan Committee
120 South Center Street
Plainfield, IN 46168
317-837-9641
scholarships@triangle.org
http://www.triangle.org/tef/programs/scholarships
Scholarship Name: Triangle Education Foundation
    Scholarship. *Academic Area: Engineering (open).
    *Age Group: Graduate students. *Eligibility:
    Applicants must be graduate student-members who
    are currently studying engineering and other "hard
    sciences." They also must demonstrate financial
    need and active involvement in their chapters on
    campus or in the community. Most scholarships
    require a minimum GPA of 3.0 on a 4.0 scale.
    Eligibility requirements vary. Visit the foundation's
    Web site for specific scholarship eligibility
    requirements. The scholarship is also available to
    undergraduate students. *Application Process:
    Applicants must submit a completed application,
    two letters of recommendation, and transcripts.
    Visit the foundation's Web site to download an
    application. *Amount: $1,000 to $5,000. *Deadline:
    February 15.

MEDIA ARTS—UNDERGRADUATE

The following financial aid resources are available to students who are interested in studying media arts and related fields at the undergraduate level.

Academy of Television Arts and Sciences
Fred Rogers Memorial Scholarship
Attn: Michele Fowble
5220 Lankershim Boulevard
North Hollywood, CA 91601-3109
818-754-2802
http://www.emmys.tv/foundation/rogersscholar.php
Scholarship Name: Fred Rogers Memorial Scholarship.
*Academic Area: Education, film/video, media arts (open). *Age Group: Undergraduate students. *Eligibility: Applicants must be undergraduates at accredited colleges or universities who are pursuing degrees in early childhood education, child development/child psychology, film/television production, media arts, music, or animation. Applicants must have the ultimate goal of working in the field of children's media. Particular attention will be given to student applicants from inner city or rural communities. The scholarship is also available to graduate students. *Application Process: Applicants must submit a completed application, a personal statement, transcripts, and two letters of recommendation. Visit the academy's Web site to download an application. *Amount: $10,000. *Deadline: January 31.

American Copy Editors Society
Attn: Naomi Seldin, ACES Contest Committee Chairman
38309 Genesee Lake Road
Oconomowoc, WI 53066
518-598-0177
nbseldin@yahoo.com
http://www.copydesk.org/contest.htm
Contest Name: American Copy Editors Society Headline Contest. *Academic Area: Publishing. *Age Group: Undergraduate students. *Eligibility: Applicants should be college students who work for a student publication. Students who have been employed by professional publications, as interns or otherwise, may enter work performed while so employed in the appropriate professional category. *Application Process: Applicants should submit an entry form along with copies of headlines as they appeared in print, or screen grabs in the case of online entries. Entries should be submitted as high-quality photocopies or scans on standard letter-size paper.

Clips or tear sheets are not acceptable submission formats. Applicants should submit five copies of each complete entry, with a copy of the entry form attached to the front of each one. Visit the society's Web site to download an entry form and to view additional specifications for submissions. *Amount: $250. *Deadline: December 16.

American Copy Editors Society
Attn: Kathy Schenck
ACES Scholarships
Milwaukee Journal Sentinel
333 West State Street
Milwaukee, WI 53203
http://www.copydesk.org/scholarships.htm
Scholarship Name: American Copy Editors Society Copy Editor Scholarship. *Academic Area: Publishing. *Age Group: Undergraduate students, graduate students. *Eligibility: Applicants should be college juniors or seniors who are interested in a career in copy editing. The scholarship is also available to graduate students and post-graduate students. *Application Process: Applicants should submit five copies of the completed application and application packet materials, which includes a list of course work relevant to copy editing, an explanation of their copy editing experience, a 750-word essay, two letters of recommendation, copies of five to 10 headlines the applicant has written, and a copy of a story the applicant has edited with an explanation of the changes made and the circumstances (deadlines) under which it was edited. Visit the society's Web site to download an application. *Amount: $1,000 to $2,500. *Deadline: October 15.

Broadcast Education Association
1771 N Street, NW
Washington, DC 20036-2891
888-380-7222
beainfo@beaweb.org
http://www.beaweb.org/scholarships/description.pdf
Scholarship Name: Broadcast Education Association National Scholarships in Broadcasting. *Academic Area: Journalism. *Age Group: Undergraduate students. *Eligibility: Applicants must be full-time students who exhibit academic excellence and

potential to be outstanding electronic media professionals. Applicants must also demonstrate high integrity and a well-articulated sense of personal and professional responsibility. Visit the Association's Web site for specific eligibility requirements for individual scholarships. *Application Process: Applicants should visit the association's Web site to view a list of specific available scholarships. Applications are available by request (mail, phone, or e-mail). *Amount: $1,250 to $5,000. *Deadline: October 12.

Electronic Document Systems Foundation
Attn: EDSF Scholarship Awards
608 Silver Spur Road, Suite 280
Rolling Hills Estates, CA 90274-3616
310-265-5510
info@edsf.org
http://www.edsf.org/scholarships.cfm
Scholarship Name: Electronic Document Systems Foundation Document Communication Scholarship Program. *Academic Area: Business, communications, computer science, engineering (open), graphic design. *Age Group: Undergraduate students. *Eligibility: Applicants must be full-time students who are committed to pursuing a career in the field of electronic document communication in the areas of: document preparation, production and/or document distribution, including 1:1 marketing; graphic communication and arts; e-commerce; imaging science, printing, Web authoring, electronic publishing, computer science, engineering, or telecommunications. Applicants must also maintain a minimum 3.0 GPA. The scholarship is also available to graduate students. *Application Process: Applicants must submit 10 copies of a completed application package. Applicants must include a covering letter, their academic details, two half- to full-page essays, a list of their extracurricular professional and academic activities, transcripts, two letters of recommendation, and samples of creative work (optional) in their application packets. Visit the foundation's Web site for further details. *Amount: Varies. *Deadline: May 15.

Indiana Broadcasters Association (IBA)
3003 East 98th Street, Suite 161
Indianapolis, IN 46280
317-573-0119, 800-342-6276
indba@aol.com
http://www.indianabroadcasters.org

Scholarship Name: Indiana Broadcasters Association Scholarship for College Students. *Academic Area: Broadcasting, journalism. *Age Group: Undergraduate students. *Eligibility: Applicants must undergraduate students and Indiana residents who are currently attending IBA-member colleges/universities majoring in broadcasting, electronic media, telecommunications, or broadcast journalism. They also must be actively participating in a college broadcasting facility or working or interning for a commercial broadcasting facility. *Application Process: Applicants must submit a completed application and college transcript request form. Visit the Association's Web site to download an application and request form. *Amount: Varies. *Deadline: March 21.

Indiana Broadcasters Association (IBA)
3003 East 98th Street, Suite 161
Indianapolis, IN 46280
317-573-0119, 800-342-6276
indba@aol.com
http://www.indianabroadcasters.org
Scholarship Name: Indiana Broadcasters Association Scholarship for High School Seniors. *Academic Area: Broadcasting, journalism. *Age Group: Undergraduate students. *Eligibility: Applicants must be second semester seniors at Indiana high schools, have a GPA of at least 3.0, be residents of Indiana, and plan to attend Indiana, IBA-member colleges/universities. They also must plan to major in broadcasting, electronic media, telecommunications, or broadcast journalism. Applicants must be actively participating in a high school broadcasting facility or working or interning for a commercial broadcasting facility. They also must have received credit in a high school broadcasting, electronic media, telecommunications, or broadcast journalism course. *Application Process: Applicants must submit a completed application and high school transcript request form. Visit the association's Web site to download an application and request a form. *Amount: Varies. *Deadline: March 27.

Iowa Broadcasters Association (IBA)
PO Box 71186
Des Moines, IA 50325
515-224-7237
iowaiba@dwx.com
http://www.iowabroadcasters.com/scholar.htm

Scholarship Name: Quarton-McElroy/IBA Scholarship. *Academic Area: Broadcasting. *Age Group: Undergraduate students. *Eligibility: Applicants must be residents of Iowa, graduated from or about to graduate from an Iowa high school, and be enrolled in or enrolling full time in a broadcasting program at an IBA-approved Iowa two- or four-year college/university. Visit the association's Web site to view a list of IBA-approved colleges/universities. *Application Process: Applicants must submit a completed application, an essay, transcripts, two letters of recommendation, and a copy of the applicant's Free Application for Federal Student Aid report or Student Aid Report. Visit the association's Web site to download an application. *Amount: Up to $3,000 per year. *Deadline: April 1.

Kansas Association of Broadcasters (KAB)
Scholarship Committee
1916 Southwest Sieben Court
Topeka, KS 66611-1656
785-235-1307
info@kab.net
http://www.kab.net/Programs/StudentServices/BroadcastScholarshipProgram/default.aspx
Scholarship Name: Broadcast Scholarship Program. *Academic Area: Broadcasting. *Age Group: Undergraduate students. *Eligibility: Applicants must be Kansas residents attending or planning to attend a Kansas postsecondary institution and pursue full-time study in broadcasting or a related curriculum. Applicants must maintain at least a 2.5 GPA. High school seniors and college undergraduates may apply. *Application Process: Applicants must submit seven copies of a completed application, three letters of recommendation, and an essay. Visit the association's Web site to download an application. *Amount: Varies. *Deadline: May 1.

Michigan Association of Broadcasters Foundation
MABF/abc12 Broadcasting Scholarship
819 North Washington Avenue
Lansing, MI 48906
800-YOUR-MAB
mabf@michmab.com
http://www.michmab.com/MABF/staoverview.html
Scholarship Name: Michigan Association of Broadcasters Foundation/abc12 Broadcasting Scholarship. *Academic Area: Broadcasting. *Age Group: Undergraduate students. *Eligibility: Applicants must be college students currently pursuing careers in broadcast-related fields in the state of Michigan. *Application Process: Applicants must submit a cover letter, a resume, letters of recommendation, and an essay. *Amount: $1,000. *Deadline: December 15.

Michigan Association of Broadcasters Foundation
MABF/WOOD-TV8 Educational Scholarship
819 North Washington Avenue
Lansing, MI 48906
800-YOUR-MAB
mabf@michmab.com
http://www.michmab.com/MABF/staoverview.html
Scholarship Name: Michigan Association of Broadcasters Foundation/WOOD-TV8 Educational Scholarship. *Academic Area: Broadcasting. *Age Group: Undergraduate students. *Eligibility: Applicants must be college student currently pursuing a career in a broadcast-related field in the state of Michigan. *Application Process: Applicants must submit a cover letter, a resume, letters of recommendation, and an essay. *Amount: $1,000. *Deadline: December 15.

Michigan Association of Broadcasters Foundation
MABF/WXYZ-TV Broadcasting Scholarship
819 North Washington Avenue
Lansing, MI 48906
800-YOUR-MAB
mabf@michmab.com
http://www.michmab.com/MABF/staoverview.html
Scholarship Name: Michigan Association of Broadcasters Foundation/WXYZ-TV Broadcasting Scholarship. *Academic Area: Broadcasting. *Age Group: Undergraduate students. *Eligibility: Applicants must be college students currently pursuing careers in broadcast-related fields in the state of Michigan. *Application Process: Applicants must submit a cover letter, a resume, letters of recommendation, and an essay. *Amount: $1,000. *Deadline: December 15.

Minnesota State Arts Board
Park Square Court, Suite 200
400 Sibley Street
St. Paul, MN 55101-1928
800-8MN-ARTS
msab@arts.state.mn.us
http://www.arts.state.mn.us/grants/artist_initiative.htm
Scholarship Name: Artist Initiative Grant. *Academic Area: Media arts, performing arts (open), visual arts (open), writing. *Age Group: Open. *Eligibility:

Applicants must be Minnesota residents, U.S. citizens or permanent residents, and at least 18 years old. Applicants must intend to expand their professional development in music, photography, media arts/new media, literary arts, dance, theater, or visual arts. *Application Process: Applicants must submit a completed application, work samples, artist plan, budget, and a resume. Visit the Arts Board's Web site to obtain specifications for work samples and artist plan, and to download an application. *Amount: $2,000 to $6,000. *Deadline: September 15.

Missouri Broadcasters Association

1025 Northeast Drive
Jefferson City, MO 65109
573-636-6692
http://www.mbaweb.org/TopStories.aspx?id=9
Scholarship Name: Missouri Broadcasters Association Scholarship Fund. *Academic Area: Broadcasting. *Age Group: Undergraduate students. *Eligibility: Applicants must be Missouri residents currently attending a Missouri college, university, or an accredited tech/trade school. Applicants may also be graduating high school seniors who have been admitted to a Missouri institution of higher learning. Applicants must be enrolled or planning to enroll in a broadcast or related curriculum, which provides training and expertise applicable to a broadcast operation. They also must be full-time students and maintain at least a 3.0 GPA. *Application Process: Applicants must submit a completed application and three letters of recommendation. Ten copies of both the application and the letters of recommendation are required. Contact the association to request an application. *Amount: Varies. *Deadline: March 31.

National Association of Farm Broadcasters

Attn: Terry Henne, Chairman, NAFB Scholarship Program
WSGW Radio
1795 Tittabawassee Road
Saginaw, MI 48604
989-752-3456
terry.henne@gte.net
http://nafb.com/DesktopDefault.aspx?tabid=26
Scholarship Name: National Association of Farm Broadcasters College Scholarship. *Academic Area: Communications science, journalism. *Age Group: Undergraduate students. *Eligibility: Applicants must be college juniors who are actively pursuing a degree in communications or journalism, with a specialty in agricultural broadcasting. The scholarship is also available to graduate students. *Application Process: Applicants should submit a completed application along with a biographical form, transcripts, a statement detailing their career activities and interests, and personal references. Visit the association's Web site to download an application. *Amount: $2,500 and $3,000. *Deadline: April 30.

National Cattlemen's Foundation

Attn: Beef Industry Scholarship
9110 East Nichols Avenue, Suite 300
Centennial, CO 80112
303-850-3347
ncf@beef.org
http://www.nationalcattlemensfoundation.org/SCHOLARSHIP.aspx
Scholarship Name: Beef Industry Scholarship. *Academic Area: Agriculture, communications, education. *Age Group: Undergraduate students. *Eligibility: Applicants must be enrolled full time in a two- or four-year institution of higher learning with an intent on majoring in a field related to the beef industry—education, communications, production, or research. They must also demonstrate commitment to the beef industry through classes, internships, or life experiences. High school seniors may also apply for this scholarship. *Application Process: Applicants should submit a completed application along with a one-page letter expressing career goals, two letters of recommendation, and a 750-word essay. *Visit the association's Web site to download an application. *Amount: $1,500, plus expenses paid to attend the organization's annual convention and trade show. *Deadline: September 30.

National Institute for Labor Relations Research

5211 Port Royal Road, Suite 510
Springfield, VA 22151
703-321-9606
research@nilrr.org
http://www.nilrr.org/scholarships.htm
Scholarship Name: William B. Ruggles Right to Work Journalism Scholarship. *Academic Area: Journalism. *Age Group: Undergraduate students. *Eligibility: Applicants must be college students majoring in journalism or a related major who demonstrate academic achievement and an interest in the work of the institute. The scholarship is also available to

graduate students. *Application Process: Applicants should submit a completed application, transcripts (or letter of college acceptance, and a 500-word essay on the principles of voluntary unionism and transcripts (or letter of college acceptance). Applications should be submitted between October 1 and December 31. Visit the institute's Web site to download an application. *Amount: $2,000. *Deadline: December 31.

National Press Photographers Foundation
3200 Croasdaile Drive, Suite 306
Durham, NC 27705
919-383-7246
info@nppa.org
http://www.nppa.org/professional_development/students/scholarships
Scholarship Name: National Press Photographers Foundation Scholarship. *Academic Area: Journalism, photojournalism. *Age Group: Undergraduate students. *Eligibility: Applicants must be full-time college students or students returning to college to finish their formal education. They also must demonstrate dedication to photojournalism, academic ability, and financial need. The scholarship is also available to graduate students. *Application Process: Applicants must submit a completed application and portfolio including six or more photos (still photographers), three tear sheets (picture editors), or three short stories (video journalists). Visit the foundation's Web site to download an application and for further application details. *Amount: Varies. *Deadline: March 1.

The Newspaper Guild-CWA
David S. Barr Award
501 Third Street, NW
Washington, DC 20001-2797
202-434-7177
http://www.newsguild.org/awards/barr.php
Award Name: David S. Barr Award. *Academic Area: Broadcasting, journalism. *Age Group: Undergraduate students. *Eligibility: Entries must be published work printed or broadcast between January 1 and December 31 of the previous year. High school students, undergraduate students, and graduate students may apply for this award. *Application Process: Applicants should submit a signed, completed application along with one original copy of the entry and four photocopies or tapes of their

work. A summary of the work and how that work helped right a wrong, corrected an injustice, or promoted justice and fairness should also be included with the entry. Visit the guild's Web site to download an application. *Amount: $500 (high school students); $1,500 (college students). *Deadline: January 31.

Oklahoma Association of Broadcasters
6520 North Western, Suite 104
Oklahoma City, OK 73116
405-848-0771
info@oabok.org
http://www.oabok.org/Careers/scholarships.html
Scholarship Name: Ken R. Greenwood Student Assistance Fund. *Academic Area: Broadcasting. *Age Group: Undergraduate students. *Eligibility: Applicants must be broadcast students attending a college/university in the state of Oklahoma who demonstrate financial need. *Application Process: Applicants must submit a request for financial assistance along with a letter from the applicant's department head or professor. Contact the association for further application details. *Amount: Up to $250. *Deadline: Varies.

Oklahoma Association of Broadcasters
6520 North Western, Suite 104
Oklahoma City, OK 73116
405-848-0771
info@oabok.org
http://www.oabok.org/Careers/scholarships.html
Scholarship Name: Oklahoma Association of Broadcasters Education Foundation Scholarship Program. *Academic Area: Broadcasting. *Age Group: Undergraduate students. *Eligibility: Applicants must be juniors or seniors enrolled in an Oklahoma college or university broadcast program and majoring in broadcasting. They also must maintain a minimum B average in all courses, take at least 12 academic hours of coursework during the scholarship year, and plan to enter the broadcasting profession upon graduation. *Application Process: Applicants must submit a completed application. Visit the association's Web site in October to download an application. *Amount: $1,000. *Deadline: December 16.

Overseas Press Club Foundation
Attn: William J. Holstein, President
40 West 45th Street
New York, NY 10036

212-626-9220
foundation@opcofamerica.org
http://www.opcofamerica.org
Scholarship Name: Overseas Press Club Foundation Scholarship. *Academic Area: Journalism. *Age Group: Undergraduate students. *Eligibility: Applicants must aspire to become foreign correspondents. The scholarship is also available to graduate students. *Application Process: Applicants should submit a cover letter, a resume, and an essay. The essay should be no longer than 500 words and concentrate on an area of the world or an international issue that is in keeping with the applicant's interests. Visit the foundation's Web site for further information that should be included in the cover letter and resume. *Amount: $2,000. *Deadline: December 1.

Quill and Scroll Society
Scholarship Committee
University of Iowa
School of Journalism and Mass Communication
100 Adler Journalism Building, Room E346
Iowa City, IA 52242
319-335-3457
quill-scroll@uiowa.edu
http://www.uiowa.edu/~quill-sc/Scholarships/index.html
Scholarship Name: Edward J. Nell Memorial Scholarships in Journalism. *Academic Area: Journalism. *Age Group: Undergraduate students. *Eligibility: Applicants must be high school seniors who are national winners in either the Yearbook Excellence Contest or the International Writing/Photography Contest. *Application Process: Applicants must submit a completed application, official transcripts, a cover letter, five selections of published work, and letters of endorsement from their principal, counselor, and/or adviser. Visit the society's Web site to download an application. *Amount: $500 to $1,500. *Deadline: May 10.

Radio-Television News Directors Foundation (RTNDF)
Attn: Irving Washington
RTNDF Scholarships
1600 K Street, NW, Suite 700
Washington, DC 20006
202-467-5218
irvingw@rtndf.org
http://www.rtnda.org/asfi/scholarships/undergrad.shtml

Scholarship Name: The George Foreman Tribute to Lyndon B. Johnson Scholarship. *Academic Area: Broadcasting, journalism. *Age Group: Undergraduate students. *Eligibility: Applicants must be enrolled full-time sophomores, juniors, or seniors at the University of Texas-Austin and interested in pursuing a career in electronic journalism. Several scholarships are available, but applicants may only apply for one scholarship through the foundation. *Application Process: Applicants should submit a completed application along with a resume, a one-page statement detailing their career goals, and a letter of reference from their dean or faculty advisor. One to three samples of the applicant's journalistic skills, totaling 15 minutes or less, should also be submitted on audiocassette or videotape (VHS only), along with a script and a statement describing the role the applicant played in each story. Any additional credits for others working on the stories should also be included. Visit the foundation's Web site to download an application. *Amount: $6,000. *Deadline: May 8.

Radio-Television News Directors Foundation (RTNDF)
Attn: Irving Washington
RTNDF Scholarships
1600 K Street, NW, Suite 700
Washington, DC 20006
202-467-5218
irvingw@rtndf.org
http://www.rtnda.org/asfi/scholarships/undergrad.shtml
Scholarship Name: The Lou and Carole Prato Sports Reporting Scholarship. *Academic Area: Broadcasting, journalism. *Age Group: Undergraduate students. *Eligibility: Applicants must be full-time college sophomores, juniors, or seniors who are pursuing careers in radio or television sports reporting. Several scholarships are available, but applicants may only apply for one scholarship through the foundation. *Application Process: Applicants should submit a completed application along with a resume, detailing their career goals, and a letter of reference from their dean or faculty advisor. One to three samples of the applicant's journalistic skills, totaling 15 minutes or less, should also be submitted on audiocassette or videotape (VHS only), along with a script and a statement describing the role the applicant played in each story. Any additional credits for others working on the stories should also be included. Visit the

foundation's Web site to download an application. *Amount: $1,000. *Deadline: May 8.

Radio-Television News Directors Foundation (RTNDF)
Attn: Irving Washington
RTNDF Scholarships
1600 K Street, NW, Suite 700
Washington, DC 20006
202-467-5218
irvingw@rtndf.org
http://www.rtnda.org/asfi/scholarships/undergrad.shtml
Scholarship Name: The Mike Reynolds Journalism Scholarship. *Academic Area: Broadcasting, journalism. *Age Group: Undergraduate students. *Eligibility: Applicants must be enrolled full-time college sophomores, juniors, or seniors who have good writing ability, excellent grades, a dedication to the news business, strong interest in pursuing a career in electronic journalism, and a demonstrated need for financial assistance. Several scholarships are available, but applicants may only apply for one scholarship through the foundation. *Application Process: Applicants should submit a completed application along with a resume, a one-page statement detailing their career goals, and a letter of reference from the student's dean or faculty advisor. One to three samples of the applicant's journalistic skills, totaling 15 minutes or less, should also be submitted on audiocassette or videotape (VHS only), along with a script and a statement describing the role the applicant played in each story. Any additional credits for others working on the stories should also be included. Visit the foundation's Web site to download an application. *Amount: $1,000. *Deadline: May 8.

Radio-Television News Directors Foundation (RTNDF)
Attn: Irving Washington
RTNDF Scholarships
1600 K Street, NW, Suite 700
Washington, DC 20006
202-467-5218
irvingw@rtndf.org
http://www.rtnda.org/asfi/scholarships/undergrad.shtml
Scholarship Name: Presidents' Scholarship. *Academic Area: Broadcasting, journalism. *Age Group: Undergraduate students. *Eligibility: Applicants must be enrolled full-time college sophomores, juniors, or seniors who are pursuing careers in radio and television news. Several scholarships are available,

but applicants may only apply for one scholarship through the foundation. *Application Process: Applicants should submit a completed application along with a resume, a one-page statement detailing their career goals, and a letter of reference from the student's dean or faculty advisor. One to three samples of the applicant's journalistic skills, totaling 15 minutes or less, should also be submitted on audiocassette or videotape (VHS only), along with a script and a statement describing the role the applicant played in each story. Any additional credits for others working on the stories should also be included. Visit the foundation's Web site to download an application. *Amount: $2,500. *Deadline: May 8.

Society for Technical Communication
Attn: Scott DeLoach, Scholarships
901 North Stuart Street, Suite 904
Arlington, VA 22203-1802
404-522-0003
scott@userfirst.net
http://www.stc.org/scholarshipInfo_national.asp
Scholarship Name: Society for Technical Communication International Scholarship Program. *Academic Area: Communications science. *Age Group: Undergraduate students. *Eligibility: Applicants must be full-time undergraduate students who are pursuing established degree programs in some area of technical communication. Applicants pursuing other communications-related majors, such as general journalism, electronic communication engineering, computer programming, creative writing, or entertainment are not eligible. Applicants must have completed at least one year of postsecondary education and should have at least one full year of academic work remaining to complete their degree programs, although under exceptional circumstances an award may be granted to a student for the final half-year. The scholarship is also available to graduate students. *Application Process: Applicants must submit a completed application, an essay, official transcripts, and two letters of recommendation. Visit the society's Web site to download an application. *Amount: $1,500. *Deadline: February 15.

Society of Professional Journalists-Mid-Florida Pro Chapter
Attn: Dr. Bonnie Jefferis, Coordinator of Mass Communications

St. Petersburg College
2465 Drew Street
Clearwater, FL 33756
JefferisB@spcollege.edu
http://www.spj.org/midflorida/danielleinfo.htm
Scholarship Name: Danielle Cipriani TV News
Scholarship. *Academic Area: Broadcasting,
journalism. *Age Group: Undergraduate students.
*Eligibility: Applicants must be residents of the
Mid-Florida Pro Chapter region (between Gainesville
and Sarasota). They also must be television news or
television production majors at a Florida college or
university. *Application Process: Applicants must
submit a completed application, a career goals
statement, a work sample (15 minutes or less) on VHS
tape or DVD, and two letters of recommendation. Visit
the society's Web site to download an application.
*Amount: $1,000. *Deadline: November 1.

MEDIA ARTS—GRADUATE

The following financial aid resources are available to students who are interested in studying the media arts and related fields at the graduate level.

Academy of Television Arts and Sciences
Fred Rogers Memorial Scholarship
c/o Michele Fowble
5220 Lankershim Boulevard
North Hollywood, CA 91601-3109
818-754-2802
http://www.emmys.tv/foundation/rogersscholar.php
Scholarship Name: Fred Rogers Memorial Scholarship. *Academic Area: Education, film/video, media arts (open). *Age Group: Graduate students. *Eligibility: Applicants must be graduate students (master's or Ph.D.) at accredited colleges or universities who are pursuing degrees in early childhood education, child development/child psychology, film/television production, music, and animation. Applicants must have the ultimate goal of working in the field of children's media. Particular attention will be given to student applicants from inner city or rural communities. The scholarship is also available to undergraduate students.*Application Process: Applicants must submit a completed application, a personal statement, transcripts, and two letters of recommendation. Visit the academy's Web site to download an application. *Amount: $10,000. *Deadline: January 31.

American Copy Editors Society
Attn: Kathy Schenck
ACES Scholarships
Milwaukee Journal Sentinel
333 West State Street
Milwaukee, WI 53203
http://www.copydesk.org/scholarships.htm
Scholarship Name: American Copy Editors Society Copy Editor Scholarship. *Academic Area: Publishing. *Age Group: Graduate students, post-graduate students. *Eligibility: Applicants should be potential professional copy editors, either still in college, or graduating students who have accepted full-time copy editing jobs or internships. The scholarship is also available to undergraduate students. *Application Process: Applicants should submit five copies of the completed application and application packet materials, which includes: a list of course work relevant to copy editing, an explanation of their copy editing experience, a 750-word essay,

two letters of recommendation, copies of five to 10 headlines the applicant has written, and a copy of a story the applicant has edited with an explanation of the changes made and the circumstances (deadlines) under which it was edited. Visit the society's Web site to download an application. *Amount: $1,000 to $2,500. *Deadline: October 15.

National Association of Farm Broadcasters
Attn: Terry Henne, Chairman, NAFB Scholarship Program
WSGW Radio
1795 Tittabawassee
Saginaw, MI 48604
989-752-3456
terry.henne@gte.net
http://nafb.com/DesktopDefault.aspx?tabid=26
Scholarship Name: National Association of Farm Broadcasters College Scholarship. *Academic Area: Broadcasting, journalism. *Age Group: Graduate students. *Eligibility: Applicants must be graduate students actively pursuing a degree in communication or journalism, with a specialty in agricultural. The scholarship is also available to undergraduate students. *Application Process: Applicants should submit a completed application along with a biographical form, transcripts, a statement detailing their career activities and interests, and personal references. Visit the foundation's Web site to download an application. *Amount: $2,500 and $3,000. *Deadline: April 30.

National Institute for Labor Relations Research
5211 Port Royal Road, Suite 510
Springfield, VA 22151
703-321-9606
research@nilrr.org
http://www.nilrr.org/scholarships.htm
Scholarship Name: William B. Ruggles Right to Work Journalism Scholarship. *Academic Area: Journalism. *Age Group: Graduate students. *Eligibility: Applicants must be college students majoring in journalism or a related major who demonstrate academic achievement and an interest in the work of the institute. The scholarship is also available to undergraduate students. *Application Process: Applicants should submit a completed application,

transcripts (or letter of college acceptance), and a 500-word essay on the principles of voluntary unionism. Applications should be submitted between October 1 and December 31. Visit the institute's Web site to download an application. *Amount: $2,000. *Deadline: December 31.

National Press Photographers Foundation

3200 Croasdaile Drive, Suite 306
Durham, NC 27705
919-383-7246
info@nppa.org
http://www.nppa.org/professional_development/students/scholarships

Scholarship Name: National Press Photographers Foundation Scholarship. *Academic Area: Photojournalism. *Age Group: Graduate students. *Eligibility: Applicants must be full-time college students or students returning to college to finish their formal education. They also must demonstrate dedication to photojournalism, academic ability, and financial need. The scholarship is also available to undergraduate students. *Application Process: Applicants must submit a completed application and portfolio including six or more photos (still photographers), three tear sheets (picture editors), or three short stories (video journalists). Visit the foundation's Web site to download an application and for further application details. *Amount: Varies. *Deadline: March 1.

The Newspaper Guild-CWA

David S. Barr Award
501 Third Street, NW
Washington, DC 20001-2797
202-434-7177
http://www.newsguild.org/awards/barr.php

Award Name: David S. Barr Award. *Academic Area: Broadcasting, journalism. *Age Group: Graduate students. *Eligibility: Entries must be published work printed or broadcast between January 1 and December 31 of the previous year. The award is also available to high school seniors and undergraduate students. *Application Process: Applicants should submit a completed, signed application along with one original copy of the entry and four photocopies or tapes. A summary of the work and how that work helped right a wrong, corrected an injustice, or promoted justice and fairness should also be included with the entry. Visit the association's Web

site to download an application. *Amount: $1,500. *Deadline: January 31.

Overseas Press Club Foundation

Attn: William J. Holstein, President
40 West 45th Street
New York, NY 10036
212-626-9220
foundation@opcofamerica.org
http://www.opcofamerica.org

Scholarship Name: Overseas Press Club Foundation Scholarship. *Academic Area: Journalism. *Age Group: Graduate students. *Eligibility: Applicants must aspire to become foreign correspondents. The scholarship is also available to undergraduate students. *Application Process: Applicants should submit a cover letter, a resume, and an essay. The essay should be no longer than 500 words and concentrate on an area of the world or an international issue that is in keeping with the applicant's interests. Visit the foundation's Web site for further information that should be included in the cover letter and resume. *Amount: $2,000. *Deadline: December 1.

Radio-Television News Directors Foundation (RTNDF)

Attn: Irving Washington
RTNDF Scholarships
1600 K Street, NW, Suite 700
Washington, DC 20006
202-467-5218
irvingw@rtndf.org
http://www.rtnda.org/asfi/scholarships/graduate.shtml

Scholarship Name: Abe Schechter Graduate Scholarship. *Academic Area: Broadcasting, journalism. *Age Group: Graduate students. Eligibility: Applicants must be enrolled, or incoming, full-time graduate students who are interested in pursuing a career in electronic journalism. *Application Process: Applicants should submit a completed application along with a resume, a one-page statement detailing their career goals, and a letter of reference from the their dean or faculty adviser. Visit the association's Web site to download an application. *Amount: $2,000. *Deadline: May 8.

Society for Technical Communication

Contact: Scott DeLoach, Scholarship Selection Committee
901 North Stuart Street, Suite 904
Arlington, VA 22203

703-522-0003
scott@userfirst.net
http://www.stc.org/scholarshipInfo_national.asp
Scholarship Name: Society for Technical Communication International Scholarship Program. *Academic Area: Communications science, computer science, graphic design. *Age Group: Graduate students. *Eligibility: Applicants must be full-time students pursuing graduate degrees in technical writing, editing, graphical design, interface design, or Web design. The scholarship is also available to undergraduate students. *Application Process: Applicants must submit a completed application, official college transcripts, and two letters of recommendation. Visit the society's Web site to download an application. *Amount: $1,500. *Deadline: February 15.

Society of Satellite Professionals International
Attn: Tamara Bond, Membership Director
The New York Information Technology Center
55 Broad Street, 14th Floor
New York, NY 10004
212-809-5199, ext. 16
tbond@sspi.org
http://www.sspi.org/displaycommon.cfm?an=1&subart iclenbr=56
Scholarship Name: Society of Satellite Professionals International Scholarship. *Academic Area: Broadcasting, business, law, government, meteorology, satellite technology. *Age Group: Graduate students. *Eligibility: Applicants must demonstrate academic and leadership achievement, commitment to pursuing education and career opportunities in the satellite industry or a field making direct use of satellite technology, and show potential for a significant contribution to the satellite communications industry. The scholarship is also available to high school seniors and undergraduate students. *Application Process: The application process is divided into two parts. Applicants who successfully pass stage one of the application process will be invited to apply for stage two. To apply for stage one, applicants should submit a completed application along with current transcripts. Information about stage two of the process will be provided to applicants who pass stage one. Visit the society's Web site to download an application. *Amount: $2,000 to $5,000. *Deadline: February 28 (for stage one).

United Methodist Communications
Scholarship Committee
Communications Resourcing Team-UMCom
PO Box 320
Nashville, TN 37202-0320
888-278-4862
scholarships@umcom.org
http://umcom.org/pages/news.asp?class=6&ID=427&typ e=2&product_id=0
Fellowship Name: Stoody-West Fellowship. *Academic Area: Journalism. *Age Group: Graduate students. *Eligibility: Applicants must be graduate students planning to pursue a degree in religious journalism. Applicants must be attending or planning to attend an accredited U.S. college or university. They also must demonstrate Christian commitment and involvement in the life of the United Methodist Church. *Application Process: Applicants must submit a completed application, official transcripts, three letters of recommendation, a personal photo, three writing samples, and a personal statement. Visit the organization's Web site to download an application. *Amount: $6,000. *Deadline: March 15.

Women's Basketball Coaches Association (WBCA)
Contact: Amy Lowe, WBCA Awards Program Manager
4646 Lawrenceville Highway
Lilburn, GA 30047-3620
770-279-8027, ext. 102
alowe@wbca.org
http://www.wbca.org/RobertsAward.asp
Scholarship Name: Robin Roberts/WBCA Broadcasting Scholarship. *Academic Area: Communications science, journalism. *Age Group: Graduate students. *Eligibility: Applicants must be female collegiate basketball players intending to pursue graduate study and careers in sports communication or journalism. *Application Process: Applicants must submit a nomination form (to be completed by WBCA member coaches), a letter of recommendation, proof of academic major and GPA, and a list of campus activities. Nomination forms are made available at the WBCA's Web site in January. Nominations must be made through the online nomination form. *Amount: $4,000, plus $1,000 for travel to the national convention. *Deadline: Contact the association for more information.

MEDICINE/HEALTH CARE—UNDERGRADUATE

The following financial aid resources are available to students who are interested in studying medicine/health care or related fields at the undergraduate level.

American Academy of Orthotists and Prosthetists
Orthotic and Prosthetic Education and Development Fund
526 King Street, Suite 201
Alexandria, VA 22314
703-836-0788, ext. 206
scholarship@oandp.org
http://www.oandp.org/education/professional_development/mckeever_scholarship.asp
Scholarship Name: Dan McKeever Scholarship. *Academic Area: Medicine (orthotics and prosthetics). *Age Group: Undergraduate students. *Eligibility: Applicants must have completed their junior year in an accredited orthotics and prosthetics bachelor's degree program. Applicants must also maintain at least a 3.0 GPA and demonstrate financial need. *Application Process: Applicants must submit a completed application, official transcripts, a recent W-2 or letter from their employer, a letter of recommendation, and a 200-word essay. Visit the academy's Web site to download an application. *Amount: $1,000. *Deadline: May 31.

American Academy of Orthotists and Prosthetists
Orthotic and Prosthetic Education and Development Fund
526 King Street, Suite 201
Alexandria, VA 22314
703-836-0788, ext. 206
scholarship@oandp.org
http://www.oandp.org/education/professional_development/chagnon_scholarship.asp
Scholarship Name: Ken Chagnon Scholarship. *Academic Area: Medicine (orthotics and prosthetics). *Age Group: Undergraduate students. *Eligibility: Applicants must be college students enrolled in an accredited orthotics and prosthetics technician program, and show exceptional technical aptitude Applicants must contribute to their own education financially, and demonstrate financial need. *Application Process: Applicants must submit a completed application, a recent W-2 or letter from employer, a letter of recommendation, and

a 200-word essay. Visit the academy's Web site to download an application. *Amount: $500. *Deadline: January 31.

American Alliance for Health, Physical Education, Recreation and Dance (AAHPERD)
Attn: Deb Callis
1900 Association Drive
Reston, VA 20191-1598
800-213-7193, ext. 405
dcallis@aahperd.org
http://www.aahperd.org/aahperd/template.cfm?template=presidents_scholarships.html
Scholarship Name: Ruth Abernathy Presidential Scholarship. *Academic Area: Medicine (open). *Age Group: Undergraduate students. *Eligibility: Applicants must be current members of AAHPERD (or join at time of application) who are majoring in the field of health, physical education, recreation, or dance. They must also be full-time students with a junior or senior status at a baccalaureate-granting college or university, maintain a 3.5 out of 4.0 GPA, demonstrate exceptional leadership abilities, and participate in school/community service activities. *Application Process: Applicants should submit a completed application along with a photocopy of the AAHPERD membership card or membership application form, three letters of recommendation, official transcripts, and a short biographical sketch. Materials should be mailed to the appropriate district contact. Visit the alliance's Web site to download application and to locate the district contact. *Amount: $1,000 plus a three-year AAHPERD membership. *Deadline: October 15.

American Assembly for Men in Nursing Foundation
11 Cornell Road
Latham, NY 12110-1499
518-782-9400, ext. 346
aamn@aamn.org
http://www.aamn.org/aamnfoundationscholarships.htm
Scholarship Name: American Assembly for Men in Nursing Foundation Scholarship. *Academic

Area: Nursing (open). *Age Group: Undergraduate students. *Eligibility: Applicants must be male students currently enrolled in nursing education programs. Applicants must maintain a minimum 2.75 GPA. A graduate scholarship is also available. *Application Process: Applicants must submit a completed application and essay. Contact the foundation to learn when scholarships are being offered and obtain further information regarding application requirements and details. *Amount: $1,000. *Deadline: Varies.

American Association of Colleges of Nursing
One Dupont Circle, NW, Suite 530
Washington, DC 20036
202-463-6930
info@campuscareercenter.com
http://aacn.campusrn.com/scholarships/scholarship_rn.asp
Scholarship Name: CampusRN/American Association of Colleges of Nursing Scholarship. *Academic Area: Nursing (open). *Age Group: Undergraduate students. *Eligibility: Applicants must be completing an RN to baccalaureate program or enrolled in an accelerated baccalaureate degree nursing program. Applicants should be Campus RN members who possess at least a 3.25 GPA. Special consideration is given to students pursuing a nursing faculty career. A scholarship is awarded every two months. The scholarship is also available to graduate students. *Application Process: Applicants should submit a completed application and submit an online profile on CampusRN. Visit the association's Web site to download an application and to complete the online profile. *Amount: $2,500. *Deadline: January 1, March 1, May 1, July 1, September 1, November 1.

American Association of Colleges of Nursing
Attn: Robert Rosseter
One Dupont Circle, NW, Suite 530
Washington, DC 20036
202-463-6930, ext. 231
rrosseter@aacn.nche.edu
http://www.aacn.nche.edu/Media/NewsReleases/2004/04LydiasScholarship.htm
Scholarship Name: Lydia's Professional Uniforms/American Association of Colleges of Nursing Excellence in Academics Nursing Scholarship. *Academic Area: Nursing (open). *Age Group: College juniors. *Eligibility: Applicants should be full-time students attending an accredited Bachelor of Science in Nursing program and possess a GPA of at least 3.5. *Application Process: Applicants must submit a completed application and a 250-word essay describing career aspirations and financial need. Visit the association's Web site to download an application. Applications should be submitted by email. *Amount: $2,500. *Deadline: August 1, November 1.

American Association of Colleges of Nursing
Attn: Pam Malloy
One Dupont Circle, NW, Suite 530
Washington, DC 20036-1120
202-463-6930
http://www.aacn.nche.edu/Education/financialaid.htm
Scholarship Name: Monster Healthcare-American Association of Colleges of Nursing, Nursing Faculty Scholarship. *Academic Area: Nursing (education). *Age Group: Undergraduate students. *Eligibility: Applicants must be U.S. citizens or permanent residents who are full-time students enrolled in or accepted into either a baccalaureate-to-doctoral degree or a doctor of nursing practice program. The purpose of this scholarship is to increase the number of doctoral nursing faculty instructors; the applicant must intend to teach. The school of nursing that the applicant attends must provide an agreement letter from the dean to match at least 50 percent of the tuition at their academic institution. If positions are available, awardees must be willing to work at least 10 hours a week while enrolled in the doctoral program so that they can maintain clinical skills and obtain health care benefits. Evidence must be provided that a mentor/adviser agrees to work with the applicant throughout the student's entire formal education process. *Application Process: Applicants should submit a completed application and all associated forms along with two letters of recommendation, a one-page letter describing their personal and professional interest in nursing and nursing education, official transcripts, a curriculum vitae, and a letter of acceptance to nursing school. Visit the association's Web site to download an application. *Amount: $25,000. *Deadline: September 30.

American Association of Neuroscience Nurses/ Neuroscience Nursing Foundation (NNF)
NNF Scholarship Program
4700 West Lake Avenue
Glenview, IL 60025

888-557-2266
info@aann.org
http://www.aann.org/nnf

Scholarship Name: NNF Scholarship Program. *Academic Area: Nursing (neuroscience). *Age Group: Undergraduate students. *Eligibility: Applicants must be registered nurses pursuing studies to advance careers in neuroscience nursing at the undergraduate level. Applicants must also maintain a minimum 3.0 GPA. A graduate scholarship is also available. *Application Process: Applicants must submit one copy of application Form A and four copies of Form B and supporting materials. Supporting materials include a letter of acceptance or evidence of enrollment in the school applicants are attending or plan to attend, official transcripts, copy of current specialty certification card(s), copy of current RN license, resume, and personal statement. Visit the foundation's Web site to download an application. *Amount: $1,500. *Deadline: January 15.

American College of Nurse-Midwives (ACNM) Foundation
Basic Midwifery Student Scholarship
8403 Colesville Road, Suite 1550
Silver Spring, MD 20910
240-485-1800
http://www.midwife.org/support.cfm?id=274

Scholarship Name: Basic Midwifery Student Scholarship. *Academic Area: Nursing (midwifery). *Age Group: Undergraduate students. *Eligibility: Applicants must be enrolled in an accredited basic midwifery program and have successfully completed one semester or module. They must also be members of ACNM, show academic achievement, and demonstrate financial need. *Application Process: Applicants must submit a completed application, a brief statement of career goals and plans, a financial assessment form, a statement of financial need, and one letter of recommendation from a faculty member. Applicant's program director must also complete the Program Director Form. Visit the foundation's Web site to download an application. *Amount: Varies. *Deadline: March 18.

American College of Nurse-Midwives (ACNM) Foundation
8403 Colesville Road, Suite 1550
Silver Spring, MD 20910
240-485-1800

http://www.midwife.org/support.cfm?id=275

Scholarship Name: Mary Keller Scholarship Fund Award. *Academic Area: Nursing (midwifery). *Age Group: Undergraduate students. *Eligibility: Applicants must be current residents of Michigan, enrolled in the nurse-midwife program at Case Western Reserve University, and agree to submit a data collection form to the ACNM Foundation within one year of scholarship award. They must also be members of ACNM, show academic achievement, and demonstrate financial need. *Application Process: Applicants must submit a completed application, a brief statement of their career goals and plans, a financial assessment form, a statement of financial need, and one letter of recommendation from a faculty member. Visit the college's Web site to download an application. *Amount: Awards vary. *Deadline: March 18.

American Dental Association (ADA) Foundation
211 East Chicago Avenue
Chicago, IL 60611
312-440-2547
adaf@ada.org
http://www.ada.org/ada/prod/adaf/prog_scholarship_prog.asp

Scholarship Name: Allied Dental Health Scholarship - Dental Hygiene. *Academic Area: Medicine (dental hygiene). *Age Group: Undergraduate students. *Eligibility: Applicants must be entering their final year of study and currently attending a dental hygiene program accredited by the Commission on Dental Accreditation, maintain a minimum grade point average of 3.0 on a 4.0 scale, and demonstrate a minimum financial need of at least $1,000. *Application Process: Applicants must submit a completed application along with Academic Achievement Record Form and Financial Needs Assessment Form signed by school officials, a copy of the school's letter of acceptance, and two completed reference forms. Applicants must also submit a typed, biographical sketch questionnaire. Application forms for all ADA foundation scholarships are available at dental schools and allied dental health programs and are disbursed by school officials. *Amount: Up to $1,000. *Deadline: August 15.

American Dental Hygienists' Association (ADHA)
ADHA Institute for Oral Health
Scholarship Award Program

444 North Michigan Avenue, Suite 3400
Chicago, IL 60611
800-735-4916
institute@adha.net
http://www.adha.org/institute/Scholarship/index.htm
Scholarship Name: American Dental Hygienists'
Association Institute for Oral Health Scholarship
Program. *Academic Area: Medicine (dental hygiene).
*Age Group: College sophomores, juniors, and
seniors. *Eligibility: Applicants should be enrolled in
accredited dental hygiene programs in the United
States and have completed at least one year in the
program and a minimum 3.0 GPA on a 4.0 scale.
Applicants should also be active members of the
Student American Dental Hygienists' Association or
the ADHA. Documented financial need of at least
$1,500 is required. The scholarship is also available to
graduate students. *Application Process: Applicants
should submit a completed application along with
all required supporting materials. Visit the institute's
Web site for a detailed listing of required materials.
A downloadable application is also available via
the institute's Web site. *Amount: $1,000 to $2,000.
*Deadline: June 30.

American Foundation for Pharmaceutical Education
One Church Street, Suite 202
Rockville, MD 20850
301-738-2160
afpe@att.net
http://www.afpenet.org/programs.htm
Scholarship Name: American Foundation for
Pharmaceutical Education Gateway To Research
Scholarship.*Academic Area: Pharmaceutical
science. *Age Group: Undergraduate students.
*Eligibility: Applicants must be enrolled in a
baccalaureate degree program and have completed
at least one year of the degree program. All
applicants must be enrolled for at least one
full academic year after initiation of the award.
Applicants must be nominated by faculty in a
school of pharmacy accredited by the American
Council on Pharmaceutical Education or faculty
in any college awarding baccalaureate degrees
who are actively undertaking research in the
pharmaceutical sciences. Applicants must be U.S.
citizens or permanent residents. The scholarship is
also available to pharmacy preprofessional degree
students. *Application Process: Applicants must
submit a completed application, a copy of their

faculty advisor's curriculum vitae, official transcripts,
a letter of intent, and two completed Statements of
Recommendation and Evaluation Forms. Visit the
foundation's Web site to download an application
and required forms. *Amount: $4,000. *Deadline:
January 27.

American Health Care Association
Attn: Adrienne Riaz-Khan
1201 L Street, NW
Washington, DC 20005
202-898-6332
http://www.ahca.org/about/scholarship.htm
Scholarship Name: James D. Durante Nurse
Scholarship. *Academic Area: Nursing (assisted
living). *Age Group: Undergraduate students.
*Eligibility: Applicants must work for a long-term
care facility that is a member of the American Health
Care Association or the National Center for Assisted
Living, and be enrolled in/accepted to an accredited
LPN or RN school of nursing program. *Application
Process: Applicants must submit a completed
application, three letters of recommendation, and
a personal statement. Contact the association to
obtain an application and for further application
details. *Amount: $500. *Deadline: Varies.

**American Health Information Management
Association (AHIMA) Foundation of Research and
Education (FORE)**
233 North Michigan Avenue, Suite 2150
Chicago, IL 60601-5800
312-233-1131
info@ahima.org
http://www.ahima.org/fore/programs.asp
Scholarship Name: FORE Merit Scholarship. *Academic
Area: Medicine (information management). *Age
Group: Undergraduate students. *Eligibility:
Applicants must have at least one full semester of
classes remaining in their course of study at the time
the award is granted. Applicants must be members
of AHIMA and maintain a minimum 3.0 GPA.
Applicants must also demonstrate a commitment
to volunteerism and the health information
management profession. The scholarship is also
available to graduate students. *Application Process:
Applicants should submit a completed application
along with transcripts and references. An application
is available for download each January at the
foundation's Web site. *Amount: $1,000 to $5,000.

*Deadline: Contact the foundation for deadline information.

American Holistic Nurses Association (AHNA)

AHNA Headquarters
PO Box 2130
Flagstaff, AZ 86003-2130
800-278-2462, ext. 10
info@ahna.org
http://www.ahna.org/edu/assist.html
Scholarship Name: Charlotte McGuire Scholarship. *Academic Area: Nursing (holistic). *Age Group: Undergraduate students. *Eligibility: Applicants must be pursuing a holistic nursing education and maintain a minimum 3.0 GPA. Applicants must have experience and interest in healing and holistic nursing practice. They must also be current members of AHNA. The scholarship is also available to graduate students. *Application Process: Applicants must submit a completed application, a financial statement, official transcripts, an essay, and two sponsorship letters. Visit the association's Web site to download an application. *Amount: Varies. *Deadline: March 15.

American Horticultural Therapy Association (AHTA)

3570 East 12th Avenue, Suite 206
Denver, CO 80206
303-322-2482, 800-634-1603
http://www.ahta.org/grantsAwards/awards.html
Scholarship Name: Ann Lane Mavromatis Scholarship. *Academic Area: Therapy (horticulture). *Age Group: Undergraduate students. *Eligibility: Applicants should have a declared major in the field of horticultural therapy or a related field with course work supporting the field of horticultural therapy, membership in the AHTA, a high level of academic achievement, evidence of financial need, and personal involvement in horticultural therapy through contribution to the development of the horticultural therapy program at their college or university or through participation in extracurricular horticultural therapy activities with a local, state, or national horticultural therapy organization. The scholarship is also available to graduate students. *Application Process: Initial nominations must be made by July. Nomination forms are available on the association's Web site in May of each year. Visit the association's Web site to download a nomination form. After being nominated, a follow-up

application, requesting more detailed and specific information, will be sent directly to the applicant. *Amount: $500. *Deadline: Contact the association for specific deadline information.

American Kinesiotherapy Association (AKTA)

Attn: J. T. Magee Jr.
Scholarship Committee Chairman
1816 Maple Shade Lane
Richmond, VA 23227
800-296-2582
ccbkt@aol.com
http://www.akta.org/scholarship.htm
Scholarship Name: Lou Montalvano Memorial Scholarship. *Academic Area: Medicine (kinesiotherapy). *Age Group: Undergraduate. *Eligibility: Applicants must demonstrate academic excellence, exceptional promise as clinicians and educators, intention to pursue certification and careers in kinesiotherapy, and potential for professional leadership. They must be currently enrolled as undergraduate students in an association-accredited kinesiotherapy program and current members of the AKTA. The scholarship is also available to graduate students *Application Process: Applicants must submit a completed application, a cover letter, three recommendation forms, and official transcripts. Visit the association's Web site to download an application and recommendation forms. *Amount: $500. *Deadline: May 1.

American Medical Technologists (AMT)

710 Higgins Road
Park Ridge, IL 60068-5765
800-275-1268
http://www.amt1.com/site/epage/9668_315.htm
Scholarship Name: American Medical Technologists Member Scholarship. *Academic Area: Medicine (medical technology). *Age Group: Undergraduate students. *Eligibility: Applicant must be a member of the AMT and enrolled in a school accredited by an accrediting agency recognized by the U.S. Department of Education. Applicant's course of study must lead to a career in a discipline certified by AMT. Applicants must also provide evidence of financial need or career goals. *Application Process: Applicants must submit a completed application, official transcripts, two letters of personal reference, and a personal statement. Visit the organization's

Web site to download an application. *Amount: One $2,500 and three $1,000 scholarships. *Deadline: April 1.

American Medical Technologists (AMT)

710 Higgins Road
Park Ridge, IL 60068-5765
800-275-1268
http://www.amt1.com/site/epage/9664_315.htm
Scholarship Name: American Medical Technologists Student Scholarship. *Academic Area: Medicine (medical technology). *Age Group: Undergraduate students. *Eligibility: Applicant must be enrolled in a school accredited by an accrediting agency recognized by the U.S. Department of Education. Applicant's course of study must lead to a career in a discipline certified by AMT. Applicants must also provide evidence of financial need or career goals. High school seniors may apply. *Application Process: Applicants must submit a completed application, official transcripts, two letters of personal reference, and a personal statement. Visit the organization's Web site to download an application. *Amount: $500. *Deadline: April 1.

American Psychiatric Nurses Association (APNA)

1555 Wilson Boulevard, Suite 602
Arlington, VA 22209
703-243-2443
arushton@apna.org
http://www.apna.org/awards/janssenprogram.html
Scholarship Name: Janssen Student Scholarship Program. *Academic Area: Nursing (psychiatric). *Age Group: Undergraduate students. *Eligibility: Applicants must be nursing students pursuing studies in psychiatric mental health care. Graduate students may also apply. Contact the association for full eligibility requirements. *Application Process: Contact APNA in December for specific details about the scholarship. *Amount: Awards vary. *Deadline: Contact APNA for details.

American School Health Association

Attn: Pamela Dean
7263 State Route 43
PO Box 708
Kent, OH 44240
330-678-1601
pdean@ashaweb.org
http://www.ashaweb.org/pdfs/scholapp05.pdf

Scholarship Name: American School Health Association Scholarship. *Academic Area: Medicine (pediatric or adolescent dentistry or medicine, school health education, school nursing. *Age Group: Undergraduate students. *Eligibility: Applicants must be college juniors or seniors enrolled full-time at an institute of higher education and maintain at least a 3.0 GPA. Applicants must have declared a major in school health education, school nursing, or pediatric or adolescent medicine or dentistry. Applicants with other school health specializations will be considered only if accompanied by a letter from the applicant's academic advisor stating the program's relationship to school health. The scholarship is also available to graduate students. *Application Process: Applicants must submit one original and seven copies of a completed application, resume, transcripts, personal statement, and three letters of recommendation. *Amount: $500. *Deadline: April 4.

American Society for Clinical Laboratory Science

Attn: Joe Briden, Scholarship Coordinator
7809 South 21st Drive
Phoenix, AZ 85041-7736
301-657-2768
http://www.ascls.org/leadership/awards/amt.asp
Scholarship Name: Alpha Mu Tau Undergraduate Scholarship. *Academic Area: Medicine (clinical laboratory science). *Age Group: Undergraduate students. *Eligibility: Applicants must be college juniors or seniors and U.S. citizens attending a National Accrediting Agency for Clinical Laboratory Sciences-accredited undergraduate clinical laboratory science program. They must be in, or entering into, their last year of study when the scholarship is awarded. *Application Process: Applicants must submit a completed application, letter of admission to program, two performance sheets, two letters of recommendation, a personal objectives statement, and transcripts. Original applications should be submitted along with four photocopies. Visit the society's Web site to download an application. *Amount: Up to $1,500. *Deadline: April 1.

American Society for Clinical Laboratory Science

Attn: Joe Briden, Scholarship Coordinator
7809 South 21st Drive
Phoenix, AZ 85041-7736

301-657-2768
http://www.ascls.org/leadership/awards/amt.asp
Scholarship Name: Dorothy Morrison Undergraduate Scholarship. *Academic Area: Medicine (clinical laboratory science). *Age Group: Undergraduate students. *Eligibility: Applicants must be college juniors or seniors and U.S. citizens attending a National Accrediting Agency for Clinical Laboratory Sciences-accredited undergraduate clinical laboratory science program, and in or entering their last year of study. *Application Process: Applicants must submit a completed application, the letter of admission to program, two performance sheets, two letters of recommendation, a 500-word personal objectives statement, and transcripts. Original applications should be submitted along with four photocopies. Visit the society's Web site to download an application. *Amount: Up to $2,000. *Deadline: April 1.

American Society for Clinical Laboratory Science
Attn: Joe Briden, Scholarship Coordinator
7809 South 21st Drive
Phoenix, AZ 85041-7736
301-657-2768
http://www.ascls.org/leadership/awards/amt.asp
Scholarship Name: Ruth M. French Undergraduate Scholarship. *Academic Area: Medicine (clinical laboratory science). *Age Group: Undergraduate students. *Eligibility: Applicants must be college juniors or seniors and U.S. citizens attending a National Accrediting Agency for Clinical Laboratory Sciences-accredited undergraduate clinical laboratory science program. They must not complete their study before the award date of the scholarship. The scholarship is also available to graduate students. *Application Process: Applicants must submit a completed application, the letter of admission to program, two performance sheets, two letters of recommendation, a personal objectives statement, and transcripts. Original applications should be submitted along with four photocopies. Visit the society's Web site to download an application. *Amount: Up to $3,000. *Deadline: April 1.

American Society for Clinical Pathology (ASCP)
Dade Behring Student Scholarship Program
2100 West Harrison Street
Chicago, IL 60612
312-738-1336

info@ascp.org
http://www.ascp.org/careerlinks/scholarships/default.aspx
Scholarship Name: Dade Behring Scholarship. *Academic Area: Medicine (medical technology). *Age Group: Undergraduate students. *Eligibility: Applicants must be enrolled in their third or fourth and final clinical year of education in a medical technologist program. To be eligible for these scholarships, applicants must be enrolled in a National Accrediting Agency for Clinical Laboratory Sciences-accredited program, be either a U.S. citizen or a permanent resident, and maintain a minimum GPA of 2.5 on a 4.0 scale. They must also demonstrate leadership skills and a commitment to community service. *Application Process: Applicants should submit a completed application along with official transcripts, three letters of recommendation, a 500-word essay, a list of community activities and leadership experiences, and two self-addressed, stamped legal-sized envelopes. Visit the society's Web site to download an application. *Amount: $2,500. *Deadline: November 11.

American Society for Clinical Pathology (ASCP)
33 West Monroe, Suite 1600
Chicago, IL 60603
312-541-4999, 800-267-2727
info@ascp.org
http://www.ascp.org/careerlinks/scholarships/default.aspx
Scholarship Name: ASCP Phlebotomy Scholarship. *Academic Area: Medicine (phlebotomy). *Age Group: Undergraduate students. *Eligibility: Applicants must be enrolled in or recent graduates of (within the past six months) a National Accrediting Agency for Clinical Laboratory Sciences-approved phlebotomy training program, which is also approved by the applicant's state department of health sciences. The program must meet the BOR Route 2 eligibility criteria. Applicants also must demonstrate leadership skills and a commitment to community service. *Application Process: Applicants should submit a completed application along with two letters of recommendation, a 500-word essay, a list of their community activities and leadership experiences, and two self-addressed, stamped legal-sized envelopes. Visit the society's Web site in the summer to download an application. *Amount: $500. *Deadline: November 1.

American Society for Clinical Pathology (ASCP)
33 West Monroe, Suite 1600
Chicago, IL 60603
312-541-4999, 800-267-2727
info@ascp.org
http://www.ascp.org/careerlinks/scholarships/default.
    aspx
Scholarship Name: ASCP Scholarship and Roche
    Diagnostics Scholarship: *Academic Area: Medicine
    (laboratory science). *Age Group: Undergraduate
    students. *Eligibility: Applicants must be in their
    final clinical year of study in cytotechnologist,
    histotechnician, histotechnologist, medical
    laboratory technician, or medical technologist
    programs. Applicants must be enrolled in a
    National Accrediting Agency for Clinical Laboratory
    Sciences- or Commission on Accreditation of Allied
    Health Education Programs-accredited laboratory
    science program, be either a United States citizen
    or a permanent resident, and maintain a minimum
    GPA of 3.0 GPA on a 4.0 scale. He or she must also
    demonstrate leadership skills and a commitment to
    community service. *Application Process: Applicants
    should submit a completed application along with
    official transcripts, three letters of recommendation,
    a 500-word essay, list of their community activities
    and leadership experiences, and two self-addressed,
    stamped legal-sized envelopes. Visit the society's
    Web site in the summer to download an application.
    *Amount: $1,000 to $2,000. *Deadline: November 1.

**American Society of Electroneurodiagnostic
    Technologists**
Attn: Sheila R. Davis, Executive Director
426 West 42nd Street
Kansas City, MO 64111
816-931-1120
sheila@aset.org
http://www.aset.org/foundation/education_
    scholarships.php
Grant Name: American Society of Electroneurodiagnostic
    Technologists Foundation Student Education Grant.
    *Academic Area: Medicine (electroneurodiagnostic
    technology). *Age Group: Undergraduate
    students. *Eligibility: Applicants must be enrolled
    full-time in a Commission on Accreditation of
    Allied Health Education Programs-accredited
    electroneurodiagnostic (END) school or already
    employed in the END field. Applicants must plan
    on attending a continuing education program or a

two- or four-year college offering END programs.
They must also display scholastic achievement
and interest in serving as future faculty in the END
profession. Early career professionals are also eligible
to apply. *Application Process: Applicants must
submit a completed application, personal statement,
outline of proposed program of study, official copies
of transcripts, and two letters of recommendation.
*Amount: Up to $1,500. *Deadline: July 1.

**American Society of Radiologic Technologists (ASRT)
    Education and Research Foundation**
Scholarship Program
15000 Central Avenue, SE
Albuquerque, NM 87123-3917
800-444-2778, ext. 2541
foundation@asrt.org
http://www.asrt.org/content/ASRTFoundation/
    AwardsandScholarships/Awards_Scholarships.aspx
Scholarship Name: Elekta Radiation Therapy Educators
    Scholarship Program. *Academic Area: Medicine
    (education, radiologic sciences). *Age Group:
    Undergraduate students. *Eligibility: Applicants
    must be educator therapists who are pursuing a
    baccalaureate degree to enhance their position
    as a program director, faculty member, clinical
    coordinator, or clinical instructor. They must be
    graduates of an accredited program in radiation
    therapy. Applicants must also be current ASRT
    members and registered by the American Registry
    of Radiologic Technologists (ARRT), or hold an
    unrestricted state license. Applicants must have
    worked in a clinical or didactic setting as a radiation
    therapy educator for at least one of the past five
    years. The scholarship is also available to graduate
    students. *Application Process: Applicants must
    submit a completed application, a written applicant
    interview, two completed evaluation forms, a
    resume, letter verifying employment as a radiation
    therapy educator for at least one of the past five
    years, and a copy of their current ARRT card or
    unrestricted state license. Visit the society's Web site
    to download an application and evaluation forms.
    *Amount: $5,000. *Deadline: February 1.

**American Society of Radiologic Technologists (ASRT)
    Education and Research Foundation**
Scholarship Program
15000 Central Avenue, SE
Albuquerque, NM 87123-3917

800-444-2778, ext. 2541

foundation@asrt.org

http://www.asrt.org/content/ASRTFoundation/
AwardsandScholarships/Awards_Scholarships.aspx

Scholarship Name: Jeanette C. and Isadore N. Stern Scholarship. *Academic Area: Medicine (education, medicine [management], medicine [radiologic sciences]). *Age Group: Undergraduate students. *Eligibility: Applicants must have applied to an accredited certificate program related to radiologic sciences or plan to pursue an associate or baccalaureate degree in radiologic sciences. They must be graduates of an accredited program in the radiologic sciences. Applicants must also be current ASRT members and registered by the American Registry of Radiologic Technologists (ARRT), or hold an unrestricted state license. They must have worked in a clinical or didactic setting in the radiologic sciences profession for at least one of the past five years. The scholarship is also available to graduate students. *Application Process: Applicants must submit a completed application, a written applicant interview, two completed evaluation forms, a resume, a letter verifying employment as a radiation therapy educator for at least one of the past five years, and a copy of their current ARRT card or unrestricted state license. Visit the society's Web site to download an application and evaluation forms. *Amount: Up to $1,000. *Deadline: February 1.

American Society of Radiologic Technologists (ASRT) Education and Research Foundation

Scholarship Program

15000 Central Avenue, SE

Albuquerque, NM 87123-3917

800-444-2778, ext. 2541

foundation@asrt.org

http://www.asrt.org/content/ASRTFoundation/
AwardsandScholarships/Awards_Scholarships.aspx

Scholarship Name: Jerman-Cahoon Student Scholarship. *Academic Area: Medicine (radiologic science). *Age Group: Undergraduate students. *Eligibility: Applicants must be currently enrolled in an entry-level radiologic sciences program. Applicants must be U.S. citizens, nationals, or permanent residents. Applicants must also have maintained a 3.0 GPA and demonstrate financial need. *Application Process: Applicants must submit a completed application, official transcripts, an evaluation form, and an essay. Visit the society's

Web site to download an application and evaluation forms. *Amount: Up to $2,500. *Deadline: February 1.

American Society of Radiologic Technologists (ASRT) Education and Research Foundation

Scholarship Program

15000 Central Avenue, SE

Albuquerque, NM 87123-3917

800-444-2778, ext. 2541

foundation@asrt.org

http://www.asrt.org/content/ASRTFoundation/
AwardsandScholarships/Awards_Scholarships.aspx

Scholarship Name: Monster Medical Imaging Educators Scholarship Program. *Academic Area: Medicine (radiologic science). *Age Group: Undergraduate students. *Eligibility: Applicants must be educators who are pursuing their baccalaureate degree to enhance their position as a medical imaging program director, faculty member, clinical coordinator, or clinical instructor. Applicants must be graduates of an accredited program in medical imaging. Applicants must also be current ASRT members and registered by the American Registry of Radiologic Technologists (ARRT), or hold an unrestricted state license. They must have worked in a clinical or didactic setting as a medical imaging educator for at least one of the past five years. The scholarship is also available to graduate students. *Application Process: Applicants must submit a completed application, a written applicant interview, two completed evaluation forms, a resume, a letter verifying employment as a radiation therapy educator for at least one of the past five years, and a copy of current ARRT card or unrestricted state license. Visit the society's Web site to download an application and evaluation forms. *Amount: $5,000. *Deadline: February 1.

American Society of Radiologic Technologists (ASRT) Education and Research Foundation

Scholarship Program

15000 Central Avenue, SE

Albuquerque, NM 87123-3917

800-444-2778, ext. 2541

foundation@asrt.org

http://www.asrt.org/content/ASRTFoundation/
AwardsandScholarships/Awards_Scholarships.aspx

Scholarship Name: Siemens Clinical Advancement Scholarship. *Academic Area: Medicine (radiologic science). *Age Group: Undergraduate students. *Eligibility: Applicants must have applied to an accredited certificate program related to radiologic sciences or plan to study for an associate or baccalaureate degree with the intention of furthering their clinical practice in radiologic sciences. Applicants must be graduates of an accredited program in the radiologic sciences, current ASRT members and registered by the American Registry of Radiologic Technologists (ARRT), or hold an unrestricted state license. Applicants must have worked in a clinical or didactic setting in the radiologic sciences profession for at least one of the past five years. The scholarship is also available to graduate students. *Application Process: Applicants must submit a completed application, written applicant interview, two completed evaluation forms, a resume, a letter verifying employment as a radiation therapy educator for at least one of the past five years, and a copy of current ARRT card or unrestricted state license. Visit the society's Web site to download an application and evaluation forms. *Amount: $3,000. *Deadline: February 1.

American Society of Radiologic Technologists (ASRT) Education and Research Foundation
Scholarship Program
15000 Central Avenue, SE
Albuquerque, NM 87123-3917
800-444-2778, ext. 2541
foundation@asrt.org
http://www.asrt.org/content/ASRTFoundation/ AwardsandScholarships/Awards_Scholarships.aspx
Scholarship Name: Varian Radiation Therapy Student Scholarship. *Academic Area: Medicine (radiologic science). *Age Group: Undergraduate students. *Eligibility: Applicants must be enrolled in an entry-level radiation therapy program. They must be U.S. citizens, nationals, or permanent residents. Applicants must also have maintained a 3.0 GPA, specifically in radiation therapy core curriculum, and demonstrate financial need. *Application Process: Applicants must submit a completed application, official transcripts, evaluation form, and an essay. Visit the society's Web site to download an application and evaluation form. *Amount: $5,000. *Deadline: February 1.

Association of Perioperative Registered Nurses Foundation
Attn: Ingrid Bendzsa
2170 South Parker Road, Suite 300

Denver, CO 80231-5711
800-755-2676, ext. 328
ibendzsa@aorn.org
http://www.aorn.org/foundation/scholarships.asp
Scholarship Name: Association of Perioperative Registered Nurses Foundation Scholarship. *Academic Area: Nursing (perioperative). *Age Group: Undergraduate students. *Eligibility: Applicants must be pursuing a bachelor's degree in perioperative nursing. Applicants must maintain a 3.0 out of 4.0 GPA and demonstrate financial need. The scholarship is also available to graduate students. *Application Process: Applicants should submit a completed application along with transcripts. Visit the foundation's Web site for additional application procedures. Applications are available for download from the foundation's Web site beginning in January of each year. *Amount: Awards vary. *Deadline: May 1.

Association of Surgical Technologists (AST)
Scholarship Department
6 West Dry Creek Circle
Littleton, CO 80120
800-637-7433
Kfrey@ast.org
http://www.ast.org/Content/Education/Scholarships.htm
Scholarship Name: AST National Honor Society Scholarship. *Academic Area: Medicine (surgery). *Age Group: Undergraduate students. *Eligibility: Applicants must be members of the AST National Honor Society and in the process of or beginning the process of completing a Commission on Accreditation of Allied Health Education Programs-accredited surgical assisting program. Applicants must also maintain at least a minimum 3.0 GPA. *Application Process: Applicants must submit a completed application and resume. Visit the association's Web site to download an application. *Amount: $1,000. *Deadline: September 1.

Association of Surgical Technologists (AST)
Scholarship Department
Foundation for Surgical Technology
6 West Dry Creek Circle
Littleton, CO 80120
800-637-7433
Kfrey@ast.org
http://www.ast.org/Content/Education/Scholarships.htm
Scholarship Name: Foundation for Surgical Technology Advanced Education Scholarship/Medical Mission

Scholarship. *Academic Area: Medicine (surgery). *Age Group: Undergraduate students. *Eligibility: Applicants must be active AST members who are pursuing advanced surgical technology education or who are seeking to perform medical missionary work. *Application Process: Applicants must submit a completed application, documented history of their AST involvement, official documentation of their education or mission program (including official course outline, fees, and transcripts, if applicable), and two letters of recommendation. Visit the association's Web site to download an application. *Amount: Varies. *Deadline: Varies.

Association of Surgical Technologists (AST)

Scholarship Department
Foundation for Surgical Technology
6 West Dry Creek Circle
Littleton, CO 80120
800-637-7433
Kfrey@ast.org
http://www.ast.org/Content/Education/Scholarships.htm

Scholarship Name: Foundation for Surgical Technology Surgical Technology Student Scholarship. *Academic Area: Medicine (surgery). *Age Group: Undergraduate students. *Eligibility: Applicants must be currently enrolled in a surgical technology program accredited by the Commission on Accreditation of Allied Health Education Programs. Applicants must demonstrate superior academic ability and have financial need. *Application Process: Applicants must submit a completed application, official transcripts, an instructor evaluation form, and mentor section. Applicants should submit their applications to their instructor, who will complete the instructor evaluation form and return the complete application packet to the Foundation for Surgical Technology. Visit the AST's Web site to download an application and required forms. *Amount: Varies. *Deadline: April 1.

Association of Surgical Technologists (AST)

Scholarship Department
6 West Dry Creek Circle
Littleton, CO 80120
800-637-7433
Kfrey@ast.org
http://www.ast.org/Content/Education/Scholarships.htm

Scholarship Name: Thomson Delmar Learning Surgical Technology Scholarship. *Academic Area: Medicine (surgery). *Age Group: Undergraduate students. *Eligibility: Applicants must submit evidence of enrollment in a Commission on Accreditation of Allied Health Education Programs-accredited program or of acceptance into the program. They must also maintain at least a 2.5 GPA. *Application Process: Applicants must submit a completed application and personal statement. Visit the association's Web site to download an application. *Amount: $1,000. *Deadline: April 1.

Association of Zoo Veterinary Technicians

Laurie Page-Peck Scholarship Fund
Attn: Sarah Snead
The Wildlife Center of Virginia
PO Box 1557
Waynesboro, VA 24431
540-942-9453
vettech@wildlifecenter.org
http://www.azvt.org/azvteducation.htm

Scholarship Name: Laurie Page-Peck Scholarship Fund. *Academic Area: Medicine (veterinary and medical technology). *Age Group: Undergraduate students. *Eligibility: Applicants must be veterinary or medical technology students with an active interest in zoo veterinary technology. Applicants submitting papers for the scholarship must be enrolled in a veterinary or medical technology program or in an internship or other learning situation. If the applicant is enrolled in a veterinary technician program in the United States, the program must be accredited by the American Veterinary Medical Association. *Application Process: Applicants must submit topic proposals to the scholarship committee for approval. Proposals must be made in abstract form (200 words or less). Contact Sarah Snead at The Wildlife Center of Virginia for further application details. *Amount: Up to $1,000. *Deadline: Varies.

Daughters of the American Revolution (DAR)

Attn: Scholarships
1776 D Street, NW
Washington, DC 20006-5303
202-628-1776
http://www.dar.org/natsociety/edout_scholar.cfm

Scholarship Name: Madeline Pickett (Halbert) Cogswell Nursing Scholarship. *Academic Area: Nursing (open). *Age Group: Undergraduate students. *Eligibility: Applicants must be citizens of the United States who are accepted or enrolled in an accredited nursing school in the United States. They also must demonstrate financial need and be members, descendents of members, or eligible for membership in the DAR. *Application Process: All applicants must obtain a letter of sponsorship from their local DAR chapter. Applicants should send a stamped, self-addressed business size envelope to obtain the name and address of their state scholarship chairman and an application. Visit the organization's Web site for the mailing address. *Amount: $500. *Deadline: February 15, August 15.

Daughters of the American Revolution (DAR)
Attn: Scholarships
1776 D Street, NW
Washington, DC 20006-5303
202-628-1776
http://www.dar.org/natsociety/edout_scholar.cfm
Scholarship Name: Mildred Nutting Nursing Scholarship. *Academic Area: Nursing (open). *Age Group: Undergraduate students. *Eligibility: Applicants must be citizens of the United States who are attending an accredited school of nursing in the United States. Preference will be given to candidates from the greater Lowell, Massachusetts area. *Application Process: All applicants must obtain a letter of sponsorship from their local DAR chapter. Applicants should send a stamped, self-addressed business size envelope to obtain the name and address of their state scholarship chairman and an application. Visit the organization's Web site for the mailing address. *Amount: $500. *Deadline: February 15, August 15.

Daughters of the American Revolution (DAR)
Attn: Scholarships
1776 D Street, NW
Washington, DC 20006-5303
202-628-1776
http://www.dar.org/natsociety/edout_scholar.cfm
Scholarship Name: Occupational/Physical Therapy Scholarship. *Academic Area: Therapy (art), therapy (music), therapy (occupational), therapy (physical). *Age Group: Undergraduate students. *Eligibility: Citizens of the United States who are attending an accredited school of occupational therapy (including art, music, or physical therapy) in the United States may apply. Applicants must demonstrate financial need. *Application Process: All applicants must obtain a letter of sponsorship from their local

DAR chapter. Applicants should send a stamped, self-addressed business size envelope to obtain the name and address of their state scholarship chairman and an application. Visit the organization's Web site for the mailing address. *Amount: $500. *Deadline: February 15, August 15.

Emergency Nurses Association
915 Lee Street
Des Plaines, IL 60016-6569
847-460-4004, 800-900-9659
foundation@ena.org
http://www.ena.org/foundation/grants
Scholarship Name: Emergency Nurses Association Foundation Scholarship. *Academic Area: Nursing (emergency care). *Age Group: Undergraduate students. *Eligibility: Visit the association's Web site for updates on eligibility requirements. Information is posted in December of each year. The scholarship is also available to graduate students. *Application Process: Applicants should contact the association for further information, or visit its Web site in late December. *Amount: Awards vary. *Deadline: Contact the association for deadline information.

Foundation of the National Student Nurses' Association (FNSNA)
45 Main Street, Suite 606
Brooklyn, NY 11201
718-210-0705
http://www.nsna.org
Scholarship Name: FNSNA Nursing Student Scholarship. *Academic Area: Nursing (general). *Age Group: Undergraduate students. *Eligibility: Applicants must be U.S. citizens currently enrolled in state-approved schools of nursing or pre-nursing in associate degree, baccalaureate, or diploma programs. Awards are based on academic achievement, financial need, and involvement in nursing student organizations and community activities related to health care. Graduating high school seniors are not eligible. The scholarship is also available to graduate students. *Application Process: Applicants must submit a completed application, along with official transcripts and a $10 processing fee. The application is available from August though January at the association's Web site. *Amount: Scholarships range from $1,000 to $5,000. *Deadline: January 13.

Health Occupations Students of America (HOSA)
6021 Morriss Road, Suite 111
Flower Mound, TX 75028
800-321-HOSA
http://www.hosa.org/member/scholar.html
Scholarship Name: Health Occupations Students of America Scholarship. *Academic Area: Medicine (open). *Age Group: Undergraduate students. *Eligibility: Applicants must be enrolled in a health occupations/health science education program and be a member of HOSA. *Application Process: Applicants must submit a completed application; transcripts; proof of acceptance; a list of leadership activities, awards, and community involvement; three letters of recommendation; and a personal statement. Visit HOSA's Web site to download an application. *Amount: Varies. *Deadline: April 15.

International Order of the King's Daughters and Sons
Attn: Director, Health Careers Scholarship Department
PO Box 1040
Chautauqua, NY 14722-1040
716-357-4951
iokds5@alltel.net
http://www.iokds.org/scholarship.html
Scholarship Name: Health Careers Scholarship. *Academic Area: Medicine (open). *Age Group: Undergraduate students. *Eligibility: Applicants must be U.S. or Canadian citizens enrolled full-time at an accredited college/university. Applicants must be preparing for careers in medicine, dentistry, nursing, pharmacy, physical or occupational therapy, and medical technologies. R.N. students must have completed their first year of schooling. Pre-med students are not eligible to apply. Applicants seeking M.D. or D.D.S. degrees must apply for at least the second year of medical or dental school. The scholarship is also available to graduate students. *Application Process: Contact the order for further application details and to request an application. *Amount: $1,000. *Deadline: April 1.

Michigan Association of Nurse Anesthetists
Attn: Mary Collins
c/o American Association of Nurse Anesthetists (AANA)
   Foundation
222 South Prospect Avenue
Park Ridge, IL 60068-4011
847-692-7050
mcollins@aana.com

http://www.miana.org/scholarships/grant_application.
   doc
Scholarship Name: Al Jarvis Research Scholarship. *Academic Area: Nursing (anesthesia). *Age Group: Undergraduate students. *Eligibility: Applicants must be members of the AANA, enrolled in a nurse anesthesia educational program in Michigan, and be in good academic standing. The scholarship is also available to graduate students. *Application Process: Applicants must submit a completed abstract, a copy of institutional investigation committee/review board approval, a letter of support from their research advisor or program director, and an estimate of the anticipated value of their research findings to nurse anesthesia. Visit the association's Web site for detailed information about the abstract and application process. *Amount: $2,500. *Deadline: August 1.

National Environmental Health Association (NEHA)/American Academy of Sanitarians (AAS)
Attn: Scholarship Coordinator, NEHA/AAS Scholarship
720 South Colorado Boulevard, Suite 970, South Tower
Denver, CO 80246-1904
303-756-9090
cdimmitt@neha.org
http://www.neha.org/scholarship/scholarship.html
Scholarship Name: National Environmental Health Association/American Academy of Sanitarians Scholarship. *Academic Area: Public health. *Age Group: Undergraduate students. *Eligibility: College juniors and seniors who are enrolled in an Environmental Health Accreditation Council (EHAC) or a NEHA Institutional/Educational or Sustaining Member school may apply. Visit the association's Web site for a list of accredited programs and/or schools. The scholarship is also available to graduate students. *Application Process: Applicants must submit a completed application along with official transcripts, two faculty letters of recommendation, and one letter of recommendation from an active NEHA member. Visit the association's Web site to download an application. *Amount: $1,000. *Deadline: February 1.

National Gerontological Nursing Association
7794 Grow Drive
Pensacola, FL 32514
800-723-0560
ngna@puetzamc.com

http://http://www.ngna.org/pdfs/MOP%20Scholarship.
pdf

Scholarship Name: Mary Opal Wolanin Undergraduate
Scholarship. *Academic Area: Nursing (gerontology).
*Age Group: Undergraduate students. *Eligibility:
Applicants must be enrolled full or part time in a
nationally accredited U.S. school of nursing and
maintain at least a 3.0 GPA. Applicants must also
intend to work in a gerontology/geriatric setting
after graduation. Graduate students may also
apply for the scholarship. *Application Process:
Applicants must submit a completed application,
two letters of recommendation, official transcripts, a
personal statement no longer than 300 words, and a
statement of financial support. Visit the association's
Web site to download an application. *Amount:
$1,500. *Deadline: June 1.

National Health Service Corps
2099 Gaither Road, Suite 600
Rockville, MD 20850
800-221-9393
callcenter@hrsa.gov
http://nhsc.bhpr.hrsa.gov/join_us/scholarships.asp

Scholarship Name: National Health Service Corps
Scholarship. *Academic Area: Medicine (open).
*Age Group: Undergraduate students. *Eligibility:
Applicants must be committed to providing
primary health care in communities of greatest
need. Applicants must be U.S. citizens enrolled, or
accepted for enrollment, in a fully accredited U.S.
allopathic or osteopathic medical school, family
nurse practitioner program, nurse-midwifery
program, physician assistant program, or dental
school. The scholarship is also available to graduate
students. *Application Process: Contact the NHSC to
request an application and for further application
details. *Amount: Paid tuition and monthly stipend
for up to four years of education. *Deadline: Varies.

Oncology Nursing Society Foundation
125 Enterprise Drive
Pittsburgh, PA 15275-1214
412-859-6100
foundation@ons.org
http://onsfoundation.org/?p=12909

Scholarship Name: Oncology Nursing Society
Foundation Bachelor's Scholarship. *Academic Area:
Nursing (oncology). *Age Group: Undergraduate
students. *Eligibility: Applicants must be enrolled

in or have been accepted into a bachelor of nursing
degree program at an accredited school of nursing.
Applicants must have an interest in and commitment
to oncology nursing. Applications are accepted for
both RN and non-RN applicants, however, eligibility
requirements vary. Contact the foundation or visit
the foundation's Web site for specific eligibility
requirements. *Application Process: Applicants
must submit one original and three copies of a
completed application and transcripts, along with
a $5 application fee. Visit the foundation's Web
site to download an application. *Amount: $2,000.
*Deadline: February 1.

Pedorthic Footwear Foundation
7150 Columbia Gateway Drive, Suite G
Columbia, MD 21046-1151
info@pedorthics.org
http://www.pedorthics.org/pages.
cfm?page=scholarship.html

Scholarship Name: Pedorthic Footwear Foundation
Scholarship for Pedorthic Education. *Academic
Area: Medicine (orthotics and prosthetics,
pedorthics, podiatry). *Age Group: Undergraduate
students. *Eligibility: Applicants must be at least 18
years old and have at least a high school diploma
or equivalent. They must have prior experience
related to footwear or foot care. Applicants are
expected to sit for the certification exam within
two years of completing course work supported by
the foundation scholarship. The scholarship is also
available to medical students. *Application Process:
Applicants must submit a completed application
and three letters of recommendation. Visit the
foundation's Web site to download an application.
*Amount: Varies. *Deadline: January 15.

Society of Diagnostic Medical Sonography
2745 North Dallas Parkway, Suite 350
Plano, TX 75093-8730
214-473-8057, 800-229-9506
foundation@sdms.org
http://www.sdms.org/foundation/general.asp

Scholarship Name: Society of Diagnostic Medical
Sonography Educational Foundation General
Scholarship. *Academic Area: Medicine
(sonography). *Age Group: Undergraduate
students. *Eligibility: Applicants must attend or be
accepted in an ultrasound program accredited by
the Commission on Accreditation of Allied Health

Education Programs or the Canadian Medical Association. They must also demonstrate academic excellence and financial need. High school seniors may also apply. *Application Process: Applicants must submit a completed application, a Need Analysis Form, a copy of current Student Aid Report (SAR), and ACT/SAT scores and/or official transcripts. Visit the society's Web site to download an application. *Amount: $500. *Deadline: March 31, July 31, and November 30.

Society of Diagnostic Medical Sonography

2745 North Dallas Parkway, Suite 350
Plano, TX 75093-8730
214-473-8057, 800-229-9506
foundation@sdms.org
http://www.sdms.org/foundation/presidential.asp
Scholarship Name: Society of Diagnostic Medical Presidential Scholarship. *Academic Area: Medicine (sonography). *Age Group: Undergraduate students. *Eligibility: Applicants must display a high level of academic excellence and maintain the drive to work in the ultrasound profession. High school seniors may also apply. *Application Process: Applicants must submit a completed application, a Need Analysis Form, a copy of current Student Aid Report (SAR), and ACT/SAT scores and/or official transcripts. Visit the society's Web site to download an application. *Amount: $1,500. *Deadline: July 31.

Society of Diagnostic Medical Sonography

2745 North Dallas Parkway, Suite 350
Plano, TX 75093-8730
214-473-8057, 800-229-9506
foundation@sdms.org
http://www.sdms.org/foundation/dubinsky.asp
Scholarship Name: Trudy Dubinsky Memorial Scholarship. *Academic Area: Medicine (sonography). *Age Group: Undergraduate students. *Eligibility: Applicants must exhibit dedication, professionalism, and love of ultrasound. High school seniors may also apply. *Application Process: Applicants must submit a completed application, a Need Analysis Form, a copy of current Student Aid Report (SAR), and ACT/SAT scores and/or official transcripts. Visit the society's Web site to download an application. *Amount: Between $500 and $1,000. *Deadline: July 31.

Society of Gastroenterology Nurses and Associates (SGNA)

Attn: SGNA Awards Committee
401 North Michigan Avenue
Chicago, IL 60611-4267
312-321-5165, 800-245-7462
http://sgna.org/resources/RNadvancing.doc
Scholarship Name: Society of Gastroenterology Nurses and Associates RN Advancing Education Scholarship. *Academic Area: Nursing (gastroenterology). *Age Group: Undergraduate students. *Eligibility: Applicants must be registered nurses working in gastroenterology who are pursing advanced education (B.S.N. or higher). Applicants may be full- or part-time nursing students, and must be members of the SGNA who maintain at least a 3.0 GPA. The scholarship is also available to graduate students. *Application Process: Applicants should submit a completed application along with a 500-word essay (see application for topic), two letters of recommendation, and transcripts. This organization awards the scholarship as a reimbursement. Applicants must submit a final copy of their transcripts to verify maintenance of the required 3.0 GPA. Amount: $1,000 (part-time students), $2,500 (full-time students). *Deadline: July 31.

Society of Gastroenterology Nurses and Associates (SGNA)

Attn: SGNA Awards Committee
401 North Michigan Avenue
Chicago, IL 60611-4267
312-321-5165, 800-245-7462
http://sgna.org/resources/RNscholarship.doc
Scholarship Name: Society of Gastroenterology Nurses and Associates RN General Education Scholarship. *Academic Area: Nursing (gastroenterology). *Age Group: Undergraduate students. *Eligibility: Applicants must be full-time, currently enrolled nursing students in accredited nursing programs who are maintaining at least a 3.0 GPA. *Application Process: Applicants should submit a completed application along with a two-page typed essay (see application for topic), two letters of recommendation, and transcripts. This organization awards the scholarship as a reimbursement. Applicants must submit a final copy of their transcripts to verify that maintenance of the required 3.0 GPA. *Amount: $2,500. *Deadline: July 31.

MEDICINE/HEALTH CARE—GRADUATE

The following financial aid resources are available to students who are interested in studying medicine/health care and related fields at the graduate level and beyond.

American Academy of Nurse Practitioners (AANP) Foundation
PO Box 10729
Glendale, AZ 85318
623-376-9467
foundation@aanp.org
http://www.aanpfoundation.org
Scholarship Name: American Academy of Nurse Practitioners Foundation Scholarships. *Academic Area: Nursing (nurse practitioner). *Age Group: Graduate students. *Eligibility: Applicants must be current AANP student or full members and formally admitted to and taking classes in a fully accredited graduate program. Visit the AANP Foundation Web site for specific scholarship eligibility requirements. *Application Process: Applicants must contact the AANP Foundation to request application materials and obtain application details. Applicants must pay a $10 application fee. *Amount: Varies. *Deadline: Varies.

American Academy of Periodontology (AAP)
Attn: Sharon K. Mellor, CAE, Executive Director
AAP Educator Scholarship
737 North Michigan Avenue, Suite 800
Chicago, IL 60611
800-282-4867, ext. 3256
sharon@perio.org
http://www.perio.org/foundation/educator-scholarship.htm
Scholarship Name: American Academy of Periodontology Educator Scholarship. *Academic Area: Medicine (dentistry). *Age Group: Post-doctoral scholars. *Eligibility: Applicants must have been accepted into or currently enrolled in a U.S. periodontal postdoctoral training program, intend to enter full-time teaching at a U.S. program, and be student members of the AAP at the time the scholarship is granted. *Application Process: Applicants must submit a completed application, transcripts, a curriculum vitae, a letter of nomination, two letters of recommendation, and an essay. Visit AAP's Web site to download an application. *Amount: $50,000. *Deadline: July 1.

American Academy of Periodontology (AAP)
Attn: Sharon K. Mellor, CAE, Executive Director
Tarrson Regeneration Scholarship

737 North Michigan Avenue, Suite 800
Chicago, IL 60611
800-282-4867, ext. 3256
sharon@perio.org
http://www.perio.org/foundation/tar-reg.html
Scholarship Name: Tarrson Regeneration Scholarship. *Academic Area: Medicine (dentistry). *Age Group: Postdoctoral scholars. *Eligibility: Applicants must be students who have been accepted into an accredited U.S. periodontal postdoctoral training program or first-year residents within the first six months of their periodontal postdoctoral training program. *Application Process: Applicants must submit a completed application, a proposal abstract, transcripts, two letters of recommendation, an essay, and a curriculum vitae. Contact the AAP to request an application. *Amount: $37,000 per year, for up to three years. *Deadline: July 15.

American Alliance for Health, Physical Education, Recreation and Dance (AAHPERD)
Attn: Deb Callis
1900 Association Drive
Reston, VA 20191-1598
703-476-3400, 800-213-7193, ext. 405
dcallis@aahperd.org
http://www.aahperd.org/aahperd/template.cfm?template=presidents_scholarships.html
Scholarship Name: Ruth Abernathy Graduate Scholarship. *Academic Area: Medicine (open), performing arts (dance), physical education. *Age Group: Graduate students. *Eligibility: Applicants must be current members of the AAHPERD (or join at time of application) who are majoring in the field of health, physical education, recreation, or dance. They also must also be full-time students who have completed at least one semester of a graduate or doctoral program, maintain a 3.5 out of 4.0 GPA, demonstrate exceptional leadership abilities, and participate in community service activities. *Application Process: Applicants should submit a completed application along with a photocopy of their AAHPERD membership card or membership application form, three letters of recommendation, official transcripts from all graduate work completed, and a short biographical sketch. Materials should be

mailed to the appropriate district contact. Applicants should visit the alliance's Web site to download an official application and to determine their district contact. *Amount: $1,500, plus a three-year AAHPERD membership. *Deadline: October 15.

American Assembly for Men in Nursing Foundation
PO Box 130220
Birmingham, AL 35213
205-802-7551
aamn@aamn.org
http://www.aamn.org/aamnfoundationscholarships.htm
Scholarship Name: American Assembly for Men in Nursing Foundation Scholarship. *Academic Area: Nursing (general). *Age Group: Graduate students. *Eligibility: Applicants must be male students currently enrolled in nursing education programs. They also must maintain a minimum 2.75 GPA. *Application Process: Applicants must submit a completed application and essay. Contact the foundation to learn when scholarships are being offered and obtain further information regarding application requirements and details. *Amount: $1,000. *Deadline: Varies.

American Association of Colleges of Nursing
One Dupont Circle, NW, Suite 530
Washington, DC 20036-1120
202-463-6930
info@campuscareercenter.com
http://aacn.campusrn.com/scholarships/scholarship_rn.asp
Scholarship Name: CampusRN/American Association of Colleges of Nursing Scholarship Fund. *Academic Area: Nursing. *Age Group: Graduate students. *Eligibility: Applicants must be enrolled in a master's or doctoral program or enrolled in an accelerated master's degree nursing program. They also should be Campus RN members who possess at least a 3.25 GPA. Special consideration is given to students pursuing a nursing faculty career. A scholarship is awarded every two months. The scholarship is also available to undergraduate students. *Application Process: Applicants should submit a completed application and submit an online profile on CampusRN. Visit the association's Web site to download an application and to fill out an online profile. *Amount: $2,500. *Deadline: January 1, March 1, May 1, July 1, September 1, and November 1.

American Association of Colleges of Nursing
Attn: Pam Malloy
One Dupont Circle, NW, Suite 530
Washington, DC 20036-1120
202-463-6930
http://www.aacn.nche.edu/Education/financialaid.htm
Scholarship Name: Monster Healthcare-American Association of Colleges of Nursing Faculty Scholarship. *Academic Area: Nursing (education). *Age Group: Graduate students. *Eligibility: Applicants must be U.S. citizens or permanent residents who are full-time students enrolled in or accepted into either a baccalaureate to doctoral degree or a doctor of nursing practice program. The purpose of this scholarship is to increase the number of doctoral nursing faculty instructors—the applicant must intend to teach. The school of nursing that the applicant attends must provide an agreement letter from the dean to match at least 50 percent of the tuition at their academic institution. If positions are available, awardees must be willing to work at least 10 hours a week while enrolled in the doctoral program so that they can maintain clinical skills and obtain health care benefits. Evidence must be provided that a mentor/adviser agrees to work with the applicant throughout the student's entire formal education process. The scholarship is also available to undergraduate students. *Application Process: Applicants should submit a completed application and all associated forms along with two letters of recommendation, a one-page letter describing their personal and professional interest in nursing and nursing education, official transcripts, a curriculum vitae, and a letter of acceptance to nursing school. Visit the association's Web site to download an application. *Amount: $25,000. *Deadline: September 30.

American Association of Neuroscience Nurses/ Neuroscience Nursing Foundation
NNF Scholarship Programs
4700 West Lake Avenue
Glenview, IL 60025
888-557-2266
info@aann.org
http://www.aann.org/nnf
Scholarship Name: Neuroscience Nursing Foundation Scholarship Program. *Academic Area: Nursing (neuroscience). *Age Group: Graduate students. *Eligibility: Applicants must be registered nurses

pursuing studies to advance their careers in neuroscience nursing at the undergraduate or graduate level. They also must also maintain a minimum 3.0 GPA. *Application Process: Applicants must submit one copy of application Form A and four copies of Form B and supporting materials. They also must submit a letter of acceptance or evidence of enrollment at the school applicants are attending or plan to attend, official transcripts, a copy of their current specialty certification card(s), a copy of their current RN license, a curriculum vitae, and a personal statement. Visit the foundation's Web site to download an application. *Amount: $1,500. *Deadline: January 15.

American Dental Association (ADA) Foundation
211 East Chicago Avenue
Chicago, IL 60611
312-440-2547
adaf@ada.org
http://www.ada.org/ada/prod/adaf/prog_scholarship_prog.asp
Scholarship Name: Dental Student Scholarship. *Academic Area: Medicine (dentistry). *Age Group: Dental students. *Eligibility: Applicants must be entering second-year students at the time of application and currently attending or enrolled at a dental school accredited by the Commission on Dental Accreditation, maintain a minimum grade point average of 3.0 on a 4.0 scale, and demonstrate a minimum financial need of $2,500. *Application Process: Applicants must submit a completed application along with academic achievement record form and financial needs assessment form signed by school officials, a copy of their school's letter of acceptance, and two completed reference forms. They also must also submit a typed, biographical sketch questionnaire. Application forms for all ADA Foundation scholarships are available at dental schools and allied dental health programs and are disbursed by school officials. *Amount: Up to $2,500. *Deadline: July 31.

American Dental Education Association (ADEA)
Attn: Monique Morgan
ADEA Awards Selection Committee
1400 K Street, NW, Suite 1100
Washington, DC 20005
202-289-7201
MorganM@adea.org
http://www.adea.org/Awards/default.htm

Scholarship Name: ADEA/Listerine Preventive Dentistry Scholarship. *Academic Area: Medicine (dentistry). *Age Group: Dental students. *Eligibility: Applicants must be enrolled full time at a U.S. dental school, nominated by their dean, and demonstrate a strong interest in preventative dentistry. They also must also be individual members of the ADEA. *Application Process: Applicants must submit four copies of the completed application form, a letter from their dean, a two-page personal statement, and a curriculum vitae. Visit the association's Web site to download an application. *Amount: $2,500. *Deadline: December 9.

American Dental Education Association (ADEA)
Attn: Monique Morgan
ADEA Awards Selection Committee
1400 K Street, NW, Suite 1100
Washington, DC 20005
202-289-7201
MorganM@adea.org
http://www.adea.org/Awards/default.htm
Scholarship Name: ADEA/Oral-B Laboratories Scholarship for Dental Hygiene Students Pursuing Academic Careers. *Academic Area: Medicine (dentistry). *Age Group: Dental students. *Eligibility: Applicants must have graduated from an accredited dental hygiene program with an associate's degree or certificate to practice dental hygiene. Applicants must be enrolled part time or full time in a degree completion program for a bachelor's or graduate degree at an ADEA-member institution. Applicants must also maintain a commitment to pursuing an academic career and be individual members of the ADEA. Priority will be given to students enrolled in bachelor's degree-completion programs. *Application Process: Applicants must submit four copies of the completed application, academic transcripts, a copy of a valid license to practice dental hygiene in the United States, a personal statement, letters of nomination, and a letter of recommendation. *Amount: $2,000. *Deadline: December 9.

American Dental Education Association (ADEA)
Attn: Monique Morgan
ADEA Awards Selection Committee
1400 K Street, NW, Suite 1100
Washington, DC 20005
202-289-7201

MorganM@adea.org

http://www.adea.org/Awards/default.htm

Scholarship Name: ADEA/Sigma Phi Alpha Linda DeVore Scholarship. *Academic Area: Medicine (dentistry). *Age Group: Dental students. *Eligibility: Applicants must be bachelor's, master's, or doctoral dental hygiene, education, or public health students enrolled part time or full time. They also must demonstrate a commitment to leadership, be in good academic standing, and be individual members of the ADEA. *Application Process: Applicants must submit four copies of the completed application, academic transcripts, a personal statement, a letter of nomination, and a letter of support. Visit the association's Web site to download an application. *Amount: $1,000. Deadline: December 9.

American Dental Hygienists' Association (ADHA)

ADHA Institute for Oral Health

Scholarship Award Program

444 North Michigan Avenue, Suite 3400

Chicago, IL 60611

800-735-4916

institute@adha.net

http://www.adha.org/institute/Scholarship/index.htm

Scholarship Name: ADHA Institute Scholarship Program. *Academic Area: Medicine (dental hygiene). *Age Group: Graduate students. *Eligibility: Applicants should have completed at least one year in a dental hygiene program and be active members of the Student ADHA or the ADHA. They should also have a minimum 3.0/4.0 GPA. Documented financial need of at least $1,500 is required for some scholarships. The scholarship is also available to undergraduate students. *Application Process: Applicants should submit a completed application along with all required supporting materials. Visit the association's Web site for a detailed listing of scholarships and required materials. A downloadable application is also available via the association's Web site. *Amount: $1,000 to $2,000. *Deadline: June 30.

American Foundation for Pharmaceutical Education (AFPE)

One Church Street, Suite 202

Rockville, MD 20850

301-738-2160

info@afpenet.org

http://www.afpenet.org/programs.htm

Scholarship Name: AFPE First Year Graduate Scholarships. *Academic Area: Pharmaceutical sciences. *Age Group: Graduate students. *Eligibility: Applicants must pursue an advanced degree/Ph.D. in a college of pharmacy graduate program in the pharmaceutical sciences. Eligibility requirements vary by specific scholarship. Visit the foundation's Web site to learn more about specific scholarship requirements. Applicants must be U.S. citizens. *Application Process: Applicants must submit a completed application, official transcripts, personal statement, and letters of recommendation (two to three). Visit the foundation's Web site for more specific scholarship application details and to download an application. *Amount: Varies. *Deadline: Varies.

American Foundation for Pharmaceutical Education (AFPE)

One Church Street, Suite 202

Rockville, MD 20850

301-738-2160

info@afpenet.org

http://www.afpenet.org/programs.htm

Scholarship Name: AFPE "Gateway To Research" Scholarship. *Academic Area: Pharmaceutical sciences. *Age Group: Graduate students. *Eligibility: Each applicant, to be selected by a faculty member, must be enrolled in a Pharm.D. program, have completed at least two years of college, and be enrolled in at least the first year of the professional pharmacy curriculum. All applicants must be enrolled for at least one full academic year after initiation of the award. Students enrolled in joint Pharm.D./Ph.D. programs may not apply. The scholarship is also available to undergraduate students. Applicants must be nominated by faculty in a school of pharmacy accredited by the American Council on Pharmaceutical Education or faculty in any college awarding baccalaureate degrees who are actively undertaking research in the pharmaceutical sciences. Applicants must be U.S. citizens or permanent residents. *Application Process: Applicants must submit a completed application, official transcripts, and two completed statements of recommendation and evaluation forms. Visit the foundation's Web site to download an application and required forms. *Amount: $5,000. *Deadline: January 27.

American Health Information Management Association (AHIMA) Foundation of Research and Education
233 North Michigan Avenue, Suite 2150
Chicago, IL 60601-5800
312-233-1131
info@ahima.org
http://www.ahima.org/fore/programs.asp
Scholarship Name: Merit Scholarship. *Academic Area: Medicine (information management). *Age Group: Graduate students. *Eligibility: Applicants must have at least one full semester of classes remaining in their course of study at the time the award is granted. They also must be members of the AHIMA, maintain a minimum of a 3.0 GPA, and demonstrate a commitment to volunteerism and the health information management profession. The scholarship is also available to undergraduate students. *Application Process: Applicants should submit a completed application along with transcripts and references. Visit the foundation's Web site to download an application. *Amount: $1,000 to $5,000. *Deadline: Contact the foundation for deadline information.

American Holistic Nurses Association (AHNA)
AHNA Headquarters
PO Box 2130
Flagstaff, AZ 86003-2130
800-278-2462, ext. 10
info@ahna.org
http://www.ahna.org/edu/assist.html
Scholarship Name: Charlotte McGuire Scholarship. *Academic Area: Nursing (holistic). *Age Group: Graduate students. *Eligibility: Applicants must be pursuing a holistic nursing education, maintain a minimum 3.0 GPA, have experience and interest in healing and holistic nursing practice, and be current members of the AHNA. The scholarship is also available to undergraduate students. *Application Process: Applicants must submit a completed application, official transcripts, an essay, and two sponsorship letters. Visit the association's Web site to download an application. *Amount: Varies. *Deadline: March 15.

American Horticultural Therapy Association (AHTA)
3570 East 12th Avenue, Suite 206
Denver, CO 80206
303-322-2482, 800-634-1603
http://www.ahta.org/grantsAwards/awards.html
Scholarship Name: Ann Lane Mavromatis Scholarship. *Academic Area: Therapy (horticulture). *Age Group: Graduate students. *Eligibility: Applicants should have a declared major in the field of horticultural therapy or a related field with course work supporting the field of horticultural therapy, membership in the AHTA, a high level of academic achievement, evidence of financial need, and personal involvement in horticultural therapy through contribution to the development of the horticultural therapy program at their college or university or through participation in extracurricular horticultural therapy activities with a local, state, or national horticultural therapy organization. The scholarship is also available to undergraduate students. *Application Process: Initial nominations must be made by July. Nomination forms are available on the association's Web site in May of each year. Visit the association's Web site to download a nomination form. After being nominated, a follow-up application, requesting more detailed and specific information, will be sent directly to the applicant. *Amount: $500. *Deadline: Contact the association for specific deadline information.

American Kinesiotherapy Association (AKTA)
Attn: J.T. Magee Jr.
AKTA Scholarship Committee Chairman
1816 Maple Shade Lane
Richmond, VA 23227
800-296-2582
ccbkt@aol.com
http://www.akta.org/scholarship.htm
Scholarship Name: Lou Montalvano Memorial Scholarship. *Academic Area: Medicine (kinesiology). *Age Group: Graduate students. *Eligibility: Applicants must demonstrate academic excellence, exceptional promise as clinicians and educators, an intention to pursue certification and careers in kinesiotherapy, and potential for professional leadership. They also must be currently enrolled in an AKTA-accredited kinesiotherapy program and current members of the AKTA. The scholarship is also available to undergraduate students. *Application Process: Applicants must submit a completed application, a cover letter, three recommendation forms, and official transcripts. Visit the association's Web site to download an application and recommendation form. *Amount: $500. *Deadline: May 1.

American Medical Association (AMA) Foundation
Attn: Dina Lindenberg, Program Officer
515 North State Street
Chicago, IL 60610
312-464-4193, 800-621-8335
dina.lindenberg@ama-assn.org
http://www.ama-assn.org/ama/pub/category/14772.
html
Scholarship Name: AMA Foundation Physicians of
Tomorrow Scholarship. *Academic Area: Medicine
(physicians). *Age Group: Medical students.
*Eligibility: Applicants must be rising fourth-year
medical students who demonstrate academic
achievement and/or financial need. *Application
Process: Medical schools are granted one to three
nominations based on enrollment. Contact the AMA
Foundation program officer for further application
details. *Amount: $10,000. *Deadline: May 31.

American Medical Association (AMA) Foundation
Attn: Dina Lindenberg, Program Officer
515 North State Street
Chicago, IL 60610
312-464-4193, 800-621-8335
dina.lindenberg@ama-assn.org
http://www.ama-assn.org/ama/pub/category/14772.
html
Scholarship Name: AMA Foundation Scholars Fund.
*Academic Area: Medicine (physicians). *Age Group:
Medical students. *Eligibility: Applicants must be
medical students who demonstrate financial need
and academic excellence. *Application Process:
Applicants are nominated by their medical school
deans. Contact the AMA Foundation program officer
for further application details. *Amount: $1,000
(minimum). *Deadline: May 31.

American Occupational Therapy Foundation
Attn: Jane Huntington, Scholarship Coordinator
4720 Montgomery Lane
PO Box 31220
Bethesda, MD 20827-1220
301-652-6611
jhuntington@aotf.org
http://www.aotf.org/html/general_information.shtml
Scholarship Name: American Occupational Therapy
Foundation Scholarship. *Academic Area: Therapy
(occupational). *Age Group: Graduate students.
*Eligibility: Applicants must be enrolled in an
entry-level post-baccalaureate occupational therapy

educational program or occupational therapy
assistant program. *Application Process: Applicants
should submit a completed application along
with letters of reference and transcripts. Visit the
foundation's Web site for further information and to
download an application. *Amount: $375 to $5,000.
*Deadline: January 15.

American School Health Association
Attn: Pamela Dean
7263 State Route 43
PO Box 708
Kent, OH 44240
330-678-1601
pdean@ashaweb.org
http://www.ashaweb.org/pdfs/scholapp05.pdf
Scholarship Name: American School Health Association
Scholarship. *Academic Area: Medicine (dentistry),
medicine (education), medicine (school), medicine
(school health). *Age Group: Graduate students.
*Eligibility: Applicants must be enrolled full time
at an institute of higher education and maintain
at least a 3.0 GPA. They also must have declared a
major in school health education, school nursing,
or pediatric or adolescent medicine or dentistry.
Applicants with other school health specializations
will be considered only if they include, with the
application, a letter from their academic adviser
stating the program's relationship to school health.
The scholarship is also available to undergraduate
students. *Application Process: Applicants must
submit one original and seven copies of a completed
application, a resume, transcripts, a personal
statement, and three letters of recommendation.
*Amount: $500. *Deadline: April 4.

American Society for Clinical Laboratory Science
Attn: Joe Briden, AMTF Scholarship Coordinator
7809 South 21st Drive
Phoenix, AZ 85041-7736
301-657-2768
http://www.ascls.org/leadership/awards/amt.asp
Scholarship Name: Alpha Mu Tau Graduate Scholarship.
*Academic Area: Medicine (clinical laboratory
science). *Age Group: Graduate students. *Eligibility:
Applicants must be U.S. citizens who are accepted
into or are enrolled in an approved master's
or doctoral program in areas related to clinical
laboratory science including clinical laboratory
education or management programs. Applicants

cannot complete their education before the scholarship is awarded. Applicants must also be U.S. citizens or permanent residents. *Application Process: Applicants should submit a typewritten or computer-generated application along with two letters of recommendation, a 500-word personal objectives statement, and transcripts. Original applications should be submitted along with four photocopies. Visit the society's Web site to download an application. *Amount: $1,000 for part-time students; $2,000 for full-time students. *Deadline: April 1.

American Society for Clinical Laboratory Science
Attn: Joe Briden, AMTF Scholarship Coordinator
7809 South 21st Drive
Phoenix, AZ 85041-7736
301-657-2768
http://www.ascls.org/leadership/awards/amt.asp
Scholarship Name: Ruth M. French Graduate or Undergraduate Scholarship. *Academic Area: Medicine (clinical laboratory science). *Age Group: Graduate students. *Eligibility: Applicants must be U.S. citizens attending a National Accrediting Agency for Clinical Laboratory Sciences-accredited graduate clinical laboratory science program and must not complete their study before the award date of the scholarship. The scholarship is also available to undergraduate students. *Application Process: Applicants should submit a typewritten or computer-generated application along with two letters of recommendation, a 500-word personal objectives statement, and transcripts. Original applications should be submitted along with four photocopies. Visit the society's Web site to download an application. *Amount: $3,000. *Deadline: April 1.

American Society of Radiologic Technologists (ASRT) Education and Research Foundation
Scholarship Program
15000 Central Avenue, SE
Albuquerque, NM 87123-3917
800-444-2778, ext. 2541
foundation@asrt.org
http://www.asrt.org/content/ASRTFoundation/AwardsandScholarships/ElektaSch.aspx
Scholarship Name: Elekta Radiation Therapy Educators Scholarship. *Academic Area: Medicine (radiologic science). *Age Group: Graduate students. *Eligibility: Applicants must be educator therapists who are

pursuing a master's or doctoral degree to enhance their position as a program director, faculty member, clinical coordinator, or clinical instructor. They also must be graduates of an accredited program in radiation therapy, current ASRT members, registered by the American Registry of Radiologic Technologists (ARRT) or hold an unrestricted state license, and worked in a clinical or didactic setting as a radiation therapy educator for at least one of the past five years. The scholarship is also available to undergraduate students. *Application Process: Applicants must submit a completed application, a written applicant interview, two completed evaluation forms, a resume, a letter verifying their employment as a radiation therapy educator for at least one of the past five years, and copy of current their ARRT card or unrestricted state license. Visit the society's Web site to download an application and evaluation form. *Amount: $5,000. *Deadline: February 1.

American Society of Radiologic Technologists (ASRT) Education and Research Foundation
Scholarship Program
15000 Central Avenue, SE
Albuquerque, NM 87123-3917
800-444-2778, ext. 2541
foundation@asrt.org
http://www.asrt.org/Content/ASRTFoundation/AwardsandScholarships/AmershamManagementScholarship.aspx
Scholarship Name: GE Healthcare Management Scholarship. *Academic Area: Medicine (management), medicine (radiologic science). *Age Group: Graduate students. *Eligibility: Applicants must have applied to an accredited advanced degree program related to management and intend to further their careers in radiologic sciences. They also must be graduates of accredited programs in radiologic sciences, current ASRT members, registered by the American Registry of Radiologic Technologists (ARRT) or hold an unrestricted state license, and have worked in a clinical or didactic setting in the radiologic sciences profession for at least one of the past five years. *Application Process: Applicants must submit a completed application, a written applicant interview, two completed evaluation forms, a resume, a letter verifying their employment as a radiation therapy educator for at least one of the past five years, and copy of their

current ARRT card or unrestricted state license. Visit the society's Web site to download an application and evaluation form. *Amount: Up to $5,000. *Deadline: February 1.

American Society of Radiologic Technologists (ASRT) Education and Research Foundation

Scholarship Program
15000 Central Avenue, SE
Albuquerque, NM 87123-3917
800-444-2778, ext. 2541
foundation@asrt.org
http://www.asrt.org/content/ASRTFoundation/
AwardsandScholarships/Stern.aspx
Scholarship Name: Jeanette C. and Isadore N. Stern Scholarship Program. *Academic Area: Medicine (radiologic science). *Age Group: Graduate students. *Eligibility: Applicants must have applied to an accredited certificate program related to radiologic sciences or plan to study for a master's or doctoral degree with the intention of furthering their clinical practice in radiologic sciences. They also must be graduates of an accredited program in the radiologic sciences, current ASRT members, registered by the American Registry of Radiologic Technologists (ARRT) or hold an unrestricted state license, and have worked in a clinical or didactic setting in the radiologic sciences profession for at least one of the past five years. The scholarship is also available to undergraduate students. *Application Process: Applicants must submit a completed application, a written applicant interview, two completed evaluation forms, a resume, a letter verifying their employment as a radiation therapy educator for at least one of the past five years, and a copy of their current ARRT card or unrestricted state license. Visit the society's Web site to download an application and evaluation form. *Amount: $1,000. *Deadline: February 1.

American Society of Radiologic Technologists (ASRT) Education and Research Foundation

Scholarship Program
15000 Central Avenue, SE
Albuquerque, NM 87123-3917
800-444-2778, ext. 2541
foundation@asrt.org
http://www.asrt.org/content/ASRTFoundation/
AwardsandScholarships/MonsterSch.aspx
Scholarship Name: Monster Medical Imaging Educators Scholarship. *Academic Area: Medicine

(management), medicine (radiologic science). *Age Group: Graduate students. *Eligibility: Applicants must be educators who are pursuing their master's or doctoral degree to enhance their position as a medical imaging program director, faculty member, clinical coordinator, or clinical instructor. They also must be graduates of an accredited program in medical imaging, current ASRT members, registered by the American Registry of Radiologic Technologists (ARRT) or hold an unrestricted state license, and have worked in a clinical or didactic setting as a medical imaging educator for at least one of the past five years. The scholarship is also available to undergraduate students. *Application Process: Applicants must submit a completed application, a written applicant interview, two completed evaluation forms, a resume, a letter verifying their employment as a radiation therapy educator for at least one of the past five years, and copy of their current ARRT card or unrestricted state license. Visit the society's Web site to download an application and evaluation form. *Amount: $5,000. *Deadline: February 1.

American Society of Radiologic Technologists (ASRT) Education and Research Foundation

Scholarship Program
15000 Central Avenue, SE
Albuquerque, NM 87123-3917
800-444-2778, ext. 2541
foundation@asrt.org
http://www.asrt.org/content/ASRTFoundation/
AwardsandScholarships/Siemens.aspx
Scholarship Name: Siemens Clinical Advancement Scholarship Program. *Academic Area: Medicine (radiologic science). *Age Group: Graduate students. *Eligibility: Applicants must have applied to an accredited certificate program related to radiologic sciences or plan to study for a master's or doctoral degree with the intention of furthering their clinical practice in radiologic sciences. They also must be medical imaging and radiation therapy professionals seeking to enhance their clinical practice skills and ability to provide excellent patient care, graduates of an accredited program in the radiologic sciences, current ASRT members, registered by the American Registry of Radiologic Technologists (ARRT) or hold an unrestricted state license, and have worked in a clinical or didactic setting in the radiologic sciences profession for at least one of the past five years.

The scholarship is also available to undergraduate students. *Application Process: Applicants must submit a completed application, a written applicant interview, two completed evaluation forms, resume, a letter verifying their employment as a radiation therapy educator for at least one of the past five years, and a copy of their current ARRT card or unrestricted state license. Visit the society's Web site to download an application and evaluation form. *Amount: $3,000. *Deadline: February 1.

Association of Perioperative Registered Nurses (AORN) Foundation

Attn: Ingrid Bendzsa, Executive Assistant
2170 South Parker Road, Suite 300
Denver, CO 80231-5711
800-755-2676, ext. 328
ibendzsa@aorn.org
http://www.aorn.org/foundation/scholarships.asp
Scholarship Name: AORN Foundation Scholarship Program. *Academic Area: Nursing (perioperative). *Age Group: Graduate students. *Eligibility: Applicants must be enrolled in CCNE- or NLNAC-accredited nursing programs, pursuing perioperative nursing master's or doctoral degrees. They also must maintain a 3.0 out of 4.0 GPA and exhibit financial need. The scholarship is also available to undergraduate students. *Application Process: Applicants should submit a completed application along with transcripts. Visit the foundation's Web site for additional application procedures. Applications are available for download from the foundation's Web site beginning in January of each year. *Amount: Awards vary. *Deadline: May 1.

Daughters of the American Revolution (DAR)

Attn: Scholarships
1776 D Street, NW
Washington, DC 20006-5303
202-628-1776
http://www.dar.org/natsociety/edout_scholar.cfm
Scholarship Name: Alice W. Rooke Scholarship. *Academic Area: Medicine (physician). *Age Group: Medical students. *Eligibility: Applicants must be citizens of the United States who demonstrate high scholastic standing and character and who have been accepted into or are pursuing an approved course of study to become a medical doctor (not pre-med) at an approved, accredited medical school. *Application Process: All applicants must obtain a letter of sponsorship from their local DAR chapter.

Applicants should send a stamped, self-addressed business size envelope to obtain the name and address of their state scholarship chairman and an application. Visit the organization's Web site for the mailing address. *Amount: $5,000, renewable annually for a total of $20,000. *Deadline: April 15.

Daughters of the American Revolution (DAR)

Attn: Scholarships
1776 D Street, NW
Washington, DC 20006-5303
202-628-1776
http://www.dar.org/natsociety/edout_scholar.cfm
Scholarship Name: Irene and Daisy MacGregor Memorial Scholarship. *Academic Area: Medicine (physician), nursing (psychiatric). *Age Group: Medical Students. *Eligibility: Applicants must be citizens of the United States who demonstrate high scholastic standing and character and who have been accepted into or are pursuing an approved course of study to become a medical doctor (not pre-med) at an approved, accredited medical school. Alternately, applicants may attend an approved course of study in the field of psychiatric nursing, graduate level, at accredited medical schools, colleges, or universities. A preference for females is stated if applicants are "equally qualified." *Application Process: All applicants must obtain a letter of sponsorship from their local DAR chapter. Applicants should send a stamped, self-addressed business size envelope to obtain the name and address of their state scholarship chairman and an application. *Amount: $5,000, renewable annually for a total of $20,000. *Deadline: April 15.

Daughters of the American Revolution (DAR)

Attn: Scholarships
1776 D Street, NW
Washington, DC 20006-5303
202-628-1776
http://www.dar.org/natsociety/edout_scholar.cfm
Scholarship Name: Occupational/Physical Therapy Scholarship. *Academic Area: Therapy (art), therapy (music), therapy (occupational), therapy (physical). *Age Group: Graduate students. *Eligibility: Applicants must be citizens of the United States who are attending an accredited school of therapy in the United States. They also must demonstrate financial need. The scholarship is also available to undergraduate students. *Application Process: All applicants must obtain a letter of sponsorship from their local DAR chapter. Applicants should send a

stamped, self-addressed business size envelope to obtain the name and address of their state scholarship chairman and an application. Visit the organization's Web site for the mailing address. *Amount: $500. *Deadline: February 15, August 15.

Emergency Nurses Association (ENA)
915 Lee Street
Des Plaines, IL 60016-6569
847-460-4004, 800-900-9659
foundation@ena.org
http://www.ena.org/foundation/grants
Scholarship Name: ENA Foundation Scholarship. *Academic Area: Nursing (emergency). *Age Group: Graduate students. *Eligibility: Visit the association's Web site for updates on eligibility requirements. Information is posted in December of each year. The scholarship is also available to undergraduate students. *Application Process: Applicants should contact the association for further information, or visit the Web site after December. *Amount: Awards vary. *Deadline: Contact the association for deadline information.

Evangelical Lutheran Church in America (ELCA)
Attn: Nancy Gruthusen
Division for Higher Education and Schools
8765 West Higgins Road
Chicago, IL 60631-4194
773-380-2850, 800-638-3522
Nancy_Gruthusen@elca.org
http://www.elca.org/education/torrison.html
Scholarship Name: Torrison Scholarship. *Academic Area: Medicine (physicians). *Age Group: Medical students. *Eligibility: Applicants must be ELCA members who have been accepted into medical school. They also should demonstrate strong academic merit and express an interest in working toward developing cures for currently incurable diseases. *Application Process: An ELCA minister, who is either on or off campus, must nominate applicants. Once an applicant has been formally nominated, an official application packet will be mailed. Visit the church's Web site for additional information about the nomination process. *Amount: $5,000. *Deadline: March 15.

Institute for Operations Research and Management Science
Attn: George Miller
Altarum
PO Box 134001

Ann Arbor, MI 48113
734-302-4640
george.miller@altarum.org
http://www.informs.org/Prizes/scholarships.html
Scholarship Name: Seth Bonder Scholarship for Applied Operations Research in Health Services. *Academic Area: Medicine (research). *Age Group: Graduate students. *Eligibility: Applicants must be students pursuing doctoral studies in health operations research or a related discipline. The scholarship is open to both U.S. citizens and international students. *Application Process: Applicants must submit three copies of a curriculum vitae, two letters of recommendation, a personal statement, and a two-page summary of their research proposal. *Amount: Up to $5,000. *Deadline: July 1.

International Order of The King's Daughters and Sons
Attn: Director, Health Careers Scholarship Department
PO Box 1040
Chautauqua, NY 14722-1040
http://www.iokds.org/scholarship.html
Scholarship Name: Health Careers Scholarship Program. *Academic Area: Medicine (dentistry), medicine (medical technology), medicine (physician), nursing (open), pharmaceutical sciences, therapy (occupational), therapy (physical). *Age Group: Graduate students. *Eligibility: Applicants must be U.S. or Canadian citizens enrolled full time at an accredited college/university who are preparing for careers in medicine, dentistry, nursing, pharmacy, physical or occupational therapy, and medical technologies. Registered nursing students must have completed the first year of schooling. Pre-med students are not eligible to apply. Applicants seeking to become physicians or dentists must apply for at least the second year of medical or dental school. Undergraduate students may apply for select scholarships in the program. *Application Process: Contact the order for further application details and to request an application. *Amount: $1,000. *Deadline: April 1.

March of Dimes
Education Services
1275 Mamaroneck Avenue
White Plains, NY 10605
profedu@marchofdimes.com
http://www.marchofdimes.com/professionals/685_1368.asp

Scholarship Name: March of Dimes Graduate Nursing Scholarship. *Academic Area: Nursing (neonatal), nursing (women's health). *Age Group: Graduate students. *Eligibility: Applicants must be registered nurses enrolled in a graduate program in maternal-child nursing at the master's or doctoral level. They also must have at least one academic term to complete after May of the year in which the scholarship is awarded, and be members of at least one of the following professional organizations: the Association of Women's Health, Obstetric and Neonatal Nurses; the American College of Nurse-Midwives; or the National Association of Neonatal Nurses. Previous recipients and March of Dimes employees and their family members are not eligible. *Application Process: Applicants must submit a completed application, a letter of recommendation (from a faculty member), and an essay. Visit the organization's Web site to download an application. *Amount: $5,000. *Deadline: January 16.

Medical University of South Carolina
Attn: Ms. Nancy Carder, Special Programs Office
165 Cannon Street, #402D, PO Box 250851
Charleston, SC 29425
843-792-1469
cardern@musc.edu
http://www.musc.edu/specialprograms
Fellowship Name: Nuclear Engineering and Health Physics Fellowship Program. *Academic Area: Engineering (nuclear), physics (health). *Age Group: Graduate students. *Eligibility: Applicants should have an undergraduate degree in the physical sciences, life sciences, or engineering. They also should be U.S. citizens or permanent residents, have at least one full year of graduate study remaining, and attend a participating university. Visit the organization's Web site for a list of participating universities. *Application Process: Applicants should submit a completed application along with three letters of reference, official transcripts, and official GRE scores. Fellowship awardees are required to serve a three-month practicum. Visit the organization's Web site to download an application. *Amount: $1,700 monthly stipend. *Deadline: January 31.

Myasthenia Gravis Foundation of America Inc.
National Office
1821 University Avenue W, Suite S256
St. Paul, MN 55104-2897
651-917-6256, 800-541-5454
mgfa@myasthenia.org
http://www.myasthenia.org/research/MGFA_
StudentFellowship.pdf
Fellowship Name: Student Fellowship. *Academic Area: Medicine (physician), medicine (research). *Age Group: Graduate students, medical students. *Eligibility: Applicants must be interested in researching the scientific basis of myasthenia gravis or related neuromuscular conditions as well as dedicated to the humane care of laboratory animals. They also must intend to include minorities in their research study populations. *Application Process: Applicants should submit a letter of interest along with a summary of their proposed research and its significance, a proposed budget, a curriculum vitae, and a letter of recommendation from a sponsor who has approved the proposed research study. *Amount: $3,000. *Deadline: March 15.

National Association of School Nurses (NASN)
Attn: Advancement Award Chair
PO Box 1300
Scarborough, ME 04070-1300
207-883-2117, 877-627-6476
nasn@nasn.org
http://www.nasn.org/Default.aspx?tabid=86
Scholarship Name: NASN Educational Advancement Award. *Academic Area: Nursing (school). *Age Group: Graduate students. *Eligibility: Applicants must be currently employed school nurses who are NASN members wishing to advance their education beyond a bachelor's degree. *Application Process: Applicants must submit a completed application, a photocopy of their state RN license, and written verification of current employment as a school nurse. Visit the association's Web site to download an application. *Amount: $1,500. *Deadline: October 15.

National Gerontological Nursing Association
7794 Grow Drive
Pensacola, FL 32514-7072
800-723-0560
ngna@puetzamc.com
http://www.ngna.org/all.php?l=resources&x=8
Scholarship Name: Mary Opal Wolanin Graduate Scholarship. *Academic Area: Nursing (gerontology). *Age Group: Graduate students. *Eligibility: Applicants must be nursing students with a major in gerontology/geriatric nursing, enrolled in a

minimum of six credits at nationally accredited nursing program in the United States, and maintain at least a 3.0 GPA. *Application Process: Applicants must submit a completed application, two letters of recommendation, official transcripts, a personal statement no longer than 300 words, and a statement of financial need. Visit the association's Web site to download an application. *Amount: $1,500. *Deadline: June 1.

National Health Service Corps (NHSC)
2099 Gaither Road, Suite 600
Rockville, MD 20850
800-221-9393
callcenter@hrsa.gov
http://nhsc.bhpr.hrsa.gov/join_us/scholarships.asp
Scholarship Name: National Health Service Corps Scholarship Program. *Academic Area: Medicine (dental), medicine (physician assisting), medicine (physicians), nursing (midwifery), nursing (nurse practitioner). *Age Group: Graduate students. *Eligibility: Applicants must be committed to providing primary health care in communities of greatest need. They also must be U.S. citizens enrolled, or accepted for enrollment, in a fully accredited U.S. allopathic or osteopathic medical school, family nurse practitioner program, nurse-midwifery program, physician assistant program. Undergraduate students may apply for select scholarships in this program, or dental school. *Application Process: Contact the NHSC to request an application and for further application details. *Amount: Paid tuition and monthly stipend. *Deadline: Varies.

Nurses Educational Funds (NEF) Inc.
304 Park Avenue South, 11th Floor
New York, NY 10010
212-590-2443
info@n-e-f.org
http://www.n-e-f.org
Scholarship Name: NEF Scholarship. *Academic Area: Nursing (open). *Age Group: Graduate students. *Eligibility: Applicants must be baccalaureate-prepared registered nurses who are in need of scholarship assistance for graduate study. Applicants must be U.S. citizens and members of a professional nursing association. They also must either be enrolled full time in a National League for Nursing Accrediting Commission- or Commission

on Collegiate Nursing Education-accredited nursing master's degree program or enrolled full or part time in a doctoral program in nursing or a nursing related field. *Application Process: Applicants must submit a completed application, a $20 application processing fee, proof of nursing registration, proof of nursing association membership, proof of U.S. citizenship, a goal statement essay, reference forms, and official transcripts. Visit the NEF's Web site to download an application and required forms. *Amount: Varies. *Deadline: March 1.

Oncology Nursing Society Foundation
RIDC Park West
125 Enterprise Drive
Pittsburgh, PA 15275-1214
412-859-6100
foundation@ons.org
http://onsfoundation.org/?p=12909
Scholarship Name: Oncology Nursing Society Foundation Doctoral Scholarship. *Academic Area: Nursing (oncology). *Age Group: Graduate students. *Eligibility: Applicants must be currently enrolled in, or applying to, a doctoral nursing degree or related program. They also must be interested in and committed to oncology nursing and in continuing their education by pursuing a doctoral degree in nursing. Applicants must also have current licenses to practice as registered nurse. *Application Process: Applicants must submit one original and three copies of a completed application, transcripts, and two letters of recommendation. Applicants must also submit a $5 application fee. Visit the foundation's Web site to download an application. *Amount: $2,000-$5,000. *Deadline: February 1.

Oncology Nursing Society Foundation
125 Enterprise Drive
Pittsburgh, PA 15275
412-859-6100
foundation@ons.org
http://onsfoundation.org/?p=12909
Scholarship Name: Oncology Nursing Society Foundation Master's and Post-Masters Nurse Practitioner Certificate Scholarship. *Academic Area: Nursing (oncology). *Age Group: Graduate students. *Eligibility: Applicants must be currently enrolled in, or applying to, a master's nursing degree or post-masters nurse practitioner certificate program at a Nursing Accrediting Commission- or Commission on

Collegiate Nursing Education-accredited accredited School of Nursing. Applicants must be interested in and committed to oncology nursing and have a current license to practice as a registered nurse. *Application Process: Applicants must submit one original and three copies of a completed application and transcripts. Applicants must also submit a $5 application fee. Visit the foundation's Web site to download an application. *Amount: $3,000. *Deadline: February 1.

Pedorthic Footwear Foundation

7150 Columbia Gateway Drive, Suite G
Columbia, MD 21046-1151
info@pedorthics.org
http://www.pedorthics.org/pages.
cfm?page=scholarship.html
Scholarship Name: Pedorthic Footwear Foundation Scholarships . *Academic Area: Medicine (pedorthics), medicine (podiatry). *Age Group: Under graduate students. *Eligibility: Applicants must have prior experience related to footwear or foot care. Contact the foundation for more information regarding eligibility requirements. *Application Process: Applicants must submit a completed application and three letters of recommendation. Visit the foundation's Web site to download an application. *Amount: Varies. *Deadline: January 15.

Society of Gastroenterology Nurses and Associates (SGNA)

Attn: SGNA Awards Committee
401 North Michigan Avenue
Chicago, IL 60611-4267
312-321-5165, 800-245-7462
http://sgna.org/resources/RNadvancing.doc
Scholarship Name: Society of Gastroenterology Nurses and Associates RN Advancing Education Scholarship. *Academic Area: Nursing (gastroenterology). *Age Group: Graduate students. *Eligibility: Applicants must be registered nurses working in gastroenterology who are pursing advanced education (BSN or higher). Applicants may be full- or part-time nursing students, and must be members of the SGNA who maintain at least a 3.0 GPA. *Application Process: Applicants should submit a completed application along with a 500-word essay (see application for topic), two letters of recommendation, and transcripts. This organization awards the scholarship as a reimbursement.

Applicants must submit a final copy of their transcripts to verify maintenance of the required 3.0 GPA. Amount: $1,000 (part-time students), $2,500 (full-time students). *Deadline: July 31.

Student American Veterinary Medical Association (SAVMA)

1931 North Meacham Road, Suite 100
Schaumburg, IL 60173
847-925-8070
avmainfo@avma.org
http://www.avma.org/noah/members/savma/
committees/ivsrc_scholarship_guidelines.pdf
Scholarship Name: International Veterinary Student Relations Committee International Exchange Scholarship. *Academic Area: Medicine (veterinary). *Age Group: Veterinary students. *Eligibility: Applicants must demonstrate a strong desire to participate in a veterinary-related international exchange. They also must be SAVMA members and have completed their international exchange within one year of the application deadline. *Application Procedure: Applicants must submit a completed application, a letter of intention, a letter of recommendation, and an estimated budget. They also must contact the SAVMA international exchange officer prior to application submittal. Visit the association's Web site to download an application. *Amount: $500. *Deadline: January 15.

UNICO National Inc.

Attn: Joan Tidona, Scholarship Director
271 U.S. Highway West
Fairfield, NJ 07004
201-933-7982
jntidona@verizon.net
http://www.unico.org/scholarships.html
Scholarship Name: Dr. Benjamin Cottone Memorial Scholarship. *Academic Area: Medicine (physician). *Age Group: Medical students. *Eligibility: UNICO touts itself as the largest Italian-American service organization in the United States. Italian-American medical students are eligible to apply. *Application Process: Applicants should contact the scholarship director to receive additional information and an application. (Note: The scholarship director distributes all rules and announcements regarding available scholarships.) *Amount: $5,000. *Deadline: Contact the scholarship director for deadline information.

OPEN TO ALL MAJORS— UNDERGRADUATE

The following financial aid resources are open to undergraduate students of all majors. Check specific listings for eligibility requirements.

All-Ink.com College Scholarship Program
PO Box 50868
Provo, UT 84605-0868
Education@All-Ink.com
http://www.all-ink.com/scholarship.aspx
Scholarship Name: All-Ink.com College Scholarship. *Academic Area: Open. *Age Group: Undergraduate students. *Eligibility: Applicants must be enrolled in or planning to attend an accredited college or university program. They must also be United States citizens and maintain at least a 2.5 GPA. High school seniors may apply. The scholarship is also available to graduate students. *Application Process: Applicants must submit an online application, which includes an essay on who has had the greatest impact on their life, and an essay on what they hope to achieve after completing college. No mailed applications will be accepted. Visit the company's Web site to apply. *Amount: Awards vary. *Deadline: December 31.

American Association of Police Polygraphists (AAPP)
PO Box 657
Waynesville, OH 45068-0657
888-743-5479
nom@policepolygraph.org
http://www.policepolygraph.org/downloads/scholarshipform.pdf
Scholarship Name: American Association of Police Polygraphists Scholarship. *Academic Area: Open. *Age Group: Undergraduate students. *Eligibility: Applicants must be a child, grandchild, niece, nephew, or adopted/dependent child under the age of 23 with at least one parent or grandparent serving as a full, life, or honorably retired AAPP member in good standing. If the said member's parent/grandparent is deceased, the member must have been in good standing of the AAPP at the time of death. High school seniors may also apply. *Application Process: Applicants must submit a completed application, official transcripts, two letters of recommendation, and a personal statement. Visit the association's Web

site to download an application. *Amount: Varies. *Deadline: March 31.

American Automobile Association (AAA)
Attn: Justin McNaull
202-942-2079
aaatravelchallenge@national.aaa.com
http://www.aaa.com/travelchallenge
Contest Name: AAA Travel High School Challenge. *Academic Area: Open. *Age Group: High school freshmen, sophomores, juniors, or seniors. *Eligibility: Applicants must be U.S. residents attending high school (home schooling is included) who are at least 13 years of age and who have an interest in geography. *Application Process: Applicants should register via the organization's Web site for the first round, online test. The top five contestants from each state go on to compete in individual state competitions in March. These exams are administered as written examinations. The winner from each state receives a paid trip, along with a guardian, to the national competition in Orlando, Florida. Interested applicants should visit the company's Web site in the fall to register for the first-round test, take practice tests, and to obtain a complete set of instructions. *Amount: Up to $25,000. *Deadline: Applicants may register any time up until the online test date, but are advised to register early to avoid high Web site traffic.

American Fire Sprinkler Association
9696 Skillman Street, Suite 300
Dallas, TX 75243-8264
214-349-5965
afsainfo@firesprinkler.org
http://www.afsascholarship.org
Scholarship Name: American Fire Sprinkler Association Scholarship. *Academic Area: Open. *Age Group: Undergraduate students. *Eligibility: Applicants must be high school seniors in the United States who plan to further their education at a college/university or certified trade school in the United States. *Application Process: Applicants must read

the "Fire Sprinkler Essay" (approximately 3000 words) about automatic fire sprinklers and take a 10-question multiple-choice test. For each question answered correctly, students will receive one entry into the scholarship drawing. Visit the association's scholarship Web site to enter the scholarship contest. *Amount: $5,000. *Deadline: September 1 and April 12.

American Foreign Service Association (AFSA)
Attn: Lori Dec, Scholarship Director
2101 E Street, NW
Washington, DC 20037
202-944-5504
dec@afsa.org
http://www.afsa.org/scholar/index.cfm
Award Name: American Foreign Service Association Merit Award. *Academic Area: Open. *Age Group: Undergraduate students. *Eligibility: High school seniors who have at least one parent who is a member of AFSA or Associates of the American Foreign Service Worldwide and maintain a 2.0 GPA on a 4.0 scale may apply. This competition rewards academic and/or art accomplishments. *Application Process: Applicants should submit a completed application along with official transcripts, two letters of recommendation, and an essay. Visit the association's Web site for further information about essay topics and to download an application. *Amount: $1,500. *Deadline: February 6.

American Police Hall of Fame
6350 Horizon Drive
Titusville, FL 32780
321-264-0911
policeinfo@aphf.org
http://www.aphf.org/scholarships.html
Scholarship Name: The Police Family Survivor's Fund. *Academic Area: Open. *Age group: Undergraduate students. *Eligibility: Applicants must be sons or daughters of officers killed in the line of duty. High school seniors may also apply. *Application Process: Contact the American Police Hall of Fame and Museum for application details. *Amount: $1,500 per year. *Deadline: Varies.

American Radio Relay League Foundation
Attn: Scholarship Program
225 Main Street
Newington, CT 06111

860-594-0397
foundation@arrl.org
http://www.arrl.org/arrlf
Scholarship Name: American Radio Relay League Foundation Scholarship. *Academic Area: Open. *Age Group: Undergraduate students. *Eligibility: Applicants must hold a valid ham radio license. Eligibility requirements vary. Visit the foundation's Web site to obtain specific scholarship eligibility requirements. *Application Process: Applicants must submit a completed application and official transcripts. They must also submit up to three letters of recommendation and an introductory letter (optional). Visit the foundation's Web site to download an application. *Amount: Up to $10,000. *Deadline: February 1.

American Society of Travel Agents Foundation
1101 King Street, Suite 200
Alexandria, VA 22314
703-739-2782
scholarship@astahq.com
http://www.astanet.com/education/scholarshiph.asp
Scholarship Name: Joseph R. Stone Scholarship. *Academic Area: Open. *Age Group: Undergraduate students. *Eligibility: Applicants must be undergraduate students and have at least one parent employed in the travel industry (i.e., hotel, car rental, airlines, travel agency, etc.). They must also maintain a minimum 2.5 GPA and be residents, citizens, or legal aliens of the United States or Canada. *Application Process: Applicants must submit one original and three copies of a completed application and all supporting materials. They must also submit proof of enrollment, an official printed description of their curricula and statement of tuition, a personal essay, and proof of their parent's or guardian's employment. Visit the foundation's Web site to download an application. *Amount: $2,400. *Deadline: August 30.

Books and Scholarships LLC
Elwood Grimes Literary Scholarship
4525 Cherry Forest Circle
Louisville, KY 40245
http://www.booksandscholarships.com/Scholarship%20EGL.htm
Scholarship Name: Elwood Grimes Literary Scholarship. *Academic Area: Open. *Age Group: Undergraduate students. *Eligibility: Applicants must be graduating

high school seniors or college students who are U.S. citizens and attending or planning to attend college at least part time. The scholarship is also available to graduate students. *Application Process: Applicants must submit a completed application along with a copy of a letter of college acceptance and a 500 (or more)-word essay. The essay must be about Elwood Grimes' book, The Rambled Soul of a 21st Century Man. *Amount: Awards vary. Up to $5,000 distributed among first, second, and third place winners. *Deadline: September 30.

California Teachers Association (CTA)

CTA Scholarship Committee
Attn: Manuel Ayan, Human Rights Department
PO Box 921
Burlingame, CA 94011-0921
650-697-1400
http://www.cta.org/InsideCTA/ScholarshipsWorkshops/
ScholarshipsWorkshops.htm
Scholarship Name: California Teachers Association Scholarship for Dependent Children. *Academic Area: Open. *Age Group: Undergraduate students. *Eligibility: Applicants must be dependents of an active, retired, or deceased CTA member. They also must be claimed as dependents on their parents' current IRS forms, maintain at least a 3.5 GPA, and be high school seniors or current college students. *Application Process: Applicants must submit a completed application, two letters of recommendation, and official transcripts. Visit the association's Web site to download an application. *Amount: $2,000. *Deadline: January 27.

Career College Foundation

c/o Peterson's, a part of the Thomson Corporation
Princeton Pike Corporate Center
2000 Lenox Drive
PO Box 67005
Lawrenceville, NJ 08648
202-336-6711
scholarships@career.org
http://www.careercollegefoundation.com
Scholarship Name: Imagine America Scholarship. *Academic Area: Open. *Age Group: Undergraduate students. *Eligibility: Applicants must be graduating high school seniors from the United States or Puerto Rico. Students must meet the standard admissions requirements of the participating career college

to which they apply. Applicants must maintain a minimum 2.5 GPA and demonstrate likelihood of successful completion of postsecondary education, financial need, and voluntary community service during their senior year. *Application Process: Applicants must submit an online application. Applicants should contact their guidance counselors or the foundation for further details. *Amount: $1,000. *Deadline: Varies.

CareerFitter.com

918-477-2280
admin3@careerfitter.com
http://www.careerfitter.com/scholarship/index.htm
Scholarship Name: CareerFitter.com Scholarship. *Academic Area: Open. *Age Group: Undergraduate students. *Eligibility: Applicants must be U.S. citizens or permanent residents who are enrolled in or accepted into a college or university and who maintain a minimum 2.5 GPA. The scholarship is also available to graduate students. *Application Process: Applicants should apply online via the company's Web site. The application includes a 250-word essay in which the applicant must address the question, "What is the perfect career for you, and why?" *Amount: Awards vary. *Deadline: Deadlines vary by semester and by fund availability.

Central Intelligence Agency

Office of Public Affairs
Washington, DC 20505
800-368-3886
http://www.odci.gov/employment/jobs/students_
scholar.html
Scholarship Name: Undergraduate Scholarship Program. *Academic Area: Open. *Age Group: Undergraduate students. *Eligibility: Applicants must be high school seniors or college sophomores who are U.S. citizens and will be at least 18 years old by April 1. They must also achieve a minimum of 1000 SAT or 21 ACT score and a minimum 3.0 GPA. Applicants must demonstrate financial need and meet the same employment standards of permanent CIA employees, successfully completing both security and medical processing. Applicants must also be available to work in the Washington, D.C., area during periods of employment. *Application Process: Applicants must submit a completed application, SAT/ACT scores, names and ages of

all family dependents and gross family income for current and previous years, a copy of their current FAFSA form, transcripts, and two letters of recommendation. Applicants must also pass a medical and psychological exam, polygraph interview, and extensive background investigation. Visit the CIA's Web site to submit an online application. *Amount: Up to $18,000 per calendar year. *Deadline: November 1.

Coca-Cola Scholars Foundation
PO Box 442
Atlanta, GA 30301-0442
800-306-2653
questions@coca-colascholars.org
https://www.coca-colascholars.org/cokeWeb/jsp/scholars/FourYearInstructions.jsp
Scholarship Name: Coca-Cola Scholars Program Scholarship. *Academic Area: Open. *Age Group: Undergraduate students. *Eligibility: Applicants must be high school seniors who are U.S. citizens, U.S. nationals, U.S. residents, temporary residents, refugees, asylees, Cuban-Haitian entrants, or humanitarian parolees. They must also maintain a minimum 3.0 GPA and plan to attend an accredited U.S. postsecondary institution. *Application Process: Applicants must submit an online application. The Coca-Cola Scholars Foundation will contact applicants requesting further application materials if the application advances. *Amount: Up to $20,000. *Deadline: October 31.

Coca-Cola Scholars Foundation
PO Box 442
Atlanta, GA 30301-0442
800-306-2653
questions@coca-colascholars.org
https://www.coca-colascholars.org/cokeWeb/jsp/scholars/TwoYearInstructions.jsp
Scholarship Name: Coca-Cola Two-Year Colleges Scholarship. *Academic Area: Open. *Age Group: Undergraduate students. *Eligibility: Applicants must be U.S. citizens or permanent residents, maintain a minimum 2.5 GPA, and plan to enroll in at least two courses during the next term at a two-year, degree granting institution. They must also have completed a minimum of 100 hours of community service in the 12 months prior to nomination. *Application Process: Applicants are nominated by their two-year, degree granting institution. Applicants are encouraged to visit their institution's

financial aid office for details. *Amount: $1,000. *Deadline: May 31.

CollegeNET Scholarship Review
805 SW Broadway, Suite 1600
Portland, OR 97205
http://www.collegenet.com/finaid/cn_scholar/info/results
Scholarship Name: CollegeNET Scholarship. *Academic Area: Open. *Age Group: Undergraduate students. *Eligibility: Applicants must write an essay on a topic designated by CollegeNET. Applicants must apply to college online using a CollegeNET hosted application. Applicants must be accepted and thereafter enrolled in a college/university to which they applied via CollegeNET. Applicants are nominated to participate in the CollegeNet Scholarship competition by their college/university. High school seniors may apply for this scholarship. *Application Process: Visit CollegeNET's Web site for further application details. *Amount: $5,000 to $10,000. *Deadline: March 31.

Corporation for National and Community Service
1150 Connecticut Avenue, NW, Suite 1100
Washington, DC 20036
866-291-7700
info@studentservicescholarship.org
http://www.nationalservice.org/scholarships
Scholarship Name: Presidential Freedom Scholarship. *Academic Area: Open. *Age Group: Undergraduate students. *Eligibility: Applicants must be high school juniors or seniors who have contributed at least 100 hours of service within the 12 months prior to certifying, be U.S. citizens or permanent residents, and attend a public, private, charter, or parochial school located within one of the 50 states, the District of Columbia, an Indian tribal nation, a U.S. territory, or a Department of Defense school. Applicants must not have been previous Presidential Freedom Scholarship recipients. *Application Process: Contact the corporation or your guidance counselor for application details. *Amount: $1,000. *Deadline: July 1.

Daughters of the American Revolution (DAR)
Committee Services Office
Attn: Scholarships
1776 D Street, NW
Washington, DC 20006-5303
202-628-1776
http://www.dar.org/natsociety/edout_scholar.cfm

Scholarship Name: General Scholarship. *Academic Area: Open. *Age Group: Undergraduate students. *Eligibility: Applicants must demonstrate academic excellence, commitment to a field of study, and financial need. No prior affiliation with DAR is necessary. The scholarship is open to both females and males. *Application Process: All applicants must obtain a letter of sponsorship from their local DAR chapter. Applicants should send a stamped, self-addressed business size envelope to obtain the name and address of their state scholarship chairman and an application. Visit the organization's Web site to obtain the address. *Amount: Awards vary. *Deadline: Deadlines vary.

Daughters of the American Revolution (DAR)

Committee Services Office
Attn: Scholarships
1776 D Street, NW
Washington, DC 20006-5303
202-628-1776
http://www.dar.org/natsociety/edout_scholar.cfm

Scholarship Name: Lillian and Arthur Dunn Scholarship. *Academic Area: Open. *Age Group: Undergraduate students. *Eligibility: Applicants must be sons or daughters of members of the DAR, citizens of the United States, and attending an accredited college or university in the United States. The scholarship is open to both females and males. *Application Process: All applicants must obtain a letter of sponsorship from their local DAR chapter. Applicants should send a stamped, self-addressed business size envelope to obtain the name and address of their state scholarship chairman and an application. *Amount: $2,000, renewable for four years of undergraduate study plus additional years of graduate study, if applicable. *Deadline: February 15.

David and Dovetta Wilson Scholarship Fund

115-67 237th Street
Elmont, NY 11003-39926
800-759-7512
http://www.wilsonfund.org/home.shtml

Scholarship Name: David and Dovetta Wilson Scholarship. *Academic Area: Open. *Age Group: Undergraduate students. *Eligibility: Applicants must be high school graduating seniors who are active participants in community or religious activities and who demonstrate financial need. *Application Process: Applicants should submit a completed application along with a copy of their high school transcript, three letters of recommendation, a W-2 or copy of standard financial aid form, a photo, and a $20 application fee. Visit the fund's Web site to download an application. *Amount: Up to $1,000. *Deadline: March 31.

Davis-Putter Scholarship Fund

PO Box 7307
New York, NY 10116-7307
http://www.davisputter.org

Scholarship Name: Davis-Putter Scholarship Fund. *Academic Area: Open. *Age Group: Undergraduate students. *Eligibility: Applicants must be currently enrolled in an accredited degree-granting institution, exhibit a history of working for social and economic justice, and demonstrate financial need. The scholarship is also available to graduate students. *Application Process: Applicants must submit a completed application along with a personal statement not to exceed 1,000 words describing their activism and perspectives on social change, transcripts, two letters of support, financial aid statements, and a headshot photograph. All application materials should be submitted along with two photocopies, comprising three complete packets. Visit the fund's Web site to download an application and for additional information about social justice activism. *Amount: Up to $6,000. *Deadline: April 1.

Discover Financial Services

Attn: Discover Card Tribute Award Scholarship Program
PO Box 30943
Salt Lake City, UT 84130-0943
http://www.discoverfinancial.com/data/philanthropy/tribute.shtml

Scholarship Name: Discover Card Tribute Award Scholarship. *Academic Area: Open. *Age Group: Undergraduate students. *Eligibility: Applicants must be high school juniors enrolled in accredited public or private high schools in the U.S. who have maintained at least a 2.75 GPA throughout their freshman and sophomore years. Applicants must demonstrate special talent, leadership, and community service while overcoming significant challenges. *Application Process: Visit Discover Financial Service's Web site to obtain application details for next year's award. *Amount: $2,500 and $25,000. *Deadline: Varies.

EasyAid.com

PO Box 124
Youngtown, AZ 85363

questions@easyaid.com
http://www.easyaid.com/scholarship_form.html
Scholarship Name: Frank O'Neill Memorial Scholarship.
*Academic Area: Open. *Age Group: Undergraduate students. *Eligibility: Applicants must be attending a college, university, trade school, or technical institute and must not be receiving a full-tuition scholarship or waiver from another source. Residents of the United States and international students may apply. The scholarship is also available to graduate students. *Application Process: Applicant must apply via EasyAid.com. Mailed submissions are not accepted. Applicants should submit their personal contact information and an essay (maximum of 1,000 words) on "how one person in particular has influenced your life in a positive way." Visit the company's Web site to apply. *Amount: $1,000. *Deadline: March 31. Additional deadlines for upcoming semesters are posted after the spring deadline has passed.

Education Is Freedom Foundation
2711 North Haskell Avenue
Dallas, TX 75204
866-EIF-EDUCATE
http://www.educationisfreedom.com/default.asp
Scholarship Name: Education is Freedom National Scholarship. *Academic Area: Open. *Age Group: Undergraduate students. *Eligibility: Applicants must be high school graduating seniors who are U.S. residents, maintain a GPA of at least 3.0, and will be enrolling in a full-time undergraduate program at an accredited two- or four-year college or university. They should also demonstrate financial need, a history of extracurricular activities and/or leadership roles, and an employment history. *Application Process: Applicants should apply online via the organization's Web site between November 1 and January 15. No mailed applications are permitted. Visit the organization's Web site to register and apply online. *Amount: $2,000. *Deadline: January 15.

Elder & Leemaur Publishers
PO Box 4169
Blaine, WA 98213
http://www.elpublishers.com/content/AboutUWS.php
Scholarship Name: University Writing Scholarship.
*Academic Area: Open. *Age Group: Undergraduate students. *Eligibility: Applicants should be graduating high school seniors or undergraduate students attending (or planning to attend) college in the United States or Canada. *Application Process: Applicants must submit an essay, up to 500 words, responding to one of the topics posted on the company's Web site. Visit the company's Web site to view the current topics. Authors of top essays will receive scholarships and possible publication opportunities. *Amount: $500 (minimum). *Deadline: March 1.

Foundation for the Preservation of Honey Bees Inc.
4-H Beekeeping Essay Contest
PO Box 1337
Jesup, GA 31598-1337
912-427-4233
info@abfnet.org
http://abfnet.org/?page_id=73
Contest Name: 4-H Beekeeping Essay Contest.
*Academic Area: Open. *Age Group: High school students. *Eligibility: Applicants must be active 4-H Club members who have not previously placed first, second, or third at the national level. *Application Process: Applicants must submit a 750- to 1,000-word essay and a brief biographical sketch. Visit the foundation's Web site for further application details. Applicants must submit essays to their state 4-H Office. State winners will then be sent to the foundation for consideration. *Amount: $50 to $250. *Deadline: Varies.

Golf Course Superintendents Association of America (GCSAA)
Attn: Amanda Howard
1421 Research Park Drive
Lawrence, KS 66049-3859
800-472-7878, ext. 4424
ahoward@gcsaa.org
http://www.gcsaa.org/students/scholarships/default.asp
Grant Name: Par Aide's Joseph S. Garske Collegiate Grant Program. *Academic Area: Open. *Age Group: Undergraduate students. *Eligibility: Applicants must be graduating high school seniors and be accepted at institutions of higher learning for the upcoming year. The grant program is available for children of GCSAA members who have been active members for five or more consecutive years. *Application Process: Contact Amanda Howard for application materials. *Amount: $2,500. *Deadline: March 15.

Hawaii Education Association (HEA)
1649 Kalakaua Avenue
Honolulu, HI 96826

808-949-6657, 866-653-9372
hea.office@heaed.com
http://www.heaed.com/HEA_Scholarships.html
Scholarship Name: High School Senior Scholarship.
*Academic Area: Open. *Age Group: Undergraduate students. *Eligibility: Applicants must be the children of HEA members (parent(s) must have been members for at least one year), and high school graduating seniors who plan to enroll in a two- or four-year college or university. *Application Process: Applicants should submit a completed application along with high school transcripts, a 300-word personal statement, a financial aid form, and three recommendations from teachers. Visit the association's Web site to download an application. *Amount: $1,000. *Deadline: April 1.

Hawaii Education Association (HEA)

1649 Kalakaua Avenue
Honolulu, HI 96826
808-949-6657, 866-653-9372
hea.office@heaed.com
http://www.heaed.com/HEA_Scholarships.html
Scholarship Name: Undergraduate College Student Scholarship. *Academic Area: Open. *Age Group: Undergraduate students. *Eligibility: Applicants must be the children of HEA members (parent(s) must have been members for at least one year), and enrolled full time in a two- or four-year college or university. *Application Process: Applicants should submit a completed application along with college transcripts, a 300-word personal statement, a financial aid form, and a recommendation from a college faculty member. Visit the association's Web site to download an application. *Amount: $1,000. *Deadline: April 1.

Horatio Alger Association of Distinguished Americans

99 Canal Center Plaza
Alexandria, VA 22314
703-684-9444
https://www.horatioalger.com/scholarships/apply.cfm
Scholarship Name: Horatio Alger Scholarship Program. *Academic Area: Open. *Age Group: Undergraduate students. *Eligibility: Applicants must be full-time high school seniors with plans to enter college no later than the fall following graduation. They must have a strong commitment to pursuing a bachelor's degree in an accredited institution, demonstrate

critical financial need and involvement in co-curricular and community activities, and maintain a minimum 2.0 GPA. They must also be U.S. citizens, or in the process of obtaining U.S. citizenship, and reside in the U.S. or attend a Department of Defense school. *Application Process: Applicants must submit a completed application and copy of the front page of their parent/guardian's individual tax return. Visit the association's Web site to complete an online application. *Amount: Varies. *Deadline: Varies.

Indiana State Teachers Association (ISTA)

ISTA Scholarships
150 West Market Street, Suite 900
Indianapolis, IN 46204-2875
317-263-3400, 800-382-4037
http://www.ista-in.org/sam.cfm?xnode=1467
Scholarship Name: ISTA Career Scholarship. *Academic Area: Open. *Age Group: Undergraduate students. *Eligibility: Applicants must be graduating high school seniors in Indiana who are planning to attend a college or university and who have a parent or legal guardian who is an active member of the ISTA. They also must demonstrate academic achievement, community involvement, cocurricular activity involvement, and leadership ability. *Application Process: Applicants should submit a completed application along with current official high school transcripts, three letters of recommendation, and a typed essay (topic outlined on the application). Visit the association's Web site to download an application. *Amount: $1,000, renewable for three additional years. *Deadline: March 3.

Jack Kent Cooke Foundation

44325 Woodridge Parkway
Lansdowne, VA 20176
703-723-8000, 800-8498-6478
jkc@jackkentcookefoundation.org
http://www.jackkentcookefoundation.org/jkcf_web/content.aspx?page=SchProg
Grant Name: September 11 Grant. *Academic Area: Open. *Age Group: Undergraduate students. *Eligibility: Applicants must be the dependant or spouse of a person killed or permanently disabled in the September 11 attacks on the Pentagon or World Trade Center, the crash of United Airlines Flight 93 in Pennsylvania, or the September and October 2001 anthrax attacks. Applicants must be able to demonstrate unmet financial need. *Application

Process: Applicants should submit a completed application form along with a financial information statement; a cost of attendance worksheet; a copy of their billing statement from their college, university, or trade school; an official copy of their birth certificate (dependants) or marriage certificate (spouses); a letter from a physician (for those with a permanently disabled family member); and income tax returns. Visit the foundation's Web site to download all required forms. *Amount: Up to $15,000/semester. These grants are not renewable, but applicants may reapply. *Deadline: February 17.

Jack Kent Cooke Foundation
44325 Woodridge Parkway
Lansdowne, VA 20176
703-723-8000, 800-498-6478
jkc-u@act.org
http://www.jackkentcookefoundation.org/jkcf_web/
     content.aspx?page=SchProg
Scholarship Name: Undergraduate Transfer
     Scholarship. *Academic Area: Open. *Age Group:
     Undergraduate students. *Eligibility: Applicants
     must be currently enrolled in a two-year program
     (or recent graduates) and plan to transfer to a four-
     year institution. Applicants must have a 3.5 GPA on
     a 4.0 scale, demonstrate unmet financial need, and
     also must receive a nomination from their school
     representative. Visit the foundation's Web site for
     a listing of representatives, by state and school.
     *Application Process: Applicants must submit a
     completed application and supporting materials.
     However, applicants must be nominated for this
     scholarship and cannot submit materials without
     having been nominated first. Application packet
     materials consist of an original plus four copies
     of the application, financial information forms, a
     nominee survey form, official transcripts, and two
     signed, sealed letters of recommendation. Visit the
     foundation's Web site to download the required
     forms. *Amount: Up to $30,000. *Deadline: Contact
     the foundation for details.

Junior Achievement (JA)
One Education Way
Colorado Springs, CO 80906
888-4-JA-ALUM
scholarships@ja.org
http://studentcenter.ja.org/aspx/PayCollege/
     ScholarshipSearch.aspx

Scholarship Name: Hugh B. Sweeny Award Scholarship.
     *Academic Area: Open. *Age Group: Undergraduate
     students. *Eligibility: Applicants must be high school
     seniors who are graduating before June 30 of the year
     in which the scholarship is awarded and demonstrate
     extraordinary results in impacting the community
     through entrepreneurship and similar initiatives.
     They must also be qualified, upon graduation, to
     enroll at an accredited postsecondary educational
     institution, including trade school or community
     college; maintain a minimum 3.0 GPA; exemplify
     achievement, citizenship, creativity, leadership,
     and motivation; and demonstrate financial need.
     Applicants must also have completed JA Company
     Program or JA Economics. *Application Process:
     Applicants must submit a completed application,
     three letters of recommendation, a 500-word essay,
     official transcripts, SAT/ACT scores, and proof of
     family income. Visit the JA Web site to download an
     application. *Amount: $5,000. *Deadline: February 1.

Junior Achievement (JA)
Joe Francomano Scholarship
One Education Way
Colorado Springs, CO 80906
888-4-JA-ALUM
scholarships@ja.org
http://studentcenter.ja.org/aspx/PayCollege/
     ScholarshipSearch.aspx
Scholarship Name: Joe Francomano Scholarship.
     *Academic Area: Open. *Age Group: Undergraduate
     students. *Eligibility: Applicants must be high
     school seniors who are graduating before June 30
     of the year in which the scholarship is awarded,
     maintain a minimum 3.0 GPA, and be qualified,
     upon graduation, to enroll at an accredited four-year
     college or university. They must also demonstrate
     academic achievement, leadership skills, and financial
     need. Applicants must also have completed JA
     Company Program or JA Economics. *Application
     Process: Applicants must submit a completed
     application, three letters of recommendation, a
     personal essay addressing a topic determined by
     JA, official transcripts, SAT/ACT scores, and proof of
     family income. Visit the JA Web site to download an
     application. *Amount: $20,000. *Deadline: February 1.

Kansas Association of Broadcasters (KAB)
Attn: Scholarship Committee
1916 Southwest Sieben Court

Topeka, KS 66611
785-235-1307
harriet@kab.net
http://www.kab.net/Programs/StudentServices/
BroadcastScholarshipProgram/default.aspx
Scholarship Name: KAB Broadcast Scholarship Program. *Academic Area: Open. *Age Group: Undergraduate students. *Eligibility: Applicants must be Kansas residents who are attending or planning to attend (by the fall semester) a Kansas post-secondary institution (two-year or four-year college or vocational-tech/trade school). If attending a four-year college, applicants must be entering their junior year; if attending a two-year school, applicants must be entering their sophomore year. They must be enrolled or planning to enroll in a broadcast or related curriculum and maintain a 2.5 GPA. *Applicants must submit seven copies of a completed application and an essay. Application must be signed by college radio/TV department head or high school adviser/counselor, certifying the applicant meets the eligibility criteria. Visit the association's Web site to download an application. *Amount: Amount varies. *Deadline: May 1.

National Association for Campus Activities
Attn: Dionne Ellison, Scholarship Coordinator
13 Harbison Way
Columbia, SC 29212
803-732-6222
dionnee@naca.org
http://www.naca.org/NACA/Schools/Scholarships
Scholarship Name: National Association for Campus Activities Student Leadership Scholarship. *Academic Area: Open. *Age Group: Undergraduate students. *Eligibility: Because there are several scholarships offered by this association, applicants should visit the association's Web site for detailed eligibility requirements for individual scholarships. Most scholarships require residence or college attendance in a specific region of the United States, demonstration of leadership skills, and a commitment to community service. Graduate students are eligible for some scholarships offered by the association. *Application Process: Applicants should submit a completed application along with two letters of recommendation, a resume detailing their leadership activities, and verification of college enrollment status. Some scholarships may require additional application materials. Visit the association's Web site for a complete listing of scholarships and to download applications. *Amount: Awards vary. *Deadline: Deadlines vary.

National FFA Organization
PO Box 68960
Indianapolis, IN 46268-0960
317-802-6060
scholarships@ffa.org
http://www.ffa.org/programs/scholarships/index.html
Scholarship Name: National FFA Collegiate Scholarship Program. *Academic Area: Open. *Age Group: Undergraduate students. *Eligibility: Applicants must be current FFA members and current high school seniors or full-time undergraduate students. Scholarships are given for a wide variety of experiences, career goals, and higher education plans. Different awards may be used at colleges, universities, and postsecondary agricultural programs. Specific eligibility criteria for individual awards can be found by visiting the association's Web site. *Application Process: Applicants should submit a completed application and relevant supporting materials, according to scholarship specifications. Visit the association's Web site to download an application. *Amount: Awards vary. *Deadline: February 15.

National Utility Contractors Association (NUCA)
Attn: Jill Glei, Director of Education
4301 North Fairfax Drive, Suite 360
Arlington, VA 22203
703-358-9300
jill@nuca.com
http://www.nuca.com/i4a/pages/index.cfm?pageid=432
Scholarship Name: Antonio M. Marinelli Founders Scholarship. *Academic Area: Open. *Age Group: Undergraduate students. *Eligibility: Applicants must be high school seniors, have parents or legal guardians who are employed by a NUCA-member company, and plan to begin their freshman year in a college or university in the fall. They also must demonstrate academic excellence and interest in extracurricular activities and community service. *Application Process: Contact the Association for application details. *Amount: $2,500. *Deadline: Varies.

National Utility Contractors Association (NUCA)
Attn: Jill Glei, Director of Education
4301 North Fairfax Drive, Suite 360

Arlington, VA 22203
703-358-9300
jill@nuca.com
http://www.nuca.com/i4a/pages/index.cfm?pageid=432
Scholarship Name: D.A. Foster Memorial Scholarship.
*Academic Area: Open. *Age Group: Undergraduate
students. *Eligibility: Applicants must be high school
seniors, have parents or legal guardians who are
employed by a NUCA-member company, and plan to
begin their freshman year in a college or university
in the fall. They also must demonstrate academic
excellence and interest in extracurricular activities
and community service. *Application Process:
Contact the association for application details.
*Amount: $2,000 per year for four years. *Deadline:
Varies.

National Utility Contractors Association (NUCA)
Attn: Jill Glei, Director of Education
4301 North Fairfax Drive, Suite 360
Arlington, VA 22203
703-358-9300
jill@nuca.com
http://www.nuca.com/i4a/pages/index.cfm?pageid=432
Scholarship Name: NUCA $4,000 Scholarship.
*Academic Area: Open. *Age Group: Undergraduate
students. *Eligibility: Applicants must be high school
seniors, have parents or legal guardians who are
employed by a NUCA-member company, and plan to
begin their freshman year in a college or university
in the fall. They also must demonstrate academic
excellence and interest in extracurricular activities
and community service. *Application Process:
Contact the association for application details.
*Amount: $1,000 per year for four years. *Deadline:
Varies.

National Utility Contractors Association (NUCA)
Attn: Jill Glei, Director of Education
4301 North Fairfax Drive, Suite 360
Arlington, VA 22203
703-358-9300
jill@nuca.com
http://www.nuca.com/i4a/pages/index.cfm?pageid=432
Scholarship Name: National Utility Contractors
Association $1,000 Scholarship. *Academic Area:
Open. *Age Group: Undergraduate students.
*Eligibility: Applicants must be high school seniors,
have parents or legal guardians who are employed by
a NUCA-member company, and plan to begin their

freshman year in a college or university in the fall.
They also must demonstrate academic excellence and
interest in extracurricular activities and community
service. *Application Process: Contact the association
for application details. *Amount: $500 per year for two
years. *Deadline: Varies.

OP Loftbed
PO Box 573
Thomasville, NC 27361-0573
866-5OP-LOFT
http://www.oploftbed.com/scholarship/index.php
Scholarship Name: OP Loftbed Scholarship. *Academic
Area: Open. *Age Group: Undergraduate students.
*Eligibility: Applicants must be college students
or high school seniors who plan to attend college.
*Application Process: Applicants should submit
a completed application along with answers to
proposed questions, which change every year. Some
recent applications have asked, "In 100 words or less,
write something that will make the judges laugh
out loud," and "Tell us about the best gift you have
ever given someone or that someone else gave to
you." Visit the company's Web site to download an
application. *Amount: $500. *Deadline: Visit the
company's Web site for deadline updates.

Orange County Mensa
Attn: Larry Grannis, Scholarship Coordinator
PO Box 11191
Santa Ana, CA 92711-1191
scholarships@acmensa.org
http://www.ocmensa.org
Scholarship Name: Orange County Mensa Essay
Contest/Scholarship. *Academic Area: Open.
*Age Group: Undergraduate students. *Eligibility:
Applicants do not have to be Mensa members, but
they must reside in a zip code within the area that
this section of Mensa serves. Applicants must also
be enrolled in or plan to enroll in a degree program
at a college or university. The scholarship is also
available to graduate students. *Application Process:
Applicants should visit the organization's Web site
to determine eligibility based on zip code. Once the
organization verifies zip code eligibility, applicants
will be allowed to download an application.
Applicants must submit the application along with
an essay, up to 550 words, explaining their academic
goals. *Amount: $300 to $1,000. *Deadline: Contact
the organization for deadline information.

Papercheck.com

866-693-EDIT

scholarships@papercheck.com

http://www.papercheck.com/scholarship.asp

Scholarship Name: The Charles Shafae' Scholarship Fund. *Academic Area: Open. *Age Group: Undergraduate students. *Eligibility: Applicants must be enrolled at an accredited four-year college or university in the United States, carry a status of "good standing," maintain a GPA of at least 3.2, and be U.S. citizens. *Application Process: Applicants must submit, online, a 1,000-word essay covering a specific topic listed at the company's Web site. The essay should include at least three outside sources and must be written using Modern Language Association (MLA) style. Visit the company's Web site for a detailed description of the essay topic. *Amount: $500. *Deadline: January 1.

The Roothbert Fund Inc.

475 Riverside Drive, Room 252

New York, NY 10115

212-870-3116

mail@roothbertfund.org

http://www.roothbertfund.org/scholarships.php

Scholarship Name: Roothbert Fund Scholarship. *Academic Area: Open. *Age Group: Undergraduate students. *Eligibility: Applicants must demonstrate financial need and openly profess that they are motivated by spiritual values. Applicants should be a resident of one of the following states: Maine, New Hampshire, Vermont, Rhode Island, Massachusetts, Connecticut, New York, New Jersey, Pennsylvania, Ohio, Delaware, Maryland, District of Columbia, Virginia, West Virginia, or North Carolina. They also should demonstrate academic achievement and be willing and able to participate in an in-person interview in New York, New Haven (Connecticut), Philadelphia, or Washington, D.C., should they be chosen for an interview (transportation is not provided). Preference is given to applicants pursuing careers in education. Visit the fund's Web site to read more about its spirituality mission. The scholarship is also available to graduate students. *Application Process: Applicants should submit a completed application along with three letters of recommendation, transcripts, and two essays (outlined on the application). Visit the fund's Web site to download an application after November 1. *Amount: $2,000 to $3,000. *Deadline: February 1.

Salute to Education Inc.

PO Box 833425

Miami, FL 33283

305-476-7709

steinfo@stescholarships.org

http://www.stescholarships.org/SC_categories.html

Scholarship Name: Salute to Education Leadership/Service Scholarship. *Academic Area: Open. *Age Group: Undergraduate students. *Eligibility: Applicants must be graduating high school seniors who attend a Miami-Dade or Broward County, Florida, high school and who also reside in one of these counties. They must also be legal residents of the United States, have a minimum weighted GPA of 3.0, demonstrate a commitment to service by participating in at least one school or community organization, and intend to pursue a college degree at an accredited institution after graduation. Applicants must demonstrate exemplary commitment to community service through documented participation and leadership in local, state, and national civic organizations. *Application Process: Applicants must apply online. Supporting materials should be mailed as detailed on the online application. *Amount: $1,000. *Deadline: Visit the organization's Web site for updated deadline information.

Seattle Jaycees

Scholarship Committee

109 West Mercer Street

Seattle, WA 98119

206-286-2014

sjc_scholarships@yahoo.com

http://www.seattlejaycees.org

Scholarship Name: Seattle Jaycees Scholarship. *Academic Area: Open. *Age Group: Undergraduate students. *Eligibility: Applicants must be enrolled in or accepted into a postsecondary educational institution in the state of Washington (though prior residency in Washington is not required). They must also demonstrate exemplary commitment to involvement and service to the community, display leadership qualities and managerial skills in matters relating to civic activism, and exhibit academic achievement as well as achievement in other areas of work and life. The scholarship is also available to graduate students. *Application Process: Applicants should submit a completed application along with a one-page essay, three letters of recommendation, and official transcripts. Visit the organization's Web site to download an application. *Amount: Awards vary. *Deadline: April 1.

Sheriff's Association of Texas
Attn: Scholarship Program
1601 South IH 35
Austin, TX 78741-2503
512-445-5888
info@txsheriffs.org
http://www.txsheriffs.org
Scholarship Name: Sheriffs' Association of Texas Scholarship Program. *Academic Area: Open. *Age Group: Undergraduate students. *Eligibility: Applicants must be enrolled in a college/university and be under 25 years of age at the time of application. Applicants must be full-time students, maintain a minimum 2.5 GPA, have completed at least one semester of study, and not have been convicted of a crime that would make an individual ineligible for employment in his/her field of study. Many scholarships are available to children/grandchildren of a Texas Sheriff's office employee or students pursuing criminal justice careers. Eligibility requirements vary. Visit the association's Web site to obtain specific scholarship eligibility requirements. *Application Process: Applicants must submit a completed application, current transcripts, proof of enrollment, and personal statement. Visit the association's Web site to download an application. *Amount: Varies. *Deadline: March 1 and October 15.

StraightForward Media
http://www.straightforwardmedia.com/scholarships/index.php
Scholarship Name: StraightForward Media Scholarships. *Academic Area: Open. *Age Group: Undergraduate students. *Eligibility: Applicants should be enrolled in an institution of higher education. This organization offers 22 different scholarships encompassing a variety of majors and categories—anything from minority scholarships to science major scholarships to get-out-of-debt scholarships. Visit the company's Web site for a complete listing of eligibility requirements. Select scholarships are also available to graduate students. *Application Process: Applicants should visit the company's Web site to apply online. Scholarships are awarded quarterly, and applicants may apply each quarter if they are not selected in a previous quarter. Applicants need to submit personal contact information and a short essay online. *Amount: $500 and up. *Deadline: Quarterly (on or around January 15, April 15, July 15, October 15, depending on the scholarship). Visit the company's Web site to confirm details.

SuperCollege.com
4546 B10 El Camino Real, Suite 281
Los Altos, CA 94022
650-618-2221
http://www.supercollege.com
Scholarship Name: SuperCollege.com Scholarship. *Academic Area: Open. *Age Group: Open. *Eligibility: Applicants must be U.S. citizens or legal residents attending or planning to attend any accredited college or university in the United States. *Application Process: Applicants must submit an online application and personal essay. Visit SuperCollege.com's Web site to complete and submit an application. *Amount: $500 to $2,500. *Deadline: July 31.

Syracuse Teachers Association Inc.
Attn: Len Fonte
c/o the STA office
905 Butternut Street
Syracuse, NY 13208
http://www.syracuseteachers.org/scholarship.pdf
Scholarship Name: Syracuse Teachers Association Scholarship. *Academic Area: Open. *Age Group: Undergraduate students. *Eligibility: Applicants must be children of Syracuse Teachers Association members, high school graduating seniors, and intend to pursue postsecondary education at an accredited institution. They should also demonstrate academic achievement and financial need. *Application Process: Applicants should submit a completed application along with transcripts. Visit the association's Web site to download an application. *Amount: $4,000 ($500 per semester for four years). *Deadline: May 2.

Tall Clubs International (TCI)
5906 Meyers Drive
Cincinnati, OH 45215
888-468-2552
http://www.tall.org/scholarships.cfm?CFID=711698&CFTOKEN=29135668
Scholarship Name: Tall Clubs International Student Scholarship. *Academic Area: Open. *Age Group: Undergraduate students. *Eligibility: Applicants

must be tall students who are under 21 years of age and attending their first year of college in the following fall. Applicants must meet the TCI height requirement minimums of 5'10" for women and 6'2" for men. High school seniors and recent graduates may apply. *Application Process: Applicants must be nominated by their local TCI member club. Visit the club's Web site to find your local member club and obtain further application details. *Amount: $1,000. *Deadline: Contact your local member club for details.

Target

612-304-6073
http://target.com/target_group/community_giving/scholarships.jhtml

Scholarship Name: Target All-Around Scholarship. *Academic Area: Open. *Age Group: Undergraduate students. *Eligibility: Applicants must be enrolled in a full-time undergraduate course of study at a two- or four-year school in the United States. High school seniors and undergraduate students age 24 or younger are eligible to apply for the scholarship. This program is not offered in Alaska, Hawaii, Puerto Rico, or outside the United States. Applicants must also demonstrate a commitment to volunteer community service. *Application Process: Applicants must apply online. No hard-copy paper applications accepted. Applicants should submit their online application, which includes detailed sections on community volunteer service, volunteer leadership awards and honors, and academic achievement (minimum 2.0 GPA). Applicants must also submit an essay on volunteer service and an appraisal form completed by a volunteer supervisor or leader. Visit the corporation's Web site to apply. *Amount: $1,000 (600 scholarships), $25,000 (one scholarship). *Deadline: November 1.

UNICO National Inc.

Attn: Joan Tidona, Scholarship Director
271 U.S. Highway West
Fairfield, NJ 07004
201-933-7982
jntidona@verizon.net
http://www.unico.org/scholarships.html

Scholarship Name: UNICO National Scholarships. *Academic Area: Open. *Age Group: Undergraduate students. *Eligibility: UNICO touts itself as the largest Italian American service organization in the United States. Italian American graduating high school

seniors, college undergraduates, and graduate students may apply for scholarships awarded for college study. *Application Process: Applicants should contact the scholarship director to receive additional information and an application. (Note: The scholarship director distributes all rules and announcements regarding available scholarships.) *Amount: $1,500. *Deadline: Contact the scholarship director for deadline information.

Veterans of Foreign Wars (VFW)

VFW National Headquarters
Attn: Veterans' Tribute Scholarship
406 West 34th Street, Suite 902
Kansas City, MO 64111
816-756-3390
SWilson@vfw.org
http://www.vfw.org/index.cfm?fa=cmty.leveld&did=1589

Scholarship Name: Veterans' Tribute Scholarship. *Academic Area: Open. *Age Group: Undergraduate students. *Eligibility: Applicants must be children and grandchildren, ages 15 through 18, of living U.S. military veterans, as well as those currently serving active duty, in the Reserves, and/or the National Guard. *Application Process: Applicants must submit a completed application, a school report card, a letter of recommendation, and appropriate military service verification documentation. Visit the VFW Web site to download an application. *Amount: $3,000 to $10,000. *Deadline: December 31.

Wal-Mart Foundation

Attn: Scholarship Program Administrators
PO Box 22492
Nashville, TN 37202
866-524-7385
http://www.walmartfoundation.org/wmstore/goodworks/scripts/index.jsp

Scholarship Name: Higher REACH Scholarship. *Academic Area: Open. *Age Group: Undergraduate students. *Eligibility: Applicants must be nontraditional students who have been employed by Wal-Mart Stores Inc. for at least one year as of February 1 and out of high school for at least one year. *Application Process: Applicants must provide evidence of financial need, academic transcripts, a personal essay, and job performance evaluation. Applicants can obtain further application details from their Wal-Mart/SAM'S CLUB personnel manager. *Amount: Up to $2,000. *Deadline: January 20.

Wal-Mart Foundation
Attn: Scholarship Program Administrators
PO Box 22117
Nashville, TN 37202
866-851-3372
http://www.walmartfoundation.org/wmstore/ goodworks/scripts/index.jsp
Scholarship Name: Sam Walton Community Scholarship. *Academic Area: Open. *Age Group: Undergraduate students. *Eligibility: Applicants must be graduating high school seniors and must not be an associate of Wal-Mart Stores Inc., or be the child/dependent of an associate of Wal-Mart Stores Inc. They must also be enrolled in an accredited U.S. college or university and have a minimum 2.5 GPA. *Application Process: Applicants must provide evidence of financial need, ACT/SAT scores, and academic transcripts. Applicants are only allowed to apply to one Wal-Mart/SAM'S CLUB location. Local scholarship winners are automatically entered into statewide competitions. State scholarship winners are then entered into a national scholarship competition. Applicants should contact their local Wal-Mart/SAM'S CLUB for application details. *Amount: $1,000 (local awards), $4,000 (state awards), $25,000 (national award). *Deadline: January 20.

Wal-Mart Foundation
Attn: Associate Scholarship Coordinator
702 SW 8th Street
Bentonville, AK 72716-0150
800-530-9925
http://www.walmartfoundation.org/wmstore/ goodworks/scripts/index.jsp
Scholarship Name: Wal-Mart Associate Scholarship. *Academic Area: Open. *Age Group: Undergraduate students. *Eligibility: Applicants must be graduating high school seniors employed by Wal-Mart Stores Inc. for at least one year as of application date, or children of associates who are considered ineligible for the Walton Family Foundation Scholarship, due to parent's length of employment or less than full-time employment status. *Application Process: Applicants must provide evidence of financial need, ACT/SAT scores, and academic transcripts. Applicants can obtain further application details on from their Wal-Mart/SAM'S CLUB personnel manager. *Amount: $2,000. *Deadline: January 20.

Wal-Mart Foundation
Attn: Walton Scholarship Coordinator
702 SW 8th Street
Bentonville, AK 72716-0150
800-530-9925
http://www.walmartfoundation.org/wmstore/ goodworks/scripts/index.jsp
Scholarship Name: Walton Foundation Scholarship. *Academic Area: Open. *Age Group: Undergraduate students. *Eligibility: Applicants must be graduating high school seniors and the children/legal dependents of Wal-Mart Stores Inc. associates who have been employed full time (34 hours per week or more) for at least one year as of January 20. *Application Process: Applicants must provide evidence of financial need, ACT/SAT scores, and academic transcripts. Applicants can obtain further application details from their Wal-Mart/SAM'S CLUB personnel manager. *Amount: $10,000. *Deadline: January 20.

OPEN TO ALL MAJORS—GRADUATE

The following financial aid resources are available to graduate students pursuing study in any academic field.

All-Ink.com College Scholarship Program
1460 North Main Street, Suite #2
Spanish Fork, UT 84660
888-567-6511
Education@All-Ink.com
http://www.all-ink.com/scholarship.aspx
Scholarship Name: All-Ink.com College Scholarship Program. *Academic Area: Open. *Age Group: Graduate students. *Eligibility: Applicants must be enrolled in or planning to attend an accredited college or university program. They also must be United States citizens or permanent residents and maintain at least a 2.5 GPA. The scholarship is also available to high school seniors and undergraduate students. *Application Process: Applicants must submit an online application, which includes a 50- to 200-word essay on who has had the greatest impact on their lives, and a 50- to 200-word essay on what they hope to achieve in their personal and professional lives after completing college. No mailed applications will be accepted. Visit the company's Web site to apply. *Amount: Awards vary. *Deadline: December 31.

American Radio Relay League Foundation Inc.
225 Main Street
Newington, CT 06111
860-594-0397
foundation@arrl.org
http://www.arrl.org/arrlf/scholgen.html
Scholarship Name: American Radio Relay League Foundation Scholarship Program. *Academic Area: Open. *Age Group: Graduate students. *Eligibility: Applicants must hold a valid ham radio license. Eligibility requirements vary. Visit the foundation's Web site to obtain specific scholarship eligibility requirements. The scholarship program is also available to undergraduate students.*Application Process: Applicants must submit a completed application and official transcripts. Applicants may submit up to three letters of recommendation and an application covering letter (optional). Visit the foundation's Web site to download an application. *Amount: Up to $10,000. *Deadline: February 1.

Books and Scholarships LLC
Elwood Grimes Literary Scholarship
4525 Cherry Forest Circle
Louisville, KY 40245
http://www.booksandscholarships.com/
    Scholarship%20EGL.htm
Scholarship Name: Elwood Grimes Literary Scholarship. *Academic Area: Open. *Age Group: Graduate students. *Eligibility: Applicants must be college students who are U.S. citizens and attending or planning to attend college at least part time. The scholarship is also available to high school seniors and undergraduate students. *Application Process: Applicants must submit a completed application along with a copy of a letter of college acceptance and a 500 (or more)-word essay. The essay must be written about Elwood Grimes' book, The Rambled Soul of a 21st Century Man. *Amount: Awards vary. Up to $5,000 distributed among first, second, and third place winners. *Deadline: September 30.

CareerFitter.com
918-477-2280
admin3@careerfitter.com
http://www.careerfitter.com/scholarship/index.htm
Scholarship Name: CareerFitter.com Scholarship. *Academic Area: Open. *Age Group: Graduate students. *Eligibility: Applicants must be U.S. citizens or permanent residents who are enrolled in or accepted into a college or university and who maintain a minimum 2.5 GPA. The scholarship is also available to undergraduate students. *Application Process: Applicants should apply online via the company's Web site. The application includes a 250-word essay in which the applicant must address the question, "What is the perfect career for you, and why?" *Amount: Awards vary. *Deadline: Deadlines vary by semester and by fund availability.

CollegeNET Scholarship Review
805 SW Broadway, Suite 1600
Portland, OR 97205
http://www.collegenet.com/finaid/cn_scholar/info/
    results

Scholarship Name: CollegeNET Scholarship. *Academic Area: Open. *Age Group: Graduate students. *Eligibility: Applicants must write an essay on a topic designated by CollegeNET, apply to college online using a CollegeNET hosted application before a specified date, and be accepted and thereafter enrolled in a college/university to which they applied via CollegeNET. Applicants are nominated to participate in the CollegeNet Scholarship competition by their college/university. The scholarship is also available to high school seniors and undergraduate students. *Application Process: Visit CollegeNET's Web site for further application details. *Amount: $5,000 to $10,000. *Deadline: March 31.

Daughters of the American Revolution (DAR)
Attn: Scholarships
1776 D Street, NW
Washington, DC 20006-5303
202-628-1776
http://www.dar.org/natsociety/edout_scholar.cfm
Scholarship Name: Lillian and Arthur Dunn Scholarship. *Academic Area: Open. *Age Group: Graduate students. *Eligibility: Applicants must be sons or daughters of members of the DAR, citizens of the United States, and attending an accredited college or university in the United States. The scholarship is also available to undergraduate students. *Application Process: All applicants must obtain a letter of sponsorship from their local DAR chapter. Applicants should send a stamped, self-addressed business size envelope to obtain the name and address of their state scholarship chairman and an application. *Amount: $2,000. *Deadline: February 15.

Davis-Putter Scholarship Fund
PO Box 7307
New York, NY 10116-7307
http://www.davisputter.org
Scholarship Name: Davis-Putter Scholarship Fund. *Academic Area: Open. *Age Group: Graduate students. *Eligibility: Applicants must be currently enrolled in an accredited degree-granting institution, exhibit a history of working for social and economic justice, and demonstrate financial need. The scholarship is also available to undergraduate students. *Application Process: Applicants must submit a completed application along with a personal statement not to exceed 1,000 words

describing their activism and perspectives on social change, transcripts, two letters of support, financial aid statements, and a headshot photograph. All application materials should be submitted along with two photocopies, comprising three complete packets. Visit the fund's Web site to download an application and for additional information about social justice activism. *Amount: Up to $6,000. *Deadline: April 1.

EasyAid.com
PO Box 124
Youngtown, AZ 85363
questions@easyaid.com
http://www.easyaid.com/scholarship_form.html
Scholarship Name: Frank O'Neill Memorial Scholarship. *Academic Area: Open. *Age Group: Graduate students. *Eligibility: Applicants must be attending a college, university, or trade school and must not be receiving a full-tuition scholarship or waiver from another source. Residents of the United States and international students may apply. The scholarship is also available to undergraduate students. *Application Process: Applicant must apply via EasyAid.com. Mailed submissions are not accepted. Applicants should submit their personal contact information and an essay (maximum of 1,000 words) on "how one person in particular has influenced your life in a positive way." Visit the company's Web site to apply. *Amount: $1,000. *Deadline: March 31. Additional deadlines for upcoming semesters are posted after the spring deadline has passed.

Jack Kent Cooke Foundation
44325 Woodridge Parkway
Lansdowne, VA 20176
703-723-8000, 800-498-6478
jkc-g@act.org
http://www.jackkentcookefoundation.org/jkcf_web/content.aspx?page=SchProg
Scholarship Name: Graduate Scholarship. *Academic Area: Open. *Age Group: Graduate students. *Eligibility: Applicants must be college seniors or recent graduates from an accredited college or university, have a 3.5 GPA on a 4.0 scale, be planning to attend graduate school full time, and demonstrate unmet financial need. They must also receive a nomination from their school representative. Visit the foundation's Web site for a listing of representatives, by state and school. *Application Process: Applicants must submit a completed application and supporting

materials. However, applicants must be nominated for this scholarship and cannot submit materials without having been nominated first. Application packet materials consist of an original plus four copies of the application, financial information forms, a nominee survey form, official transcripts, and two signed, sealed letters of recommendation. Visit the foundation's Web site to download all of the required forms. *Amount: Up to $50,000. *Deadline: May 1.

Josephine De Kármán Fellowship Trust

Attn: Judy McClain, Secretary
PO Box 3389
San Dimas, CA 91773
909-592-0607
http://www.dekarman.org/Default.htm
Fellowship Name: Josephine De Kármán Fellowship. *Academic Area: Open. *Age Group: Graduate students. *Eligibility: Applicants should be entering seniors in their undergraduate year up through Ph.D. candidates who will defend their dissertations by June. Special consideration is given to candidates who are studying the humanities. Applicants must also be foreign students who are already enrolled in a university in the United States. Contact the organization for additional eligibility information. The fellowship is also available to undergraduate students. *Application Process: Applicants should submit a completed application along with official transcripts and two letters of recommendation. Visit the organization's Web site to download an application. *Amount: $16,000 (graduates). *Deadline: January 31.

National Association for Campus Activities (NACA)

Attn: Dionne Ellison, Scholarship Coordinator
13 Harbison Way
Columbia, SC 29212
803-732-6222
dionnee@naca.org
http://www.naca.org/NACA/Schools/Scholarships
Scholarship Name: NACA Student Leadership Scholarship. *Academic Area: Open. *Age Group: Graduate students. *Eligibility: Because there are several scholarships offered by this association, applicants should visit the association's Web site for detailed eligibility requirements for individual scholarships. Most scholarships require residence or college attendance in a specific region of the United States, demonstration of leadership skills, and a commitment to community service. Undergraduate students are eligible for some scholarships offered by the association. *Application Process: Applicants should submit a completed application along with two letters of recommendation, a resume detailing their leadership activities, and verification of college enrollment status. Some scholarships may require additional application materials. Visit the association's Web site for a complete listing of scholarships and to download applications. *Amount: Awards vary. *Deadline: Deadlines vary.

National Society of Collegiate Scholars (NSCS)

1900 K Street, NW, Suite 890
Washington, DC 20006
202-265-9000, 800-989-6727
http://www.nscs.org/memberbenefits/ScholarshipOpportunities/grad/index.cfm
Scholarship Name: NSCS-GEICO Graduate School Scholarship. *Academic Area: Open. *Age Group: Graduate students. *Eligibility: Applicants must be NSCS members who are accepted into a graduate or Ph.D. program, beginning in the fall. *Application Process: Applications become available February 1 of each year. Visit the society's Web site in February to download an application. *Amount: $5,000. *Deadline: Contact NSCS for deadline information.

National Society of Collegiate Scholars (NSCS)

1900 K Street, NW, Suite 890
Washington, DC 20006
202-265-9000, 800-989-6727
http://www.nscs.org/memberbenefits/ScholarshipOpportunities/MeritAward/index.cfm
Award Name: NSCS Merit Award. *Academic Area: Open. *Age Group: Graduate students. *Eligibility: Applicants must be new NSCS members who demonstrate academic excellence and engaged citizenship. The scholarship is also available to undergraduate students. *Application Process: There isn't an application process. Contact the society for information on how new members are nominated for this award. *Amount: $1,000. *Deadline: Contact the society for nomination deadline information.

Orange County Mensa

Attn: Larry Grannis, Scholarship Coordinator
PO Box 11191
Santa Ana, CA 92711-1191
scholarships@acmensa.org
http://www.ocmensa.org

Scholarship Name: Orange County Mensa Essay Contest/Scholarship. *Academic Area: Open. *Age Group: Graduate students. *Eligibility: Applicants do not have to be Mensa members, but they must reside in a zip code within the area that this section of Mensa serves. Applicants must also be enrolled in or plan to enroll in a degree program at a college or university. The scholarship is also available to undergraduate students. *Application Process: Applicants should visit the organization's Web site to determine eligibility based on zip code. Once the organization verifies zip code eligibility, applicants will be allowed to download an application. Applicants must submit the application along with an essay, up to 550 words, explaining their academic goals. *Amount: $300 to $1,000. *Deadline: Contact the organization for deadline information.

Professional Bowlers Association
Attn: Billy Welu Bowling Scholarship
719 Second Avenue, Suite 701
Seattle, WA 98104
206-332-9688
http://www.pba.com/corporate/scholarships.asp
Scholarship Name: Billy Welu Scholarship. *Academic Area: Open. *Age Group: Graduate students. *Eligibility: Applicants must be amateur bowlers who are matriculating college students maintaining at least a 2.5 GPA. They also should demonstrate academic achievement and a love of bowling. The scholarship is also available to undergraduate students. *Application Process: Applicants should submit a completed application along with transcripts and an essay that does not exceed 500 words. Visit the organization's Web site to download an application. *Amount: $1,000. *Deadline: May 31.

The Roothbert Fund Inc.
475 Riverside Drive, Room 252
New York, NY 10115
212-870-3116
mail@roothbertfund.org
http://www.roothbertfund.org/scholarships.php
Scholarship Name: Roothbert Fund Scholarship. *Academic Area: Open. *Age Group: Graduate students. *Eligibility: Applicants must demonstrate financial need and openly profess that they are motivated by spiritual values. Applicants should be residents of one of the following states: Maine, New Hampshire, Vermont, Rhode Island, Massachusetts, Connecticut, New York, New Jersey, Pennsylvania, Ohio, Delaware, Maryland, District of Columbia, Virginia, West Virginia, or North Carolina. They also should demonstrate academic achievement and be willing and able to participate in an in-person interview in New York, New Haven (Connecticut), Philadelphia, or Washington, D.C., should they be chosen for an interview (transportation is not provided). Preference is given to applicants pursuing careers in education. Visit the fund's Web site to read more about its spirituality mission. The scholarship is also available to undergraduate students. *Application Process: Applicants should submit a completed application along with three letters of recommendation, transcripts, and two essays (outlined on the application). Visit the fund's Web site to download an application after November 1. *Amount: $2,000 to $3,000. *Deadline: February 1.

Seattle Jaycees
Scholarship Committee
109 West Mercer Street
Seattle, WA 98119
206-286-2014
sjc_scholarships@yahoo.com
http://www.seattlejaycees.org
Scholarship Name: Seattle Jaycees Scholarship. *Academic Area: Open. *Age Group: Graduate students. *Eligibility: Applicants must be enrolled in or accepted into a postsecondary educational institution in the state of Washington (though prior residency in Washington is not required). They must also demonstrate exemplary commitment to involvement and service to the community, display leadership qualities and managerial skills in matters relating to civic activism, and exhibit academic achievement as well as achievement in other areas of work and life. The scholarship is also available to undergraduate students. *Application Process: Applicants should submit a completed application along with a one-page essay, three letters of recommendation, and official transcripts. Visit the organization's Web site to download an application. *Amount: Awards vary. *Deadline: April 1.

Sheriffs' Association of Texas
Attn: Scholarship Program
1601 South IH 35
Austin, TX 78741-2503
512-445-5888
info@txsheriffs.org
http://www.txsheriffs.org

Scholarship Name: Sheriffs' Association of Texas Scholarship Program. *Academic Area: Open. *Age Group: Graduate students. *Eligibility: Applicants must be enrolled in a college/university and be less than 25 years of age at the time of application. They also must be full-time students, maintain a minimum 2.5 GPA, and have completed at least one semester of study. Applicants must not have been convicted of a crime, which would make an individual ineligible for employment in his/her field of study. Many scholarships are available to children/grandchildren of a Texas Sheriff's office employee or students pursuing criminal justice careers. Eligibility requirements vary. Visit the association's Web site to obtain specific scholarship eligibility requirements. Some scholarships in this program are available to undergraduate students. *Application Process: Applicants must submit a completed application, current transcripts, proof of enrollment, and a personal statement. Visit the association's Web site to download an application. *Amount: Varies. *Deadline: March 1 and October 15.

StraightForward Media
http://www.straightforwardmedia.com/scholarships/index.php
Scholarship Name: StraightForward Media Scholarships. *Academic Area: Open. *Age Group: Graduate students. *Eligibility: Applicants should be enrolled in an institution of higher education. This organization offers 22 different scholarships encompassing a variety of majors and categories—anything from minority scholarships to science major scholarships to get-out-of-debt scholarships. Visit the company's Web site for a complete listing of eligibility requirements. Select scholarships are also available to undergraduate students. *Application Process: Applicants should visit the company's Web site to apply online. Scholarships are awarded quarterly, and applicants may apply each quarter if they are not selected in a previous quarter. Applicants need to submit personal contact information and a short essay online. *Amount: $500 and up. *Deadline: Quarterly (On or around January 15, April 15, July 15, October 15, depending on the scholarship) Visit the company's Web site to confirm details.

SuperCollege.com
4546 B10 El Camino Real, Suite 281
Los Altos, CA 94022
650-618-2221
http://www.supercollege.com

Scholarship Name: SuperCollege.com Scholarship. *Academic Area: Open. *Age Group: Graduate students. *Eligibility: Applicants must be U.S. citizens or legal residents attending or planning to attend any accredited college or university in the United States. The scholarship is also available to high school seniors and undergraduate students. *Application Process: Applicants must submit an online application and a personal essay. Visit SuperCollege.com's Web site to complete and submit an application. *Amount: $500 to $2,500. *Deadline: July 31.

UNICO National Inc.
Attn: Joan Tidona, Scholarship Director
271 U.S. Highway West
Fairfield, NJ 07004
201-933-7982
jntidona@verizon.net
http://www.unico.org/scholarships.html
Scholarship Name: UNICO National Scholarships. *Academic Area: Open. *Age Group: Graduate students. *Eligibility: UNICO touts itself as the largest Italian-American service organization in the United States. Italian-American graduating high school seniors, college undergraduates, and graduate students may apply for scholarships awarded for college study. *Application Process: Applicants should contact the scholarship director to receive additional information and an application. (Note: The scholarship director distributes all rules and announcements regarding available scholarships.) *Amount: $1,500. *Deadline: Contact the scholarship director for deadline information.

United Daughters of the Confederacy
328 North Boulevard
Richmond, VA 23220-4009
804-355-1636
hqudc@rcn.com
http://www.hqudc.org
Scholarship Name: Graduate Scholarship. *Academic Area: Open. *Age Group: Graduate students. *Eligibility: Applicants must be of lineal descent of an eligible Confederate soldier, maintain at least a 3.0 GPA, and be admitted to a college or university graduate program. Applicants should visit the organization's Web site for specific details about acceptable Confederate lineage as well as any additional eligibility requirements for individual scholarships. *Application Process: Applicants should submit a completed, original application along with

original transcripts, recommendation forms, a copy of their birth certificate, and a lineage form. One complete set of originals should be included (with the exception of a photocopied birth certificate) along with four additional photocopied sets of these materials. Additionally, a wallet-sized photograph, completed checklist, and Confederate ancestor's proof of service are required. Visit the organization's Web site to download an application. *Amount: Awards vary. *Deadline: March 15.

Wal-Mart Foundation
Wal-Mart Stores Inc.
Bentonville, AK 72716-8611
800-914-8385

http://www.walmartfoundation.org/wmstore/goodworks/scripts/index.jsp
Scholarship Name: Higher REACH Scholarship. *Academic Area: Open. *Age Group: Open. *Eligibility: Applicants must be nontraditional students who have been employed by Wal-Mart Stores Inc. for at least one year as of February 1 and out of high school for at least one year. *Application Process: Applicants must provide evidence of financial need, academic transcripts, a personal essay, and a job performance evaluation. Applicants can obtain further application details on Pipeline, the WIRE, or from their Wal-Mart/SAM'S CLUBS personnel manager. *Amount: Up to $2,000. *Deadline: January 20.

PERFORMING ARTS— UNDERGRADUATE

The following financial aid resources are available to students who are interested in studying the performing arts at the undergraduate level.

Alabama Commission on Higher Education
PO Box 302000
Montgomery, AL 36130-2000
334-242-1998
http://www.ache.state.al.us/StudentAsst/Programs.htm
Scholarship Name: Junior and Community College Performing Arts Scholarship. *Academic Area: Performing arts (open). *Age Group: Undergraduate students. *Eligibility: Applicants must be full-time students attending a public junior or community college in Alabama who also have a demonstrated performing arts talent. They must also participate in a competitive audition process. *Application Process: Applicants should contact the financial aid office at the school they plan to attend to request an application and audition information. *Amount: Full tuition. *Deadline: Contact the financial aid office at your school for deadline information.

Alaska State Council on the Arts (ASCA)
411 West 4th Avenue, Suite 1E
Anchorage, AK 99501-2343
907-269-6610
aksca_info@eed.state.ak.us
http://www.eed.state.ak.us/aksca/Grants3.htm
Grant Name: Career Opportunity Grant. *Academic Area: Performing arts (dance), performing arts (music-open), performing arts (theatre). *Age Group: Adults. *Eligibility: Applicants must be Alaskan residents, at least 18 years old, and desire to increase their development as an artist and to further their artistic careers. They must not be enrolled as full-time students. Applicants must demonstrate artistic merit by submitting a work sample. *Application Process: Applicants should apply online. They also should submit video or DVD samples of their work and a printed copy of the ASCA Grants Online application profile page. Visit the council's Web site to apply. *Amount: $100 to $1,000. *Deadline: March 1, June 1, September 1, December 1.

Alaska State Council on the Arts
411 West 4th Avenue, Suite 1E
Anchorage, AK 99501-2343
907-269-6610
aksca_info@eed.state.ak.us
http://www.eed.state.ak.us/aksca/Grants3.htm
Fellowship Name: Connie Boochever Artist Fellowship. *Academic Area: Education, performing arts (open), media arts, visual arts (open), writing. *Age Group: Adults. *Eligibility: Applicants must be Alaska residents, at least 18 years old, and emerging artists who are pursuing their art form on an ongoing basis. Applicants may not be enrolled as full-time students and must not have received a grant in the last two years. *Application Process: Applicants should submit a complete application packet including supporting materials verifying the quality of their work (through visual representation, resume, and recommendations). This grant is offered to artists pursing different art forms in two-year, rotating cycles. Applicants should visit the council's Web site to see if they will qualify for the current discipline that is being offered. Visit the council's Web site for more details. *Amount: $2,500. *Deadline: Contact the council for deadline information.

Alaska State Council on the Arts
411 West 4th Avenue, Suite 1E
Anchorage, AK 99501-2343
907-269-6610
aksca_info@eed.state.ak.us
http://www.eed.state.ak.us/aksca/Grants3.htm
Grant Name: Master Artist and Apprenticeship Grant. *Academic Area: Performing arts (dance), performing arts (music-instrumental), performing arts (voice), visual arts (crafts), visual arts (painting), visual arts (sculpting). *Age Group: Adults. *Eligibility: Applicants must be residents of Alaska, at least 18 years old, have an interest in traditional Alaska Native art, and desire the opportunity to develop their skills in an Alaskan Native art form. They must also have demonstrated experience working in the art form for which they are applying and must have identified a master artist under whom they would like to serve as an apprentice. Applicants may not be enrolled as full-time students during the period of the grant.

*Application Process: Applicants should submit a complete application packet, which includes supporting material verifying the quality of the apprentice's work (through visual representation, resume, and recommendations), quality of the master artist's work (through visual representation, resume, and recommendations), a description of the project and the skills that will be taught and learned, and a complete itemized budget. Visit the council's Web site for more details. *Amount: Up to $2,000. *Deadline: The first of the month prior to the applicant's planned apprenticeship.

American Cinema Editors

100 Universal City Plaza
Building 2352 B, Room 202
Universal City, CA 91608
818-777-2900
http://www.ace-filmeditors.org/newace/abt_
    StudentEdit.html
Contest Name: American Cinema Editors Student Editing Competition. *Academic Area: Film/television. *Age Group: Open. *Eligibility: Applicants must be among the first 50 entrants who send in an entry request along with a $125 entry fee. *Application Process: Applicant should submit his or her name, address, area code and phone number, e-mail address, physical mailing address for receipt of package during daytime hours, name and address of school, the complete name of the applicant's instructor, as well as the entry fee by check or credit card. If paying by credit card, include the name of the cardholder, type of card, and the card number and expiration date. Visit the organization's Web site for further information. *Amount: Plaque plus publicity in Hollywood trade papers. *Deadline: October (contact the organization for detailed deadline information).

American Society of Cinematographers (ASC)

ASC Student Awards
1313 North Vine Street
Hollywood, CA 90028
323-969-4333
http://www.theasc.com/awards/index.html
Award Name: American Society of Cinematographers Jordan Cronenweth Heritage Award. *Academic Area: Film/television. *Age Group: Undergraduate students. *Eligibility: Applicants must be in their final year of a cinematography program or recent graduates (within one year). Graduate students are also eligible for this award. *Application Process: Applicants should submit a completed application along with a nomination form signed by the dean or department chair, a resume, a 500-word personal statement, one film submission (for which the applicant is the sole cinematographer), and the same film on Beta SP. The application packet should be shipped via Fed Ex or UPS. Visit the society's Web site to download an application and nomination form. *Amount: All expenses paid to attend the ASC Awards ceremony. *Deadline: November 1.

American String Teachers Association (ASTA)

American String Teachers Association /Auday-Giormenti
    Double Bass Competition
4153 Chain Bridge Road
Fairfax, VA 22030
703-279-2113
asta@astaweb.com
http://www.astaweb.com/competitions/
    BassCompetition.htm
Contest Name: American String Teachers Association /Auday-Giormenti Double Bass Competition. *Academic Area: Performing arts (music-instrumental). *Age Group: High school students, undergraduate students. *Eligibility: Applicants must be between the ages of 12 and 21 and either the applicant or his or her teacher must be a member of the ASTA. *Application Process: Applicants must submit a completed application packet, plus three copies (of all materials). Application packet consists of a completed application along with an audio CD and a videotape of a specific concerto/concertos. Visit the association's Web site for a list of approved selections. Applicants must also submit a second piece of their own choice, which should be contrasting in style to the required selection. A $25 entry fee is also required. *Amount: An Auday-Giormenti Viennese model double bass, a brief performance at the ASTA National Conference, and a commemorative plaque. *Deadline: November 1.

American String Teachers Association (ASTA)

Merle J. Isaac Composition Contest
Attn: James Nacy, Composition Contest Chair
4153 Chain Bridge Road
Fairfax, VA 22030
636-537-4300, ext. 4752
iamacellist@sbcglobal.net
http://www.astaweb.com/competitions/MerleIsaac.htm

Contest Name: Merle J. Isaac Composition Contest. *Academic Area: Performing arts (music-composition). *Age Group: Open. *Eligibility: Applicants must be composers who are interested in submitting an unpublished composition that would be suitable for performance at the middle school/junior high grade levels or the high school level. *Application Process: Applicants should submit a completed application along with six copies of the score and one set of parts, including winds. A $25 application fee is also required. *Amount: $1,500, plus aid in publication and national publicity. *Deadline: April 1.

American String Teachers Association (ASTA)

Attn: Michael Carrera, Chair, ASTA National Solo
  Competition
4153 Chain Bridge Road
Fairfax, VA 22030
703-279-2113
Carrera@ohio.edu
http://www.astaweb.com

Contest Name: National Solo Competition. *Academic Area: Performing arts (music-instrumental). *Age Group: High school students, undergraduate students. *Eligibility: Applicants for the junior division must be under the age of 19 and applicants for the senior division must be ages 19 to 25. Applicants must be soloists on one of the following instruments: violin, viola, cello, double bass, classical guitar, or harp. Applicants must be ASTA members or current students of ASTA members. Graduate students are also eligible for this competition. *Application Process: Applicants must first register for their state competition. Finalists from the state competition advance to the national competition. Applicants should contact their ASTA State Competition Chairs for information about entering their state competition. A complete list of these state chairs is available on ASTA's Web site. Detailed information about repertoire choices for the national event is listed on the Web site. Visit the Web site to read more about the competition and to locate your state contact. *Amount: Prizes to be determined. *Deadline: Deadlines vary.

Arizona Commission on the Arts

417 West Roosevelt Street
Phoenix, AZ 85003-1326
602-255-5882
info@azarts.gov

http://www.azarts.gov/artists/grants.htm

Grant Name: Career Advancement and Project Grants. *Academic Area: Performing arts (open), visual arts (open). *Age Group: Adults. *Eligibility: Applicants must be residents of Arizona, at least 18 years old, and not enrolled for more than three credit hours at a college or university. They must be seeking funds to advance their professional artistic careers or to help them complete a worthy artistic endeavor. Applicants must be able to provide documentation of Arizona residency. This organization provides three different kinds of grants for individuals. Eligibility requirements may vary slightly. *Application Process: Applicants should submit a completed application along with the appropriate supporting materials. Supporting materials include visual documentation of work samples (slides, video, etc.), resume, and a project narrative. Visit the commission's Web site to download an application and to view additional information about individual grants. *Amount: $500 to $5,000 (depending on the type of grant). *Deadline: Deadlines vary.

Arkansas Arts Council

1500 Tower Building, 323 Center Street
Little Rock, AR 72201
501-324-9766
info@arkansasarts.com
http://www.arkansasarts.com/grants

Grant Name: Individual Artists Fellowship. *Academic Area: Performing arts (open), visual arts (open). *Age Group: Adults. *Eligibility: Applicants must be residents of Arkansas who are at least 25 years old. They must have lived in Arkansas for at least one year to qualify and cannot be degree-seeking students or have received the award previously. Categories rotate yearly, so interested candidates should contact the council for information on the area in which they are taking applications for the current year. *Application Process: Applicants should contact the council for information on the application process. Applications are also periodically available at the council's Web site for download. *Amount: Awards vary. *Deadline: May 12.

Choristers Guild

Attn: Memorial Scholarship Committee
2834 West Kingsley Road
Garland, TX 75041-2498
972-271-1521

customerservice@mailcg.org
http://www.choristersguild.org/news.html
Scholarship Name: Choristers Guild College Scholarship.
*Academic Area: Performing arts (music-religious).
*Age Group: Undergraduate students. *Eligibility:
Applicants must be college juniors or seniors who are
pursuing a degree that will lead to a career in music
ministry. Applicants should be able to demonstrate
talent and leadership as well as financial need.
Preference is given to applicants who want to work
with children and youth. Graduate students may
also apply for the scholarship. *Application Process:
Applicants should submit a completed application
along with transcripts and a photograph. Visit the
guild's Web site to download an application. *Amount:
$1,000. *Deadline: February 1.

Connecticut Association of Schools/Connecticut Interscholastic Athletic Conference
Attn: Dr. Robert F. Carroll
30 Realty Drive
Chesire, CT 06410
203-250-1111
bcarroll@casciac.org
http://www.casciac.org/hsawards.shtml
Scholarship Name: Bruce Eagleson Memorial Scholarship.
*Academic Area: Performing arts (open), visual
arts (open). *Age Group: Undergraduate students.
*Eligibility: Applicants must be graduating high
school seniors who are accepted into a college degree
program in the visual or performing arts. They must be
residents of Connecticut, graduating from Connecticut
high schools, and have demonstrated involvement
showcasing their artistic work in shows, exhibits, or
performances. Applicants must also be committed to
community and public service and must demonstrate
financial need. *Application Process: Applicants should
submit a completed application along with two letters
of recommendation, a letter of college acceptance,
a 250-word personal statement, a video or photo
representation of artistic ability, and a statement
outlining financial need and expected college costs.
Visit the association's Web site to download an
application. *Amount: $10,000 (one award), $5,000 (two
awards). *Deadline: March 17.

Connecticut Commission on Culture and Tourism
Attn: Tamara Dimitri
One Financial Plaza
755 Main Street

Hartford, CT 06103
860-256-2720
tdimitri@ctarts.org
http://www.cultureandtourism.org/cct/cwp/view.
asp?a=2207&q=293740&cctPNavCtr=|43595|
Fellowship Name: Individual Artists Fellowship.
*Academic Area: Film/television, performing arts
(choreography), performing arts (composition),
visual arts (open), writing. *Age Group: Adults.
*Eligibility: Applicants must be Connecticut
residents who have lived within the state for at
least one year. Applicants must not be degree-
seeking college students and cannot have received
the award previously. Categories rotate yearly, so
interested candidates should visit the organization's
Web site to see which category is available for
the current year. *Application Process: Applicants
should contact the commission for information
on the application process. Application materials
are available in July of each year. *Amount: $2,500
and $5,000. *Deadline: September (contact the
commission for exact deadlines).

Delaware Division of the Arts
820 North French Street
Wilmington, DE 19801
302-577-8278
delarts@state.de.us
http://www.artsdel.org/grants/artistgrants.shtml
Grant Name: Grants for Individual Artists. *Academic
Area: Media arts, performing arts (open), visual arts
(open), writing. *Age Group: Adults. *Eligibility:
Applicants must be Delaware residents, at least
18 years old, and have lived in the state for at least
one year. They must not be enrolled in a degree-
granting program. This organization offers more
than one kind of grant for individual artists. Visit
the organization's Web site for additional eligibility
requirements for individual grants. *Application
Process: Applicants should submit a completed
application along with a one-page narrative, a
budget, a resume, and work samples (examples
of appropriate submissions are listed on the
application). Visit the organization's Web site to
download an application. *Amount: Awards vary.
*Deadline: Deadlines vary by grant.

Florida Division of Cultural Affairs
Attn: Morgan Barr
R.A. Gray Building, 3rd Floor

500 South Bronough Street
Tallahassee, FL 32399-0250
850-245-6470
mhbarr@dos.state.fl.us
http://www.florida-arts.org/grants/forindividuals.htm
Grant Name: Grants for Individual Artists. *Academic Area: Media arts, performing arts (dance), performing arts (music-general), performing arts (theatre), visual arts (open), writing. *Age Group: Adults. *Eligibility: Applicants must be Florida residents, at least 18 years old, and not be enrolled in any degree program. This organization offers more than one kind of grant for individual artists. Applicants must not have received a grant from the same organization in the previous grant period. Some grants are offered on a rotating categorical basis, with visual arts and media arts grouped together for one year and performing arts and literary arts in the next year. Visit the organization's Web site for additional eligibility requirements for individual grants. *Application Process: Applicants should submit a completed application along with supporting materials. Visit the organization's Web site for additional information on the application process. *Amount: Awards vary. *Deadline: Deadlines vary by individual award.

Florida State Music Teachers Association (FSMTA)
Attn: Gloria Bolivar, VP Competitive Events
13202 Dorchester Drive
Seminole, FL 33776
727-397-1771
http://www.fmta.org/awards.html
Scholarship Name: FSMTA Scholarships and Awards. *Academic Area: Performing arts (music-general). *Age Group: High school students, undergraduate students. *Eligibility: Applicants must reside in Florida and have expertise in musical performance. Applicants should contact their local music teachers for additional information on eligibility requirements. Graduate students also may apply for scholarships and awards from the association. *Application Process: Applicants should contact their local music teachers or the FSMTA for information on the application process. The association offers many scholarships and awards for varying types of performance and the application process/competition dates will vary. *Amount: $50 to $600. *Deadline: Varies.

Glenn Miller Birthplace Society
107 East Main Street, PO Box 61
Clarinda, IA 51632
712-542-2461
caldrich@clarinda.k12.ia.us
http://www.glennmiller.org/scholar.htm
Scholarship Name: Glenn Miller Scholarship Competition. *Academic Area: Performing arts (music-instrumental), performing arts (voice). *Age Group: Undergraduate students. *Eligibility: Applicants must be graduating high school seniors or first-year college students who intend to major in music in college and pursue some form of musical career. *Application Process: Applicants must submit an audition CD or tape (approximately 10 minutes in length) and a personal statement. Finalists (10 vocalists and 10 instrumentalists) will be chosen to compete in Clarinda, Iowa, in early June of each year. Applicants must agree to travel to the competition at their own expense. A first, second, and third place award will be awarded in both categories. Visit the society's Web site for additional information on the application and competition. *Amount: $3,000; $2,000; $1,000. *Deadline: March 15.

Hawaii State Foundation on Culture and the Arts
Attn: Fay Ann Chun, Individual Artists Program Coordinator
250 South Hotel Street, 2nd Floor
Honolulu, HI 96813
808-586-9965
hsfca2006awards@yahoo.com
http://www.state.hi.us/sfca
Fellowship Name: Individual Artist Fellowship. *Academic Area: Performing arts (open), visual arts (open). *Age Group: Adults. *Eligibility: Applicants must be residents of Hawaii, at least 18 years old, and recognized in their communities as professional artists. They must be financially compensated for their work as part of their livelihood and able to provide documentation of their artistic experience for at least the last five years. Visit the organization's Web site for a complete list of eligibility requirements in each visual arts or performing arts category. *Application Process: Applicants should submit a completed application along with an artist statement form, a resume form, three references and a reference form, and work samples. The process for submitting appropriate work samples is explained in depth on the application form. Visit the organization's Web

site for additional information on the application process. *Amount: Awards vary. *Deadline: Contact the organization for deadline information.

Idaho Commission on the Arts
PO Box 83720
Boise, ID 83720-0008
208-334-2119
info@arts.idaho.gov
http://www.arts.idaho.gov/grants/indoverview.aspx
Grant Name: Grants for Individual Artists. *Academic Area: Media arts, performing arts (open), visual arts (open), writing. *Age Group: Adults. *Eligibility: Applicants must be residents of Idaho who demonstrate artistic excellence and a professional artistic history. This organization offers several grants and fellowships, many of which are offered on a rotating scale according to artistic discipline. Visit the organization's Web site for further information. *Application Process: Applicants should submit a completed application along with supporting materials, including a resume, an artist statement, and work samples. Visit the organization's Web site for a checklist of supporting materials for each type of grant or fellowship. *Amount: $3,500 (approximate). *Deadline: January 31.

Illinois Arts Council
James R. Thompson Center
100 West Randolph, Suite 10-500
Chicago, IL 60601
314-814-4991
rose@arts.state.il.us
http://www.state.il.us/agency/iac/Guidelines/guidelines.htm
Fellowship Name: Artist Fellowship Program. *Academic Area: Film/television, media arts, performing arts (choreography), performing arts (composition), visual arts (crafts), visual arts (photography), visual arts (open). *Age Group: Adults. *Eligibility: Applicants must be residents of Illinois who can provide proof that they've resided within the state for at least one year. They must be U.S. citizens or permanent residents and not be enrolled in any degree program. Applicants must not have received funds from this fellowship in the two preceding years. These fellowships are offered on a rotating basis according to artistic discipline. Applicants in the disciplines of choreography, crafts, ethnic and folk arts, media arts, new performance

forms, prose, and scriptwriting may apply in even-numbered years, and applicants in interdisciplinary/computer art, music composition, photography, poetry, and visual arts can apply in odd-numbered years. Visit the organization's Web site for further information. *Application Process: Applicants should submit a completed application along with a work sample sheet, work samples, a one-page artistic resume, and a one-page artist statement. Work samples must not be more than four years old. A detailed explanation of work sample submission procedures is explained on the application. Visit the organization's Web site to download an application. *Amount: $700 and $7,000. *Deadline: September 1.

Indiana Arts Commission
Attn: Monica Peterson
150 West Market Street, Suite 618
Indianapolis, IN 46204
317-232-1279
mpeterson@iac.in.gov
http://www.in.gov/arts/grants/program_iap.html
Grant Name: Grants for Individual Artists. *Academic Area: Media arts, performing arts (open), visual arts (open), writing. *Age Group: Adults. *Eligibility: Applicants must be at least 18 years old and be residents of Indiana who have lived in the state for at least one full year preceding the application. They must also remain an Indiana resident during the grant period, not be enrolled in any degree program, and not have received this award in the preceding year. Applicant must apply as an individual and not as part of a collaborative project. Visit the commission's Web site for further information. *Application Process: Applicants should submit a completed application along with a formal letter stating the reasons for consideration and supporting materials. A detailed explanation of how to submit supporting materials is included on the application. Visit the commission's Web site to download an application. *Amount: $1,000. *Deadline: February 3.

Iowa Arts Council
Attn: Bruce Williams
600 East Locust
Des Moines, IA 50319-0290
515-281-4006
Bruce.Williams@iowa.gov
http://www.iowaartscouncil.org/funding/artist-project-grant/index.shtml

Grant Name: Artist Major Grants and Mini Grants. *Academic Area: Performing arts (open), visual arts (open). *Age Group: Adults. *Eligibility: Applicants must be at least 18 years old and have lived in Iowa for at least one full year preceding the application. Applicants must not be students and not have received two Iowa Arts Council grants within the same fiscal year of this proposed grant activity. This program also includes applicants from select bordering communities. Visit the council's Web site for the border state policy. Eligibility requirements may differ slightly for major and mini grants. Visit the council's Web site for additional eligibility requirements. *Application Process: Applicants must submit an online application on the state's new eGRANT system. The application will include information on the proposed project, a budget, a personal narrative, a work sample form and work samples, a service contract, and a project timeline. Visit the council's Web site to apply online. *Amount: $1,500 (mini grant); $10,000 (major grant). *Deadline: April 1.

Kentucky Arts Council
Attn: Lori Meadows
Capital Plaza Tower, 500 Mero Street, 21st Floor
Frankfort, KY 40601-1987
502-564-3747, ext. 482, 888-833-2787, ext. 482
Lori.Meadows@ky.gov
http://artscouncil.ky.gov/guide/prog3/asf_gdl.htm
Fellowship Name: Al Smith Individual Artist Fellowship Program. *Academic Area: Media arts, performing arts (open), visual arts (open), writing. *Age Group: Adults. *Eligibility: Applicants must be U.S. citizens or permanent residents, residents of Kentucky (who have lived in the state for at least one year), at least 18 years old, and demonstrate artistic excellence and professional achievement. They must remain Kentucky residents during the period for which they receive funding. Applicants must be professional artists who are creating their own work, and not interpreting the work of others. *Application Process: Applicants should submit a completed application along with supporting materials. Supporting materials include a narrative essay, proof of residency, work samples and an index of work samples, and an optional resume. Detailed descriptions of how to submit work samples are listed on the application. This fellowship is offered in alternating disciplines every other year.

Writers, choreographers, musical composers, and interdisciplinary artists may apply in even-numbered years, and visual and media artists may apply in odd-numbered years. Visit the organization's Web site to download an application. *Amount: $7,500; $1,000 professional assistance awards given to some applicants who do not receive the Individual Artist Fellowships. *Deadline: August 15 (intent to apply deadline); September 15 (application deadline).

Maine Arts Commission
Attn: Donna McNeil, Contemporary Art & Public Art Associate
193 State Street, 25 State House Station
Augusta, ME 04333-0025
207-287-2726
Donna.McNeil@maine.gov
http://www.mainearts.com/Grants/index.shtml
Fellowship Name: Individual Artist Fellowship. *Academic Area: Media arts, performing arts (open), visual arts (open), writing. *Age Group: Adults. *Eligibility: Applicants must be residents of Maine, at least 18 years old, and not enrolled as full-time students in a field relating to the application. They must have lived in Maine for at least two years and demonstrate artistic excellence. Artists in all mediums are encouraged to apply. *Application Process: Applicants should submit a completed application along with one set of labeled artistic materials (instructions are located on the application), a biographical information sheet, and a self-addressed stamped postcard and envelope. Visit the commission's Web site to download an application. *Amount: $13,000. *Deadline: June 9.

Massachusetts Cultural Council
10 Saint James Avenue, 3rd Floor
Boston, MA 02116-3803
617-727-3668, 800-232-0960
mcc@art.state.ma.us
http://www.massculturalcouncil.org/programs/artistgrants.html
Grant Name: Artist Grants Program. *Academic Area: Media arts, performing arts (open), visual arts (open), writing. *Age Group: Adults. *Eligibility: Applicants must be residents of Massachusetts, at least 18 years old, and not be enrolled as students in degree programs. Applicants must demonstrate artistic excellence. Categories in which applicants may apply rotate every other year. Applicants should visit

the organization's Web site to view the eligibility requirements for the current application period. *Application Process: Applicants should submit a completed application along with supporting materials. Visit the council's Web site to download an application and a description of how to submit work samples. *Amount: $5,000. *Deadline: December. Visit the council's Web site for deadline information.

Mississippi Arts Commission

Attn: Judi Cleary, Director of Grants & Programs
Woolfolk Building
501 North West Street, Suite 701B
Jackson, MS 39201
601-359-6034
jcleary@arts.state.ms.us
http://www.mswholeschools.org/mac/grants/for-individuals.html

Fellowship Name: Artist Fellowship. *Academic Area: Media arts, performing arts (open), visual arts (open), writing. *Age Group: Adults. *Eligibility: Applicants must be residents of Mississippi, at least 18 years old, and maintain residency in Mississippi for the duration of the fellowship. They must demonstrate artistic excellence and earn at least part of their income from their artistic discipline. Applicants should consider their artistic endeavors as a career and should devote significant time to this work. Full-time students are not eligible for this fellowship. Categories in which applicants may apply rotate every other year. Applicants should visit the organization's Web site to view the eligibility requirements for the current application period. *Application Process: Applicants should submit a completed application along with an artist narrative, a resume, and work samples. Visit the organization's Web site to download an application and a description of how to submit work samples in each category. *Amount: Up to $5,000. *Deadline: March 1.

Missouri Music Teachers Association

Attn: Carol A. Borgstadt, Executive Secretary
29327 Highway PP
Concordia, MO 64020
http://missourimta.org/auditions.php

Contest Name: Missouri Music Teachers Association Competitions. *Academic Area: Performing arts (music-open). *Age Group: High school students, undergraduate students. *Eligibility: Applicants must possess a musical talent. For further eligibility

requirements in each of the many categories, visit the association's Web site or contact your local music teacher. *Application Process: Applicants should visit the association's Web site to determine the dates of district events and their application deadlines. Participants compete in district events before proceeding to state finals. Many musical categories and age group categories are available. *Amount: Awards vary. *Deadline: Deadlines vary by district.

Montana Arts Council

PO Box 202201
Helena, MT 59620-2201
406-444-6430
mac@mt.gov
http://www.art.state.mt.us/artists/artists.asp

Grant Name: Opportunity and Professional Development Grants. *Academic Area: Performing arts (open), visual arts (open). *Age Group: Adults. *Eligibility: Applicants must be at least 18 years old and residents of Montana for at least one year. Full-time students are not eligible for these grants. Applicants should visit the council's Web site to view additional eligibility requirements for specific grants and specific artistic mediums. These grants require the applicant to match the funds with an equal dollar amount of their own funds or funds that they have raised for a given artistic endeavor. *Application Process: Applicants should submit a completed application along with an artist narrative, a project synopsis, a complete budget, and a resume. Visit the council's Web site to download an application. *Amount: $750 to $1,000. *Deadline: Deadlines vary.

National Association of Pastoral Musicians (NPM)

NPM Scholarships
962 Wayne Avenue, Suite 210
Silver Spring, MD 20910-4461
240-247-3000
npmsing@npm.org
http://www.npm.org/Membership/scholarship.htm

Scholarship Name: Academic Scholarships. *Academic Area: Performing arts (music-religious). *Age Group: Undergraduate students. *Eligibility: Applicants must be members of the NPM, enrolled in a degree program related to pastoral music, intend to work as a pastoral musician for at least two years, and demonstrate financial need. *Application Process: Applicants should submit a letter of application containing all of their contact information as well as pertinent biographical information, a CD or cassette recording that demonstrates their performance skills, two letters of recommendation, and a financial need statement. Visit the association's Web site to download a financial need statement and for further information about the many scholarships awarded in this category. *Amount: $500 to $4,500. *Deadline: March 3.

National Opera Association (NOA)

Vocal Competition
PO Box 60869
Canyon, TX 79016-0001
806-651-2857
rhansen@mail.wtamu.edu
http://www.noa.org

Scholarship Name: National Opera Association Vocal Competition-Scholarship Division. *Academic Area: Performing arts (voice). *Age Group: Undergraduate students. *Eligibility: Applicants must be currently enrolled undergraduate students between the ages of 18 and 24. They must have a teacher or opera director who is a member of the NOA, or they must attend an institution that is a NOA member. Graduate students may also enter this competition. *Application Process: Applicants must submit a completed application, a copy of legal proof of age, a resume photo, a $20 entry fee, and a cassette tape or CD of two arias from the repertoire list that have been recorded after January 1. Visit the association's Web site to download an application and to obtain further contest details. *Amount: $500 to $2,000. *Deadline: October 15.

National Religious Music Week Alliance

201 Dayton Street
Hamilton, OH 45011
513-844-1500
musicweek@aol.com
http://www.religiousmusicweek.com/scholar.html

Scholarship Name: National Religious Music Week Alliance Scholarship. *Academic Area: Performing arts (music-religious). *Age Group: Undergraduate students. *Eligibility: Applicants must be pursuing a degree that will lead to a career in music ministry. They should also be able to demonstrate academic achievement. Graduate students also may apply for this scholarship. *Application Process: Applicants should visit the alliance's Web site in January of each year, when the new application is available for

download. Applicants should apply by submitting a completed application along with any supporting materials. *Amount: $2,500. *Deadline: Contact the alliance for deadline information.

National Television Academy

Attn: Luke Smith, Scholarship Coordinator
111 West 57th Street, Suite 600
New York, NY 10019
212-586-8424
scholarship@emmyonline.tv
http://www.emmyonline.org/emmy/scholarship.html

Scholarship Name: John Cannon Memorial Scholarship. *Academic Area: Communications science, film/television. *Age Group: Undergraduate students. *Eligibility: Applicants should be graduating high school seniors who are interested in pursuing a career in television or a related field at a four-year college or university. *Application Process: Applicants should submit a completed application along with a career-aspirations essay and a creative essay. For additional information about the scholarship specifications, visit the academy's Web site. Applications are also available for download. *Amount: $40,000. *Deadline: December 12.

Nevada Arts Council

Attn: Fran Morrow, Artist Services Program Coordinator
716 North Carson Street, Suite A
Carson City, NV 89701
775-687-7106
fkmorrow@clan.lib.nv.us
http://dmla.clan.lib.nv.us/docs/arts/programs/grants/grantsforartists.htm

Grant Name: Grants for Artists. *Academic Area: Media arts, performing arts (open), visual arts (open), writing. *Age Group: Adults. *Eligibility: Applicants must be at least 21 years old and residents of the state of Nevada for at least one year (and reside in the state of Nevada for the duration of the grant period). They must be U.S. citizens or legal permanent residents who are practicing professional artists and who demonstrate artistic excellence and merit. Applicants must not be full-time students. This organization offers more than one type of grant. Visit the organization's Web site to view additional eligibility requirements for specific grants. *Application Process: Applicants should submit a completed application along with five copies of the work sample list, work samples required for their category (detailed on the application), and a resume. Visit the organization's Web site to download an application.*Amount: $500 to $5,000. *Deadline: Deadlines vary by grant. Visit the organization's Web site to view current deadlines.

New Hampshire State Council on the Arts

2 1/2 Beacon Street, 2nd Floor
Concord, NH 03301-4974
603-271-2789
http://www.state.nh.us/nharts/grants/artists/index.htm
Grant/Fellowship Name: Grants and Fellowships for Artists. *Academic Area: Media arts, performing arts (open), visual arts (open), writing. *Age Group: Adults. *Eligibility: Applicants must be at least 18 years old and residents of New Hampshire for at least one year (and reside in the state for the duration of the grant or fellowship period). They must demonstrate a commitment to artistic excellence and possess artistic merit. Applicants must not be full-time students. This organization offers more than one type of grant. Visit the organization's Web site to view additional eligibility requirements for specific awards. *Application Process: Applicants should submit a completed application along with answers to the required narrative questions, a resume, and work samples required for their category (detailed at the council's Web site). Visit the council's Web site to download an application.*Amount: $250 to $5,000. *Deadline: Deadlines vary by award. Visit the council's Web site to view current deadlines.

New Jersey State Council on the Arts

Attn: Rebecca Scolian
c/o Mid Atlantic Arts Foundation
201 North Charles Street, Suite 401
Baltimore, MD 21201
410-539-6656, ext. 101
rebecca@midatlanticarts.org
http://www.njartscouncil.org/program7.html
Fellowship Name: Artist Fellowship. *Academic Area: Media arts, performing arts (open), visual arts (open), writing. *Age Group: Adults. *Eligibility: Applicants must be at least 18 years old and residents of New Jersey for at least one year (and reside in the state for the duration of the fellowship period). They must demonstrate a commitment to artistic excellence and possess artistic merit. Applicants must not be full-time students in a degree program. Visit the organization's Web site to view additional eligibility

requirements for the category in which they intend to apply. *Application Process: Applicants should submit a completed application along with two copies of their resume, work samples, and a descriptive cover page. Visit the council's Web site to download an application. *Amount: $7,800 to $12,000. *Deadline: July 15.

North Carolina Arts Council

Department of Cultural Resources
Grants Office
226 East North Street
Raleigh, NC 27699-4632
919-733-2111
ncarts@ncmail.net
http://www.ncarts.org/freeform_scrn_template.
    cfm?ffscrn_id=47&menu_sel=4&sub_sel=15
Grant/Fellowship Name: Artist Grants and Fellowships. *Academic Area: Media arts, performing arts (open), visual arts (open), writing. *Age Group: Adults. *Eligibility: Applicants must be at least 18 years old, residents of the state of North Carolina for at least one year (and reside in the state for the duration of the fellowship period), and U.S. citizens or permanent residents. Applicants must demonstrate a commitment to artistic excellence and possess artistic merit. They must not be full-time students in a degree program. Applicants should visit the council's Web site to view additional eligibility requirements for the category in which they intend to apply. More than one type of fellowship and grant is offered by this organization. Visit the council's Web site for complete listings. *Application Process: Applicants should submit a completed application online, via eGRANT, by first submitting an electronic artist registration form. Applicants must also submit an artist narrative, a resume, a work sample with a descriptive cover page, work samples required for their category (detailed on the council's Web site). Visit the council's Web site to apply. *Amount: $500 to 8,000. *Deadline: Deadlines vary.

Oregon Arts Commission

Attn: Shannon Planchon
775 Summer Street, NE, Suite 200
Salem, OR 97301-1284
503-986-0086
shannon.planchon@state.or.us
http://www.oregonartscommission.org/grants/
    commission_grant_programs.php

Fellowship/Grant Name: Individual Artists Fellowship Grant. *Academic Area: Media arts, performing arts (open), visual arts (open), writing. *Age Group: Adults. *Eligibility: Applicants must have been residents of Oregon for at least one year and demonstrate a commitment to artistic excellence and artistic merit. These grants are offered on a rotating basis by artistic discipline. Visit the commission's Web site for more information. *Application Process: Applicants should submit a completed application and supplementary materials. Applications are available for download from the commission's Web site in July of each year. Applicants must also submit their supporting materials according to the requirements posted for each art form. Visit the commission's Web site for additional information. *Amount: $3,000. *Deadline: October 16.

Oregon Music Teachers Association (OMTA)
Attn: Victoria Buhn, Education Chair
2100 Ridgeway Drive
Eugene, OR 97401-1724
541-683-5231
virginiabuhn@earthlink.net
http://www.oregonmta.org/Forms.html
Scholarship Name: Jane Thomas Memorial Scholarship. *Academic Area: Performing arts (music-open). *Age Group: High school students. *Eligibility: Applicants must be attending high school in Oregon, as an Oregon teacher who is a member of the OMTA must nominate them. Applicants must possess a musical ability, financial need, and a commitment to the musical community. *Application Process: Applicants should contact the OMTA for information about the application process. An application is available for download from the association's Web site along with a list of requirements that the applicant's teacher must submit (i.e., student's syllabus level, teacher's evaluation of the student's financial need, musical ability, musical community involvement, and a copy of the teacher's OMTA membership card). Ask your music teacher or OMTA representative for additional information. *Amount: Awards vary. *Deadline: May 31.

Pennsylvania Council on the Arts
Attn: Kerry Swartz, Administrative Assistant
717-787-6883, ext, 3030
keswartz@state.pa.us
http://www.pacouncilonthearts.org/pca.cfm?id=9&level=Third&sid=13

Fellowship Name: Individual Artist Fellowship. *Academic Area: Media arts, performing arts (open), visual arts (open), writing. *Age Group: Adults. *Eligibility: Applicants must be current residents of Pennsylvania, and have been residents there for at least two years. They must not be high school students or degree-seeking students. Applicants may not apply for a fellowship if they received one during the previous award period. The council awards fellowships on a rotating basis according to artistic discipline. Applicants should visit the council's Web site to view additional eligibility requirements for the category in which they intend to apply. In even-numbered years applications are accepted in arts commentary, crafts, folk and traditional arts (craft traditions), literature (fiction or creative nonfiction), media arts (narrative and animation), music (jazz, blues, world, or non-classical composition), theatre (new performance forms, and visual arts (photography, sculpture). Applicants in dance (choreography), folk and traditional arts (performing traditions), literature (poetry), media arts (documentary and experimental), music (classical composition), theatre (scriptworks), and visual arts (painting and printmaking) should apply in odd-numbered years. *Application Process: Applicants should submit a completed application along with program-specific work samples and supporting materials. Visit the council's Web site for details on these requirements in individual categories. Applicants should mail their applications to the specified organization, which differs based on artistic discipline. The main office does not accept application packets. *Amount: $5,000 and $10,000. *Deadline: The first business day in August.

Princess Grade Foundation-USA
150 East 58th Street, 25th Floor
New York, NY 10155
212-317-1470
info@pgfusa.org
http://www.pgfusa.com/awards/grants/index.html
Scholarship/Fellowship Name: Princess Grace Foundation Scholarships and Fellowships. *Academic Area: Film/television, performing arts (choreography), performing arts (dance), performing arts (theatre). *Age Group: Open. *Eligibility: The foundation offers numerous scholarships, apprenticeships, and fellowships to applicants of varying ages and stages of education. All applicants should be U.S. citizens or permanent residents who

are pursuing careers in the performing arts. Visit the foundation's Web site for specific eligibility requirements for specific awards in choreography, dance, film, theatre, and playwriting. *Application Process: Applicants should download the relevant application form from the foundation's Web site and submit the application along with supporting materials. *Amount: Awards vary. *Deadline: Deadlines vary depending on category.

Salute to Education Inc.

PO Box 833425
Miami, FL 33283
305-476-7709
steinfo@stescholarships.org
http://www.stescholarships.org/SC_categories.html
Scholarship Name: Salute to Education Performing Arts Scholarship. *Academic Area: Performing arts (open). *Age Group: Undergraduate students. *Eligibility: Applicants must be graduating high school seniors who attend a Miami-Dade or Broward County, Florida, high school. They must be legal residents of the United States, live in Miami-Dade or Broward County, have a minimum weighted GPA of 3.0, demonstrate a commitment to service by participating in at least one school or community organization, and intend to pursue a college degree at an accredited institution after graduation. Applicants must excel in an area of the performing arts such as theatre, dance, or instrumental or vocal music. They should also demonstrate active involvement in, and exceptional aptitude for, school and extracurricular performing arts activities. *Application Process: Applicants must apply online. Supporting materials should be mailed as detailed on the online application. *Amount: $1,000. *Deadline: Visit the organization's Web site for updated deadline information.

South Carolina Arts Commission

1800 Gervais Street
Columbus, SC 29201
803-734-8696
http://www.state.sc.us/arts/grants/artists/fellowships.htm
Fellowship/Grant Name: Individual Artist Fellowship Grant. *Academic Area: Media arts, performing arts (open), visual arts (open), writing. *Age Group: Adults. *Eligibility: Applicants must be at least 18 years old, have resided in South Carolina for at least two years, demonstrate a commitment to artistic excellence, and

possess artistic merit. Full-time students in a degree program are not eligible for this fellowship. Applicants should visit the organization's Web site to view additional eligibility requirements for the category in which they intend to apply. Fellowships are offered in different categories each year. Visit the commission's Web site to see if your discipline qualifies for the current year's awards. *Application Process: Applicants should submit an application along with supporting materials and an artist resume. For a detailed explanation of supporting materials in each artistic category, visit the commission's Web site. Applications are accepted for specific artistic disciplines each year and the current year's artistic areas are posted on the commission's Web site. Visit the commission's Web site to download an application. *Amount: $2,500. *Deadline: May 15.

South Dakota Arts Council

800 Governors Drive
Pierre, SD 57501-2294
605-773-3131
sdac@state.sd.us
http://www.artscouncil.sd.gov/Pubs/guide/Guide%20t o%20Grants%2006%2007/ArtistGrants/grantsartists.htm
Grant Name: Individual Artist Grant. *Academic Area: Media arts, performing arts (open), visual arts (open), writing. *Age Group: Adults. *Eligibility: Applicants must be at least 18 years old, have resided in South Dakota for at least two years, demonstrate a commitment to artistic excellence, and possess artistic merit. Full-time students in a degree program are not eligible for this grant. *Application Process: Applicants should submit an application along with supporting materials and an artist resume. Additional supporting materials such as newspaper reviews of the artist's work may also be submitted. For a detailed explanation of supporting materials in each artistic category, visit the council's Web site. Applications are accepted in all artistic disciplines. Visit the council's Web site to download an application. *Amount: $1,000 and $3,000. *Deadline: March 1.

Tennessee Arts Commission

Attn: Rod Reiner, Deputy Director
Citizens Plaza Building
401 Charlotte Avenue
Nashville, TN 37243-0780

615-741-2093
rod.reiner@state.tn.us
http://www.arts.state.tn.us/grantprograms.htm
Fellowship Name: Individual Artist Fellowship.
*Academic Area: Media arts, performing arts (open), visual arts (open), writing. *Age Group: Adults. *Eligibility: Applicants must be residents of Tennessee with a valid Tennessee mailing address. They must demonstrate that art is part of their livelihood and that they make a significant portion of their income from their art. Full-time students in a degree program are not eligible for this fellowship. Applicants should visit the commission's Web site to view the categories for which the organization is accepting applications for the current year. Disciplines vary by year. *Application Process: Applicants should submit an online application along with supporting materials. A new eGRANT system is now being used. Applicants should apply online, print a copy of the completed application, and submit the copy with the required supporting work samples. For a detailed explanation of supporting materials in each artistic category, visit the commission's Web site. *Amount: $5,000. *Deadline: January 30.

Texas Music Teachers Association
1106 Clayton Lane 240 W
Austin, TX 78723
512-419-1352
tmta@tmta.org
http://tmta.org/activity.html
Scholarship/Award Name: Texas Music Teachers Association Whitlock Memorial Scholarship Award. *Academic Area: Performing arts (music-open). *Age Group: Undergraduate students. *Eligibility: Applicants must be high school students who possess musical ability and who reside in Texas. Contact the association or your local music teacher for additional eligibility requirements. *Application Process: Applicants should contact the association or their local music teacher for information on how to register for the competition that results in the disbursement of scholarship funds. *Amount: $100. *Deadline: Contact the association for deadline information.

Vermont Arts Council
Attn: Michele Bailey, Director of Creation & Foundation Programs
136 State Street, Drawer 33
Montpelier, VT 05633-6001

802-828-3294
mbailey@vermontartscouncil.org
http://www.vermontartscouncil.org/grants/documents/for_artists.html
Grant Name: Grants for Artists. *Academic Area: Media arts, performing arts (open), visual arts (open), writing. *Age Group: Adults. *Eligibility: Applicants must be at least 18 years of age and have lived in Vermont for at least one year prior to application. Full-time students in a degree program are not eligible for these grants. The council offers more than one type of individual grant. Visit its Web site to learn more. All grants require a 1:1 cash match. Applicants will need to raise equal funds in order to be eligible for an award. *Application Process: Applicants should submit a completed application along with an artist narrative, a project timeline, a budget, supporting work samples, proof of Vermont residency, and a $10 application fee. Applicants should visit the council's Web site for complete details on how to submit work samples. *Amount: $250 to $5,000. *Deadline: Deadlines vary. Visit the council's Web site for detailed information.

Virginia Commission for the Arts
223 Governor Street
Lewis House, Second Floor
Richmond, VA 23219
804-225-3132
arts@arts.virginia.gov
http://www.arts.virginia.gov/artist%20fellowships.htm
Fellowship Name: Artist Fellowship. *Academic Area: Media arts, performing arts (open), visual arts (open), writing. *Age Group: Adults. *Eligibility: Applicants must be at least 18 years of age and legal residents of Virginia who plan to reside in the state for the duration of the fellowship period. Applicants must not be full-time students in a degree program. This organization offers fellowships in rotating disciplines. In one year applicants may apply in categories such as playwriting and sculpture. Two new categories will be chosen for the following year. Interested applicants should visit the commission's Web site to view the current categories, or contact the organization for more information. *Application Process: Applicants should submit a completed application along with an information page, an artist narrative, work samples, and a resume. Applicants should visit the commission's Web site for complete details on how to submit work samples in each category. *Amount: $5,000. *Deadline: August 1.

West Virginia Commission on the Arts

Attn: Jeff Pierson, Individual Artist Coordinator
The Cultural Center
1900 Kanawha Boulevard East
Charleston, WV 25305-0300
304-558-0240, ext. 717
jeff.pierson@wvculture.org
http://www.wvculture.org/arts/grants/fy06artistfellow.
    pdf
Fellowship Name: Artist Fellowships. *Academic Area:
    Performing arts (open), visual arts (open), writing.
    *Age Group: Adults. *Eligibility: Applicants must be
    at least 18 years old and residents of West Virginia
    for at least one year. Full-time students in a degree
    program are not eligible for these fellowships.
    Fellowships are offered in varying categories, which
    rotate on a yearly basis. Applicants should visit the
    commission's Web site to view additional eligibility
    requirements for the category in which they intend
    to apply and to see if applications are currently being
    accepted in their artistic discipline. *Application
    Process: Applicants should submit two copies of the
    completed application along with work samples (as
    specified for the category), a resume, and a self-
    addressed, stamped envelope and postcard. Visit the
    commission's Web site to download an application.
    *Amount: $3,500. *Deadline: September 1.

Wisconsin Arts Board

101 East Wilson Street, First Floor
Madison, WI 53702
608-266-0190
http://www.arts.state.wi.us/static/fellwshp.htm
Fellowship Name: Artist Fellowship Awards. *Academic
    Area: Media arts, performing arts (open), visual arts
    (open), writing. *Age Group: Adults. *Eligibility:
    Applicants must be at least 18 years old and
    residents of Wisconsin for at least one year. Those
    attending a college degree program are not eligible

for these fellowships. Fellowships are offered in
varying categories, which rotate on a yearly basis.
In even-numbered years, applicants may apply in
the categories of literary arts, music composition,
choreography, and performance art. Visual and
media arts applicants may apply in odd-numbered
years. *Application Process: Applicants apply
online via the eGRANT system. Hard copies of the
application and work samples must also be mailed.
Applicants should visit the board's Web site for
additional updates. This program is currently under
review, and procedures may change. *Amount:
$8,000. *Deadline: September 15.

Wisconsin Music Teachers Association (WMTA) Foundation

Attn: Gail A. Heywood, President
1531 Main Street
Rudolph, WI 54475-0084
heywood@tznet.com
http://www.wmta.net/collegiatefoundgrant.htm
Grant Name: Wisconsin Music Teachers Association
    Collegiate Foundation Grant. *Academic Area:
    Performing arts (music-open). *Age Group:
    Undergraduate students. *Eligibility: Applicants
    must be full-time music majors at an accredited
    Wisconsin college or university and nominated
    by a WMTA member (faculty member). Applicants
    must intend to use the money for a specific, special
    program that is not related to the earning of their
    academic degree (workshops, conventions, camps,
    etc.). *Application Process: Applicants should submit
    a letter of application describing the activity they
    would like to use the money for and the reason
    this activity is relevant to the applicant's study
    of music, a current curriculum vitae, and two
    letters of recommendation. One of the letters of
    recommendation should be from the nominating
    faculty member. *Amount: $200. *Deadline: March 1.

PERFORMING ARTS—GRADUATE

The following financial aid resources are available to students who are interested in studying the performing arts at the graduate level.

Alaska State Council on the Arts (ASCA)
411 West 4th Avenue, Suite 1E
Anchorage, AK 99501-2343
907-269-6610
aksca_info@eed.state.ak.us
http://www.eed.state.ak.us/aksca/Grants3.htm
Grant Name: Career Opportunity Grant. *Academic Area: Performing arts (dance), performing arts (music-open), performing arts (theatre). *Age Group: Adults. *Eligibility: Applicants must be Alaskan residents, at least 18 years old, and desire to increase their development as an artist and to further their artistic careers. They must not be enrolled as full-time students. Applicants must demonstrate artistic merit by submitting a work sample. *Application Process: Applicants should apply online. They should also submit video or DVD samples of their work and a printed copy of the ASCA Grants Online application profile page. Visit the council's Web site to apply. *Amount: $100 to $1,000. *Deadline: March 1, June 1, September 1, December 1.

Alaska State Council on the Arts (ASCA)
411 West 4th Avenue, Suite 1E
Anchorage, AK 99501-2343
907-269-6610
aksca_info@eed.state.ak.us
http://www.eed.state.ak.us/aksca/Grants3.htm
Fellowship Name: Connie Boochever Artist Fellowship. *Academic Area: Education, performing arts (open), media arts, visual arts (open), writing. *Age Group: Adults. *Eligibility: Applicants must be Alaska residents, at least 18 years old, and emerging artists who are pursuing their art form on an ongoing basis. Applicants may not be enrolled as full-time students and must not have received a grant in the last two years. *Application Process: Applicants should submit a complete application packet including supporting materials verifying the quality of their work (through visual representation, resume, and recommendations). This grant is offered to artists pursing different art forms in two-year, rotating cycles. Applicants should visit the council's Web site to see if they will qualify for the current discipline that is being offered. Visit the council's Web site for

more details. *Amount: $2,500. *Deadline: Contact the council for deadline information.

Alaska State Council on the Arts
411 West 4th Avenue, Suite 1E
Anchorage, AK 99501-2343
907-269-6610
aksca_info@eed.state.ak.us
http://www.eed.state.ak.us/aksca/Grants3.htm
Grant Name: Master Artist and Apprenticeship Grant. *Academic Area: Performing arts (dance), performing arts (music-instrumental), performing arts (voice), visual arts (crafts), visual arts (painting), visual arts (sculpting). *Age Group: Adults. *Eligibility: Applicants must be residents of Alaska, at least 18 years old, have an interest in traditional Alaska Native art, and desire the opportunity to develop their skills in an Alaskan Native art form. They must have demonstrated experience working in the art form for which they are applying and must have identified a master artist under whom they would like to serve as an apprentice. Applicants may not be enrolled as full-time students during the period of the grant. *Application Process: Applicants should submit a complete application packet, which includes supporting material verifying the quality of the apprentice's work (through visual representation, resume, and recommendations), quality of the master artist's work (through visual representation, resume, and recommendations), a description of the project and the skills that will be taught and learned, and a complete itemized budget. Visit the council's Web site for more details. *Amount: Up to $2,000. *Deadline: The first of the month prior to the applicant's planned apprenticeship.

American Cinema Editors
100 Universal City Plaza
Building 2352 B, Room 202
Universal City, CA 91608
818-777-2900
http://www.ace-filmeditors.org/newace/abt_StudentEdit.html
Contest Name: American Cinema Editors Student Editing Competition. *Academic Area: Film/

television. *Age Group: Open. *Eligibility: Applicants must be among the first 50 entrants who send in an entry request along with a $125 entry fee. *Application Process: Applicant should submit his or her name, address, area code and phone number, e-mail address, physical mailing address for receipt of package during daytime hours, name and address of school, the complete name of the applicant's instructor, as well as the entry fee by check or credit card. If paying by credit card, include the name of the cardholder, type of card, and the card number and expiration date. Visit the organization's Web site for further information. *Amount: Plaque plus publicity in Hollywood trade papers. *Deadline: October (contact the organization for detailed deadline information).

American Society of Cinematographers (ASC)
ASC Student Awards
1313 North Vine Street
Hollywood, CA 90028
323-969-4333
http://www.theasc.com/awards/index.html
Award Name: American Society of Cinematographers Jordan Cronenweth Heritage Award. *Academic Area: Film/television. *Age Group: Graduate students. *Eligibility: Applicants must be in their final year of a cinematography program or recent graduates (within one year). The award is also available to undergraduate students and recent graduates. *Application Process: Applicants should submit a completed application along with a nomination form signed by the dean or department chair, a resume, a 500-word personal statement, one film submission (for which the applicant is the sole cinematographer), and the same film on Beta SP. The application packet should be shipped via Fed Ex or UPS. Visit the society's Web site to download an application and nomination form. *Amount: All expenses paid to attend the ASC Awards ceremony. *Deadline: November 1.

American String Teachers Association (ASTA)
Merle J. Isaac Composition Contest
Attn: James Nacy, Composition Contest Chair
4153 Chain Bridge Road
Fairfax, VA 22030
636-537-4300, ext. 4752
iamacellist@sbcglobal.net
http://www.astaweb.com/competitions/MerleIsaac.htm

Contest Name: Merle J. Isaac Composition Contest. *Academic Area: Performing arts (music-composition). *Age Group: Open. *Eligibility: Applicants must be composers who are interested in submitting an unpublished composition that would be suitable for performance at the middle school/junior high grade levels or the high school level. *Application Process: Applicants should submit a completed application along with six copies of the score and one set of parts, including winds. A $25 application fee is also required. *Amount: $1,500, plus aid in publication and national publicity. *Deadline: April 1.

American String Teachers Association (ASTA)
Attn: Michael Carrera, Chair, ASTA National Solo Competition
4153 Chain Bridge Road
Fairfax, VA 22030
703-279-2113
Carrera@ohio.edu
http://www.astaweb.com/2007/SoloComp.html
Contest Name: National Solo Competition. *Academic Area: Performing arts (music-instrumental). *Age Group: Graduate students. *Eligibility: Applicants must be between the ages of 19 to 25. Applicants must be soloists on one of the following instruments: violin, viola, cello, double bass, classical guitar, or harp. Applicants must also be ASTA members or current students of ASTA members. High school students and undergraduate students may also participate in this competition. *Application Process: Applicants must first register for their state competition. Finalists from the state competition advance to the national competition. Applicants should contact their ASTA State Competition Chairs for information about entering their state competition. A complete list of these state chairs is available on ASTA's Web site. Detailed information about repertoire choices for the national event is listed on the Web site. Visit the Web site to read more about the competition and to locate your state contact. *Amount: Prizes to be determined. *Deadline: Deadlines vary.

Arizona Commission on the Arts
417 West Roosevelt Street
Phoenix, AZ 85003-1326
602-255-5882
info@azarts.gov
http://www.azarts.gov/artists/grants.htm

Grant Name: Career Advancement and Project Grants. *Academic Area: Performing arts (open), visual arts (open). *Age Group: Adults. *Eligibility: Applicants must be residents of Arizona, at least 18 years old, and not enrolled for more than three credit hours at a college or university. They must be seeking funds to advance their professional artistic careers or to help them complete a worthy artistic endeavor. Applicants must be able to provide documentation of Arizona residency. This organization provides three different kinds of grants for individuals. Eligibility requirements may vary slightly. *Application Process: Applicants should submit a completed application along with the appropriate supporting materials. Supporting materials include visual documentation of work samples (slides, video, etc.), resume, and a project narrative. Visit the commission's Web site to download an application and to view additional information about individual grants. *Amount: $500 to $5,000 (depending on the type of grant). *Deadline: Deadlines vary.

Arkansas Arts Council

1500 Tower Building, 323 Center Street
Little Rock, AR 72201
501-324-9766
info@arkansasarts.com
http://www.arkansasarts.com/grants

Grant Name: Individual Artists Fellowship. *Academic Area: Performing arts (open), visual arts (open). *Age Group: Adults. *Eligibility: Applicants must be residents of Arkansas who are at least 25 years old. They must have lived in Arkansas for at least one year to qualify and cannot be degree-seeking students or have received the award previously. Categories rotate yearly, so interested candidates should contact the council for information on the area in which they are taking applications for the current year. *Application Process: Applicants should contact the council for information on the application process. Applications are also periodically available at the council's Web site for download. *Amount: Awards vary. *Deadline: May 12.

Choristers Guild

Attn: Memorial Scholarship Committee
2834 West Kingsley Road
Garland, TX 75041-2498
972-271-1521
customerservice@mailcg.org
http://www.choristersguild.org/news.html

Scholarship Name: Choristers Guild College Scholarship. *Academic Area: Performing arts (music-religious). *Age Group: Graduate students. *Eligibility: Applicants must be pursuing a degree that will lead to a career in music ministry. Applicants should be able to demonstrate talent and leadership as well as financial need. Preference is given to applicants who want to work with children and youth. Undergraduate students may also apply for this scholarship. *Application Process: Applicants should submit a completed application along with transcripts and a photograph. Visit the guild's Web site to download an application. *Amount: $1,000. *Deadline: February 1.

Connecticut Commission on Culture and Tourism

Attn: Tamara Dimitri
One Financial Plaza
755 Main Street
Hartford, CT 06103
860-256-2720
tdimitri@ctarts.org
http://www.cultureandtourism.org/cct/cwp/view.asp?a=2207&q=293740&cctPNavCtr=|43595|

Fellowship Name: Individual Artists Fellowship. *Academic Area: Film/television, performing arts (choreography), performing arts (composition), visual arts (open), writing. *Age Group: Adults. *Eligibility: Applicants must be Connecticut residents who have lived within the state for at least one year. Applicants must not be degree-seeking college students and cannot have received the award previously. Categories rotate yearly, so interested candidates should visit the organization's Web site to see which category is available for the current year. *Application Process: Applicants should contact the commission for information on the application process. Application materials are available in July of each year. *Amount: $2,500 and $5,000. *Deadline: September (contact the commission for exact deadlines).

Delaware Division of the Arts

820 North French Street
Wilmington, DE 19801
302-577-8278
delarts@state.de.us
http://www.artsdel.org/grants/artistgrants.shtml

Grant Name: Grants for Individual Artists. *Academic Area: Media arts, performing arts (open), visual arts (open), writing. *Age Group: Adults. *Eligibility:

Applicants must be Delaware residents, at least 18 years old, and have lived in the state for at least one year. They must not be enrolled in a degree-granting program. This organization offers more than one kind of grant for individual artists. Visit the organization's Web site for additional eligibility requirements for individual grants. *Application Process: Applicants should submit a completed application along with a one-page narrative, a budget, a resume, and work samples (examples of appropriate submissions are listed on the application). Visit the organization's Web site to download an application. *Amount: Awards vary. *Deadline: Deadlines vary by grant.

Florida Division of Cultural Affairs
Attn: Morgan Barr
R.A. Gray Building
500 South Bronough Street, 3rd Floor
Tallahassee, FL 32399-0250
850-245-6470
mhbarr@dos.state.fl.us
http://www.florida-arts.org/grants/forindividuals.htm
Grant Name: Grants for Individual Artists. *Academic Area: Media arts, performing arts (dance), performing arts (music-general), performing arts (theatre), visual arts (open), writing. *Age Group: Adults. *Eligibility: Applicants must be Florida residents, at least 18 years old, and not be enrolled in any degree program. This organization offers more than one kind of grant for individual artists. Applicants must not have received a grant from the same organization in the previous grant period. Some grants are offered on a rotating categorical basis, with visual arts and media arts grouped together for one year and performing arts and literary arts in the next year. Visit the organization's Web site for additional eligibility requirements for individual grants. *Application Process: Applicants should submit a completed application along with supporting materials. Visit the organization's Web site for additional information on the application process. *Amount: Awards vary. *Deadline: Deadlines vary by individual award.

Florida State Music Teachers Association (FSMTA)
Attn: Gloria Bolivar, VP Competitive Events
13202 Dorchester Drive
Seminole, FL 33776
727-397-1771
http://www.fmta.org/awards.html

Scholarship Name: Florida State Music Teachers Association Scholarships and Awards. *Academic Area: Performing arts (music-general). *Age Group: Graduate students. *Eligibility: Applicants must reside in Florida and have expertise in musical performance. Applicants should contact their local music teachers for additional information on eligibility requirements. High school students and undergraduate students may also apply for scholarships and awards from the association. *Application Process: Applicants should contact their local music teachers or the FSMTA for information on the application process. The association offers many scholarships and awards for varying types of performance and the application process/competition dates will vary. *Amount: $50 to $600. *Deadline: Varies.

Hawaii State Foundation on Culture and the Arts
Attn: Fay Ann Chun, Individual Artists Program Coordinator
250 South Hotel Street, 2nd Floor
Honolulu, HI 96813
808-586-9965
hsfca2006awards@yahoo.com
http://www.state.hi.us/sfca
Fellowship Name: Individual Artists Fellowship. *Academic Area: Performing arts (open), visual arts (open). *Age Group: Adults. *Eligibility: Applicants must be residents of Hawaii, at least 18 years old, and recognized in their communities as professional artists. They must be financially compensated for their work as part of their livelihood and able to provide documentation of their artistic experience for at least the last five years. Visit the organization's Web site for a complete list of eligibility requirements in each visual arts or performing arts category. *Application Process: Applicants should submit a completed application along with an artist statement form, a resume form, three references and a reference form, and work samples. The process for submitting appropriate work samples is explained in depth on the application form. Visit the organization's Web site for additional information on the application process. *Amount: Awards vary. *Deadline: Contact the organization for deadline information.

Idaho Commission on the Arts
PO Box 83720
Boise, ID 83720-0008
208-334-2119

info@arts.idaho.gov
http://www.arts.idaho.gov/grants/indoverview.aspx
Grant Name: Grants for Individual Artists. *Academic
Area: Media arts, performing arts (open), visual arts
(open), writing. *Age Group: Adults. *Eligibility:
Applicants must be residents of Idaho who
demonstrate artistic excellence and a professional
artistic history. This organization offers several
grants and fellowships, many of which are offered on
a rotating scale according to artistic discipline. Visit
the organization's Web site for further information.
*Application Process: Applicants should submit
a completed application along with supporting
materials, including a resume, an artist statement,
and work samples. Visit the organization's Web
site for a checklist of supporting materials for
each type of grant or fellowship. *Amount: $3,500
(approximate). *Deadline: January 31.

Illinois Arts Council
James R. Thompson Center
100 West Randolph, Suite 10-500
Chicago, IL 60601
314-814-4991
rose@arts.state.il.us
http://www.state.il.us/agency/iac/Guidelines/guidelines.
htm
Fellowship Name: Artist Fellowship Program.
*Academic Area: Film/television, media arts,
performing arts (choreography), performing
arts (composition), visual arts (crafts), visual arts
(photography), visual arts (open). *Age Group:
Adults. *Eligibility: Applicants must be residents of
Illinois who can provide proof that they've resided
within the state for at least one year. They must be
U.S. citizens or permanent residents and not be
enrolled in any degree program. Applicants must
not have received funds from this fellowship in the
two preceding years. These fellowships are offered
on a rotating basis according to artistic discipline.
Applicants in the disciplines of choreography, crafts,
ethnic and folk arts, media arts, new performance
forms, prose, and scriptwriting may apply in even-
numbered years, and applicants in interdisciplinary/
computer art, music composition, photography,
poetry, and visual arts can apply in odd-numbered
years. Visit the organization's Web site for further
information. *Application Process: Applicants should
submit a completed application along with a work
sample sheet, work samples, a one-page artistic

resume, and a one-page artist statement. Work
samples must not be more than four years old. A
detailed explanation of work sample submission
procedures is explained on the application. Visit the
organization's Web site to download an application.
*Amount: $700 and $7,000. *Deadline: September 1.

Indiana Arts Commission
Attn: Monica Peterson
150 West Market Street, Suite 618
Indianapolis, IN 46204
317-232-1279
mpeterson@iac.in.gov
http://www.in.gov/arts/grants/program_iap.html
Grant Name: Grants for Individual Artists. *Academic
Area: Media arts, performing arts (open), visual arts
(open), writing. *Age Group: Adults. *Eligibility:
Applicants must be at least 18 years old and
residents of Indiana who have lived in the state for
at least one full year preceding the application. They
must remain an Indiana resident during the grant
period, not be enrolled in any degree program, and
not have received this award in the preceding year.
Applicant must apply as an individual and not as part
of a collaborative project. Visit the commission's Web
site for further information. *Application Process:
Applicants should submit a completed application
along with a formal letter stating the reasons for
consideration and supporting materials. A detailed
explanation of how to submit supporting materials
is included on the application. Visit the commission's
Web site to download an application. *Amount:
$1,000. *Deadline: February 3.

Iowa Arts Council
Attn: Bruce Williams
600 East Locust
Des Moines, IA 50319-0290
515-281-4006
Bruce.Williams@iowa.gov
http://www.iowaartscouncil.org/funding/artist-project-
grant/index.shtml
Grant Name: Artist Major Grants and Mini Grants.
*Academic Area: Performing arts (open), visual arts
(open). *Age Group: Adults. *Eligibility: Applicants
must be at least 18 years old and have lived in Iowa
for at least one full year preceding the application.
Applicants must not be students and not have
received two Iowa Arts Council grants within the
same fiscal year of this proposed grant activity.

This program also includes applicants from select bordering communities. Visit the council's Web site for the border state policy. Eligibility requirements may differ slightly for major and mini grants. Visit the council's Web site for additional eligibility requirements. *Application Process: Applicants must submit an online application on the state's new eGRANT system. The application will include information on the proposed project, a budget, a personal narrative, a work sample form and work samples, a service contract, and a project timeline. Visit the council's Web site to apply online. *Amount: $1,500 (mini grant); $10,000 (major grant). *Deadline: April 1.

Kentucky Arts Council

Attn: Lori Meadows
Capital Plaza Tower
500 Mero Street, 21st Floor
Frankfort, KY 40601-1987
502-564-3747 (or 888-833-2787), ext. 482
Lori.Meadows@ky.gov
http://artscouncil.ky.gov/guide/prog3/asf_gdl.htm
Fellowship Name: Al Smith Individual Artist Fellowship Program. *Academic Area: Media arts, performing arts (open), visual arts (open), writing. *Age Group: Adults. *Eligibility: Applicants must be U.S. citizens or permanent residents, residents of Kentucky (who have lived in the state for at least one year), at least 18 years old, and demonstrate artistic excellence and professional achievement. They must remain Kentucky residents during the period for which they receive funding. Applicants must be professional artists who are creating their own work, not just interpreting the work of others. *Application Process: Applicants should submit a completed application along with supporting materials. Supporting materials include a narrative essay, proof of residency, work samples and an index of work samples, and an optional resume. Detailed descriptions of how to submit work samples are listed on the application. This fellowship is offered in alternating disciplines every other year. Writers, choreographers, musical composers, and interdisciplinary artists may apply in even-numbered years, and visual and media artists may apply in odd-numbered years. Visit the organization's Web site to download an application. *Amount: $7,500; $1,000 professional assistance awards given to some applicants who do not receive the Individual Artist

Fellowships. *Deadline: August 15 (intent to apply deadline); September 15 (application deadline).

Maine Arts Commission

Attn: Donna McNeil, Contemporary Art & Public Art Associate
193 State Street, 25 State House Station
Augusta, ME 04333-0025
207-287-2726
Donna.McNeil@maine.gov
http://www.mainearts.com/Grants/index.shtml
Fellowship Name: Individual Artist Fellowship. *Academic Area: Media arts, performing arts (open), visual arts (open), writing. *Age Group: Adults. *Eligibility: Applicants must be residents of Maine, at least 18 years old, and not enrolled as full-time students in a field relating to the application. They must have lived in Maine for at least two years and demonstrate artistic excellence. Artists in all mediums are encouraged to apply. *Application Process: Applicants should submit a completed application along with one set of labeled artistic materials (instructions are located on the application), a biographical information sheet, and a self-addressed stamped postcard and envelope. Visit the commission's Web site to download an application. *Amount: $13,000. *Deadline: June 9.

Massachusetts Cultural Council

10 Saint James Avenue, 3rd Floor
Boston, MA 02116-3803
617-727-3668, 800-232-0960
mcc@art.state.ma.us
http://www.massculturalcouncil.org/programs/artistgrants.html
Grant Name: Artist Grants Program. *Academic Area: Media arts, performing arts (open), visual arts (open), writing. *Age Group: Adults. *Eligibility: Applicants must be residents of Massachusetts, at least 18 years old, and not be enrolled as students in degree programs. Applicants must demonstrate artistic excellence. Categories in which applicants may apply rotate every other year. Applicants should visit the organization's Web site to view the eligibility requirements for the current application period. *Application Process: Applicants should submit a completed application along with supporting materials. Visit the council's Web site to download an application and a description of how to submit work samples. *Amount: $5,000.

*Deadline: December. Visit the council's Web site for deadline information.

Mississippi Arts Commission
Attn: Judi Cleary, Director of Grants & Programs
Woolfolk Building
501 North West Street, Suite 701B
Jackson, MS 39201
601-359-6034
jcleary@arts.state.ms.us
http://www.mswholeschools.org/mac/grants/for-individuals.html
Fellowship Name: Artist Fellowship. *Academic Area: Media arts, performing arts (open), visual arts (open), writing. *Age Group: Adults. *Eligibility: Applicants must be residents of Mississippi, at least 18 years old, and maintain residency in Mississippi for the duration of the fellowship. They must demonstrate artistic excellence and earn at least part of their income from their artistic discipline. Applicants should consider their artistic endeavors as a career and should devote significant time to this work. Full-time students are not eligible for this fellowship. Categories in which applicants may apply rotate every other year. Applicants should visit the organization's Web site to view the eligibility requirements for the current application period. *Application Process: Applicants should submit a completed application along with an artist narrative, a resume, and work samples. Visit the organization's Web site to download an application and a description of how to submit work samples in each category. *Amount: Up to $5,000. *Deadline: March 1.

Montana Arts Council
PO Box 202201
Helena, MT 59620-2201
406-444-6430
mac@mt.gov
http://www.art.state.mt.us/artists/artists.asp
Grant Name: Opportunity and Professional Development Grants. *Academic Area: Performing arts (open), visual arts (open). *Age Group: Adults. *Eligibility: Applicants must be at least 18 years old and residents of Montana for at least one year. Full-time students are not eligible for these grants. Applicants should visit the council's Web site to view additional eligibility requirements for specific grants and specific artistic mediums. These grants require the applicant to match the funds with an equal dollar amount of their own funds or funds that they have raised for a given artistic endeavor. *Application Process: Applicants should submit a completed application along with an artist narrative, a project synopsis, a complete budget, and a resume. Visit the council's Web site to download an application. *Amount: $750 to $1,000. *Deadline: Deadlines vary.

National Association of Pastoral Musicians (NPM)
NPM Scholarships
962 Wayne Avenue, Suite 210
Silver Spring, MD 20910-4461
240-247-3000
npmsing@npm.org
http://www.npm.org/Membership/scholarship.htm
Scholarship Name: Academic Scholarships. *Academic Area: Performing arts (music-religious). *Age Group: Graduate students. *Eligibility: Applicants must be members of the NPM, enrolled in a degree program related to pastoral music, intend to work as a pastoral musician for at least two years, and demonstrate financial need. *Application Process: Applicants should submit a letter of application containing all of their contact information as well as pertinent biographical information, a CD or cassette recording that demonstrates their performance skills, two letters of recommendation, and a financial need statement. Visit the association's Web site to download a financial need statement and for further information about the many scholarships awarded in this category. *Amount: $500 to $4,500. *Deadline: March 3.

National Opera Association
Vocal Competition
PO Box 60869
Canyon, TX 79016-0001
806-651-2857
rhansen@mail.wtamu.edu
http://www.noa.org
Scholarship Name: National Opera Association Vocal Competition-Scholarship Division. *Academic Area: Performing arts (voice). *Age Group: Graduate students. *Eligibility: Applicants must be currently enrolled students between the ages of 18 and 24. They must have a teacher or opera director who is a member of the NOA, or they must attend an institution that is a NOA member. Undergraduate students may also participate in this competition. *Application Process: Applicants must submit a

completed application, a copy of legal proof of age, a resume photo, a $20 entry fee, and a cassette tape or CD of two arias from the repertoire list that have been recorded after January 1. Visit the association's Web site to download an application and to obtain further contest details. *Amount: $500 to $2,000. *Deadline: October 15.

National Religious Music Week Alliance
201 Dayton Street
Hamilton, OH 45011
513-844-1500
musicweek@aol.com
http://www.religiousmusicweek.com/scholar.html
Scholarship Name: National Religious Music Week Alliance Scholarship. *Academic Area: Performing arts (music-religious). *Age Group: Graduate students. *Eligibility: Applicants must be pursuing a degree that will lead to a career in music ministry. They should also be able to demonstrate academic achievement. Undergraduate students may also apply for this scholarship. *Application Process: Applicants should visit the alliance's Web site in January of each year, when the new application is available for download. Applicants should apply by submitting a completed application along with any supporting materials. *Amount: $2,500. *Deadline: Contact the alliance for deadline information.

Nevada Arts Council
Attn: Fran Morrow, Artist Services Program Coordinator
716 North Carson Street, Suite A
Carson City, NV 89701
775-687-7106
fkmorrow@clan.lib.nv.us
http://dmla.clan.lib.nv.us/docs/arts/programs/grants/grantsforartists.htm
Grant Name: Grants for Artists. *Academic Area: Media arts, performing arts (open), visual arts (open), writing. *Age Group: Adults. *Eligibility: Applicants must be at least 21 years old and residents of the state of Nevada for at least one year (and reside in the state of Nevada for the duration of the grant period). They must be U.S. citizens or legal permanent residents who are practicing professional artists and who demonstrate artistic excellence and merit. Applicants must not be full-time students. This organization offers more than one type of grant. Visit the organization's Web site to view additional eligibility requirements for specific grants.

*Application Process: Applicants should submit a completed application along with five copies of the work sample list, work samples required for their category (detailed on the application), and a resume. Visit the organization's Web site to download an application.*Amount: $500 to $5,000. *Deadline: Deadlines vary by grant. Visit the organization's Web site to view current deadlines.

New Hampshire State Council on the Arts
2 1/2 Beacon Street, 2nd Floor
Concord, NH 03301-4974
603-271-2789
http://www.state.nh.us/nharts/grants/artists/index.htm
Grant/Fellowship Name: Grants and Fellowships for Artists. *Academic Area: Media arts, performing arts (open), visual arts (open), writing. *Age Group: Adults. *Eligibility: Applicants must be at least 18 years old and residents of New Hampshire for at least one year (and reside in the state for the duration of the grant or fellowship period). They must demonstrate a commitment to artistic excellence and possess artistic merit. Applicants must not be full-time students. This organization offers more than one type of grant. Visit the organization's Web site to view additional eligibility requirements for specific awards. *Application Process: Applicants should submit a completed application along with answers to the required narrative questions, a resume, and work samples required for their category (detailed at the council's Web site). Visit the council's Web site to download an application.*Amount: $250 to $5,000. *Deadline: Deadlines vary by award. Visit the council's Web site to view current deadlines.

New Jersey State Council on the Arts
Attn: Rebecca Scolian
c/o Mid Atlantic Arts Foundation
201 North Charles Street, Suite 401
Baltimore, MD 21201
410-539-6656, ext. 101
rebecca@midatlanticarts.org
http://www.njartscouncil.org/program7.html
Fellowship Name: Artist Fellowship. *Academic Area: Media arts, performing arts (open), visual arts (open), writing. *Age Group: Adults. *Eligibility: Applicants must be at least 18 years old and residents of New Jersey for at least one year (and reside in the state for the duration of the fellowship period). They must

demonstrate a commitment to artistic excellence and possess artistic merit. Applicants must not be full-time students in a degree program. Visit the organization's Web site to view additional eligibility requirements for the category in which they intend to apply. *Application Process: Applicants should submit a completed application along with two copies of their resume, work samples, and a descriptive cover page. Visit the council's Web site to download an application.*Amount: $7,800 to $12,000. *Deadline: July 15.

North Carolina Arts Council
Department of Cultural Resources
Grants Office
226 East North Street
Raleigh, NC 27699-4632
919-733-2111
ncarts@ncmail.net
http://www.ncarts.org/freeform_scrn_template.
    cfm?ffscrn_id=47&menu_sel=4&sub_sel=15
Grant/Fellowship Name: Artist Grants and Fellowships.
    *Academic Area: Media arts, performing arts (open),
    visual arts (open), writing. *Age Group: Adults.
    *Eligibility: Applicants must be at least 18 years old,
    residents of the state of North Carolina for at least
    one year (and reside in the state for the duration
    of the fellowship period), and U.S. citizens or
    permanent residents. Applicants must demonstrate
    a commitment to artistic excellence and possess
    artistic merit. They must not be full-time students
    in a degree program. Applicants should visit the
    council's Web site to view additional eligibility
    requirements for the category in which they intend
    to apply. More than one type of fellowship and grant
    is offered by this organization. Visit the council's
    Web site for complete listings. *Application Process:
    Applicants should submit a completed application
    online, via eGRANT, by first submitting an electronic
    artist registration form. Applicants must also submit
    an artist narrative, a resume, a work sample with a
    descriptive cover page, and work samples required
    for their category (detailed on the council's Web
    site). Visit the council's Web site to apply. *Amount:
    $500 to 8,000. *Deadline: Deadlines vary.

Oregon Arts Commission
Attn: Shannon Planchon
775 Summer Street, NE, Suite 200
Salem, OR 97301-1284
503-986-0086
shannon.planchon@state.or.us
http://www.oregonartscommission.org/grants/
    commission_grant_programs.php
Fellowship/Grant Name: Individual Artists Fellowship
    Grant. *Academic Area: Media arts, performing
    arts (open), visual arts (open), writing. *Age Group:
    Adults. *Eligibility: Applicants must have been
    residents of Oregon for at least one year and
    demonstrate a commitment to artistic excellence
    and artistic merit. These grants are offered on
    a rotating basis by artistic discipline. Visit the
    commission's Web site for more information.
    *Application Process: Applicants should submit
    a completed application and supplementary
    materials. Applications are available for download
    from the commission's Web site in July of each
    year. Applicants must also submit their supporting
    materials according to the requirements posted for
    each art form. Visit the commission's Web site for
    additional information.*Amount: $3,000. *Deadline:
    October 16.

Pennsylvania Council on the Arts
Attn: Kerry Swartz, Administrative Assistant
717-787-6883
keswartz@state.pa.us
http://www.pacouncilonthearts.org/pca.cfm?id=9&level
    =Third&sid=13
Fellowship Name: Individual Artist Fellowship.
    *Academic Area: Media arts, performing arts (open),
    visual arts (open), writing. *Age Group: Adults.
    *Eligibility: Applicants must be current residents
    of Pennsylvania, and have been residents there for
    at least two years. They must not be high school
    students or degree-seeking students. Applicants
    may not apply for a fellowship if they received one
    during the previous award period. The council
    awards fellowships on a rotating basis according
    to artistic discipline. Applicants should visit the
    council's Web site to view additional eligibility
    requirements for the category in which they intend
    to apply. In even-numbered years, applications
    are accepted in arts commentary, crafts, folk and
    traditional arts (craft traditions), literature (fiction
    or creative nonfiction), media arts (narrative and
    animation), music (jazz, blues, world, or nonclassical
    composition), theatre (new performance forms,
    and visual arts (photography, sculpture). Applicants
    in dance (choreography), folk and traditional arts

(performing traditions), literature (poetry), media arts (documentary and experimental), music (classical composition), theatre (scriptworks), and visual arts (painting and printmaking) should apply in odd-numbered years. *Application Process: Applicants should submit a completed application along with program-specific work samples and supporting materials. Visit the council's Web site for details on these requirements in individual categories. Applicants should mail their applications to the specified organization, which differs based on artistic discipline. The main office does not accept application packets.*Amount: $5,000 and $10,000. *Deadline: The first business day in August.

Princess Grace Foundation-USA
150 East 58th Street, 25th Floor
New York, NY 10155
212-317-1470
info@pgfusa.org
http://www.pgfusa.com/awards/grants/index.html
Scholarship/Fellowship Name: Princess Grace Foundation Scholarships and Fellowships. *Academic Area: Film/television, performing arts (choreography), performing arts (dance), performing arts (theatre). *Age Group: Open. *Eligibility: The foundation offers numerous scholarships, apprenticeships, and fellowships to applicants of varying ages and stages of education. All applicants should be U.S. citizens or permanent residents who are pursuing careers in the performing arts. Visit the foundation's Web site for specific eligibility requirements for specific awards in choreography, dance, film, theatre, and playwriting. *Application Process: Applicants should download the relevant application form from the foundation's Web site and submit the application along with supporting materials. *Amount: Awards vary. *Deadline: Deadlines vary depending on category.

South Carolina Arts Commission
1800 Gervais Street
Columbus, SC 29201
803-734-8696
http://www.state.sc.us/arts/grants/artists/fellowships.htm
Fellowship/Grant Name: Individual Artist Fellowship Grant. *Academic Area: Media arts, performing arts (open), visual arts (open), writing. *Age Group: Adults. *Eligibility: Applicants must be at least 18 years old, have resided in South Carolina for at least two years, demonstrate a commitment to artistic excellence, and possess artistic merit. Full-time students in a degree program are not eligible for this fellowship. Applicants should visit the organization's Web site to view additional eligibility requirements for the category in which they intend to apply. Fellowships are offered in different categories each year. Visit the commission's Web site to see if your discipline qualifies for the current year's awards. *Application Process: Applicants should submit an application along with supporting materials and an artist resume. For a detailed explanation of supporting materials in each artistic category, visit the commission's Web site. Applications are accepted for specific artistic disciplines each year and the current year's artistic areas are posted on the commission's Web site. Visit the commission's Web site to download an application. *Amount: $2,500. *Deadline: May 15.

South Dakota Arts Council
800 Governors Drive
Pierre, SD 57501-2294
605-773-3131
sdac@state.sd.us
http://www.artscouncil.sd.gov/Pubs/guide/Guide%20to%20Grants%2006%2007/ArtistGrants/grantsartists.htm
Grant Name: Individual Artist Grant. *Academic Area: Media arts, performing arts (open), visual arts (open), writing. *Age Group: Adults. *Eligibility: Applicants must be at least 18 years old, have resided in South Dakota for at least two years, demonstrate a commitment to artistic excellence, and possess artistic merit. Full-time students in a degree program are not eligible for this grant. *Application Process: Applicants should submit an application along with supporting materials and an artist resume. Additional supporting materials such as newspaper reviews of the artist's work may also be submitted. For a detailed explanation of supporting materials in each artistic category, visit the council's Web site. Applications are accepted in all artistic disciplines. Visit the council's Web site to download an application. *Amount: $1,000 and $3,000. *Deadline: March 1.

Tennessee Arts Commission
Attn: Rod Reiner, Deputy Director
Citizens Plaza Building
401 Charlotte Avenue

Nashville, TN 37243-0780
615-741-2093
rod.reiner@state.tn.us
http://www.arts.state.tn.us/grantprograms.htm
Fellowship Name: Individual Artist Fellowship.
*Academic Area: Media arts, performing arts (open),
visual arts (open), writing. *Age Group: Adults.
*Eligibility: Applicants must be residents of Tennessee
with a valid Tennessee mailing address. They must
demonstrate that art is part of their livelihood and
that they make a significant portion of their income
from their art. Full-time students in a degree program
are not eligible for this fellowship. Applicants
should visit the commission's Web site to view the
categories for which the organization is accepting
applications for the current year. Disciplines vary by
year. *Application Process: Applicants should submit
an online application along with supporting materials.
A new eGRANT system is now being used. Applicants
should apply online, print a copy of the completed
application, and submit the copy with the required
supporting work samples. For a detailed explanation
of supporting materials in each artistic category,
visit the commission's Web site. *Amount: $5,000.
*Deadline: January 30.

Vermont Arts Council
Attn: Michele Bailey, Director of Creation & Foundation
Programs
136 State Street, Drawer 33
Montpelier, VT 05633-6011
802-828-3294
mbailey@vermontartscouncil.org
http://www.vermontartscouncil.org/grants/documents/
for_artists.html
Grant Name: Grants for Artists. *Academic Area: Media
arts, performing arts (open), visual arts (open),
writing. *Age Group: Adults. *Eligibility: Applicants
must be at least 18 years of age and have lived in
Vermont for at least one year prior to application.
Full-time students in a degree program are not
eligible for these grants. The council offers more
than one type of individual grant. Visit its Web site
to learn more. All grants require a 1:1 cash match.
Applicants will need to raise equal funds in order
to be eligible for an award. *Application Process:
Applicants should submit a completed application
along with an artist narrative, a project timeline, a
budget, supporting work samples, proof of Vermont
residency, and a $10 application fee. Applicants

should visit the council's Web site for complete
details on how to submit work samples.*Amount:
$250 to $5,000. *Deadline: Deadlines vary. Visit the
council's Web site for detailed information.

Virginia Commission for the Arts
223 Governor Street
Lewis House, Second Floor
Richmond, VA 23219
804-225-3132
arts@arts.virginia.gov
http://www.arts.virginia.gov/artist%20fellowships.htm
Fellowship Name: Artist Fellowship. *Academic Area:
Media arts, performing arts (open), visual arts (open),
writing. *Age Group: Adults. *Eligibility: Applicants
must be at least 18 years of age and legal residents
of Virginia who plan to reside in the state for the
duration of the fellowship period. Applicants must
not be full-time students in a degree program.
This organization offers fellowships in rotating
disciplines. In one year applicants may apply in
categories such as playwriting and sculpture. Two
new categories will be chosen for the following year.
Interested applicants should visit the commission's
Web site to view the current categories, or contact
the organization for more information. *Application
Process: Applicants should submit a completed
application along with an information page, an artist
narrative, work samples, and a resume. Applicants
should visit the commission's Web site for complete
details on how to submit work samples in each
category. *Amount: $5,000. *Deadline: August 1.

West Virginia Commission on the Arts
Attn: Jeff Pierson, Individual Artist Coordinator
The Cultural Center
1900 Kanawha Boulevard East
Charleston, WV 25305-0300
304-558-0240, ext. 717
jeff.pierson@wvculture.org
http://www.wvculture.org/arts/grants/fy06artistfellow.
pdf
Fellowship Name: Artist Fellowships. *Academic Area:
Performing arts (open), visual arts (open), writing.
*Age Group: Adults. *Eligibility: Applicants must be
at least 18 years old and residents of West Virginia
for at least one year. Full-time students in a degree
program are not eligible for these fellowships.
Fellowships are offered in varying categories, which
rotate on a yearly basis. Applicants should visit the

commission's Web site to view additional eligibility requirements for the category in which they intend to apply and to see if applications are currently being accepted in their artistic discipline. *Application Process: Applicants should submit two copies of the completed application along with work samples (as specified for the category), a resume, and a self-addressed, stamped envelope and postcard. Visit the commission's Web site to download an application. *Amount: $3,500. *Deadline: September 1.

Wisconsin Arts Board
101 East Wilson Street, First Floor
Madison, WI 53702
608-266-0190
http://www.arts.state.wi.us/static/fellwshp.htm
Fellowship Name: Artist Fellowship Award. *Academic Area: Media arts, performing arts (open), visual arts (open), writing. *Age Group: Adults. *Eligibility: Applicants must be at least 18 years old and residents of Wisconsin for at least one year. Those attending a college degree program are not eligible for these fellowships. Fellowships are offered in varying categories, which rotate on a yearly basis. In even numbered years, applicants may apply in the categories of literary arts, music composition, choreography, and performance art. Visual and media arts applicants may apply in odd-numbered years. *Application Process: Applicants apply online via the eGRANT system. Hard copies of the application and work samples must also be mailed. Applicants should visit the board's Web site for additional updates. This program is currently under review, and procedures may change. *Amount: $8,000. *Deadline: September 15.

SCIENCE—UNDERGRADUATE

The following financial aid resources are available to students who are interested in studying science and related fields at the undergraduate level.

American Dietetic Association (ADA)
Attn: ADA Foundation, Education Team
120 South Riverside Plaza, Suite 2000
Chicago, IL 60606-6995
800-877-1600, ext. 5400
education@eatright.org
http://www.eatright.org/cps/rde/xchg/ada/hs.xsl/
    career_394_ENU_HTML.htm
Scholarship Name: American Dietetic Association
    Foundation Scholarships. *Academic Area: Food
    sciences. *Age Group: Undergraduate students.
    *Eligibility: Applicants must be members of the ADA
    who are juniors or seniors in a baccalaureate program
    in dietetics or the second year of study in a dietetic
    technician program, or a dietetic internship program.
    Some scholarships may require specific dietetic
    practice group membership and residency in a specific
    state. Some scholarships are also available to graduate
    students. *Application Process: Applicants should visit
    the ADA Web site to download an application or to
    seek membership and specific scholarship information.
    Amount: $500 to $5,000. *Deadline: Contact the
    association for deadline information.

American Institute of Professional Geologists (AIPG)
Attn: Education Committee Chair
1400 West 122nd Avenue, Suite 250
Westminster, CO 80234
303-412-6205
aipg@aipg.org
http://www.aipg.org/StaticContent/anonymous/
    Sections/Section%20Serv/AIPGScholarship_poster_
    booth.pdf
Scholarship Name: American Institute of Professional
    Geologists Scholarship Program. *Academic Area: Earth
    science, geology. *Age Group: Undergraduate students.
    *Eligibility: Applicants must be college sophomores,
    juniors, or seniors; majoring in geology or earth
    science; attending a four-year accredited institution
    in the United States; and participating student
    members of the AIPG (may apply for membership
    with application). Winners of the scholarships must
    also agree to submit a 600- to 800-word article for
    publication in The *Professional Geologist.* *Application
    Process: Applicants should submit a letter of interest,
    which includes name, address, e-mail address, and

telephone number, along with proof of enrollment in
a geological sciences program, transcripts, a one-page
essay on why they want to become a geologist, and
a letter of support from a faculty member. *Amount:
$1,000. *Deadline: February 15.

American Institute of Wine and Food (AIWF)
213-37 39th Avenue, Box 216
Bayside, NY 11361
800-274-2493
info@aiwf.org
http://www.aiwf.org/site/scholarships.html
Scholarship Name: American Institute of Wine and
    Food Scholarship Program. *Academic Area: Food
    sciences. *Age Group: Open. *Eligibility: Applicants
    should be working or interested in fields related
    to the AIWF mission of "enhancing the quality of
    life through education about what we eat and
    drink." *Application Process: Applicants should
    visit the institute's Web site for a listing of available
    scholarships by chapter. Only select chapters
    offer scholarships. Contact your local chapter for
    additional application information. *Amount: Awards
    vary. *Deadline: Contact the appropriate local
    chapter for deadline information.

American Meteorological Society
Attn: Freshman Scholarship Program
45 Beacon Street
Boston, MA 02108
617-227-2426, ext. 246
dfernand@ametsoc.org
http://www.ametsoc.org/amsstudentinfo/scholfeldocs/
    index.html
Scholarship Name: American Meteorological Society
    Freshman Undergraduate Scholarship Program.
    *Academic Area: Hydrology, marine sciences,
    meteorology. *Age Group: Undergraduate students.
    *Eligibility: Applicants must be high school seniors
    entering their freshman year of college in the fall
    of the next academic year, full-time students, and
    planning to pursue a degree in the atmospheric
    or related oceanic or hydrologic sciences. They
    also must have maintained at least a 3.0 GPA and
    be U.S. citizens or hold permanent resident status.
    *Application Process: Applicants must submit a

completed application, official transcripts, a letter of recommendation, a copy of their SAT/ACT scores, and an essay. Visit the society's Web site to download an application. *Amount: Varies. *Deadline: February 10.

American Meteorological Society
Undergraduate Scholarship Program
45 Beacon Street
Boston, MA 02108
617-227-2426, ext. 246
dfernand@ametsoc.org
http://www.ametsoc.org/amsstudentinfo/scholfeldocs/index.html
Scholarship Name: American Meteorological Society Undergraduate Scholarship Program. *Academic Area: Hydrology, marine sciences, meteorology. *Age Group: Undergraduate students. *Eligibility: Applicants must be full-time students entering their final year of undergraduate study at an accredited U.S. institution. They also must be majoring in the atmospheric or related oceanic or hydrologic science, and/or must show clear intent to make the atmospheric or related sciences their career. Applicants must have maintained at least a 3.25 GPA and demonstrate financial need. *Application Process: Applicants must submit a completed application, three letters of recommendation, and official transcripts. Visit the society's Web site to download an application. *Amount: Varies. *Deadline: February 10.

Annie's Homegrown
Annie's Scholarship Applications
564 Gateway Drive
Napa, CA 94558
800-288-1089
cfc@annies.com
http://www.annies.com/programs/ess.html
Scholarship Name: Annie's Environmental Studies Scholarship. *Academic Area: Environmental science. *Age Group: Undergraduate students. *Eligibility: Applicants must be full-time students beginning or returning to an accredited two- or four-year technical or college program in the United States. Students must be focusing on classes in the environmental studies field and have at least one more year before completing their degree. High school seniors, undergraduate students, and graduate students with more than one year in their program are welcome to apply. *Application Process: Applicants must submit an online fact sheet along with a one-paragraph

personal statement explaining what they currently do and what they are planning to do to change the world. Applicants should also submit official transcripts and two letters of reference. Visit the company's Web site to fill out an online fact sheet. *Amount: $1,000. *Deadline: July 1.

Armed Forces Communications and Electronics Association (AFCEA) Educational Foundation
Attn: Norma Corrales, Director, Scholarships and Awards Program
4400 Fair Lakes Court
Fairfax, VA 22033-3899
703-631-6149, 800-336-4583, ext. 6149
scholarship@afcea.org
http://www.afcea.org/education/scholarships/undergraduate/pub1.asp
Scholarship Name: Armed Forces Communications and Electronics Association Distance Learning/Online Scholarship. *Academic Area: Computer science, engineering (aerospace), engineering (chemical), engineering (computer), engineering (electrical), physics, mathematics. *Age Group: Undergraduate students. *Eligibility: Applicants must be U.S. citizens currently enrolled in full-time distance learning or online programs majoring in mathematics, physics, electrical, chemical, systems or computer engineering, and computer science. Applicants must have completed at least 30 semester hours of study (or equivalent) to be eligible to apply. Applicants must also have completed at least two semesters of calculus. *Application Process: Applicants must submit a completed application. Applications are available on the foundation's Web site each December. *Amount: $1,000. *Deadline: June 1.

Armed Forces Communications and Electronics Association Educational Foundation
Attn: Fred H. Rainbow, Vice President and Executive Director
4400 Fair Lakes Court
Fairfax, VA 22033-3899
703-631-6149, 800-336-4583, ext. 6149
scholarship@afcea.org
http://www.afcea.org/education/scholarships/undergraduate/pub3.asp
Scholarship Name: AFCEA Lockheed Martin Orincon IT Scholarship. *Academic Area: Computer science, engineering (aerospace), engineering (chemical), engineering (computer), engineering (electrical),

physics, mathematics. *Age Group: Undergraduate students. *Eligibility: Applicants must be U.S. citizens attending an accredited four-year college or university in the greater San Diego, California, area. Applicants must be enrolled full time as sophomores or juniors majoring in electrical, computer, chemical, systems or aerospace engineering, computer science, physics, or mathematics. Applicants must also maintain at least a 3.5 GPA. Students enrolled in distance learning or online programs are not eligible to apply. *Application Process: Applicants must submit a completed application, at least two letters of recommendation, and official transcripts. Applications are available on the foundation's Web site each January. *Amount: $3,000. *Deadline: May 1.

Armed Forces Communications and Electronics Association Educational Foundation

Attn: Fred H. Rainbow, Vice President and Executive Director
4400 Fair Lakes Court
Fairfax, VA 22033-3899
703-631-6149, 800-336-4583, ext. 6149
scholarship@afcea.org
http://www.afcea.org/education/scholarships/undergraduate/pub2.asp

Scholarship Name: General John A. Wickham Scholarship. *Academic Area: Computer science, engineering (aerospace), engineering (chemical), engineering (computer), engineering (electrical), physics, mathematics. *Age Group: Undergraduate students. *Eligibility: Applicants must be U.S. citizens attending an accredited four-year college or university. They also must be enrolled full time as sophomores or juniors majoring in electrical, computer, chemical, systems or aerospace engineering, computer science, physics, or mathematics and maintain at least a 3.5 GPA. Students enrolled in distance learning or online programs are not eligible to apply. *Application Process: Applicants must submit a completed application, at least two letters of recommendation, and official transcripts. Applications are available on the foundation's Web site each January. *Amount: $2,000. *Deadline: May 1.

Armed Forces Communications and Electronics Association Educational Foundation

Attn: Fred H. Rainbow, Vice President and Executive Director
4400 Fair Lakes Court
Fairfax, VA 22033-3899
703-631-6149, 800-336-4583, ext. 6149
scholarship@afcea.org
http://www.afcea.org/education/scholarships/undergraduate/Bragunier.asp

Scholarship Name: William E. "Buck" Bragunier Scholarship for Outstanding Leadership. *Academic Area: Computer science, engineering (aerospace), engineering (chemical), engineering (computer), engineering (electrical), physics, mathematics. *Age Group: Undergraduate students. *Eligibility: Applicants must be U.S. citizens attending an accredited four-year college or university in the greater San Diego, California, area. Applicants must also demonstrate academic excellence and a commitment to university and/or local community leadership. They also must be enrolled full time as sophomores or juniors majoring in electrical, computer, chemical, systems or aerospace engineering, computer science, physics, or mathematics and maintain at least a 3.5 GPA. Students enrolled in distance learning or online programs are not eligible to apply. *Application Process: Applicants must submit a completed application, at least two letters of recommendation, and official transcripts. Applications are available on the foundation's Web site each January. *Amount: $2,000. *Deadline: May 1.

Cartography and Geographic Information Society (CaGIS)

CaGIS Scholarship Committee
c/o American Congress on Surveying and Mapping
6 Montgomery Village Avenue, Suite 403
Gaithersburg, MD 20879
240-632-9716, ext. 109
ilse.genovese@acsm.net
http://www.acsm.net/cagis/05scholarship.html

Scholarship Name: Cartography and Geographic Information Society Scholarship. *Academic Area: Geosciences. *Age Group: Undergraduate students. *Eligibility: Applicants must be enrolled full time in a four-year undergraduate degree program in cartography or geographic information science. They also should demonstrate academic achievement and show commitment to professional activities. Financial need will be considered, if necessary, to break ties. The scholarship is also available to graduate students. *Application Process: Applicants should submit a completed application along with three letters of recommendation and a 500-word statement of educational objectives, future study or research plans and professional activities, and financial need. Proof of membership in the CaGIS/ACSM is also required (or a membership application). Three copies of the application packet should be sent. *Amount: $1,000. *Deadline: January 22.

Entomological Foundation
9332 Annapolis Road, Suite 210
Lanham, MD 20706
301-731-4535
april@entfdn.org
http://www.entsoc.org/awards/student/bioquip.htm
Scholarship Name: BioQuip Undergraduate Scholarship. *Academic Area: Entomology. *Age Group: Undergraduate students. *Eligibility: Applicants must have been enrolled as an undergraduate student in entomology (or related degree if their university does not offer an entomology degree) at a college or university in the United States, Mexico, or Canada in the fall prior to the application deadline. Applicants must also have accumulated a minimum of 90 college credit hours by September 1 following the application deadline, and either completed two junior-level entomology courses or have a research project in entomology. Preference will be given to students with demonstrated financial need. *Application Process: Applicants must submit a completed application, a curriculum vitae (including all the information requested in the curriculum vitae template on the foundation's Web site), a letter of nomination, a personal statement, three letters of recommendation, and official transcripts. Visit the foundation's Web site to download and/or submit an application. *Amount: $2,000. *Deadline: July 1.

Experimental Aircraft Association (EAA)
EAA Scholarship Department
PO Box 3086
Oshkosh, WI 54903-3086
920-426-6823
scholarships@eaa.org
http://www.eaa.org/education/scholarships
Scholarship Name: Payzer Scholarship. *Academic Area: Biological sciences, engineering (open), mathematics, and physical sciences. *Age Group: Undergraduate students. *Eligibility: Applicants must be accepted or enrolled in an accredited college, university, or postsecondary school that emphasizes technical information. Applicants must be majoring in and pursuing a professional career in engineering, mathematics, or the physical or biological sciences. Applicants must be well rounded and involved in school/community activities and aviation. Applicants must also be current members of EAA or recommended by a current EAA member. *Application Process: Applicants must visit the Association's Web site to submit an online application. *Amount: $5,000. *Deadline: March 1.

Georgia Science Teachers Association (GSTA)
Attn: Bob Farmer, GSTA Awards Chair
Cedartown High School
167 Frank Lott Drive
Cedartown, GA 30125
770-748-0490
bfarmer@polk.k12.ga.us
http://www.georgiascienceteacher.org/awards.htm
Scholarship Name: Science Adventure Student Scholarship. *Academic Area: Science. *Age Group: Junior high school students, high school students, undergraduate students. *Eligibility: Applicants must be in grades six though 12 or pursuing undergraduate study at a school in Georgia. They also must have an interest in attending a science conference or event to further their science education. *Application Process: Applicants should submit a letter with their name and contact information; the names of their parents, science teacher, and principal; and school name, address, and phone number. Applicants can apply as individuals or as a group. They also should include in this letter a description of the program they hope to attend and why they want to attend, the cost of the program for each participant (including travel), and a description of how the applicants will share their experience when they return. Applicants must also submit two letters of recommendation. Recipients of the award must agree to write an article for publication in The Georgia Science Teacher. Contact the association for further information. *Amount: Up to $2,000. *Deadline: October 25.

Institute of Food Technologists (IFT)
Attn: Elizabeth Plummer
IFT Scholarship Department
525 West Van Buren, Suite 1000
Chicago, IL 60607
312-782-8424
ejplummer@ift.org

http://www.ift.org/cms/?pid=1000444

Scholarship Name: Institute of Food Technologists Freshman/Sophomore Scholarship. *Academic Area: Food sciences. *Age Group: Undergraduate students. *Eligibility: Applicants must be high school seniors, high school graduates entering college for the first time, or college freshmen enrolled in or planning to enroll in an approved program in food science/technology. *Application Process: Applicants must submit a completed application, official transcripts, a recommendation form (freshmen), and a recommendation letter (sophomores). Visit the IFT's Web site to download an application and recommendation form. *Amount: $1,000 to $1,500. *Deadline: Varies by age group.

Institute of Food Technologists (IFT)
Attn: Elizabeth Plummer
IFT Scholarship Department
525 West Van Buren, Suite 1000
Chicago, IL 60607
312-782-8424
ejplummer@ift.org
http://www.ift.org/cms/?pid=1001271

Scholarship Name: Institute of Food Technologists Junior/Senior Scholarship. *Academic Area: Food sciences. *Age Group: Undergraduate students. *Eligibility: Applicants must be college sophomores, juniors, or seniors pursuing a degree in food science or food technology at an accredited educational institution. *Application Process: Applicants must submit a completed application, official transcripts, a recommendation letter, and a statement from their department head. Visit the IFT's Web site to download an application. Applications must be submitted to the applicant's department head. *Amount: $1,000 to $2,500. *Deadline: February 1.

Marine Technology Society (MTS)
MTS Student Scholarship
5565 Sterrett Place, Suite 108
Columbia, MD 21044
410-884-5330
mtsmbrship@erols.com
http://www.mtsociety.org/education/student_scholarships.cfm

Scholarship Name: Charles H. Bussmann Scholarship. *Academic Area: Marine sciences. *Age Group: Undergraduate students. *Eligibility: Applicants must be full-time undergraduate students studying a marine-related field. Applicants must be MTS members. The scholarship is also available to graduate students. *Application Process: Applicants must submit contact details, a personal statement, a biographical sketch, official transcripts, one academic letter of recommendation, and one personal reference. *Amount: $2,500. *Deadline: April 17.

Marine Technology Society (MTS)
MTS Student Scholarship
5565 Sterrett Place, Suite 108
Columbia, MD 21044
410-884-5330
mtsmbrship@erols.com
http://www.mtsociety.org/education/student_scholarships.cfm

Scholarship Name: MTS Student Scholarship Award. *Academic Area: Marine sciences. *Age Group: Undergraduate students. *Eligibility: Applicants must be full-time students (MTS or non-MTS) enrolled in academic institutions who are studying marine-related fields. High school seniors and undergraduate students are eligible for this scholarship. *Application Process: Applicants must submit contact information, a personal statement, a biographical sketch, official transcripts, one academic letter of recommendation, and one personal reference. *Amount: $2,000. *Deadline: April 17.

Marine Technology Society (MTS)
Attn: Chuck Richards, ROV Scholarship Committee Chair
Chuck Richards, ROV Scholarship Committee Chair
c/o C.A. Richards and Associates Inc.
777 North Eldridge Parkway, Suite 280
Houston, TX 77079
410-884-5330
chuck@carichards.com
http://www.mtsociety.org/education/student_scholarships.cfm

Scholarship Name: Remotely Operated Vehicle (ROV) Student Scholarship. *Academic Area: Marine sciences. *Age Group: Undergraduate students. *Eligibility: Applicants must be MTS members and full-time students in academic institutions majoring in marine-related fields. They also must possess an interest in underwater work that furthers the use of remotely operated vehicles. The scholarship is also available to high school students and graduate students. *Application Process: Applicants must submit contact information, biography, official transcripts, a one-page essay, an academic letter of recommendation, and three personal references. *Amount: Up to $10,000. *Deadline: April 17.

Maryland Agriculture Teachers Association

Attn: Ms. Jamie Picardy, MATA Consultant
403 Oakington Road
PO Box 536
Havre de Grace, MD 21078
410-939-9030, 800-205-9737
jpicardy@maefonline.com
http://iaa.umd.edu/MATA/elcScholars.htm
Scholarship Name: Elmer L. Cooper Scholarship. *Academic Area: Agriculture, education. *Age Group: Undergraduate students. *Eligibility: Applicants must be high school seniors. There are two scholarships available in this program. One is for a high school senior who intends on becoming an agriculture teacher, and the other is for an outstanding FFA member who intends on majoring in any area of agriculture. *Application Process: Applicants should contact the association to receive an application. *Amount: Awards vary. *Deadline: Contact the association for deadline information.

National Aeronautics and Space Administration (NASA)

NASA Headquarters
NASA Education Program
Office of Education
Code N
Washington, DC 20546-0001
202-358-0103
http://education.nasa.gov/divisions/higher/overview/
F_pathfinder_scholarship.html
Scholarship Name: NASA Science and Technology Scholarship Program. *Academic Area: Computer science, engineering (open), life sciences, mathematics, and physical sciences. *Age Group: Undergraduate students. *Eligibility: Applicants must be undergraduate students pursuing degrees in engineering, mathematics, computer science, physical science, or life science. *Application Process: Contact the NASA Education Program for details. *Amount: Up to $20,000. *Deadline: Varies.

National Cattlemen's Foundation

Beef Industry Scholarship
9110 East Nichols Avenue, Suite 300
Centennial, CO 80112

303-850-3347
ncf@beef.org
http://www.nationalcattlemensfoundation.org/
SCHOLARSHIP.aspx
Scholarship Name: Beef Industry Scholarship. *Academic Area: Agriculture, communications, education. *Age Group: Undergraduate students. *Eligibility: Applicants must be enrolled full time in a two- or four-year institution of higher learning with an intent on majoring in a field related to the beef industry—education, communications, production, or research. They must also demonstrate commitment to the beef industry through classes, internships, or life experiences. High school seniors, may also apply for this scholarship. *Application Process: Applicants should submit a completed application along with a one-page letter expressing career goals, two letters of recommendation, and a 750-word essay. *Visit the association's Web site to download an application. *Amount: $1,500, plus expenses paid to attend the organization's annual convention and trade show. *Deadline: September 30.

National Environmental Health Association (NEHA)/ American Academy of Sanitarians (AAS)

Attn: Scholarship Coordinator, NEHA/AAS Scholarship
720 South Colorado Boulevard, Suite 970, South Tower
Denver, CO 80246-1904
303-756-9090
cdimmitt@neha.org
http://www.neha.org/scholarship/scholarship.html
Scholarship Name: NEHA/AAS Scholarship. *Academic Area: Environmental science. *Age Group: Undergraduate students. *Eligibility: Applicants must be college juniors or seniors enrolled in an Environmental Health Accreditation Council or a NEHA institutional/educational or sustaining member school. Visit the association's Web site for a list of accredited programs and/or schools. The scholarship is also available to graduate students. *Application Process: Applicants must submit a completed application along with official transcripts, two faculty letters of recommendation, and one letter of recommendation from an active NEHA member. Visit the association's Web site to download an application. *Amount: $1,000. *Deadline: February 1.

National Fish and Wildlife Foundation

Attn: Lauren Guite
1120 Connecticut Avenue, NW, Suite 900

Washington, DC 20036
202-857-0166
lauren.guite@nfwf.org
http://www.nfwf.org/programs/budscholarship
Scholarship Name: Budweiser Conservation Scholarship. *Academic Area: Biology, environmental science, geography, natural resources, political science, social sciences, public policy. *Age Group: Undergraduate students. *Eligibility: Applicants must be U.S. citizens, at least 21 years old, and enrolled in an accredited college or university in the United States. They also must apply during their sophomore or junior years. The scholarship is also available to graduate students. *Application Process: Applicants should submit a completed application along with a 1,500-word essay, a research proposal and/or abstract, official transcripts, and three letters of recommendation. Visit the foundation's Web site to download an application. *Amount: Up to $10,000. *Deadline: January 27.

National Ground Water Research and Educational Foundation
Attn: Lee Salvator
601 Dempsey Road
Westerville, OH 43081
800-551-7379
lsalvator@ngwa.org
http://www.ngwa.org/about/auxsch.cfm
Scholarship Name: National Ground Water Research and Educational Foundation Len Assante Scholarship Fund. *Academic Area: Environmental science. *Age Group: Undergraduate students. *Eligibility: Applicants must be high school seniors or undergraduate students, planning to or currently attending school full time, and entering or pursuing a field of study that serves, supports, or promotes the ground water industry. Applicants must also have maintained a minimum 2.5 GPA. *Application Process: Applicants must submit a completed application and official transcripts. Visit the foundation's Web site to download an application. *Amount: Varies. *Deadline: April 1.

National Oceanic Atmospheric Administration (NOAA)
NOAA/Hollings Scholarship
Oak Ridge Institute for Science and Education
PO Box 117, MS 36
Oak Ridge, TN 37831

202-482-3384
noaa.education@noaa.gov
http://www.orau.gov/noaa/HollingsScholarship
Scholarship Name: Ernest F. Hollings Scholarship Program. *Academic Area: Marine sciences. *Age Group: Undergraduate students. *Eligibility: Applicants must be undergraduate students studying ocean and marine sciences who will be juniors in the fall academic term at an accredited college/university in the United States or U.S. territories. They also must be U.S. citizens and maintain at least a 3.0 GPA. *Application Process: Applicants must submit a completed application, two reference forms (to be completed and submitted by referees), and official transcripts. Visit NOAA's Web site to download an application. *Amount: Up to $8,000. *Deadline: May 23.

National Weather Association
1697 Capri Way
Charlottesville, VA 22911-3534
434-296-9966
NatWeaAsoc@aol.com
http://www.nwas.org/award.html
Scholarship Name: AccuWeather Undergraduate Scholarship in Meteorology. *Academic Area: Meteorology. *Age Group: Undergraduate students. *Eligibility: Applicants must be entering their sophomore year or a higher grade and majoring in operational meteorology (forecasting, broadcasting, or consulting). Applicants classified as seniors must have one more fall semester to complete after the scholarship is awarded. *Application Process: Applicants must submit a completed application, official transcripts, two letters of recommendation, and a personal statement. Visit the association's Web site to download an application. *Amount: $1,000. *Deadline: May 15.

National Weather Association
1697 Capri Way
Charlottesville, VA 22911-3534
434-296-9966
NatWeaAsoc@aol.com
http://www.nwas.org/award.html
Scholarship Name: Arthur C. Pike Scholarship in Meteorology. *Academic Area: Meteorology. *Age Group: Undergraduate students. *Eligibility: Applicants must be undergraduate students pursuing a degree and career in meteorology.

Applicants must be at least in their junior year of study. Those classified as seniors must have one more fall semester to complete after the scholarship is awarded. The scholarship is also available to graduate students. *Application Process: Applicants must submit a completed application, official transcripts, two letters of recommendation, and a personal statement. Visit the association's Web site to download an application. *Amount: $1,000. *Deadline: April 15.

Salute to Education Inc.

PO Box 833425
Miami, FL 33283
305-476-7709
steinfo@stescholarships.org
http://www.stescholarships.org/SC_categories.html
Scholarship Name: Salute to Education Natural Science Scholarship. *Academic Area: Natural resources. *Age Group: Undergraduate students. *Eligibility: Applicants must be graduating high school seniors who attend a Miami-Dade or Broward County, Florida, high school and who also reside in one of these counties. Applicants must be legal residents of the United States, have a minimum weighted GPA of 3.0, demonstrate a commitment to service by participating in at least one school or community organization, and intend to pursue a college degree at an accredited institution after graduation. They should also participate in peer tutoring, science clubs, and academic competitions as well as be able to submit written samples of science projects that have resulted in theory generation from experimentation. *Application Process: Applicants must apply online. Supporting materials should be mailed as detailed on the online application. *Amount: $1,000. *Deadline: Visit the organization's Web site for updated deadline information.

Society for Mining, Metallurgy, and Exploration (SME)

Attn: Mary O'Shea, Scholarship Coordinator
8307 Shaffer Parkway
Littleton, CO 80127
303-973-9550, 800-763-3132
http://www.smenet.org/education/Students/sme_scholarships.cfm
Scholarship Name: Environmental Division Scholarship. *Academic Area: Engineering (mining), environmental science. *Age Group: Undergraduate

students. *Eligibility: Applicants must be SME student members in good standing, currently enrolled in an Accreditation Board for Engineering and Technology accredited course of study, and have completed their sophomore year. Applicants must also be recommended by the departmental chairperson. *Application Process: Applicants should contact the scholarship coordinator via an online form to receive an application. Visit the society's Web site for further information. *Amount: Up to $2,000. *Deadline: October 30.

Society for Mining, Metallurgy, and Exploration (SME)

Attn: Mary O'Shea, Scholarship Coordinator
8307 Shaffer Parkway
Littleton, CO 80127
303-973-9550, 800-763-3132
http://www.smenet.org/education/Students/sme_scholarships.cfm
Scholarship Name: Gerald V. Henderson Industrial Minerals Memorial Scholarship. *Academic Area: Economics, engineering (mining), geology. *Age Group: Undergraduate students. *Eligibility: Applicants must be SME student members in good standing, currently enrolled in an Accreditation Board for Engineering and Technology accredited course of study, and have completed their sophomore year. They also must be recommended by the departmental chairperson. *Application Process: Applicants should contact the scholarship coordinator via an online form to receive an application. Visit the society's Web site for further information. *Amount: Up to $2,000. *Deadline: October 15.

Society for Mining, Metallurgy, and Exploration (SME)

Attn: Mary O'Shea, Scholarship Coordinator
8307 Shaffer Parkway
Littleton, CO 80127
303-973-9550, 800-763-3132
http://www.smenet.org/education/Students/sme_scholarships.cfm
Scholarship Name: SME Mining & Exploration Division Scholarship. *Academic Area: Engineering (mining), geology. *Age Group: Undergraduate students. *Eligibility: Applicants must be SME student members in good standing, currently enrolled in an Accreditation Board for Engineering and Technology accredited course of study, and have completed their sophomore

year. Applicants must also be recommended by the departmental chairperson. *Application Process: Applicants should contact the scholarship coordinator via an online form to receive an application. Visit the society's Web site for further information. *Amount: $1,500. *Deadline: November 30.

Society for Range Management (SRM)
10030 West 27th Avenue
Wheat Ridge, CO 80215-6601
303-986-3309
vskiff@rangelands.org
http://www.rangelands.org/education_masonicscholarship.shtml

Scholarship Name: SRM Masonic-Range Science Scholarship. *Academic Area: Range management. *Age Group: Undergraduate students. *Eligibility: Applicants must be high school seniors, college freshmen, or college sophomores planning to major in or presently majoring in range science and/or a closely related field. They also must be planning to attend or be currently in attendance at a college or university with a range science program. Applicants must be sponsored by a member of the SRM, the National Association of Conservation Districts, or the Soil and Water Conservation Society. *Application Process: Applicants must submit a completed application form, transcripts, a certified copy of their SAT/ACT scores, and two letters of recommendation. Visit the society's Web site to download an application. *Amount: Varies. *Deadline: January 15.

Society of Exploration Geophysicists
PO Box 702740
Tulsa, OK 74170-2740
918-497-5500
scholarships@seg.org
http://seg.org/business/foundation/scholarships/index.shtml

Scholarship Name: Society of Geophysics Foundation Scholarships. *Academic Area: Geophysics. *Age Group: Undergraduate students. *Eligibility: Applicants must intend to pursue an academic curriculum and career in exploration geophysics. Other eligibility requirements for specific scholarships may be set forth by the sponsors of those awards. Contact the foundation for more information regarding specific scholarships. Scholarships are available for high school seniors, undergraduate students, and graduate students

*Application Process: Applicants must submit a completed application, official transcripts, and two letters of recommendation. Visit the foundation's Web site to download an application. *Amount: $500 to $14,000. *Deadline: February 1.

Society of Physics Students (SPS)
SPS Scholarship Committee
One Physics Ellipse
College Park, MD 20740
301-209-3100
sps@aip.org
http://www.spsnational.org/programs/spsscholarships.htm

Scholarship Name: Herbert Levy Memorial Scholarship. *Academic Area: Physics. *Age Group: Undergraduate students. *Eligibility: Applicants must be able to demonstrate a high level of scholarship, potential for continued scholastic development, and active participation in SPS programs. Applicants should be college juniors and seniors and demonstrate financial need. *Application Process: Applicants should submit a completed application along with official transcripts and two letters of recommendation. Visit the society's Web site to download an application. *Amount: $2,000. *Deadline: February 15.

Society of Physics Students (SPS)
SPS Scholarship Committee
One Physics Ellipse
College Park, MD 20740
301-209-3100
sps@aip.org
http://www.spsnational.org/programs/spsscholarships.htm

Scholarship Name: Peggy Dixon Two-Year Scholarship. *Academic Area: Physics. *Age Group: Undergraduate students. *Eligibility: Applicants must demonstrate a high level of scholarship, potential for continued scholastic development, and active participation in SPS programs. This scholarship is intended for students who are transitioning from a two-year college into a physics bachelor's degree program. *Application Process: Applicants should submit a completed application along with official transcripts and two letters of recommendation. Visit the society's Web site to download an application. *Amount: $2,000. *Deadline: February 15.

Society of Physics Students (SPS)
SPS Scholarship Committee
One Physics Ellipse
College Park, MD 20740
301-209-3100
sps@aip.org
http://www.spsnational.org/programs/spsscholarships.htm
Scholarship Name: Society of Physics Students Future Teacher Scholarship. *Academic Area: Education, physics. *Age Group: Undergraduate students. *Eligibility: Applicants must be college juniors and seniors who demonstrate a high level of scholarship and active participation in SPS programs. They also must be participating in a teacher education program and plan to pursue a career in physics education. *Application Process: Applicants should submit a completed application along with official transcripts, two letters of recommendation, and a statement from an advisor verifying participation in a teacher education program. Visit the society's Web site to download an application. *Amount: $2,000. *Deadline: February 15.

Society of Physics Students (SPS)
SPS Scholarship Committee
One Physics Ellipse
College Park, MD 20740
301-209-3100
sps@aip.org
http://www.spsnational.org/programs/spsscholarships.htm
Scholarship Name: Society of Physics Leadership Scholarship. *Academic Area: Physics. *Age Group: Undergraduate students. *Eligibility: Applicants must demonstrate a high level of scholarship, potential for continued scholastic development, and active participation in SPS programs. College juniors or seniors may apply. *Application Process: Applicants should submit a completed application along with official transcripts and two letters of recommendation. Visit the society's Web site to download an application. *Amount: $2,000 and $5,000. *Deadline: February 15.

SCIENCE—GRADUATE

The following financial aid resources are available to students who are interested in studying science and related fields at the graduate level.

Air & Waste Management Association

One Gateway Center, 3rd Floor
420 Fort Duquesne Boulevard
Pittsburgh, PA 15222
412-232-3444, 800-270-3444
info@awma.org
http://www.awma.org/education/images/
ScholarshipFlyer2006-2007.pdf

Scholarship Name: Air & Waste Management Association Scholarship. *Academic Area: Environmental science. *Age Group: Graduate students. *Eligibility: Applicants must be full-time graduate students pursuing careers in fields related to air quality, waste management, or environmental management/policy/law. *Application Process: Applicants should contact the association to request an application. *Amount: $2,000 to $7,500. *Deadline: January 13.

American Dietetic Association (ADA)

Attn: ADA Foundation, Education Team
120 South Riverside Plaza, Suite 2000
Chicago, IL 60606-6995
800-877-1600, ext. 5400
education@eatright.org
http://www.eatright.org/cps/rde/xchg/ada/hs.xsl/
career_394_ENU_HTML.htm

Scholarship Name: American Dietetic Association Foundation Scholarships. *Academic Area: Food sciences. *Age Group: Graduate students. *Eligibility: Applicants must be members of the ADA who are attending a dietetics graduate program. Some scholarships may require specific dietetic practice group membership and residency in a specific state. Scholarships are also available for undergraduate students.*Application Process: Applicants should visit the ADA Web site to download an application or to seek membership and specific scholarship information. Amount: $500 to $5,000. *Deadline: Contact the association for deadline information.

American Institute of Wine and Food (AIWF)

213-37 39th Avenue, Box 216
Bayside, NY 11361
800-274-2493
info@aiwf.org
http://www.aiwf.org/site/scholarships.html

Scholarship Name: American Institute of Wine and Food Scholarship Program. *Academic Area: Food sciences. *Age Group: Open. *Eligibility: Applicants should be working or interested in fields related to the AIWF mission of "enhancing the quality of life through education about what we eat and drink." *Application Process: Applicants should visit the institute's Web site for a listing of available scholarships by chapter. Only select chapters offer scholarships. Contact your local chapter for additional application information. *Amount: Awards vary. *Deadline: Contact the appropriate local chapter for deadline information.

Annie's Homegrown

Annie's Scholarship Applications
564 Gateway Drive
Napa, CA 94558
800-288-1089
cfc@annies.com
http://www.annies.com/programs/ess.html

Scholarship Name: Annie's Environmental Studies Scholarship. *Academic Area: Environmental science. *Age Group: Graduate students. *Eligibility: Applicants must be full-time students beginning or returning to an accredited technical or college program in the United States. Students must be focusing on classes in the environmental studies field and have at least one more year before completing their degree. The scholarship is also available to high school seniors and undergraduate students. *Application Process: Applicants must submit an online fact sheet along with a one-paragraph personal statement explaining what they currently doing and what they are planning to do to change the world. Applicants should also submit official transcripts and two letters of reference. Visit the company's Web site to fill out the online fact sheet. *Amount: $1,000. *Deadline: July 1.

Association of Engineering Geologists (AEG)

Attn: Paul Santi, Department of Geology and Geological Engineering
Colorado School of Mines
Berthoud Hall
Golden, CO 80401

303-273-3108

psanti@mines.edu

http://www.aegfoundation.org/index2.php

Scholarship Name: Marliave Fund/Scholarship. *Academic Area: Engineering (geological). *Age Group: Graduate students. *Eligibility: Applicants must be presently enrolled full-time in a college or university degree program that is directly applicable to engineering geology or geological engineering. They also must also be student members of the AEG. *Application Process: Applicants must submit a completed application form along with official transcripts of all undergraduate and graduate work, copies of pertinent publications and abstracts, three letters of reference, and a statement detailing their career goals. Visit the association's Web site to download an application. The application package must be submitted through the applicant's major professor, AEG student chapter adviser, or department chair. *Amount: Awards vary. *Deadline: April 15.

Association of Engineering Geologists (AEG)

Attn: Robert A. Larson, Martin L. Stout Scholarship Committee Chair

13376 Azores Avenue

Sylmar, CA 91342

818-362-0363

ralarson@rampageusa.com

http://www.aegfoundation.org/index2.php

Scholarship Name: Martin L. Stout Scholarship. *Academic Area: Engineering (geological). *Age Group: Graduate students. *Eligibility: Applicants should be graduate students with an environmental or engineering geology emphasis. Student membership in the AEG is required at the time of the award. Applicants who are not currently student members may submit a membership application and dues to AEG headquarters with a copy included with their scholarship application. The scholarship is also available to undergraduate students. *Application Process: Applicants should submit an original completed application form along with four photocopies. Confidential evaluations submitted on the appraisal of applicant form are required from each of two professors who have knowledge of the applicant's achievements. These forms must accompany the application in envelopes sealed by the professors. Visit the association's Web site to download an application. *Amount: $1,000. *Deadline: February 1.

Cartography and Geographic Information Society (CaGIS)

CaGIS Scholarship Committee

c/o American Congress on Surveying and Mapping

6 Montgomery Village Avenue, Suite 403

Gaithersburg, MD 20879

240-632-9716, ext. 109

ilse.genovese@acsm.net

http://www.acsm.net/cagis/05scholarship.html

Scholarship Name: Cartography and Geographic Information Society Scholarship. *Academic Area: Geosciences. *Age Group: Graduate students. *Eligibility: Applicants must be enrolled full time in a graduate degree program in cartography or geographic information science. They also should demonstrate academic achievement and show commitment to professional activities. Financial need will be considered, if necessary, to break ties. The scholarship is also available to undergraduate students. *Application Process: Applicants should submit a completed application along with three letters of recommendation and a 500-word statement of educational objectives, future study or research plans and professional activities, and financial need. Proof of membership in CaGIS/American Congress on Surveying and Mapping is also required (or a membership application). Three copies of the application packet should be sent. *Amount: $1,000. *Deadline: January 22.

Marine Technology Society (MTS)

MTS Student Scholarship

5565 Sterrett Place, Suite 108

Columbia, MD 21044

410-884-5330

mtsmbrship@erols.com

http://www.mtsociety.org/education/student_scholarships.cfm

Scholarship Name: Charles H. Bussmann Scholarship. *Academic Area: Marine science. *Age Group: Graduate students. *Eligibility: Applicants must be full-time graduate students studying a marine related field, as well as MTS members. The scholarship is also available to undergraduate students. *Application Process: Applicants must submit contact information, a personal statement, a biographical sketch, official transcripts, one academic letter of recommendation, and one personal reference. *Amount: $2,500. *Deadline: April 17.

Marine Technology Society (MTS)

Attn: Chuck Richards, ROV Scholarship Committee Chair
c/o C.A. Richards and Associates Inc.
777 North Eldridge Parkway, Suite 280
Houston, TX 77079
410-884-5330
chuck@carichards.com
http://www.mtsociety.org/education/student_scholarships.cfm

Scholarship Name: Remotely Operated Vehicle (ROV) Student Scholarship. *Academic Area: Marine science. *Age Group: Graduate students. *Eligibility: Applicants must be MTS members and full-time students in academic institutions majoring in marine-related fields. They also must possess an interest in underwater work that furthers the use of remotely operated vehicles. The scholarship is also available to undergraduate students. *Application Process: Applicants must submit contact information, a biography, official transcripts, a one-page essay, one academic letter of recommendation, and three personal references. *Amount: Up to $10,000. *Deadline: April 17.

National Environmental Health Association (NEHA)/ American Academy of Sanitarians (AAS)

Attn: Scholarship Coordinator, NEHA/AAS Scholarship
720 South Colorado Boulevard, Suite 970, South Tower
Denver, CO 80246-1904
303-756-9090
cdimmitt@neha.org
http://www.neha.org/scholarship/scholarship.html

Scholarship Name: NEHA/AAS Scholarship. *Academic Area: Environmental science. *Age Group: Graduate students. *Eligibility: Applicants must be enrolled in a graduate program in environmental health sciences and/or public health. Visit the association's Web site for a list of accredited programs and/or schools. The scholarship is also available to undergraduate students. *Application Process: Applicants must submit a completed application along with official transcripts, two faculty letters of recommendation, and one letter of recommendation from an active NEHA member. Visit the association's Web site to download an application. *Amount: $1,000. *Deadline: February 1.

National Ground Water Association (NGWA)

Attn: Michelle Islam
601 Dempsey Road
Westerville, OH 43081
800-551-7379
mislam@ngwa.org
http://www.ngwa.org/about/schship_api-ngwa.cfm

Scholarship Name: American Petroleum Institute/ NGWA Scholarship. *Academic Area: Environmental Science. *Age Group: Graduate students. *Eligibility: Applicants must be pursuing a Master of Science or Doctor of Philosophy degree in a subsurface environmental science-related graduate program at an accredited university. Preference is given to those submissions whose graduate research activities are related to some aspect of petroleum hydrocarbon corrective action, or to techniques for other types of contaminants that may have relevance to petroleum hydrocarbons/motor fuels. *Application Process: Applicants must submit a completed application and a one-page research proposal. Visit the association's Web site to download an application. *Amount: $3,000. *Deadline: July 1.

National Weather Association

1697 Capri Way
Charlottesville, VA 22911-3534
434-296-9966
NatWeaAsoc@aol.com
http://www.nwas.org/award.html

Scholarship Name: Arthur C. Pike Scholarship in Meteorology. *Academic Area: Meteorology. *Age Group: Graduate students. *Eligibility: Applicants must be graduate students pursuing a degree and career in meteorology. The scholarship is also available to undergraduate students. *Application Process: Applicants must submit a completed application, official transcripts, two letters of recommendation, and a personal statement. Visit the association's Web site to download an application. *Amount: $1,000. *Deadline: April 15.

Society of Exploration Geophysicists (SEG)

PO Box 702740
Tulsa, OK 74170-2740
918-497-5500
scholarships@seg.org
http://seg.org/business/foundation/scholarships/index.shtml

Scholarship Name: SEG Foundation Scholarships. *Academic Area: Geophysics. *Age Group: Graduate students. *Eligibility: Applicants must intend to pursue an academic curriculum and career in exploration geophysics. Other eligibility requirements for specific scholarships may be set forth by the sponsors of those awards. Contact the foundation for more information regarding specific scholarships. Scholarships are also available for undergraduate students. *Application Process: Applicants must submit a completed application, official transcripts, and two letters of recommendation. Visit the foundation's Web site to download an application. *Amount: $500 to $14,000. *Deadline: February 1.

SOCIAL SCIENCES—UNDERGRADUATE

The following financial aid resources are available to students who are interested in studying the social sciences or related fields at the undergraduate level.

Academy of Television Arts and Sciences
Fred Rogers Memorial Scholarship
Attn: Michele Fowble
5220 Lankershim Boulevard
North Hollywood, CA 91601-3109
818-754-2802
http://www.emmys.tv/foundation/rogersscholar.php
Scholarship Name: Fred Rogers Memorial Scholarship.
  *Academic Area: Education, film/video, media arts,
  psychology. *Age Group: Undergraduate students.
  *Eligibility: Applicants must be undergraduates
  at accredited colleges or universities who are
  pursuing degrees in early childhood education,
  child development/child psychology, film/television
  production, media arts, music, or animation.
  Applicants must have the ultimate goal of working
  in the field of children's media. Particular attention
  will be given to student applicants from inner
  city or rural communities. The scholarship is also
  available to graduate students. *Application Process:
  Applicants must submit a completed application,
  a personal statement, transcripts, and two letters
  of recommendation. Visit the academy's Web site
  to download an application. *Amount: $10,000.
  *Deadline: January 31.

American Foreign Service Association (AFSA)
Attn: Lori Dec, Scholarship Director
2101 E Street, NW
Washington, DC 20037
202-944-5504, 800-704-AFSA
dec@afsa.org
http://www.afsa.org/scholar/winners05.cfm
Award Name: American Foreign Service Association
  Academic and Art Merit Awards. *Academic
  Area: Performing arts (dance), performing arts
  (open), visual arts (open), writing. *Age Group:
  Undergraduate students. *Eligibility: Applicants
  must be high school seniors who have one or more
  parents who are U.S. government Foreign Service
  employees and members of the AFSA or Associates
  of the American Foreign Service Worldwide.
  They also must maintain a 2.0 GPA on a 4.0 scale.
  This competition rewards academic and artistic
  accomplishments. *Application Process: Applicants
  should submit a completed application along with

official transcripts, two letters of recommendation,
and an essay. Visit the association's Web site
for further information about essay topics and
to download an application. *Amount: $1,500.
*Deadline: February 6.

Association of Former Intelligence Officers
AFIO Scholarships Committee
6723 Whittier Avenue, Suite 303A
McLean, VA 22101-4533
703-790-0320
afio@afio.com
http://www.afio.com/sections/academic/scholarship.
  html
Scholarship Name: Harold and Maria Ransburg
  American Patriot Undergraduate Scholarships.
  *Academic Area: International studies. *Age Group:
  Undergraduate students. *Eligibility: Applicants
  must be entering their sophomore or junior year of
  college and studying intelligence, foreign affairs,
  and/or national security studies. They also must
  be U.S. citizens. The scholarship is also available to
  graduate students. *Application Process: Applicants
  must submit a cover letter, a resume, transcripts, one
  letter of recommendation, and a recent photograph.
  *Amount: $1,500 to $3,000. Deadline: August 30.

California School Library Association (CSLA)
Attn: Chair, Jewel Gardiner Memorial Fund
717 K Street, Suite 515
Sacramento, CA 95814
916-447-2684
csla@pacbell.net
http://schoolibrary.org/awa/scholarships.htm
Scholarship Name: Jewel Gardiner Memorial
  Scholarship. *Academic Area: Library sciences.
  *Age Group: Undergraduate students. *Eligibility:
  Applicants must be enrolled in an accredited library
  media teacher program in Northern California.
  They also must demonstrate academic excellence.
  Preference is given to current CSLA (and CSLA
  National Section) members and applicants with
  teaching experience. The scholarship is also
  available to graduate students. *Application Process:
  Applicants must submit a completed application, an
  essay, and two letters of recommendation. Visit the

association's Web site to download an application. *Amount: $1,000. *Deadline: August 1, November 1, and May 1.

California School Library Association
1001 26th Street
Sacramento, CA 95816
916-447-2684
csla@pacbell.net
http://schoolibrary.org/awa/scholarships.htm
Scholarship Name: Southern Section Library Media Teacher Scholarship. *Academic Area: Library sciences. *Age Group: Undergraduate students. *Eligibility: Applicants must be students seeking to work in the library media field in a school setting, enrolled in an accredited school library media credential program, residents of Southern California, and members of the California School Library Association. The scholarship is also available to graduate students. *Application Process: Applicants must submit a completed application, proof of enrollment, and three letters of recommendation. Visit the association's Web site to download an application. *Amount: $1,500. *Deadline: March 11.

California School Library Association (CSLA)
1001 26th Street
Sacramento, CA 95816
916-447-2684
csla@pacbell.net
http://schoolibrary.org/awa/scholarships.htm
Scholarship Name: Southern Section Paraprofessional Scholarship. *Academic Area: Library sciences. *Age Group: Undergraduate students. *Eligibility: Applicants must be school library paraprofessionals who wish to obtain certification in order to serve as a school library technician. They also must be enrolled in a two-year paraprofessional program, residents of Southern California, CSLA members, and currently employed in a school, district, or county office of education. *Application Process: Applicants must submit a completed application, proof of enrollment, and three letters of recommendation. Visit the association's Web site to download an application. *Amount: $250. *Deadline: January 31.

California School Library Association (CSLA)
1001 26th Street
Sacramento, CA 95816
916-447-2684

csla@pacbell.net
http://schoolibrary.org/awa/scholarships.htm
Scholarship Name: Southern Section Paraprofessional-to-LMT Scholarship. *Academic Area: Library sciences. *Age Group: Undergraduate students. *Eligibility: Applicants must be school library paraprofessionals enrolled in a bachelor's degree program that is preparing them to become library media teachers. Applicants must be working or have worked in the last three years in a school, district, or county office of education. They must be CSLA members , Southern California residents, and intend to work as library media teachers in California upon completion of their studies. The scholarship is also available to graduate students. *Application Process: Applicants must submit a completed application, proof of enrollment, and three letters of recommendation. Visit the association's Web site to download an application. *Amount: $500. *Deadline: January 31.

Connecticut Funeral Directors Association
Attn: John Cascio
350 Silas Deane Highway, Suite 202
Wethersfield, CT 06109
860-721-0234, 800-919-CFDA
connfda@aol.com
http://www.ctfda.org/html/scholarship.html
Scholarship Name: Family Support Services Scholarship. *Academic Area: Counseling, medicine (open), medicine (psychiatry), mortuary science, nursing (open), psychology, social work. *Age Group: Undergraduate students. *Eligibility: Applicants must be high school seniors or college students interested in pursuing careers in a profession that provides emotional or medical support to families (i.e. counseling, social services, psychology, psychiatry, nursing, medicine, social, gerontology, and funeral service). They also must be legal residents of the state of Connecticut and maintain at least a B average throughout high school. *Application Process: Applicants must submit a completed application, transcripts, and an essay. Visit the association's Web site to download an application. *Amount: $500. *Deadline: April 14.

Daughters of the American Revolution (DAR)
Attn: Scholarships
1776 D Street, NW
Washington, DC 20006-5303

202-628-1776
http://www.dar.org/natsociety/edout_scholar.cfm
Scholarship Name: American History Scholarship.
*Academic Area: Economics, government, history, political science. *Age Group: Undergraduate students. *Eligibility: Applicants must be high school seniors intending to have a concentrated study of a minimum of 24 credit hours in American history and American government. U.S. Citizens residing abroad may apply through a Units Overseas Chapter. *Application Process: All applicants must obtain a letter of sponsorship from their local DAR chapter. Applicants should send a stamped, self-addressed business size envelope to obtain the name and address of their state scholarship chairman and an application. American History Scholarship applications are first judged on the state level. Only state winners are eligible for judging on the division level. Division level first- and second-place winners are judged at the national level. *Amount: $2,000, renewable for four years of college. *Deadline: February 1.

Daughters of the American Revolution (DAR)
Attn: Scholarships
1776 D Street, NW
Washington, DC 20006-5303
202-628-1776
http://www.dar.org/natsociety/edout_scholar.cfm
Scholarship Name: Enid Hall Griswold Memorial Scholarship. *Academic Area: Economics, government, history, political science. *Age Group: Undergraduate students. *Eligibility: Applicants must be U.S. citizens who are accepted into or currently attending an accredited college or university in the United States. *Application Process: All applicants must obtain a letter of sponsorship from their local DAR chapter. Applicants should send a stamped, self-addressed business size envelope to obtain the name and address of their state scholarship chairman and an application. *Amount: $1,000. *Deadline: February 15.

Government Finance Officers Association
Attn: Scholarship Committee
203 North LaSalle Street, Suite 2700
Chicago, IL 60601-1210
312-977-9700
http://www.gfoa.org/services/scholarships.shtml
Scholarship Name: George A. Nielsen Public Investor Scholarship. *Academic Area: Business administration, finance, government, public policy. *Age Group: Undergraduate students. *Eligibility: Applicants must be employees of a local government or public entity planning to enroll or currently enrolled in an undergraduate program in public administration, finance, or business administration. They also must have been employed by a state, local government, or other public entity for at least one year and be citizens or permanent residents of the United States or Canada. The scholarship is also available to graduate students. *Application Process: Applicants must submit a completed application, a statement describing their work experience, transcripts, a resume, and an employer's letter of recommendation. Visit the association's Web site to download an application. *Amount: $2,500 to $5,000. *Deadline: February 3.

International Union of Police Associations (IUPA), AFL-CIO
Scholarship Program
1549 Ringling Boulevard, Suite 600
Sarasota, FL 34236
941-487-2560
iupa@iupa.org
http://www.iupa.org
Scholarship Name: Edward J. Kiernan Memorial Scholarship. *Academic Area: Criminal justice, labor relations. *Age Group: Undergraduate students. *Eligibility: Applicants must be high school seniors who intend on pursuing a career in law enforcement, labor relations, or a related field. They also must be accepted in a course of study at an accredited college/university and have a parent or guardian who is a member of a union affiliated with the IUPA, AFL-CIO. Children of retired members will be considered only if those members are per capita paying members in good standing. *Application Process: Applicant must submit a completed application, a letter of recommendation, official transcripts, and SAT/ACT scores. Visit the IUPA's Web site to download an application. *Amount: $2,500. *Deadline: April 30.

J. Edgar Hoover Foundation
Attn: Chairman
PO Box 5914
Hilton Head, SC 29938
mail@jedgarhooverfoundation.org
http://www.jedgarhooverfoundation.org/scholar/scholar.html

Scholarship Name: J. Edgar Hoover Foundation Scholarship. *Academic Area: Criminal justice. *Age Group: Undergraduate students. *Eligibility: Applicants must be undergraduate students who are pursuing degrees in law, enforcement studies, or forensic sciences, and demonstrate financial need. The scholarship is also available to graduate students. *Application Process: Applicants must submit a completed application and two letters of recommendation. Visit the foundation's Web site to download an application. *Amount: $500 to $1,000. *Deadline: April 1.

Klingon Language Institute
Kor Memorial Scholarship
PO Box 634
Flourtown, PA 19031
http://www.kli.org/scholarship
Scholarship Name: Kor Memorial Scholarship. *Academic Area: Foreign languages. *Age Group: Undergraduate students. *Eligibility: Applicants must be full-time students, studying in the field of language study, making progress toward a degree, and demonstrating academic achievement. Familiarity with Klingon or other constructed languages is not required, but creative, innovative applicants are preferred. Graduate students may also apply for this scholarship. *Application Process: Applicants must ask their department chair or dean to nominate them for the award (the department head or dean can only nominate one person per year). Applicants should submit a nominating letter from the chair or dean of the their department that describes the applicant's accomplishments and career potential. Applicants should also submit two letters of recommendation from faculty members (in addition to the nominating letter), a brief personal statement, and a resume or curriculum vitae that describes any awards or community service. Visit the organization's Web site for additional information. *Amount: $500. *Deadline: June 1.

National Federation of Paralegal Associations Inc.
Attn: Scholarship Chair
PO Box 2016
Edmonds, WA 98020
425-967-0045
info@paralegals.org
http://www.paralegals.org/associations/2270/files/2006_
   Thomson_West_Scholarship.pdf

Scholarship Name: National Federation of Paralegal Associations/Thomson West Scholarship. *Academic Area: Law. *Age Group: Undergraduate students. *Eligibility: Applicants must be enrolled or accepted into a paralegal education program or a college-level program with emphasis on paralegal studies, maintain a 3.0/4.0 GPA, and demonstrate a commitment to campus, community, and paralegal program leadership activities. *Application Process: Applicants should submit a completed application along with a letter of recommendation from their program director, official transcripts, and an essay (not to exceed four pages). Visit the federation's Web site to download an application. *Amount: $1,500, $3,500, and $5,000. *Deadline: February 1.

National Fish and Wildlife Foundation
Attn: Lauren Guite
1120 Connecticut Avenue, NW, Suite 900
Washington, DC 20036
202-857-0166
lauren.guite@nfwf.org
http://www.nfwf.org/programs/budscholarship
Scholarship Name: Budweiser Conservation Scholarship. *Academic Area: Biology, environmental science, geography, natural resources, political science, public policy, social sciences. *Age Group: Undergraduate students. *Eligibility: Applicants must be U.S. citizens, at least 21 years old, and enrolled in an accredited college or university in the United States. They must apply during their sophomore or junior years. The scholarship is also available to graduate students. *Application Process: Applicants should submit a completed application along with a 1,500-word essay, a research proposal and/or abstract, official transcripts, and three letters of recommendation. Visit the foundation's Web site to download an application. *Amount: Up to $10,000. *Deadline: January 27.

National Organization for Human Service (NOHS)
Attn: Judith Townes, Education Committee Chair
Brookdale Community College
765 Newman Springs Road
Lincroft, NJ 07738-1597
512-692-9361
jtownes@brookdalecc.edu
http://www.nohse.com/scholarship.html
Scholarship Name: David C. Maloney Scholarship. *Academic Area: Human services. *Age Group:

Undergraduate students. *Eligibility: Applicants must be current student members of the NOHS, enrolled in an acknowledged associate, baccalaureate, or master's degree human services studies program, and maintain a 3.0/4.0 GPA. Special consideration will be made for applicants with special needs and/or minority status. *Application Process: Applicants must submit transcripts, a current resume, a personal statement, a copy of their current NOHS membership card, and two letters of recommendation. Visit the NOHS Web site for further application details. *Amount: Varies. *Deadline: May 1.

National Security Agency (NSA)
STOKES Application
9800 Savage Road, Suite 6779
Ft. George G. Meade, MD 20755-6779
410-854-4725
http://www.nsa.gov/careers/students_4.cfm?#stokes
Scholarship Name: Stokes Educational Scholarship Program. *Academic Area: Computer /electrical engineering, computer science, foreign languages, mathematics. *Age Group: Undergraduate students. *Eligibility: Applicants must be high school seniors or college students who are citizens of the United States. They must have a minimum SAT score of 1600 or ACT score of 25 and at least a 3.0 GPA out of 4.0. Applicants must work during the summer at the NSA in areas related to the course of study. Selected winners are required to work for the NSA after college graduation for at least one-and-one-half times the length of study. (Note: Applicants must maintain at least a 3.0 GPA on a 4.0 scale each semester after their freshman year.) *Application Process: Applicants must submit a resume online during open season and submit, by mail, a letter of recommendation from a teacher, counselor, or advisor, a one-page essay, and an official high school or college transcript. They should also submit a photocopy of their SAT/ACT scores and up to three pages of supplemental information, if desired. Visit the agency's Web site for additional information on specific major categories. *Amount: Full tuition. *Deadline: November 30.

National Sheriffs' Association (NSA)
Attn: Tim Woods
NSA Scholarship Program
1450 Duke Street
Alexandria, VA 22314
800-424-7827
http://www.sheriffs.org/nsa-scholarship.shtml
Scholarship Name: NSA Scholarship. *Academic Area: Criminal justice. *Age Group: Undergraduate students. *Eligibility: Applicants must be applying to, or enrolled in, an undergraduate program majoring in a criminal justice-related subject area. They also must be either employed by a sheriff's office or the son/daughter of an individual employed by a sheriff's office. The scholarship is also available to graduate students. *Application Process: Applicants must submit a completed application, transcripts, two letters of recommendation, an endorsement statement from sheriff of applicant's county, a short essay, and a statement of financial need. Visit the association's Web site to download an application. *Amount: $1,000. *Deadline: March 1.

National Stone, Sand & Gravel Association
Jennifer Curtis Byler Scholarship
1605 King Street
Alexandria, VA 22314
703-525-8788
info@NSSGA.org
http://www.nssga.org/careerscholarships/scholarships.cfm
Scholarship Name: Jennifer Curtis Byler Scholarship. *Academic Area: Public policy. *Age Group: Undergraduate students. *Eligibility: Applicants must be graduating high school seniors or college students already enrolled in public affairs majors. They must be sons or daughters of an aggregates company employee and demonstrate commitment to a career in public affairs. *Application Process: Applicants must submit a completed application, a letter of recommendation (academic), and a personal statement. One additional letter of recommendation from an employer should be included if the applicant has work experience in public affairs. Visit the association's Web site to download an application. *Amount: Varies. *Deadline: May 31.

Parapsychology Foundation Inc.
PO Box 1562
New York, NY 10021
212-628-1550
info@parapsychology.org
http://www.parapsychology.org/dynamic/040000.html
Award Name: Charles T. and Judith A. Tart Student Incentive Award for Parapsychological Research.

*Academic Area: Parapsychology. *Age Group: Undergraduate students. *Eligibility: Applicants must have specific research goals in the field of parapsychology. Graduate students also may apply for this award. *Application Process: Applicants must purchase an application packet from the foundation's Web site for $3. Visit the foundation's Web site for more information or to purchase the application. *Amount: $500. *Deadline: Contact the foundation for deadline information.

Parapsychology Foundation Inc.
PO Box 1562
New York, NY 10021
212-628-1550
info@parapsychology.org
http://www.parapsychology.org/dynamic/040000.html
Scholarship Name: Eileen J. Garrett Scholarship. *Academic Area: Parapsychology. *Age Group: Undergraduate students. *Eligibility: Applicants must be completing a degree program in parapsychology or conducting research in parapsychology as part of a degree requirement. Graduate students also may apply for this scholarship. *Application Process: Applicants must purchase an application packet from the foundation's Web site for $3. Visit the foundation's Web site for more information or to purchase the application. *Amount: $3,000. *Deadline: Contact the foundation for deadline information.

Phi Chi Theta Educational Foundation
Attn: Mary Ellen Lewis, Co-Chair
1886 South Poplar Street
Denver, CO 80224-2271
303-757-2535
FoundationScholarship@phichitheta.org
http://www.phichitheta.org/foundation/programs.htm
Scholarship Name: Phi Chi Theta Educational Foundation Scholarship. *Academic Area: Business, economics. *Age Group: Undergraduate students. *Eligibility: Applicants must be members of Phi Chi Theta in good standing who have completed at least one semester or two quarters of college work in the United States. They also must be enrolled in classes for the upcoming year. The scholarship is also available to graduate students. *Application Process: Applicants should submit a completed application along with an essay, a statement of their career goals, a description of their contributions to Phi Chi Theta, a list of school and community involvement

areas, official transcripts, and two letters of recommendation. Visit the foundation's Web site to download an application. *Amount: $500 to $1,000. *Deadline: May 1.

Salute to Education Inc.
PO Box 833425
Miami, FL 33283
305-476-7709
steinfo@stescholarships.org
http://www.stescholarships.org/SC_categories.html
Scholarship Name: Salute to Education Social Science Scholarship. *Academic Area: Open. *Age Group: Undergraduate students. *Eligibility: Applicants must be graduating high school seniors who attend a Miami-Dade or Broward County, Florida, high school and who also reside in one of these counties. They must be legal residents of the United States, have a minimum weighted GPA of 3.0, demonstrate a commitment to service by participating in at least one school or community organization, and intend to pursue a college degree at an accredited institution after graduation. Applicants must demonstrate exceptional knowledge in the subjects of history, economics, psychology, political science, or social studies through participation in community or civic related activities. *Application Process: Applicants must apply online. Supporting materials should be mailed as detailed on the online application. *Amount: $1,000. *Deadline: Visit the organization's Web site for updated deadline information.

Scholastic
The Scholastic Art & Writing Awards
557 Broadway
New York, NY 10012
212-343-6493
A&WGeneralInfo@scholastic.com
http://www.scholastic.com/artandwritingawards
Award Name: Scholastic Art and Writing Award. *Academic Area: English/literature, visual arts (open), writing. *Age Group: Middle school students, high school students. *Eligibility: Applicants must be currently enrolled in grades seven through 12 at public, private, parochial, or home-schools in the United States, U.S. territories, or U.S.-sponsored schools abroad. Applicants from Canada are eligible to participate as part of the Region at Large. Students are eligible to enter various art categories including drawing, photography, animation, mixed

media, painting, art portfolio, ceramics and glass, computer art, design, digital imagery, photography portfolio, sculpture, printmaking, and video and film. Writing categories include journalism, dramatic script, humor, novel writing, personal essay/memoir, poetry, science fiction/fantasy, short story, short-short story, general writing portfolio, and nonfiction portfolio. Visit Scholastic's Web site to obtain specific award eligibility requirements. *Application Process: Applicants must submit a completed application, art or writing submission piece or portfolio, and letter of recommendation (graduating students only). Visit Scholastic's Web site to download an application and for further application details. *Amount: Up to $10,000. *Deadline: Varies.

Society for Mining, Metallurgy, and Exploration (SME)

Attn: Mary O'Shea, Scholarship Coordinator
8307 Shaffer Parkway
Littleton, CO 80127
303-973-9550, 800-763-3132
http://www.smenet.org/education/Students/sme_scholarships.cfm

Scholarship Name: Gerald V. Henderson Industrial Minerals Memorial Scholarship. *Academic Area: Economics, engineering (mining), geology. *Age Group: Undergraduate students. *Eligibility: Applicants must be SME student members in good standing, currently enrolled in an Accreditation Board for Engineering and Technology accredited course of study, and have completed their sophomore year. They also must be recommended by the departmental chairperson. *Application Process: Applicants should contact the scholarship coordinator via an online form to receive an application. Visit the society's Web site for further information. *Amount: Up to $2,000. *Deadline: October 15.

Society of Satellite Professionals International (SSPI)

Attn: Tamara Bond, Membership Director
The New York Information Technology Center
55 Broad Street, 14th Floor
New York, NY 10004
212-809-5199, ext. 16

tbond@sspi.org
http://www.sspi.org/displaycommon.cfm?an=1&subarticlenbr=56

Scholarship Name: SSPI Scholarship Program. *Academic Area: Broadcasting, business, law, government, meteorology, satellite technology. *Age Group: Undergraduate students. *Eligibility: Applicants must demonstrate academic and leadership achievement, a commitment to pursuing education and career opportunities in the satellite industry or a field making direct use of satellite technology, and show potential for a significant contribution to the satellite communications industry. High school seniors and undergraduate students may apply. *Application Process: The application process is divided into two parts. Applicants who successfully pass stage one of the application process will be invited to apply for stage two. To apply for stage one, applicants should submit a completed application along with current transcripts. Information about stage two of the process will be provided to applicants who pass stage one. Visit the society's Web site to download an application. *Amount: $2,000 to $5,000. *Deadline: February 28 (for stage one).

Washington Crossing Foundation

Attn: Eugene C. Fish, Esquire, Vice Chairman
PO Box 503
Levittown, PA 19058-0503
215-949-8841
info@gwcf.org
http://gwcf.org/applicants

Scholarship Name: National Washington Crossing Foundation Scholarship Award. *Academic Area: Government. *Age Group: Undergraduate students. *Eligibility: Applicants must be U.S. citizens who are high school seniors planning on a career in government service in the United States. *Application Process: Applicants must submit a completed application, a one-page essay, a letter of recommendation from their high school principal or guidance counselor, official transcripts, and national testing scores. Visit the foundation's Web site to download an application. *Amount: $1,000 to $20,000. *Deadline: January 15.

SOCIAL SCIENCES—GRADUATE

The following financial aid resources are available to students who are interested in studying the social sciences and related fields at the graduate level.

Academy of Television Arts and Sciences
Fred Rogers Memorial Scholarship
Attn: Michele Fowble
5220 Lankershim Boulevard
North Hollywood, CA 91601-3109
818-754-2802
http://www.emmys.tv/foundation/rogersscholar.php
Scholarship Name: Fred Rogers Memorial Scholarship.
*Academic Area: Education, film/video, media arts (open). *Age Group: Graduate students. *Eligibility: Applicants must be graduate students (master's or Ph.D.) at accredited colleges or universities who are pursuing degrees in early childhood education, child development/child psychology, film/television production, music, and animation. Applicants must have the ultimate goal of working in the field of children's media. Particular attention will be given to student applicants from inner city or rural communities. The scholarship is also available to undergraduate students. *Application Process: Applicants must submit a completed application, a personal statement, transcripts, and two letters of recommendation. Visit the academy's Web site to download an application. *Amount: $10,000. *Deadline: January 31.

American Association of Law Libraries (AALL)
Attn: Chair, Scholarships Committee
53 West Jackson Boulevard, Suite 940
Chicago, IL 60604
312-939-4764
membership@aall.org
http://www.aallnet.org/services/sch_edu.asp
Scholarship Name: AALL Educational Scholarships.
*Academic Area: Library sciences. *Age Group: Graduate students. *Eligibility: Applicants must intend to pursue a career as a law librarian. Applicants must also demonstrate financial need. Five different AALL Educational Scholarship tracks are available depending on the educational background and future degree sought by applicants. Visit the association's Web site for further information on specific eligibility requirements. *Application Process: Applicants must submit a completed application, official transcripts, a letter of acceptance, three letters of recommendation, and a personal statement. Visit

the association's Web site to download an application and for further application details. *Amount: Varies. *Deadline: April 1.

American Association of Law Libraries (AALL)
Attn: Chair, Scholarships Committee
53 West Jackson Boulevard, Suite 940
Chicago, IL 60604
312-939-4764
membership@aall.org
http://www.aallnet.org/services/sch_connolly.asp
Scholarship Name: James F. Connolly LexisNexis Academic & Library Solutions Scholarship.
*Academic Area: Library sciences. *Age Group: Graduate students. *Eligibility: Applicants must be library school graduates with meaningful law library experience, who are pursuing degrees in accredited law schools with the intention of having a career in law librarianship. Applicants must not have more than 36 semester (54 quarter) credit hours remaining before qualifying for the degree. They also must demonstrate financial need. Preference is given to applicants who have demonstrated an interest in government documents. *Application Process: Applicants must submit a completed application, official transcripts, a letter from their law school detailing their academic status, three letters of recommendation, and a personal statement. Visit the association's Web site to download an application. *Amount: $3,000. *Deadline: April 1.

American Intellectual Property Law Education Foundation
485 Kinderkamack Road, 2nd Floor
Oradell, NJ 07649
201-634-1870
http://www.aiplef.org/scholarships
Award Name: Jan Jancin Award. *Academic Area: Law.
*Age Group: Law students. *Eligibility: Any law student attending a law school that offers at least one intellectual property course is eligible. *Application Process: The dean or appropriate faculty member of each law school will determine which student, who has taken an intellectual property class, best exemplifies excellence in the field of intellectual property law. The dean or delegated faculty member must nominate a

candidate by sending a letter identifying the student candidate along with a brief summary of the student's achievements in intellectual property law, together with a paragraph or two explaining why the student is considered deserving of the award. The student must also submit a one-page summary discussing personal achievements in the field of intellectual property law. Visit the foundation's Web site for further information and to download a nomination form. *Amount: $5,000. *Deadline: June 12.

American Polygraph Association (APA)
PO Box 8037
Chattanooga, TN 37414-0037
423-892-3992, 800-APA-8037
manager@polygraph.org
http://www.polygraph.org/williamyankee.htm
Scholarship Name: William J. Yankee Memorial Scholarship. *Academic Area: Criminal justice. *Age Group: Graduate students. *Eligibility: Applicants must have a four-year degree from an accredited college or university, plan to attend an APA-accredited basic polygraph examiner training course, and qualify for APA membership upon completion of training. *Application Process: Applicants must submit a covering letter, a resume, and essay of up to 1,000 words on detection of deception, interviewing, interrogation, or related fields. *Amount: $5,000. *Deadline: June 1.

American Psychological Association of Graduate Students
750 First Street, NE
Washington, DC 20002-4242
202-336-6014
apags@apa.org
http://www.apa.org/apags/members/schawrdsintro.html
Scholarship Name: American Psychological Association of Graduate Students Scholarships. *Academic Area: Psychology. *Age Group: Graduate students. *Eligibility: Applicants must be graduate student members of the association who are enrolled at least half time as a student in good standing at a regionally accredited university. Undergraduates, APAGS officers, subcommittee, and/or task force chairs are not eligible to apply. *Application Process: Applicants must submit a completed application and supporting documents. Visit the association's Web site to learn more about supporting documents needed for specific scholarships and to download

an application. *Amount: Varies. *Deadline: May 1 (unless otherwise indicated on application).

Association of Former Intelligence Officers (AFIO)
Attn: AFIO Scholarships Committee
6723 Whittier Avenue, Suite 303A
McLean, VA 22101-4533
703-790-0320
afio@afio.com
http://www.afio.com/sections/academic/scholarship.html
Scholarship Name: Al Ponte Graduate Scholarship. *Academic Area: International studies. *Age Group: Graduate students. *Eligibility: Applicants must be graduate students who are studying international relations and/or intelligence. They must also U.S. citizens and either AFIO members or children/grandchildren of AFIO members or of serving intelligence personnel. Applicants must not be in their second year of graduate study. *Application Process: Applicants must submit a covering letter, a resume, transcripts, one letter of recommendation, and a recent photograph. *Amount: $1,250. *Deadline: August 30.

Association of Former Intelligence Officers (AFIO)
Attn: AFIO Scholarships Committee
6723 Whittier Avenue, Suite 303A
McLean, VA 22101-4533
703-790-0320
afio@afio.com
http://www.afio.com/sections/academic/scholarship.html
Scholarship Name: Harold and Maria Ransburg American Patriot Graduate Scholarship. *Academic Area: International studies. *Age Group: Graduate students. *Eligibility: Applicants must be graduate students who are studying intelligence, foreign affairs, and/or national security. Applicants must be U.S. citizens in their first year of graduate school. The scholarship is also available to undergraduate students. *Application Process: Applicants must submit a cover letter, a resume, transcripts, one letter of recommendation, and a recent photograph. *Amount: $1,500 to $3,000. *Deadline: August 30.

California Library Association (CLA)
717 20th Street, Suite 200
Sacramento, CA 95814
916-447-8541

208 Social Sciences—Graduate

info@cla-net.org

http://www.cla-net.org/awards/begun.php

Scholarship Name: Begun Scholarship. *Academic Area: Library sciences. *Age Group: Graduate students. *Eligibility: Applicants must be currently enrolled in an American Library Association-accredited master's of library and information science or information studies program in California. They also must be California residents who have completed their core course work and demonstrate a commitment to becoming a children's or young adult librarian in a California public library. Applicants must be U.S. citizens and maintain at least a 3.0 GPA. *Application Process: Applicants must submit a completed application, an official record of courses taken, two letters of recommendation, a resume, a personal statement, and an essay. Visit the association's Web site to download an application. *Amount: $3,000. *Deadline: July 15.

California Library Association

717 20th Street, Suite 200

Sacramento, CA 95814

916-447-8541

info@cla-net.org

http://www.cla-net.org/awards/rspf.php

Fellowship Name: California Library Association Reference Service Press Fellowship. *Academic Area: Library sciences. *Age Group: Graduate students. *Eligibility: Applicants must be college seniors, college graduates, or graduate students with no more than eight credits completed in an accredited master's of library science program. They also must be California residents attending or planning to attend an American Library Association-accredited library school master's program within the United States. Applicants may also be residents of states other than California who attend or are planning to attend an accredited library school master's program in California. And they must be interested in pursuing a career in reference or information service librarianship. Upon receipt of the scholarship, the recipient must enroll in at least three reference or information service classes. *Application Process: Applicants must submit a completed application, official transcripts, documentation of acceptance into an accredited master's of library science program, a personal statement, two letters of recommendation, and an essay. *Amount: $3,000. *Deadline: June 15.

California School Library Association (CSLA)

Attn: Chair, Jewel Gardiner Memorial Fund

717 K Street, Suite 515

Sacramento, CA 95814

916-447-2684

csla@pacbell.net

http://schoolibrary.org/awa/scholarships.htm

Scholarship Name: Jewel Gardiner Memorial Scholarship. *Academic Area: Library sciences. *Age Group: Graduate students. *Eligibility: Applicants must be enrolled in an accredited library media teacher program in Northern California. They also must demonstrate academic excellence. Preference is given to current CSLA (and CSLA National Section) members and applicants with teaching experience. The scholarship is also available to undergraduate students. *Application Process: Applicants must submit a completed application, an essay, and two letters of recommendation. Visit the association's Web site to download an application. *Amount: $1,000. *Deadline: August 1, November 1, and May 1.

California School Library Association (CSLA)

Attn: Rebecca Johnston, President, Southern Section

7160 Cloverhill Drive

Highland, CA 92346

909-389-2500, ext. 4210

rebecca_johnston@redlands.k12.ca.us

http://schoolibrary.org/awa/scholarships.htm

Scholarship Name: Southern Section Library Media Teacher Scholarship. *Academic Area: Library sciences. *Age Group: Graduate students. *Eligibility: Applicants must be students seeking to work in the library media field in a school setting. They also must be enrolled in an accredited school library media credential program or a school library media teachers master's program, Southern California residents, and CSLA members. The scholarship is also available to undergraduate students. *Application Process: Applicants must submit a completed application, proof of enrollment, and three letters of recommendation. Visit the association's Web site to download an application. *Amount: $1,500. *Deadline: February 15.

California School Library Association (CSLA)

Attn: Southern Section Scholarship Chairperson

1766 North El Molino Avenue

Pasadena, CA 91104

916-447-2684

csla@pacbell.net
http://schoollibrary.org/awa/scholarships.htm
Scholarship Name: Southern Section Paraprofessional-to-LMT Scholarship. *Academic Area: Library sciences. *Age Group: Graduate students. *Eligibility: Applicants must be school library paraprofessionals enrolled in advanced degree program that prepare them to serve as library media teachers. They also must be CSLA members who are working or have worked in the last three years in a school, district, or county office of education, and be residents of Southern California who intend to work as library media teachers in California upon completion of their studies. The scholarship is also available to undergraduate students. *Application Process: Applicants must submit a completed application, proof of enrollment, and three letters of recommendation. Visit the association's Web site to download an application. *Amount: $500. *Deadline: January 31.

Daughters of the American Revolution (DAR)
Attn: Scholarships
1776 D Street, NW
Washington, DC 20006-5303
202-628-1776
http://www.dar.org/natsociety/edout_scholar.cfm
Scholarship Name: J.E. Caldwell Centennial Scholarship. *Academic Area: History. *Age Group: Graduate students. *Eligibility: Applicants must be U.S. citizens who are attending an accredited college or university in the United States. They also must be outstanding students pursuing a course of graduate study in the field of historic preservation. *Application Process: All applicants must obtain a letter of sponsorship from their local DAR chapter. Applicants should send a stamped, self-addressed business size envelope to obtain the name and address of their state scholarship chairman and an application. Visit the organization's Web site for the mailing address. *Amount: $2,000. *Deadline: February 15.

Government Finance Officers Association
Attn: Scholarship Committee
203 North LaSalle Street, Suite 2700
Chicago, IL 60601-1210
312-977-9700
http://www.gfoa.org/services/scholarships.shtml
Scholarship Name: George A. Nielsen Public Investor Scholarship. *Academic Area: Business, finance. *Age Group: Graduate students. *Eligibility: Applicants must be employees of a local government or public entity planning to enroll in a graduate program in public administration, finance, or business administration. They also must have been employed by a state, local government, or other public entity for at least one year, and be citizens or permanent residents of the United States or Canada. The scholarship is also available to undergraduate students. *Application Process: Applicants must submit a completed application, a statement describing their work experience, transcripts, a resume, and an employer's letter of recommendation. Visit the association's Web site to download an application. *Amount: $2,500 to $5,000. *Deadline: February 3.

Government Finance Officers Association
Attn: Scholarship Committee
203 North LaSalle Street, Suite 2700
Chicago, IL 60601-1210
312-977-9700
http://www.gfoa.org/services/scholarships.shtml
Scholarship Name: Public Employee Retirement Research and Administration Scholarship. *Academic Area: Business, finance, social sciences. *Age Group: Graduate students. *Eligibility: Applicants must be full- or part-time students enrolled in graduate programs in public administration, finance, business, or social sciences. They also must aim to prepare for a career in state and local government focusing on public-sector retirement benefits and be citizens or permanent residents of the United States or Canada. *Application Process: Applicants must submit a completed application, a statement detailing their proposed career plan, transcripts, a resume, and a letter of recommendation (from an academic adviser or dean). Visit the association's Web site to download an application. *Amount: $4,000. *Deadline: February 3.

J. Edgar Hoover Foundation
Attn: Chairman
PO Box 5914
Hilton Head, SC 29938
mail@jedgarhooverfoundation.org
http://www.jedgarhooverfoundation.org/scholar/scholar.html
Scholarship Name: J. Edgar Hoover Foundation Scholarship. *Academic Area: Criminal justice. *Age

Group: Graduate students. *Eligibility: Applicants must be graduate students who are pursuing advanced degrees in law, enforcement studies, or forensic sciences and demonstrate financial need. The scholarship is also available to undergraduate students. *Application Process: Applicants must submit a completed application and two letters of recommendation. Visit the foundation's Web site to download an application. *Amount: $500 to $1,000. *Deadline: April 1.

Klingon Language Institute

Kor Memorial Scholarship
PO Box 634
Flourtown, PA 19031
http://www.kli.org/scholarship

Scholarship Name: Kor Memorial Scholarship. *Academic Area: Foreign languages. *Age Group: Undergraduate students. *Eligibility: Applicants must be full-time students, studying in the field of language study, and making progress towards a degree. They should also demonstrate academic achievement. Familiarity with Klingon or other constructed languages is not required, but creative, innovative applicants are preferred. Graduate students may also apply for this scholarship. *Application Process: Applicants must ask their department chair or dean to nominate them for the award (the department head or dean can only nominate one person per year). Applicants should submit a nominating letter from the chair or dean of the their department that describes the applicant's accomplishments and career potential. Applicants should also submit two letters of recommendation from faculty members (in addition to the nominating letter), a brief personal statement, and a resume or curriculum vitae that describes any awards or community service. Visit the organization's Web site for additional information. *Amount: $500. *Deadline: June 1.

Medical Library Association (MLA)

Attn: Lisa C. Fried
Professional Development Department
65 East Wacker Place, Suite 1900
Chicago, IL 60601-7246
312-419-9094, ext. 28
mlapd2@mlahq.org
http://www.mlanet.org/awards/grants

Scholarship Name: MLA Scholarship. *Academic Area: Library sciences. *Age Group: Graduate students. *Eligibility: Applicants must be entering an American Library Association-accredited graduate library school or must have completed no more than half of his or her graduate program at the time the award is made in February. They also must be citizens or permanent residents of the United States or Canada wishing to study health sciences librarianship. *Application Process: Applicants must submit nine copies of a completed application form and personal statement. Applicants must also submit a single copy of two to three letters of recommendation, official transcripts, and library school's catalog or Web page stating the number of credits needed for applicant's degree. Visit the association's Web site to download an application. *Amount: Up to $5,000. *Deadline: December 1.

National Association of Social Workers (NASW)

750 First Street, NE, Suite 700
Washington, DC 20002-4241
202-408-8600, ext. 504
naswfoundation@naswdc.org
http://www.naswfoundation.org/gosnell.asp

Scholarship Name: Consuelo W. Gosnell Memorial Master of Social Work Scholarship. *Academic Area: Social work. *Age Group: Graduate students. *Eligibility: Applicants must demonstrate a commitment to working with, and/or maintain a special affinity with, American Indian/Alaska Native or Hispanic/Latino populations in the United States. Candidates who demonstrate a commitment to working with public or voluntary nonprofit agencies or with local grassroots groups in the United States are also eligible. Applicants must be NASW members, have applied to or have been accepted into accredited master's in social work programs, and maintain at least a 3.0 GPA. *Application Process: Applicants must submit a copy of their current NASW membership card, a completed application, a personal statement, a statement of merit and need for the award, two letters of recommendation, official transcripts, a letter of acceptance from the program (if not currently enrolled), a signed release of information, a letter from their academic adviser (for candidates applying for continued funding only), and an application checklist. Visit the association's Web site to download an application. *Amount: $1,000 to $4,000. *Deadline: March 17.

National Association of Social Workers (NASW)

750 First Street, NE, Suite 700
Washington, DC 20002-4241
202-408-8600, ext. 504

naswfoundation@naswdc.org

http://www.naswfoundation.org/lyons.asp

Scholarship Name: Verne LaMarr Lyons Memorial Master of Social Work Scholarship. *Academic Area: Social work. *Age Group: Graduate students. *Eligibility: Applicants must possess interest and/or demonstrate ability in health/mental health practice and a commitment to working in African American communities. Applicants must be NASW members, have applied to or have been accepted into accredited master's in social work programs, and maintain at least a 3.0 GPA. *Application Process: Applicants must submit a copy of their current NASW membership card, a completed application, a personal statement, two letters of recommendation, official transcripts, a letter of acceptance from the program (if not currently enrolled), a signed release of information, letter from their academic adviser (for candidates applying for continued funding only), and an application checklist. Visit the association's Web site to download an application. *Amount: $1,000. *Deadline: March 17.

National Fish and Wildlife Foundation

Attn: Lauren Guite

1120 Connecticut Avenue, NW, Suite 900

Washington, DC 20036

202-857-0166

lauren.guite@nfwf.org

http://www.nfwf.org/programs/budscholarship

Scholarship Name: Budweiser Conservation Scholarship. *Academic Area: Biology, environmental science, geography, natural resources, political science, public policy, social sciences. *Age Group: Graduate students. *Eligibility: Applicants must be U.S. citizens, at least 21 years old, and enrolled in an accredited college or university in the United States. They must apply during their sophomore or junior years. The scholarship is also available to undergraduate students. *Application Process: Applicants should submit a completed application along with a 1,500-word essay, a research proposal and/or abstract, official transcripts, and three letters of recommendation. Visit the foundation's Web site to download an application. *Amount: Up to $10,000. *Deadline: January 27.

National Organization for Human Service (NOHS)

Attn: Jonathan Appel, Education Committee Chair

Brookdale Community College

176 Wentz Street

Tiffin, OH 44883-2044

jappel37@yahoo.com

http://www.nohse.com/scholarship.html

Scholarship Name: David C. Maloney Scholarship. *Academic Area: Human services. *Age Group: Graduate students. *Eligibility: Applicants must be current student members of the NOHS and enrolled in an acknowledged master's degree human services studies program. Special consideration will be made for applicants with special needs and/or minority status. The scholarship is also available to undergraduate students. *Application Process: Applicants must submit a completed application along with transcripts, a current resume, a personal statement, a copy of their current NOHS membership card, and two letters of recommendation. Visit the NOHS Web site for further application details. *Amount: Varies. *Deadline: May 1.

National Sheriffs' Association

Attn: Tim Woods

NSA Scholarship Program

1450 Duke Street

Alexandria, VA 22314

800-424-7827

http://www.sheriffs.org/nsa-scholarship.shtml

Scholarship Name: National Sheriffs' Association Scholarship. *Academic Area: Criminal justice. *Age Group: Graduate students. *Eligibility: Applicants must be applying to, or enrolled in, a graduate program majoring in a criminal justice-related subject area. They also must also be either employed by a sheriff's office or the son/daughter of an individual employed by a sheriff's office. The scholarship is also available to undergraduate students. *Application Process: Applicants must submit a completed application, transcripts, two letters of recommendation, an endorsement statement from sheriff of applicant's county, a short essay, and a statement of financial need. Visit the association's Web site to download an application. *Amount: $1,000. *Deadline: March 1.

Parapsychology Foundation Inc.

PO Box 1562

New York, NY 10021

212-628-1550

info@parapsychology.org

http://www.parapsychology.org/dynamic/040000.html

Award Name: Charles T. and Judith A. Tart Student Incentive Award for Parapsychological Research.

*Academic Area: Parapsychology. *Age Group: Undergraduate students. *Eligibility: Applicants must have specific research goals in the field of parapsychology. Graduate students also may apply for this award. *Application Process: Applicants must purchase an application packet from the foundation's Web site for $3. Visit the foundation's Web site for more information or to purchase the application. *Amount: $500. *Deadline: Contact the foundation for deadline information.

Parapsychology Foundation Inc.
PO Box 1562
New York, NY 10021
212-628-1550
info@parapsychology.org
http://www.parapsychology.org/dynamic/040000.html
Scholarship Name: Eileen J. Garrett Scholarship. *Academic Area: Parapsychology. *Age Group: Undergraduate students. *Eligibility: Applicants must be completing a degree program in parapsychology or conducting research in parapsychology as part of a degree requirement. Graduate students also may apply for this scholarship. *Application Process: Applicants must purchase an application packet from the foundation's Web site for $3. Visit the foundation's Web site for more information or to purchase the application. *Amount: $3,000. *Deadline: Contact the foundation for deadline information.

Phi Chi Theta Educational Foundation
Attn: Mary Ellen Lewis, Co-Chair
1886 South Poplar Street
Denver, CO 80224-2271
303-757-2535
FoundationScholarship@phichitheta.org
http://www.phichitheta.org/foundation/foundation.htm
Scholarship Name: Phi Chi Theta Educational Foundation Scholarship. *Academic Area: Business, economics. *Age Group: Graduate students. *Eligibility: Applicants must be members of Phi Chi Theta in good standing, who have completed at least one semester or two quarters of college work in the United States. Applicants must be enrolled in classes for the upcoming year. The scholarship is also available to undergraduate students. *Application Process: Applicants should submit a completed application along with an essay, a statement detailing their career goals, a description of their

contributions to Phi Chi Theta, a list of school and community involvement areas, official transcripts, and two letters of recommendation. Visit the foundation's Web site to download an application. *Amount: $500 to $1,000. *Deadline: May 1.

Society of Satellite Professionals International
Attn: Tamara Bond, Membership Director
The New York Information Technology Center
55 Broad Street, 14th Floor
New York, NY 10004
212-809-5199, ext. 16
tbond@sspi.org
http://www.sspi.org/displaycommon.cfm?an=1&subart iclenbr=56
Scholarship Name: Society of Satellite Professionals International Scholarship. *Academic Area: Broadcasting, business, law, government, meteorology, satellite technology. *Age Group: Graduate students. *Eligibility: Applicants must demonstrate academic and leadership achievement, commitment to pursuing education and career opportunities in the satellite industry or a field making direct use of satellite technology, and show potential for a significant contribution to the satellite communications industry. The scholarship is also available to high school seniors and undergraduate students. *Application Process: The application process is divided into two parts. Applicants who successfully pass stage one of the application process will be invited to apply for stage two. To apply for stage one, applicants should submit a completed application along with current transcripts. Information about stage two of the process will be provided to applicants who pass stage one. Visit the society's Web site to download an application. *Amount: $2,000 to $5,000. *Deadline: February 28 (for stage one).

Special Libraries Association (SLA)
331 South Patrick Street
Alexandria, VA 22314-3501
703-647-4900
sla@sla.org
http://www.sla.org/content/learn/scholarship/sch-index/index.cfm
Scholarship Name: Plenum Scholarship. *Academic Area: Library sciences. *Age Group: Graduate students. *Eligibility: Applicants must be members of the SLA and have worked in a special library.

Preference will be given to those who display an aptitude for and interest in special library work, who show promise of accomplishment, and who are judged capable of making specific contributions to the library profession. Applicants must be doctoral candidates who have dissertation topic approval and are enrolled in a course of study by the time the award is given. *Application Process: Applicants must submit five copies of a completed application, a personal statement, official transcripts, evidence of financial need and dissertation topic approval, and three letters of recommendation. Visit the association's Web site to download an application. *Amount: $1,000. *Deadline: October 31.

Special Libraries Association (SLA)
331 South Patrick Street
Alexandria, VA 22314-3501
703-647-4900
sla@sla.org
http://www.sla.org/content/learn/scholarship/sch-index/index.cfm
Scholarship Name: SLA Scholarship. *Academic Area: Library sciences. *Age Group: Graduate students. *Eligibility: Applicants must be college graduates or college seniors with an interest in special librarianship. Extra consideration will be given to SLA members and to persons who have worked in and for special libraries. Preference will be given to those who display an aptitude for and interest in special library work. *Application Process: Applicants must submit five copies of a completed application, a personal statement, official transcripts, a letter or provisional acceptance or evidence of enrollment, three letters of recommendation, and evidence of financial need. Visit the association's Web site to download an application. *Amount: $6,000. *Deadline: October 31.

Texas Library Association (TLA)
Attn: Stephany Compton, CULD Scholarship Committee Chair
Texas Woman's University
PO Box 425528
Denton, TX 76204-5528
940-898-3339
scompton@mail.twu.edu
http://www.txla.org/groups/culd/Scholarship.html
Scholarship Name: College and University Library Division (CULD) Scholarship. *Academic Area: Library

sciences. *Age Group: Graduate students. *Eligibility: Applicants must be accepted as graduate students at an American Library Association-accredited library education program in Texas. They also must have maintained at least a B average in the last two years of their baccalaureate program and demonstrate commitment to academic librarianship and good written communication skills. *Application Process: Applicants must submit a completed application, a personal statement, and three letters of recommendation. Visit the association's Web site to download an application. *Amount: $1,000. *Deadline: February 15.

Texas Library Association (TLA)
Attn: Mary Castle, Scholarship Chair
UTA Libraries
PO Box 19497
Arlington, TX 76019-0497
817-272-3405
castle@uta.edu
http://www.txla.org/html/awards/scholar.html
Scholarship Name: Garrett Scholarship. *Academic Area: Library sciences. *Age Group: Graduate students. *Eligibility: Applicants must be entering graduate students who have attained at least a B average throughout the last two years of a baccalaureate program. They also must be Texas residents and have been accepted as graduate students at an American Library Association-accredited library education program in Texas. Applicants must focus their studies on children's, young adult, or school librarianship. *Application Process: Applicants must submit a completed application, a resume, transcripts, a statement of academic and career goals, and three letters of recommendation. Visit the association's Web site to download an application. *Amount: $1,000. *Deadline: January 31.

Texas Library Association (TLA)
Attn: Mary Castle, Scholarship Chair
UTA Libraries
PO Box 19497
Arlington, TX 76019-0497
817-272-3405
castle@uta.edu
http://www.txla.org/html/awards/scholar.html
Scholarship Name: Jeannette Marquis Memorial MLS Scholarship. *Academic Area: Library sciences. *Age Group: Graduate students. *Eligibility: Applicants

must be must be TLA members, bilingual, enrolled in an American Library Association-accredited MLS program, and taking at least two courses a semester. They also must reside in Texas and plan to or already be working in a public or school library that serves the Latino community. The applicant's degree plan must demonstrate a commitment to public or school libraries. *Application Process: Applicants must submit a completed application, a resume, transcripts, a statement of academic and career goals, and three letters of recommendation. Visit the association's Web site to download an application. *Amount: $1,000. *Deadline: January 31.

Texas Library Association (TLA)
Attn: Robin Dwight, TASL Scholarship Committee Chair
1455 Clubhill Drive
Rockwall, TX 75087
http://www.txla.org/html/awards/scholar/taslscol.html
Scholarship Name: Texas Association of School Libraries Scholarship. *Academic Area: Library sciences. *Age Group: Graduate students. *Eligibility: Applicants must be graduate-level students pursuing course work in school librarianship for initial library certification, a degree program, or professional growth. They also must demonstrate commitment to school librarianship and good written communication skills. *Application Process:

Applicants must submit a completed application, a statement of academic and career goals, and two letters of recommendation. Visit the association's Web site to download an application. *Amount: $500. *Deadline: January 9.

Women's Basketball Coaches Association (WBCA)
Attn: Amy Lowe, WBCA Awards Program Manager
4646 Lawrenceville Highway
Lilburn, GA 30047-3620
770-279-8027, ext. 102
alowe@wbca.org
http://www.wbca.org/StonerAward.asp
Scholarship Name: Charles T. Stoner Law Scholarship Award. *Academic Area: Law. *Age Group: Graduate students. *Eligibility: Applicants must be senior female collegiate basketball players intending to pursue a career in law. *Application Process: Applicants must submit a nomination form (to be completed by WBCA member coaches), a letter of recommendation, proof of academic major and GPA, basketball statistics, and a list of academic and athletic honors and campus activities. Nomination forms are made available on the WBCA Web site each January. Nominations must be made through the online nomination form. *Amount: $1,000. *Deadline: Contact the association for more information.

VISUAL ARTS/DESIGN— UNDERGRADUATE

The following financial aid resources are available to visual artists and designers at the undergraduate level.

Alaska State Council on the Arts (ASCA)
411 West 4th Avenue, Suite 1E
Anchorage, AK 99501-2343
907-269-6610
aksca_info@eed.state.ak.us
http://www.eed.state.ak.us/aksca/Grants3.htm
Grant Name: Career Opportunity Grants. *Academic Area: Visual arts (open). *Age Group: Adults. *Eligibility: Applicants must be Alaskan residents who are at least 18 years old. They must not be enrolled as full-time students and have not received this grant in the preceding year. Applicants must desire to increase their development as an artist and to further their artistic careers. They also must demonstrate artistic merit by submitting a work sample. *Application Process: Applicants should apply online. Applicants should also submit up to 10 images of recent artwork and a printed copy of the ASCA Grants Online application profile page. Visit the association's Web site to apply. *Amount: $100 to $1,000. *Deadline: March 1, June 1, September 1, December 1.

Alaska State Council on the Arts
411 West 4th Avenue, Suite 1E
Anchorage, AK 99501-2343
907-269-6610
aksca_info@eed.state.ak.us
http://www.eed.state.ak.us/aksca/Grants3.htm
Fellowship Name: Connie Boochever Artist Fellowship. *Academic Area: Education, performing arts (open), media arts, visual arts (open), writing. *Age Group: Adults. *Eligibility: Applicants must be Alaska residents, at least 18 years old, and emerging artists who are pursuing their art form on an ongoing basis. Applicants may not be enrolled as full-time students and must not have received a grant in the last two years. *Application Process: Applicants should submit a complete application packet including supporting materials verifying the quality of their work (through visual representation, resume, and recommendations). This grant is offered to artists pursing different art forms in two-year, rotating cycles. Applicants should visit the council's Web site to see if they will qualify for the current discipline that is being offered. Visit the council's Web site for more details. *Amount: $2,500. *Deadline: Contact the council for deadline information.

Alaska State Council on the Arts
411 West 4th Avenue, Suite 1E
Anchorage, AK 99501-2343
907-269-6610
aksca_info@eed.state.ak.us
http://www.eed.state.ak.us/aksca/Grants3.htm
Grant Name: Master Artist and Apprenticeship Grant. *Academic Area: Performing arts (dance), performing arts (music-instrumental), performing arts (voice), visual arts (crafts), visual arts (painting), visual arts (sculpting). *Age Group: Adults. *Eligibility: Applicants must be residents of Alaska, at least 18 years old, have an interest in traditional Alaska Native art, and desire the opportunity to develop their skills in an Alaskan Native art form. They must also have demonstrated experience working in the art form for which they are applying and must have identified a master artist under whom they would like to serve as an apprentice. Applicants may not be enrolled as full-time students during the period of the grant. *Application Process: Applicants should submit a complete application packet, which includes supporting material verifying the quality of the apprentice's work (through visual representation, resume, and recommendations), quality of the master artist's work (through visual representation, resume, and recommendations), a description of the project and the skills that will be taught and learned, and a complete itemized budget. Visit the council's Web site for more details. *Amount: Up to $2,000. *Deadline: The first of the month prior to the applicant's planned apprenticeship.

Arizona Commission on the Arts
417 West Roosevelt Street
Phoenix, AZ 85003-1326
602-255-5882
info@azarts.gov
http://www.azarts.gov/artists/grants.htm
Grant Name: Career Advancement and Project Grants. *Academic Area: Performing arts (open), visual arts

(open). *Age Group: Adults. *Eligibility: Applicants must be residents of Arizona, at least 18 years old, and not enrolled for more than three credit hours at a college or university. They must be seeking funds to advance their professional artistic careers or to help them complete a worthy artistic endeavor. Applicants must be able to provide documentation of Arizona residency. This organization provides three different kinds of grants for individuals. Eligibility requirements may vary slightly. *Application Process: Applicants should submit a completed application along with the appropriate supporting materials. Supporting materials include visual documentation of work samples (slides, video, etc.), resume, and a project narrative. Visit the commission's Web site to download an application and to view additional information about individual grants. *Amount: $500 to $5,000 (depending on the type of grant). *Deadline: Deadlines vary.

Arkansas Arts Council

1500 Tower Building, 323 Center Street
Little Rock, AR 72201
501-324-9766
info@arkansasarts.com
http://www.arkansasarts.com/grants

Grant Name: Individual Artists Fellowship. *Academic Area: Performing arts (open), visual arts (open). *Age Group: Adults. *Eligibility: Applicants must be residents of Arkansas who are at least 25 years old. They must have lived in Arkansas for at least one year to qualify and cannot be degree-seeking students or have received the award previously. Categories rotate yearly, so interested candidates should contact the council for information on the area in which they are taking applications for the current year. *Application Process: Applicants should contact the council for information on the application process. Applications are also periodically available at the council's Web site for download. *Amount: Awards vary. *Deadline: May 12.

Associated Landscape Contractors of America Educational Foundation

Attn: PLANET
950 Herndon Parkway, Suite 450
Herndon, VA 20170
703-736-9666, 800-395-2522
http://planetfile.objectwareinc.com/pdfs/
AEFScholarshipApp06.pdf

Scholarship Name: Associated Landscape Contractors of America Educational Foundation Scholarship. *Academic Area: Landscape architecture. *Age Group: Undergraduate students. *Eligibility: Applicants must be enrolled in a college or university that has an accredited Professional Landcare Network (PLANET) landscaping contracting curriculum and/or has a PLANET student chapter membership or is a participating PLANET Student Career Days School. *Application Process: Applicants should submit a completed application along with a copy of their transcripts and a minimum of two letters of recommendation. Visit the foundation's Web site to download an application. *Amount: Awards vary. *Deadline: January 20.

Connecticut Association of Schools/Connecticut Interscholastic Athletic Conference

Attn: Dr. Robert F. Carroll
30 Realty Drive
Chesire, CT 06410
203-250-1111
bcarroll@casciac.org
http://www.casciac.org/hsawards.shtml

Scholarship Name: Bruce Eagleson Memorial Scholarship. *Academic Area: Performing arts (open), visual arts (open). *Age Group: Undergraduate students. *Eligibility: Applicants must be graduating high school seniors who are accepted into a college degree program in the visual or performing arts. They must be residents of Connecticut, graduating from Connecticut high schools, and have demonstrated involvement showcasing their artistic work in shows, exhibits, or performances. Applicants must also be committed to community and public service and must demonstrate financial need. *Application Process: Applicants should submit a completed application along with two letters of recommendation, a letter of college acceptance, a 250-word personal statement, a video or photo representation of artistic ability, and a statement outlining financial need and expected college costs. Visit the association's Web site to download an application. *Amount: $10,000 (one award), $5,000 (two awards). *Deadline: March 17.

Connecticut Commission on Culture and Tourism

Attn: Tamara Dimitri
One Financial Plaza
755 Main Street

Hartford, CT 06103

860-256-2720

tdimitri@ctarts.org

http://www.cultureandtourism.org/cct/cwp/view.
asp?a=2207&q=293740&cctPNavCtr=|43595|

Fellowship Name: Individual Artists Fellowship.
*Academic Area: Film/television, performing arts
(choreography), performing arts (composition),
visual arts (open), writing. *Age Group: Adults.
*Eligibility: Applicants must be Connecticut
residents who have lived within the state for at
least one year. Applicants must not be degree-
seeking college students and cannot have received
the award previously. Categories rotate yearly, so
interested candidates should visit the organization's
Web site to see which category is available for
the current year. *Application Process: Applicants
should contact the commission for information
on the application process. Application materials
are available in July of each year. *Amount: $2,500
and $5,000. *Deadline: September (contact the
commission for exact deadlines).

Delaware Division of the Arts

820 North French Street

Wilmington, DE 19801

302-577-8278

delarts@state.de.us

http://www.artsdel.org/grants/artistgrants.shtml

Grant Name: Grants for Individual Artists. *Academic
Area: Media arts, performing arts (open), visual arts
(open), writing. *Age Group: Adults. *Eligibility:
Applicants must be Delaware residents, at least
18 years old, and have lived in the state for at least
one year. They must not be enrolled in a degree-
granting program. This organization offers more
than one kind of grant for individual artists. Visit
the organization's Web site for additional eligibility
requirements for individual grants. *Application
Process: Applicants should submit a completed
application along with a one-page narrative, a
budget, a resume, and work samples (examples
of appropriate submissions are listed on the
application). Visit the organization's Web site to
download an application. *Amount: Awards vary.
*Deadline: Deadlines vary by grant.

Florida Division of Cultural Affairs

Attn: Morgan Barr

R.A. Gray Building

500 South Bronough Street, 3rd Floor

Tallahassee, FL 32399-0250

850-245-6470

mhbarr@dos.state.fl.us

http://www.florida-arts.org/grants/forindividuals.htm

Grant Name: Grants for Individual Artists. *Academic
Area: Media arts, performing arts (dance),
performing arts (music-general), performing arts
(theatre), visual arts (open), writing. *Age Group:
Adults. *Eligibility: Applicants must be Florida
residents, at least 18 years old, and not be enrolled
in any degree program. This organization offers
more than one kind of grant for individual artists.
Applicants must not have received a grant from the
same organization in the previous grant period.
Some grants are offered on a rotating categorical
basis, with visual arts and media arts grouped
together for one year and performing arts and
literary arts in the next year. Visit the organization's
Web site for additional eligibility requirements for
individual grants. *Application Process: Applicants
should submit a completed application along with
supporting materials. Visit the organization's Web
site for additional information on the application
process. *Amount: Awards vary. *Deadline: Deadlines
vary by individual award.

Hawaii State Foundation on Culture and the Arts

Attn: Fay Ann Chun, Individual Artists Program
Coordinator

250 South Hotel Street, 2nd Floor

Honolulu, HI 96813

808-586-9965

hsfca2006awards@yahoo.com

http://www.state.hi.us/sfca

Fellowship Name: Individual Artists Fellowship.
*Academic Area: Performing arts (open), visual arts
(open). *Age Group: Adults. *Eligibility: Applicants
must be residents of Hawaii, at least 18 years old,
and recognized in their communities as professional
artists. They must be financially compensated for
their work as part of their livelihood and able to
provide documentation of their artistic experience
for at least the last five years. Visit the organization's
Web site for a complete list of eligibility
requirements in each visual arts or performing arts
category. *Application Process: Applicants should
submit a completed application along with an artist
statement form, a resume form, three references
and a reference form, and work samples. The

process for submitting appropriate work samples is explained in depth on the application form. Visit the organization's Web site for additional information on the application process. *Amount: Awards vary. *Deadline: Contact the organization for deadline information.

Idaho Commission on the Arts
PO Box 83720
Boise, ID 83720-0008
208-334-2119
info@arts.idaho.gov
http://www.arts.idaho.gov/grants/indoverview.aspx
Grant Name: Grants for Individual Artists. *Academic Area: Media arts, performing arts (open), visual arts (open), writing. *Age Group: Adults. *Eligibility: Applicants must be residents of Idaho who demonstrate artistic excellence and a professional artistic history. This organization offers several grants and fellowships, many of which are offered on a rotating scale according to artistic discipline. Visit the organization's Web site for further information. *Application Process: Applicants should submit a completed application along with supporting materials, including a resume, an artist statement, and work samples. Visit the organization's Web site for a checklist of supporting materials for each type of grant or fellowship. *Amount: $3,500 (approximate). *Deadline: January 31.

Illinois Arts Council
James R. Thompson Center
100 West Randolph, Suite 10-500
Chicago, IL 60601
314-814-4991
rose@arts.state.il.us
http://www.state.il.us/agency/iac/Guidelines/guidelines.htm
Fellowship Name: Artist Fellowship Program. *Academic Area: Film/television, media arts, performing arts (choreography), performing arts (composition), visual arts (crafts), visual arts (photography), visual arts (open). *Age Group: Adults. *Eligibility: Applicants must be residents of Illinois who can provide proof that they've resided within the state for at least one year. They must be U.S. citizens or permanent residents and not be enrolled in any degree program. Applicants must not have received funds from this fellowship in the two preceding years. These fellowships are offered on a rotating basis according

to artistic discipline. Applicants in the disciplines of choreography, crafts, ethnic and folk arts, media arts, new performance forms, prose, and scriptwriting may apply in even-numbered years, and applicants in interdisciplinary/computer art, music composition, photography, poetry, and visual arts can apply in odd-numbered years. Visit the organization's Web site for further information. *Application Process: Applicants should submit a completed application along with a work sample sheet, work samples, a one-page artistic resume, and a one-page artist statement. Work samples must not be more than four years old. A detailed explanation of work sample submission procedures is explained on the application. Visit the organization's Web site to download an application. *Amount: $700 and $7,000. *Deadline: September 1.

Indiana Arts Commission
Contact: Monica Peterson
150 West Market Street, Suite 618
Indianapolis, IN 46204
317-232-1279
mpeterson@iac.in.gov
http://www.in.gov/arts/grants/program_iap.html
Grant Name: Grants for Individual Artists. *Academic Area: Media arts, performing arts (open), visual arts (open), writing. *Age Group: Adults. *Eligibility: Applicants must be at least 18 years old and be residents of Indiana who have lived in the state for at least one full year preceding the application. They must remain an Indiana resident during the grant period, not be enrolled in any degree program, and not have received this award in the preceding year. Applicant must apply as an individual and not as part of a collaborative project. Visit the commission's Web site for further information. *Application Process: Applicants should submit a completed application along with a formal letter stating the reasons for consideration and supporting materials. A detailed explanation of how to submit supporting materials is included on the application. Visit the commission's Web site to download an application. *Amount: $1,000. *Deadline: February 3.

Iowa Arts Council
Attn: Bruce Williams
600 East Locust
Des Moines, IA 50319-0290
515-281-4006
Bruce.Williams@iowa.gov

http://www.iowaartscouncil.org/funding/artist-project-grant/index.shtml

Grant Name: Artist Major Grants and Mini Grants. *Academic Area: Performing arts (open), visual arts (open). *Age Group: Adults. *Eligibility: Applicants must be at least 18 years old and have lived in Iowa for at least one full year preceding the application. Applicants must not be students and not have received two Iowa Arts Council grants within the same fiscal year of this proposed grant activity. This program also includes applicants from select bordering communities. Visit the council's Web site for the border state policy. Eligibility requirements may differ slightly for major and mini grants. Visit the council's Web site for additional eligibility requirements. *Application Process: Applicants must submit an online application on the state's new eGRANT system. The application will include information on the proposed project, a budget, a personal narrative, a work sample form and work samples, a service contract, and a project timeline. Visit the council's Web site to apply online. *Amount: $1,500 (mini grant); $10,000 (major grant). *Deadline: April 1.

Kentucky Arts Council
Attn: Lori Meadows
Capital Plaza Tower, 500 Mero Street, 21st Floor
Frankfort, KY 40601-1987
502-564-3747 (or 888-833-2787), ext. 482
Lori.Meadows@ky.gov
http://artscouncil.ky.gov/guide/prog3/asf_gdl.htm

Fellowship Name: Al Smith Individual Artist Fellowship Program. *Academic Area: Media arts, performing arts (open), visual arts (open), writing. *Age Group: Adults. *Eligibility: Applicants must be U.S. citizens or permanent residents, residents of Kentucky (who have lived in the state for at least one year), at least 18 years old, and demonstrate artistic excellence and professional achievement. They must remain Kentucky residents during the period for which they receive funding. Applicants must be professional artists who are creating their own work, not just interpreting the work of others. *Application Process: Applicants should submit a completed application along with supporting materials. Supporting materials include a narrative essay, proof of residency, work samples and an index of work samples, and an optional resume. Detailed descriptions of how to submit work samples are listed on the application. This fellowship is offered in alternating disciplines every other year. Writers, choreographers, musical composers, and interdisciplinary artists may apply in even-numbered years, and visual and media artists may apply in odd-numbered years. Visit the organization's Web site to download an application. *Amount: $7,500; $1,000 professional assistance awards given to some applicants who do not receive the Individual Artist Fellowships. *Deadline: August 15 (intent to apply deadline); September 15 (application deadline).

Maine Arts Commission
Attn: Donna McNeil, Contemporary Art & Public Art Associate
193 State Street, 25 State House Station
Augusta, ME 04333-0025
207-287-2726
Donna.McNeil@maine.gov
http://www.mainearts.com/Grants/index.shtml

Fellowship Name: Individual Artist Fellowship. *Academic Area: Media arts, performing arts (open), visual arts (open), writing. *Age Group: Adults. *Eligibility: Applicants must be residents of Maine, at least 18 years old, and not enrolled as full-time students in a field relating to the application. They must have lived in Maine for at least two years and demonstrate artistic excellence. Artists in all mediums are encouraged to apply. *Application Process: Applicants should submit a completed application along with one set of labeled artistic materials (instructions are located on the application), a biographical information sheet, and a self-addressed stamped postcard and envelope. Visit the commission's Web site to download an application. *Amount: $13,000. *Deadline: June 9.

Massachusetts Cultural Council
10 Saint James Avenue, 3rd Floor
Boston, MA 02116-3803
617-727-3668, 800-232-0960
mcc@art.state.ma.us
http://www.massculturalcouncil.org/programs/artistgrants.html

Grant Name: Artist Grants Program. *Academic Area: Media arts, performing arts (open), visual arts (open), writing. *Age Group: Adults. *Eligibility: Applicants must be residents of Massachusetts, at least 18 years old, and not be enrolled as students in degree programs. Applicants must demonstrate artistic excellence. Categories in which applicants may apply rotate every other year. Applicants should visit the organization's Web site to view the eligibility requirements for the current application period. *Application Process: Applicants should submit a completed application along with supporting materials. Visit the council's Web site to download an application and a description of how to submit work samples. *Amount: $5,000. *Deadline: December. Visit the council's Web site for deadline information.

Mississippi Arts Commission

Attn: Judi Cleary, Director of Grants & Programs
Woolfolk Building, 501 North West Street, Suite 701B
Jackson, MS 39201
601-359-6030
jcleary@arts.state.ms.us
http://www.mswholeschools.org/mac/grants/for-individuals.html

Fellowship Name: Artist Fellowship. *Academic Area: Media arts, performing arts (open), visual arts (open), writing. *Age Group: Adults. *Eligibility: Applicants must be residents of Mississippi, at least 18 years old, and maintain residency in Mississippi for the duration of the fellowship. They must demonstrate artistic excellence and earn at least part of their income from their artistic discipline. Applicants should consider their artistic endeavors as a career and should devote significant time to this work. Full-time students are not eligible for this fellowship. Categories in which applicants may apply rotate every other year. Applicants should visit the organization's Web site to view the eligibility requirements for the current application period. *Application Process: Applicants should submit a completed application along with an artist narrative, a resume, and work samples. Visit the organization's Web site to download an application and a description of how to submit work samples in each category. *Amount: Up to $5,000. *Deadline: March 1.

Montana Arts Council

PO Box 202201
Helena, MT 59620-2201
406-444-6430
mac@mt.gov
http://www.art.state.mt.us/artists/artists.asp

Grant Name: Opportunity and Professional Development Grants. *Academic Area: Performing arts (open), visual arts (open). *Age Group: Adults. *Eligibility: Applicants must be at least 18 years

old and residents of Montana for at least one year. Full-time students are not eligible for these grants. Applicants should visit the council's Web site to view additional eligibility requirements for specific grants and specific artistic mediums. These grants require the applicant to match the funds with an equal dollar amount of their own funds or funds that they have raised for a given artistic endeavor. *Application Process: Applicants should submit a completed application along with an artist narrative, a project synopsis, a complete budget, and a resume. Visit the council's Web site to download an application. *Amount: $750 to $1,000. *Deadline: Deadlines vary.

Nevada Arts Council

Attn: Fran Morrow, Artist Services Program Coordinator
716 North Carson Street, Suite A
Carson City, NV 89701
775-687-7106
fkmorrow@clan.lib.nv.us
http://dmla.clan.lib.nv.us/docs/arts/programs/grants/grantsforartists.htm

Grant Name: Grants for Artists. *Academic Area: Media arts, performing arts (open), visual arts (open), writing. *Age Group: Adults. *Eligibility: Applicants must be at least 21 years old and residents of the state of Nevada for at least one year (and reside in the state of Nevada for the duration of the grant period). They must be U.S. citizens or legal permanent residents who are practicing professional artists and who demonstrate artistic excellence and merit. Applicants must not be full-time students. This organization offers more than one type of grant. Visit the organization's Web site to view additional eligibility requirements for specific grants. *Application Process: Applicants should submit a completed application along with five copies of the work sample list, work samples required for their category (detailed on the application), and a resume. Visit the organization's Web site to download an application.*Amount: $500 to $5,000. *Deadline: Deadlines vary by grant. Visit the organization's Web site to view current deadlines.

New Hampshire State Council on the Arts

2 1/2 Beacon Street, 2nd Floor
Concord, NH 03301-4974
603-271-2789
http://www.state.nh.us/nharts/grants/artists/index.htm

Grant/Fellowship Name: Grants and Fellowships for Artists. *Academic Area: Media arts, performing arts (open), visual arts (open), writing. *Age Group: Adults. *Eligibility: Applicants must be at least 18 years old and residents of New Hampshire for at least one year (and reside in the state for the duration of the grant or fellowship period). They must demonstrate a commitment to artistic excellence and possess artistic merit. Applicants must not be full-time students. This organization offers more than one type of grant. Visit the organization's Web site to view additional eligibility requirements for specific awards. *Application Process: Applicants should submit a completed application along with answers to the required narrative questions, a resume, and work samples required for their category (detailed at the council's Web site). Visit the council's Web site to download an application.*Amount: $250 to $5,000. *Deadline: Deadlines vary by award. Visit the council's Web site to view current deadlines.

New Jersey State Council on the Arts
Attn: Rebecca Scolian
c/o Mid Atlantic Arts Foundation
201 North Charles Street, Suite 401
Baltimore, MD 21201
410-539-6656, ext. 101
rebecca@midatlanticarts.org
http://www.njartscouncil.org/program7.html
Fellowship Name: Artist Fellowship. *Academic Area: Media arts, performing arts (open), visual arts (open), writing. *Age Group: Adults. *Eligibility: Applicants must be at least 18 years old and residents of New Jersey for at least one year (and reside in the state for the duration of the fellowship period). They must demonstrate a commitment to artistic excellence and possess artistic merit. Applicants must not be full-time students in a degree program. Visit the organization's Web site to view additional eligibility requirements for the category in which they intend to apply. *Application Process: Applicants should submit a completed application along with two copies of their resume, work samples, and a descriptive cover page. Visit the council's Web site to download an application.*Amount: $7,800 to $12,000. *Deadline: July 15.

New York State Art Teachers Association (NYSATA)
Attn: Janice Oldak/Art Department
Barnum Woods Elementary School
500 May Lane
East Meadow, NY 11554

516-564-6500
Artmuse5@aol.com
http://www.nysata.org/scholarships.php
Scholarship Name: Aida Snow Scholarship. *Academic Area: Visual arts (open). *Age Group: Undergraduate students. *Eligibility: Applicants must be graduating high school seniors who are students of a NYSATA member. They also must intend to pursue a degree/career in visual arts, have been accepted into an art school or a college art program, and demonstrate a commitment to the visual arts and a unique vision in their media of choice. *Application Process: Applicants should submit a completed application along with transcripts, a one-page essay describing themselves and their interest visual art, 15 slides of their work, a copy of their letter of acceptance to college or art school, and two letters of recommendation. The applicant's art teacher, who must be a member of the NYSATA, must sign the essay. All application materials must be taken to the applicant's guidance office. The guidance office staff should mail the packet from their office. Visit the association's Web site to download an application. *Amount: $500. *Deadline: May 15.

New York State Art Teachers Association (NYSATA)
Attn: Janice Oldak/Art Department
Barnum Woods Elementary School
500 May Lane
East Meadow, NY 11554
516-564-6500
Artmuse5@aol.com
http://www.nysata.org/scholarships.php
Scholarship Name: Bill Milliken Scholarship. *Academic Area: Visual arts (open). *Age Group: Undergraduate students. *Eligibility: Applicants must be graduating high school seniors who are students of a NYSATA member. They also must intend to pursue a degree/career in visual arts, have been accepted into an art school or a college art program, and demonstrate a commitment to the visual arts and a unique vision in their media of choice. The Bill Milliken Scholarship helps enable student to purchase art materials and supplies during their first year of postsecondary education. *Application Process: Applicants should submit a completed application along with transcripts, a one-page essay describing themselves and their interest in visual art, 15 slides of their work, a copy of their letter of acceptance to college or art school, and two letters of recommendation. The applicant's art teacher, who must be a member of

the NYSATA, must sign the essay. All application materials must be taken to the applicant's guidance office. The guidance office staff should mail the packet from their office. Visit the association's Web site to download an application. *Amount: $500. *Deadline: May 15.

New York State Art Teachers Association (NYSATA)
Attn: Janice Oldak/Art Department
Barnum Woods Elementary School
500 May Lane
East Meadow, NY 11554
516-564-6500
Artmuse5@aol.com
http://www.nysata.org/scholarships.php
Scholarship Name: Elaine Goldman Scholarship.
*Academic Area: Visual arts (open). *Age Group: Undergraduate students. *Eligibility: Applicants must be graduating high school seniors who are students of a NYSATA member. They must intend to pursue a degree/career in visual arts, have been accepted into an art school or a college art program, and demonstrate a commitment to the visual arts and a unique vision in their media of choice. *Application Process: Applicants should submit a completed application along with transcripts, a one-page essay describing themselves and their interest in visual art, 15 slides of their work, a copy of their letter of acceptance to college or art school, and two letters of recommendation. The applicant's art teacher, who must be a member of the NYSATA, must sign the essay. All application materials must be taken to the applicant's guidance office. The guidance office staff should mail the packet from their office. Visit the association's Web site to download an application. *Amount: $500. *Deadline: May 15.

New York State Art Teachers Association (NYSATA)
Attn: Janice Oldak/Art Department
Barnum Woods Elementary School
500 May Lane
East Meadow, NY 11554
516-564-6500
Artmuse5@aol.com
http://www.nysata.org/scholarships.php
Scholarship Name: Zara B. Kimmey Scholarship.
*Academic Area: Visual arts (open). *Age Group: Undergraduate students. *Eligibility: Applicants must be graduating high school seniors who are students of a NYSATA member. They must intend

to pursue a degree/career in visual arts, have been accepted into an art school or a college art program, and demonstrate a commitment to the visual arts and a unique vision in their media of choice. The Zara B. Kimmey Scholarship helps enable students to purchase art materials and supplies during their first year of post-secondary education. *Application Process: Applicants should submit a completed application along with transcripts, a one-page essay describing themselves and their interest in visual art, 15 slides of their work, a copy of their letter of acceptance to college or art school, and two letters of recommendation. The applicant's art teacher, who must be a member of the NYSATA, must sign the essay. All application materials must be taken to the applicant's guidance office. The guidance office staff should mail the packet from their office. Visit the association's Web site to download an application. *Amount: $1,000. *Deadline: May 15.

North Carolina Arts Council
Department of Cultural Resources
Grants Office
226 East North Street
Raleigh, NC 27699-4632
919-733-2111
ncarts@ncmail.net
http://www.ncarts.org/freeform_scrn_template.
  cfm?ffscrn_id=47&menu_sel=4&sub_sel=15
Grant/Fellowship Name: Artist Grants and Fellowships.
*Academic Area: Media arts, performing arts (open), visual arts (open), writing. *Age Group: Adults. *Eligibility: Applicants must be at least 18 years old, residents of the state of North Carolina for at least one year (and reside in the state for the duration of the fellowship period, and U.S. citizens or permanent residents. Applicants must demonstrate a commitment to artistic excellence and possess artistic merit. They must not be full-time students in a degree program. Applicants should visit the council's Web site to view additional eligibility requirements for the category in which they intend to apply. More than one type of fellowship and grant is offered by this organization. Visit the council's Web site for complete listings. *Application Process: Applicants should submit a completed application online, via eGRANT, by first submitting an electronic artist registration form. Applicants must also submit an artist narrative, a resume, a work sample with a descriptive cover page, and work samples required

for their category (detailed on the council's Web site). Visit the council's Web site to apply. *Amount: $500 to 8,000. *Deadline: Deadlines vary.

Ohio Arts Council

727 East Main Street
Columbus, OH 43205-1796
614-466-2613
http://www.oac.state.oh.us/grantsprogs/guidelines/IndividualCreativity.asp

Award Name: Individual Excellence Award. *Academic Area: Media arts, visual arts (open), writing. *Age Group: Adults. *Eligibility: Applicants must be at least 18 years old and residents of Ohio for at least one year (and reside in the state for the duration of the award period). They must demonstrate a commitment to artistic excellence and possess artistic merit in a creative art. Full-time students in a degree program are not eligible for this award. Applicants should visit the organization's Web site to view additional eligibility requirements for the category in which they intend to apply. *Application Process: Applicants should submit a completed application online. Paper applications are not accepted. Applicants must also submit their supporting materials according to the requirements posted for each art form. Visit the council's Web site for a complete list of required supporting materials and to apply. *Amount: $5,000 and $10,000. *Deadline: September 1.

Oregon Arts Commission

Attn: Shannon Planchon
775 Summer Street, NE, Suite 200
Salem, OR 97301-1284
503-986-0086
shannon.planchon@state.or.us
http://www.oregonartscommission.org/grants/commission_grant_programs.php

Fellowship/Grant Name: Individual Artist Fellowship Grant. *Academic Area: Media arts, performing arts (open), visual arts (open), writing. *Age Group: Adults. *Eligibility: Applicants must have been residents of Oregon for at least one year and demonstrate a commitment to artistic excellence and artistic merit. These grants are offered on a rotating basis by artistic discipline. Visit the commission's Web site for more information. *Application Process: Applicants should submit a completed application and supplementary materials. Applications are available for download from the commission's Web site in July of each year.

Applicants must also submit their supporting materials according to the requirements posted for each art form. Visit the commission's Web site for additional information. *Amount: $3,000. *Deadline: October 16.

Pennsylvania Council on the Arts

http://www.pacouncilonthearts.org/pca.cfm?id=9&level=Third&sid=13

Fellowship Name: Individual Artist Fellowship. *Academic Area: Media arts, performing arts (open), visual arts (open), writing. *Age Group: Adults. *Eligibility: Applicants must be current residents of Pennsylvania, and have been residents there for at least two years. They must not be high school students or degree-seeking students. Applicants may not apply for a fellowship if they received one during the previous award period. The council awards fellowships on a rotating basis according to artistic discipline. Applicants should visit the council's Web site to view additional eligibility requirements for the category in which they intend to apply. In even-numbered years, applications are accepted in arts commentary, crafts, folk and traditional arts (craft traditions), literature (fiction or creative nonfiction), media arts (narrative and animation), music (jazz, blues, world, or non-classical composition), theatre (new performance forms, and visual arts (photography, sculpture). Applicants in dance (choreography), folk and traditional arts (performing traditions), literature (poetry), media arts (documentary and experimental), music (classical composition), theatre (scriptworks), and visual arts (painting and printmaking) should apply in odd-numbered years. *Application Process: Applicants should submit a completed application along with program-specific work samples and supporting materials. Visit the council's Web site for details on these requirements in individual categories. Applicants should mail their applications to the specified organization, which differs based on artistic discipline. The main office does not accept application packets. *Amount: $5,000 and $10,000. *Deadline: The first business day in August.

Rhode Island State Council on the Arts

One Capitol Hill, 3rd Floor
Providence, RI 02908
401-222-3880
info@arts.ri.gov
http://www.arts.ri.gov/pdf/fellowship_guidelines.pdf

Grant Name: Artist Fellowship Grant. *Academic Area: Media arts, visual arts (open), writing. *Age Group: Adults. *Eligibility: Applicants must be at least 18 years old and residents of Rhode Island for at least one year prior to application. They must demonstrate a commitment to artistic excellence and possess artistic merit. Applicants must not be full-time students in a degree program. Visit the council's Web site to view additional eligibility requirements for the category in which they intend to apply. *Application Process: Applicants should submit a signed original application along with one copy, a supporting materials reference sheet, and an artist resume. For a detailed explanation of supporting materials in each artistic category, visit the council's Web site. Applications are accepted on a rotating schedule for specific artistic disciplines. Visit the council's Web site to download an application. *Amount: $1,000 and $5,000. *Deadline: Varies by discipline.

Salute to Education Inc.
PO Box 833425
Miami, FL 33283
305-476-7709
steinfo@stescholarships.org
http://www.stescholarships.org/SC_categories.html
Scholarship Name: Salute to Education Visual Arts Scholarship. *Academic Area: Visual arts (open). *Age Group: Undergraduate students. *Eligibility: Applicants must be graduating high school seniors who attend a Miami-Dade or Broward County, Florida, high school. Applicants must be legal residents of the United States, reside in Miami-Dade or Broward County, have a minimum weighted GPA of 3.0, demonstrate a commitment to service by participating in at least one school or community organization, and intend to pursue a college degree at an accredited institution after graduation. Applicants must demonstrate expression through creative works of art, knowledge of design principles, and an appreciation of art history across cultures. *Application Process: Applicants must apply online. Supporting materials should be mailed as detailed on the online application. *Amount: $1,000. *Deadline: Visit the organization's Web site for updated deadline information.

South Carolina Arts Commission
1800 Gervais Street
Columbus, SC 29201

803-734-8696
http://www.state.sc.us/arts/grants/artists/fellowships.htm
Fellowship/Grant Name: Individual Artist Fellowship Grant. *Academic Area: Media arts, performing arts (open), visual arts (open), writing. *Age Group: Adults. *Eligibility: Applicants must be at least 18 years old, have resided in South Carolina for at least two years, demonstrate a commitment to artistic excellence, and possess artistic merit. Full-time students in a degree program are not eligible for this fellowship. Applicants should visit the organization's Web site to view additional eligibility requirements for the category in which they intend to apply. Fellowships are offered in different categories each year. Visit the commission's Web site to see if your discipline qualifies for the current year's awards. *Application Process: Applicants should submit an application along with supporting materials and an artist resume. For a detailed explanation of supporting materials in each artistic category, visit the commission's Web site. Applications are accepted for specific artistic disciplines each year and the current year's artistic areas are posted on the commission's Web site. Visit the commission's Web site to download an application. *Amount: $2,500. *Deadline: May 15.

South Dakota Arts Council
800 Governors Drive
Pierre, SD 57501-2294
605-773-3131
sdac@state.sd.us
http://www.artscouncil.sd.gov/Pubs/guide/Guide%20to%20Grants%2006%2007/ArtistGrants/grantsartists.htm
Grant Name: Individual Artist Grant. *Academic Area: Media arts, performing arts (open), visual arts (open), writing. *Age Group: Adults. *Eligibility: Applicants must be at least 18 years old, have resided in South Dakota for at least two years, demonstrate a commitment to artistic excellence, and possess artistic merit. Full-time students in a degree program are not eligible for this grant. *Application Process: Applicants should submit an application along with supporting materials and an artist resume. Additional supporting materials such as newspaper reviews of the artist's work may also be submitted. For a detailed explanation of supporting materials in each artistic category, visit the council's Web site.

Applications are accepted in all artistic disciplines. Visit the council's Web site to download an application. *Amount: $1,000 and $3,000. *Deadline: March 1.

Tennessee Arts Commission
Attn: Rod Reiner, Deputy Director
Citizens Plaza Building, 401 Charlotte Avenue
Nashville, TN 37243-0780
615-741-2093
rod.reiner@state.tn.us
http://www.arts.state.tn.us/grantprograms.htm
Fellowship Name: Individual Artist Fellowship. *Academic Area: Media arts, performing arts (open), visual arts (open), writing. *Age Group: Adults. *Eligibility: Applicants must be residents of Tennessee with a valid Tennessee mailing address. They must demonstrate that art is part of their livelihood and that they make a significant portion of their income from their art. Full-time students in a degree program are not eligible for this fellowship. Applicants should visit the commission's Web site to view the categories for which the organization is accepting applications for the current year. Disciplines vary by year. *Application Process: Applicants should submit an online application along with supporting materials. A new eGRANT system is now being used. Applicants should apply online, print a copy of the completed application, and submit the copy with the required supporting work samples. For a detailed explanation of supporting materials in each artistic category, visit the commission's Web site. *Amount: $5,000. *Deadline: January 30.

UNICO National Inc.
Attn: Joan Tidona, Scholarship Director
271 U.S. Highway 46 West
Fairfield, NJ 07004
201-933-7982
jntidona@verizon.net
http://www.unico.org
Scholarship Name: Theodore Mazza Scholarship. *Academic Area: Visual arts (open). *Age Group: Undergraduate students. *Eligibility: UNICO touts itself as the largest Italian-American service organization in the United States. Italian-American graduating high school seniors or college undergraduates majoring in fine art may apply. *Application Process: Applicants should contact the scholarship director to receive additional information and an application. The scholarship director distributes all rules and announcements regarding available scholarships. *Amount: $1,500. *Deadline: Contact the scholarship director for deadline information.

Vermont Arts Council
Attn: Michele Bailey, Director of Creation & Foundation Programs
136 State Street, Drawer 33
Montpelier, VT 05633-6001
802-828-3294
mbailey@vermontartscouncil.org
http://www.vermontartscouncil.org/grants/documents/for_artists.html
Grant Name: Grants for Artists. *Academic Area: Media arts, performing arts (open), visual arts (open), writing. *Age Group: Adults. *Eligibility: Applicants must be at least 18 years of age and have lived in Vermont for at least one year prior to application. Full-time students in a degree program are not eligible for these grants. The council offers more than one type of individual grant. Visit its Web site to learn more. All grants require a 1:1 cash match. Applicants will need to raise equal funds in order to be eligible for an award. *Application Process: Applicants should submit a completed application along with an artist narrative, a project timeline, a budget, supporting work samples, proof of Vermont residency, and a $10 application fee. Applicants should visit the council's Web site for complete details on how to submit work samples. *Amount: $250 to $5,000. *Deadline: Deadlines vary. Visit the council's Web site for detailed information.

Virginia Commission for the Arts
223 Governor Street
Lewis House, Second Floor
Richmond, VA 23219
804-225-3132
arts@arts.virginia.gov
http://www.arts.virginia.gov/artist%20fellowships.htm
Fellowship Name: Artist Fellowship. *Academic Area: Media arts, performing arts (open), visual arts (open), writing. *Age Group: Adults. *Eligibility: Applicants must be at least 18 years of age and legal residents of Virginia who plan to reside in the state for the duration of the fellowship period. Applicants must not be full-time students in a degree program.

This organization offers fellowships in rotating disciplines. In one year applicants may apply in categories such as playwriting and sculpture. Two new categories will be chosen for the following year. Interested applicants should visit the commission's Web site to view the current categories, or contact the organization for more information. *Application Process: Applicants should submit a completed application along with an information page, an artist narrative, work samples, and a resume. Applicants should visit the commission's Web site for complete details on how to submit work samples in each category. *Amount: $5,000. *Deadline: August 1.

Washington State Arts Commission
Attn: Willie Smyth, Program Manager
PO Box 42675
Olympia, WA 98504-2675
360-586-2856
willies@arts.wa.gov
http://www.arts.wa.gov
Fellowship Name: Folk Arts Fellowship. *Academic Area: Visual arts (folk). *Age Group: Adults. *Eligibility: Applicants must be traditional artists, residents of Washington, and demonstrate a commitment to preserving endangered art forms. They should also demonstrate a commitment to their communities. *Application Process: Applicants should submit a completed application along with supporting work samples, which include photos or slides, audio or videotapes, exhibit brochures or clippings, and optional letters of support. Visit the commission's Web site to download an application. *Amount: $5,000. *Deadline: April 22.

West Virginia Commission on the Arts
Attn: Jeff Pierson, Individual Artist Coordinator
The Cultural Center
1900 Kanawha Boulevard East
Charleston, WV 25305-0300
304-558-0240, ext. 717
jeff.pierson@wvculture.org
http://www.wvculture.org/arts/grants/fy06artistfellow.pdf

Fellowship Name: Artist Fellowships. *Academic Area: Performing arts (open), visual arts (open), writing. *Age Group: Adults. *Eligibility: Applicants must be at least 18 years old and residents of West Virginia for at least one year. Full-time students in a degree program are not eligible for these fellowships. Fellowships are offered in varying categories, which rotate on a yearly basis. Applicants should visit the commission's Web site to view additional eligibility requirements for the category in which they intend to apply and to see if applications are currently being accepted in their artistic discipline. *Application Process: Applicants should submit two copies of the completed application along with work samples (as specified for the category), a resume, and a self-addressed, stamped envelope and postcard. Visit the commission's Web site to download an application. *Amount: $3,500. *Deadline: September 1.

Wisconsin Arts Board
101 East Wilson Street, First Floor
Madison, WI 53702
608-266-0190
http://www.arts.state.wi.us/static/fellwshp.htm
Fellowship Name: Artist Fellowship Awards. *Academic Area: Media arts, performing arts (open), visual arts (open), writing. *Age Group: Adults. *Eligibility: Applicants must be at least 18 years old and residents of Wisconsin for at least one year. Those attending a college degree program are not eligible for these fellowships. Fellowships are offered in varying categories, which rotate on a yearly basis. In even numbered years, applicants may apply in the categories of literary arts, music composition, choreography, and performance art. Visual and media arts applicants may apply in odd-numbered years. *Application Process: Applicants apply online via the eGRANT system. Hard copies of the application and work samples must also be mailed. Applicants should visit the board's Web site for additional updates. This program is currently under review, and procedures may change. *Amount: $8,000. *Deadline: September 15.

VISUAL ARTS/DESIGN—GRADUATE

The following financial aid resources are available to visual artists and designers at the graduate level.

Alaska State Council on the Arts (ASCA)
411 West 4th Avenue, Suite 1E
Anchorage, AK 99501-2343
907-269-6610
aksca_info@eed.state.ak.us
http://www.eed.state.ak.us/aksca/Grants3.htm
Grant Name: Career Opportunity Grants. *Academic Area: Visual arts (open). *Age Group: Adults. *Eligibility: Applicants must be Alaskan residents who are at least 18 years old. They must not be enrolled as full-time students and have not received this grant in the preceding year. Applicants must desire to increase their development as an artist and to further their artistic careers. They must also demonstrate artistic merit by submitting a work sample. *Application Process: Applicants should apply online. Applicants should also submit up to 10 images of recent artwork and a printed copy of the ASCA Grants Online application profile page. Visit the association's Web site to apply. *Amount: $100 to $1,000. *Deadline: March 1, June 1, September 1, December 1.

Alaska State Council on the Arts (ASCA)
411 West 4th Avenue, Suite 1E
Anchorage, AK 99501-2343
907-269-6610
aksca_info@eed.state.ak.us
http://www.eed.state.ak.us/aksca/Grants3.htm
Fellowship Name: Connie Boochever Artist Fellowship. *Academic Area: Education, performing arts (open), media arts, visual arts (open), writing. *Age Group: Adults. *Eligibility: Applicants must be Alaska residents, at least 18 years old, and emerging artists who are pursuing their art form on an ongoing basis. Applicants may not be enrolled as full-time students and must not have received a grant in the last two years. *Application Process: Applicants should submit a complete application packet including supporting materials verifying the quality of their work (through visual representation, resume, and recommendations). This grant is offered to artists pursing different art forms in two-year, rotating cycles. Applicants should visit the council's Web site to see if they will qualify for the current discipline that is being offered. Visit the council's

Web site for more details. *Amount: $2,500. *Deadline: Contact the council for deadline information.

Alaska State Council on the Arts (ASCA)
411 West 4th Avenue, Suite 1E
Anchorage, AK 99501-2343
907-269-6610
aksca_info@eed.state.ak.us
http://www.eed.state.ak.us/aksca/Grants3.htm
Grant Name: Master Artist and Apprenticeship Grant. *Academic Area: Performing arts (dance), performing arts (music-instrumental), performing arts (voice), visual arts (crafts), visual arts (painting), visual arts (sculpting). *Age Group: Adults. *Eligibility: Applicants must be residents of Alaska, at least 18 years old, have an interest in traditional Alaska Native art, and desire the opportunity to develop their skills in an Alaskan Native art form. They must also have demonstrated experience working in the art form for which they are applying and must have identified a master artist under whom they would like to serve as an apprentice. Applicants may not be enrolled as full-time students during the period of the grant. *Application Process: Applicants should submit a complete application packet, which includes supporting material verifying the quality of the apprentice's work (through visual representation, resume, and recommendations), quality of the master artist's work (through visual representation, resume, and recommendations), a description of the project and the skills that will be taught and learned, and a complete itemized budget. Visit the council's Web site for more details. *Amount: Up to $2,000. *Deadline: The first of the month prior to the applicant's planned apprenticeship.

Arizona Commission on the Arts
417 West Roosevelt Street
Phoenix, AZ 85003-1326
602-255-5882
info@azarts.gov
http://www.azarts.gov/artists/grants.htm
Grant Name: Career Advancement and Project Grants. *Academic Area: Performing arts (open), visual arts (open). *Age Group: Adults. *Eligibility: Applicants must be residents of Arizona, at least 18 years old,

and not enrolled for more than three credit hours at a college or university. They must be seeking funds to advance their professional artistic careers or to help them complete a worthy artistic endeavor. Applicants must be able to provide documentation of Arizona residency. This organization provides three different kinds of grants for individuals. Eligibility requirements may vary slightly. *Application Process: Applicants should submit a completed application along with the appropriate supporting materials. Supporting materials include visual documentation of work samples (slides, video, etc.), resume, and a project narrative. Visit the commission's Web site to download an application and to view additional information about individual grants. *Amount: $500 to $5,000 (depending on the type of grant). *Deadline: Deadlines vary.

Arkansas Arts Council
1500 Tower Building, 323 Center Street
Little Rock, AR 72201
501-324-9766
info@arkansasarts.com
http://www.arkansasarts.com/grants
Grant Name: Individual Artists Fellowship. *Academic Area: Performing arts (open), visual arts (open). *Age Group: Adults. *Eligibility: Applicants must be residents of Arkansas who are at least 25 years old. They must have lived in Arkansas for at least one year to qualify and cannot be degree-seeking students or have received the award previously. Categories rotate yearly, so interested candidates should contact the council for information on the area in which they are taking applications for the current year. *Application Process: Applicants should contact the council for information on the application process. Applications are also periodically available at the council's Web site for download. *Amount: Awards vary. *Deadline: May 12.

College Art Association
Attn: Stacy Miller, Director of Research & Career Development
275 Seventh Avenue
New York, NY 10001
212-691-1051, ext 252
smiller@collegeart.org
http://www.collegeart.org/fellowships
Fellowship Name: Professional Development Fellowship. *Academic Area: Visual arts (history), visual arts (open). *Age Group: Graduate students. *Eligibility:

Applicants must be U.S. citizens, pursuing a M.F.A. or Ph.D. in the arts, and demonstrate financial need. Applicants must belong to an underrepresented minority group in their field "due to race, religion, gender, age, national origin, sexual orientation, disability, or financial status." *Application Process: Applicants should submit a completed application along with a five-page personal statement, three letters of recommendation, a photocopy of their Free Application for Federal Student Aid, official graduate school transcripts, a description of their M.F.A. exhibition and timetable, and visual documentation of recent work along with a slide or video script. Visit the association's Web site for additional information and downloadable applications. *Amount: $5,000 and $10,000. *Deadline: January 31.

Connecticut Commission on Culture and Tourism
Attn: Tamara Dimitri
One Financial Plaza
755 Main Street
Hartford, CT 06103
860-256-2720
tdimitri@ctarts.org
http://www.cultureandtourism.org/cct/cwp/view.asp?a=2207&q=293740&cctPNavCtr=|43595|
Fellowship Name: Individual Artists Fellowship. *Academic Area: Film/television, performing arts (choreography), performing arts (composition), visual arts (open), writing. *Age Group: Adults. *Eligibility: Applicants must be Connecticut residents who have lived within the state for at least one year. Applicants must not be degree-seeking college students and cannot have received the award previously. Categories rotate yearly, so interested candidates should visit the organization's Web site to see which category is available for the current year. *Application Process: Applicants should contact the commission for information on the application process. Application materials are available in July of each year. *Amount: $2,500 and $5,000. *Deadline: September (contact the commission for exact deadlines).

Delaware Division of the Arts
820 North French Street
Wilmington, DE 19801
302-577-8278
delarts@state.de.us
http://www.artsdel.org/grants/artistgrants.shtml

Grant Name: Grants for Individual Artists. *Academic Area: Media arts, performing arts (open), visual arts (open), writing. *Age Group: Adults. *Eligibility: Applicants must be Delaware residents, at least 18 years old, and have lived in the state for at least one year. They must not be enrolled in a degree-granting program. This organization offers more than one kind of grant for individual artists. Visit the organization's Web site for additional eligibility requirements for individual grants. *Application Process: Applicants should submit a completed application along with a one-page narrative, a budget, a resume, and work samples (examples of appropriate submissions are listed on the application). Visit the organization's Web site to download an application. *Amount: Awards vary. *Deadline: Deadlines vary by grant.

Florida Division of Cultural Affairs
Attn: Morgan Barr
R.A. Gray Building, 500 South Bronough Street, 3rd Floor
Tallahassee, FL 32399-0250
850-245-6356
mhbarr@dos.state.fl.us
http://www.florida-arts.org/grants/forindividuals.htm
Grant Name: Grants for Individual Artists. *Academic Area: Media arts, performing arts (dance), performing arts (music-general), performing arts (theatre), visual arts (open), writing. *Age Group: Adults. *Eligibility: Applicants must be Florida residents, at least 18 years old, and not be enrolled in any degree program. This organization offers more than one kind of grant for individual artists. Applicants must not have received a grant from the same organization in the previous grant period. Some grants are offered on a rotating categorical basis, with visual arts and media arts grouped together for one year and performing arts and literary arts in the next year. Visit the organization's Web site for additional eligibility requirements for individual grants. *Application Process: Applicants should submit a completed application along with supporting materials. Visit the organization's Web site for additional information on the application process. *Amount: Awards vary. *Deadline: Deadlines vary by individual award.

Hawaii State Foundation on Culture and the Arts
Attn: Fay Ann Chun, Individual Artists Program Coordinator
250 South Hotel Street, 2nd Floor
Honolulu, HI 96813

808-586-9965
hsfca2006awards@yahoo.com
http://www.state.hi.us/sfca
Fellowship Name: Individual Artists Fellowship. *Academic Area: Performing arts (open), visual arts (open). *Age Group: Adults. *Eligibility: Applicants must be residents of Hawaii, at least 18 years old, and recognized in their communities as professional artists. They must be financially compensated for their work as part of their livelihood and able to provide documentation of their artistic experience for at least the last five years. Visit the organization's Web site for a complete list of eligibility requirements in each visual arts or performing arts category. *Application Process: Applicants should submit a completed application along with an artist statement form, a resume form, three references and a reference form, and work samples. The process for submitting appropriate work samples is explained in depth on the application form. Visit the organization's Web site for additional information on the application process. *Amount: Awards vary. *Deadline: Contact the organization for deadline information.

Idaho Commission on the Arts
PO Box 83720
Boise, ID 83720-0008
208-334-2119
info@arts.idaho.gov
http://www.arts.idaho.gov/grants/indoverview.aspx
Grant Name: Grants for Individual Artists. *Academic Area: Media arts, performing arts (open), visual arts (open), writing. *Age Group: Adults. *Eligibility: Applicants must be residents of Idaho who demonstrate artistic excellence and a professional artistic history. This organization offers several grants and fellowships, many of which are offered on a rotating scale according to artistic discipline. Visit the organization's Web site for further information. *Application Process: Applicants should submit a completed application along with supporting materials, including a resume, an artist statement, and work samples. Visit the organization's Web site for a checklist of supporting materials for each type of grant or fellowship. *Amount: $3,500 (approximate). *Deadline: January 31.

Illinois Arts Council
James R. Thompson Center
100 West Randolph, Suite 10-500

Chicago, IL 60601

314-814-4991

rose@arts.state.il.us

http://www.state.il.us/agency/iac/Guidelines/guidelines.htm

Fellowship Name: Artist Fellowship Program. *Academic Area: Film/television, media arts, performing arts (choreography), performing arts (composition), visual arts (crafts), visual arts (photography), visual arts (open). *Age Group: Adults. *Eligibility: Applicants must be residents of Illinois who can provide proof that they've resided within the state for at least one year. They must be U.S. citizens or permanent residents and not be enrolled in any degree program. Applicants must not have received funds from this fellowship in the two preceding years. These fellowships are offered on a rotating basis according to artistic discipline. Applicants in the disciplines of choreography, crafts, ethnic and folk arts, media arts, new performance forms, prose, and scriptwriting may apply in even-numbered years, and applicants in interdisciplinary/computer art, music composition, photography, poetry, and visual arts can apply in odd-numbered years. Visit the organization's Web site for further information. *Application Process: Applicants should submit a completed application along with a work sample sheet, work samples, a one-page artistic resume, and a one-page artist statement. Work samples must not be more than four years old. A detailed explanation of work sample submission procedures is explained on the application. Visit the organization's Web site to download an application. *Amount: $700 and $7,000. *Deadline: September 1.

Indiana Arts Commission

Attn: Monica Peterson

150 West Market Street, Suite 618

Indianapolis, IN 46204

317-232-1279

mpeterson@iac.in.gov

http://www.in.gov/arts/grants/program_iap.html

Grant Name: Grants for Individual Artists. *Academic Area: Media arts, performing arts (open), visual arts (open), writing. *Age Group: Adults. *Eligibility: Applicants must be at least 18 years old and residents of Indiana who have lived in the state for at least one full year preceding the application. They must remain an Indiana resident during the grant period, not be enrolled in any degree program, and not have received this award in the preceding year. Applicant must be applying as an individual and not as part of a collaborative project. Visit the commission's Web site for further information. *Application Process: Applicants should submit a completed application along with a formal letter stating the reasons for consideration and supporting materials. A detailed explanation of how to submit supporting materials is included on the application. Visit the commission's Web site to download an application. *Amount: $1,000. *Deadline: February 3.

Iowa Arts Council

Attn: Bruce Williams

600 East Locust

Des Moines, IA 50319-0290

515-252-6194

Bruce.Williams@iowa.gov

http://www.iowaartscouncil.org/funding/artist-project-grant/index.shtml

Grant Name: Artist Major Grants and Mini Grants. *Academic Area: Performing arts (open), visual arts (open). *Age Group: Adults. *Eligibility: Applicants must be at least 18 years old and have lived in Iowa for at least one full year preceding the application. Applicants must not be students and not have received two Iowa Arts Council grants within the same fiscal year of this proposed grant activity. This program also includes applicants from select bordering communities. Visit the council's Web site for the border state policy. Eligibility requirements may differ slightly for major and mini grants. Visit the council's Web site for additional eligibility requirements. *Application Process: Applicants must submit an online application on the state's new eGRANT system. The application will include information on the proposed project, a budget, a personal narrative, a work sample form and work samples, a service contract, and a project timeline. Visit the council's Web site to apply online. *Amount: $1,500 (mini grant); $10,000 (major grant). *Deadline: April 1.

Kentucky Arts Council

Attn: Lori Meadows

Capital Plaza Tower, 500 Mero Street, 21st Floor

Frankfort, KY 40601-1987

502-564-3747, ext. 482

Lori.Meadows@ky.gov

http://artscouncil.ky.gov/guide/prog3/asf_gdl.htm

Fellowship Name: Al Smith Individual Artist Fellowship Program. *Academic Area: Media arts, performing arts (open), visual arts (open), writing. *Age Group: Adults. *Eligibility: Applicants must be U.S. citizens or permanent residents, residents of Kentucky (who have lived in the state for at least one year), at least 18 years old, and demonstrate artistic excellence and professional achievement. They must remain Kentucky residents during the period for which they receive funding. Applicants must be professional artists who are creating their own work, not just interpreting the work of others. *Application Process: Applicants should submit a completed application along with supporting materials. Supporting materials include a narrative essay, proof of residency, work samples and an index of work samples, and an optional resume. Detailed descriptions of how to submit work samples are listed on the application. This fellowship is offered in alternating disciplines every other year. Writers, choreographers, musical composers, and interdisciplinary artists may apply in even numbered years, and visual and media artists may apply in odd numbered years. Visit the organization's Web site to download an application. *Amount: $7,500; $1,000 professional assistance awards given to some applicants who do not receive the Individual Artist Fellowships. *Deadline: August 15 (intent to apply deadline); September 15 (application deadline).

Maine Arts Commission
Attn: Donna McNeil, Contemporary Art & Public Art
    Associate
193 State Street, 25 State House Station
Augusta, ME 04333-0025
207-287-2726
Donna.McNeil@maine.gov
http://www.mainearts.com/Grants/index.shtml
Fellowship Name: Individual Artist Fellowship.
    *Academic Area: Media arts, performing arts
    (open), visual arts (open), writing. *Age Group:
    Adults. *Eligibility: Applicants must be residents
    of Maine, at least 18 years old, and not enrolled
    as full-time students in a field relating to the
    application. They must have lived in Maine for at
    least two years and demonstrate artistic excellence.
    Artists in all mediums are encouraged to apply.
    *Application Process: Applicants should submit a
    completed application along with one set of labeled
    artistic materials (instructions are located on the
    application), a biographical information sheet, and
    a self-addressed stamped postcard and envelope.

Visit the commission's Web site to download an application. *Amount: $13,000. *Deadline: June 9.

Massachusetts Cultural Council
10 Saint James Avenue, 3rd Floor
Boston, MA 02116-3803
617-727-3668, 800-232-0960
mcc@art.state.ma.us
http://www.massculturalcouncil.org/programs/
    artistgrants.html
Grant Name: Artist Grants Program. *Academic Area:
    Media arts, performing arts (open), visual arts (open),
    writing. *Age Group: Adults. *Eligibility: Applicants
    must be residents of Massachusetts, at least 18
    years old, and not be enrolled as students in degree
    programs. Applicants must demonstrate artistic
    excellence. Categories in which applicants may
    apply rotate every other year. Applicants should visit
    the organization's Web site to view the eligibility
    requirements for the current application period.
    *Application Process: Applicants should submit
    a completed application along with supporting
    materials. Visit the council's Web site to download an
    application and a description of how to submit work
    samples. *Amount: $5,000. *Deadline: December.
    Visit the council's Web site for deadline information.

Mississippi Arts Commission
Attn: Judi Cleary, Director of Grants & Programs
Woolfolk Building, 501 North West Street, Suite 701B
Jackson, MS 39201
601-359-6030
jcleary@arts.state.ms.us
http://www.mswholeschools.org/mac/grants/for-
    individuals.html
Fellowship Name: Artist Fellowship. *Academic Area:
    Media arts, performing arts (open), visual arts
    (open), writing. *Age Group: Adults. *Eligibility:
    Applicants must be residents of Mississippi, at least
    18 years old, and maintain residency in Mississippi
    for the duration of the fellowship. They must
    demonstrate artistic excellence and earn at least
    part of their income from their artistic discipline.
    Applicants should consider their artistic endeavors
    as a career and should devote significant time to
    this work. Full-time students are not eligible for
    this fellowship. Categories in which applicants may
    apply rotate every other year. Applicants should visit
    the organization's Web site to view the eligibility
    requirements for the current application period.

*Application Process: Applicants should submit a completed application along with an artist narrative, a resume, and work samples. Visit the organization's Web site to download an application and a description of how to submit work samples in each category. *Amount: Up to $5,000. *Deadline: March 1.

Montana Arts Council
PO Box 202201
Helena, MT 59620-2201
406-444-6430
mac@mt.gov
http://www.art.state.mt.us/artists/artists.asp
Grant Name: Opportunity and Professional Development Grants. *Academic Area: Performing arts (open), visual arts (open). *Age Group: Adults. *Eligibility: Applicants must be at least 18 years old and residents of Montana for at least one year. Full-time students are not eligible for these grants. Applicants should visit the council's Web site to view additional eligibility requirements for specific grants and specific artistic mediums. These grants require the applicant to match the funds with an equal dollar amount of their own funds or funds that they have raised for a given artistic endeavor. *Application Process: Applicants should submit a completed application along with an artist narrative, a project synopsis, a complete budget, and a resume. Visit the council's Web site to download an application. *Amount: $750 to $1,000. *Deadline: Deadlines vary.

Nevada Arts Council
Attn: Fran Morrow, Artist Services Program Coordinator
716 North Carson Street, Suite A
Carson City, NV 89701
775-687-7106
fkmorrow@clan.lib.nv.us
http://dmla.clan.lib.nv.us/docs/arts/programs/grants/grantsforartists.htm
Grant Name: Grants for Artists. *Academic Area: Media arts, performing arts (open), visual arts (open), writing. *Age Group: Adults. *Eligibility: Applicants must be at least 21 years old and residents of the state of Nevada for at least one year (and reside in the state of Nevada for the duration of the grant period). They must be U.S. citizens or legal permanent residents who are practicing professional artists and who demonstrate artistic excellence and merit. Applicants must not be full-time students. This organization offers more than one type of grant. Visit the organization's Web site to view additional eligibility requirements for specific grants. *Application Process: Applicants should submit a completed application along with five copies of the work sample list, work samples required for their category (detailed on the application), and a resume. Visit the organization's Web site to download an application. *Amount: $500 to $5,000. *Deadline: Deadlines vary by grant. Visit the organization's Web site to view current deadlines.

New Hampshire State Council on the Arts
2 1/2 Beacon Street, 2nd Floor
Concord, NH 03301-4974
603-271-2789
http://www.state.nh.us/nharts/grants/artists/index.htm
Grant/Fellowship Name: Grants and Fellowships for Artists. *Academic Area: Media arts, performing arts (open), visual arts (open), writing. *Age Group: Adults. *Eligibility: Applicants must be at least 18 years old and residents of New Hampshire for at least one year (and reside in the state for the duration of the grant or fellowship period). They must demonstrate a commitment to artistic excellence and possess artistic merit. Applicants must not be full-time students. This organization offers more than one type of grant. Visit the organization's Web site to view additional eligibility requirements for specific awards. *Application Process: Applicants should submit a completed application along with answers to the required narrative questions, a resume, and work samples required for their category (detailed at the council's Web site). Visit the council's Web site to download an application. *Amount: $250 to $5,000. *Deadline: Deadlines vary by award. Visit the council's Web site to view current deadlines.

New Jersey State Council on the Arts
Attn: Rebecca Scolian
c/o Mid Atlantic Arts Foundation
201 North Charles Street, Suite 401
Baltimore, MD 21201
410-539-6656, ext. 101
rebecca@midatlanticarts.org
http://www.njartscouncil.org/program7.html
Fellowship Name: Artist Fellowship. *Academic Area: Media arts, performing arts (open), visual arts (open), writing. *Age Group: Adults. *Eligibility: Applicants must be at least 18 years old and residents of New Jersey for at least one year (and reside in the state

for the duration of the fellowship period). They must demonstrate a commitment to artistic excellence and possess artistic merit. Applicants must not be full-time students in a degree program. Visit the organization's Web site to view additional eligibility requirements for the category in which they intend to apply. *Application Process: Applicants should submit a completed application along with two copies of their resume, work samples, and a descriptive cover page. Visit the council's Web site to download an application. *Amount: $7,800 to $12,000. *Deadline: July 15.

North Carolina Arts Council
Department of Cultural Resources
Grants Office
226 East North Street
Raleigh, NC 27699-4632
919-733-2111
ncarts@ncmail.net
http://www.ncarts.org/freeform_scrn_template.
cfm?ffscrn_id=47&menu_sel=4&sub_sel=15
Grant/Fellowship Name: Artist Grants and Fellowships.
*Academic Area: Media arts, performing arts (open), visual arts (open), writing. *Age Group: Adults. *Eligibility: Applicants must be at least 18 years old, residents of the state of North Carolina for at least one year (and reside in the state for the duration of the fellowship period, and U.S. citizens or permanent residents. Applicants must demonstrate a commitment to artistic excellence and possess artistic merit. They must not be full-time students in a degree program. Applicants should visit the council's Web site to view additional eligibility requirements for the category in which they intend to apply. More than one type of fellowship and grant is offered by this organization. Visit the council's Web site for complete listings. *Application Process: Applicants should submit a completed application online, via eGRANT, by first submitting an electronic artist registration form. Applicants must also submit an artist narrative, a resume, a work sample with a descriptive cover page, and work samples required for their category (detailed on the council's Web site). Visit the council's Web site to apply. *Amount: $500 to 8,000. *Deadline: Deadlines vary.

Ohio Arts Council
727 East Main Street
Columbus, OH 43205-1796

614-466-2613
http://www.oac.state.oh.us/grantsprogs/guidelines/
IndividualCreativity.asp
Award Name: Individual Excellence Award. *Academic Area: Media arts, visual arts (open), writing. *Age Group: Adults. *Eligibility: Applicants must be at least 18 years old and residents of Ohio for at least one year (and reside in the state for the duration of the award period). They must demonstrate a commitment to artistic excellence and possess artistic merit in a creative art. Full-time students in a degree program are not eligible for this award. Applicants should visit the organization's Web site to view additional eligibility requirements for the category in which they intend to apply. *Application Process: Applicants should submit a completed application online. Paper applications are not accepted. Applicants must also submit their supporting materials according to the requirements posted for each art form. Visit the council's Web site for a complete list of required supporting materials and to apply. *Amount: $5,000 and $10,000. *Deadline: September 1.

Oregon Arts Commission
Attn: Shannon Planchon
775 Summer Street, NE, Suite 200
Salem, OR 97301-1284
503-986-0086
shannon.planchon@state.or.us
http://www.oregonartscommission.org/grants/
commission_grant_programs.php
Fellowship/Grant Name: Individual Artist Fellowship Grant. *Academic Area: Media arts, performing arts (open), visual arts (open), writing. *Age Group: Adults. *Eligibility: Applicants must have been residents of Oregon for at least one year and demonstrate a commitment to artistic excellence and artistic merit. These grants are offered on a rotating basis by artistic discipline. Visit the commission's Web site for more information. *Application Process: Applicants should submit a completed application and supplementary materials. Applications are available for download from the commission's Web site in July of each year. Applicants must also submit their supporting materials according to the requirements posted for each art form. Visit the commission's Web site for additional information. *Amount: $3,000. *Deadline: October 16.

Pennsylvania Council on the Arts

http://www.pacouncilonthearts.org/pca.cfm?id=9&level
=Third&sid=13

Fellowship Name: Individual Artist Fellowship.
*Academic Area: Media arts, performing arts (open),
visual arts (open), writing. *Age Group: Adults.
*Eligibility: Applicants must be current residents
of Pennsylvania, and have been residents there for
at least two years. They must not be high school
students or degree-seeking students. Applicants
may not apply for a fellowship if they received one
during the previous award period. The council
awards fellowships on a rotating basis according
to artistic discipline. Applicants should visit the
council's Web site to view additional eligibility
requirements for the category in which they intend
to apply. In even-numbered years, applications
are accepted in arts commentary, crafts, folk and
traditional arts (craft traditions), literature (fiction
or creative nonfiction), media arts (narrative and
animation), music (jazz, blues, world, or non-classical
composition), theatre (new performance forms,
and visual arts (photography, sculpture). Applicants
in dance (choreography), folk and traditional arts
(performing traditions), literature (poetry), media
arts (documentary and experimental), music
(classical composition), theatre (scriptworks), and
visual arts (painting and printmaking) should apply
in odd-numbered years. *Application Process:
Applicants should submit a completed application
along with program-specific work samples and
supporting materials. Visit the council's Web site
for details on these requirements in individual
categories. Applicants should mail their applications
to the specified organization, which differs based on
artistic discipline. The main office does not accept
application packets. *Amount: $5,000 and $10,000.
*Deadline: The first business day in August.

Rhode Island State Council on the Arts

One Capitol Hill, 3rd Floor
Providence, RI 02908
401-222-3880
info@arts.ri.gov
http://www.arts.ri.gov/pdf/fellowship_guidelines.pdf

Grant Name: Artist Fellowship Grant. *Academic
Area: Media arts, visual arts (open), writing. *Age
Group: Adults. *Eligibility: Applicants must be at
least 18 years old and residents of Rhode Island for
at least one year prior to application. They must

demonstrate a commitment to artistic excellence
and possess artistic merit. Applicants must not be
full-time students in a degree program. Visit the
council's Web site to view additional eligibility
requirements for the category in which they intend
to apply. *Application Process: Applicants should
submit a signed original application along with
one copy, a supporting materials reference sheet,
and an artist resume. For a detailed explanation of
supporting materials in each artistic category, visit
the council's Web site. Applications are accepted on
a rotating schedule for specific artistic disciplines.
Visit the council's Web site to download an
application. *Amount: $1,000 and $5,000. *Deadline:
Varies by discipline.

South Carolina Arts Commission

1800 Gervais Street
Columbus, SC 29201
803-734-8696
http://www.state.sc.us/arts/grants/artists/fellowships.
htm

Fellowship/Grant Name: Individual Artist Fellowship
Grant. *Academic Area: Media arts, performing arts
(open), visual arts (open), writing. *Age Group: Adults.
*Eligibility: Applicants must be at least 18 years old,
have resided in South Carolina for at least two years,
demonstrate a commitment to artistic excellence, and
possess artistic merit. Full-time students in a degree
program are not eligible for this fellowship. Applicants
should visit the organization's Web site to view
additional eligibility requirements for the category in
which they intend to apply. Fellowships are offered in
different categories each year. Visit the commission's
Web site to see if your discipline qualifies for the
current year's awards. *Application Process: Applicants
should submit an application along with supporting
materials and an artist resume. For a detailed
explanation of supporting materials in each artistic
category, visit the commission's Web site. Applications
are accepted for specific artistic disciplines each year
and the current year's artistic areas are posted on the
commission's Web site. Visit the commission's Web
site to download an application. *Amount: $2,500.
*Deadline: May 15.

South Dakota Arts Council

800 Governors Drive
Pierre, SD 57501-2294
605-773-3131

sdac@state.sd.us

http://www.artscouncil.sd.gov/Pubs/guide/Guide%20t o%20Grants%2006%2007/ArtistGrants/grantsartists. htm

Grant Name: Individual Artist Grant. *Academic Area: Media arts, performing arts (open), visual arts (open), writing. *Age Group: Adults. *Eligibility: Applicants must be at least 18 years old, have resided in South Dakota for at least two years, demonstrate a commitment to artistic excellence, and possess artistic merit. Full-time students in a degree program are not eligible for this grant. *Application Process: Applicants should submit an application along with supporting materials and an artist resume. Additional supporting materials such as newspaper reviews of the artist's work may also be submitted. For a detailed explanation of supporting materials in each artistic category, visit the council's Web site. Applications are accepted in all artistic disciplines. Visit the council's Web site to download an application. *Amount: $1,000 and $3,000. *Deadline: March 1.

Tennessee Arts Commission

Attn: Rod Reiner, Deputy Director

Citizens Plaza Building, 401 Charlotte Avenue

Nashville, TN 37243-0780

615-741-2093

rod.reiner@state.tn.us

http://www.arts.state.tn.us/grantprograms.htm

Fellowship Name: Individual Artist Fellowship. *Academic Area: Media arts, performing arts (open), visual arts (open), writing. *Age Group: Adults. *Eligibility: Applicants must be residents of Tennessee with a valid Tennessee mailing address. They must demonstrate that art is part of their livelihood and that they make a significant portion of their income from their art. Full-time students in a degree program are not eligible for this fellowship. Applicants should visit the commission's Web site to view the categories for which the organization is accepting applications for the current year. Disciplines vary by year. *Application Process: Applicants should submit an online application along with supporting materials. A new eGRANT system is now being used. Applicants should apply online, print a copy of the completed application, and submit the copy with the required supporting work samples. For a detailed explanation of supporting materials in each artistic category,

visit the commission's Web site. *Amount: $5,000. *Deadline: January 30.

Vermont Arts Council

Attn: Michele Bailey, Director of Creation & Foundation Programs

136 State Street, Drawer 33

Montpelier, VT 05633-6001

802-828-3294

mbailey@vermontartscouncil.org

http://www.vermontartscouncil.org/grants/documents/ for_artists.html

Grant Name: Grants for Artists. *Academic Area: Media arts, performing arts (open), visual arts (open), writing. *Age Group: Adults. *Eligibility: Applicants must be at least 18 years of age and have lived in Vermont for at least one year prior to application. Full-time students in a degree program are not eligible for these grants. The council offers more than one type of individual grant. Visit its Web site to learn more. All grants require a 1:1 cash match. Applicants will need to raise equal funds in order to be eligible for an award. *Application Process: Applicants should submit a completed application along with an artist narrative, a project timeline, a budget, supporting work samples, proof of Vermont residency, and a $10 application fee. Applicants should visit the council's Web site for complete details on how to submit work samples. *Amount: $250 to $5,000. *Deadline: Deadlines vary. Visit the council's Web site for detailed information.

Virginia Commission for the Arts

Lewis House, 223 Governor Street, Second Floor

Richmond, VA 23219

804-225-3132

arts@arts.virginia.gov

http://www.arts.virginia.gov/artist%20fellowships.htm

Fellowship Name: Artist Fellowship. *Academic Area: Media arts, performing arts (open), visual arts (open), writing. *Age Group: Adults. *Eligibility: Applicants must be at least 18 years of age and legal residents of Virginia who plan to reside in the state for the duration of the fellowship period. Applicants must not be full-time students in a degree program. This organization offers fellowships in rotating disciplines. In one year applicants may apply in categories such as playwriting and sculpture. Two new categories will be chosen for the following year. Interested applicants should visit the commission's

Web site to view the current categories, or contact the organization for more information. *Application Process: Applicants should submit a completed application along with an information page, an artist narrative, work samples, and a resume. Applicants should visit the commission's Web site for complete details on how to submit work samples in each category. *Amount: $5,000. *Deadline: August 1.

Washington State Arts Commission
Attn: Willie Smyth, Program Manager
PO Box 42675
Olympia, WA 98504-2675
360-586-2856
willies@arts.wa.gov
http://www.arts.wa.gov
Fellowship Name: Folk Arts Fellowship. *Academic Area: Visual arts (folk). *Age Group: Adults. *Eligibility: Applicants must be traditional artists, residents of Washington, and demonstrate a commitment to preserving endangered art forms. They should also demonstrate a commitment to their communities. *Application Process: Applicants should submit a completed application along with supporting work samples, which include photos or slides, audio or videotapes, exhibit brochures or clippings, and optional letters of support. Visit the commission's Web site to download an application. *Amount: $5,000. *Deadline: April 22.

West Virginia Commission on the Arts
Attn: Jeff Pierson, Individual Artist Coordinator
The Cultural Center
1900 Kanawha Boulevard East
Charleston, WV 25305-0300
304-558-0240, ext. 717
jeff.pierson@wvculture.org
http://www.wvculture.org/arts/grants/fy06artistfellow.
pdf
Fellowship Name: Artist Fellowships. *Academic Area: Performing arts (open), visual arts (open), writing.

*Age Group: Adults. *Eligibility: Applicants must be at least 18 years old and residents of West Virginia for at least one year. Full-time students in a degree program are not eligible for these fellowships. Fellowships are offered in varying categories, which rotate on a yearly basis. Applicants should visit the commission's Web site to view additional eligibility requirements for the category in which they intend to apply and to see if applications are currently being accepted in their artistic discipline. *Application Process: Applicants should submit two copies of the completed application along with work samples (as specified for the category), a resume, and a self-addressed, stamped envelope and postcard. Visit the commission's Web site to download an application. *Amount: $3,500. *Deadline: September 1.

Wisconsin Arts Board
101 East Wilson Street, First Floor
Madison, WI 53702
608-266-0190
http://www.arts.state.wi.us/static/fellwshp.htm
Fellowship Name: Artist Fellowship Awards. *Academic Area: Media arts, performing arts (open), visual arts (open), writing. *Age Group: Adults. *Eligibility: Applicants must be at least 18 years old and residents of Wisconsin for at least one year. Those attending a college degree program are not eligible for these fellowships. Fellowships are offered in varying categories, which rotate on a yearly basis. In even numbered years, applicants may apply in the categories of literary arts, music composition, choreography, and performance art. Visual and media arts applicants may apply in odd-numbered years. *Application Process: Applicants apply online via the eGRANT system. Hard copies of the application and work samples must also be mailed. Applicants should visit the board's Web site for additional updates. This program is currently under review, and procedures may change. *Amount: $8,000. *Deadline: September 15.

VOCATIONAL EDUCATION— UNDERGRADUATE

The following financial aid resources are available to students who are interested in studying vocational education-related majors at the undergraduate level.

Aircraft Electronics Association Educational Foundation
4217 South Hocker
Independence, MO 64055
816-373-6565
info@aea.net
http://www.aea.net/EducationalFoundation/scholarship.asp?Category=4
Scholarship Name: Aircraft Electronics Association Educational Foundation Scholarship Program. *Academic Area: Aviation maintenance. *Age Group: Undergraduate students. *Eligibility: Applicants must be high school seniors or undergraduate students seeking careers in the aircraft electronics and aviation maintenance industry. Applicants must maintain a minimum 2.5 GPA on a 4.0 scale. Depending on scholarship, applicants may need to be Aircraft Electronics Association members or dependents of members. Visit the foundation's Web site to learn more about eligibility requirements for specific scholarships. *Application Process: Applicants must submit a completed application, official transcripts, a letter of recommendation, and a personal statement. Visit the foundation's Web site to review and download applications. *Amount: Varies. *Deadline: February 15.

Air Traffic Control Association
Attn: Scholarship Fund
1101 King Street, Suite 300
Alexandria, VA 22314
703-299-2430
info@atca.org
http://www.atca.org/activities/scholarships.asp
Scholarship Name: Air Traffic Control Association Scholarship. *Academic Area: Aviation. *Age Group: College students. *Eligibility: Applicants must meet one of the following four eligibility categories: (1) students enrolled half- to full-time in a two- to four-year air traffic control program at an institution approved and/or licensed by the Federal Aviation Administration (FAA) as directly supporting the FAA's college and training initiative; (2) students enrolled half- to full-time in a program leading to a bachelor's degree or higher in an aviation-related course of study; (3) full-time employees enrolled in advanced study programs to improve their skills in air traffic control or an aviation discipline; (4) U.S. citizens, children of air traffic control specialists enrolled half- to full-time in a program leading to a bachelor's degree or higher. *Application Process: Applicants should visit the association's Web site for specific eligibility requirements related to each of the four above-mentioned categories. Applicants should submit a completed application along with two letters of recommendation, transcripts, a statement of financial need, and an essay. Visit the association's Web site to download the appropriate application. *Amount: Awards vary. *Deadline: Contact the association for deadline information.

American Academy of Chefs (AAC)
180 Center Place Way
St. Augustine, FL 32095
904-824-4468, 800-624-9458
http://www.acfchefs.org/academy/aacschol2.html
Scholarship Name: American Academy of Chefs Chair's Scholarship. *Academic Area: Culinary arts. *Age Group: Undergraduate students. *Eligibility: Applicants must be full-time culinary students attending a two- or four-year accredited, postsecondary school of culinary arts (or other postsecondary culinary training program acceptable to the AAC). Applicants must have completed at least one semester, quarter or trimester, be an exemplary student, and have a career goal of becoming a chef or pastry chef. *Application Process: Applicants should submit a completed application along with two letters of recommendation, a financial aid release form, and a sealed official transcript showing GPA. Visit the academy's Web site to download an official application. *Amount: $1,000. *Deadline: July 1.

American Board of Funeral Service Education Inc.
Attn: Scholarship Committee
38 Florida Avenue
Portland, ME 04103

207-878-6530
gconnic1@main.rr.com
http://www.abfse.org/html/scholarship.html
Scholarship Name: American Board of Funeral Service Education National Scholarship Program. *Academic Area: Mortuary science. *Age Group: Undergraduate students. *Eligibility: Applicants must be U.S. citizens who have completed at least one semester (or quarter) of study in a program in funeral service or mortuary science education accredited by the American Board of Funeral Service Education. To be considered for a full award, they must have at least one term or semester remaining in their program, which will commence after the award. Partial awards may be given to students with less than one full term of study remaining. *Application process: Applicants must submit a completed application, a personal statement, a letter of recommendation, college transcripts, and federal tax form 1040. Applications can be obtained from the financial aid officer at each board college or downloaded at the board's Web site. *Amount: $250 or $500. * Deadline: March 17.

American Congress on Surveying and Mapping
Attn: Pat Canfield
6 Montgomery Village Avenue, Suite 403
Gaithersburg, MD 20879
240-632-9716, ext. 113
pat.canfield@acsm.net
http://www.acsm.net/scholar.html
Scholarship Name: American Congress on Surveying and Mapping (ACSM) Scholarships. *Academic Area: Surveying. *Age Group: Undergraduate students. *Eligibility: Applicants must be members of the ACSM, pursuing careers in surveying or mapping, and demonstrate financial need. The scholarship is also available to graduate students. *Application Process: Applicants should submit a completed application along with proof of membership in the ACSM; a brief statement of their educational objectives, professional activities, and financial need; three letters of recommendation; and official transcripts. Visit the organization's Web site for a complete list of individual scholarships, specific eligibility requirements, and a downloadable application. *Amount: $500 to $2,000. *Deadline: December 1.

American Hotel and Lodging Educational Foundation
1201 New York Avenue, NW, Suite 600
Washington, DC 20005-3931

202-289-3188
ahlef@ahlef.org
http://www.ahlef.org/scholarships_aaa_five_diamond.asp
Scholarship Name: AAA Five Diamond Hospitality Scholarship. *Academic Area: Hospitality. *Age Group: Undergraduate students. *Eligibility: Each year, AAA selects one of the four-year programs participating in the American Hotel and Lodging Educational Foundation's Annual Scholarship Grant Program to receive the award. The school then selects the scholarship recipient based upon a set of minimum eligibility criteria. Visit the foundation's Web site to learn which institution has been granted the award for the upcoming year. *Application Process: If you are attending the appointed institution, visit your dean's office to inquire about the application process. *Amount: $5,000. *Deadline: Deadlines vary.

American Hotel and Lodging Educational Foundation
1201 New York Avenue, NW, Suite 600
Washington, DC 20005-3931
202-289-3188
ahlef@ahlef.org
http://www.ahlef.org/scholarships_ecolab.asp
Scholarship Name: Academic Ecolab Scholarship. *Academic Area: Hospitality. *Age Group: Undergraduate students. *Eligibility: Applicants must be enrolled or intend to enroll fulltime in a U.S. baccalaureate or associate hospitality degree-granting program for both the upcoming fall and spring semesters. The applicant's school does not have to be affiliated with the foundation. High school seniors may apply. *Application Process: Applicants should submit a completed application along with their most recent transcripts, a copy of their college curriculum as described in the college catalog, and copies of tax form 1040. Visit the foundation's Web site to download an application or to apply directly online. *Amount: $1,000 for enrollment in a two-year program; $2,000 for enrollment in a four-year program. *Deadline: Quarterly (January 1, April 1, July 1, and October 1).

American Hotel and Lodging Educational Foundation
1201 New York Avenue, NW, Suite 600
Washington, DC 20005-3931
202-289-3188
ahlef@ahlef.org
http://www.ahlef.org/scholarships_extended_stay.asp

Scholarship Name: American Hotel and Lodging Association Extended Stay Council Scholarship. *Academic Area: Hospitality. *Age Group: Undergraduate students. *Eligibility: Applicants must have previous work experience at an extended stay property and a desire to pursue their professional careers in the extended stay segment of the hotel industry. *Application Process: Applicants should submit a completed application along with a copy of their letter of college admittance, a statement of financial need and a copy of tax form 1040, a personal essay (maximum 500 words), two letters of recommendation, and official transcripts (including high school transcripts). One original packet and three copies should be submitted. Visit the association's Web site to download an application. *Amount: $500 to $2,000. *Deadline: June 15.

American Hotel and Lodging Educational Foundation
1201 New York Avenue, NW, Suite 600
Washington, DC 20005-3931
202-289-3188
ahlef@ahlef.org
http://www.ahlef.org/scholarships_annual_grant.asp
Scholarship Name: Annual Scholarship Grant Program. *Academic Area: Hospitality. *Age Group: Undergraduate students. *Eligibility: Applicants must be attending one of the 79 universities or colleges affiliated with the American Hotel and Lodging Educational Foundation (AH&LEF). Affiliated schools are comprised of approved two- and four-year hospitality management programs in the United States. Interested applicants should contact their department or the foundation to verify eligibility. *Application Process: Applicants receiving these scholarships are selected by their respective schools—not by the Foundation. The schools are required to use a set of minimum eligibility requirements designated by AH&LEF when selecting the scholarship recipients. Some of AH&LEF's criteria include full-time enrollment status, minimum GPA of 3.0, U.S. citizenship or permanent U.S. resident status, and completion of at least one or two years of school. A few scholarships have slightly different criteria, depending on the program. Interested students should contact the dean's office at their school for more details. *Amount: Awards vary. *Deadline: Contact your dean's office for deadlines. Schools must submit their student nominations to the foundation by May 1.

American Hotel and Lodging Educational Foundation
1201 New York Avenue, NW, Suite 600
Washington, DC 20005-3931
202-289-3188
ahlef@ahlef.org
http://www.ahlef.org/scholarships_packard_memorial.asp
Scholarship Name: Arthur J. Packard Memorial Scholarship. *Academic Area: Hospitality. *Age Group: Undergraduate students. *Eligibility: The applicant's university must be an affiliated four-year program of the American Hotel and Lodging Educational Foundation, and the applicant must demonstrate outstanding academic achievement. *Application Process: Each university nominates the one student most qualified according to the criteria to compete in the competition. Students should express their interest in the scholarship to their dean's office for consideration in the nomination and application process. Visit the foundation's Web site for a listing of eligible four-year institutions. *Amount: $5,000 for first place, $3,000 for second place, and $2,000 for third place. *Deadline: April 1.

American Hotel and Lodging Educational Foundation
1201 New York Avenue, NW, Suite 600
Washington, DC 20005-3931
202-289-3188
ahlef@ahlef.org
http://www.ahlef.org/scholarships_pepsi.asp
Scholarship Name: Pepsi Scholarship. *Academic Area: Hospitality. *Age Group: Undergraduate students. *Eligibility: Applicants must be graduating seniors from the Marriott Hospitality High School located in Washington, D.C. They must also be admitted to an undergraduate hospitalityrelated degree granting program at a college or university for the upcoming academic year. *Application Process: Applicants should inquire in their principal's office for consideration of this scholarship. *Amount: Awards vary. *Deadline: Inquire at your high school principal's office for deadline information.

American Public Transportation Association (APTA)
1666 K Street, NW, Suite 1100
Washington, DC 20006
202-496-4800
pboswell@apta.com
http://www.apta.com/services/human_resources/program_guidelines.cfm
Scholarship Name: Dan M. Reichard Jr. Scholarship. *Academic Area: Business administration/

management, transportation. *Age Group: Undergraduate students. *Eligibility: Applicants must demonstrate dedication to pursuing careers in the business administration/management area of the transit industry. They must also be enrolled in a fully accredited institution, maintain at least a 3.0 GPA (B) in course work that is relevant to the industry or required of a degree program, and either be employed by or demonstrate a strong interest in entering the public transportation industry. College sophomores (30 hours or more satisfactorily completed), juniors, seniors, or those seeking advanced degrees may apply for scholarships. *Application Process: Any APTA member organization may nominate and sponsor candidates for the scholarship programs. Applicants must submit a completed application, letter of nomination, essay, three letters of recommendation, a copy of their completed Free Application for Financial Student Aid (FAFSA) form, official school transcripts, verification of enrollment, and a copy of the fee schedule. Visit the foundation's Web site to download an application. *Amount: $2,500. *Deadline: June 17.

American Public Transportation Association (APTA)
1666 K Street, NW, Suite 1100
Washington, DC 20006
202-496-4800
http://www.apta.com/services/human_resources/
program_guidelines.cfm
Scholarship Name: Jack R. Gilstrap Scholarship.
*Academic Area: Transportation. *Age Group: Undergraduate students. *Eligibility: Applicants must demonstrate dedication to pursuing careers in the transit industry and display a high level of academic/personal achievement. Applicants must be enrolled in a fully accredited institution, maintain at least a 3.0 GPA (B) in course work that is relevant to the industry or required of a degree program, and either be employed by or demonstrate a strong interest in entering the public transportation industry. College sophomores (30 hours or more satisfactorily completed), juniors, seniors, or those seeking advanced degrees may apply for scholarships. *Application Process: Any APTA member organization may nominate and sponsor candidates for the scholarship programs. Applicants must submit a completed application, a letter of nomination, an essay, three letters of

recommendation, a copy of their completed FAFSA form, official school transcripts, verification of enrollment, and copy of the fee schedule. Visit the foundation's Web site to download an application. *Amount: $2,500. *Deadline: June 17.

American Society for Enology and Viticulture (ASEV)
Attn: ASEV Scholarship Committee
PO Box 1855
Davis, CA 95617-1855
530-753-3142
society@asev.org
http://www.asev.org
Scholarship Name: American Society for Enology and Viticulture Scholarship. *Academic Area: Enology/viticulture. *Age Group: Undergraduate students. *Eligibility: Applicants must be undergraduate students enrolled in or accepted into a full-time accredited four-year college or university program. They must reside in North America (Canada, Mexico, or the United States). Applicants should be a minimum of junior status for the upcoming academic year. They must also have maintained a minimum 3.0 GPA and graduate applicants a 3.2 GPA on a 4.0 scale. Applicants must be enrolled in a major emphasizing enology or viticulture, or in a curriculum emphasizing a science basic to the wine and grape industry. The scholarship is also available to graduate students. *Application Process: Applicants must submit a completed application, a student questionnaire, a statement of intent, original transcripts, a list of courses for the upcoming year, and two original letters of recommendation. Visit the society's Web site to download an application. *Amount: Varies. *Deadline: March 1.

American Society for Horticultural Science
113 South West Street, Suite 200
Alexandria, VA 22314-2851
703-836-4606
mmcguire@ashs.org http://www.ashs.org/awards/
student.html
Award Name: American Society for Horticultural Science Scholars Award. *Academic Area: Horticulture. *Age Group: Undergraduate students. *Eligibility: Applicants must be full-time students majoring in horticulture at a four-year institution of higher education and must demonstrate commitment to the horticulture science profession and related career fields. Scholarship will also be granted based upon

the student's class standing at the time of application; excellence in academic and scholastic performance; participation in extracurricular, leadership, and research activities relating to horticulture; participation in university and community service; and related horticultural experience. *Application Process: Applicants must be nominated by the chair/head of the department in which they are majoring. Applicants must submit an application form, a 250- to 500-word essay, a resume, three reference letters, and official college transcripts. Visit the society's Web site to download an application. *Amount: $1,500. *Deadline: February 4.

American Society for Horticultural Science

Attn: Collegiate Scholars Award
113 South West Street, Suite 200
Alexandria, VA 22314-2851
703-836-4606
ashs@ashs.org
http://www.ashs.org/awards/student.html
Award Name: Collegiate Scholars Award. *Academic Area: Horticulture. *Age Group: Undergraduate students. *Eligibility: Applicants must be junior and senior undergraduates majoring in horticulture whose academic standing is in the top 15 percent of their class. Students will be selected by their departments on the basis of their scholarship achievements, leadership abilities, participation in campus/club activities, and services to their departments. *Application Process: Departments will submit their nominations to the society. Visit the society's Web site for more information. *Amount: Varies. *Deadline: February 11.

American Society for Horticultural Science

113 South West Street, Suite 200
Alexandria, VA 22314-2851
703-836-4606
mmcguire@ashs.org
http://www.ashs.org/awards/student.html
Scholarship Name: E. Ted Sims Jr. Memorial Scholarship. *Academic Area: Horticulture. *Age Group: Undergraduate students. *Eligibility: Applicants must be registered as full-time students, with junior or senior class standing beginning in the fall of the award year, who demonstrate a commitment to the horticulture profession, excellence in academic performance in the major, and participation in extracurricular activities relating to horticulture.

*Application Process: Applicants must be nominated by the chair/head of the department in which they are majoring. Applicants must submit an application form, a 250- to 500-word essay, a resume, three reference letters, and official college transcripts. Visit the society's Web site to download an application. *Amount: $1,000. *Deadline: February 4.

American Society of Transportation and Logistics

Attn: Scholarship Judging Panel
1700 North Moore Street, Suite 1900
Arlington, VA 22209-1904
703-524-5011
astl@nitl.org
http://www.astl.org/scholar.htm
Scholarship Name: L.L. Waters Scholarship. *Academic Area: Transportation. *Age Group: Undergraduate students. *Eligibility: Applicants must be in their junior year at a fully accredited four-year U.S. college or university, who are enrolled in a degree program in which transportation/logistics is their area of concentration. Applicants must demonstrate scholastic achievement and commitment to the pursuit of a professional career in transportation/logistics. The scholarship is also available to graduate students. *Application Process: Applicants must submit a completed application, a letter of intent, official transcripts, and two letters of recommendation. Visit the society's Web site to download an application. *Amount: $2,000. *Deadline: September 30.

Appraisal Institute Education Trust

Attn: Olivia Carreon
550 West Van Buren Street, Suite 1000
Chicago, IL 60607
312-335-4100
ocarreon@appraisalinstitute.org
http://www.appraisalinstitute.org/education/downloads/AIET_Info.pdf
Scholarship Name: Appraisal Institute Education Trust Scholarship. *Academic Area: Real estate. *Age Group: Undergraduate students. *Eligibility: Applicants must be U.S. citizens attending a community college or four-year college full time, and majoring in real estate appraisal, land economics, or a real estate related field. They must be sophomores, juniors, or seniors. The scholarship is also available to graduate students. *Application Process: Applicants should request further information from the

institute. Applications are available in November. *Amount: $2,000 undergraduate students, $3,000 graduate students. *Deadline: March 15.

Associated General Contractors (AGC) of America

AGC Education and Research Foundation
2300 Wilson Boulevard, Suite 400
Arlington, VA 22201
703-837-5342
sladef@agc.org
http://www.agc.org/page.ww?section=AGC+Foundation
&name=Undergraduate+Scholarships
Scholarship Name: Associated General Contractors Foundation Undergraduate Construction Education Scholarship. *Academic Area: Construction trades. *Age Group: Undergraduate students. *Eligibility: Applicants must be full-time students who are college sophomores or juniors enrolled or planning to enroll in a full-time, four- or five-year Accreditation Board for Engineering and Technology- or American Council for Construction Education-accredited construction management or construction-related engineering program. Applicants must be U.S. citizens or be documented permanent residents of the United States. *Application Process: Applications will be available in July. Applicants must submit a completed application, two evaluation forms, transcripts, and notification of receipt postcard. Visit the foundation's Web site to download an application. *Amount: $2,000 per year ($6,000 maximum for renewal). *Deadline: November 1.

Associated General Contractors (AGC) of America

AGC Education and Research Foundation
333 John Carlyle Street, Suite 200
Alexandria, VA 22314
703-548-3318
agcf@agc.org
http://www.agc.org/page.ww?section=AGC+Foundatio
n&name=James+L.+Allhands+Student+Essay+Com
petition
Scholarship Name: James L. Allhands Essay Competition. *Academic Area: Construction trades, engineering (construction). *Age Group: Undergraduate students. *Eligibility: Applicants must be senior-level students in four- or five-year Accreditation Board for Engineering Technology or American Council for Construction Education-accredited university construction management or construction-related engineering programs.

*Application Process: Applicants must submit one original and two copies of an essay (no longer than 10 pages) and an essay abstract. Visit the foundation's Web site to download an application. *Amount: $300 to $1,000. *Deadline: November 1.

Automotive Hall of Fame

Automotive Educational Fund
21400 Oakwood Boulevard
Dearborn, MI 48124
313-240-4000
http://www.automotivehalloffame.org/scholarships.php
Scholarship Name: Automotive Hall of Fame Scholarships. *Academic Area: Automotive. *Age Group: Undergraduate students. *Eligibility: Applicants must possess an automotive career interest. Applicants must be accepted (high school seniors) or attending an accredited college, university, or trade school within the United States, with satisfactory to superior academic progress, at the time of application and be enrolled full-time. Eligibility requirements vary by scholarship. Visit the Hall of Fame's Web site for specific scholarship eligibility requirements. *Application Process: Applicants must submit a completed application, official transcripts, two letters of recommendation, and a letter of acceptance to degree program. Visit the Hall of Fame's Web site to download an application. *Amount: Varies. *Deadline: May 30.

Connecticut Funeral Directors Association Inc.

Attn: John Cascio
350 Silas Deane Highway, Suite 202
Wethersfield, CT 06109
860-721-0234
connfda@aol.com
http://www.ctfda.org/html/scholarship-mortuary.html
Scholarship Name: Mortuary Science Scholarship. *Academic Area: Mortuary science. *Age Group: Undergraduate students. *Eligibility: Applicants must be students who plan to complete their education in an accredited mortuary science school and serve the public in their chosen profession in the state of Connecticut. They also must be legal residents of the state of Connecticut. *Application Process: Applicants submit a completed application, transcripts, proof of Connecticut residency, and two essays. Visit the association's Web site to download an application. *Amount: $1,000. *Deadline: November 1.

ConstructMyFuture.com

Attn: Nicole Hallada
Association of Equipment Manufacturers
111 East Wisconsin Avenue, Suite 1000
Milwaukee, WI 53202
866-AEM-0442
nhallada@aem.org
http://www.constructmyfuture.com/stu-scholarships.
html

Scholarship Name: ConstructMyFuture Scholarship.
*Academic Area: Construction trades. *Age Group:
Undergraduate students. *Eligibility: Applicants
must be planning on attending post-secondary
programs in any construction industry related field.
High school seniors may apply. *Application Process:
Interested applicants should email the contact
person listed above for information on obtaining
an application. Visit the Web site for future updates.
*Amount: Awards vary. *Deadline: Contact the
organization for deadline information.

Cosmetology Advancement Foundation

Access to Cosmetology Education Grant Program
PO Box 811, FDR Station
New York, NY 10150-0811
212-750-2412
http://www.cosmetology.org/ace2.pdf

Grant Name: Access to Cosmetology Education Grant.
*Academic Area: Cosmetology *Age Group: Open.
*Eligibility: Applicants should contact the foundation
for information about the eligibility and availability
of the grant. *Application Process: Applicants
should contact the foundation for an application
and application procedures. *Amount: Awards vary.
*Deadline: Contact the foundation for deadline
information.

The Culinary Trust

Attn: Trina Gribbins
304 West Liberty Street, Suite 201
Louisville, KY 40202
800-928-4227, ext.264
tgribbins@hqtrs.com
http://www.iacpfoundation.com/html/scholarships.html

Scholarship Name: The Culinary Trust Scholarship
Program. *Academic Area: Culinary arts. *Age Group:
Undergraduate students. *Eligibility: Applicants
must have two years of foodservice experience
(either paid or volunteer or a combination of
the two). Students and professionals may apply.

Applicants who are currently students must maintain
a 3.0 GPA. Eligibility requirements vary depending
on the specific scholarship. Visit the trust's Web site
or contact the trust to obtain detailed eligibility
requirements for specific scholarships. *Application
Process: Applicants must submit a completed
application, a two-page essay, two letters of
recommendation, a budget and tentative travel
dates (if applying for an independent research
scholarship), and $25 application fee. Visit the trust's
Web site to download an application. *Amount:
Varies. *Deadline: December 15.

Experimental Aircraft Association (EAA)

John D. Odegard School of Aerospace Sciences
University of North Dakota
PO Box 9007
Grand Forks, ND 58202-9007
800-258-1525
flyund@aero.und.edu
http://www.youngeagles.org/programs/scholarships

Scholarship Name: Clay Lacy Professional Pilot
Scholarship. *Academic Area: Aviation. *Age Group:
Undergraduate students. *Eligibility: Applicants
must plan to attend a professional pilot program
at the University of North Dakota (UND), John D.
Odegard School of Aerospace Sciences, to earn
a college degree as a professional pilot and earn
commercial, instrument, multi-engine and all
fixed-wing flight instructor ratings. Scholarship
winners must participate in flight by living on
the EAA Air Academy campus, supporting EAA
programs, activities and events. Applicants must
demonstrate financial need, attend UND, meet
FAA criteria for licensure, and must have their
private pilot's certificate to be eligible for the
scholarship. Applicants must be well rounded
and involved in school/community activities and
aviation. Applicants must also be current members
of EAA or recommended by a current EAA member.
*Application Process: Applicants must contact the
John D. Odegard School of Aerospace Science at
UND to obtain an application and for application
details. *Amount: Up to $12,500 per year. *Deadline:
Varies.

Experimental Aircraft Association (EAA)

Attn: EAA Scholarship Department
PO Box 3086
Oshkosh, WI 54903-3086

920-426-6815
scholarships@eaa.org
http://www.youngeagles.org/programs/scholarships
Scholarship Name: EAA Achievement in Aviation
Scholarship. *Academic Area: Aviation. *Age Group:
Undergraduate students. *Eligibility: Applicants
must be active in recreational aviation endeavors
and pursuing further aviation education or training.
They must also be well rounded and involved in
school/community activities and aviation. Academic
records should show that applicants have the ability
to successfully complete the program in which they
seek a scholarship. Applicants must also be current
members of EAA or recommended by a current EAA
member. *Application Process: Applicants must visit
the association's Web site to complete and submit
an online application. *Amount: $500. *Deadline:
March 1.

Experimental Aircraft Association (EAA)
Attn: EAA Scholarship Department
PO Box 3086
Oshkosh, WI 54903-3086
920-426-6815
scholarships@eaa.org
http://www.youngeagles.org/programs/scholarships
Scholarship Name: H.P. "Bud" Milligan Aviation
Scholarship. *Academic Area: Aviation. *Age Group:
Undergraduate students. *Eligibility: Applicants
must be students enrolled in an accredited aviation
program at a college, technical school, or aviation
academy. Academic records should show that
applicants have the ability to successfully complete
the program in which they seek a scholarship.
Financial need is not a requirement. Applicants
must also be well rounded and involved in school/
community activities and aviation and current
members of EAA or recommended by a current EAA
member. *Application Process: Applicants must visit
the association's Web site to complete and submit
an online application. *Amount: $1,000 (renewable).
*Deadline: March 1.

Experimental Aircraft Association (EAA)
Attn: EAA Scholarship Department
PO Box 3086
Oshkosh, WI 54903-3086
920-426-6815
scholarships@eaa.org
http://www.youngeagles.org/programs/scholarships

Scholarship Name: Herbert L. Cox Memorial
Scholarship. *Academic Area: Aviation. *Age Group:
Undergraduate students. *Eligibility: Applicants
must be accepted or attending a four-year accredited
college or university pursuing a degree leading to an
aviation profession. Applicants must demonstrate
financial need, be well rounded, and involved in
school/community activities and aviation. They must
also be current members of EAA or recommended
by a current EAA member. *Application Process:
Applicants must visit the association's Web site to
complete and submit an online application. *Amount:
$500. *Deadline: March 1.

Floriculture Industry Research and Scholarship Trust
PO Box 280
East Lansing, MI 48826-0280
517-333-4617
first@firstinfloriculture.org
http://www.firstinfloriculture.org/schl_req_app.htm
Scholarship Name: First Scholarship. *Academic Area:
Horticulture. *Age Group: Undergraduate students.
*Eligibility: Applicants must be pursuing a career in
a horticulture-related field and maintain a minimum
3.0 GPA. They must also be citizens or residents of
the United States or Canada or be enrolled in an
accredited educational institution in the United
States or Canada. *Application Process: Contact the
trust in January to obtain information on application
details. *Amount: Varies. *Deadline: May 1.

Florida Funeral Directors Association
228 Lafayette Circle
Tallahassee, FL 32303
850-224-1969, 800-226-3332
ffdamember@ffda.org
http://www.ffda.org/scholarship.html
Scholarship Name: Florida Funeral Directors
Association Scholarship. *Academic Area: Mortuary
science. *Age Group: Undergraduate students.
*Eligibility: Applicants must be students enrolled in
mortuary science programs in accredited mortuary
science schools who plan to serve the profession in
the state of Florida. They also must have completed
at least 30 hours of study and maintained at least
a 2.5 GPA. Applicants must not have received
any marks of D in any required mortuary science
classes. They also must be residents of Florida and
student members of the Florida Funeral Directors
Association. *Application Process: Applicants must

submit a completed application, transcripts, proof of Florida residency (two forms), and two 500-word essays. Visit the association's Web site to download an application. *Amount: Varies. *Deadline: Varies.

Funeral Service Foundation (FSF)

Attn: FSF Scholarship Committee
Joseph E. Hagan Memorial Scholarship
13625 Bishop's Drive
Brookfield, WI 53005-6607
877-402-5900
fsf@funeralservicefoundation.org
http://www.funeralservicefoundation.org/scholarships/
FuneralServiceFoundation-JoeHaganbio.htm

Scholarship Name: Joseph E. Hagan Memorial Scholarship. *Academic Area: Mortuary science. *Age Group: Undergraduate students. *Eligibility: Applicants must be full-time students enrolled in or accepted for enrollment in a mortuary science program accredited by the American Board of Funeral Service Education. *Application Process: Applicants must submit two copies of an application checklist, a completed application, enrollment verification, and an essay. Visit the foundation's Web site to download an application. *Amount: $1,000. *Deadline: April 30.

Funeral Service Foundation (FSF)

13625 Bishop's Drive
Brookfield, WI 53005-6607
877-402-5900
fsf@funeralservicefoundation.org
http://www.funeralservicefoundation.org/scholarships/
FuneralServiceFoundation-Keystone.htm

Scholarship Name: Key Memories™ Scholarship Essay Contest. *Academic Area: Mortuary science. *Age Group: Undergraduate students. *Eligibility: Applicants must be studying mortuary sciences at an accredited institution. *Application Process: Applicants must submit an essay covering a designated topic. Applicants can obtain applications from their faculty advisors, through the FSF Web site, or at http://www.keystonegroup.com. *Amount: $1,000. *Deadline: Varies.

Garden Club of America

Attn: Mrs. Nancy Stevenson
Grosscup Scholarship Committee
Cleveland Botanical Garden
11030 East Boulevard
Cleveland, OH 44106
Fax: 216-753-8287
http://www.gcamerica.org/scholarship/grosscup.html

Scholarship Name: Katharine M. Grosscup Scholarship. *Academic Area: Horticulture. *Age Group: Undergraduate students. *Eligibility: Applicants must be current college sophomores, juniors, or seniors majoring in horticulture or a related field. Preference is given to residents of Indiana, Kentucky, Michigan, Ohio, Pennsylvania, and West Virginia. Applicants must maintain a B average or better. The scholarship is also available to graduate students. *Application Process: Applicants must submit a completed application, two letters of recommendation, and official transcripts. Finalists must attend a personal interview in Cleveland. Visit the club's Web site to download an application. *Amount: Up to $3,000. *Deadline: February 1.

General Aviation Manufacturers Association

GAMA Education Office
1400 K Street, NW, Suite 801
Washington, DC 20005
202-393-1500
aved@GAMA.aero
http://www.gama.aero/resources/AVEducation/index.php

Award Name: Edward W. Stimpson Aviation Excellence Award. *Academic Area: Aviation. *Age Group: Undergraduate students. *Eligibility: Applicants must be high school seniors planning to attend a college or university with an aviation degree core. A 3.0 grade-point average, and community and school activities are required. *Application Process: Applicants should submit a completed application along with transcripts, letters of recommendation from teachers and school administrators, and a 750-word essay. Visit the association's Web site to download an application. *Amount: $500. *Deadline: April 28.

Hawaii Community Foundation

Attn: Scholarships
1164 Bishop Street, Suite 800
Honolulu, HI 96813
808-566-5570
http://www.hawaiicommunityfoundation.org/scholar/voced.php

Scholarship Name: Vocational Education Program. *Academic Area: Vocational education. *Age Group: Undergraduate students. *Eligibility: Applicants must be Hawaii residents who are enrolled in a vocational degree program in a select group of community colleges in Hawaii. This list is subject to change, so visit the foundation's Web site to see if your school is eligible. *Application Process: Applicants should submit a completed application along with a personal statement explaining their goals, career plans, and interests, and a letter of recommendation. Visit the foundation's Web site to download the application. *Amount: $500/semester for four semesters. *Deadline: July 1, October 2.

Helicopter Association International
Aviation Maintenance Technician Scholarship
1635 Prince Street
Alexandria, VA 22314-2818
703-683-4646
harold.summers@rotor.com
http://www.rotor.com/get.php?page=operations/awards.htm
Scholarship Name: Bill Sanderson Aviation Maintenance Technician Scholarship Award. *Academic Area: Aviation maintenance. *Age Group: Undergraduate students. *Eligibility: Applicants must be about to graduate from an FAA-approved PART 147 Aviation Maintenance Technician (AMT) school or a recent recipient of an Airframe and Powerplant certificate. *Application Process: Applicants must submit a completed two-part application. The first part of the application is to be completed by the applicant. The second part is to be completed by the AMT program director, administrator, or instructor. Visit the association's Web site to download an application. *Amount: $500 to $1,500, plus the expense of one course listed on the association's Web site. *Deadline: December 15.

H. H. Harris Foundation
30 South Wacker Drive, Suite 2300
Chicago, IL 60606
312-346-7900
JohnHH@aol.com
http://www.afsinc.org/Harris.htm
Scholarship Name: H.H. Harris Scholarship. *Academic Area: Foundry. *Age Group: Undergraduate students. *Eligibility: Applicants must be U.S. citizens and either students or professionals in the metallurgical and casting of metals field. *Application Process: Applicants should submit a completed application

and two letters of recommendation. Visit the foundation's Web site to download an application. *Amount: $1,000. *Deadline: June 30.

Hospitality Sales and Marketing Association International (HSMAI) Foundation
8201 Greensboro Drive, Suite 300
McLean, VA 22102
703-610-9024
info@hsmai.org
http://www.hsmai.org/Events/scholarship.cfm
Scholarship Name: Hospitality Sales and Marketing Association International Foundation Scholarship. *Academic Area: Hospitality. *Age Group: Undergraduate students. *Eligibility: Applicants must be either part- or full-time students pursuing careers in a hospitality management field. One scholarship is awarded to a part-time student and three are awarded to full-time students. Applicants should be members of HSMAI. The scholarship is also available to graduate students. *Application Process: HSMAI issues a call for entries for student scholarships each fall. Interested applicants should check the association's Web site for updated application information or contact the association. *Amount: Awards vary. *Deadline: Contact the association for deadline information.

Illinois Funeral Service Foundation
215 South Grand Avenue West
Springfield, IL 62704-3838
217-525-2000, 800-240-4332
info@ifda.org
http://www.ifda.org/education/scholarships.html
Scholarship Name: The Illinois Funeral Service Foundation Scholarship Program is available to students who attend one of the following schools of mortuary science: Southern Illinois University School of Mortuary Science (Carbondale), Malcolm X College (Chicago), Worsham's College, (Chicago), and Carl Sandburg College (Galesburg). *Academic Area: Mortuary science. *Age Group: Undergraduate students. *Eligibility: Applicants must be Illinois residents enrolled in one of the aforementioned mortuary science programs. The Foundation awards the scholarships directly to these institutions each year. The chosen educational institutions can then make their own eligibility requirements. *Application Process: Applicants should contact their educational institution to inquire about

scholarship availability and application details. *Amount: Varies. *Deadline: Varies.

International Association of Arson Investigators (IAAI)

Attn: Executive Director
12772 Boenker Road
Bridgeton, MO 63044
314-739-4224
jvanheest@beersanderson.com
http://www.firearson.com/ef/jcwscholar/index.asp

Scholarship Name: John Charles Wilson Scholarship Program. *Academic Area: Fire science/service, law enforcement. *Age Group: Undergraduate students. *Eligibility: Applicants must be members in good standing of the IAAI or the immediate family of a member; or the applicant must be recommended and sponsored by a member in good standing with the IAAI. Applicants must be enrolled or planning to enroll in the next scheduled semester of a two- or four-year accredited college or university that offers courses in police or fire sciences including fire investigation and related subjects. *Application Process: Applicants must complete an application, a personal statement, and submit with official transcripts. Visit the association's Web site to download an application. *Amount: $1,000. *Deadline: February 15.

International Executive Housekeepers Association Inc. (IEHA)

Attn: IEHA Scholarship Selection Committee
1001 Eastwind Drive, Suite 301
Westerville, OH 43081-3361
800-200-6342
http://www.ieha.org/education/scholarship_ieha.htm

Scholarship Name: International Executive Housekeepers Association Education/Scholarship Foundation Award. *Academic Area: Hospitality. *Age Group: Undergraduate students. *Eligibility: Applicants must be IEHA members enrolled in a program of study leading to an undergraduate degree, associate degree, or IEHA-approved certification programs that include a self-study course. *Application Process: Applicants must submit a completed application, one original and three copies of an original written manuscript concerning the housekeeping industry (i.e., inservice, management, AIDS, personal experience, hotel, healthcare, recycling, waste disposal, personnel

shortage, OSHA standards, etc), official transcripts, and letter of recommendation. Visit the association's Web site to download an application. *Amount: Up to $800. *Deadline: January 10.

International Executive Housekeepers Association (IEHA)

Attn: IEHA Scholarship Selection Committee
1001 Eastwind Drive, Suite 301
Westerville, OH 43081-3361
800-200-6342
http://www.ieha.org/education/scholarship_spartan.htm

Scholarship Name: Spartan Sponsored International Executive Housekeepers Association Scholarship Award. *Academic Area: Hospitality. *Age Group: Undergraduate students. *Eligibility: Applicants must be IEHA members or immediate family members who wish to pursue careers in executive housekeeping. *Application Process: Applicants must submit a completed application and personal statement. Visit the association's Web site to download an application. *Amount: $1,500. *Deadline: September 10.

International Food Service Executives Association (IFSEA)

IFSEA Administrative Office
836 San Bruno Avenue
Henderson, NV 89015
800-824-3732
HQ@ifsea.com
http://doclibrary.com/ASC19/DOC/scholarship5329.pdfm

Scholarship Name: International Food Service Executives Association Worthy Goal Scholarship. *Academic Area: Hospitality. *Age Group: Undergraduate students. *Eligibility: Applicants must be enrolled or accepted as a full-time student in a food service-related major at a two- or four-year college or university for the fall term. *Application Process: Applicants must submit a completed application, a personal financial statement summary, a personal statement, documentation of their work experience and leadership in student organizations, a statement of the scholarship's significance in achieving their career goals, official transcripts, and three letters of recommendation. Visit the association's Web site to download an application. *Amount: $500 to $1,000. *Deadline: February 1.

International Order of the Golden Rule

PO Box 28689
St. Louis, MO 63146-1189
800-637-8030
info@ogr.org
http://www.ogr.org/scholarships.php

Scholarship Name: Awards of Excellence Scholarship. *Academic Area: Mortuary science. *Age Group: Undergraduate students. *Eligibility: Applicants must be currently enrolled in an accredited mortuary science school and maintain at least a 3.0 GPA. They must also graduate after December 31 of the current year. *Application Process: Scholarship applications are available in January/February. Visit the organization's Web site for application details. *Amount: Varies. *Deadline: October 1.

International Order of the Golden Rule

PO Box 28689
St. Louis, MO 63146-1189
800-637-8030
info@ogr.org
http://www.ogr.org/scholarships.php

Scholarship Name: Koven L. Brown Scholarship Program. *Academic Area: Mortuary science. *Age Group: Undergraduate students. *Eligibility: Applicants must be currently enrolled in an accredited mortuary science school and maintain at least a 3.0 GPA. They must graduate after December 31 of the current year, and also demonstrate financial need. *Application Process: Applicants must submit a completed application, official transcripts, and evidence of financial need. Visit the organization's Web site to download an application. *Amount: $1,000. *Deadline: December 31.

Iowa Funeral Directors Association

2400 86th Street, Unit 22
Des Moines, IA 50322
515-270-0130, 800-982-6561
admin@iafda.org
http://www.iafda.org/displaycommon.cfm?an=1&subarticlenbr=24

Scholarship Name: Iowa Funeral Directors Association Scholarship Program. *Academic Area: Mortuary science. *Age Group: Undergraduate students. *Eligibility: Applicants must be legal Iowa residents who intend to practice funeral service in Iowa upon graduation, have completed two years and have accumulated 60 credit hours at an accredited college

or university, and be admitted to, or enrolled in, a program in funeral service or mortuary science education accredited by the American Board of Funeral Service Education. Students in coordinated programs are only eligible for an award during a period of attendance at an American Board-accredited institution. Applicants must also have at least one term or semester remaining in their programs, which will commence after the award date. Eligibility requirements vary by specific scholarship. Visit the association's Web site for specific scholarship eligibility requirements. *Application Process: Applicants must submit a completed application, transcripts, a letter of recommendation, and proof of Iowa residency. Visit the association's Web site to download an application. *Amount: $500 to $1,000. *Deadline: March 15.

ISA-The Instrumentation, Systems, and Automation Society

67 Alexander Drive
Research Triangle Park, NC 27709
919-549-8411
info@isa.org
http://www.isa.org/Content/NavigationMenu/General_Information/Careers/Scholarships/Scholarships.htm

Scholarship Name: ISA Educational Foundation Scholarship. *Academic Area: Automation. *Age Group: Undergraduate students. *Eligibility: Applicants must be enrolled full-time in an instrumentation, systems, or automation discipline at an education institution in their country of residence. They also must be in their sophomore year or higher and maintain at least a minimum 3.0 GPA. The scholarship is also available to graduate students. *Application Process: Applicants must submit one original and nine copies of a completed application, transcripts, a list of their activities and awards, an employment record, and an essay. Visit the foundation's Web site to download an application. *Amount: Varies. *Deadline: February 15.

James Beard Foundation

Attn: Scholarship Department
167 West 12th Street
New York, NY 10011
212-675-4984, ext. 311
http://www.jamesbeard.org

Scholarship Name: James Beard Foundation Scholarship. *Academic Area: Culinary arts. *Age Group: Undergraduate students. *Eligibility: Applicants must be aspiring culinary professionals who have not yet graduated from culinary school. Contact the foundation to learn more about specific scholarship eligibility requirements. *Application Process: Applicants must submit a completed application, two reference letters, a copy of the first two pages of their most recent Federal Income Tax Returns, official transcripts, an essay, and proof of residency. New scholarship applications are available each winter. Visit the foundation's Web site to download an application. *Amount: Up to $20,000. *Deadline: June 30.

Kansas Funeral Directors Association (KFDA) Foundation
PO Box 1904
Topeka, KS 66601
785-232-7789
kfda@kfda.kscoxmail.com
http://www.ksfda.org/educareer.htm
Scholarship Name: Kansas Funeral Directors Association Foundation Scholarship. *Academic Area: Mortuary science. *Age Group: Undergraduate students. *Eligibility: Applicants must be enrolled in a mortuary science program in Kansas with at least one, but no more than two semesters remaining following September 30. They also must demonstrate academic excellence, leadership, and financial need. *Application Process: Applicants must submit a completed application, transcripts, a personal statement, and a most recent tax return. Contact the KFDA to request an application. *Amount: Varies. *Deadline: September 30.

Maryland State Funeral Directors Association
Attn: Daniel T. Mulheran Memorial Scholarship
311 Crain Highway, SE
Glen Burnie, MD 21061
410-553-9106, 888-459-9693
msfda@msfda.net
http://www.msfda.net/scholarship.php
Scholarship Name: Daniel T. Mulheran Memorial Scholarship. *Academic Area: Mortuary science. *Age Group: Undergraduate students. *Eligibility: Applicants must be students who have completed at least two-thirds of their educational requirements, plan to complete their education in an accredited mortuary science school, maintain a GPQA of at least 2.5, and work in their chosen profession in the state of Maryland. *Application Process: Applicants must submit a completed application, two letters of recommendation, and two 500-word essays. Visit the association's Web site to download an application. *Amount: $1,000. *Deadline: October 1.

National Air Transportation Foundation
Dan L. Meisinger Sr. Memorial Learn to Fly Scholarship
4226 King Street
Alexandria, VA 22302
703-845-9000
http://www.nata.aero/about/sch_meisinger.jsp
Scholarship Name: Dan L. Meisinger Sr. Memorial Learn to Fly Scholarship. *Academic Area: Aviation. *Age Group: Undergraduate students. *Eligibility: Applicants must be college students currently enrolled in aviation programs with a minimum B-average or better. It is preferable for applicants to be recommended by aviation professionals and be residents of Kansas, Missouri, or Illinois. *Application Process: Applicants must submit a completed application. Visit the foundation's Web site to download an application. Contact the foundation to inquire about supporting documents necessary to accompany the application. There is a $5 application fee. *Amount: $2,500. *Deadline: Last Friday in November.

National Air Transportation Foundation
John E. Godwin Jr. Memorial Scholarship Fund
4226 King Street
Alexandria, VA 22302
703-845-9000
http://www.nata.aero/about/sch_godwin.jsp
Scholarship Name: John E. Godwin Jr. Memorial Scholarship. *Academic Area: Aviation. *Age Group: Open. *Eligibility: Applicants must be a minimum of 18 years old and be nominated and endorsed by a representative or a regular/associate member company of the National Air Transportation Association. Applicants must possess a Student Pilot certificate (or higher), with a third-class medical certificate, or with the possibility to qualify for a second-class medical certificate. They must also demonstrate a commitment to general aviation and preferably have a membership in good standing with the Civil Air Patrol. *Application Process: Applicants must submit a completed application and copies of an airman's certificate and current medical certificate. Visit the foundation's Web site to download an application. Contact the foundation to inquire about any additional supporting documents necessary to accompany the application. *Amount: $2,500. *Deadline: Last Friday in November.

National Air Transportation Foundation
Pioneers of Flight Scholarship Program
4226 King Street
Alexandria, VA 22302
703-845-9000
http://www.nata.aero/about/sch_pioneersofflight.jsp
Scholarship Name: Pioneers of Flight Scholarship
Program. *Academic Area: Aviation. *Age Group:
Undergraduate students. *Eligibility: Applicants
must be college students in their sophomore
or junior year at the time of application who are
pursuing full-time study at an accredited four-year
college or university. They must also demonstrate
interest in pursuing a career in general aviation.
*Application Process: Applicants must submit a
completed application, official transcripts, a letter
of recommendation, an essay on general aviation,
and a personal statement. Visit the foundation's Web
site to download an application. *Amount: $1,000.
*Deadline: Last Friday in December.

National Court Reporters Association (NCRA)
Foundation
Attn: Donna Gaede
8224 Old Courthouse Road
Vienna, VA 22182-3808
800-272-6272
dgaede@ncrahq.org
http://www.ncraonline.org/education/students/index.
shtml
Scholarship Name: Council on Approved Student
Education (CASE) Scholarship. *Academic Area:
Court reporting. *Age Group: Undergraduate
students. *Eligibility: Applicants must attend an
NCRA-approved court reporting program and be in
good academic standing. They must also be student
members of NCRA, and be able to write 140 to 180
words per minute. *Application Process: Applicants
must submit a completed application and a two-
page essay with references on a preselected topic.
Contact Donna Gaede for further details on how
to apply for a CASE Scholarship. *Amount: $500 to
$1,500. *Deadline: April 1.

National Court Reporters Association (NCRA)
Foundation
Attn: B.J. Shorak, Deputy Executive Director
8224 Old Courthouse Road
Vienna, VA 22182-3808
800-272-6272

bjshorak@ncrahq.org
http://www.ncraonline.org/foundation/education/sarli.
shtml
Scholarship Name: Frank Sarli Memorial Scholarship.
*Academic Area: Court reporting. *Age Group:
Undergraduate students. *Eligibility: Nominees must
be current NCRA student members and enrolled in an
NCRA-approved court reporting program. Applicants
must also pass at least one of the court reporting
program's Q & A tests at a minimum of 200 words
per minute, maintain a GPA of at least 3.5 on a 4.0
scale, demonstrate financial need, and possess all the
qualities exemplified by a professional court reporter,
including professional attitude, demeanor, dress,
and motivation. All criteria must be confirmed and
verified by the submitting court reporting program.
*Application Process: Visit the association's Web site
to download a nomination form. *Amount: $2,000.
*Deadline: March 4.

National Court Reporters Association (NCRA)
Attn: Amy Davidson
8224 Old Courthouse Road
Vienna, VA 22182-3808
800-272-6272
adavidson@ncrahq.org
http://www.ncraonline.org/education/students/index.
shtml
Grant Name: Student Member Tuition Grant. *Academic
Area: Court reporting. *Age Group: Undergraduate
students. *Eligibility: Applicants must be NCRA student
members in good standing, be in good academic
standing, and be able to write 120 to 200 words per
minute. *Application Process: Applicants can find more
information about the grant drawing in the May issue
of the NCRA's Journal of Court Reporting. Contact Amy
Davidson for further details on the Student Member
Tuition Grant. *Amount: $500. *Deadline: May 31.

National Fire Protection Association
Attn: Christine Ellis
1 Batterymarch Park
Quincy, MA 02169-7471
617-984-7244
cellis@nfpa.org
http://www.nfpa.org/categoryList.asp?categoryID=205&
URL=Learning/Public%20Education/Scholarships,%2
0awards,%20grants
Scholarship Name: George D. Miller Scholarship.
*Academic Area: Fire science/service. *Age Group:

Undergraduate students. *Eligibility: Applicants must be nominated by their college or university located in the United States or Canada. Applicants must be full- or part-time bachelor's degree candidates in a fire service or public administration program. They must be currently pursuing a career in the fire service and have completed at least one academic year of post-high school credits. They must also exhibit scholarship achievement, leadership qualities, and concern for others/volunteerism. The scholarship is also available to graduate students. *Application Process: Applicants must submit an application, a personal statement, undergraduate transcripts, and a letter of recommendation. Visit the association's Web site to download an application. *Amount: $5,000 minimum. *Deadline: April 1.

National Restaurant Association Educational Foundation

175 West Jackson Boulevard, Suite 1500
Chicago, IL 60604-2814
312-715-1010, ext. 733
scholars@foodtrain.org
http://www.nraef.org/scholarships/highschool
Scholarship Name: Academic Scholarship for High School Seniors. *Academic Area: Hospitality. *Age Group: Undergraduate students. *Eligibility: Applicants must be high school seniors, demonstrate a commitment to both a postsecondary foodservice education and a career in the restaurant and foodservice industry, maintain a minimum 2.75 GPA on a 4.0 scale, and have a minimum of 250 hours of foodservice-related work experience. They must also apply and gain acceptance to a foodservice-related, postsecondary program, either full-time or substantial part-time, and plan to enroll in a minimum of two terms for the school year. *Application Process: Applicants must submit an application, paycheck stubs, and one to three letters of recommendation from current or previous employers. Contact the association for further application details. *Amount: $2,000. *Deadline: April 21.

National Restaurant Association Educational Foundation

175 West Jackson Boulevard, Suite 1500
Chicago, IL 60604-2814
312-715-1010, ext. 733
scholars@foodtrain.org
http://www.nraef.org/scholarships/undergraduate

Scholarship Name: Academic Scholarship for Undergraduate Students. *Academic Area: Hospitality. *Age Group: Undergraduate students. *Eligibility: Applicants must be undergraduate students who have completed at least one semester and are pursuing a certificate, associate degree, or bachelor degree in a restaurant and/or foodservice-related program. They must also have a minimum 2.75 GPA on a 4.0 scale and have a minimum of 750 hours of work experience in the restaurant and food service industry. *Application Process: Applicants must submit a completed application online and post a copy of the online application, official transcripts, a copy of their college curriculum, two essays, paycheck stubs, and one to three letters of recommendation from current or previous employers. Visit the association's Web site to download and submit an application. *Amount: $2,000. *Deadline: November 18 and April 7.

National Strength and Conditioning Association (NSCA) Foundation

1885 Bob Johnson Drive
Colorado Springs, CO 80906
800-815-6826
nsca@nsca-lift.org
http://www.nsca-lift.org/Foundation
Scholarship Name: Challenge Scholarship. *Academic Area: Wellness (strength and conditioning). *Age Group: Undergraduate students. *Eligibility: Applicants must be NSCA members for at least one year prior to application deadline date. Applicants must be seeking either an undergraduate degree in a strength and conditioning-related field. The scholarship is also available to graduate students. *Application Process: Applicants must submit a covering letter of application, completed application information as listed on the foundation's Web site, a resume, original transcripts, three letters of recommendation, and a personal statement. Visit the foundation's Web site for further details. *Amount: $1,000. *Deadline: March 15.

National Strength and Conditioning Association (NSCA) Foundation

1885 Bob Johnson Drive
Colorado Springs, CO 80906
800-815-6826
nsca@nsca-lift.org
http://www.nsca-lift.org/Foundation

Scholarship Name: High School Scholarship. *Academic Area: Wellness (strength and conditioning). *Age Group: Undergraduate students. *Eligibility: Applicants must be high school seniors preparing to enter college. Students must demonstrate they have been accepted into an accredited institution with the intention to graduate with a degree in the strength and conditioning field. They must also demonstrate a record of community service and maintain a minimum 3.0 GPA based on a 4.0 system. Applicants must also sign up for NSCA membership at the time of application if they are not already members. *Application Process: Applicants must submit a covering letter of application, completed application information as listed on the foundation's Web site, original transcripts, two recommendation letters, a personal statement, a copy of their letter of acceptance to college, and information regarding their extracurricular activities and community involvement. Visit the foundation's Web site for further details. *Amount: $1,000. *Deadline: March 15.

Nebraska Funeral Directors Association
c/o Laughlin Trust Committee
201 North 8th Street, Suite 400, PO Box 93313
Lincoln, NE 68501-3313
402-423-8900
http://www.nefda.org/careers/documents/
LaughlinTrustBrochure.pdf
Scholarship Name: Nebraska Funeral Directors Association Scholarship. *Academic Area: Funeral services. *Age Group: Undergraduate students. *Eligibility: Applicants should be graduating high school seniors in Nebraska who meet pre-mortuary school educational requirements and who intend to pursue a career in mortuary science. Students who receive the scholarship must practice mortuary science in Nebraska for a minimum of three years (or repay the funds). *Application Process: Applicants should contact the association to receive an application. Written applications are required along with a letter of recommendation from an association member, transcripts, and a letter stating pre-mortuary science requirements have been met. *Amount: $1,000. *Deadline: June 30.

New Jersey State Funeral Directors Association
Attn: Scholarship Program
PO Box L
Manasquan, NJ 08736
732-974-9444
njsfda@njsfda.org
http://www.njsfda.org/education/edu_3scholar.shtml
Scholarship Name: New Jersey Funeral Service Education Corporation Scholarship. *Academic Area: Mortuary science. *Age Group: Undergraduate students. *Eligibility: Applicants must be registered in a mortuary science program, demonstrate academic achievement by maintaining at least a 2.5 GPA, and possess a commitment to funeral service. They also must be New Jersey residents who plan to work in funeral service within the state of New Jersey. *Application Process: Applicants should submit a completed application along with transcripts, two or three letters of recommendation, and a 200- to 300-word essay. Applicants must be available to attend a mandatory interview at the corporation's headquarters in July. Visit the organization's Web site to download an application. *Amount: Awards vary. *Deadline: June 30.

Oregon Funeral Directors Association
c/o Mount Hood Community College
Attn: Bill Malcom
26000 Southeast Stark Street
Gresham, OR 97030
503-491-6941
http://www.nfda.org/page.php?pID=230
Scholarship Name: Oregon Funeral Directors Association Scholarship. *Academic Area: Funeral services. *Age Group: Undergraduate students. *Eligibility: Applicants must be full-time students at Mount Hood Community College who have completed at least 35 credit hours, demonstrate financial need, and maintain at least a 3.0 GPA. *Application Process: Applicants should contact the Mount Hood Community College financial aid office to request an application. Applicants must submit two letters of recommendation from instructors. *Amount: $1,500. *Deadline: Contact the college for deadline information.

Plastics Institute of America (PIA)
333 Aiken Street
Lowell, MA 01854-3686
978-934-3130
info@plasticsinstitute.org
http://www.plasticsinstitute.org/scholarships.php
Scholarship Name: Plastics Pioneers Association Scholarship. *Academic Area: Plastics. *Age Group: Undergraduate students. *Eligibility: Applicants must be pursuing careers in any segment of the plastics industry including new technology,

education, organizational leadership, polymer development, and processing machinery innovation. They must also be U.S. citizens with strong academic records and commitment to student/community involvement. *Application Process: Applicants must submit a completed application, a resume, letter of recommendation, and a personal statement. Visit PIA's Web site to submit an online application. *Amount: $1,500. *Deadline: April 1.

Plumbing-Heating-Cooling Contractors (PHCC) Educational Foundation
American Standard Scholarship Program
PO Box 6808
Falls Church, VA 22040
800-533-7694
scholarships@naphcc.org
http://www.foundation.phccweb.org/Scholarships/ASScholarship.htm
Scholarship Name: American Standard Scholarship. *Academic Area: Construction trades. *Age Group: Undergraduate students. *Eligibility: Applicants must be enrolled in a PHCC-approved apprenticeship program, full-time certificate or degree program at an accredited two-year community college, technical college or trade school, or undergraduate degree program at an accredited four-year college or university. They must also be citizens of either the United States or Canada. High school seniors may apply. *Application Process: Applicants must submit a completed application, a personal statement, a letter of recommendation from an active member of the PHCC National Association, an academic letter of recommendation, official transcripts, and SAT/ACT scores. Visit the foundation's Web site to download an application. *Amount: $2,500. *Deadline: June 1.

Plumbing-Heating-Cooling Contractors (PHCC) Educational Foundation
A.O. Smith Scholarship Program
PO Box 6808
Falls Church, VA 22040
800-533-7694
scholarships@naphcc.org
http://www.foundation.phccweb.org/Scholarships/AOSScholarship.htm
Scholarship Name: A.O. Smith Water Heaters Scholarship. *Academic Area: Construction trades. *Age Group: Undergraduate students. *Eligibility: Applicants must be enrolled in a PHCC-approved

apprenticeship program, full-time certificate or degree program at an accredited two-year community college, technical college or trade school, or undergraduate degree program at an accredited four-year college or university. They must also be citizens of either the United States or Canada. High school seniors may apply. *Application Process: Applicants must submit a completed application, a personal statement, a letter of recommendation from an active member of the PHCC National Association, an academic letter of recommendation, official transcripts, and SAT/ACT scores. Visit the foundation's Web site to download an application. *Amount: $2,500. *Deadline: June 1.

Plumbing-Heating-Cooling Contractors (PHCC) Educational Foundation
Bradford White Scholarship Program
PO Box 6808
Falls Church, VA 22040
800-533-7694
scholarships@naphcc.org
http://www.foundation.phccweb.org/Scholarships/BWScholarship.htm
Scholarship Name: Bradford White Scholarship. *Academic Area: Construction trades. *Age Group: Undergraduate students. *Eligibility: Applicants must be enrolled in a PHCC-approved apprenticeship program or full-time certificate or degree program at an accredited two-year community college, technical college or trade school. They must also be citizens of either the United States or Canada. High school seniors may apply. *Application Process: Applicants must submit a completed application, a personal statement, a letter of recommendation from an active member of the PHCC National Association, an academic letter of recommendation, official transcripts, and SAT/ACT scores. Visit the foundation's Web site to download an application. *Amount: $2,500. *Deadline: June 1.

Plumbing-Heating-Cooling Contractors (PHCC) Educational Foundation
Delta Faucet Scholarship Program
PO Box 6808
Falls Church, VA 22040
800-533-7694
scholarships@naphcc.org
http://www.foundation.phccweb.org/Scholarships/DScholarship.htm

Scholarship Name: Delta Faucet Scholarship. *Academic Area: Construction trades. *Age Group: Undergraduate students. *Eligibility: Applicants must be enrolled in a PHCC-approved apprenticeship program, full-time certificate or degree program at an accredited two-year community college, technical college or trade school, or undergraduate degree program at an accredited four-year college or university. They must also be citizens of either the United States or Canada. High school seniors may apply. *Application Process: Applicants must submit a completed application, a personal statement, a letter of recommendation from an active member of the PHCC National Association, an academic letter of recommendation, official transcripts, and SAT/ACT scores. Visit the foundation's Web site to download an application. *Amount: $2,500. *Deadline: June 1.

Plumbing-Heating-Cooling Contractors (PHCC) Educational Foundation
Foundation Need-Based Scholarship Program
PO Box 6808
Falls Church, VA 22040
800-533-7694
scholarships@naphcc.org
http://www.foundation.phccweb.org/Scholarships/NeedScholarship.htm
Scholarship Name: PHCC Educational Foundation Need-Based Scholarship. *Academic Area: Construction trades. *Age Group: Undergraduate students. *Eligibility: Applicants must be enrolled in a PHCC-approved apprenticeship program, full-time certificate or degree program at an accredited two-year community college, technical college or trade school, or undergraduate degree program at an accredited four-year college or university. They must also be citizens of either the United States or Canada. High school seniors may apply. *Application Process: Applicants must submit a completed application, a personal statement, explanation of financial need, a letter of recommendation from an active member of the PHCC National Association, an academic letter of recommendation, official transcripts, and SAT/ACT scores. Visit the foundation's Web site to download an application. *Amount: $2,500. *Deadline: May 1.

Plumbing-Heating-Cooling Contractors (PHCC) Educational Foundation
PHCC Educational Foundation Scholarship Program
PO Box 6808
Falls Church, VA 22040
800-533-7694
scholarships@naphcc.org
http://www.foundation.phccweb.org/Scholarships/EFScholarship.htm
Scholarship Name: PHCC Educational Foundation Scholarship. *Academic Area: Construction trades. *Age Group: Undergraduate students. *Eligibility: Applicants must be enrolled in a PHCC-approved apprenticeship program, full-time certificate or degree program at an accredited two-year community college, technical college or trade school, or undergraduate degree program at an accredited four-year college or university. They must also be citizens of either the United States or Canada. High school seniors may apply. *Application Process: Applicants must submit a completed application, a personal statement, a letter of recommendation from an active member of the PHCC National Association, an academic letter of recommendation, official transcripts, and SAT/ACT scores. Visit the foundation's Web site to download an application. *Amount: $3,000 to $12,000. *Deadline: May 1.

Plumbing-Heating-Cooling Contractors (PHCC) Educational Foundation
State Water Heaters Scholarship Program
PO Box 6808
Falls Church, VA 22040
800-533-7694
scholarships@naphcc.org
http://www.foundation.phccweb.org/Scholarships/SScholarship.htm
Scholarship Name: State Water Heaters Scholarship. *Academic Area: Construction trades. *Age Group: Undergraduate students. * Eligibility: Applicants must be enrolled in a PHCC-approved apprenticeship program, full-time certificate or degree program at an accredited two-year community college, technical college or trade school, or undergraduate degree program at an accredited four-year college or university. They must also be citizens of either the United States or Canada. High school seniors may apply. *Application Process: Applicants must submit a completed application, a personal statement, a letter of recommendation from an active member of the PHCC National Association, an academic letter of recommendation, official transcripts, and SAT/ACT scores. Visit the foundation's Web site to download an application. *Amount: $2,500. *Deadline: June 1.

Print and Graphics Scholarship Foundation

Scholarship Competition
200 Deer Run Road
Sewickley, PA 15143-2600
412-741-6860, ext. 161
pgsf@piagatf.org
http://www.gain.net/employment/scholarships/annual.
html
Scholarship Name: Print and Graphics Scholarship
Foundation. *Academic Area: Printing. *Age
Group: Undergraduate students. *Eligibility:
Applicants must be interested in a career in graphic
communications, be enrolled in or intending to
enroll full-time in a two- or four-year university,
and able to maintain a 3.0 GPA. High school seniors
may apply. *Application Process: Applicants should
submit a completed application along with two
letters of recommendation, a photocopy of intended
course of study, and transcripts. Official SAT or ACT
scores should also be sent. Visit the foundation's
Web site to download an application. *Amount:
$1,000 to $1,500, renewable for up to four years.
*Deadline: March 1 (high schools students), April 1
(enrolled college students).

Professional Aviation Maintenance Association (PAMA)

PAMA Foundation Scholarships
717 Princess Street
Alexandria, VA 22314
703-683-3171
hq@pama.org
http://www.pama.org/content.asp?contentid=73
Scholarship Name: PAMA Foundation Scholarship
Program. *Academic Area: Aviation maintenance.
*Age Group: Undergraduate students. *Eligibility:
Applicants should be currently enrolled in FAR
Part 147 certificated educational institution
pursuing an Airframe & Powerplant certificate,
avionics certification, or a degree in aerospace
maintenance and management. Applicants should
also have completed 25 percent of the required
curriculum and have a B average. Demonstrated
need of financial assistance is also required.
*Application Process: Applicants should submit a
completed application along with transcripts and
letters of reference. Visit the association's Web
site to download an application. *Amount $1,000.
*Deadline: Applications accepted July 1 through
November 30.

Real Estate Educators Association (REEA)

Attn: Harwood Scholarship Committee
19 Mantua Road
Mt. Royal, NJ 08061
856-423-3215
info@reea.org
http://www.reea.org/scholarships/index.htm
Scholarship Name: REEA Harwood Scholarship.
*Academic Area: Real estate. *Age Group:
Undergraduate students. *Eligibility: Applicants
must be studying real estate at an accredited college
or university where a REEA member is an instructor.
*Application Process: Applicants should submit
a completed application along with a resume,
transcripts (which verify completion of real estate
courses), and a letter of recommendation from a real
estate instructor. Visit the association's Web site to
download an application. *Amount: $250. *Deadline:
February 28.

Salute to Education Inc.

PO Box 833425
Miami, FL 33283
305-476-7709
steinfo@stescholarships.org
http://www.stescholarships.org/SC_categories.html
Scholarship Name: Salute to Education Vocational/
Technical Scholarship. *Academic Area: Vocational
education. *Age Group: Undergraduate students.
*Eligibility: Applicants must be graduating high
school seniors who attend a Miami-Dade or Broward
County, Florida, high school and who also reside
in one of these counties. They must also be legal
residents of the United States, have a minimum
weighted GPA of 3.0, demonstrate a commitment
to service by participating in at least one school or
community organization, intend to pursue a college
degree at an accredited institution after graduation,
and demonstrate leadership potential and success
in a vocational/technical area. *Application
Process: Applicants must apply online. Supporting
materials should be mailed as detailed on the
online application. *Amount: $1,000. *Deadline: Visit
the organization's Web site for updated deadline
information.

TAPPI

Attn: Veranda Edmondson
15 Technology Parkway South
Norcross, GA 30092

770-209-7536
vedmondson@tappi.org
http://www.tappi.org/index.asp?pid=16234&ch=15
Scholarship Name: William L. Cullison Scholarship. *Academic Area: Pulp and paper. *Age Group: Undergraduate students. *Eligibility: Applicants must be college juniors and seniors who are attending a university or college that offers pulp and paper programs and/or has TAPPI student chapters (a list of institutions is available on TAPPI's Web site). Applicants must maintain a 3.5 GPA or better through the first two years in a four-year program, or the first three years in a five-year program. They must also demonstrate outstanding leadership abilities and a significant interest in the pulp and paper industry. *Application Process: Applicants should submit a completed application along with official transcripts, a list of scholarships and amounts already received, and three letters of recommendation. Visit the association's Web site to download an application. *Amount: Increments of $4,000 for the last two years of undergraduate study. *Deadline: May 1.

Tourism Cares for Tomorrow
Attn: Carolyn Viles, CTC, Program Manager
585 Washington Street
Canton, MA 02021
carolynv@tourismcares.org
http://www.ntfonline.org/TourismCares/What+We+Do/Students/Scholarships
Scholarship Name: Academy of Hospitality & Tourism Scholarship. *Academic Area: Hospitality. *Age Group: Undergraduate students. *Eligibility: Applicants must be high school seniors maintaining at least a 3.0 GPA who are enrolled in one of the national Academies of Hospitality & Tourism. *Application Process: Applicants should submit a completed application along with transcripts and a two-page essay. Visit the organization's Web site to download an application and to view the essay topic. *Amount: $1,000. *Deadline: April 1.

Tourism Cares for Tomorrow
Attn: Carolyn Viles, CTC, Program Manager
585 Washington Street
Canton, MA 02021
carolynv@tourismcares.org
http://www.ntfonline.org/TourismCares/What+We+Do/Students/Scholarships

Scholarship Name: LaMacchia Family Scholarship. *Academic Area: Hospitality. *Age Group: Undergraduate students. *Eligibility: Applicants must be students who are entering their junior or senior year at any accredited four-year college or university in Wisconsin. They also must have a GPA of at least 3.0 GPA. *Application Process: Applicants should submit a completed application along with transcripts. Visit the organization's Web site to download an application. *Amount: $1,000. *Deadline: April 1.

Tourism Cares for Tomorrow
Attn: Carolyn Viles, CTC, Program Manager
585 Washington Street
Canton, MA 02021
carolynv@tourismcares.org
http://www.ntfonline.org/TourismCares/What+We+Do/Students/Scholarships
Scholarship Name: Pat and Jim Host Scholarship. *Academic Area: Hospitality. *Age Group: Undergraduate students. *Eligibility: Applicants must have graduated from a Kentucky high school, be accepted into or enrolled in a four-year college or university in Kentucky as full-time students, and intend to major in travel and tourism. They also must have at least a 3.0 GPA. *Application Process: Applicants should submit a completed application along with two letters of recommendation and a two- to five-page essay on a topic relating to the changing role of the group tour industry. Visit the organization's Web site to download an application and to view the essay topic. *Amount: $2,500. *Deadline: April 1.

United States Aquaculture Society (USAS)
Attn: Jimmy Avery, Vice President
Professor, National Warmwater Aquaculture Center
Mississippi State University
PO Box 197
Stoneville, MS 38776
662-686-3273
javery@drec.msstate.edu
http://www.was.org/USAS-SAC/mulvihill.htm
Scholarship Name: M.P. Mulvihill Aquaculture Student Scholarship. *Academic Area: Aquaculture. *Age Group: Undergraduate students. *Eligibility: Applicants should be college juniors or seniors, U.S. citizens, and student members of the World Aquaculture Society and the USAS. They also should

demonstrate an exceptional academic history, financial need, and commitment and contributions to the field of aquaculture and/or the USAS. Graduate students may also apply for this scholarship. *Application Process: Applicants should submit a completed application along with a cover letter describing their project/major and educational/research interests, a letter from a professor in their major verifying their enrollment, a typed essay (500-word maximum) that addresses their commitment to aquaculture and the USAS, and undergraduate and graduate transcripts. Visit the society's Web site to download an application. *Amount: $1,500. *Deadline: Contact the society for information.

West Virginia Funeral Directors Association
Attn: Pat Reger
815 Quarrier Street, Suite 345
Charleston, WV 25301-2616
304-522-2031, 800-585-2351
info@wvfda.org
http://www.wvfda.org/scholarship.htm
Scholarship Name: George E. Reger Memorial Scholarship. *Academic Area: Funeral services. *Age Group: Undergraduate students. *Eligibility: Applicants must be West Virginia residents who have completed at least their first quarter at an accredited mortuary school, demonstrate financial need, exhibit academic achievement, and show a commitment to community involvement. *Application Process: Applicants should request an application from the association and submit the completed application along with transcripts, a list of extracurricular or community activities, a letter stating financial need, and a letter of recommendation. Contact the association to request an application. *Amount: $1,000. *Deadline: March 30.

Wisconsin Funeral Directors Association Foundation
Attn: Gary Langendorf
c/o Draeger Langendorf Funeral Home

4600 County Line Road
Racine, WI 53403
262-552-9000
info@wfda.org
http://www.wfda.org
Scholarship Name: Wisconsin Funeral Directors Foundation, Ltd. Scholarship. *Academic Area: Funeral services. *Age Group: Undergraduate students. *Eligibility: Applicants must be legal residents of the state of Wisconsin who are attending Milwaukee Area Technical College in West Allis, Wisconsin. They must have completed at least six months in the program and have maintained at least a 3.0 GPA. *Application Process: Applicants should submit a cover letter along with a 500-word typewritten personal statement and their transcripts. *Amount: $1,000. *Deadline: June 15.

Wisconsin State Horse Council (WSHC)
132A South Ludington Street
Columbus, WI 53925
920-623-0393
info@wisconsinstatehorsecouncil.org
http://www.wisconsinstatehorsecouncil.org/scholarship.html
Scholarship Name: Wisconsin State Horse Council Scholarship. *Academic Area: Equestrian studies. *Age Group: Undergraduate students. *Eligibility: Applicants must be planning to, or currently majoring in, any equine profession at a two-year or four-year college/university. They must also have been full-time Wisconsin residents for the past five years and be current members of the WSHC. *Application Process: Applicants must submit a completed application, three letters of recommendation, transcripts, and a current photo. Visit the council's Web site to download an application. *Amount: $500 to $1,000. *Deadline: March 1.

VOCATIONAL EDUCATION—GRADUATE

The following financial aid resources are available to students who are interested in studying vocational education or related fields at the graduate level.

Air Traffic Control Association
Attn: Scholarship Fund
1101 King Street, Suite 300
Alexandria, VA 22314
703-299-2430
info@atca.org
http://www.atca.org/activities/scholarships.asp
Scholarship Name: Air Traffic Control Association Scholarship. *Academic Area: Aviation. *Age Group: Graduate students. *Eligibility: Applicants must fit into one of the following four eligibility categories: (1) students enrolled half to full time in a two- to four-year air traffic control program at an institution approved and/or licensed by the Federal Aviation Administration (FAA) as directly supporting the FAA's college and training initiative; (2) students enrolled half to full time in a program leading to a bachelor's degree or higher in an aviation-related course of study; (3) full-time employees enrolled in advanced study programs to improve their skills in air traffic control or an aviation discipline; (4) U.S. citizens, children of air traffic control specialists enrolled half to full time in a program leading to a bachelor's degree or higher. *Application Process: Applicants should visit the association's Web site for specific eligibility requirements related to each of the four above-mentioned categories. Applicants should submit a completed application along with two letters of recommendation, transcripts, a statement of financial need, and an essay. Visit the association's Web site to download the appropriate application. *Amount: Awards vary. *Deadline: Contact the association for deadline information.

American Congress on Surveying and Mapping (ACSM)
Attn: Pat Canfield
6 Montgomery Village Avenue, Suite 403
Gaithersburg, MD 20879
240-632-9716, ext. 113
pat.canfield@acsm.net
http://www.acsm.net/scholar.html
Scholarship Name: American Congress on Surveying and Mapping Scholarships. *Academic Area: Surveying. *Age Group: Graduate students. *Eligibility: Applicants must be members of the ACSM, pursuing careers in surveying or mapping, and demonstrate financial need. Some scholarships in this program are also available to undergraduate students. *Application Process: Applicants should submit a completed application along with proof of membership in the ACSM; a brief statement detailing their educational objectives, professional activities, and financial need; at least three letters of recommendation; and official transcripts. Visit the organization's Web site for a complete list of individual scholarships, eligibility requirements, and a downloadable application. *Amount: $500 to $2,000. *Deadline: December 1.

American Industrial Hygiene Association (AIHA) Foundation
AIHF Scholarship Program
2700 Prosperity Avenue, Suite 250
Alexandria, VA 22031
703-849-8888
aihf@aiha.org
http://www.aiha.org/Content/InsideAIHA/Foundation/AIHFScholarshipProgram.htm
Scholarship Name: Graduate Scholarship Program. *Academic Area: Industrial hygiene. *Age Group: Graduate students. *Eligibility: Applicants must be AIHA student members (or applying for student, full, or associate membership), currently attending an Accreditation Board for Engineering Technology accredited program full- or part-time, majoring in a field of concentration in industrial hygiene, and enrolled in the current and following academic years. *Application Process: Applicants should submit a completed application along with a copy of their most recent cumulative industrial hygiene program GPA, typed personal statement, a list of volunteer and/or community service activities, a typed answer to an ethics-related question, and one or two letters of reference on letterhead stationery. Visit the foundation's Web site to download an application. *Amount: Up to $6,000. *Deadline: March 17.

American Public Transportation Foundation
Attn: Pamela Boswell
1666 K Street, NW, Suite 1100

Washington, DC 20006
202-496-4803
pboswell@apta.com
http://www.apta.com/services/human_resources/
  program_guidelines.cfm
Scholarship Name: Dan M. Reichard Jr. Scholarship.
  *Academic Area: Business administration,
  transportation. *Age Group: Graduate students.
  *Eligibility: Applicants must demonstrate
  dedication to pursuing careers in the business
  administration/management area of the transit
  industry. Applicants must be enrolled in a fully
  accredited institution, maintain at least a 3.0
  GPA (B) in course work that is relevant to the
  industry or required of a degree program, and
  either be employed by or demonstrate a strong
  interest in entering the public transportation
  industry. College sophomores (30 hours or more
  satisfactorily completed), juniors, seniors, or
  those seeking advanced degrees may apply for
  scholarships. *Application Process: Applicants
  must submit a completed application, a
  letter of nomination, an essay, three letters
  of recommendation, a copy of a completed
  FAFSA form, official transcripts, verification
  of enrollment, and a copy of their academic
  fee schedule. Visit the foundation's Web site
  to download an application. *Amount: $2,500
  minimum. *Deadline: June 17.

American Public Transportation Foundation
Contact: Pamela Boswell
1666 K Street, NW, Suite 1100
Washington, DC 20006
202-496-4803
pboswell@apta.com
http://www.apta.com/services/human_resources/
  program_guidelines.cfm
Scholarship Name: Jack R. Gilstrap Scholarship.
  *Academic Area: Transportation. *Age Group:
  Graduate students. *Eligibility: Applicants must
  demonstrate dedication to pursuing careers
  in the transit industry and display a high level
  of academic/personal achievement. They also
  must be enrolled in a fully accredited institution,
  maintain at least a 3.0 GPA (B) in course work
  that is relevant to the industry or required of
  a degree program, and either be employed by
  or demonstrate a strong interest in entering
  the public transportation industry. College

sophomores (30 hours or more satisfactorily
  completed), juniors, seniors, or those seeking
  advanced degrees may apply for scholarships.
  *Application Process: Applicants must submit a
  completed application, a letter of nomination, an
  essay, three letters of recommendation, a copy
  of a completed FAFSA form, official transcripts,
  verification of enrollment, and a copy of their
  academic fee schedule. Visit the foundation's Web
  site to download an application. *Amount: $2,500
  minimum. *Deadline: June 17.

American Society for Enology and Viticulture
Attn: ASEV Scholarship Committee
PO Box 1855
Davis, CA 95617-1855
530-753-3142
society@asev.org
http://www.asev.org
Scholarship Name: American Society for Enology
  and Viticulture Scholarship. *Academic Area:
  Enology and viticulture. *Age Group: Graduate
  students. *Eligibility: Applicants must be enrolled
  in or accepted into a full-time accredited college
  or university program, with a minimum 3.2 GPA.
  They must reside in North America (Canada,
  Mexico, or the United States). Applicants must
  be enrolled in a major, or in a graduate group,
  emphasizing enology or viticulture, or in a
  curriculum emphasizing a science basic to the wine
  and grape industry. The scholarship is also available
  to undergraduate students. *Application Process:
  Applicants must submit a completed application,
  a student questionnaire, a statement of intent,
  original transcripts, a list of courses they will be
  taking in the upcoming year, and two original
  letters of recommendation. Visit the society's Web
  site to download an application. *Amount: Varies.
  *Deadline: March 1.

**American Society of Transportation and Logistics
  Inc.**
Attn: Scholarship Judging Panel
1700 North Moore Street, Suite 1900
Arlington, VA 22209
703-524-5011
astl@nitl.org
http://www.astl.org/scholar.htm
Scholarship Name: L.L. Waters Scholarship. *Academic
  Area: Transportation. *Age Group: Graduate

students. *Eligibility: Applicants must be enrolled in, or accepted into, a fully accredited college or university in the pursuit of graduate studies in transportation/logistics/physical distribution as their concentration of study. They also must demonstrate scholastic achievement and commitment to the pursuit of a professional career in transportation/logistics. The scholarship is also available to undergraduate students. *Application Process: Applicants must submit a completed application, official transcripts, and two letters of recommendation. Visit the society's Web site to download an application. *Amount: $2,000. *Deadline: September 30.

American Wine Society (AWS) Educational Foundation

Attn: Les Sperling, Vice President for Student Affairs & Scholarships
1134 Prospect Avenue
Bethlehem, PA 18018-4914
610-865-2401
lhs0@lehigh.edu
http://www.americanwinesociety.org/web/scholarship_application.htm
Scholarship Name: AWS Educational Foundation Scholarship. *Academic Area: Enology and viticulture. *Age Group: Graduate students. *Eligibility: Applicants must be North American (United States, Canada, Mexico, Bahamas, or West Indies) citizens and full-time graduate students in an enology, viticulture, or wine-related graduate program at a North American institute of higher learning. They also must express their intent to make a career in one of these areas upon completion of their graduate degree. *Application Process: Applicants must submit a completed application form, official transcripts, a personal statement, a written recommendation form to be completed by an academic adviser, and two letters of recommendation. Visit the society's Web site to download an application. *Amount: $1,000 to $3,000. *Deadline: March 31.

Appraisal Institute Education Trust

Attn: Olivia Carreon, Project Coordinator
550 West Van Buren Street, Suite 1000
Chicago, IL 60607
312-335-4100
ocarreon@appraisalinstitute.org

http://www.appraisalinstitute.org/education/downloads/AIET_Info.pdf
Scholarship Name: Appraisal Institute Educational Trust Scholarship. *Academic Area: Real estate. *Age Group: Graduate students. *Eligibility: Applicants must be U.S. citizens who are majoring in real estate appraisal, land economics, or another real estate-related field at a university or college in the United States. The scholarship is also available to undergraduate students. *Application Process: Applicants should request further information from the institute. Applications are available in November. *Amount: $3,000 (graduate students). *Deadline: March 15.

Associated General Contractors (AGC) of America

AGC Education and Research Foundation
2300 Wilson Boulevard, Suite 400
Alexandria, VA 22201
703-837-5342
sladef@agc.org
http://www.agc.org/page.ww?section=AGC+Foundation&name=Graduate+Scholarships
Scholarship Name: Associated General Contractors Foundation Graduate Construction Education Scholarship. *Academic Area: Construction trades, engineering (construction). *Age Group: Graduate students, professionals. *Eligibility: Applicants who are college seniors enrolled in undergraduate construction management or construction-related engineering degree programs, or others possessing an undergraduate degree in construction management or construction-related engineering are eligible to apply. Applicants must be enrolled or planning to enroll in graduate-level construction management or construction-related engineering degree programs as full-time students. *Application Process: Applicants must submit a completed application, three evaluation forms, transcripts, and a notification of receipt postcard. Visit the organization's Web site to download an application. *Amount: $7,500. *Deadline: November 1.

Floriculture Industry Research and Scholarship Trust

PO Box 280
East Lansing, MI 48826-0280
517-333-4617
scholarships@firstinfloriculture.org
http://www.firstinfloriculture.org/schl_req_app.htm
Scholarship Name: First Scholarships. *Academic Area: Horticulture. *Age Group: Graduate students.

*Eligibility: Applicants must be pursuing a career in a horticulture-related field and maintain a minimum 3.0 GPA. They also must also be citizens or residents of the United States or Canada or be enrolled in an accredited educational institution in the United States or Canada. More than 25 First Scholarships are available, some of which are geared specifically toward undergraduate students. *Application Process: Applicants must submit a completed application along with two letters of recommendation and transcripts. *Amount: $500 to $2,000. *Deadline: May 1.

Garden Club of America

Attn: Mrs. Nancy Stevenson
Grosscup Scholarship Committee
Cleveland Botanical Garden
11030 East Boulevard
Cleveland, OH 44106
212-753-8287
http://www.gcamerica.org/scholarship/grosscup.html
Scholarship Name: Katharine M. Grosscup Scholarship. *Academic Area: Horticulture. *Age Group: Graduate students. *Eligibility: Applicants must be master's degree candidates majoring in horticulture or related field. Preference is given to residents of Indiana, Kentucky, Michigan, Ohio, Pennsylvania, and West Virginia. Applicants must maintain a B average or better. The scholarship is also available to undergraduate students. *Application Process: Applicants must submit a completed application, two letters of recommendation, and official transcripts. Finalists must attend a personal interview in Cleveland. Visit the club's Web site to download an application. *Amount: Up to $3,000. *Deadline: February 1.

Hospitality Sales & Marketing Association International (HSMAI)

8201 Greensboro Drive, Suite 300
McLean, VA 22102
703-610-9024
info@hsmai.org
http://www.hsmai.org/Events/scholarship.cfm
Scholarship Name: HSMAI Foundation Scholarships. *Academic Area: Hospitality. *Age Group: Graduate students. *Eligibility: Applicants must be either part- or full-time students pursuing careers in a hospitality management field. One scholarship is awarded to a part-time student and three are awarded to full-time students. Applicants should be student members

of the HSMAI. The scholarship is also available to undergraduate students. *Application Process: Applicants must submit a completed application, official transcripts, two letters of recommendation, a current resume, and three personal essays. *Amount: $500 and $2,000. *Deadline: May 1.

ISA-The Instrumentation, Systems, and Automation Society

67 Alexander Drive
Research Triangle Park, NC 27709
919-549-8411
info@isa.org
http://www.isa.org/Content/NavigationMenu/
    Educators_and_Students/Scholarships/Scholarships.
    htm
Scholarship Name: ISA Educational Foundation Scholarship. *Academic Area: Automation. *Age Group: Graduate students. *Eligibility: Applicants must be enrolled full time in a graduate program in an instrumentation, systems, or automation discipline at an education institution in their country of residence. They also must have completed at least one academic semester and maintain a GPA of at least 3.0. The scholarship is also available to undergraduate students. *Application Process: Applicants must submit one original and nine copies of a completed application, transcripts, a list of activities and awards, an employment record, and an essay. Visit the society's Web site to download an application. *Amount: Varies. *Deadline: February 15.

National Air Transportation Foundation

John E. Godwin Jr. Memorial Scholarship Fund
4226 King Street
Alexandria, VA 22302
703-845-9000
http://www.nata.aero
Scholarship Name: John E. Godwin Jr. Memorial Scholarship. *Academic Area: Aviation. *Age Group: Open. *Eligibility: Applicants must be a minimum of 18 years old and be nominated and endorsed by a representative or a regular/associate member company of the National Air Transportation Association. Applicants must possess a Student Pilot certificate (or higher), with a third-class medical certificate, or with the possibility to qualify for a second-class medical certificate. They also must demonstrate a commitment to general aviation and preferably have a membership in good standing

with the Civil Air Patrol. *Application Process: Applicants must submit a completed application and copies of an airman's certificate and current medical certificate. Visit the foundation's Web site to download an application. Contact the foundation to inquire about any additional supporting documents necessary to accompany the application. *Amount: $2,500. *Deadline: Last Friday in November.

National Fire Protection Association
Attn: Christine Ellis
1 Batterymarch Park
Quincy, MA 02169-7471
617-984-7244
cellis@nfpa.org
http://www.nfpa.org/categoryList.asp?categoryID=205&
 URL=Learning/Public%20Education/Scholarships,%2
 0awards,%20grants
Scholarship Name: David B. Gratz Scholarship.
 *Academic Area: Engineering (fire protection), fire science. *Age Group: Graduate students. *Eligibility: Applicants must be full- or part-time graduate students enrolled in fire science or fire engineering programs (outside of the United States or Canada) who exhibit scholarship achievement, leadership qualities, concern for others/volunteerism, and contributions to international/national fire safety activities. *Application Process: Applicants must submit an application, a personal statement (in English), undergraduate and graduate transcripts, and a letter of recommendation. Visit the association's Web site to download an application. *Amount: $5,000 minimum. *Deadline: April 1.

National Fire Protection Association
Attn: Christine Ellis
1 Batterymarch Park
Quincy, MA 02169-7471
617-984-7244
cellis@nfpa.org
http://www.nfpa.org/categoryList.asp?categoryID=205&
 URL=Learning/Public%20Education/Scholarships,%2
 0awards,%20grants
Scholarship Name: George D. Miller Scholarship.
 *Academic Area: Fire science. *Age Group: Graduate students. *Eligibility: Applicants must be nominated by their college or university, which must be located in the United States or Canada. They also must be full- or part-time master's degree candidates in a fire service or public administration program,

currently pursuing a career in the fire service, and have completed at least one academic year of post-high school credits. Applicants must also exhibit scholarship achievement, leadership qualities, and concern for others/volunteerism. The scholarship is also available to undergraduate students. *Application Process: Applicants must submit an application, a personal statement (in English), undergraduate or both undergraduate and graduate transcripts, and a letter of recommendation. Visit the association's Web site to download an application. *Amount: $5,000 minimum. *Deadline: April 1.

National Strength and Conditioning Association (NSCA) Foundation
1885 Bob Johnson Drive
Colorado Springs, CO 80906
719-632-6722, 800-815-6826
nsca@nsca-lift.org
http://www.nsca-lift.org/Foundation
Scholarship Name: Challenge Scholarship. *Academic Area: Wellness (strength and conditioning). *Age Group: Graduate students. *Eligibility: Applicants must be NSCA members seeking a graduate degree in a strength and conditioning-related field. The scholarship is also available to undergraduate students. *Application Process: Applicants must submit a cover letter of application, completed application information as listed on the foundation's Web site, a resume, original transcripts, three letters of recommendation, and a personal statement. Visit the foundation's Web site for further details. *Amount: $1,000. *Deadline: March 15.

Tourism Cares for Tomorrow
Attn: Carolyn Viles, CTC, Program Manager
585 Washington Street
Canton, MA 02021
carolynv@tourismcares.org
http://www.ntfonline.org/TourismCares/What+We+Do/
 Students/Scholarships
Scholarship Name: Liberty Scholarship. *Academic Area: Hospitality. *Age Group: Graduate students. *Eligibility: Applicants must be graduate students attending the Robert Preston Tisch Center for Hospitality, Travel, and Sports Administration at New York University. They also should demonstrate a commitment to a career in tourism, a dedication to philanthropic and volunteer work, and possess a GPA of at least 3.0. *Application Process: Applicants

should submit a completed application along with transcripts. Visit the organization's Web site for additional application information. *Amount: $10,000. *Deadline: April 1.

Tourism Cares for Tomorrow

Attn: Carolyn Viles, CTC, Program Manager
585 Washington Street
Canton, MA 02021
carolynv@tourismcares.org
http://www.ntfonline.org/TourismCares/What+We+Do/Students/Scholarships
Scholarship Name: Sustainable Tourism Scholarship. *Academic Area: Hospitality. *Age Group: Graduate Students. *Eligibility: Applicants must be tourism graduate students who are maintaining at least a 3.0 GPA at an accredited university. *Application Process: Applicants should submit a completed application, a five-page essay, a resume, and transcripts. Yearly topics for the essay question are announced via the organization's Web site. Visit the organization's Web site to download an application and to view the essay topic. *Amount: $1,000. *Deadline: April 1.

United States Aquaculture Society (USAS)

Attn: Jimmy Avery, USAS Vice President
Professor, National Warmwater Aquaculture Center
Mississippi State University
PO Box 197
Stoneville, MS 38776
662-686-3273
javery@drec.msstate.edu
http://www.was.org/USAS-SAC/mulvihill.htm
Scholarship Name: M.P. Mulvihill Aquaculture Student Scholarship. *Academic Area: Aquaculture. *Age Group: Graduate students. *Eligibility: Applicants should be U.S. citizens and student members of the World Aquaculture Society and the U.S. Aquaculture Society. They also should demonstrate an exceptional academic history, financial need, and commitment and contributions to the field of aquaculture and/or the USAS. The scholarship is also available to undergraduate students. *Application Process: Applicants should submit a completed application along with a cover letter describing their project/major and educational/research interests, a letter from a professor in their major verifying that the applicant is a current student, a typed essay (500-word maximum) that addresses the applicant's commitment to aquaculture and the U.S. Aquaculture Society, and undergraduate and graduate transcripts. Visit the society's Web site to download an application. *Amount: $1,500. *Deadline: Contact the society for official deadlines.

STUDENT PROFILE-BASED AID

DEPENDENTS OF VETERANS

The following financial aid resources are available to children and spouses of military personnel who have died or who were disabled as a result of military service, as well as those who have been declared prisoners of war or missing in action. In addition, this section lists financial aid resources for dependents of military personnel who are on active or reserve duty. Visit the "Military Scholarships" section for resources for active, reserve, and retired military personnel.

Air Force Aid Society (AFAS)
Education Assistance Department
241 18th Street, Suite 202
Arlington, VA 22202-3409
800-769-8951
dvosburg@afas.org
http://www.afas.org/Education/body_stap.cfm
Scholarship Name: General George S. Brown Spouse Tuition Assistance Program. *Academic Area: Open. *Age Group: Undergraduate students, graduate students. *Eligibility: Applicants must be spouses of active duty officers, intend to pursue higher education that will lead to better employment opportunities, and be living overseas with their spouses. They also must attend institutions that have been contracted for on-base programs and must be able to demonstrate financial need and career goals. Visit the society's Web site for an in-depth explanation of the program. *Application Process: Applicants should pick up AFAS Form 90A at their base's education office. The base office will be able to inform the applicant of additional information that may be required along with the application (this varies by office). *Amount: Up to $1,500. *Deadline: Deadlines vary. Contact your base education office for deadlines.

Air Force Aid Society
Education Assistance Department
241 18th Street, Suite 202
Arlington, VA 22202
703-607-3072, 800-429-9475
dvosburg@afas.org
http://www.afas.org/Education/body_grant.cfm
Grant Name: General Henry H. Arnold Education Grant. *Academic Area: Open. *Age Group: Undergraduate students. *Eligibility: Applicants must be dependent children of Air Force members (select categories only), spouses of Active Duty members and Title 10 AGR/Reservists, or surviving spouses of Air Force members who died while on active duty or in retirement. Applicants should visit the society's Web site to read more detailed specifications. Applicants must be high school graduates enrolled or accepted as full-time students into a college, university, or trade school approved by the U.S. Department of Education for federal aid programs. They also must maintain at least a 2.0 GPA. *Application Process: Applicants should submit a completed application along with copies of both sides of their parent's military ID card and sponsoring member's qualifying documentation. Visit the society's Web site to find out more about these additional documentation requirements and to download application forms. *Amount: $2,000. *Deadline: March 10.

American Legion Auxiliary
777 North Meridian Street, Third Floor
Indianapolis, IN 46204-1420
317-955-3845
alahq@legion-aux.org
http://www.legion-aux.org/nPresScholarship.aspx
Scholarship Name: National President's Scholarship. *Academic Area: Open. *Age Group: Undergraduate students. *Eligibility: Applicants must be high school seniors and children of veterans who served in the Armed Forces during eligibility dates specified by the legion (a complete list of dates are listed on application) and who complete 50 hours of community service during high school. They also should demonstrate leadership skills, financial need, and academic excellence. *Application Process: Applicants should submit a completed application along with four letters of recommendation, an essay not to exceed 1,000 words entitled, "My Vision of Freedom," a letter verifying community service, transcripts, ACT or SAT scores, and a statement containing verifiable dates of a parent's military service. Visit the auxiliary's Web site to download an application. *Amount: $1,000, $2,000, and $2,500. *Deadline: March 1.

American Legion Auxiliary
777 North Meridian Street, Third Floor
Indianapolis, IN 46204-1420
317-955-3845

mpotts@legion-aux.org
http://www.legion-aux.org/nontraditional.aspx
Scholarship Name: Non-Traditional Student Scholarship. *Academic Area: Open. *Age Group: Undergraduate students. *Eligibility: Students who plan to return to the classroom after an extended period of time or students who have completed at least one year of college, but are in need of financial aid to continue their education, may apply. Applicants must also be members of the American Legion, the American Legion Auxiliary, or Sons of the American Legion and be enrolled in at least six hours per semester or four hours per quarter. *Application Process: Visit the auxiliary's Web site to download an application. *Amount: $1,000 per year for four years. *Deadline: March 1.

American Legion Auxiliary
777 North Meridian Street, Third Floor
Indianapolis, IN 46204-1420
317-955-3845
alahq@legion-aux.org
http://www.legion-aux.org/spiritYouth.aspx
Scholarship Name: Spirit of Youth Scholarship for Junior Members. *Academic Area: Open. *Age Group: Undergraduate students. *Eligibility: High school seniors who have been members of the American Legion Auxiliary for the immediate past three years, and who continue their membership during the four-year scholarship period, may apply for this scholarship. Applicants must also demonstrate leadership ability and academic achievement, having maintained at least a 3.0 GPA. *Application Process: Applicants should submit a completed application along with four letters of recommendation, an essay entitled, "My Vision of Freedom," transcripts, and ACT or SAT scores. Visit the auxiliary's Web site to download an application. *Amount: $1,000 per year for four years. *Deadline: March 1.

American Legion-Iowa Auxiliary
720 Lyon Street
Des Moines, IA 50309
515-282-7987
http://www.ialegion.org/ala
Scholarship Name: Hoffman Memorial Teaching Scholarship. *Academic Area: Education. *Age Group: Undergraduate students. *Eligibility: Applicants must be high school seniors or college students, dependents of a disabled veteran, and Iowa residents who wish to pursue teaching

careers. *Application Process: Applicants must submit a completed application, transcripts, a personal statement, a 400-word essay, three letters of recommendation, and a photograph. Visit the legion's Web site to download an application. *Amount: $400. *Deadline: June 1.

American Legion-Iowa Auxiliary
720 Lyon Street
Des Moines, IA 50309
515-282-7987
http://www.ialegion.org/ala
Scholarship Name: Iowa Department Scholarship. *Academic Area: Open. *Age Group: Undergraduate students, graduate students. *Eligibility: Applicants must be high school seniors or college students, dependents of a disabled veteran, and Iowa residents who wish to pursue college study. *Application Process: Applicants must submit a completed application, transcripts, a personal statement, a 400-word essay, three letters of recommendation, and a photograph. Visit the legion's Web site to download an application. *Amount: $300. *Deadline: June 1.

American Legion-Iowa Auxiliary
720 Lyon Street
Des Moines, IA 50309
515-282-7987
http://www.ialegion.org/ala
Scholarship Name: Mary Virginia Macrae Memorial Nursing Scholarship. *Academic Area: Nursing (open). *Age Group: Undergraduate students, graduate students. *Eligibility: Applicants must be high school seniors or college students, dependents of a disabled veteran, and Iowa residents who wish to pursue nursing careers. *Application Process: Applicants must submit a completed application, transcripts, a personal statement, a 400-word essay, three letters of recommendation, and a photograph. Visit the legion's Web site to download an application. *Amount: $400. *Deadline: June 1.

American Legion-Oregon Auxiliary
PO Box 1730
Wilsonville, OR 97070-1730
503-682-3162
pcalhoun@pcez.com
Scholarship Name: American Legion-Oregon Auxiliary Scholarship. *Academic Area: Open. *Age Group:

Undergraduate students. *Eligibility: Applicants must be high school seniors or college students, children of a disabled veteran, and plan to pursue postsecondary education at a school within the state of Oregon. *Application Process: Contact the legion for application details. *Amount: Up to $1,000. *Deadline: Typically in March.

American Legion-Pennsylvania Auxiliary

PO Box 2643
Harrisburg, PA 17105-2643
717-763-7545
paalad@hotmail.com
Scholarship Name: American Legion-Pennsylvania Auxiliary Scholarship. *Academic Area: Open. *Age Group: Undergraduate students. *Eligibility: Applicants must be Pennsylvania high school seniors who are sons or daughters of disabled veterans. They also must demonstrate financial need. *Application Process: Contact the legion for application details. *Amount: Up to $600 per year. *Deadline: March 15.

Alabama Department of Veterans Affairs

RSA Plaza Building, 770 Washington Avenue, Suite 530
Montgomery, AL 36130-2755
334-242-5077
http://www.va.state.al.us/scholarship.htm
Scholarship Name: G. I. Dependents' Scholarship. *Academic Area: Open. *Age Group: Undergraduate students. *Eligibility: Children or spouses of Alabama military veterans who are disabled as a result of military service or who died while in the military are eligible to apply. Recipients must attend a college or university in the state. Children must begin their education prior to their 26th birthday; there are no age limitations for spouses. *Application Process: Applicants should contact their county veterans affairs office for more information; visit the department's Web site for the location of the office in your county. *Amount: Amounts vary, but benefits are limited to cost of tuition and fees. Awards are renewable for up to four years. *Deadline: Write or call for details.

Alaska Office of Veterans Affairs

Attn: Jerry Beale, Director
Camp Denali, PO Box 5800
Fort Richardson, AK 99505-5800
907-428-6016
jerry_beale@ak-prepared.com
http://www.ak-prepared.com/vetaffairs
Grant Name: The office provides tuition waivers for the purpose of college study. *Academic Area: Open. *Age Group: Undergraduate students. *Eligibility: Children and spouses of Alaska military veterans who died as a result of military service, or who have been declared missing in action, are eligible to apply. Applicants must be residents of Alaska and attend selected public colleges or universities in the state. *Application Process: Applicants should contact their county veterans affairs office for more information; visit the department's Web site for the location of the office in your county. *Amount: Amounts vary. *Deadline: Write or call for details.

Arkansas Department of Veterans' Affairs

Attn: James L. Miller, Director
Building 65, 2200 Fort Roots Drive, Room 119
North Little Rock, AR 72114
501-370-3820
advjmill@vba.va.gov
http://www.nasdva.com/arkansas.html
Grant Name: The department provides tuition waivers for the purpose of college study. *Academic Area: Open. *Age Group: Undergraduate students. *Eligibility: Children and the spouses of Arkansas military veterans who died as a result of military service, or who have been declared missing in action, are eligible to apply. Applicants must be residents of Arkansas and attend a public college or university in the state. *Application Process: Contact the department for details. *Amount: Free tuition. *Deadline: Write or call for details.

Army Aviation Association of America (AAAA)

755 Main Street, Suite 4D
Monroe, CT 06468-2830
203-268-2450
aaaa@quad-a.org
http://www.quad-a.org
Grant/Loan Name: Army Aviation Association of America Scholarship Grant and Loan Program. *Academic Area: Open. *Age Group: Undergraduate students, graduate students. *Eligibility: Applicants must be members of AAAA for at least one year prior to applying, spouses of AAAA members or a deceased member, or unmarried children, siblings, or grandchildren of AAAA members or deceased members. They also should demonstrate academic achievement and exceptional character.

*Application Process: Applicants should submit a completed application along with official transcripts, a photograph, proof of college admission, two references, a school recommendation, a teacher recommendation, and an academic reporting form. Visit the organization's Web site to download an application and additional forms. *Amount: $1,000 to $4,000. Applicants who don't receive grants will qualify for no-interest loans. *Deadline: May 1.

Blinded Veterans Association
477 H Street, NW
Washington, DC 20001-2694
202-371-8880
bva@bva.org
http://www.bva.org
Scholarship Name: Kathern F. Gruber Scholarship. *Academic Area: Open. *Age Group: Undergraduate students, graduate students. *Eligibility: Applicants must be the children or spouses of blind veterans. *Application Process: Contact the association for application details. *Amount: $1,000. *Deadline: Typically in April.

California Department of Veterans Affairs
Division of Veterans Services
1227 O Street
Sacramento, CA 95814
916-503-8397
http://www.cdva.ca.gov/service/feewaiver.asp
Scholarship Name: The department offers scholarships to help finance college training. *Academic Area: Open. *Age Group: Undergraduate students. *Eligibility: California children and spouses of veterans with a service-related disability are eligible for financial aid to attend a California state college, university, or community college. Applicants must demonstrate financial need. *Application Process: An application is available for download at the department's Web site. Contact the department for details. *Amount: Full scholarships for tuition and fees, plus a stipend of $100 a month are awarded. *Deadline: Contact the department for information.

Coast Guard Mutual Assistance (CGMA)
Attn: CWO Kimberly A. Smith
2100 2nd Street, SW, Room B-442
Washington, DC 20593-0001
202-267-2085, 800-881-2462
kasmith@comdt.uscg.milhttp://www.cgmahq.org/Assistance/Frame.htm

Grant Name: Supplemental Education Grant. *Academic Area: Open. *Age Group: Undergraduate students. *Eligibility: Applicants must be enrolled in an undergraduate degree program or vocational/tech program approved by the U.S. Department of Veteran Affairs or Department of Education. They may also be seeking a GED, with intentions of pursuing a college education. Applicants should visit the organization's Web site for a detailed definition of a CGMA client. The following groups are eligible for this grant: active duty members of the U.S. Coast Guard, retired U.S. Coast Guard military personnel, civilian employees of the U.S. Coast Guard, U.S. Coast Guard Reserve members, U.S. Coast Guard Auxiliary members, Public Health Service Officers serving with the U.S. Coast Guard, and family members of the aforementioned groups. *Application Process: Applicants should submit a completed application, receipts for qualifying items (the grant pays for specific school-related expenses), and proof of enrollment. Visit the organization's Web site for a complete list of eligible expenses and to download an application. Applicants should submit their completed documents to their nearest CGMA representative. A complete list of CGMA representatives, by state, is available at the organization's Web site. *Amount: $160. *Deadline: Contact your local CGMA representative for deadline information.

Coast Guard Mutual Assistance (CGMA)
Attn: CWO Kimberly A. Smith
2100 2nd Street, SW, Room B-442
Washington, DC 20593-0001
202-267-2085, 800-881-2462
kasmith@comdt.uscg.milhttp://www.cgmahq.org/Assistance/Frame.htm
Loan Name: Supplemental Student Loan Program. *Academic Area: Open. *Age Group: Undergraduate students. *Eligibility: Applicants must demonstrate unmet financial need, after other sources of maximum assistance from the Coast Guard Tuition Assistance Program have been utilized. The following groups are eligible for this grant: active duty members of the U.S. Coast Guard, retired U.S. Coast Guard military personnel, civilian employees of the U.S. Coast Guard, U.S. Coast Guard Reserve members, U.S. Coast Guard Auxiliary members, Public Health Service Officers serving with the U.S. Coast Guard, and family members of the aforementioned groups. *Application Process: Applicants should submit a completed

application along with a copy of the front and back of the member's valid Coast Guard identification card, a copy of a signed tuition assistance authorization form, or a copy of documentation that shows other sources of Coast Guard assistance have been temporarily suspended. Visit the organization's Web site to download an application. Applications should be turned in to the nearest CGMA representative. A complete list of CGMA representatives is available at the organization's Web site. *Amount: Up to $700. *Deadline: None.

Coast Guard Mutual Assistance (CGMA)

Attn: CWO Kimberly A. Smith
2100 2nd Street, SW, Room B-442
Washington, DC 20593-0001
202-267-2085, 800-881-2462
kasmith@comdt.uscg.milhttp://www.cgmahq.org/
    Assistance/Frame.htm

Loan Name: Vocational and Technical Training Student Loan Program. *Academic Area: Vocational education. *Age Group: Undergraduate students. *Eligibility: Applicants must be CGMA members, their spouses, or their dependent children who are enrolled in a vocational education program and who demonstrate financial need. *Application Process: Applicants should submit a completed application along with proof of enrollment and a copy of the front and back of the member's Coast Guard identification card. Visit the organization's Web site to download an application. Applications should be submitted to the closest CGMA representative. Visit the Web site for a list of CGMA representatives by state. *Amount: Up to $1,500. *Deadline: Applicants must submit the application no later than 30 days after the course begins.

Delaware Commission of Veterans Affairs

Robbins Building, 802 Silver Lake Boulevard, Suite 100
Dover, DE 19904
302-739-2792, 800-344-9900
http://www.state.de.us/veteran

Grant Name: The commission provides tuition waivers for the purpose of college study. *Academic Area: Open. *Age Group: Undergraduate students. *Eligibility: Children of Delaware military veterans who died as a result of military service, or who have been declared missing in action, are eligible to apply. Applicants must be residents of Delaware, be at least 16 and not older than 24, and attend a public college or university in the state. *Application Process:

Contact the commission for details. *Amount: $525 or the amount of tuition per academic year, whichever is greater. *Deadline: Contact the commission for details.

Elks National Foundation (ENF)

Scholarship Department
2750 North Lakeview Avenue
Chicago, IL 60614-1889
773-755-4732
scholarship@elks.org
http://www.elks.org/enf/scholars/eefgrants.cfm

Grant Name: Emergency Educational Fund Grant Program. *Academic Area: Open. *Age Group: Undergraduate students. *Eligibility: Applicants must be high school seniors or college students who are children/stepchildren of deceased or totally disabled Elks members. Applicants must be under 23 and demonstrate financial need. *Application Process: Applicants may request an Emergency Educational Fund Grant application from the ENF. All applications, new and renewal, must be submitted to, and processed by, the lodge where the Elk parent or stepparent is or was a member. *Amount: Up to $4,000. *Deadline: December 31.

Fleet Reserve Association (FRA)

Attn: FRA Scholarship Administrator
125 North West Street
Alexandria, VA 22314-2754
703-683-1400, 800-FRA-1924
http://www.fra.org/Content/fra/AboutFRA/Scholarships/
    default.htm

Scholarship Name: Fleet Reserve Association Scholarship. *Academic Area: Open. *Age Group: Undergraduate students, graduate students. *Eligibility: Applicants must be FRA members or the spouses, children, or grandchildren of FRA members (current and former members of the Navy, Marine Corps, and Coast Guard) in good standing or of a member in good standing at the time of death. Applicants must demonstrate academic achievement, leadership potential, and financial need. *Application Process: Applicants should submit a completed application along with completed transcript request forms and an essay. Financial information on the application (along with all other sections) should be completed in its entirety to be considered. Visit the association's Web site to download an application. *Amount: $5,000. *Deadline: April 15.

Fleet Reserve Association (FRA)
Attn: FRA Scholarship Administrator
125 North West Street
Alexandria, VA 22314-2754
703-683-1400, 800-FRA-1924
http://www.fra.org/Content/fra/AboutFRA/Scholarships/
  default.htm
Scholarship Name: Glenn F. Glezen Scholarship.
  *Academic Area: Open. *Age Group: Undergraduate
  students, graduate students. *Eligibility: Applicants
  must be FRA members, or the spouses, children,
  or grandchildren of FRA members (current and
  former members of the Navy, Marine Corps, and
  Coast Guard) in good standing or of a member in
  good standing at the time of death. They must also
  demonstrate academic achievement, leadership
  potential, and financial need. Preference is given to
  students pursuing master's or doctorate degrees.
  *Application Process: Applicants should submit
  a completed application along with completed
  transcript request forms and an essay. Financial
  information on the application (along with all
  other sections) should be completed in its entirety
  to be considered. Visit the association's Web site
  to download an application. *Amount: $5,000.
  *Deadline: April 15.

Fleet Reserve Association (FRA)
Attn: FRA Scholarship Administrator
125 North West Street
Alexandria, VA 22314-2754
703-683-1400, 800-FRA-1924
http://www.fra.org/Content/fra/AboutFRA/Scholarships/
  default.htm
Scholarship Name: Robert W. Nolan Emeritus
  Scholarship. *Academic Area: Open. *Age Group:
  Undergraduate students, graduate students.
  *Eligibility: Applicants must be the spouses, children,
  or grandchildren of FRA members (current and
  former members of the Navy, Marine Corps, and
  Coast Guard) in good standing or of a member in
  good standing at the time of death. They must also
  demonstrate academic achievement, leadership
  potential, and financial need. Applicants may also
  be FRA members. Preference is given to students
  pursuing master's or doctorate degrees. *Application
  Process: Applicants should submit a completed
  application along with completed transcript request
  forms and an essay. Financial information on the
  application (along with all other sections) should be
  completed in its entirety to be considered. Visit the

association's Web site to download an application.
  *Amount: $5,000. *Deadline: April 15.

Fleet Reserve Association (FRA)
Attn: FRA Scholarship Administrator
125 North West Street
Alexandria, VA 22314-2754
703-683-1400, 800-FRA-1924
http://www.fra.org/Content/fra/AboutFRA/Scholarships/
  default.htm
Scholarship Name: Schuyler S. Pyle Scholarship.
  *Academic Area: Open. *Age Group: Undergraduate
  students, graduate students. *Eligibility: Applicants
  must be the spouses, children, or grandchildren
  of FRA members (current and former members of
  the Navy, Marine Corps, and Coast Guard) in good
  standing or of a member in good standing at the
  time of death. They must also demonstrate academic
  achievement, leadership potential, and financial need.
  Applicants may also be FRA members. *Application
  Process: Applicants should submit a completed
  application along with completed transcript request
  forms and an essay. Financial information on the
  application (along with all other sections) should be
  completed in its entirety to be considered. Visit the
  association's Web site to download an application.
  *Amount: $5,000. *Deadline: April 15.

Fleet Reserve Association (FRA)
Attn: FRA Scholarship Administrator
125 North West Street
Alexandria, VA 22314-2754
703-683-1400, 800-FRA-1924
http://www.fra.org/Content/fra/AboutFRA/Scholarships/
  default.htm
Scholarship Name: Stanley A. Doran Memorial
  Scholarship. *Academic Area: Open. *Age Group:
  Undergraduate students, graduate students.
  *Eligibility: Applicants must be the children of FRA
  members (current and former members of the Navy,
  Marine Corps, and Coast Guard) in good standing or
  of a member in good standing at the time of death.
  They must also demonstrate academic achievement,
  leadership potential, and financial need. *Application
  Process: Applicants should submit a completed
  application along with completed transcript request
  forms and an essay. Financial information on the
  application (along with all other sections) should be
  completed in its entirety to be considered. Visit the
  association's Web site to download an application.
  *Amount: Awards vary. *Deadline: April 15.

Fleet Reserve Association (FRA)
Attn: W. R. Holcombe
Walter E. Beale Scholarship
4911 Fennell Court
Suffolk, VA 23435
800-FRA-1924
prp.inc2@verizon.net
http://www.fra.org/Content/fra/AboutFRA/Scholarships/
   default.htm
Scholarship Name: Walter E. Beale Scholarship.
   *Academic Area: Aviation, engineering
   (aeronautical). *Age Group: Undergraduate students,
   graduate students. *Eligibility: Applicants must
   be FRA members (current and former members of
   the Navy, Marine Corps, and Coast Guard) or the
   spouses, children, or grandchildren of FRA members
   who are majoring in aeronautical engineering or
   aviation. They must also demonstrate academic
   achievement, leadership potential, and financial
   need. *Application Process: Applicants must request
   an application by mail or e-mail. Applications must
   be submitted along with any additional required
   documentation by the deadline. *Amount: Awards
   vary. *Deadline: April 15.

Florida Department of Education
Office of Student Financial Assistance
1940 North Monroe Street, Suite 70
Tallahassee, FL 32303-4759
888-827-2004
http://www.firn.edu/doe/bin00065/cddvfactsheet.htm
Scholarship Name: Children of Deceased or Disabled
   Veterans or Children of Servicemen Classified as
   Prisoners of War or Missing in Action Scholarship.
   *Academic Area: Open. *Age Group: Undergraduate
   students. *Eligibility: Children of Florida military
   veterans who died or were disabled as a result of
   military service, or who have been declared missing
   in action, are eligible to apply. Applicants must be
   residents of Florida, between the ages of 16 and 22,
   and pursuing or planning to pursue at least six credit
   hours at an approved postsecondary Florida public
   college or university. *Application Process: Applicants
   must complete the Florida Financial Aid Application,
   which is available at the department's Web site.
   Contact the department for details. *Amount: Tuition
   and fees are covered. *Deadline: April 1.

Force Recon Association (FRA)
Scholarship Committee
Attn: Dr. Wayne M. Lingenfelter, Chairman

2992 Calle Gaucho
San Clemente, CA 92673
http://www.forcerecon.com
Scholarship Name: Force Recon Association
   Scholarship. *Academic Area: Open. *Age Group:
   Undergraduate students, graduate students.
   *Eligibility: Applicants must members in good
   standing of the Force Recon Association, family
   members of members, or family members of a
   deceased member. They also must be pursuing any
   kind of postsecondary education and demonstrate
   academic achievement and exceptional character.
   *Application Process: Applicants should submit
   a completed application along with a personal
   statement detailing their career plans, copies
   of official transcripts, and three letters of
   recommendation. Visit the association's Web site to
   download an application. *Amount: Awards vary.
   *Deadline: Two weeks prior to the annual meeting.

Grantham University
7200 NW 86th Street, Suite M
Kansas City, MO 64153
800-955-2527
admissions@grantham.edu
http://www.grantham.edu/scholarships.htm
Scholarship Name: Military Education Scholarship
   for Family Members. *Academic Area: Open. *Age
   Group: Undergraduate students, graduate students.
   *Eligibility: Applicants must be military spouses or
   children of a family member in any branch of the
   U.S. military (active duty or reserve) who intend to
   pursue a degree program at Grantham University.
   *Application Process: Applicants should visit the
   university's Web site to download an application
   packet. Application forms are downloadable as
   zip files; you'll need the appropriate program to
   open the files. Contact the university if you would
   like an application mailed to you. An application
   and additional supporting materials should be
   submitted. *Amount: Awards vary. *Deadline:
   Contact the university for deadline information.

Illinois Department of Veterans' Affairs
833 South Spring Street, PO Box 19432
Springfield, IL 62794-9432
217-782-6641
http://www.state.il.us/agency/dva/vetben.htm
Scholarship Name: Children of Veterans Scholarship.
   *Academic Area: Open. *Age Group: Undergraduate
   students. *Eligibility: Applicants must be the

children of veterans who served during WWI, WWII, Korean War, the Vietnam Conflict, or any time after August 2, 1990. The children of deceased or disabled veterans are given preference. This scholarship is awarded to attend the University of Illinois, and applicants must be residents of Illinois. *Application Process: Applicants should contact the university's financial aid office for information on the application process. Applicants apply directly through the university. *Amount: Full tuition for four consecutive years. *Deadline: Contact the financial aid office for deadline information.

Illinois Department of Veterans' Affairs
833 South Spring Street, PO Box 19432
Springfield, IL 62794-9432
217-782-6641
http://www.state.il.us/agency/dva/vetben.htm
Scholarship Name: MIA/POW Scholarship. *Academic Area: Open. *Age Group: Undergraduate students. *Eligibility: Applicants must be the dependents of a veteran who has either died (as the result of service) or has been declared a prisoner of war or missing in action by the U.S. Department of Defense or U.S. Department of Veterans Affairs. The veteran may also have been permanently disabled from service-connected causes with 100 percent disability. Illinois residency at the time of service is also required. *Application Process: Applicants should contact the Illinois Department of Veterans' Affairs for information on the application process. *Amount: Full tuition, plus fees at state-supported Illinois colleges and universities (for four years of study). *Deadline: Contact the Illinois Department of Veterans' Affairs for deadline information.

Indiana Department of Veterans' Affairs
302 West Washington Street, Room E120
Indianapolis, IN 46204-2738
317-232-3910, 800-400-4520
http://www.in.gov/veteran/sso/brochure/remission.html
Scholarship Name: Remission of Fees for the Child of a Disabled Veteran or POW/MIA. *Academic Area: Open. *Age Group: Undergraduate students. *Eligibility: Children of Indiana veterans who died or who are permanently disabled, or who have been declared a prisoner of war or missing in action, as a result of military service are eligible to apply. Applicants must be residents of Indiana and attend a college or university in the state. *Application

Process: Visit the department's Web site to download an application. Contact the department for details. *Amount: Amounts vary, but benefits are limited to cost of tuition and fees. *Deadline: Contact the department for details.

Iowa Commission of Veterans Affairs
Camp Dodge, Building A6A
7700 NW Beaver Drive
Johnston, IA 50131-1902
515-242-5331
info@icva.state.ia.us
http://www.iowava.org/asp/orphan.asp
Scholarship Name: War Orphans Educational Aid. *Academic Area: Open. *Age Group: Undergraduate students. *Eligibility: Children of Iowa veterans who died as a result of military service are eligible to apply. Applicants must be residents of Iowa and attend selected public colleges or universities in the state. *Application Process: Contact the department to obtain an application. Applicants must submit a completed application, a copy of their birth certificate, a copy of their veteran parent's death certificate, and verification that they have lived in Iowa for two years prior to making application.. *Amount: $600 per calendar year, with a lifetime maximum benefit of $3,000. *Deadline: Contact the commission for details.

Kansas Commission on Veterans' Affairs
Jayhawk Towers, 700 Southwest Jackson Street, Suite 701
Topeka, KS 66603-3743
785-296-3976
http://www.kcva.org
Grant Name: The commission provides tuition waivers for the purpose of college study. *Academic Area: Open. *Age Group: Undergraduate students. *Eligibility: Children of Kansas veterans who are deceased as a result of military service, or missing in action, are eligible to apply. Applicants must be residents of Kansas and attend a public college or university in the state. *Application Process: Contact the commission for details. *Amount: Full tuition. *Deadline: Contact the commission for details.

Kentucky Department of Veterans Affairs
1111 Louisville Road
Frankfort, KY 40601
502-564-9203, 800-572-6245
jennifer.waddell@ky.gov
http://www.kdva.net/tuitionwaiver.htm

Grant Name: Tuition Waiver Program. *Academic Area: Open. *Age Group: Undergraduate students. *Eligibility: Kentucky residents who are children or spouses of disabled veterans are eligible. Applicants must plan to attend or be currently attending a public college or university in the state. *Application Process: Visit the department's Web site to download an application, which must be submitted with the following documents: applicant's birth certificate, marriage certificate (spouses only), death certificate (if military parent is deceased), and veteran's discharge papers (if the military parent is disabled). *Amount: Full tuition. *Deadline: Contact the department for details.

Louisiana Department of Veterans Affairs
Capitol Station, PO Box 94095
Baton Rouge, LA 70804-9095
225-922-0500
http://www.vetaffairs.com
Scholarship Name: State Aid Program-Dependents Educational Assistance. *Academic Area: Open. *Age Group: Undergraduate students. *Eligibility: Children and spouses of Louisiana veterans who are disabled or deceased as a result of wartime active duty service are eligible to apply. Child applicants must be between the ages of 16 and 25; spouses must use the aid within 10 years of becoming eligible for the program. Applicants must plan to or currently attend one of the state's public colleges and universities. *Application Process: Visit the department's Web site for details. *Amount: Full tuition. *Deadline: Contact the department for details.

Maine Bureau of Veterans' Services
117 State House Station
Augusta, ME 04333-0117
207-626-4464
http://www.mainebvs.org/VDEB%20eligibility.htm
Scholarship Name: Veterans Dependents Educational Benefits Program. *Academic Area: Open. *Age Group: Undergraduate students, graduate students. *Eligibility: Maine residents who are children or spouses of a veteran who is deceased or severely disabled as a result of military duty may apply. Children must be at least 16 years of age, but not over 25, at the time of application. *Application Process: Applicants must submit a completed application and a copy of their certificate (child applicant) or marriage certificate (spouse applicant)

Visit the bureau's Web site to download an application.*Amount: Full tuition. *Deadline: Call or write for information.

Marine Corps Scholarship Foundation
PO Box 3008
Princeton, NJ 08543-3008
800-292-7777
mcsfnj@mcsf.org
http://www.marine-scholars.org
Scholarship Name: Combined Marine and Navy Corpsman Scholarship. *Academic Area: Open. *Age Group: Undergraduate students. *Eligibility: Applicants must be the son or daughter of a marine or navy corpsman. Visit the foundation's Web site for specific eligibility requirements regarding the parent's (or grandparent's) service. Additionally, the total family gross income may not exceed $63,000. High school seniors and undergraduate students may apply for this scholarship. *Application Process: Applicants should submit a completed application along with their Student Aid Report, tax returns, a certificate of service, transcripts, and a 300-word essay. Visit the foundation's Web site to download an official application. *Amount: Awards vary. *Deadline: March 1 (high school seniors), April 15 (undergraduate students).

Maryland Higher Education Commission
Office of Student Financial Assistance
Attn: Edward T. Conroy Memorial Scholarship Program
839 Bestgate Road, Suite 400
Annapolis, MD 21401-3013
410-260-4500, 800-974-0203
osfamail@mhec.state.md.us
http://www.mhec.state.md.us/financialAid/ProgramDescriptions/prog_conroy.asp
Scholarship Name: Edward T. Conroy Memorial Scholarship. *Academic Area: Open. *Age Group: Undergraduate students, graduate students. *Eligibility: Children or spouses of a permanently disabled Maryland veteran, a disabled state or local public safety employee, or a deceased victim of the September 11 terrorist attacks may apply. Applicants must be enrolled or plan to enroll in a Maryland college or university. Visit the commission's Web site for further eligibility requirements. *Application Process: Visit the commission's Web site to download an application. *Amount: Tuition and fees not to exceed $8,550. *Deadline: July 15.

Massachusetts Department of Veterans' Services
454 Broadway Street, Suite 200
Revere, MA 02151
617-727-9420
osfa@osfa.mass.edu
http://www.state.ma.us/veterans
Grant Name: Massachusetts Public Service Grant
Program. *Academic Area: Open. *Age Group:
Undergraduate students, graduate students.
*Eligibility: Children and spouses of Massachusetts
veterans who were killed in action or who died
from service-related injuries may apply. Applicants
must plan to attend a public institution in the
state of Massachusetts. Children and widows of
Massachusetts police officers, fire fighters, and
corrections officers killed in the line of duty or who
died from service-related injuries may also apply.
*Application Process: Visit the department's Web
site for more information. *Amount: Up to $2,500.
*Deadline: Contact the department for details.

**Michigan Department of Military and Veterans
Affairs**
3411 Martin Luther King Jr. Boulevard
Lansing, MI 48906
517-483-5469
http://www.michigan.gov/dmva/0,1607,7-126-2362-
11891--,00.html
Grant Name: Tuition Grant. *Academic Area: Open.
*Age Group: Undergraduate students. *Eligibility:
Children or spouses of Michigan veterans who
died or who are permanently disabled as a result
of military service are eligible to apply. Applicants
must be residents of Michigan for at least 12 months
prior to application, be between the ages of 16 and
25, have a GPA of at least 2.25, and attend a college
or university in the state full time. *Application
Process: Visit the department's Web site to download
an application. *Amount: Up to $2,800 annually.
*Deadline: Contact the department for details.

Military Intelligence Corps Association (MICA)
Attn: MICA Scholarship Committee
PO Box 13020
Fort Huachuca, AZ 85670-3020
scholarship@micorps.org
http://www.micorps.org/scholarship.htm
Scholarship Name: MICA Scholarship Program.
*Academic Area: Open. *Age Group: Undergraduate
students. *Eligibility: Applicants must be

dependents (children or spouse) of a military
intelligence soldier who is on active duty, reserve,
or retired. Applicants (or family members) must
be active members of MICA, pursuing their first
undergraduate degree, and accepted into a college
or university. *Application Process: Applicants
must submit a completed application along with
three letters of recommendation, a one-page essay
detailing their educational goals, high school or
GED transcripts, proof of college acceptance, and a
photocopy of the appropriate military identification.
Visit the association's Web site to download an
application. *Amount: $500 to $1,000. *Deadline:
May 15.

Minnesota Department of Veterans Affairs
State Veterans Service Building
20 West 12th Street, Room 206C
St. Paul, MN 55155-2006
651-296-2562
http://www.mdva.state.mn.us/education.htm
Grant Name: War Orphan Education Assistance.
*Academic Area: Open. *Age Group: Undergraduate
students. *Eligibility: Dependents of Minnesota
veterans who have died while on active duty or as
a result of a service-related condition may apply.
Applicants must be residents of Minnesota for at
least two years prior to application and plan to
or currently attend a public college or university
in Minnesota.*Application Process: Visit the
department's Web site for details.*Amount: Tuition
waiver plus $750 per year for fees, books and
supplies, and/or room and board. *Deadline: Contact
the department for details.

Mississippi State Veterans Affairs Board
PO Box 5947
Pearl, MS 39288-5947
601-576-4850
grice@vab.state.ms.us
http://www.vab.state.ms.us/booklet.htm#Educational
Grant Name: The department provides tuition waivers
for the purpose of college study. *Academic Area:
Open. *Age Group: Undergraduate students,
graduate students. *Eligibility: Children of Mississippi
veterans who are officially classified as being either
a prisoner of a foreign government or missing in
action can receive an eight-semester scholarship at
a Mississippi public college or university. Applicants
must be residents of Mississippi.*Application Process:

Visit the board's Web site for details.*Amount: Contact the board for details. *Deadline: Contact the board for details.

Navy-Marine Corps Relief Society (NMCRS)
NMCRS Education Division
875 North Randolph Street, Suite 225
Arlington, VA 22203
703-696-4960
education@hq.nmcrs.org
http://www.nmcrs.org/education.html
Scholarship Name: Dependents of Deceased Service Members Scholarship. *Academic Area: Open. *Age Group: Undergraduate students. *Eligibility: Applicants must be unmarried children or unmarried spouses who are military dependents of deceased service members, and who are enrolled as full-time undergraduate students in a program that participates in the U.S. Department of Education's Title IV financial aid program. They also must maintain at least a 2.0 GPA, demonstrate financial need, and possess a current military dependent's Uniformed Services Identification and Privilege Card. *Application Process: Applicants must submit a completed application along with the eligibility application form, a family financial data form, a grade point average verification form, transcripts, a copy of the dependent's Uniformed Services Identification and Privilege Card, and a copy of the relevant death report. Visit the organization's Web site to download the application and forms. *Amount: Up to $3,000. *Deadline: March 1.

Navy-Marine Corps Relief Society (NMCRS)
NMCRS Education Division
875 North Randolph Street, Suite 225
Arlington, VA 22203
703-696-4960
education@hq.nmcrs.org
http://www.nmcrs.org/education.html
Scholarship Name: Spouse Tuition Aid Program. *Academic Area: Open. *Age Group: Undergraduate students, graduate students. *Eligibility: Applicants must be spouses of active duty service members who are residing with that active duty service member outside of the United States. They also must be pursuing postsecondary education at an on-base educational program. *Application Process: Applicants should contact their nearest Navy-Marine Corps Relief Society Office for details

on the application process. This scholarship is administered locally (in overseas locations). Visit the organization's Web site for a listing of Navy-Marine Corp Relief Society offices. *Amount: Up to $1,500 (undergraduate students); up to $1,750 (graduate students). *Deadline: Contact your local NMCRS office for deadline information.

Navy-Marine Corps Relief Society (NMCRS)
NMCRS Education Division
875 North Randolph Street, Suite 225
Arlington, VA 22203
703-696-4960
education@hq.nmcrs.org
http://www.nmcrs.org/education.html
Scholarship Name: USS Tennessee Scholarship Fund. *Academic Area: Open. *Age Group: Undergraduate students. *Eligibility: Applicants must be dependent children of active duty or retired service members who have served aboard the USS Tennessee. They also must be enrolled as full-time undergraduate students in a program that participates in the U.S. Department of Education's Title IV financial aid program. Applicants must maintain at least a 2.0 GPA and demonstrate financial need. *Application Process: Applicants must submit a completed application along with a family financial data form, a grade point average verification form, and transcripts. Visit the organization's Web site to download the application and forms. *Amount: Up to $2,000. *Deadline: March 1.

Navy-Marine Corps Relief Society (NMCRS)
NMCRS Education Division
4015 Wilson Boulevard, 10th Floor
Arlington, VA 22203
703-696-4960
education@hq.nmcrs.org
http://www.nmcrs.org/education.html
Scholarship/Loan Name: Vice Admiral E. P. Travers Scholarship and Loan Program. *Academic Area: Open. *Age Group: Undergraduate students. *Eligibility: Applicants must be dependent children of active duty and retired Navy-Marine Corps personnel, or spouses of active duty Navy and Marine Corps personnel who are enrolled as full-time undergraduate students in a program that participates in the U.S. Department of Education's Title IV financial aid program. Applicants must maintain at least a 2.0 GPA and demonstrate

financial need. *Application Process: Applicants must submit a completed application along with the family financial data form, a grade point average verification form, and transcripts. Visit the organization's Web site to download the application and forms. *Amount: Up to $2,000 (grant); up to $3,000 (loan). *Deadline: March 1.

Nebraska Department of Veterans' Affairs

301 Centennial Mall South, 6th Floor, PO Box 95083
Lincoln, NE 68509-5083
402-471-2458
http://www.nebraskaveteran.com

Grant Name: The department provides tuition waivers for the purpose of college study. *Academic Area: Open. *Age Group: Undergraduate students. *Eligibility: Children or spouses of Nebraska veterans who died or who are permanently disabled as a result of military service are eligible to apply. Applicants must be residents of Nebraska and attend a college or university in the state. Visit the department's Web site for further eligibility requirements. *Application Process: Visit the department's Web site for details. *Amount: Full tuition. *Deadline: Contact the department for details.

New Hampshire State Veterans Council

275 Chestnut Street, Room 321
Manchester, NH 03101-2411
603-624-9230, 800-622-9230
nhviold@vba.va.gov
http://www.nh.gov/nhveterans/bene.html

Grant Name: The council provides tuition waivers for the purpose of college study. *Academic Area: Open. *Age Group: Undergraduate students. *Eligibility: Children of New Hampshire veterans who are deceased as a result of a service-connected disability or declared missing in action are eligible to apply. Applicants must be residents of New Hampshire and attend a public college or university in the state. *Application Process: Contact the council for details. *Amount: Full tuition (children of those missing in action); up to $2,500 (children of those deceased as a result of a disability). *Deadline: Contact the council for details.

New Mexico Department of Veterans' Services (NMDVS)

PO Box 2324
Santa Fe, NM 87504

505-827-6300, 866-433-8387
alan.martinez@state.nm.us
http://www.state.nm.us/veterans/

Scholarship Name: Children of Deceased Veterans Scholarship. *Academic Area: Open. *Age Group: Undergraduate students. *Eligibility: Applicants must be the children of a veteran of the Armed Forces who died as a result of fighting during a period of armed conflict. Children of National Guard members and state police officers who were killed while on active duty are also eligible. The veteran must have been a resident of the state of New Mexico at the time he or she entered the armed forces. Applicants must also be between the ages of 16 and 26, attend a state-supported institution, and demonstrate academic achievement and financial need. *Application Process: Applicants should contact the NMDVS office for details on the application process. *Amount: Tuition, room and board, fees, and books. *Deadline: Contact the NMDVS for deadline information.

New York State Division of Veterans' Affairs

c/o New York State Higher Education Services Corporation
99 Washington Avenue
Albany, NY 12255
518-473-1574, 888-697-4372
http://www.hesc.com/bulletin.nsf
http://www.veterans.state.ny.us/benefits.htm

Scholarship Name: Children of Veterans Award. *Academic Area: Open. *Age Group: Undergraduate students, graduate students. *Eligibility: Applicants must be the children of parent(s) who served in the U.S. armed forces during a period of war or national emergency and who were either killed or suffered a 40 percent or more disability due to that service. The parent may also have been classified as missing in action or a prisoner of war. New York residency, either currently, or at the time of death is required of the veteran. Applicants should visit the organization's Web site for a complete list of approved service dates. *Application Process: Applicants should submit a Child of Veteran Award Supplement form to the New York State Higher Education Service Corporation (HESC) to establish eligibility. This should be done before applying for payment. Contact the HESC by phone to request the form. *Amount: $450 per year. *Deadline: May 1.

New York State Division of Veterans' Affairs
c/o New York State Higher Education Services
    Corporation
99 Washington Avenue
Albany, NY 12255
518-473-1574, 888-697-4372
http://www.hesc.com/bulletin.nsf/
http://www.veterans.state.ny.us/benefits.htm
Scholarship Name: Military Service Recognition
    Scholarship. *Academic Area: Open. *Age Group:
    Undergraduate students. *Eligibility: Applicants must
    be the children, spouses, or financial dependents of
    individuals who either died or became permanently
    disabled while serving in conflict or a military training
    operation on or after August 2, 1990. Veterans who
    became severely or permanently disabled during this
    time, either in combat or as the result of a military
    training accident, are also eligible. The veteran must
    be, or have been, a New York resident at the time of
    the incident. *Application Process: Applicants should
    submit a supplement form to the New York State
    Higher Education Service Corporation to establish
    eligibility. Visit the corporation's Web site to download
    the form or contact the corporation by phone to
    request the form. *Amount: Full undergraduate
    tuition, room and board, fees, and books (at state-
    sponsored schools). Individuals attending private
    schools will receive the current state-school rates only.
    *Deadline: May 1.

North Carolina Division of Veterans Affairs
325 North Salisbury Street
Raleigh, NC 27699-1315
919-733-3851
http://www.nasdva.com/northcarolina.html
Grant Name: The division offers tuition waivers to help
    finance college training. *Academic Area: Open. *Age
    Group: Undergraduate students. *Eligibility: North
    Carolina residents who are children of disabled
    veterans, or those who died in combat or as a result
    of combat-related injuries are eligible. Children of
    soldiers declared missing action or prisoners of war
    may also apply. *Application Process: Contact the
    division for details. Amount: Contact the division for
    details. *Deadline: Contact the division for details.

North Dakota Department of Veterans Affairs
1411 32nd Street South, PO Box 9003
Fargo, ND 58106-9003
701-239-7165, 866-634-8387

http://www.nd.gov/veterans/benefits/waiver.html
Grant Name: The department offers tuition/fee waivers
    to help finance college. *Academic Area: Open.
    *Age Group: Undergraduate students. *Eligibility:
    North Dakota residents who are children of disabled
    veterans, those who died in combat, those who died
    as a result of combat-related injuries, or those who
    are have been declared missing in action are eligible.
    *Application Process: Contact the department for
    details. *Amount: Full tuition. *Deadline: Contact the
    department for details.

Paralyzed Veterans of America
801 18th Street, NW
Washington, DC 20006-3517
800-424-8200, ext. 619
info@pva.org
http://www.pva.org
Grant Name: Educational Scholarship. *Academic
    Area: Open. *Age Group: Undergraduate students,
    graduate students. *Eligibility: Organization
    members and their dependents under 24 years of
    age pursuing college degrees are eligible to apply.
    *Application Process: Contact the organization for
    details. *Amount: $1,000 (full time); $500 (part time).
    *Deadline: Contact the organization for details.

**Pennsylvania Department of Military and Veterans
    Affairs**
Fort Indiantown Gap, Building P-O-47
Annville, PA 17003-5002
717-861-8901
http://www.dmva.state.pa.us/dmvanew
Grant Name: The department offers tuition waivers to
    help finance college training. *Academic Area: Open.
    *Age Group: Undergraduate students, graduate
    students. *Eligibility: Pennsylvania residents who are
    children of disabled veterans or those who died in
    combat or as a result of combat-related industries are
    eligible. *Application Process: Contact the department
    for details. *Amount: Tuition waivers are awarded.
    *Deadline: Contact the department for details.

Scholarships for Military Children Program
Career Opportunities Through Education
407 South White Horse Pike
Audubon, NJ 08106
856-573-9400
militaryscholar@scholarshipmanagers.com
http://www.militaryscholar.org

Scholarship Name: Scholarships for Military Children. *Academic Area: Open. *Age Group: Undergraduate students. *Eligibility: Applicants must be the children of active duty, reserve or guard, retired, or deceased military personnel; unmarried; under the age of 23; and have maintained at least a 3.0 GPA in high school. They must also have a military dependent identification card and be enrolled in, or planning to enroll in, a full-time undergraduate program. Applicants attending a two-year school must be able to show that classes are being transferred to a four-year institution. *Application Process: Applicants should submit a completed application along with transcripts, a letter of recommendation, and a typed essay (topic explained on the application). Applications must be turned in to the applicant's local commissary. Applicants may mail applications to a local commissary, but applications must be received by the deadline (postmarked by the deadline is not acceptable). Visit the organization's Web site to download an application, or request an application in person at your local commissary. *Amount: $1,500 (minimum). *Deadline: February 22.

Society of the First Infantry Division Foundation
1933 Morris Road
Blue Bell, PA 19422
888-342-4733
Soc1ID@aol.com
http://www.bigredone.org
Scholarship Name: DePuy Scholarship. *Academic Area: Open. *Age Group: Undergraduate students. *Eligibility: Applicants must have a parent who was killed while serving in combat (with the 1st Infantry Division) or in peacetime training accidents. *Application Process: There is no formal application process. When the foundation is notified of a casualty with dependent children, the foundation mails a letter to the next-of-kin notifying them that educational assistance will be provided when the children are old enough to receive postsecondary education. Applicants who have been notified that they qualify should contact the foundation. *Amount: Awards vary. *Deadline: None.

Society of the First Infantry Division Foundation
1933 Morris Road
Blue Bell, PA 19422
888-342-4733
Soc1ID@aol.com
http://www.bigredone.org

Scholarship Name: Huebner/Zimmerman Scholarship. *Academic Area: Open. *Age Group: Undergraduate students. *Eligibility: Applicants must be high school seniors who have a parent or grandparent who has served in the First Infantry Division of the United States Army. They also must demonstrate academic achievement and have well-defined career objectives. *Application Process: Applicants should submit a completed application along with a 200-word essay (topic explained on application), a copy of their high school transcripts, standardized test scores (SAT or ACT), a letter of acceptance from a college or university, two letters of recommendation, and proof of parent's or grandparent's service with the First Infantry Division. Males must also provide proof of registration with the Selective Service. Visit the organization's Web site to download an application. *Amount: $1,000 per year for four years. *Deadline: June 1.

South Carolina State Office of Veterans' Affairs
1205 Pendleton Street, Suite 369
Columbia, SC 29201
803-255-4255
va@oepp.sc.gov
http://www.govoepp.state.sc.us/vetaff.htm
Grant Name: Tuition Assistance for Certain War Veterans' Children. *Academic Area: Open. *Age Group: Undergraduate students, graduate students. *Eligibility: Children of South Carolina veterans who died in combat, those who died as a result of combat-related injuries, those who are disabled as a result of service, or those who are have been declared missing in action are eligible to apply. Applicants must be residents of South Carolina and attend a public college or university in the state. *Application Process: Visit the office's Web site to download an application and for more information on the application process. *Amount: Full tuition. *Deadline: Contact the office for details.

South Dakota Department of Military and Veteran Affairs (DMVA)
Soldiers & Sailors Memorial Building, 425 East Capitol Avenue
Pierre, SD 57501-5070
605-773-3269
andy.gerlach@state.sd.us
http://mva.sd.gov/Default.asp?navid=11
Scholarship Name: Free Tuition for Children of Veterans Who Die During Service. *Academic Area: Open.

*Age Group: Undergraduate students. *Eligibility: Applicants must be the children of a veteran who was either killed in action or died as a result of active-duty service. Applicants must be under the age of 25 and be a resident of South Dakota, and the veteran parent must also have been a resident of South Dakota for at least six months prior to entering the service. *Application Process: Applicants should request an application from their school's financial aid office, their local veterans representative, or the DMVA. The completed application should be submitted to the Sioux Falls VA Regional Office. *Amount: Full tuition at state-supported schools. *Deadline: Contact the DMVA office for deadline information.

South Dakota Department of Military and Veteran Affairs (DMVA)

Soldiers & Sailors Memorial Building, 425 East Capitol Avenue
Pierre, SD 57501-5070
605-773-3269
andy.gerlach@state.sd.us
http://mva.sd.gov/Default.asp?navid=11
Scholarship Name: Free Tuition for Dependents of POWs and MIAs. *Academic Area: Open. *Age Group: Undergraduate students. *Eligibility: Applicants must be the children or spouses of service members who are listed as missing in action or prisoners of war. Applicants are eligible for this award only if they are not eligible for equal or greater federal benefits. *Application Process: Applicants should request an application from their school's financial aid office, their local veterans representative, or the DMVA. The completed application should be submitted to the Sioux Falls VA Regional Office. *Amount: Full tuition at state-supported schools. *Deadline: Contact the DMVA office for deadline information.

Tailhook Educational Foundation

9696 Businesspark Avenue
San Diego, CA 92131-1643
858-689-9223, 800-269-8267
thookassn@aol.com
http://www.tailhook.org
Scholarship Name: Tailhook Educational Foundation Scholarship. *Academic Area: Open. *Age Group: Undergraduate students. *Eligibility: Applicants must be individuals who are serving or have served on a U.S. Navy aircraft carrier in the ship's company or the air wing, or their dependent

children. They also must already be accepted into an undergraduate program at a college or university, and have demonstrated academic achievement in their high school careers. *Application Process: Applicants should submit a completed application along with SAT or ACT scores, a personal essay detailing their career goals, high school and college transcripts, an acceptance letter to college, and summary of achievements. Visit the foundation's Web site to download an application. *Amount: $2,000 to $3,000. *Deadline: March 15.

Tennessee Department of Veterans Affairs

Attn: Donald L. Samuels, Public Information Officer
215 Eighth Avenue North
Nashville, TN 37243
615-741-6663
Donald.Samuels@state.tn.us
http://www.state.tn.us/veteran
Scholarship Name: The department offers scholarships to help finance college. *Academic Area: Open. *Age Group: Undergraduate students, graduate students. *Eligibility: Children of disabled military service veterans whose disability occurred as the result of active service are eligible. Applicants must reside in Tennessee. *Application Process: Contact the department for details. *Amount: Full tuition. *Deadline: Contact the department for details.

Virginia Department of Veterans Services

Poff Federal Building, 270 Franklin Road, SW, Room 503
Roanoke, VA 24011
540-857-7101
pmignard131@worldnet.att.net
http://www.vdva.vipnet.org/education_benefits.htm
Grant Name: Survivors and Dependents Educational Assistance Program. *Academic Area: Open. *Age Group: Undergraduate students, graduate students. *Eligibility: Children of Virginia veterans who are deceased or disabled as a result of military service are eligible to apply. Applicants must be residents of Virginia and plan to or currently attend a public college or university in the state. *Application Process: Visit the department's Web site for more information. *Amount: Varies. *Deadline: Contact the department for details.

Virginia Department of Veterans Services

Poff Federal Building, 270 Franklin Road, SW, Room 503
Roanoke, VA 24011

540-857-7101

http://www.vdva.vipnet.org/education_benefits.htm

Grant Name: Virginia War Orphans Education Program. *Academic Area: Open. *Age Group: Undergraduate students, graduate students. *Eligibility: Children of Virginia veterans who are deceased, disabled, or declared missing in action as a result of military service are eligible to apply. Applicants must be residents of Virginia; at least 16 years of age, but no more than 25 years of age; and plan to or currently attend a public college or university in the state. *Application Process: Visit the department's Web site to download an application. *Amount: Full tuition. *Deadline: Contact the department for details.

Washington Department of Veterans Affairs

Republic Building, 505 East Union, #150, PO Box 41155

Olympia, WA 98504-1155

360-586-1070, 800-562-2308

http://www.dva.wa.gov

Grant Name: The department provides tuition waivers for the purpose of college study. *Academic Area: Open. *Age Group: Undergraduate students, graduate students. *Eligibility: Children of Washington veterans who are disabled as a result of military service are eligible to apply. Applicants must be residents of Washington and attend public colleges or universities in the state. *Application Process: Contact the department for details. *Amount: Varies based on degree of disability and length of service. *Deadline: Contact the department for details.

Wisconsin Department of Veterans Affairs

30 West Mifflin Street, PO Box 7843

Madison, WI 53703

608-266-1311, 800-947-8387

wdvaweb@dva.state.wi.us

http://dva.state.wi.us/Ben_personalloans.asp

Loan Name: Personal Loan Program. *Academic Area: Open. *Age Group: Undergraduate students, graduate students. *Eligibility: Veterans, spouses of deceased veterans, and children of deceased veterans who are seeking a loan to pursue postsecondary education may apply. Applicants must plan to attend a public institution in the state of Wisconsin. *Application Process: Visit the department's Web site to download an application. *Amount: Up to $25,000. *Deadline: Contact the department for details.

Wisconsin Department of Veterans Affairs

30 West Mifflin Street, PO Box 7843

Madison, WI 53703

608-266-1311, 800-947-8387

wdvaweb@dva.state.wi.us

http://dva.state.wi.us/Ben_education.asp

Grant Name: Wisconsin G.I. Bill. *Academic Area: Open. *Age Group: Undergraduate students, graduate students. *Eligibility: Spouses and children of veterans who died in the line of duty or who have substantial service-connected disabilities may apply. Applicants must plan to attend a public institution in the state of Wisconsin. Child applicants must be between the ages of 18 and 25; spouses must use the waiver within 10 years of eligibility for the program. *Application Process: Visit the department's Web site to download an application. *Amount: Free tuition for spouses and children; 50-percent tuition reduction for veterans. *Deadline: Contact the department for details.

LESBIAN, GAY, BISEXUAL, AND TRANSGENDER STUDENTS

The following financial aid resources are available to lesbian, gay, bisexual, and transgender (LGBT) students or supporters of the LGBT community at the undergraduate and graduate levels.

Bread and Roses Community Fund
Lax Scholarship Fund
1500 Walnut, Suite 1305
Philadelphia, PA 19102
215-731-1107, ext. 207
lax@breadrosesfund.org
http://www.breadrosesfund.org/grants/lax.html
Scholarship Name: Jonathan Lax Scholarship for Gay Men. *Academic Area: Open. *Age Group: Undergraduate students, graduate students. *Eligibility: Applicants must be openly gay men who are either from the Philadelphia, Pennsylvania area or who plan to attend school in the Philadelphia area. The counties of residence (or school attendance) that qualify include Camden, Chester, Bucks, Delaware, Montgomery, and Philadelphia. Applicants must aspire to be role models for other gay men. *Application Process: Applicants must apply online through the fund's Web site. The online application requires a statement of income as well as a personal statement. Transcripts and references must be mailed separately. Visit the fund's Web site to apply. *Amount: $20,000 (at least one per year) or $5,000 (multiple awards). *Deadline: January 16.

Children of Lesbians and Gays Everywhere (COLAGE)
Attn: COLAGE Scholarship Committee
3543 18th Street, #1
San Francisco, CA 94110
415-861-5437
colage@colage.org
http://www.colage.org/scholarship.html
Scholarship Name: Lee Dubin Scholarship. *Academic Area: Open. *Age Group: Undergraduate students. *Eligibility: Applicants must have one or more lesbian, gay bisexual, or transgender parents or guardians, be enrolled or accepted into an accredited college or university, and maintain at least a 2.0 GPA. They also should possess a commitment to the lesbian, gay, bisexual, and transgender community and demonstrate economic need. *Application Process: Applicants should submit a completed application along with proof of enrollment in a college or university, a copy of their transcripts or report card, a financial need worksheet, a statement of financial need, and a recent photograph. Visit the organization's Web site to download an application. *Amount: $1,000. *Deadline: April 15.

Deaf Queer Resource Center (DQRC)
Attn: Deaf Queer Youth Scholarship Fund Selection Committee
PO Box 14431
San Francisco, CA 94114
scholarships@deafqueer.org
http://www.deafqueer.org/communities/youth/scholarships/index.html
Scholarship Name: DQRC Deaf Queer Youth Scholarship Fund. *Academic Area: Open. *Age Group: Undergraduate students, graduate students. *Eligibility: Applicants must be U.S. citizens who are deaf or hard of hearing; identify as lesbian, gay, bisexual, transgender, intersex, or queer; be out about their sexual orientation; currently enrolled in college or high school, and who are under the age of 25. They also must maintain at least a 2.5 GPA. *Application Process: Applicants should submit a completed application along with proof of enrollment in college or high school, a copy of their school transcripts, a letter of recommendation, two recent photos, and a written or video essay (topic explained at length on the application). Visit the center's Web site to download an application. *Amount: $250 to $500. *Deadline: July 15.

Duke University
Attn: Kerry Poynter, Interim Director
Center for Lesbian, Gay, Bisexual, and Transgender Life
02 West Union Building
Box 90958
Durham, NC 27708
919-684-6607
Kpoynter@duke.edu
http://lgbt.studentaffairs.duke.edu/programs_services/programs/Scholarship/index.html

Scholarship Name: Carolina's Gay & Lesbian Scholarship. *Academic Area: Open. *Age Group: Undergraduate students. *Eligibility: Applicants must be from North or South Carolina and either currently enrolled at Duke University or high school students planning to attend Duke University. Applicants must openly identify themselves as gay or lesbian, demonstrate financial need, and possess a commitment to involvement in the lesbian, gay, bisexual, and transgender community. *Application Process: Applicants should submit a completed application along with transcripts and any additional supporting materials. Visit the university's Web site to download an application or request further information by e-mail. *Amount: Awards vary. *Deadline: Contact the university for deadline information.

eQuality Scholarship Collaborative
PO Box 191311
San Francisco, CA 94119-1311
equality@planetoutcast.net
http://www.glsen-sfeb.org/scholarship/index.htm
Scholarship Name: Bobby Griffith Memorial Scholarship. *Academic Area: Open. *Age Group: Undergraduate students. *Eligibility: Applicants must be graduating high school seniors from Contra Costa county in California who have demonstrated academic achievement and who have applied to a two- or four-year college, university, or trade school. They also must actively promote understanding of and equality for LGBT individuals. Applicants should demonstrate leadership ability, service to the LGBT and queer community, and financial need. *Application Process: Applicants should submit a completed application along with transcripts, an essay (topic outlined on the application), and a letter of recommendation. Visit the organization's Web site to download an application. *Amount: $2,000. *Deadline: February 28.

eQuality Scholarship Collaborative
PO Box 191311
San Francisco, CA 94119-1311
equality@planetoutcast.net
http://www.glsen-sfeb.org/scholarship/index.htm
Scholarship Name: eQuality Scholarships. *Academic Area: Open. *Age Group: Undergraduate students. *Eligibility: Applicants must be graduating high school seniors in northern and central California

who have demonstrated academic achievement and who have applied to a two- or four-year college, university, or trade school. They also must actively promote understanding of and equality for LGBT individuals. Applicants should demonstrate leadership ability, service to the LGBT and queer community, and financial need. *Application Process: Applicants should submit a completed application along with transcripts, an essay (topic outlined on the application), and a letter of recommendation. Visit the organization's Web site to download an application. *Amount: $2,000 to $2,500. *Deadline: February 28.

eQuality Scholarship Collaborative
KP Pride
PO Box 30573
Oakland, CA 94604
510-987-4148
eQuality@planetoutcast.net
http://www.glsen-sfeb.org/scholarship/index.htm
Scholarship Name: Permanente Medical Group Scholarship. *Academic Area: Medicine (physician). *Age Group: Medical students. *Eligibility: Applicants must either be attending medical school in California or be California residents who are attending medical school within the United States. They must be active participants in promoting understanding of and equality for lesbian, gay, bisexual, and transgender individuals. Applicants should also be able to demonstrate academic achievement. *Application Process: Applicants should submit a completed application along with an essay (described on the application), official transcripts, and one letter of reference. Visit the organization's Web site to download an application. *Amount: $2,000. *Deadline: March 1.

First Friday Breakfast Club
Attn: Eric Burmeister, Scholarship Chair
666 Walnut Street, Suite 2500
Des Moines, IA 50309
515-273-9406
ericb@regencyhomes-usa.com
http://www.ffbciowa.org/scholarship.htm
Scholarship Name: First Friday Breakfast Club Scholarship. *Academic Area: Open. *Age Group: Undergraduate students. *Eligibility: Applicants must be high school seniors in the state of Iowa who have contributed to increasing awareness of gay

and lesbian issues in their school and community. In short, applicants must strive to reduce homophobia and increase tolerance of gay and lesbians. *Application Process: Applicants must submit an application that includes an essay (detailed on the application form) as well as academic transcripts. Visit the club's Web site to download an application. *Amount: Up to $3,000. *Deadline: March 31.

Gay and Lesbian Business Association of Santa Barbara

PO Box 90907
Santa Barbara, CA 93190
805-961-3970
glba@prideguide.net
http://prideguide.net/glba/default.htm
Scholarship Name: This association offers multiple scholarship opportunities for gays and lesbians. *Academic Area: Open. *Age Group: Undergraduate students, graduate students. *Eligibility: Applicants must be attending a college or university in Santa Barbara county, California, demonstrate financial need, and a commitment to gay and lesbian community involvement. They also should ultimately strive to make a contribution to the gay and lesbian community in the Santa Barbara area. *Application Process: Applicants should submit an autobiography, academic transcripts, and two letters of recommendation. Contact the association for further information on the application process. *Amount: Awards vary. *Deadline: Deadlines vary.

Gay Asian Pacific Alliance

Attn: Hao Thai, Scholarship Coordinator
Horizons Foundation
870 Market Street, Suite 728
San Francisco, CA 94102
415-398-2333
hao@gapa.org
http://www.gapa.org
Scholarship Name: George Choy Memorial/Gay Asian Pacific Alliance Scholarship. *Academic Area: Open. *Age Group: Undergraduate students, graduate students. *Eligibility: Applicants must be at least 25 percent Asian/Pacific Islander and planning to attend or currently attending college or university in one of nine Bay Area counties (Alameda, Contra Costa, Marin, Napa, San Francisco, San Mateo, Santa Clara, Solano, and Sonoma). Priority is given to openly lesbian, gay, bisexual, or transgender

individuals who are actively involved in the lesbian, gay, bisexual, and transgender community. Applicants must also maintain a GPA of at least 2.75. *Application Process: Applicants should submit a completed application along with a 500-word essay (described on the application form), transcripts, and a letter of recommendation. Visit the alliance's Web site to download an application. *Amount: $1,000. *Deadline: August 1.

Gay, Lesbian and Straight Education Network-Chicago (GLSEN)

Attn: Aren Drehobl
961 West Montana
Chicago, IL 60614
773-472-6469, ext. 235
drehobl@glsenchicago.org
http://www.glsenchicago.org/scholarship.html
Scholarship Name: GLSEN Chicago Scholarship. *Academic Area: Open. *Age Group: Undergraduate students. *Eligibility: Applicants must be high school seniors who have contributed to lesbian, gay, bisexual, transgender, or queer (LGBTQ) activism in their schools. An applicant's sexual orientation is not an issue for these scholarships, but applicants must be activists promoting LGBTQ issues. This organization offers several scholarships, some of which have additional eligibility requirements. Visit the organization's Web site for a complete listing of eligibility requirements for each scholarship. *Application Process: Applicants should submit a completed application along with a separate sheet indicating any awards and/or honors, academic achievements, examples of activism or school activities, and school and community LGBTQ-related projects they have led or participated in. Applicants should also submit their academic transcripts. Visit the organization's Web site to download an application. *Amount: $500 to $1,000. *Deadline: April 18.

Greater Seattle Business Association (GSBA)

GSBA and Pride Foundation Scholarships
2150 North 107th Street, Suite 205
Seattle, WA 98133-9009
206-363-9188
office@thegsba.org
http://www.thegsba.org/scholarshipprogram.php
Scholarship Name: GSBA/Pride Foundation Scholarship. *Academic Area: Open. *Age Group: Undergraduate

students. *Eligibility: Applicants must be residents of the state of Washington (but may study anywhere) who hold a strong conviction of civil and human rights for all people. Preference is given to applicants who are self-identified LGBT, members of LGBT families, or individuals who have strongly supported the LGBT community. *Application Process: Applicants should submit a completed application along with two letters of reference, transcripts, and additional applicable materials. Each packet must contain one set of originals plus seven sets of photocopied materials. Visit the association's Web site in the fall to download an application. *Amount: Awards vary. *Deadline: January 13.

Imperial Court de San Diego

c/o San Diego Lesbian, Gay, Bisexual, or Transgender Center
3909 Center Street
San Diego, CA 92101
619-692-2077
Jygzz1@aol.com
http://www.imperialcourtsandiego.org/GrantsPrograms.html
Scholarship Name: Nicole Murray-Ramirez Student Scholarship Program. *Academic Area: Open. *Age Group: Undergraduate students, graduate students. *Eligibility: This organization offers general scholarships along with scholarships for specific communities and specific college majors. Applicants should contact the organization by e-mail for eligibility requirements. *Application Process: Applicants should contact the organization by e-mail to request information about the application process. *Amount: Awards vary. *Deadline: Contact the organization for deadline information.

Imperial Court of the Rocky Mountain Empire

White Rose Scholarship Foundation
PO Box 100811
Denver, CO 80250-0811
whiterosecressywest@denvercourt.org
http://www.denvercourt.org/modules/wfchannel/index.php?pagenum=6
Scholarship Name: White Rose Scholarship. *Academic Area: Open. *Age Group: Undergraduate students. *Eligibility: Applicants should be U.S. citizens and residents of the state of Colorado (for at least one year) who demonstrate academic achievement by maintaining at least a 3.0 GPA. They also should be able to demonstrate financial need, a commitment

to community service, and be enrolled in or accepted into an accredited college, university, or vocational school. *Application Process: Applicants should submit a completed application along with a copy of current transcripts (high school or college) and two letters of recommendation. Applications are available in July of each year and can be obtained by contacting the organization by e-mail. *Amount: Awards vary. *Deadline: January 31.

Imperial Royal Sovereign Court of the Desert Empire Inc.

Attn: Scholarship Committee
PO Box 46481
Las Vegas, NV 89114-6481
http://www.desertempire.org/TnTScholarship.htm
Scholarship Name: T-n-T Scholarship. *Academic Area: Open. *Age Group: Undergraduate students, graduate students. *Eligibility: Applicants must be pursing postsecondary education within Nevada and should be able to demonstrate involvement in human and civil rights movements. Applicants must have resided in Nevada for a minimum of two years. *Application Process: Applicants should submit an application and an essay (up to 1,000 words) that expresses their commitment to their studies, goals, and activism. Visit the organization's Web site to download an application. *Amount: $500. *Deadline: October 31.

Imperial Sovereign Court of Seattle and the Olympic and Rainier Empire

J.C./Graytop Memorial Scholarship Fund
Attn: Scholarship Committee
1122 East Pike Street, PMB #1300
Seattle, WA 98122
http://www.imperialcourtofseattle.com/jcgraytop.htm
Scholarship Name: J.C./Graytop Memorial Scholarship. *Academic Area: Open. *Age Group: Undergraduate students. *Eligibility: Applicants must be high school seniors or currently enrolled undergraduates who have maintained at least a 2.5 GPA, are residents of Washington, and have a demonstrated commitment to diversity and promoting human rights in the gay and lesbian community. *Application Process: Applicants should submit a completed application form, certified (sealed) high school transcripts (or GED scores), college transcripts (for those already attending college), an essay (described on application), and two letters of recommendation. Visit the organization's Web site to download an

application. *Amount: Awards vary. *Deadline: January 20.

Imperial Sovereign Gem Court of Boise, Idaho, Inc.
Attn: Taylor Maid, Court Secretary
PO Box 6338
Boise, ID 83707-6338
208-353-6615
1taylor@idgemcourt.org
http://www.idgemcourt.org/
Funds%20&%20Applications.htm
Scholarship Name: Imperial Sovereign Gem Court of Boise, Idaho Inc. Scholarship. *Academic Area: Open. *Age Group: High school students, undergraduate students. *Eligibility: Applicants must be residents of Idaho who are seeking enrollment in high school or postsecondary education and who are self-identified, and openly gay. Applicants should demonstrate a commitment to community service and the gay community. *Application Process: Applicants should submit an application, which can be found on the organization's Web site. *Amount: $100 to $1,000. *Deadline: July 17.

International Foundation for Gender Education
Transgender Scholarship and Education Legacy Fund
PO Box 540229
Waltham, MA 02454-0229
781-899-2212
http://www.tself.org
Scholarship Name: Transgender Scholarship and Education Legacy Fund. *Academic Area: Education, medicine (open), law, religion, social work. *Age Group: Undergraduate students, graduate students. *Eligibility: Applicants must openly identify themselves as transgender individuals and must be living full time in a gender or sex role different from that which they were born. They also must be planning to attend a college or university in the next academic year and must be seeking a career in a "helping and caring" profession in the United States or Canada. *Application Process: Applicants should submit a completed application along with a list of references, two letters of recommendation, and transcripts (high school, college, or GED certificate). Visit the foundation's Web site to download an official application. *Amount: Awards vary. *Deadline: February 1.

LEAGUE at AT&T Foundation
Attn: Charles Eader, President
One AT&T Way, Room 4B214J

Bedminster, NJ 07921
703-713-7820
attleague@aol.com
http://www.league-att.org/foundation/fscholarships.html
Scholarship Name: Academic Scholarship. *Academic Area: Open. *Age Group: Undergraduate students. *Eligibility: Applicants must be graduating high school seniors in the United States who have been accepted at a two- or four-year college or university. They also must attend school full time; identify themselves as gay, lesbian, bisexual, or transgender; maintain at least a 3.0 GPA in high school; and be actively involved in their communities. *Application Process: Applicants should submit a completed application along with high school transcripts, two 250-word essays (described on the application form), three letters of recommendation, and a college acceptance letter. Visit the foundation's Web site to download an application. *Amount: $1,500. *Deadline: April 22.

LEAGUE at AT&T Foundation
Attn: Charles Eader, President
One AT&T Way, Room 4B214J
Bedminster, NJ 07921
703-713-7820
attleague@aol.com
http://www.league-att.org/foundation/fscholarships.html
Scholarship Name: Matthew Shepard Scholarship. *Academic Area: Open. *Age Group: Undergraduate students. *Eligibility: Applicants must have demonstrated exceptional leadership abilities in promoting understanding and diversity in their schools and communities. They also must be graduating high school seniors in the United States who have been accepted at a two- or four-year college or university. Applicants must attend school full time, identify themselves as gay, lesbian, bisexual, or transgender, and maintain at least a 3.0 GPA in high school. *Application Process: Applicants should submit a completed application along with high school transcripts, two 250-word essays (described on the application form), three letters of recommendation, and a college acceptance letter. Visit the foundation's Web site to download an application. *Amount: $2,500. *Deadline: April 22.

National Gay and Lesbian Task Force
Messenger-Anderson Journalism Scholarship and Internship Program

90 William Street, Suite 1201
New York, NY 10038
thetaskforce@thetaskforce.org
http://www.thetaskforce.org/aboutus/
   messengerguidelines.cfm
Scholarship Name: Messenger-Anderson Journalism
   Scholarship and Internship Program. *Academic
   Area: Journalism. *Age Group: Undergraduate
   students. *Eligibility: Applicants must be high
   school seniors or current undergraduate students
   who identify themselves as lesbian, gay, bisexual, or
   transgender and who are member of the National
   Gay and Lesbian Task Force. (Note: Applicants may
   send the $20 membership fee with the scholarship
   application if they are not already members). They
   also must be attending or planning to attend an
   accredited four-year college or university and
   pursuing a degree and/or career in journalism.
   Applicants must also maintain at least a 2.8 GPA
   and agree to complete an eight-week summer
   internship at one of the task force office in New
   York City. *Application Process: Applicants should
   submit a completed application along with official
   transcripts (one sealed original and five photocopies
   of an original), an essay (detailed on the application
   form), journalistic work sample (six copies), and three
   letters of recommendation. Visit the task force's Web
   site to download an official application. *Amount:
   $5,000 (first year), (renewable for $2,500 for two
   additional years), plus an internship. *Deadline:
   February 24.

National Lesbian and Gay Journalists Association
Attn: Jason Lloyd Clement
1420 K Street, NW, Suite 910
Washington, DC 20005
202-588-9888, ext. 12
jlclement@nlgja.org, aaronsaward@nlgja.org
http://www.nlgja.org/students/student_index.html
Scholarship Name: Leroy F. Aarons Scholarship.
   *Academic Area: Journalism. *Age Group:
   Undergraduate students, graduate students.
   *Eligibility: Applicants must be high school seniors
   accepted to a community college or four-year
   institution, current undergraduate students, or
   current undergraduate students accepted into a
   graduate program in journalism. They also must be
   U.S. citizens or permanent residents who attend
   school full time and who are committed to fair
   and accurate coverage of the lesbian and gay

community. *Application Process: Applicants should
submit a completed application along with a one-
page resume, five work samples, sealed transcripts,
three letters of recommendation, a letter of college
acceptance (high school students), and a 1,000-
word third-person autobiography. One original set
should be submitted along with five photocopied
sets. Visit the association's Web site to download an
application. *Amount: $5,000. *Deadline: February 1.

National Women's Studies Association (NWSA)
University of Maryland
7100 Baltimore Avenue, Suite 502
College Park, MD 20740
301-403-0524
nwsaoffice@nwsa.org
http://www.nwsa.org
Scholarship Name: NWSA Lesbian Caucus Scholarship.
   *Academic Area: Women's studies. *Age Group:
   Graduate students. *Eligibility: Students must be
   working on a thesis or dissertation in lesbian studies
   and must be able to demonstrate financial need.
   *Application Process: Applicants should submit a
   completed application form, a two- to three-page
   abstract of the work in progress, and three letters of
   recommendation. Visit the association's Web site to
   download an application. *Amount: $500. *Deadline:
   February 15.

Ohio State University
Gay, Lesbian, Bisexual, and Transgender Alumni Society
Attn: Erica Claman
1800 Cannon Drive, Suite 700
Columbus, OH 43210
614-457-5413
claman.3@osu.edu
http://www.osuglbt.org/scholarship.html
Scholarship Name: Undergraduate Scholarship.
   *Academic Area: Open. *Age Group: Undergraduate
   students. *Eligibility: Applicants must be currently
   enrolled students at The Ohio State University.
   Students who have completed at least 45 credit
   hours must have a GPA of at least 2.5, and students
   with less than 45 credit hours must have a GPA of
   at least 2.0. Four separate scholarships are awarded
   with varying eligibility criteria. Applicants must
   have made some contribution to the gay, lesbian,
   bisexual, and transgender community and/or
   the HIV/AIDS community. Visit the society's Web
   site for detailed specific eligibility requirements.

*Application Process: Applicants should apply online and must also submit a letter of recommendation. Visit the society's Web site to apply online. *Amount: $1,200. *Deadline: February 28.

Parents, Families and Friends of Lesbians and Gays (PFLAG)

Attn: Judy Hoff, National Scholarship Administrator
PFLAG National Scholarships Program
1726 M Street, Suite 400
Washington, DC 20036
202-467-8180, ext 219
schools@pflag.org
http://www.pflag.org/index.php?id=122
Scholarship Name: PFLAG National Scholarships Program. *Academic Area: Open. *Age Group: Undergraduate students. *Eligibility: Applicants must be graduating high school seniors who have applied to a two- or four-year degree-granting college or university. They also must either identify as LGBT or be supporters of and demonstrate a commitment to the LGBT community. This association awards numerous scholarships and some of them have additional eligibility requirements. Visit the association's Web site for a complete listing of scholarships and requirements. *Application Process: Applicants should submit a completed application along with unofficial high school transcripts, an essay (detailed on the application), and two reference forms that certify the applicant's contribution to or involvement in the lesbian, gay, bisexual, and transgender community. Visit the association's Web site to download an application. *Amount: $1,000 and $2,500. *Deadline: February 14.

The Point Foundation

Bryan L. Knapp Scholarship
PO Box 565
Genoa, NV 89411
866-33-POINT
info@thepointfoundation.org
http://www.thepointfoundation.org/scholarships/knapp.html
Scholarship Name: Bryan L. Knapp Scholarship. *Academic Area: Open. *Age Group: Undergraduate students. *Eligibility: Applicants must be from the New York City-area and attending Cornell University in Ithaca, New York. They also must demonstrate leadership ability, scholastic achievement, and a desire to "make a difference." Applicants must be

self-identified LGBT who demonstrate a commitment to the LGBT community. Applicants should visit the foundation's Web site to read about Bryan L. Knapp's life achievements in order to better understand the type of applicant who will be selected for this scholarship. Applicants who receive scholarships agree to maintain at least a 3.5 GPA. *Application Process: Applicants must apply online. Visit the foundation's Web site to receive step-by-step application guidelines and to apply. Applicants will be assigned a PIN number when they have successfully made an online submission, and this PIN number must be written on all additional supporting materials that must be mailed. These materials include two to three letters of recommendation, official school transcripts, standardized test scores, a recent photo, and an optional resume/curriculum vitae. *Amount: $5,000 to $28,000. *Deadline: March 1.

The Point Foundation

Carlos Enrique Cisneros Scholarship
PO Box 565
Genoa, NV 89411
866-33-POINT
info@thepointfoundation.org
http://www.thepointfoundation.org/scholarships/cisneros.html
Scholarship Name: Carlos Enrique Cisneros Scholarship. *Academic Area: Open. *Age Group: Undergraduate students, graduate students. *Eligibility: Applicants must attend American University in Washington, D.C., and must demonstrate leadership ability, scholastic achievement, and a desire to "make a difference." They also must be self-identified LGBT individuals who demonstrate a commitment to the LGBT community. Applicants should visit the foundation's Web site to read about Carlos Enrique Cisneros's life achievements in order to better understand the type of applicant who will be chosen for this scholarship. Applicants who receive scholarships agree to maintain at least a 3.5 GPA. *Application Process: Applicants must apply online. Visit the foundation's Web site to receive step-by-step application guidelines and to apply. Applicants will be assigned a PIN number when they have successfully made an online submission, and this PIN number must be written on all additional supporting materials that must be mailed. These materials include two to three letters of recommendation, official school transcripts, standardized test scores, a recent photo, and an

optional resume/ curriculum vitae. *Amount: $5,000 to $28,000. *Deadline: March 1.

The Point Foundation
Merle Aronson Scholarship
PO Box 565
Genoa, NV 89411
866-33-POINT
info@thepointfoundation.org
http://www.thepointfoundation.org/scholarships/
aronson.html
Scholarship Name: Merle Aronson Scholarship.
*Academic Area: Open. *Age Group: Undergraduate students, graduate students. *Eligibility: Applicants must demonstrate leadership ability, scholastic achievement, and a desire to "make a difference." They also must have a commitment to the LGBT community either by involvement on an advocacy basis alone or as a self-identified LGBT individual. Applicants should visit the foundation's Web site to read about Merle Aronson's life achievements in order to better understand the type of applicant who will be chosen for this scholarship. Applicants who receive scholarships agree to maintain at least a 3.5 GPA. *Application Process: Applicants must apply online. Visit the foundation's Web site to receive step-by-step application guidelines and to apply. Applicants will be assigned a PIN number when they have successfully made an online submission, and this PIN number must be written on all additional supporting materials that must be mailed. These materials include two to three letters of recommendation, official school transcripts, standardized test scores, a recent photo, and an optional resume/curriculum vitae. *Amount: $5,000 to $28,000. *Deadline: March 1.

The Point Foundation
mtvU + The Point Foundation Scholarship
PO Box 565
Genoa, NV 89411
866-33-POINT
info@thepointfoundation.org
http://www.thepointfoundation.org/scholarships/mtvu.
html
Scholarship Name: mtvU + The Point Foundation Scholarship. *Academic Area: Open. *Age Group: Undergraduate students, graduate students. *Eligibility: Applicants must demonstrate leadership ability, scholastic achievement, participation in extracurricular activities, emotional or financial

need, and a desire to "make a difference." They also must have a commitment to the LGBT community either by involvement on an advocacy basis alone or as a self-identified LGBT individual, and attend an mtvU school. Applicants should visit the foundation's Web site to view a complete list of mtvU schools by state. Applicants who receive scholarships agree to maintain at least a 3.5 GPA. *Application Process: Applicants must apply online. Visit the foundation's Web site to receive step-by-step application guidelines and to apply. Applicants will be assigned a PIN number when they have successfully made an online submission, and this PIN number must be written on all additional supporting materials that must be mailed. These materials include two to three letters of recommendation, official school transcripts, standardized test scores, a recent photo, and an optional resume/curriculum vitae. *Amount: $10,000. *Deadline: March 1.

The Point Foundation
Point Scholarship
PO Box 565
Genoa, NV 89411
866-33-POINT
info@thepointfoundation.org
http://www.thepointfoundation.org/scholarships/
scholarship.html
Scholarship Name: The Point Scholarship. *Academic Area: Open. *Age Group: Undergraduate students, graduate students. *Eligibility: Applicants must demonstrate leadership ability, scholastic achievement, and a desire to "make a difference." Applicants must show a commitment to the LGBT community either by involvement on an advocacy basis alone or as a self-identified LGBT individual. Applicants who receive scholarships agree to maintain at least a 3.5 GPA and to promote the mission of The Point Foundation. *Application Process: Applicants must apply online. Visit the foundation's Web site to receive step-by-step application guidelines and to apply. Applicants will be assigned a PIN number when they have successfully made an online submission, and this PIN number must be written on all additional supporting materials that must be mailed. These materials include two to three letters of recommendation, official school transcripts, standardized test scores, a recent photo, and an optional resume/curriculum vitae. *Amount: $5,000 to $28,000. *Deadline: March 1.

The Point Foundation
Walter M. Decker Scholarship
PO Box 565
Genoa, NV 89411
866-33-POINT
info@thepointfoundation.org
http://www.thepointfoundation.org/scholarships/
 decker.html
Scholarship Name: Walter M. Decker Scholarship.
 *Academic Area: Open. *Age Group: Undergraduate
 students, graduate students. *Eligibility: Applicants
 must demonstrate leadership ability, scholastic
 achievement, and a desire to "make a difference."
 Applicants must have a commitment to the LGBT
 community either by involvement on an advocacy
 basis alone or as a self-identified LGBT individual.
 Applicants should visit the foundation's Web site
 to read about Walter M. Decker's life achievements
 in order to better understand the type of applicant
 who will be selected for this scholarship. Applicants
 who receive scholarships agree to maintain at least
 a 3.5 GPA. *Application Process: Applicants must
 apply online. Visit the foundation's Web site to
 receive step-by-step application guidelines and to
 apply. Applicants will be assigned a PIN number
 when they have successfully made an online
 submission, and this PIN number must be written
 on all additional supporting materials that must be
 mailed. These materials include two to three letters
 of recommendation, official school transcripts,
 standardized test scores, a recent photo, and an
 optional resume/curriculum vitae. *Amount: $5,000
 to $28,000. *Deadline: March 1.

Pride Foundation
1122 East Pike Street, PMB #1001
Seattle, WA 98122
206-323-3318, 800-735-7287
info@pridefoundation.org
http://www.pridefoundation.org/our_programs/
 scholarships/funds/
Scholarship Name: Pride Foundation Scholarships.
 *Academic Area: Open. *Age Group: Undergraduate
 students, graduate students. *Eligibility: Applicants
 must be residents of Alaska, Idaho, Montana,
 Oregon, or Washington (but may study anywhere)
 who hold a strong conviction in civil and human
 rights for all people. Preference is given to applicants
 who are self-identified LGBT, members of LGBT
 families, or individuals who have strongly supported
 the LGBT community. Applicants should visit the

association's Web site to view a complete listing
 of the scholarships and their additional eligibility
 requirements. *Application Process: Applicants
 should submit a completed application along with
 two letters of reference, transcripts, and additional
 applicable materials. Each packet must contain
 one set of originals plus seven sets of photocopied
 materials. Visit the foundation's Web site to
 download an application. *Amount: $500 to $10,000.
 *Deadline: January 13.

Queer Foundation
Attn: Joseph Dial, Executive Director
3213 West Wheeler Street, #145
Seattle, WA 98199
206-999-8740
jdial@post.harvard.edu
http://home.comcast.net/~threepennynovel/
 queerfoundation/scholarships.html
Scholarship Name: Queer Foundation Scholarship.
 *Academic Area: Humanities (queer theory). *Age
 Group: Undergraduate students. *Eligibility:
 Applicants must be lesbian, gay, bisexual,
 transgender, or queer (LGBTQ) high school
 graduating seniors who demonstrate a desire to
 contribute to the LGBTQ community and who are
 interested in competing in an essay contest in which
 a topic of importance in the LGBTQ community is
 addressed. *Application Process: Applicants should
 submit a completed application by mail along with
 their essay. Visit the foundation's Web site for further
 information about the essay topic. Applicants should
 also e-mail their essay to the executive director.
 Selected applicants will be required to participate
 in an interview and background check. *Amount:
 $1,000. *Deadline: April 1.

**Society for the Psychological Study of Lesbian and
 Gay Issues**
http://www.apadivision44.org/honors
Scholarship Name: Bisexual Foundation Scholarship.
 *Academic Area: Psychology. *Age Group: Graduate
 students. *Eligibility: Applicants must be graduate
 students who are pursuing advanced research
 opportunities on the psychology of bisexuality. They
 also must be full-time graduate students in their
 school's department of psychology. *Application
 Process: Applicants should submit a completed
 application along with an application coversheet, a
 project description (in APA style, 10-page maximum),
 a budget worksheet, and two self-addressed

stamped envelopes. Five copies of this packet should be submitted. Visit the society's Web site for detailed information about project description specifications and to download an application. *Amount: $2,000. *Deadline: February 1.

Society for the Psychological Study of Lesbian and Gay Issues

http://www.apadivision44.org/honors

Scholarship Name: Malyon-Smith Scholarship. *Academic Area: Psychology. *Age Group: Graduate students. *Eligibility: Applicants must be graduate students who are pursuing advanced research opportunities on the psychology of sexual orientation and gender identity. They also must be full-time graduate students in their school's department of psychology. *Application Process: Applicants should submit a completed application along with an application coversheet, a project description (in APA style, 10-page maximum), a budget worksheet, and two self-addressed stamped envelopes. Five copies of this packet should be submitted. Visit the society's Web site for detailed information about project description specifications and to download an application. *Amount: $1,000. *Deadline: February 1.

Society of Lesbian and Gay Anthropologists (SOLGA)

Contact: Ellin Lewin, SOLGA Scholarship Chair
Department of Women's Studies
University of Iowa
210 Jefferson Building
Iowa City, IA 52242
319-335-1610
ellen-lewin@uiowa.edu.
http://sscl.berkeley.edu/~afaweb/
     Payne%20Prize%20SOLGA.htm

Award Name: Kenneth W. Payne Student Prize. *Academic Area: Anthropology. *Age Group: Graduate students. *Eligibility: Graduate students who have completed an outstanding work on a lesbian, gay, bisexual, or transgendered topic in anthropology are eligible to apply. *Application Procedure: Papers should be no more than 40 typed, double-spaced pages. Contact the scholarship chair for further information. *Amount: $300. *Deadline: August 1.

University of New Hampshire

Attn: Paula M. DiNardo, Chair
Student Awards Committee
114 Hood House
Durham, NH 03824
603-862-3485
paula.dinardo@unh.edu
http://www.unh.edu/awards

Award Name: Bill Kidder Fund Award. *Academic Area: Open. *Age Group: Undergraduate students, graduate students. *Eligibility: Applicant must be a University of New Hampshire student who has worked to increase tolerance and understanding of sexual orientation on campus. *Application Process: Applications are accepted by online nomination only between the dates of January 3 and March 1. Visit the university's Web site to nominate a candidate or to request further information. *Amount: Awards vary. *Deadline: March 1.

University of Puget Sound

Student Services Office, WSC 203
1500 North Warner #1082
Tacoma, WA 98416
253-879-3374
lperez@ups.edu
http://www2.ups.edu/dsa/lgbt/scholarship.htm

Scholarship Name: Puget Sound Lesbian, Gay, Bisexual, and Transgender Leadership Scholarship Fund. *Academic Area: Open. *Age Group: Undergraduate students. *Eligibility: Applicants must be enrolled for the fall semester at the University of Puget Sound and be sophomores, juniors, or seniors during the academic year for which they are applying. They also must demonstrate leadership ability in campus and community events promoting the LGBT community and must demonstrate academic achievement. *Application Process: Applicants should submit a completed application along with a resume of LGBT leadership activities and a short essay (described on the application). Visit the university's Web site to download an application or visit its student services office in person to pick one up. *Amount: Up to $2,000. *Deadline: April 8.

ZAMI

PO Box 2502
Decatur, GA 30031
404-370-0920
audrelordescholarship@zami.org
http://www.zami.org/application.htm

Scholarship Name: Audre Lorde Scholarship. *Academic Area: Open. *Age Group: Undergraduate students, graduate students. *Eligibility: Applicants must be self-identified lesbians or gay men of color who are open about their sexuality to their families, friends, and communities. They also may be graduating high school seniors or students currently attending a college, university, or technical school in the United States. Applicants must be accepted or registered at a postsecondary institution and must have a cumulative GPA (high school or college) of at least 2.5. These eligibility requirements are strictly enforced. ZAMI also strongly encourages lesbians and gay men who are 40 years old (or older) to apply.

*Application Process: Applicants should submit a completed application along with transcripts, an acceptance letter (entering freshmen or transfer students), two essays (detailed on the application), three letters of recommendation, and a headshot photo. Scholarship winners must attend the scholarship award ceremony to receive the award (transportation, lodging, and all other expenses are paid for by ZAMI). Visit the organization's Web site to download an application. *Amount: $1,000. *Deadline: May 1.

INDEXES

LOCATIONS INDEX

LOCATIONS INDEX

MAJORS INDEX

MAJORS INDEX

ORGANIZATIONS INDEX

ORGANIZATIONS INDEX